P9-AQA-369

# WORLD AFFAIRS
## National and International Viewpoints

# WORLD AFFAIRS

## National and International Viewpoints

The titles in this collection were selected
from the Council on Foreign Relations' publication:
*The Foreign Affairs 50-Year Bibliography*

Advisory Editor
RONALD STEEL

# The EARTH
# and the STATE

## A Study of Political Geography
### BY
## DERWENT WHITTLESEY

### ARNO PRESS
**A NEW YORK TIMES COMPANY**
New York • 1972

Reprint Edition 1972 by Arno Press Inc.

Reprinted from a copy in The Wesleyan University
Library

World Affairs: National and International Viewpoints
ISBN for complete set: 0-405-04560-3
See last pages of this volume for titles.

Manufactured in the United States of America

∽∾∽∾∽∾∽∾∽∾∽∾∽∾∽∾

**Library of Congress Cataloging in Publication Data**

**Whittlesey**, Derwent Stainthorpe, 1890-1956.
    The earth and the state.

    (World affairs:  national and international
viewpoints)
    Reprint of the 1939 ed.
    1. Geopolitics.  I.  Title.  II.  Series.
JC319.W45  1972          327'.1011          72-4308
ISBN 0-405-04597-2

# The EARTH and the STATE

## A Study of Political Geography

BY

## DERWENT WHITTLESEY

NEW YORK
HENRY HOLT AND COMPANY

075658

COPYRIGHT, 1939
BY
HENRY HOLT AND COMPANY, INC.

PRINTED IN THE
UNITED STATES OF AMERICA

# Foreword

POLITICAL geography is perhaps the oldest kind of geography. Paradoxically, there is even yet neither a universally accepted approach to the subject nor a consensus as to its content. I have therefore indulged in the pleasurable procedure of pioneering along lines that seem to me germinant.

For me the differentiation of political phenomena from place to place over the earth is the essence of political geography. Among these political features the state ranks first. The character of a state is intimately bound up with the particular earth conditions in which it evolves. Once in being, a system of government and the political concepts that express it are not confined to the region of its origin, but may spread to other areas and so create some degree of political uniformity over contrasted regions. In a very real sense the modern national state, which originated in Western Europe, has migrated to all parts of the globe. Nevertheless, in the process it has been much modified.

In any one place the interplay of government and nature is dynamic and subject to ceaseless change. For example, the European state of classical antiquity or of the middle ages differed in character from the European state today. Some understanding of the processes of alteration is basic to a grasp of the political geography of the present era. This is especially true of the states of Western Europe, where lie the roots of the political system currently dominant over much of the earth, and of Central Europe, which has wholeheartedly adopted the concept of the national state worked out by its western neighbors.

Because of the leading role played by Western and Central Europe in the political geography of the world today, the central theme of this book is the areal differentiation of governments (states) in that part of the Eurasian continent. Corollary and inextricably bound to this central theme is the extension of the European system of government to the ends of the earth.

iii

The transference has been accomplished in three ways. European people have migrated, with their political principles and practices, to new environments. European states have imposed their political system upon peoples of other origin in the form of colonial domination. And a few non-European peoples have imitated the European mode of governance wholly or in part.

Migration of Europeans to new environments has been most notable in the Americas. Australia-New Zealand, much smaller and less diverse, have received lesser streams of migrants. Contrasts between North and South America exemplify all the chief aspects of this phase of European expansion. I have therefore treated these continents on a scale commensurate with the discussion of Europe itself, leaving Australia-New Zealand to briefer mention as part of the British Empire.

The prime scene of imposition of European political forms upon non-Europeans is Africa, a veritable laboratory of colonial experimentation. For that reason, and also because it has been neglected by students of political geography, I have treated Africa at unconventional length. The distinctive geopolitical character of colonial areas in other parts of the world is brought out in considering them as subject to exploitation under the Western European mode of governance. In this way I have discussed South Asia and the Pacific realm, as well as strategic islands in other parts of the world.

Imitation of the Western European political system by outsiders has occurred chiefly in the vast expanse of country between the western boundary of Russia and the Pacific Ocean. That Japan has been an imitator is generally accepted. Russia, in view of its great extent in Asia, the much longer association of its nucleus with Asia than with Western and Central Europe, and the trend of its political life since the World War, can readily be recognized as essentially Asiatic, rather than European, in character. In this light it appears as an imitator of European political forms, rather than a partaker of them. Indeed, the Western European system has been so radically altered in areas under Russian and Japanese influence as to raise the question whether that system has merely been more notably modified there than elsewhere, or whether it has actually been rejected. Until time answers that question, it appears to me fruitless to attempt analysis of the political geography of those states on the same scale as the rest of the world. Just now both Japan and the Soviet state are following courses out of harmony with the European political order that they once appeared to have adopted. They, and the Japanese sphere in China, have been withdrawn from the interdependent world that evolved under the aegis of Western

European nations — both in the utilization of their natural resources and in their political procedures, internal and external. If this withdrawal proves permanent, it will amount to the establishment of new modes of government, and so will break down the uniform, worldwide political system of European origin to which our age is accustomed. But it is quite as likely that the withdrawal is temporary, and that the pattern of politics will in time merge with that of nations in other areas, where experimentation in government is likewise going forward. For these reasons I have discussed Russia, China, and Japan only as they figure in the world structure of political affairs.

While the study of states is the chief topic of political geography, it is not the only phase of the subject. Every state is implemented with law, and the differentiation of law from place to place is a topic only less significant than that of the state itself. The law alters with time, as do the states it serves. Embedded in the contemporary legal systems of the world are vestiges of several modes of governance belonging to the past. The law also may spread from one environment to another. Nearly all current codes have been stamped with some impress of legal systems indigenous to Western Europe, consequent to the spread of European political forms round the world. Some of these non-European codes show signs of reasserting themselves, and there is always the possibility that radical alterations in any legal code may be brought about by changing conditions in the technology and the economic geography of humankind. Students of political geography have paid little attention to the law as a part of their subject. I have treated it mainly in two chapters, following the discussions of the states of the world.

In short, in this book I have sought to lay hold of the areal differentiation of the world's principal states and legal codes, insofar as these political phenomena are firmly established and their character clear. I have left to the future the detailed consideration of states and legal systems now in violent flux.

D. W.

Harvard University,
    August, 1939

# Analytical Table of Contents

075658

## Chapter 5

## Chapter 6

079838

## Chapter 7

# A CONFLICT OF MARITIME AND INTERIOR IN-TERESTS – GERMANY

## Chapter 8

# EAST CENTRAL EUROPE EXEMPLIFIED IN ITS CAPITALS

## Chapter 9

# THE MEDITERRANEAN REALM

## Chapter 10

# GEOPOLITICAL STRUCTURES IN ITALY . 279

## Chapter 11

# AFRICA, AN EXPLOITABLE CONTINENT 304

## Chapter 12

# GEOPOLITICAL ANTITHESIS IN THE AMERICAS

## Chapter 13

# LATIN AMERICA

## Chapter 14

# LATIN-AMERICAN BOUNDARIES AND CAPITALS

## Chapter 15

# THE ANTECEDENT BOUNDARY BETWEEN THE AMERICAS

## Chapter 16

# THE GEOPOLITICAL STRUCTURE OF NORTH AMERICA

## Chapter 17

# EARTH IMPRESS ON POLITICAL THOUGHT

# CONTENTS

## Chapter 18

## EARMARKS OF POLITICAL GEOGRAPHY

## BIBLIOGRAPHY

## GLOSSARY

## INDEX

# List of Maps

## A NOTE ON THE MAPS

All the maps have been prepared expressly for this book. Three of them have been modified from maps previously published to illustrate articles of mine on political geography. These and, with the exceptions noted below, all the others have been drafted by Edward A. Schmitz. His masterly execution of my specifications has far surpassed the labor of routine drafting, and to his critical suggestions and his skilled pen should be attributed much of the effectiveness of the maps.

Four of the maps are the work of other hands. Figure 39 is an excerpt from a publication of the American Geographical Society. Figure 35 is drawn on a base prepared by my student, Edward A. Ackerman. Figures 3 and 21 were drawn for me by another student, Harley L. Stowell.

## CHAPTER ONE

# Geographic Features of the State

GEOGRAPHY concerns itself with the areal arrangement of phenomena on the earth. The size and shape of areas and their location, when distributed on a map make a pattern, whether of soils or of crops, of climates or of nations. Some areal patterns describe earth conditions: climate, landforms, and the natural resources — soils, waters, minerals, natural vegetation, and native animal life. These earth conditions combine in infinite variety to constitute the natural environment of human society, the manifold human habitat. Man further diversifies the natural variety of the earth by tracing upon it areal patterns of his own devising: evidences of modes of settlement, whether clustered in cities or villages or disseminated over farm or in forest; mosaics of areas utilized to carry on economic pursuits — agriculture, fishing, mining, manufacture, trade; distributions of items in the landscape contrived for the social life of mankind — areas devoted to temples and churches, theaters and playing fields, schools and graveyards; and finally, political patterns, intended to facilitate economic and social life by providing devices for regulating the interrelations of territorial groups and of individuals within such groups.

The primary political pattern superposed on the earth is that of states.[1] This book, in treating of Political Geography, is bound to give attention to the degree of correspondence between the pattern of states and the patterns of the natural environment, ranging from coincidence to complete discrepancy. It must further inquire into the geographic structure of states and the organic relation between political and natural phenomena. In brief, its subject is geopolitical [2] patterns and structures. Most of the chapters that follow are devoted to particu-

[1] Throughout this book " state " when not capitalized is used to signify a sovereign political entity. When capitalized, it refers to constituent members of a federation, as the forty-eight States of our own nation.

[2] " Geopolitical " is a portmanteau adjective used throughout this volume instead of the cumbersome " politico-geographical."

1

lar states in different parts of the world, to groups of states similar in their geographic relations, or to areas deserving treatment as a whole because they possess in common some basic natural feature compelling in its political implications.

Nearly the whole earth is incorporated in or subject to states which are postulated on territorial spread. That is to say, the state occupies area. The concept of territoriality — that government occupies space and administers the people and natural resources of that space — is the outgrowth of life in two sorts of regions. In humid climates of the middle latitudes society is generally sedentary and people and place become intimately interrelated through long collaboration. In the low latitudes territoriality appears chiefly in dry regions, where the compulsion to irrigate the thirsty soil creates social groups firmly welded to the land.

While sedentary states vary greatly in their size, shape, and location, and therefore describe a crazy-quilt pattern, they all have in common certain structural features that may be considered geopolitical.

Typically, each one has crystallized about a nuclear core that fostered integration. Europe affords numerous examples. The basin of the Thames River expanded to make England, and the Île de France evolved into the French nation of today. Switzerland grew from a core of mountain valleys bordering the " Lake of the Four Forest Cantons " when they found their lake in the path of trade flowing between north and south Europe over the St. Gotthard Pass. Norway is the fringe of lowlands along a semicircle of fjord coast, connected between Oslo and Trondheim by habitable inland valleys that describe a chord of the arc.

In nearly all states the nuclear core is also the most populous part — its ecumene.[1] The ecumene is the portion of the state that supports the densest and most extended population and has the closest mesh of transportation lines. By inference such a region is capable of supporting a relatively dense population because it is more richly endowed by nature than the rest of the state. The endowment may be confined to a single resource, such as metals in Bolivia, a state handicapped by location, climate, landforms, soils, and natural vegetation. It may comprise

---

[1] The term " ecumene " is Mark Jefferson's, who defines it as the land within ten miles of a railroad; *Economic Geography* 4 (1928), 127–131, and *Geografiska Annaler* 16 (1934), 146–158. Limitation to railroad lines is a fairly accurate representation for the occidental world of the present day (or of the day just passing). To define the ecumene as it exists in all parts of the earth and in the long view of human history, every type of transportation route in being should be included. The zones in effective contact with the routes, be they wide or narrow, in conjunction with the areas of densest population, approximate the ecumene. No accurate world-map superimposing transportation zones on population density has been constructed. Figure 1 is a crude version of it.

a combination of natural advantages. Argentina's ecumene is blessed by fertile soil, flat land, and mild climate — an endowment favorable to tillage and stock raising, but limited to these pursuits. A somewhat different but equally propitious environment for agriculture, coupled with a favorable situation for trade, abundant forests, and ultimately the unearthing of coal, made the English Plain leader in Britain, a state based on a natural endowment of uncommonly great variety.

In some instances a growing state absorbs areas with natural endowments equal or superior to its original core. In such states the ecumene expands, or in rare instances migrates. The ecumene of the United States incorporates most of the humid country east of the Great Plains, an area several times the size of the seaboard core. The mountain valleys that saw the birth of the Serb state scarcely belong to the contemporary ecumene of Yugoslavia, which focuses on its larger fluvial plains.

Either the ecumene or the nuclear core is likely to contain the capital of the state. Paris, London, and a score of other capitals are focal in the original organizing center and in the ecumene as well. Shift of the ecumene from the nuclear core sometimes carries the capital with it, as in the case of Bern in Switzerland. More commonly such a shift leaves the capital offside the ecumene, tenacious of its location in the organizing center. Washington and Berlin are examples. The capital of Australia lies between two nuclear cores of the federated States comprising the nation. All the exceptional cases cited are capitals of federations in which recent origin, compromise among the component sections, or shifts in the ecumene have occasioned the atypical location of the capital. Centralized or unitary states tend strongly to set up their capitals either centrally within the ecumene or on the side of it toward the most exposed frontier. Whether centrality or military strategy predominates in locating a capital depends on the state of public security at the time the site is fixed. Berlin began as an outpost of the German " push to the east "; Madrid was chosen as being central in the Iberian Peninsula. Under political stress, such as external war or internal dissension, central authority is strengthened and the capital is aggrandized, wherever it be located.

Government lays hands in a special way upon its capitals. The focusing of roads, railroads, and canals upon the seat of government is partly the result of economic evolution, but it is often encouraged by political aid. Berlin, for instance, is not the center of Germany to the degree indicated by its hub of communication lines. The location of some capitals has been shifted in harmony with migrating political power.

This has been a notable feature of the hill-land of the Western Balkans, where half a dozen places have served as capitals. Once fixed, capitals become the pets of government. On them public money is frequently lavished beyond present needs, even beyond the natural desire of the people to dress up their capital city. Delhi, Peiping, Berlin, Rome (both ancient and modern), are notable examples of generous expenditure. All these cities are splendid to look at, and each looks very different from the ordinary commercial city. Minor capitals have been garnished in proportion to their funds. Nearly every German quondam state has an imitation Versailles, and the forty-eight democratic United States of America have spent staggering sums to house their governments. Washington and Canberra, as purely political, fiat towns, are the clearest beneficiaries of political favor, but even London, primarily a world port and the leading manufacturing city of Britain, is impressively the capital of a nation and an empire. The spaciousness of modern capitals — Washington, " city of magnificent distances "; Paris with its broad boulevards; Rome, roomy enough to accommodate the national capital, the papal see, and the exhumed capital of the classical empire — are all made possible by the security which central authority affords. Some governments which have spent overmuch on dressing up their capital cities have been overthrown not long after. By their very splendor Athens of Pericles and Versailles of the later Bourbons contributed to the undoing of their sponsors.

The state is made up of component units, each of which, like the state itself, comprises a specific area. They range from quasi-independent nations, as in the British " Commonwealth of Nations," to districts purely administrative, laid out and closely supervised by the central authority, as in France, Yugoslavia, Rumania, and many other countries. There are several other types of components, intermediate to the extremes: units hoary with local tradition but subordinate to the central authority, such as the counties of England; former independent entities recently federated but imposing fixed limitations on the central power, such as the Australian States; and former sovereignties which retain different and slowly altering degrees of authority within a federal union, such as Switzerland and the United States of America. There is a marked tendency for traditional components to retain their local color, particularly if they more or less correspond to natural regions. The provinces of France were abolished as legal entities by the Revolution at the end of the 18th century, but most of them are still current in the life of the people. If you ask a French citizen the name of his " pays," he responds with a province name of the *ancien régime* —

Normandie or Provence or Limousin — never with the department in which he holds legal residence. The component units of the United States which retain most pronounced individuality occupy relatively unified environments. California, the region of Mediterranean climate, Louisiana, on the Mississippi Delta, and tropical, peninsular Florida come to mind. In the northeast, where the states are small and obviously only pieces of a larger regional unity, a resident is apt to think of himself as a New Englander. Regional diversity within a larger political unity is made possible by communication effective enough to link distinctive regions without destroying their individuality — a quality which is rooted in some degree of physical isolation or in contrasts in natural environment.

The state is marked off from its neighbors by political boundaries. It is habitual to think of such boundaries as lines, and so they generally are in the contemporary occidental state and its colonies. Yet everywhere until recently, and in parts of the earth today, political boundaries are vaguely defined zones. This is common where central authority is weak and local interests stand paramount, at least along frontiers. Examples are the mountain and desert (landward) boundaries of China. Until the 17th century so centralized a state as France had no incontestable linear land boundaries. Zonal boundaries actually represent the conditions of the habitat more precisely than do lines, because few linear boundaries exist in nature. The seacoast is very nearly a line, yet even there a zone separates high and low tidemarks. The Pyrenees, often cited as an ideal mountain boundary, are occupied all summer by flocks and herds from both flanks of the range, and from time immemorial the herdsmen have been accustomed to fraternize on their common pastures, and to subscribe to treaties regulating joint use of the grazing ground. Drawing political lines in boundary zones of intermingling works hardship on the border peoples. Nevertheless, linear boundaries are generally preferred, as expressing a human concept more readily grasped and more convenient for the general public than the zone. Today only the most inaccessible frontiers, in interior South America and Asia, remain both undefined by treaty and unmarked on the ground.

The political boundary may be of many sorts. Quite commonly it follows some feature of the landscape, in which case it may be called naturally marked. Naturally marked boundaries include streams, lakes and marshes, crests of ranges, and watersheds. The Rhine, the Great Lakes, the Pyrenees, the Amazon-Orinoco water-parting are examples. During recent centuries many boundaries have been defined by geodetic lines. These may be drawn somewhere within boundary zones marked by nature. A political boundary *line* through the midst of a desert, a wide marsh, or a forest is related to the natural feature, but cannot be observed unless marked by the hand of man. To rectify this deficiency the Chinese built their wall, and the United States and Canada carve lines through the forests. Other boundary lines bear no relation to natural features. In cases where two states gradually push their borders outward, such a line may mark a military stalemate, as does the Paraguay-Bolivian boundary, a line between established villages, as in many post-war boundaries of East Central Europe, or a conquest of mineral or other resources, as in (Franco-German) Lorraine, and Acré, once contested by Brazil's neighbors. Other linear boundaries of recent origin have been defined antecedent to settlement. This is common in the new continents, e.g., the forty-ninth parallel in Western United States. Whatever the character of a linear boundary, it is almost certain to work hardship upon some of the people settled along it. In epochs of well-consolidated central authority, this is generally held to be less vexatious than a zonal boundary, which would conform to conditions of local communities but would give rise to continual friction between the central authorities concerned. The character and utility of political boundaries is closely linked with the existing degree of centralization in government.

In many states particular districts give rise to particular political problems. Where such problems perennially rise to plague governments, they are likely to be based on conditions of the natural environment. Critical zones of friction are commonest along political boundaries. More than one state is involved, and the border peoples are likely to merge or interpenetrate in a zone rather than to cleave along any possible linear boundary. In some cases the border people feel themselves distinct from both of their dominant neighbors. The Basques and the Catalans of the Pyrenees are cases in point. Possession in common of a natural resource, such as a navigable stream, is a fruitful source of friction. Adjacence to exceptionally valuable areas, such as a mineralized district, a rich commercial city, or a fertile lowland, awakens the cupidity of the country which is cut off from the desirable item by no barrier stronger than a political line. Lorraine, Flanders, and Alsace furnish examples of friction arising from these causes.

Another type of problem area is the region so handicapped by nature as to be a liability on the balance sheets of the state which embraces it. Such are the North Country of Canada and the desert of Australia. Such a region tends to be a breeder of poverty and all its train of evils, in an ever descending spiral. It sometimes occurs that problem areas are created, or at any rate accentuated, by the very fact that regions of meager resources are coupled politically with favored regions. The abandonment of rocky farms in New England followed upon the opening of the prairie soils in the Middle West to any New England farmer who could transport himself thither. The former leadership of New England in textile manufacturing and its present adversity resulting from loss of much business to the South are alike the result of New England's partnership in the federal union. Not only the pattern and the structure of political areas, but also the laws by which political areas are governed are to some extent conditioned by natural environment. They in turn modify the utilization of earth resources. E.g., the Netherlands, at the mouth of the chief river system of Western Europe and terminal to the world's most active ocean trade routes, naturally developed a government favorable to shipping. In turn Dutch laws stimulate commerce by establishing free ports, subsidizing lines of vessels, and encouraging international banking.

Geopolitical patterns and structures, then, are the fabric of political geography. The basic political pattern, that of states, corresponds in varying degrees with the several patterns of natural environment. Every state is distinguished by its unique geopolitical structure. Yet the elements of this structure are common to all. The nuclear core, within which the state is organized, and about which its territory accretes, possesses qualifications that lend themselves to political integration. The ecumene in any period is the part of the state best endowed by nature to support a dense population. The location, the site, the size, and the functions of the capital are intimately conditioned by the natural wealth and the political character of the state. The component areas vary no less than different states themselves. Their composite nature, set in various political frames, gives rise to sectionalism. Boundaries are perhaps the most discussed of all the geographic features of the state. Problem areas and other critical districts compel the rulers of each state to give them particular attention. In them may germinate the seeds that ultimately destroy the state itself. The functioning of every state operates through the laws. These may be in harmony with the natural environment or discordant to it. In the long run the most successful laws conform to basic conditions of the habitat, although they may by their action ameliorate or otherwise modify minor natural conditions, and alter the incidence of local environment.

## CHAPTER TWO

# The State and Communication

## THE RIGHT OF A STATE TO "SPACE"

BECAUSE every infant is born into a state, mankind grows up with an unreasoned conviction that his country or people is immutable, a force inseparably linked to a specific portion of the earth's surface. This feeling transformed into argument underlies many of the attempts to make political geography serve the purposes of this or that particular state — emotional efforts which have been rationalized into the dogma known as Geopolitics. The brutal, temporary dissection of territory incidental to warfare, and the more permanent and hardly less rude dismemberment produced by dictated peace terms do not dislodge this faith that the state is inherently entitled to its proper space, to its "place in the sun." Even the stubborn fact that two different states may lay equal claim to the same border zone fails to undermine the devotion of the opposing nationals to their respective articles of faith.

In their favor is the powerful impulsion of the inhabitants of every distinctive region to form a more perfect union. The Gaul recognized and later unified by the Romans reappeared after centuries of disruption as the Western Kingdom of Charlemagne's progeny, and again after another breakdown, still more firmly integrated as modern France. China, whatever its status at the moment, has repeatedly achieved some degree of political unity, to express the integrity of its ecumene. China proper is little more than the densely populated territory lying between the sea and the great semicircle of desert and mountain — a harsh and thinly inhabited environment — that marks its landward borders. This urge to coalesce is spurred by the community of feeling which springs from the use of common resources, and above all by ease of communication among the parts of the area. Throughout history, periods of political disintegration have generally coincided with times when transport was slow, dangerous, and costly. If the sequence of political units in any region is traced, states are seen as mutable, almost fluid objects, shrinking and growing, forming varied combinations, disappearing.

So clearly outlined an area as the Italian Peninsula has been politically unified less than 75 years in the past 16 centuries, and only 700 years in the whole course of its recorded history, which reaches back nearly three millennia. The powerful, unified Italian territory of today was labelled, just prior to the advent of the railroad and the telegraph, " merely a geographical expression." At that time its ungainly length, crosshatched by mountain ranges, was divided among more than half a dozen independent states, and all its fertile northeast was property of the Austrian Empire. In fact this represented for Italy a high degree of unity. From the breakup of Roman union until after the Renaissance nearly every valley in hilly Tuscany was the seat of a state practically, if not nominally, independent. The gentle terrain of the Po Plain was a kaleidoscope of shifting boundaries, as its merchant cities squabbled among themselves, while Pope and Emperor, Spain, France, and Austria contested there for exclusive domination over the peninsula that none ever achieved. The map must be rolled back to the days of the Roman Empire, with its network of paved roads, to find an earlier era when the whole of Italy was unified. And before the Roman legions hammered the peninsula into unity with the impact of their marching feet, separatism not unlike that of the middle ages prevailed, reaching back into the misty period in which history merges with legend. The Romans were the first people to unify Italy, and the 19th century Italians were the second. Each possessed a new means of overland transportation and communication, and no other of the inhabitants of the peninsula ever held this key to political success — for the Roman nation the road and the courier; for the Italian nation the railroad and the telegraph, the automobile road and the telephone, the airplane and the radio.

## THE SIZE OF STATES

The status of communication is particularly critical in periods when states are taking shape, and has much to do with determining the size of political units. Improvement in the means of communication kept step with expansion of the little city-state, Rome, into an empire reaching from the Scottish border to the Plateau of Iran. " All roads lead to Rome " was no idle boast; it was the slogan of Roman statehood.

Gradual improvement in communication during the later middle ages narrowed the barrier boundaries between European feudal states, extinguished many of them, and sketched the outlines of the national states which constitute the political Europe of today. The most persistent and least frequently contested national boundaries on the continent have been those which correspond to enduring breaks in the flow of communication, such as the Baltic Sea, the Pyrenees Mountains, and the ranges of forested hills on the north and west margins of Bohemia. The boundary zones of acutest contemporary discord lie where interruptions to communication have been eliminated by the increasingly proficient technology of passing centuries. As a result of draining marshes, felling forests, and laying railroads and all-weather highways across the remnants of these obstacles, once-dreaded coniferous sand barrens and impassable tidal and fresh water marshes have lost much of their barrier character, although most of them remain districts of sparse population. By tunnelling for lines of rails, even mountain ranges have been diminished.

The peopling by Europeans of that most unified of continents, North America, was overtaken and rushed to completion by the age of railroads. Middle and South America were first occupied by Europeans a century earlier than North America, and the segregated peripheral settlements have never been brought into contact because the interior stubbornly balked railroad building. In English-speaking North America there are but two political units today, compared to twenty in Latin America (Ch. 12).

It is obvious that there exists no significant relation between the power or vitality of a state and its area. Netherlands contains less than 13,000 square miles, Bolivia more than half a million, yet Netherlands is much the stronger. Some sorts of regions are positive handicaps to effective functioning of the state to which they belong. A political unit should be envisaged in terms of its climate, landforms, and natural resources, rather than its area. These are its true measures as an apportionment of the earth's resources. In a crude way variation in population density is a clue to the degree to which a state is favored by nature. Wide allowance must be made for differences in standard of living and in prevailing technology in the use of earth's resources. Java, about half as large as New Zealand, holds nearly thirty times as many people; that Java and New Zealand inherit the earth in the ratio of 60:1 is patently absurd. Nevertheless, the ecumene is presumably the part of the earth that society has found best suited to its needs. The ecumene of each state may be thought of as the region or regions which are well-peopled and given internal coherence by a network of transportation lines (Fig. 1). It is distinguished from sparsely populated or uninhabited parts of the same country, penetrated only here and there by routes. Efficient transportation consolidates political areas, whether the Roman Empire or the United States of America. The lack of ready means of circulation is a source of political weakness whatever the density of population, as the plight of China proves.

THE EARTH'S LARGEST POLITICAL ENTITIES

A comparison of the very large states with respect to both total area and ecumene, serves to point up the insignificance of area unaccompanied by population and access (Table I).

TABLE I. AREAS, POPULATIONS, AND COMMUNICATIONS OF THE LARGER STATES

| State | Area | Population | Railroad Mileage | Road Mileage | Waterway Mileage | Airline Mileage | Telegraph Mileage | Telephone Mileage |
|---|---|---|---|---|---|---|---|---|
| Russia......... | 8,095,728 | 165,847,100 | 44,761 | 847,360 | 68,200 | 59,760 | 334,243 | 7,893 |
| China and Mongolia......... | 3,529,258 | 424,785,537 | 8,131 | 59,886 | | 8,246 | 61,395 | Along railroads |
| Canada........ | 3,466,556 | 10,376,786 | 42,552 | ? | 2,700 | ? | 52,907 | 5,120,610 |
| Brazil.......... | 3,275,510 | 41,560,147 | 29,945 | 78,205 | 21,944 | 49,779 | 37,776 | ? |
| U.S.A.......... | 3,026,789 | 122,775,046 | 252,871 | 3,009,066 | ? | 66,153,000 (flown) | 251,888 | 65,121,000 |
| Australia....... | 2,974,581 | 6,806,752 | 27,089 | ? | 0 | 21,588 | ? | ? |
| India.......... | 1,575,187 | 338,170,632 | 43,128 | ? | ? | ? | 108,635 | ? |

Note: — The question marks indicate lack of data.

The United States of America possesses the largest ecumene on earth. It comprises at least half a dozen distinct natural and economic regions. They are complementary in character and form a well-knit combination of sections, each retaining its own individuality while sharing in the common lot. The state could scarcely have held together, in spite of the initial unity of its population, had it not been for the timely invention of the railroad and the telegraph. Before the railroad era, building canals and improving navigation on rivers was the most vital issue in national political life. Around it grew the sectionalism which in time threatened the existence of the political federation. Railroads diminished the interval of time necessary to people the Middle West with easterners. The prospect of railroads kept the restive Pacific coast loyal during the trying period of Civil War, the struggle which decided the issue of political unity in the " United " States. That war itself was fought along lines determined mainly by the novel strategy of railroads, rivers being relegated to second place. The North profited greatly by the ease with which it could place troops and supplies on its front lines by means of the rails. A little later, railroads made it profitable to grow wheat in the heart of the continent, where climate verges on semi-aridity and the summers are short. Railroads laid the groundwork for converting the still drier grazing country of the nomadic Indian into livestock ranches. This extended the ecumene, reduced the area of sparse population, and narrowed the gap between the populous regions based on opposite coasts of the continent. Two generations after the first railroads pushed westward from the Atlantic seaboard, the automobile recreated the highway web which the rails had eclipsed, and airlines further strengthened the bonds between the sections.

Accompanying and reinforcing the transportational revolution were other technological novelties which aided the consolidation of the American nation by encouraging farming of several contrasting natural environments and mutual exchange of their distinctive products. The cotton gin, the plow with steel shoe and self-scouring moldboard, harvesters of several sorts, the threshing machine, and refrigeration, all combined to give the new transportation system heavy traffic in agricultural products. At the same time manufacturing was stepped up to unparalleled output with the task of making the machines of agriculture and transportation. Mass production was made possible by gauging each mechanical part to standardized specifications.

All these economic revolutions took place in Western Europe as fully as in North America. But in Europe the states were politically mature and their boundaries were pretty well crystallized in terms of the slow communication of the early modern era — stagecoach and canal. Western and Central Europe remain divided into states incommensurate in size, if not in resources, with the current forms of transportation. The United States, with national boundaries once believed by most people to be too remote to endure, proved to be just the right scale for a modern state. Its extensive lands consigned by nature to scanty population are mainly mountain ranges and intermont deserts. Although large, they are not disproportionate to the ecumene, and they are traversed by lines of transportation and communication.

The Dominion of Canada, although slightly exceeding the United States in area, must be dropped from the group of very large countries if its ecumene be substituted for its political area. The Canadian ecumene consists of four distinct areas, each of which may be looked upon as an extension of a region from adjacent United States. The political separation of these regional units began with enmity sown by the American Revolution along the Atlantic seaboard. This was followed by projecting into the western wilderness a pioneer boundary line antecedent to settlement. Never subsequently disputed except to adjust details, it stands as the most notable peaceable boundary line on earth, some 4,000 miles long. Approximately 45 percent of it is land boundary and is dotted with markers; in much of the forest areas a narrow vista is cut along the line as well. Were it not for this, the boundary would be unrecognizable along most of its length.

The integrity of the boundary has however been supported by railroad and telegraph lines which parallel it at no great distance. Only the promise of a transcontinental railroad drew the six Canadian provinces into their " more perfect union " [1]; only the fulfillment of that promise prevented secession of the remote regions at both extremities. This east-west band of rails proved an economic, as well as a political, success, because it fitted into the basic pattern of transportation in North America — a festoon of lines connecting the interior with the eastern seaboard and trans-Atlantic trade, later extended to the Pacific coast and serving as a link in the girdle of trade routes encircling the northern hemisphere.

Except for the narrow belt bordering the United States, Canada is a wilderness of tundra and coniferous forest inhabited by a few aborigines and scattered trappers, miners, and woodsmen. Few rails and no roads penetrate the vast north country, where the sole means of access are likely to be canoes and a few larger vessels on the many lakes and streams and airplanes sailing over the obstructions of terrain. In the center of the continent, where this refractory land touches and crosses the national border, it is traversed only by three slender threads of rails.

Much like Canada in possessing a high percentage of wilderness, and even in the ratio of population to area, is Australia. For contrast the ecumene is peripheral, and the interior wilderness is handicapped by aridity instead of by cold and scanty, infertile soil. As in Canada, the isolated southwest has been linked to the populous southeast by a railroad. Its function is wholly political, because neither passengers nor freight are likely to use it in preference to the parallel and nearby seaway. Its success is questionable, in view of continued discontent in West Australia with a government located on the opposite side of the continent. As late as 1933, West Australia recorded itself on referendum vote as being in favor of secession from the Commonwealth of Australia. A more central railroad is being built from south to north, as a further aid in linking the habitable peripheral segments of the continent. With improved connections to the north coast, it is hoped to

---

[1] The British North America Act of 1867 created the Dominion of Canada from the three Maritime Provinces, Quebec, Ontario, and British Columbia. The three Prairie Provinces came into existence subsequently.

stimulate settlement there. Australia lags far behind Canada in railroad construction, a contrast which is emphasized by the fact that several of the colonies which later coalesced into the federal commonwealth built their lines to different gauges, thus hampering interstate traffic. This again calls attention to the peripheral character of the Australian ecumene, in which the value of transcontinental and inter-colonial rail connection was realized late. Parts, if not all the northern fringe of the continent are clearly habitable for peoples who occupy much the same natural environment in Insulindia, on the mainland of Asia, and in Africa. It is vacant today because the Australian government steadfastly refuses to permit settlement by other than white peoples.

Both Canada and Australia have undergone a change of attitude toward their wild land. Formerly each nation divided it among the constituent provinces of the federation with the expectation that in time it would be occupied and set up as new constituent units, in the manner of the United States. Today vast areas have been taken under the wing of the federal government, to be administered indefinitely as " territories."

Brazil is another of the New World countries possessing a very large area of which only a small fraction is ecumene. With a slightly smaller area than Canada, it has more than four times the population. Its railroad mileage is less than two-thirds that of Canada, and more nearly equals Australia's. This may be attributed in part to the difficult highland terrain in the section of Brazil suitable for European settlers and to the seacoast along two fronts and the broad riverways of the Amazon, Paraná, and Rio Grande do Sul — systems which penetrate and connect vast areas and so obviate the long trunk rails so conspicuous in most other states of equivalent area. The few inhabitants of the interior lowlands live close to the rivers, which serve their needs adequately. The unused areas are either the dense forests of rainy low latitudes, or the grassland, seeded with thickets and with scattered trees, characteristic of low latitude climates in which drouth alternates with rainy seasons.

Each of the several well-settled districts along the hot and humid Brazilian coast is linked to the nearest seaport. Those south of the eastern tip of the continent may be considered as part of the Brazilian ecumene. Toward the south end of the country, the coastal fringe merges into the indisputable inhabited core. There latitude and altitude combine to offset tropical heat and moisture and a considerable railroad net has opened the country. A few nerve ends of this net make tenuous contact with the Paraná riverway, and with the rail system of the Pampa. Nearly the whole of the landward boundary is so beset by swamp, rain forest, or mountain ranges that transcontinental railroad lines, in the North American, Australian, or Russian sense, are not projected even by the optimistic.

Russia's ecumene is on the same grand scale as that of the United States, and its total population is not much greater. In it the people are more evenly spread, and there are no large areas so densely occupied as the urbanized cores of North America. In Russia the mesh of the transportation net is much coarser.

The Russian ecumene lacks a seafront contact with the outside world, except for outlets on the Black Sea and the Gulf of Finland, both deeply recessed behind several other states which are in a position to deny access to Russian ports. Landward it lies adjacent to the states of Central Europe, with which its railroad net is in contact at several points. The twofold weakness of the position is admitted in a number of ways. Whenever the state is strong it pushes ruthlessly across its neighbors in efforts to gain political control of ports in closer touch with the open sea. Its railroad gauge differs from that of adjacent European countries, except in one instance of an outlet line to an ice-free port on the Baltic. At the present time Russia is depopulating a band from 1,500 to 3,000 feet wide along its eastern border. Villages are being moved to the interior, and hereafter the land in the defense zone can be used only subject to military authorities.

The sparsely inhabited lands of Soviet Russia, added to the ecumene, form an area more than twice as large as the territory of any other state on earth. All these lands lie marginal to the ecumene, and there has been less necessity to join them with rails and other lines of communication than in North America or Australia. Nevertheless, the Trans-Siberian Railroad is the longest line on earth, and in telegraph mileage, Russia compares with the United States. Rails, highways, and airlines are ramifying to the outlying areas. The wastes are of two sorts: tundra and forest much like the Canadian northland, and deserts not very different from those of the United States. Penetration of the Arctic border, as well as the ecumene, is greatly facilitated by rivers which are navigable in summer, the total mileage being twenty-five times that of Canada's used waterways. It is possible that parts of the region as yet beyond the ecumene, may some day be drawn into it. It is also possible that some of the remoter areas may be lost because they are military liabilities. Events have proved that Russia's hold on its Pacific coast, tenuous at best, must be maintained in the face of Japanese opposition, and is held only by aid of the railroad.

The two remaining political units of major size, India and China, are embedded in the flanks of Asia. They contrast strikingly with the rest in their much larger populations — both absolutely and in ratio to their total areas. The ecumene of each state therefore occupies a large fraction of its total area, although in China the transportation pattern only barely suggests the fact.

India appears strikingly a unit on a physical map of Asia because it is so sharply demarked by the lofty Himalayas and the lesser ranges which carry this barrier boundary to the sea on either flank. Despite the unremitting effort of many centuries, however, the lower lying area of plains and hills south of the mountains was never politically unified until the end of the 17th century, when the Mogul emperors, originally nomads from Central Asia, and itinerant as long as they lived in India, succeeded in holding nearly all of it for a few decades. This feat they accomplished by means of a well-maintained east-west highway across the northern plains, from which branch roads ran southward into the peninsula. The Mogul conquest was shortlived; its relaxed hold had already permitted the rise of many quasi-independent states by the time Europeans began to knock at the coastal portals of the subcontinent.

The first unification effective over a considerable period is that accomplished by the British. Though British domination began in 1757, it was not India-wide until a century later, when British India was created and effective British suzerainty over the Native States was established (1858).

British rule has succeeded where all its predecessors failed, in considerable part because of the mobility of the rulers. This has increased with the speeding up of communication, especially by means of railroads. Today India's rail mileage ranks with that of Russia and Canada, and is surpassed only in the United States. Mobility enables a hundred thousand British to conquer and administer 340,000,000 Indians, to rejuvenate their northern blood in the cool Himalayan foothills during the most enervating season, and to make frequent stays in Europe. Increased facilities for exchange have given every Indian community a stake in world trade. Famines are no longer dreaded, since local failure of the monsoon is mitigated by the importation of food from luckier regions. If today groups of Indians are becoming restive and demanding political independence, their sense of unity has been engendered by the railroads, which have for the first time in history enabled Indians by the million to get away from their native villages and to become conscious of their fellow countrymen. Occidental organization has for the first time made it possible for India to realize to the full the values inherent in its large area and an ecumene not much smaller, although less well endowed, than those of the United States and Russia.

China, more or less unified several times during its long history,[1] stands today the symbol of political disruption. Hardly a month passes that the newspapers do not blazon some new phase of internal strife or of invasion by aggressive enemies. Each local " warlord " attempts to rule the small district he can overawe with his army, but none is able to achieve domination over his rivals. The only real solidarity prevails in the compact basins of the Si Kiang and the Upper Yangtze, both unified by a navigable waterway and circumscribing hills of scantier population. The Yangtze and Hwangho river systems are, in contrast, divided into segments. Szechwan, roughly the basin of the Upper Yangtze, is unified and defended by surrounding rugged mountains, through which the river rushes in a gorge. In their lower courses the Yangtze and the Hwangho deltas merge into a single lowland. These basins, together with the hill-land of the Upper Hwangho, make up the ecumene of China. Rivers are much used for transportation, and in recent years a good many miles of highway have been built, but the railroad mileage is less than a third as great as that of Brazil or Australia, and scarcely 3 percent of that of the United States. In earlier centuries political unity was effected from a capital in this great lowland of the lower rivers. Its effectiveness seems to have depended on the navigable streams supplemented by the Grand Canal which connected them. The central government of the 20th century took shape in the same vital region, and made its seat historic Nanking, a word which means " southern capital." Yet today waterways are not enough. Without a web of rails or motor roads a region so large and so populous as China resists integration. Few of its myriad people have ever seen anything of their country beyond the confines of their village, and perhaps the nearest market town. Without transportation lines the central government cannot muster the resources on which it must rely to dispatch troops to put down insurrections, to succor the famine-stricken with grain from districts of plenty, or to ward off invaders. The significance of Peking, repeatedly the " northern capital," is that of an advance base for successive foreign dynasties, intruders from the north.

[1] First during the Han Dynasty, which covers the four centuries immediately before and after the time of Christ; next during the 7th century of our era under Tang rulers; then in the Sung period, during the 12th and 13th centuries; under the Mongols, 1280–1368; in the Ming period which followed for three centuries; and finally under the Manchus, who lost their throne along with Chinese unity under the impact of European aggression, a generation ago.

Beyond the ecumene lie sparsely peopled regions of highland and desert. Some of these have lately fallen under the sway of Japan and Russia. Their connection with China is tenuous, being effected by the slow and intermittent means of camel caravans.

Comparing in area and in population with India, having a climate more stimulating to effort, possessing both coal and iron, and looking back upon a history of half a dozen long periods of political unity, four of them achieved by local rulers, in contrast to the one ephemeral union of India superposed from outside, modern China has lacked the power or has missed the opportunity to bind itself into a firm unit with steel. It seems likely that real unity will be delayed until an adequate transportation system has been constructed. Quite possibly this will be done, as it has been done in India, by an outside power.

If, in the Americas, Australia, and Asia, the correspondence of ecumene and communication lines is so inseparably interwoven with political unity, it may be asked why Europe, with the densest rail web in the world, has taken no real steps toward unity. The answer is probably to be found in chronology. Western and Central Europe had become crystallized into national states before the railroad era dawned. Roads and waterways there were, each navigable system contributing mightily to the unification of the country which built it. When the railroads came, they first supplemented, then partly supplanted the earlier highways and waterways. Italy and Germany, incompletely unified before the age of rails, used this new mode of transportation to win the campaigns which effected their unification, and expanded their somewhat arbitrary political capitals into economic capitals by making them the hubs of the national railroad systems. For a time the potent pocketbook values of free exchange of goods appeared to be dissolving some of the lesser barriers of nationality as communication ramified and accelerated. The World War measured the weakness of this force when pitted against national feeling. The conclusion of the war left Europe with more states than it had at the outbreak of hostilities.

### GEOPOLITICAL IMMATURITY

A good many states, both small and large, are geopolitically immature. Some have not fully populated their ecumene, some have failed to crisscross it with a close mesh of communication lines (Fig. 2), or have not extended lines into parts of their political area doomed by nature to sparse population. None of the very large countries has attained geopolitical maturity, except the United States. In Europe the

treaties closing the World War dismembered the communication systems of several states, and lopped off border zones of others. In most
cases the ends were left severed or barely articulated, because movement across new boundaries was either stopped or greatly diminished.
In other places bits of different states were pieced together to form political units. After two decades many of the splices show clearly on the
landscape. Many needed links still wait to be forged. Thus it happens
that several states in Central Europe, both small and medium sized,
have not yet remodelled themselves to fit their new areas.

Outside Europe immature states are likely to be in process of growth.
They have not yet filled out to their boundaries. Several of the very
large states already discussed belong to this group. So do many smaller
states of the new continents, Australia, Africa, and the Americas. Except for a few short segments, every national boundary in Latin America lies far from settlements larger than hamlets. Friction between these
countries is nearly always engendered by the discovery of some valuable
resource, generally an extractive commodity, along an ill-defined
boundary. In many cases the ecumene of one or the other claimant
country is so remote as to handicap defense of its claims by show of military force. In many of these states the ecumene makes up a very small
percentage of the total area. In others it is scattered about different
parts of the country, sometimes separated by formidable barriers of
terrain.

All states so hampered by low ratio of ecumene to total area were
able to develop little political strength so long as integration depended
chiefly on waterways and coach roads. Even the railroad and its hand-
maid the telegraph — the modes of communication which have borne
the brunt of political unification during the past century — could offset natural handicaps only locally. The advent of internal combustion
engines and wireless transmission of messages has done much to emancipate these areas from servitudes imposed by nature.

In many deserts, mountains, and steppes, surfaced roads cost less to
build and to maintain than railroads, and the motor car has lent a new
significance to the highway for the first time since the Romans made
the road their chief political emissary. It is too early to measure the
effect of motor roads on the status of nations. Thus far there has been
a strong inclination for states to foster a road pattern essentially parallel to railroad systems already constructed instead of striking out into
country not yet tapped by other efficient transportation. This is especially true in difficult terrain where jungle, marsh, desert, or ruggedness
interpose much the same barriers to road builders as the railroad men

faced a little earlier. Through mountains the valley routes are few and peremptory, and motor roads commonly interlace with railroads, although they can include steeper grades and sharper curves. Across deserts the shortcuts between oases and water holes are almost as definitive for the motor vehicle as for the camel. In rain forests the cuts through the vegetation already made for the rails can be widened at relatively low cost to accommodate a road alongside; and across large swamps the narrows selected for rails and already traversed by causeways similarly offer the least difficult routes for highways. Whatever the reason for parallel construction, the result is to divide the traffic, scarcely heavy enough in most of these handicapped regions to support a single route, and to open up very little new country. Where motor roads have been built to supplement and feed existing railroads, development of new countries has been hastened. Telegraph and telephone wires are likely to accompany the motor roads into new territory.

In the most extreme environments, airplanes and radio have recently sprung into prominence as offering communication less bound to the land than railroad or highway, telegraph or telephone. These new agents of communication can follow direct lines, besides being fast and requiring *pieds à terre* in spots only, rather than in continuous lines. Because flying reduces the time required for the traject to a small fraction of that needed to traverse even the speediest terrestrial routes, states formerly handicapped by territory unsuited to rails or roads now find themselves suddenly knit into closer unity than was deemed possible anywhere on earth, only a few years ago. Nowhere is this more striking than in Peru. Lima, its capital, communicates by rail and road only with its immediate mountain hinterland, and with one or two nearby oases. To reach other oases of the coast has required a sea voyage; to get to most parts of the high plateau an ocean trip is supplemented by a tedious railroad journey; the few who needed to move themselves or their goods between the capital and the upper (Peruvian) Amazon had to choose between adding an arduous trip by horseback and canoe to the sea and rail journey, or going around the continent and up the Amazon River — a journey of 6,000 miles and four weeks. Today any place in Peru equipped with an air field can be reached from Lima in less than ten hours. The oases are being doubly linked to the capital by the construction of motor roads.

It is in precisely the least developed parts of the earth where air communication is most prized. Every Latin American country maintains internal mail, passenger, and express service to its principal sections, besides linking the main centers in international flights. The regular air service which skirts or traverses the whole of Latin America has for the first time placed all these republics in close juxtaposition, a relationship existing in only two cases before the days of flying — Argentina and Uruguay, and Guatemala and El Salvador.

In Africa fewer air routes are regularly flown, although landing fields and supplies are numerous for those who wish to charter planes. In that continent the number of people who can afford to fly is small, and the initiative in organizing regular service must come from the European countries which govern the continent for their own ends. These authorities do not always desire the attenuation of barrier boundaries entailed by air service. Regular flights across the Sahara by way of its Atlantic margin are incidental to the route linking Europe and southern South America. The Cape-to-Cairo route, still only a dream as a railroad, is regularly flown, and it has branches, the longest of which traverses the Sudan, and connects with points on the west coast.

Russia and Canada depend almost exclusively on planes to reach their north country, especially in winter.

The world map of regular air routes (Fig. 2) suggests the important role they play in the business of colonies. Just as land routes have aided in consolidating the adjacent regions of each political entity, whether a home state or a colony, so air routes are knitting together the discrete parts of each colonial empire. But unless the number of travellers enormously increases, the political advantages will be restricted chiefly to such obvious matters as the quick quelling of incipient revolt and the facile movement of officials in the discharge of their regular duties. The intangible power of popular intermingling, which has made the cheap railroad a chief agent of regional reformation, cannot operate in the case of expensive air travel. Perhaps the British Commonwealth of Nations, European in origin but widely scattered, stands to profit more than other empires by this quickened pace of communication. Certainly the daily contact with "home" through the radio diminishes the remoteness of the Dominions from the mother country.

At the same time the barrier boundaries between states, including the colonies of different powers, are losing a part of their barrier quality, due to the ease with which they can be vaulted by a gas-propelled Pegasus. The danger of friction along boundaries is by so much increasing. The countries of Western and Central Europe find themselves painfully small in comparison to the giant leaps of this new horse of the air. Nearly every capital lies within a few minutes of one or more neighbor's frontier. The possibility of hurling bombs and spreading poison gas upon unprotected populations on the far side of any boundary has already become a nightmare in every region where threat of war lurks behind the daily routine.

In peacetime, flying is restricted in order to reduce provocative incidents to a minimum. Along most frontiers civilian planes may cross national boundaries only by way of specified gates. Some of these are as narrow as a mile and a half. An excuse for this is the need to check on all vehicles entering or leaving the country. A further reason is to protect frontier fortifications from being spied upon by potential enemies. In some countries whole districts are forbidden to fliers. These are ammunition dumps and other bases of military or naval activity. In order to minimize international nuisances arising from air transport in a continent of small nations, many countries have subscribed to uniform rules for handling both passengers and freight.

As the telegraph grew up to aid the dispatching of railroad trains, so the radio is indispensable in dispatching air liners. And as the telegraph proved its utility to the general public which lives near rails, so the radio is coming to be the communication link for peoples remote from wires. In so far as knowledge is power, radio communication is a means of coordinating the several parts of a state, and a new weapon in the hands of government. Already the radio is daily used for propaganda by most of the governments of Europe, and very often it is directed to the end of undermining the authority of its rivals, especially among subject peoples or discontented minorities.

The full effect of air travel and radio communication can be gauged only after they have become more fully developed. If the past is any sort of guide to the future, the state will always remain closely identified with whatever means of transportation and communication are current. It is hard to believe that states of small size which have expanded their ecumene to their very confines, will find it easy to function successfully in a world in which the convenient size for a state is half a continent. In the cross-currents of military efficiency, national antipathy, and closer intercourse, all three powerfully intensified by new means of communication, the national state which took shape in the days of dirt tracks for horses and oxen, poled boats on the rivers, and sailing vessels along the coasts, would appear to be an anachronism.

## THE SIZE VERSUS THE FORM OF THE IDEAL STATE

The ideal size of the state varies with the efficacy of communication, the level of material technology, and the ecumene. These are active agents in creating and altering political boundaries.

In contrast, the shape of a state and the salient features of pattern and structure within it appear to fit an unchanging formula.

a. The ideal state should be chunky rather than elongate. This minimizes the amount of transportation and frontier paraphernalia required, and favors military defense.

b. It should have its densest population (ecumene) in the center, diminishing gradually to the borders. By concentrating the market area, this further reduces the mileage covered in transporting people, goods, and messages. It also minimizes friction along the frontier, assuming that the fewest disputes arise where there are the fewest potential disputants.

c. It should have naturally marked barrier boundaries. Such barriers may be permanent ice, deserts, oceans, rugged terrain, infertile or rocky soil, marshy or jungly vegetation; not lakes, gulfs, straits, and streams. A barrier boundary aids defense, runs through sparsely peopled country, is crossed by few lines of transportation.

d. It should be self-contained, with no large surpluses or deficits of any essential commodity.

Obviously no state of the present day fulfills these ideals. The scattering of essential minerals without reference to the other natural conditions conducive to dense population makes self-containment impossible even to the largest states. The rarity of satisfactory barrier boundaries restricts their fortunate possessors to a small number. The unevenness of the distribution of climate, landforms, soil, and surface and ground water results in uneven distribution of populations of any given density. Finally the conformation of the major natural divisions of any continent produces some geographic regions irretrievably elongate, with corresponding elongate ecumene, if not total political area.

However difficult it is to meet the ideal qualifications, large states come closer to achieving them than small states. Yet it must not be lost to sight that in the world today the material conditions of political existence function only in the presence of the emotion of nationality. This feeling, the outgrowth of decades and centuries of communal living, expresses a political pattern of the past almost everywhere. The national emotions of another day, engendered in a world geared to making a living in small units by human labor and a little aid from animals, have been overtaken by material advancement which has redoubled the ideal size of states and placed a premium on natural resources from beyond established national boundaries. To this extent the habitat has been modified by human ingenuity. Yet, be the state large or small, the pattern of its communication conforms in considerable degree to surface conditions.

## CHAPTER THREE

# Political Geography and Localized Resources

SIZE and form constitute the frame within which a state may function. Its power and reach are more precisely commensurate with its ecumene. Regions where nature's provision for human society is ample and accessible are the parts of a country which support the densest population and the most widely ramified communication system. Earth resources, particularly arable land and useful minerals, are strongly localized, so that some areas " have " while others " have not." This distribution is mutable by human ingenuity only within very narrow limits. E.g., tiny patches in desert areas may be irrigated; low-grade coal may be converted into briquettes which burn more readily. A far wider range in the utilization of the earth's resources is afforded by advances in technology. The value of any resource is limited by man's knowledge of how to avail himself of it, i.e., by the current stage of technology. The technology of any place or period primarily refers to the state of the arts, but more broadly it includes also the technique of government, always intimately linked with the utilization of material resources.

The extent to which resources are utilized varies from place to place. In earlier times there was no effective intercourse among the grand divisions of the earth, and each evolved a technology commensurate with local opportunities. Aboriginal peoples of nearly all the low-latitude lowlands and the entire Americas and Australia have been so severely handicapped that they. have remained primitive both in economic and political life. Peoples of the Orient developed great skill in farming and in crafts — to the limit set by hand labor. Their simple rural society has made ineffective attempts to integrate large areas into political unity. The Occident utilized its more accessible resources to create the machine society of today, with its well-organized states, large and small, and its political efficiency. Worldwide trade and colonization have done much to blur the distinctions among the continents which grew up before the ocean became a highway. Nevertheless, the low latitudes, most of the Orient, and the Occident (now including most of the new continents) remain at different technological levels, and their consequent density of population and standard of living are so different as to render comparison between them difficult.

It is unsafe to assume that economic and political centers are tied to fixed regions determined by the distribution of resources. On the contrary, novel utilization of natural resources may shift the ecumene as well as alter the structure of economic and political life. The wide range possible within a single area is sharply illustrated in the part of America which lies north of Mexico. There three well-marked stages of technological control have functioned within the period of record.

The first occupance of the North American continent known to history is that of the American Indians. The most advanced groups lived in the arid southwest, the very region which today is most dependent upon its neighbors. The desert Amerinds practiced irrigation agriculture which yielded little or no surplus staple food, lived in scattered but fixed and compact communities, joined in cooperative control of their water supply, and produced skilled craftsmen who worked in wool, pottery, silver, and semi-precious stones. The tribes of the more humid regions of the continent depended chiefly upon extractive industry — hunting, fishing, and collecting from forest or grassland. Products gathered from nature's store they supplemented by crude plantings of a few crops. Their mode of subsistence required frequent shifting of habitations and demanded much land. Tools and weapons were of stone, although the native copper of the Lake Superior district was known to them. Clothing, shelter, and canoes (their only contrivance for transportation) were extracted from nature. The densest settlement and the most elaborate technology were found in the southeast, where an abundance of rain and mild winters accelerate vegetational growth and minimize the shelter needed. The dry-subtropical (Californian) part of the Pacific coast was inhabited by the most primitive tribes on the continent — folk who subsisted on nuts, roots, reptiles, and insects. Throughout the continent tribal groups knew each other only as enemies, and peaceable trade was limited to short truces for obtaining localized supplies of flint and other material for implements and weapons. The total population of the continent is estimated to have been only about 300,000.

The Europeans who came to the Atlantic seaboard and later to the dry southwest brought with them technologies much alike but differentiated as between the agriculture practiced in Northwest Europe and on Mediterranean shores. They combined extraction of indigenous resources with agriculture based on imported seeds and stock plus the maize, beans, squash, and turkeys of the Amerinds. From the beginning it was hoped to produce surpluses for sale, but except on the coastal plain south of Chesapeake Bay, exports were confined for some time to goods extracted from the forests. At first weapons and implements were imported from Europe, but before long local wood, iron, and lead were being converted by handcrafts of European origin into the simple items required to carry on subsistence farming, and into vehicles and boats adapted from European models to serve in trade and in pioneering. The population was many times as dense as that of the supplanted Amerinds, and the separate seaboard settlements gradually expanded toward each other and finally into the interior basin of the continent. Market towns and small cities grew up to care for increasing commercial intercourse, and household crafts occupied both farm- and towns-folk in hours spared from farming, trade, and housework. The total population at the opening of the 19th century was a little over 5,000,000. The Atlantic seaboard was the prime ecumene, with rapidly growing, somewhat isolated settlements in the eastern half of the Mississippi Basin and a small and distinct settlement on the dry-subtropical Pacific coast. Even in the east the component units of the two nations which covered the area felt themselves to be real entities. Federation did not yet exist in Canada, and in the United States it had slight hold on the individual.

The complex occupance of English-speaking North America today requires no recapitulation. In every aspect of the utilization of local resources it has surpassed the limits dreamed of by the pioneers. American society lives in a world of exchange, both among its constituent regions and with outside areas. Particularly it reaches out to the corners of the earth to obtain the few items, chiefly minerals and low-latitude crops, which are not obtainable within its borders. Centralization of government has been proceeding apace for nearly a century and is accelerating. The total population is about 135,000,000.

The area not excessively peopled by this number is the same as that which furnished a more meager existence for 300,000 Amerinds. Yet its natural resources have considerably diminished through use and misuse. The annual increments of minerals and other commodities from abroad are presumably balanced by outgo of items of North American origin. Only two things have changed. Europeans brought with them domestic animals and seeds of crop plants which greatly enlarged the productivity of the new continent. They also brought with them a technology vastly superior to the best the Amerinds knew. These contributions of plants and animals, knowledge and skill, applied to the virgin resources of North America, worked the transformation from subsistence economy to the commercial and manufactural society of today.

In any stage of technology the force a state can exert and the ramifications of economic life from which its political strength derives, are limited by the available natural resources — available in the primary sense of existing within the state boundaries, and available in the relative sense of being physically accessible and technologically usable. In the present-day world every state possesses such a variety of environmental conditions and resources that several economic pursuits are carried on within its borders. Farmers, miners, fishermen, manufacturers, traders, and professional men are engaged in gaining a living by specific means, and they are at the same time members of the state. In their political capacity they express themselves in a variety of ways, two of which lie always in the background of their acts. They desire political action favorable to their several businesses, including the utilization of natural resources on which their livelihood is based, and they think in terms of the region or district in which they live and work.

The larger and more diverse the state, the more complex the economic and regional interests seeking to find expression in the national government. These varied ambitions become blurred or cancel each other when transformed into political aspirations. To distinguish from such a confusion any clear political translation of natural environment or economic interests is all but impossible. It can be accomplished, if at all, only in careful regional surveys which take into account all the diverse aspects of the local geography. One such is the force of habit which holds each local unit to a traditional loyalty, even when its political adherence bears no relation to its current economic life. In such cases the explanation may be found in the economic geography of the past. The persistence of conservative and liberal districts in the United States unaltered through upheavals in which old parties disappear and new ones rise is an example of habitual political action. In France many districts of incorrigibly monarchic, republican, or radical temper have survived from the *ancien régime*, notwithstanding complete reorganization of administrative districts at the time of the Revolution.

It may be taken for granted that every major mode of economic land occupance ramifies into politics, no matter how well concealed the connections may be. A few of the more clear-cut cases will serve to illustrate the participation of localized resources in government.

## EXTRACTIVE RESOURCES

Of all the natural resources minerals are the most persistently and conspicuously in politics. Primitive peoples are accustomed to agree upon truces to permit enemy tribes to obtain stone, obsidian, or metal needed for tools and weapons, from the few and scattered deposits known. States of all eras have exerted cunning and force to obtain exclusive control of valuable minerals. The particular items wanted vary with advancing technology, either becoming more numerous and being required in ever-larger quantities, or disappearing from the coveted list. Thus all the flints used in guns are now made by two men, but in the past score of years no less than 25 minerals have been added to the commercial group. Some of the most vexatious political issues of the day have literally arisen from the ground, when new values have been unearthed in unclaimed territory or on political borders. The issue of Lorraine iron ore as between France and Germany is a case in point. The discovery of petroleum on the Texas-Oklahoma border precipitated legal settlement of a boundary question until then ignored.

The perennial politics of minerals lies in their character as the items chiefly used in making tools and weapons. Therefore the state that controls the items currently in vogue for those purposes can forge ahead fastest in material civilization and is in a superior position for making war.

It is impossible to increase the sum total of mineral resources, because ores and rocks are being concentrated in the earth's crust so slowly that the life of the human race is ephemeral by comparison. Fixed limits to supply incite bitter political rivalry for the known deposits, and even for territory where deposits are believed to exist. As the rate of consumption increases, the rivalry is intensified. The past quarter century has brought to the surface a full half of all minerals ever mined. At the same time the possibility of making new finds of major importance diminishes. The geologic structure of the earth has been pretty well canvassed, to the end that the general areas which can conceivably yield metals, coal and petroleum, and valuable earths are mapped out. Increasing knowledge tends to reduce the estimates as to available reserves rather than to increase them.

The unique role of minerals in human society is accentuated by the fact that no other major class of resources is so sharply localized. This is obvious in the case of rarities like potash, produced in only two districts, one in Germany, the other in France; nickel, almost all of which

075658

comes from one district in eastern Ontario, Canada; tin, derived principally from the Malay Peninsula and the high Andes of Southern Bolivia, with a little from the Nigerian Plateau and a few other spots. It is almost equally true of many common minerals, such as copper and iron, which are widely scattered over the earth, but which are produced only in the few districts where there are geologic concentrations of easily smelted ore, or where the combination of several minerals permits profitable production of the aggregate, although extraction of only one would not pay. Because of the large scale of manufacture and the requirement that mines yield large increments, many small mineral deposits are unused although well known. They may even have been worked in days of smaller-scale industry. In countries which have adopted a policy of self-sufficiency at all costs, some small deposits are being used, at unit costs above the world price level established by the large-scale and efficient producers.

Another peculiarity of the geography of minerals is the lack of correspondence between their distribution and the distribution of population. This calls attention to the fact that the ecumene is typically found where the combination of climate, landforms, soil, and waters stimulates agriculture and trade. In other words, people live where the present-day natural environment is favorable to a well-founded livelihood. Nearly all mineral deposits are the product of earth conditions long since superseded, and in most cases the conditions producing valuable minerals are not the same as those ideal for human occupance of the land. Where minerals of the required sorts happen to lie accessible within or close to the ecumene, they make possible an advanced technology. Great Britain was able to take the lead in the Industrial Revolution because its small waterpower sites, easily harnessed to run machines, its coal for steam engines, and iron ore and limestone needed for steel making, all lay within the ecumene (Fig. 3). Later on, other countries which had slightly less favorable combinations of natural conditions imitated the English prototype. Many countries have been unable to create large-scale manufacturing, in spite of strenuous efforts of their governments. Those which have failed most signally lack the favorable combination of minerals within the ecumene. For example, Brazil is superlatively endowed with iron ore, but has been unable to utilize it or even export it because it lies well inland on rugged terrain, and unprofitably remote from coal or any other means of smelting.

One of the principal objectives in exploration and colonization has nearly always been the discovery of useful minerals. Prospectors have been the vanguard in the settlement of many a region. In numerous

FIG. 3. Population and critical natural resources in Great Britain at the outset of the Industrial Revolution.

Upland masses are depicted pictorially. Waterpower is most abundant on the margins of the more rugged highlands.

cases, miners' finds have led a state to lay claim to territory beyond its borders, even beyond the seas. Many valuable mineral deposits lie outside the ecumene, but not too far away to warrant mining them. To transport them to markets requires extensions of existing transportation systems, and many lines, especially railroads, constructed for this purpose can also be put to the service of general traffic. The state is thereby integrated and, where the conditions for trade or agriculture are not too adverse, permanent settlements grow up along the routes. Denver, Colorado, is an outfitting point for mines which has become a considerable metropolis and a State capital. Minerals have pulled railroads into rain forests, up mountain heights, and across deserts and Arctic wastes. Once built they serve the government by linking remote regions to the ecumene.

The apportionment of minerals by states bears less relation to population than does that of any other natural resource. All the minerals required in great quantity are many fold more abundant in the basin of the North Atlantic Ocean than in any other equal area. It is not a coincidence that the first four of the Great Powers (France, Germany, Great Britain, the United States) face that basin, and that both Italy and Russia have made or are making violent efforts to obtain unhampered access to it. The one remaining Great Power (Japan) controls the only considerable development of varied minerals in a populous region outside the North Atlantic Basin.

In the recurrent struggles for political supremacy among the more powerful states, the demand for an equal share in the world's minerals pushes increasingly to the foreground. Such a demand cannot be met in the middle latitudes without disrupting empires and creating new zones of friction. Even if an equitable redistribution of minerals were politically feasible, it would be physically impossible, because some deposits are unique and others are not divisible among the number of eager contestants. None of the Great Powers of the moment is self-sufficient in all vital minerals, or even in all major ones. The United States comes out best. Nevertheless it lacks chromite and manganese among the commodities used in large quantity, and nickel, tin, and three or four other minerals used in small amounts. The British Empire is short on petroleum and copper. The other powers are wanting in larger numbers of major items. Some of the lesser minerals such a pyrites, sulphur, and the steel alloys, are critical in the manufacturing industry on which a nation must rely for prosperity in peace and for success in war. The concept of autarchy becomes from the standpoint of minerals a chimera. That does not make it any the less a political philosophy seriously threatening the continued peace of the nations, because a people imbued with the false hope that it can become self-sufficient in material resources is likely to support its government in initiating war.

All extractive industries are similar in character to mining, but none of them is so bound up with the ambitions of government. Yet wherever nature's bounty can be reaped without replacement, man is prone to seize upon it, especially if it lies in an unclaimed area. This is particularly true of seafishing. Long before the freedom of the seas had been established as beginning three miles from land, men living on many-harbored coasts were accustomed to fish off their own shores. Before Columbus discovered America, Bretons and Basques appear to have fished along all the shores and on all the banks of the North Atlantic, as far west as the Grand Bank of Newfoundland. With the establishment of the three-mile limit, inshore waters became territorial preserves. Open-sea fishing is impossible without a land base, either for marketing a fresh catch, or for drying, salting, and other handling. This has led to numerous international agreements governing fishing on the high seas. Some of the most notable regulate the use of the Atlantic North American waters. French ownership of two islands off the coast of Newfoundland is a vestige of the time when France was shorn of its continental possessions but could not be deprived of the right of its nationals to fish on the banks. To extinguish similar rights on the coast of Newfoundland itself, Great Britain sacrificed the entire hinterland of the easiest line of ingress to West Africa. The history of the United States and Maritime Canada is checkered with international disputes and settlements concerning fishing.

The conflict between fishermen inshore and fishermen on the high sea reaches a climax in the case of marine forms which spend their life in open waters but come inshore to spawn or breed. On the American coast of the North Pacific salmon and seals are the two chief marine resources, and both have this habit. To preserve the salmon industry governments have made it illegal to take the fish after they reach a line marked by stakes, off each river mouth. The great temptation to poach in the safety zone, teeming during the annual run of the fish, incites to international disputes when the poachers are citizens of a foreign state. Pursuit of fish of these waters within the three-mile limit by Japanese fishermen is a current cause of diplomatic interchange between the governments concerned.

The one important breeding ground of that species of seal which produces the fur most prized, is the Pribilof group of islands in the Bering Sea. It is easy to kill the animals on the high sea as they make their way toward these islands. In response to intense demand for the fur the habit of killing the young with the mother had well-nigh exterminated the species when the interested governments, the United States, Great Britain, Japan, and Russia, made a treaty whereby each agreed to prohibit their nationals from taking seals on the high seas, and to respect a patrol maintained by the United States as owner of the islands. Similar agreements among interested nations restrict the killing of seals in both the North and South Atlantic. One of the chief reasons for claiming sovereignty over parts of the Antarctic continent is to lay a foundation for regulating sealing and whaling in those waters.

## Agricultural Land Occupance

Apart from extractive industries, clear-cut examples of the political geography of land occupance are few, because other resources are less localized than those which are subject to extraction. Of husbandry, two types are sufficiently uniform and isolated to serve as samples — commercial plantation crop tillage and commercial grain farming (Fig. 4). They illustrate limitations of governmental control more clearly than do extractive industries.

Every plantation region is in politics from its inception. A plantation begins as a device of middle-latitude business men to obtain from the low latitudes, crop products which cannot be grown at home. Their option on the necessary land involves either seizure in the name of their home government or dickering with the local (foreign) government. As the business evolves, much capital becomes fixed in the form of land, crop plantings, buildings, and machinery, and a good many outsiders come in to carry on the business. Sooner or later this arrangement generates friction: between indigenes and interlopers, both administrators and laborers; between planting interests and the interests of distant, middle-latitude consumers. Social and economic friction is promptly transferred to the governments represented, because a prime function of government is to settle quarrels.

Every crop which occupies only a small part of the acreage environmentally suited to its growth, presses toward overproduction under any political system. In an uncontrolled world market, relative costs and prices rectify a disturbed balance between supply and demand at the expense of the marginal growers. This action is hampered and delayed in the case of many plantation-grown crops by tariffs, drawbacks, and subsidies which confine movements to narrow, charted channels between which there are no spillways for regularizing the flow. Only

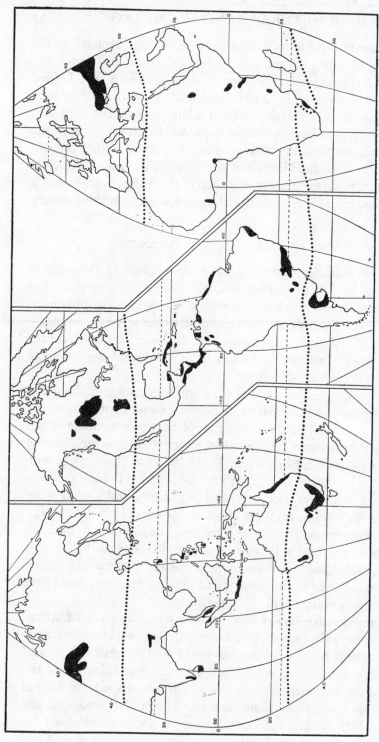

FIG. 4. Regions of plantation type agriculture (between the dash lines) and of commercial wheat farming (north and south of the dash lines) are shown in solid black.

Sugar cane is grown in many plantation areas, and is dominant in the West Indies, Coastal Brazil, the Philippines, and Java. Rubber is confined to the Middle East — Ceylon, the Malay Peninsula, and Sumatra.

The base used is modified from Robert B. Hall's outline map, published by John Wiley & Sons, Inc.

when overproduction has become a long-pent flood can these channels be overflowed; then ensues an inundation of the world markets which destroys reasonable profits to all growers.

Not all plantation areas and not all plantation crops exemplify clearly their political geography. Rubber and sugar perhaps best represent the interplay between crop and politics. In addition, rubber production began as an extractive industry, and so illustrates the continuity of politics in the changeover from extraction to plantation.

## RUBBER

The substance which had already been known in Europe and North America for more than sixty years as an eraser (rubber), entered upon its commercial career in 1823. In that year a vessel bringing West Indian sugar to the rum distilleries of Boston imported waterproof shoes of rubber, crudely made by Amerinds. In England in the same year MacIntosh made waterproof garments by inserting a layer of rubber between two pieces of woolen cloth. For half a century technological progress and markets advanced slowly and in jumps (Table II). Raw material was extracted from many different plants of all the low-latitude continents, but one of them, hevea, a tall tree of the rain forest of the Amazon Basin ultimately became the dominant contributor to the small market. Rubber gathering was the first industry to change northern Brazil from an unexplored wilderness to a source of profit. Rubber, as its only source of wealth, supported the local governments by paying export taxes. These increased in pace with rising demand, and fluctuated, ordinarily between 20 and 25 percent ad valorem, but in some years amounting to a third of the market value of the crop. To protect the quasi-monopoly it was legally forbidden to export trees and seeds of the hevea, by all odds the most productive source of rubber known.

By the 1870s rubber was used in many forms and had become a commodity of importance in world markets. Its price remained high. In 1876, instigated by the government of British India, a British subject succeeded in smuggling hevea seeds out of Brazil, and by the end of that year young trees were growing in Ceylon. Thus Brazilian rubber producers, greedy to charge all the traffic would bear and backed by their government, drove the industry afield to other regions where hevea could be grown as a plantation crop.

For a quarter century little was done to utilize the Ceylonese plantings, while the advent of the pneumatic tire and bicycle stimulated a steady increase in the output of the Amazon and caused a small war.

TABLE II. A CRITICAL CHRONOLOGY OF THE RUBBER INDUSTRY

| | |
|---|---|
| 1770. | Priestley discovered rubber as an eraser. |
| 1823. | Amerind-made rubber shoes brought to Boston by sugar (rum) vessel. Mackintosh waterproofed cloth by inserting a layer of rubber between two layers of woolen. |
| 1827. | Forty tons shipped from Pará. |
| 1839. | Goodyear successful in vulcanizing — still elastic, but not tacky. |
| 1846. | Rubber tires (hard) being made in England. Pneumatic tires patented in England, France, and U. S. in 1845 but not made. |
| 1860. | Plantation of ficus elastica in Java. |
| 1876. | Hevea seeds taken to Kew Gardens. |
| 1876. | First plantation of hevea seeds in Ceylon. |
| 1870s. | Electrical industry began to grow. Rubber used for insulation. |
| 1888. | First manufacture of pneumatic tires. Britain allowed new patent; France and United States did not. |
| 1889. | Amazonas an autonomous State. |
| 1898. | Pneumatic tires first made for automobiles. |
| 1900. | First plantation rubber shipped from the Middle East. |
| 1903. | Acré brought under Brazilian flag. |
| 1905–06. | Brazilians attempted to corner the rubber market. |
| 1906. | Marks and Oenslager learned to use accelerators — to make low-grade rubber nearly as good as Pará fine, and to decrease time required for vulcanization. |
| 1909–10. | Brazilians again caused rubber market to soar by speculative means. |
| 1909. | Pará government enacted laws to favor concessionaires by following means: reduction of export duties and transportation charges; encouragement of plantations by granting 99-year leases; protection of fruitful trees. |
| 1911. | Amazonas government enacted similar laws. |
| 1912. | Brazilian federal government followed suit with laws to favor planting and a plan to build railroads. Wild rubber reached maximum output. |
| 1914. | Exports of plantation rubber exceeded exports of wild rubber. |
| 1914–18. | War held back production, due to lack of shipping and government regulation to prevent Central Powers from getting a supply. |
| 1920. | Voluntary restriction affecting 70% of the plantations. |
| 1920. | Cord tire introduced generally; uses as much rubber as fabric tire, but lasts much longer. |
| 1922. | Stevenson plan for restriction in British territory passed by Parliament. |
| 1924. | Use of reclaimed rubber put on solid foundation. |
| 1924. | Balloon tire introduced. Uses 30% more rubber than cord tire. |
| 1928. | Stevenson law abrogated. |
| 1929. | World economic depression. |
| 1934. | Cartel established among 98% of all rubber producers. |

Brazil controlled without question the original Pará district near the mouth of the Amazon. The other richly endowed region lay on the upper waters of the river, along a frontier which had never been defined, so remote and valueless had it been and of so little interest to possible national owners. With rubber prices rising, Brazil, Bolivia, and Peru contested hotly for the territory on their mutual borders. After clashes, especially between Brazil and Bolivia, which led the local rubber gatherers to set up the independent State of Acré, Brazil bought out Bolivian claims in 1903, and after two more years restored order by military force (Ch. 14 and Fig. 68).

While this " war " was raging, the value of the territory was sharply declining through loss of its market, although nobody realized it at the time. In 1898 pneumatic tires were first used for automobiles — the beginning of a demand which soon exceeded all others combined. In 1900 the first rubber from planted hevea reached the Occident from the Middle East.[1] So little did Brazilian producers sense their peril that during the first decade of the new century they attempted two corners of the rubber market, more than doubling the price on the first occasion, and more than quadrupling it on the second. The State governments reaped their share of the profit in the shape of export taxes.

About the time of the second of these booms the government of the State of Pará enacted laws to prevent destruction of wild trees by over-tapping and to encourage plantations. Concessions for 99 years were to be let, and to planters export duties and transportation charges were to be reduced. In 1911 the other principal rubber producing State, Amazonas, followed suit, and in 1912 the Brazilian Federal Government passed an act to favor planting and looking toward building railroads in the rubber region. It is noteworthy that these laws emphasized plantations, an indication that Brazil was at last conscious of the need to reduce costs of production and to meet competition from the descendants of those smuggled hevea seeds of 1876. It seems unlikely that such efforts as these would have achieved their intention at any time. The Indians of the Amazon country have never been numerous enough to furnish the necessary labor, nor have they or any other Brazilian laborers the skill which would enable them to compete with laborers of the Middle East in plantation production. It is noteworthy that none of these laws provides for reduction of the export tax, or prevention of speculative price raising, the only two legal restrictions which would give plantations in the Middle East serious competition.

In 1912 the production of wild rubber reached its maximum and in 1914 the path of its descent was crossed by the rising exports of the plantation product. Today Brazil produces nearly all the wild rubber on the market, with an output averaging a little less than half the peak production. This is but 2 percent of the world's supply, so rapidly has the plantation product shot up. That Brazil does not drop out altogether seems to be due to the high quality of " Pará fine " rubber and to the presence of experienced gatherers who have no better means of earning a meager living. The production is unresponsive to market fluc-

[1] Since the commencement of automobile manufacture, so much of the world's rubber has been consumed by the United States, that New York prices are taken as setting values. By Middle East is meant the region which includes India and Ceylon, the Indo-China peninsula, and the Netherlands Indies.

tuations, because the productive trees are far inland, and so much time is required to start additional tapping that only a long-term rise in the price can accomplish it.

The rapid increase in plantation-grown rubber which began to flood the market in 1914 was the result of feverish planting when prices were forced up by the first (1906) Brazilian corner. The lag represents the seven years required for the young trees to come to the age for tapping. A further burst in output marked fruition of the next wave of planting — inspired by the second corner (1910). Thereafter began a period of experimental regulation in the plantation districts that illustrates most of the difficulties suffered by commercial plantation crop tillage.

After the price slump that ended the second corner, the price decreased only slightly for almost a decade, in spite of a phenomenal increase in supplies. The equally phenomenal increase in consumption in the United States almost kept pace with output, in spite of shrinkage in European consumption (by the Central Powers and Russia) during the World War. Toward the end of the war, lack of shipping caused consuming governments to reduce importations and to fix the price. These regulations were effective, because all the important consumers were politically allied and had legal machinery for cooperating. With the close of the war this machinery became inoperative. The decline in exports in 1918 due to control, was offset in 1919, when nearly twice as much rubber was shipped as in the preceding year.

The peace ended the restriction on imports. As the reign of normal supply and demand reinstated its sway, prices fell below cost of production, in the face of reduced purchases and flooding the market with accumulated supplies. Production had outstripped consumption with dramatic suddenness. In an effort to avert ruin, planters reduced costs somewhat, but they could not discharge labor quickly, since it is brought in from the Madras coast or from Java under three-year indenture. Most of their overhead charges also inexorably continued.

Voluntary restriction of output, already tried by some planters when stock on hand was accumulating during the war, was then assented to by planters who controlled 70 percent of the acreage in bearing. The agreed 25 percent reduction is supposed to have amounted in fact to only 10 percent, and after one season's trial most Dutch and Ceylonese planters, and many in British Malaya, were unwilling to continue, because they found that native and Chinese growers maintained and even increased their output. These small growers, stimulated by war prices, had entered the field in accountable measure (in 1920, 3 percent of the world output in the Netherlands Indies alone). This they were able to do because of the abundant suitable land to be had for nothing or for a nominal payment.

Before the day of rubber, much of the land on Sumatra, Borneo, and the Malay Peninsula, was lightly peopled by migrant farmers who shifted their fields as the soil became exhausted. To plant a few hevea trees, along with food crops customarily grown or in abandoned clearings, promised to provide a little cash at the cost of nothing but a little work. In a few years the new source of rubber produced a threatening percentage of the world supply. Here, as is characteristic in the humid low latitudes, demands of an occidental market gave rise to two novel and competing modes of farming — plantations and plantings by indigenes. The small producers, numerous and widely scattered through the forest, cannot be organized to restrict tapping. Quite the contrary, in an effort to keep their cash income at its wonted level as prices fall, they tap more often and begin on trees only five or even three years old, instead of the seven allowed by large planters. Voluntary restriction had the effect of transferring an increasing percentage of the world's rubber supply from commercial plantations to native plantings.

Pleas for political regulation of rubber growing, first addressed to the British colonial government before the trial of voluntary restriction, redoubled after that attempt failed. In 1922 the British government set up legal restriction. The output of 1920 was taken as a standard and growers were compelled to restrict their export to a fixed percentage of the base, to be determined in advance with each season. The Dutch colonies refused to participate, asserting that they could not police the widely scattered small holdings and the long indented coasts of their islands. Their output, more than a quarter of the world total, added to the small amount reaching the market from wild-rubber gatherers, left almost exactly two-thirds of the world supply theoretically under restriction.

By improving stock and other scientific methods, Dutch planters had learned to reduce costs of production and so suffered less than the British from the depressed prices. Once restriction was in force British official exports fell off. In response the world price doubled, jumping from 14 to 35 cents. Exports from the Dutch islands promptly rose and the price sagged again. Some of this increase was the inevitable harvest of plantings made during the war, when the neutral Dutch could pay more attention to rubber plantations than could nationals of a British Empire absorbed in war. A share of it came from native small growers in the Dutch islands, who doubled their output between 1920 and

1926. Harassed British planters charged that these native growers were overtapping their trees, but continued production indicates that they did not damage their orchards. Instead, they ingeniously plant the trees close together so that shade will keep the weeds down; then as the trees grow, the orchard is thinned by tapping weaklings to death.

A part of the increased supply of rubber came from British territory in spite of restriction. During the first six months after the law went into effect, villages sprang up on the Dutch Sumatra coast where no villages had ever been. Independent Siam's increase in exports was unmatched by corresponding expansion of production. British planters found that their trees had been clandestinely tapped. It is charged that some connived at this circumvention of the law. A coastguard fleet was unable to stop smuggling along these coasts, pocked with snug smugglers' havens in forest-fringed lagoons and bays.

In the face of restriction total world output continued to rise. Quite clearly control of two-thirds of the area in a crop is not enough to insure monopoly, if the crop is confined to only a small percentage of the available acreage. The attempt was entirely successful in only one respect — it engendered bad feeling among the three principal national groups concerned. British planters felt that the Dutch had let them down, Dutch planters were quietly enjoying an expanding output, and American manufacturers let their stocks of crude rubber fall very low. One of them, Firestone, vociferously combatted restriction and sought a place under American control where he could start his own plantations.

Then came the balloon tire, requiring 30 percent more rubber than ordinary cords. The sudden demand upon depleted stocks forced the New York prices from less than 19 cents a pound in July, 1924, to $1.23 a year later. British planters were legally permitted to export all they could produce, and attributed their sudden prosperity to the legal restriction. The price level legally allowed as the minimum was raised from 30 to 42 cents. American manufacturers who had been apathetic to the slight price rise of the first years, became bitter. Firestone began planting rubber in Liberia and Ford in the Amazon Basin, both regions being environmentally suited to the hevea and exempt from British political domination. The methods of reclaiming used rubber were improved. From less than a fifth of the total consumed by American rubber factories at the beginning of restriction, reclaimed rubber rose to more than half the total in 1928. British political manipulation thus acted as a protector of an infant industry — but under the Stars and Stripes. A United States Congressional investigation was undertaken. Recriminations were published on both sides of the Atlantic.

Meanwhile the Dutch continued to increase their output. Exports from Dutch territory in 1926 were double the figure of 1922, and threatened to overtake British output, which had again receded with falling prices. At the beginning of 1928, the price, after remaining at about 40 cents for two years, had dropped to less than 20 cents. Thereupon the restrictions upon British output were withdrawn, and the attempt to defeat natural environment with law was acknowledged a failure.

Planting new trees had not been forbidden by the restrictive law, and heavy additions during the boom of 1924 showed results in increased yields of the early 1930s. This occurred in the teeth of a world-wide economic depression and prices again dropped. Once more agitation to limit production took effect. In 1934 a cartel of producers was formed for the purpose of setting a limit to planting and to fix quarterly quotas on the amount of rubber permitted to reach the market. This group is said to represent 98 percent of the world's rubber producers, and must therefore include most of the small growers of Malaya.

With the apparent recession of the depression in 1937, the price of rubber topped 25 cents and the quota was raised to 90 percent of the established base. Then came a second drop in business, particularly in the United States, and the price fell to 14 cents, necessitating reduction in the marketable quota. To quiet resentment among planters it has been proposed to increase the number of trees which may be planted. This obviously is a short-sighted policy.

From the vicissitudes of the rubber industry, it seems clear that a crop which nature is capable of supplying in many times the quantity demanded by the world market is chronically bidding for regulation. Voluntary restriction by the growers themselves contains less dynamite than government control. Neither appears to be effective for any long period.

## SUGAR

Sugar cane antedates the plantation crop system by centuries. So ancient was its cultivation in South Asia from slips, that it lost its power to propagate by seeds. It was one of the garden crops grown by Moors in irrigated patches all about the Mediterranean Sea. From these spots it was driven, along with the Moors, by the less sophisticated societies of Central Asia and Northern Europe. In the Occident it survived only in the islands off West Africa (including the Azores). There during the 15th century, Portuguese entrepreneurs succeeded in growing it with the help of slave labor, a circumstance which justifies the claim that it is the earliest of plantation crops.

It came into its own, however, only with the introduction of slave labor from Africa to the relatively healthful, alternately wet and dry, low latitudes of the Americas. Up to this time the output had been measured in hundredweights and sold for medicine or as a luxury to the wealthy. A little before 1600 the Portuguese had been able to launch sugar planting on the coast of Pernambuco, Brazil, combining their knowledge of the business acquired in the Atlantic islands, slaves from the African mainland, and favorable natural environment on that part of the South American coast which had been adjudged to Portugal a century earlier through ignorance of New World geography (Ch. 13).

Of land suitable for cane growing there was superabundance, even when sugar ceased to be a luxury and became a customary food in the middle latitudes. Yet for a century and a half after the business began to flourish the colonial nations of Western Europe fought almost continually for the few producing districts which were exceptionally favored by nature for exploitation from a base overseas. The first struggle was precipitated by the Dutch, who seized Pernambuco along with whatever else Portuguese they could lay hands on. After a quarter century, they were expelled from the Brazilian coast, and the main theater of sugar production shifted to the Antilles, where sugar cane had already been successfully grown. There the original Spanish claimants and Dutch, French, English, and Danes struggled with each other for possession of the sugar islands. Vestiges of the numerous changes of title among the contestants exist in the complicated political map of today, and in the speech of the colored inhabitants, who may speak the language of their rulers, but just as likely some other — English in Dutch or Danish islands and French in British islands, with a strong salting of Spanish words in all.

The Caribbean islands shared the advantage of accessibility to ships trading into the Spanish Main, since the defeat of the Armada no longer exclusively Spanish. At the outset the Lesser Antilles were even more in demand than the Greater. They could produce all the sugar Europe could then consume. They were notably fertile, with soils formed either from coral limestone or from lavas extruded from volcanoes. Their very smallness was a triple advantage. They were relatively free from diseases rife in the continental rain forests, and planters who lived on the sultry west coasts could easily get relief by visiting places swept by the invigorating, easterly trade winds. Almost every plantation could have its own little port, to serve merchant shipping and also war vessels in case of need to intimidate the servile population. During the 18th century the Greater Antilles rose to preeminence,

Haiti taking the lead until its seizure by the slaves, when it was superseded by Jamaica. The governorship of Jamaica was the most prized
gift within the power of the British Colonial Office, even while Great
Britain still controlled the North American seaboard. Cuba, the largest
island of all and today the world's leading sugar producer, did not come
into its own until the 20th century. Some notion of national participation in sugar production at this period is given by the following table.

TABLE III. SUGAR EXPORTS UNDER EUROPEAN FLAGS, LATE 18TH
CENTURY *

|  | Metric Tons |
|---|---|
| French Colonies (1788) . . . . . . . . . . | 93,045 |
| English Colonies (1781–1785) yearly average . . | 78,029 |
| Danish Colonies (1768) . . . . . . . . . . . | 20,550 |
| Spanish Cuba (1790) . . . . . . . . . . . . | 13,993 |
| Portuguese Brazil (1796) . . . . . . . . . | 34,276 |
| Dutch Colonies (1785) . . . . . . . . . . . | 8,892 |
| Total . . . . . . . . . . . . . . . . . . | 248,785 |

* Reese, J. J.: De Suikerhandel van Amsterdam (Haarlem, 1908), p. 225.

Besides suffering from wars, sugar planting was restricted by laws calculated to make the business of the colonies profitable to the mother
countries. The heavy duties on sugar imported from British Antilles
to British mainland North American colonies interrupted free movement of goods to the nearest market, and played a part in bringing on
the American Revolution. Increasing demand in Europe operated
along with wars and legal restrictions to keep prices high, and the industry gave evidences of expanding to new areas, notably the Indian
Ocean islands Mauritius and Réunion, much like the Antilles in size
and climate. In Central European countries without colonies experiments with substitute sources of sugar were undertaken. The 19th century saw the cumulation of these efforts in large-scale extraction from
beets, and a succession of politically induced ups and downs in the
sugar industry unparalleled among major crops.

The struggle between Great Britain and Napoleon stopped legal importations and effectively checked smuggling into the considerable
fraction of Europe dominated by France. The exclusion of cane sugar,
bulky for its value, was pretty complete, and caused intense dissatisfaction. A few years earlier experiments on sugar production from local
plants had been begun in the Elbe and Oder valleys. By fostering this
work Napoleon launched the industry in France, and his embargoes on

imports gave it great impetus in Germany, the land of its origin. After the restoration of normal trade, these infant industries were kept alive by high tariffs. In France, which had sugar-producing colonies, the tariff was withdrawn after three decades, but by that time world production of cane sugar had fallen off, due to the abolition of slavery in British sugar islands a decade earlier. This tided the French beet sugar business over until cane sugar once more became a threatening competitor. Then protection was again accorded to beet sugar.

The abolition of slavery dealt sugarcane planting a heavy blow, because the planters had to readjust to a wage scale, and many of the freed Negroes refused, for some years, to work in the cane fields. Abolition, which spread over half a century,[1] kept the American cane industry in upheaval. To replace the slaves Chinese and British Indian coolies were imported into some regions, but without marked success. After abolition, Britain levied an import duty on sugar from places where slavery was still in force. It is perhaps significant that this duty was revoked in the year slavery came to an end in the French possessions.

While the planting of sugar cane was languishing, sugar beets were being grown increasingly in continental northern Europe. German states led by Prussia, having no colonies, fenced out cane sugar by replacing revenue-producing duties with protective tariffs. The loss of revenue was made up by an excise tax on the amount of sugar turned out by home mills. Thanks to improved manufacturing processes and rapidly rising sugar content in the beets by plant-breeding, the manufacturers came to have a surplus on which they paid no tax. Similar systems were in operation in Austria-Hungary, Russia, and France. During the period when cane sugar production was low, consumption continued to increase rapidly in its two chief markets, the United States and the United Kingdom. Exports of beet sugar expanded to satisfy the need. Between 1875 and 1885 Germany increased exports from 22 percent of its total production to 60 percent. By this time, the Antilles (except Cuba, a minor producer) were reconstructing their business on a basis of hired labor and large central factories with efficient machinery. Java increased production and reestablished propagation of cane plants from seed; from this experimentation came many new and valuable types of cane, resistant to disease and high in sugar content.

---

[1] The dates of abolition in the principal cane producing areas are as follows:

| | | | |
|---|---|---|---|
| British Possessions | ..1834 | Puerto Rico | .......1873 |
| French Possessions | .1848 | Danish Possessions | .1876 |
| Dutch Possessions | ..1863 | Cuba | ............1880 |
| Louisiana | .........1863 | Brazil | ...........1888 |

In 1884–85 the politically induced overexpansion of beet growing caused prices to fall. In the following year the British government, in the interests of its sugar producing colonies, including British India, convened a meeting of the beet-sugar producing countries to consider abrogation of the bounties, drawbacks on excises, and other laws which encouraged dumping beet sugar on the British market. Nothing came of it. The producing countries were unwilling to sacrifice the business which these laws protected, although they kept the price high at home. For example, Russia protected its home production of beet sugar by tariff and dumped the surplus on to the world market at a much lower rate than the home consumer paid. During the 1890s Central European producers began doing the same thing by means of agreements (cartels). Sugar became cheaper than ever for the British manufacturers of jams, chocolate, and biscuits.

Curiously enough, while beet-sugar output was increasing under the stimulus of bounties and drawbacks, cane-sugar production likewise advanced. The United States, to protect its home producers of both beet and cane, levied an extra duty on all bounty sugar equivalent to the bounty it received. At the same time it put sugar on the free list, with a bounty of two cents a pound to protect the domestic industry. The Hawaiian Islands, for fifteen years favored by a reciprocity treaty, had been increasing cane-sugar production with American capital. The new law threatened the industry. Agitation resulted in a revolt of American settlers against the native régime, who set up the Republic of Hawaii and petitioned to be annexed to the United States. This event was delayed until 1898, when the imperialistic elements in the United States were in control of the government. In the same year war broke out between Spain and the United States over the sugar island, Cuba.

The role of sugar in the relations between the United States and Cuba has been masterful. Ever since the independent establishment of the United States, men have been expecting Cuba to gravitate into the political orbit of the adjacent mainland. The anticipated event was postponed until American interests in Cuban sugar production had laid the foundation by creating a strong economic structure of American investments in Cuba. American apathy toward the Cuban insurrection of the 1870s contrasts sharply with American armed intervention in the insurrection of the 1890s. The Spanish-American War was in fact only the latest of a long series of international wars precipitated over West Indian sugar. When the peace established Cuba as a republic instead of a colony, many Americans felt that their country had been cheated.

By treaty in 1903 the two nations agreed to reciprocity in the exchange of certain commodities, sugar among them. This insured Cuban preference in the large and expanding American market by allowing a 20 percent reduction in the duty. It also encouraged investment of American capital in Cuba and insured its safety by a clause in the same treaty granting to the United States the right to intervene in Cuban political crises. This right was invoked repeatedly during the thirty years before it was abrogated in 1934. Therein lies proof of the reality of Cuban dependence on the United States. At first military forces were sent in, later individual Americans were able to cope with emergencies. Regardless of the political status, sugar keeps the two countries locked in an economic embrace which neither can break without wrecking the economic structure of the sugar island.

An unforeseen outcome of the war over Cuba was annexation by the United States of Puerto Rico and the Philippines, both suited to cane growing. Puerto Rican sugar has entered the United States free of duty since 1901. Philippine sugar was at first allowed a 25 percent reduction on the duty, a fixed quantity was allowed free entry in 1909, and all restrictions were removed in 1913.

In 1895 Japan annexed Formosa and thereafter discriminated against other sugar by means of a tariff. Queensland and Natal had protection in their respective Australian and South African markets. In 1899 British India placed a tariff on bounty sugar similar to that operative in the United States, and for the same reason.

As a result of these protective laws in countries outside Europe, the beet overproducers were finding themselves in an intolerable position. In 1901 Belgium called another conference on sugar, of all the European producers, and the consumers Great Britain and Sweden. Britain, now desirous of obtaining the support of all its colonies for waging the Boer War, threatened to follow the precedent of the United States and British India unless the bounty was reduced enough to kill cartels. A five-year agreement was then signed by all important European producers except Russia to abolish bounties and to fix a maximum difference between tariffs and excises  Bounty sugar was to be taxed by signatory importers to the amount of the bounty. With modifications this agreement was continued until the World War broke rudely upon all international agreements. During this interval Germany, France, and Belgium reduced the excise, whereupon consumption rose to make the income to the state as high as before. With the incentive to export gone, beet sugar decreased in the world market in favor of cane, which costs less to produce, political manipulation aside.

The World War turned the momentarily stable situation topsy-turvy. With few exceptions the sugar beet areas ceased to contribute to the world supply. The Central Powers continued to produce for themselves, although as time passed scarcity of labor made production increasingly difficult. Russia's output was unavailable outside the national boundaries. The Belgian, and most of the French beet fields lay in the territory seized by the German armies or in the western theater of the war. Upon the cane regions devolved the job of supplying Western Europe as well as the new demands of the fighting forces. Java, far away, could contribute less and less as shipping declined and had to be kept in the Atlantic trade. In the later war years Javanese stocks accumulated, due to shortage of shipping. The Antilles once more came to the fore, especially Cuba. There the industry was in the hands of capital from the United States, and large-scale machine methods were in vogue. Much virgin land had never been cleared of bush, because Cuba was the least developed of the Antilles before it became independent at the beginning of the century. Throughout the war forest land was feverishly cleared, and plantings of every other sort were torn out to make room for sugar, now soaring to hitherto undreamed prices.

The war over, all Europe began to buy Cuban sugar, pending the restoration of national beet industries. For a time even the surplus from Java did not satiate the market. Later, as the demand began to wane, the powerful United States companies which controlled Cuban production accumulated stocks in order to maintain prices, which actually advanced for more than a year after the war was over to thrice its war-controlled price. Under this stimulus Cubans continued to plant cane. When the reckoning came, the price of sugar fell in twelve months from 24 cents a pound to less than 5 cents, a figure below the cost of production in the most efficient Cuban mills. Marginal land has been more or less out of production ever since. Cuba, a vast sugar plantation, is tied fast to its chief market, the United States. Unfortunately for the Republic of Cuba, American interests in sugar are linked with production in territory which flies the American flag; tariffs protect Louisiana, a marginal cane producer, and the costly beet growing of central and western United States. During the fifteen years after the war the United States increased its tariff three times, with the result that protected production in its low-latitude territories jumped — nearly doubling in Hawaii and Puerto Rico, and quadrupling in the Philippines, where the introduction of efficient methods increased production with little expansion of planting.

Cuba tried every means of control, including restrictions on output.

The measures failed to lift prices to a profitable level in the face of world overproduction, which was constantly increasing because of the United States tariff, the British bounty, initiated at the close of the war in the form of imperial preference, and the reestablishment of political favors for nationally grown beets in continental European countries. In 1931 most of the growers of surplus sugar — both beet and cane — signed an agreement by which they limited themselves to established quotas. Cuba agreed to reduce its crop by about a third. The plan failed, partly because countries which can produce enough for themselves did not participate. Cuba was thrown into the convulsions of political revolution.

By a law of 1934 the United States government reduced the tariff and arranged for quotas from its domestic producers, in order to let Cuba share the market. As every tariff since 1890 has been high enough to increase domestic production, the laying of quotas is the first check domestic beet and cane sugar received. This law has brought improvement in the economic conditions of Cuba, but like its predecessors, it cannot reach the roots of the trouble — the existence of far more sugar land than is needed to supply the world's population with all the sugar it can buy, and the complications injected by the political strategy of producing nations.

The so-called world market for sugar is in fact circumscribed by legal restrictions calculated to foster nationalistic production. The tendency appears everywhere in Europe. Each sugar producer tries to meet its needs from the homeland soil, at no matter what cost, by tariffs, excises, or a combination of these. This springs from the desire to be self-dependent in the production of major crops — an ambition born as twin of commercial agriculture in Western and Central Europe, an ambition intensified since the World War by the drive toward national isolation pursued in most continental countries. France, embarrassed by heavy home production of beet sugar and wine, restricts, by a system of quotas, the production of both sugar and rum in its cane-growing possessions. Even the United Kingdom has attempted to develop a domestic beet-sugar business by means of governmental aid. Outside Europe many countries favor the flag. The United States draws its supply from its own soil, its colonies, and its pseudo-colony, Cuba. Japan depends on Formosa. The members of the British Empire have endeavored to improve the fortunes of British domains which produce sugar by setting up preferential tariffs. Through them Australia is supplied by Queensland, South Africa by Natal, Canada by British West Indies, India in part by Mauritius, and Britain by various colonies.

Because sugar beets are raised on high-priced land, generally in congested regions, the crop would appear to be uneconomic. And so it is, considered by itself, because beet sugar is probably never laid down to the consumer for as low actual cost as is the most efficient product of cane, despite its origin in the market region and the consequent offset in transportation charges. It so happens however that the deep plowing, intensive weeding, and thorough loosening of the soil which beet production entails, so improves tilth that a succeeding yield of a crop in rotation which is not weeded (usually the principal bread grain) is enhanced perhaps 25 percent. Thus the desire to be self-sufficient in sugar is reinforced by the still stronger urge to be as nearly self-sufficient as possible in staple cereals. The tops and pulp of the beets and the lees of molasses make useful stock feed, especially for the dairy cows which figure largely in the agricultural system of northern Europe. To complete the circle, the additional animals reared on these by-products furnish manure invaluable in maintaining crop yields and in sustaining the weak structure of the none too fertile soils of that part of the world. Possessed of these virtues, sugar-beet production has been the solicitude of governments situated (as all continental Europe is) in a potential war zone.

Java alone supplies a really foreign market. By rigid political limitation of the output and the good luck of a dense population, cane yields and costs of production are there kept down to a level which gives Javan sugar ingress to India and to the whole of populous South and East Asia, except territory controlled by Japan. The low cost of producing sugar in Java is the rock on which all proposals for world limitation founder, for behind the actual market lies the potential market of the United Kingdom, accessible whenever the world price rises above Javan production costs plus the charge for transportation halfway around the globe.

As long as the present political organization of the earth, based on national subdivision, persists, there seems little likelihood that sugar production will be allowed to pursue the course natural to it if only economic geography were operative. While the consumer continues to pay prices higher than necessary, the producer will continue to lose money periodically, in order that political exigency may be served. Beets will continue to be grown on land which might be used more efficiently, considering the labor and capital involved, and low-grade soils in drouthy climates will continue to be planted to cane, while lands admirably suited to sugar cane remain under virgin forest because they lack political favor.

## WHEAT

To find another type of agricultural land occupance that is chronically engrossed in political agitation comparable to the plantation industry, it is necessary to go to the commercial grain farming regions of the middle latitudes. At first thought no contrast could be greater than that between the spots of plantation crops grown in clearings in the humid low-latitude bush with the aid of much hand labor, and wheat grown by the largest-scale farm machinery in replacement of natural grasses, over vast expanses of sub-humid continental climate in middle latitudes. Wheat is one of the most widely grown of all crops, being of some importance in every climate except the coldest and rainiest types. Therefore no one sort of region has a semi-monopoly as is characteristic with plantation crop tillage. Instead of being a luxury, or a commodity of inelastic demand because of the rigid size of its market, wheat is " the staff of life," staple food grain of occidental peoples, and widely used in the Orient and in the low latitudes as well. An annual, it is little affected by the lag between planting and marketing so upsetting to growers of rubber, coffee, and the other tree crops of plantations, and even the perennial field crops such as sugar and cotton.

In spite of these antitheses, there are a few similarities, and they are critical. Wheat of commercial grain farms, like most plantation crops, is the sole cash reliance of the grower. It is produced a long way from its market. It is compelled to meet competition from other areas under different political control. To these must be added a circumstance uncommon in plantation crop regions — extreme unreliability of rainfall and consequent high uncertainty of outturn.

About two-fifths of the world's wheat is consumed in the region of its origin, and of that a large fraction never crosses a national border. Some of it, as in Mediterranean and Danubian Europe and parts of India and East Central North America, is produced where the natural environment approaches the ideal. Some is planted under the protection of tariffs in countries of Northwest Europe not especially suited to the crop, but whose people are willing to make sacrifices in order to be assured of home production in case of war. In all these areas outturn is fairly reliable, as farm crops of the middle latitudes go. This two-fifths of the world's crop may therefore be looked upon as a unit apart from the output from commercial grain farms. Yet it is not wholly distinct, because the total yield does fluctuate and by so much affects prices in the world market.

The remaining three-fifths of the world crop is grown in regions devoted primarily to wheat produced for sale (Fig. 4). It finds a varied market. A very little is consumed by the small local population, but nearly all is shipped to an open market made up of occidental countries which can grow little or no wheat, which do not supply all their needs from the home fields despite tariffs, or which lay no duty. In ordinary times, with wheat at about $1.00 a bushel (a price which has remained fairly stable for more than a century) most of the land well suited to wheat growing is either under that crop or some other in an established rotation of which wheat is the dominant member. In emergencies, such as a war, when the price advances sharply, marginal lands are sown to wheat.

With minor exceptions all the regions exporting wheat raise it as the dominant crop. Their climates are similar, in that each lies on the dry margin of humid middle latitudes in a climate characterized by hot summers. To date none of these regions has been able to devise an agricultural system varying from a simple formula: wheat, the main cash crop, grown in most years; flax, a minor cash crop, grown as a groundbreaker on virgin soil and sometimes in rotation; oats, to feed the draft animals and to serve in rotation; fallow every so many years, at least in the drier regions; few animals, except beasts for draft, even these being in competition with tractors in the new continents and with man-power in the Old World. In effect, such a region is almost solely dependent on wheat. The highly productive chernozem soils which make up the choicer lands of all these regions postpone the evil day when profitable returns cease because of depletion of the soil. But already, fifty years or less after turning the sod in all the new continents, output is diminishing and return per acre is low.

Unable to alter the mode of land occupance, and faced with diminishing returns, every commercial wheat region is also subject to sharp fluctuations of precipitation. In favorable years the rainfall nourishes a generous crop of wheat; in years of deficiency it causes partial or complete crop failure.

Because the wheat regions are so widely dispersed crop failure in some is likely to be countered by abundant yield in others. For this reason the consumer is guaranteed flour at a not too widely fluctuating cost. The farmer enjoys no such stability. If his output is low, he may discover that bumper crops in other regions hold prices down, so that his small contribution brings in a beggarly pittance; or in years of high yield wheat may be so cheap that it will cost more to ship it to the market than its sale will realize. The unpredictable competitive contribution of the several commercial grain regions is further complicated by the size of the crop in the countries which produce for home consumption.

Because of these variables in wheat production, all resting at base on rainfall, the commercial grain farmer is subjected to cruel ups and downs. Being human, he tends to anticipate bumper crops every year. Also, being human, he is likely to extend himself in times of prosperity, so that adversity catches him with debts which he cannot pay off. Faced with famine, as often in Russia, he succumbs; faced with financial ruin, as in most of the new continents, he looks about for means of retrieving his dire straits.

He sees a complex human machinery and himself in its toils. The bankers who have made him loans appear to him usurers, and the credit system of the country which backs them is a device specially created to " crucify him on a cross of gold." The wheat exchanges in distant cities, by their distribution of consumer risk through buying for future delivery, seem to have been making money out of his losses. The brokers who buy his crop at harvest time and store it until it can be marketed, are sharpers taking advantage of his need for ready cash. The railroad lines, sole avenues by which his remote inland crop can reach the consuming world, are monopolistic ogres which league to maintain exorbitant freight rates. Without these devices of economic society, wheat could never have been produced in the commercial grain regions, but abuses lend color to the agonized farmer's charges. What recourse has he? The government! Let laws regulate the evils, not only to correct abuses in the operation of marketing, but also to perfect faulty human machinery, and even to complete the job by changing the climate. The wheat regions of the Great Plains of North America furnish a concrete illustration of the interplay of wheat and politics. Few, if any, other agricultural regions are so unwilling to accept the verdicts of the successive seasons, and so prone to embrace political panaceas for economic ills and the shortcomings of nature.

## Laws and Localized Resources

That governments should attempt to regulate and guide the utilization of the earth's resources is natural. Their success is measured by the degree to which the resource is localized. Unless a single state has a monopoly of a commodity, regulation is likely to be defeated by the refusal of other states to cooperate. In some cases treaties can be substituted for internal law, to take care of cases involving more than one nation. The extractive industries are more readily subjected to governmental regulation than is agriculture. Among agricultural products, those saleable only after intricate processing can be controlled by government most readily.

The essential element in successful regulation of the use of natural resources is harmony between the law and the environment. A Massachusetts law passed early in the 19th century provided that land must be divided equally among the children of deceased parents. Because the niggardly soil proved quite incapable of supporting an increasing number of farm families, this law hastened farm abandonment, in a period which coincided with the opening of the Middle West to settlement.

The homestead laws of the United States government initially provided for farms of 160 acres. This was merely a mathematical subdivision of the rectilinear land survey which was used for Ohio and territories farther west. By good fortune it happened to coincide with the amount of land necessary to maintain a farm family on the fertile soil of the humid Middle West. (Even today the average farm in this region, the Corn Belt, is about 150 acres). As homesteaders moved farther west into subhumid and semiarid country 160 acres proved to be too little to support a family. Subsequent doubling of the allotments came too late. Most of the choice land had already been subdivided into parcels inappropriately small, considering the climate. Before many years homesteads were being abandoned by the disillusioned and defeated pioneers. To encourage railroad construction, the federal government habitually granted to railroad companies alternate sections (square miles) of land along proposed rights-of-way. This further complicated subdivision of the country, and in the arid Great Basin proved to be pernicious. There livestock ranches are the only feasible farms except in irrigated districts. A successful ranch must exceed a section of land in area, and it must comprise waterholes and have access to the railroad. By creating a checkerboard of government and railroad holdings on a rigid pattern of small rectangles, the law made it difficult to sell the land in the first place, and awkward for ranchers to operate on it once they had acquired units of it. Overgrazing is directly related to this discordant land system.

By virtue of the continuous pressure it exerts, the natural environment can sometimes bring a set of laws into harmony with itself. This has occurred in twelve of the western United States with respect to the laws governing the utilization of streams and lakes. The English settlers on the North American Atlantic seaboard brought with them the

English common law, a legal code which fits the humid lands of eastern United States. As people pushed westward they carried this code with them, until it has become the basic law for all the States (except Louisiana, which inherited French law). In humid regions the chief use for streams, aside from watering stock and the like, is navigation. In order to maintain navigability the English common law declares that each abutting property owner has a right to undiminished flow of water past his land. In regions which have long periods without rain, especially during the warm season, the chief use for water is to irrigate land otherwise useless or uncertain in crop production. Few streams in regions with dry seasons are navigable in any case, and even when they are, their value for irrigation is higher than their value as shipways. The Roman law, originating in a land of summer drouth, recognizes this and permits the withdrawal of water under specified conditions, chief of which is the right of the first comer to continue to withdraw his quota. In parts of California and other States once Mexican, the Roman law was introduced by the Spaniards. Elsewhere the English common law stood in the way of irrigation projects and in parts of California it superseded the Roman law when Americans rushed in to find gold. One by one the States of the dry west have supplanted the English rule of riparian rights with a law akin to the Roman.

The importance of concord between the law and the natural conditions is increasing with the gradual abandonment of laissez faire in government, and the substitution therefor of regulations, some of which are very detailed. Aside from regulations which are dictated by the exigencies of the moment or by political wire-pulling, there are two movements on foot in the world today which look toward improved utilization of the earth and its resources. Both of these movements are reactions against the failure of laissez faire government to keep pace with swiftly changing modes of economic land use. Each can fulfill its destiny only by increasing the political regulation of man's use of the earth.

One of these movements, conservation of natural resources, looks toward the optimum utilization of the earth's resources. It would replace waste in the extractive industries with utilization at the highest level of efficiency known to society. It would replace soil erosion with soil replenishment. It would put underground and surface waters to their best use. It would protect extractable resources from destructive exploitation.

The other movement, land planning, seeks to look ahead and to provide a material framework for human living which will yield the maximum comfort and convenience possible in every environment. It undertakes to classify land and other natural resources as to character and quality. Then it would find means of putting each sort of land to the best possible use. This may involve resettlement of families and communities, converting an area from farmland to timber or to pasture land, laying out routes and cities, and any other devices for handling the natural environment as intelligently as human knowledge permits.

The principal stumbling block to both conservation and land planning is the character of human society. Communities and individuals often find themselves unhappy in following what they may recognize as their wisest course. Perhaps the great majority can see no merit in schemes which may not turn out as hoped, particularly if they require present sacrifice for the sake of future realization. Minorities, spurred by powerful stimulants, power or greed or fanaticism, are likely to set themselves against far-seeing plans, precisely because such plans interfere with personal objectives. Such minorities easily translate their obstruction into political terms. Under any form of government, public-spirited projects for conserving natural resources and for planning wise utilization of land are prone to be diverted to the benefit of individuals or small groups, instead of the welfare of society as a whole. Both movements are phases of the evolution of political society, and should be viewed in their long-range setting.

The history of political society can be resolved into a repetition of a simple formula: first, the establishment of a government adequate to cope with pressing problems arising from an expanded utilization of earth resources; second, a prolonged struggle to instill in this effective but brutal government a recognition of human values; third, the renewed extension of technologic control over material means of existence, and once more the compulsion to find a political formula which will facilitate the functioning of the new economic life. Although it is always impossible to place the present accurately in the perspective of the past and the prospect of the future, it is a tenable hypothesis that the tremendous strides in material control which mark the past few decades have outmoded the governments ushered in with the modern era. If so, the current swing to despotism is an effort to find a political technology competent to deal with such complex problems as conservation and land planning. Insofar as this movement oversweeps the world, society is compelled to begin once more the painful endeavor to reassert human values for which despotic rule has little place.

## CHAPTER FOUR

# The Oceans as International Areas

THE utilization of natural resources, and particularly those notably localized within one or another state, is markedly affected by the opportunities for trade. Under primitive conditions transportation by water takes precedence of overland movement, but water routes are likely to be confined to rivers and lakes and to coastal waters, especially those of inclosed seas. The full fruition of possessing valuable resources comes only with transport across the oceans. It thus occurs that the ocean lanes of traffic are themselves valuable assets, and the power to control some or all the ocean ways is a political perquisite of no little importance.

## THE OCEANS THE SEAT OF SEAPOWER

The ocean is the incentive to colonial expansion, the avenue of colonial traffic, and the seat of colonial power. It occupies two-thirds of the earth's surface, and thereby relegates the lands to a marginal position facing its vast expanse. A large fraction of the earth's population lives on lowlands adjacent to the sea. This is clearly shown if a map of the earth's ecumene be consulted (Fig. 1). Of all the continents, only Europe and North America possess extensive inland tracts able to support dense populations.

So long as subsistence economy prevails, each continent lives to itself and looks upon the ocean as the unknown realm of dangers. As a society solves its problem of subsistence and slowly accumulates surpluses, trade swells from intermittent trickles to floods that cut new channels. When it reaches the ocean it is released to the ends of the earth (Fig. 2).

In the commercial sense, the Discoveries by Europeans of the other continents attained their objective when they disclosed the oceanic articulation of regions which, although facing the sea, had remained unaware of each other. Many of these regions contrast sharply in climate, soil, terrain, and natural resources — unaltering differences that lay permanent foundations for trade. All of them had lived their discrete lives so long that they stood at every conceivable economic level, from the most primitive bushmen subsisting on roots and insects to the refined civilizations of the Orient. Even if two coasts were identical in climate and similar in natural resources, as in the case of Mediterranean Europe and California, different economic levels provide a basis for commercial exchange so long as they last.

Commercial objectives were prime incentives to the opening of the oceanway, and commercial opportunities quickly created contacts for Europe with both the legendary ancient Orient on the opposite corner of Eurasia and the new continents heretofore unknown. From the outset governments have cast their aegis over these commercial ventures. They have backed exploration, chartered commercial companies, protected their nationals in hazardous foreign parts, and set their yokes on them, almost regardless of their proved value. It is inevitable that friction should have been engendered by this sudden confrontation of coasts hitherto belonging to different worlds. It is natural that European states, possessing the technologic means of reaching the other worlds, should also have possessed the power to dominate nearly all the new lands which they discovered. It is not surprising that in time such of these lands as possess resources equivalent to those of Europe should emancipate themselves from subjection to Europe. In this tug-of-war across the seas, competition among the colonial powers, most of them European, has complicated the struggle, frequently to the detriment of their cause. Seapower generally comes to be associated with colonial success, although it has often been built up in order to cope with enemies nearer home and sometimes primarily to gain prestige.

It is the nature of seapower to be absolute, as landpower rarely is. Control of the sea can function in two spheres, a lesser and a greater. It can be sufficient to protect the coast of the country which has created it. Since a navy must depend slavishly upon a base for refueling, revictualing, and refitting, a relatively small operating unit can ward off invaders from a considerable coast. Moreover, coast guns, having the advantages of land emplacements, appear to be invincibly superior to war vessels of any and all sorts. A coast well defended requires of the supplementary navy only the work of keeping open the lanes of communication with the outside world. To wield seapower capable of carrying on offensive warfare, a nation must have enough more units than the enemy to operate along the enemy coast and keep its opponents shut off from the ocean trade routes. In theory this means more units than any presumptive combination of enemies, and includes the units of allies who can be counted upon. Seapower in the sense of ruling the ocean implies ability to maintain communication lines to the nearest base.

The evolution of seapower during the past half millennium has re-oriented all the continents, placing certain critical points in the fore-front of world politics. During its progress it has reflected the changing material resources of society, and shifted from one state to another in conformity to the distribution of those resources.

### SEAPOWER IN A CHANGING WORLD

When navigators timidly pushed beyond the coastal fringes of Europe, including the Mediterranean and Baltic enclosed waters, they carried with them the concept of the closed sea. Every body of water was considered the private preserve of the nation which controlled its entrances. This was a doctrine as old as seafaring. The two nations which made the first great discoveries (Portugal with its route to the Orient via Africa, and Spain with its crossing of the Atlantic to the Americas) were rather less concerned to occupy the coasts they had discovered than to acquire a monopoly of the trade. To obtain this they invoked the ancient dogma of the closed sea, and to bolster their claims obtained from the Papacy a demarcation of the non-European world into two hemispheres, one for each. The substance of this demarcation was solemnly engrossed in a treaty, and evidence that the two parties took it seriously exists today in mutually exclusive national exploitation — a Portuguese-speaking Brazil embedded in Spanish-speaking South America, and conversely the Spanish Philippines in the East Indies, formerly a Portuguese trade sphere. Unfortunately for these contracting states, the oceans could not be policed well enough to exclude greedy competitors who wished to share in the profits of the new overseas commerce. Still more unfortunately, the Protestant Reformation, itself an expression of the very mental awakening which launched the Discoveries, soon destroyed the papal sanctions in considerable sections of maritime Europe. Some of the reformed countries challenged the validity of closure of the seas by legal restrictions. Before the papal demarcation had found expression in effective occupation of much of the newly discovered land, the Portuguese found their lucrative oriental trade sharply cut by Dutch competition, and the Spanish-ruled sea was limited to the periodic movements of the bullion fleet heavily convoyed by men-of-war, through narrow lanes perennially harried by English freebooters. The dogma of the closed sea was bound to lose its force in the presence of the open ocean, and at the same time commercial competition and raiding on the high seas were supplemented by more or less effective occupation of many overseas coasts by one or another nation of Northwestern Europe.

### REORIENTATION OF THE CONTINENTS TO FACE THE SEA

Except for the utilization of enclosed seas for trade, most traffic adhered to land routes before the Discoveries. The few goods which moved about in Africa, Asia, and Europe, followed streams, mountain passes, and the coasts of inland seas. The still fewer commodities which moved from one continent to another crossed the forbidding intervening deserts by caravan. Trade in the Americas and Australia appears to have been slight and confined to the most prized articles, such as salt, shells, flint, and other items imperatively needed by a primitive society. Only the inhabitants of the thickly strewn islets of the Southeast Pacific appear to have mastered the art of navigation beyond sight of land, and they were restricted to quiet waters and small boats.

The Discoveries turned the continents inside out. European coast towns throve, especially those facing the Atlantic. European traders established stations on or near the coasts of Africa, Asia, and the Americas. In the new continents the merchants offered arms, cloths, and gewgaws for goods which might be extracted from the natural environment by indigenous craft or labor. Later they dispatched men inland to obtain larger and more varied consignments at even lower cost. In the Orient the coastal stations dispensed gold and particularly silver for the pepper, silk, and luxury goods of complex and industrious civilizations. India has been likened to a great sink capable of swallowing occidental silver century after century.

### ISLANDS AS SPRINGBOARDS

In this reorientation of the continents from isolated units to interdependent neighbors, islands and rivers have played significant roles. Islands figure far more conspicuously than either their size or their resources appear to warrant. Their qualities of unity, isolation, and strategic location lend them this political significance. Islands fringing the coasts of continents in process of being broached, make ideal advance bases for expanding political power.

Archipelagoes piecemeal, can be conquered, subjected by relatively small detachments of mariners and soldiers, and assimilated for purposes of trade and production by the invading nations. The two chief archipelagoes in this category are the West and East Indies. It is not coincidence that these were among the first European conquests after voyages west and southeast disclosed them. In the primitive and somewhat inimical Americas, the islands were for a time the only lands occupied, and certain of them remained throughout the heyday of Spanish rule the concentration points for the overseas trade. Meanwhile they served as outfitting bases for the spectacular conquests of the mainlands that quickly succeeded domination of the islands themselves. In the Orient the invaders faced less physical danger than in the Americas, but greater difficulty in establishing effective political control. There the separate islands succumbed to European rule before the larger and less vulnerable blocks of mainland. Neither East nor West Indies have been subjected as units, and they have rarely owed allegiance to the same European master as controlled the nearby mainlands.

A far more intimate relation of island to mainland persists between islands close to shore (such as Manhattan) and the hinterland. At the outset such islands can be utilized as natural defense points. They are small enough to be easily conquered and effectively controlled by little groups of invading mariners and soldiers, whose disadvantage in numbers is only partly offset by superior technology of warfare. Once firmly ensconced in fortified positions on the island, the interlopers make it a base of operations against the mainland, and a haven in case of forced retreat. For trading also such an island offers initial advantages. If it lies in a river mouth or near the mainland shore it shelters a belt of calm water in which the ships from the home country can safely anchor, and across which forces attacking the mainland can easily make their way. This use of the islands may be transitory, because once the mainland is subjugated it becomes the more convenient and commodious location for trading towns. If the mainland lacks harbors, or if trade is carried on for a long time unaccompanied by political domination of the mainland, island springboards may become sites of permanent settlements. For entrepôt business, in which goods are collected for reexportation, islands serve quite as well as mainland sites, because most entrepôt traffic is water-borne. Frontier trade of the sort usual in the early decades or centuries of a newly established commercial connection is likely to make large use of the entrepôt.

Most onshore islands belong to one of three types. Least common and most prized are rocky outliers of the mainland. These are likely to be associated with volcanic action, coral reefs, or coasts in which hills or mountains rise abruptly from the sea. Such islands generally provide deep water harborage, terrain easily defended, and dry and windswept sites for habitations — the last a real merit in humid climates, especially in low latitudes. Along fjord coasts islands are commonly selected for settlements because they furnish sites for port towns more suitable than either the steep side-walls or the shallow heads of the fjords themselves. Because the nature of the terrain commits the trade of such coasts permanently to ships, island sites for trading towns are not at a disadvantage. Bergen, Sitka, and Ancud are examples from the three principal coastlines of this type. Bergen has been linked to the interior by rail, but the line is less a commercial venture than a political device.

More widely distributed over the face of the earth than fjord coasts are sandbars built by waves and currents in front of the mainland, from which they are separated by lagoons and tidal marshes. In some cases the lagoons provide harborage and lead to streams by which the interior may be penetrated. Elsewhere it may be difficult or impossible for ocean-going ships to cross the shallow bars over which the lagoons discharge their surplus water. Most lagoon coasts have fended off early settlement or have been occupied only where no alternative offers. The chief exceptions are those of Upper Guinea and of the United States South with adjacent Mexico. Wherever possible, as at Charleston, Savannah, St. Augustine, and Corpus Christi in America and St. Louis, Bathurst, Bissau, and Lagos in Africa, early settlers took advantage of the harbors formed by river mouths, to pass the bars and settle on the lagoons, facing deep water but preferably backed by a protecting maze of creeks or swamps. Along much of Upper Guinea the streams cannot cut through the bars, except during the rainy season, and the heavy surf makes it impossible for ships to enter them. Hence many towns there have grown up on the bar, in spite of the handicap of lightering goods and passengers through the surf. They have the advantage of facing the sea breeze and their sandy soil affords dry sites — great advantages in regions within or near the Tropics.

The third group of onshore islands are those which form the fringe of delta mosaics. These have the advantage of immediate contact with the interior by way of the river, generally a large stream if it has created a delta in open ocean. Delta islands are flat, muddy, and marshy, however, and in low latitudes subject to most insect-borne diseases as well as motionless and often humid atmosphere. Delta islands are likely to be larger than required either by military or commercial needs. As a rule the marshy expanses not utilized include bayous, and, depending on the climate, either grassy tidal marsh or jungly swamp. These serve as natural defenses against human enemies. Some deltaic distributaries are impaired as commercial arteries by shallow bars across their mouths. Where bases for conquest and trade occupy the outermost islands the settlements may have to be abandoned when one distributary wanes in volume and its bar shallows, while another waxes and cuts a channel through the sediment off its mouth. Many stations on the outer Niger have risen and fallen in a single generation. On the Zambesi, Quelimane had long been the established port when, less than half a century ago, the more direct Chinde mouth of the stream was found to be deep enough to carry the traffic. Settlements located farther upstream have a choice of outlet and have generally been more stable. New Orleans on the Mississippi, Calcutta on the Ganges, and Shanghai on the Yangtze are notable examples of delta ports with long histories.

Few onshore islands have remained in different hands from the adjacent mainland for long, because their principal political function is to serve as springboards for conquest. The exceptions are in the middle-latitude Orient, where a densely populated and advanced state has resisted conquest. There, island concessions granted to foreign traders remain useful so long as the mainland lags behind the overseas trading nations in protecting lives and property of foreigners. The most striking example is British Hong Kong at the mouth of the Si River, main artery of trade in South China (Fig. 5). Located on an outlier of the mountainous mainland north of the Si Valley, it has the advantages of a deep-water harbor accommodating ships of all sizes, a more airy site than the mainland affords, and a hill station for residential use. A railroad connects the harbor with Canton, the metropolis of the Si delta. The advantages of Hong Kong's site are thrown into sharp relief by a comparison with the Portuguese holding at Macao, on the outer fringe of the Si delta. Macao has been in European hands nearly 300 years longer than Hong Kong. The town is on a peninsular fragment of a large deltaic island and faces two small ones, and shares the humid heat of the mainland, as delta locations are wont to do. When it was established its harbor was deep enough, but it has shoaled and until new construction was recently finished could accommodate only small ships.

A number of islands have been utilized briefly as advance bases and

then abandoned. These include Raleigh's ill-fated Roanoke settlement in a lagoon of the Carolina coast, San Juan de Ulloa, in the
lee of which Cortes anchored before landing on the opposite main-

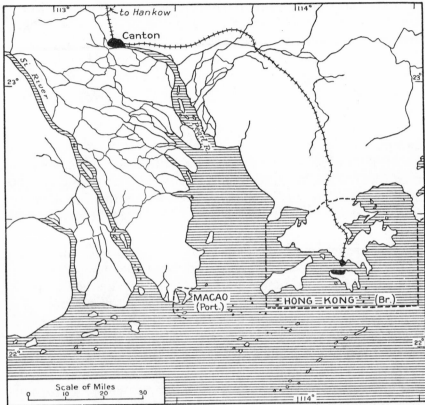

Fig. 5. The lower Si River, showing Canton, Macao, and Hong Kong.
Most of the outer islands are high and precipitous. Shoals abound in the river mouths.

land to invade Mexico, and a number of decadent trading posts on the
coast of Upper Guinea.

Islands which have maintained their utility are most numerous in
the low latitudes, perhaps because in addition to their military security, they are less unhealthful than the nearby mainland, and because
in the low latitudes entrepôt business is likely to persist longer than in
middle latitudes, ordinarily colonized by Europeans. As settlement
proceeds the islands cease to be precarious footholds on unfriendly
coasts, and serve as naval, military, and commercial bases for penetration of the mainland. As the island establishment succeeds in extending its control to the mainland coast and its hinterland, military defense becomes secondary to trade. When this occurs the islands,

originally chosen for safety, may have to compete with mainland sites equal or superior as trading stations. Insularity is a commercial handicap except for entrepôt business, although salubrity of climate and interests which have capital fixed in buildings on the original site may oppose the change. If the span to shore is short, it may be bridged, and the community can then spill onto the mainland. This has occurred at Recife in Brazil, where the island of original settlement is now chiefly the port, at Lagos in Nigeria, where port facilities, manufacturing plants, and residential quarters have spread to the mainland, and in many other places, notably New York.

Where the island lies too far at sea to permit bridge connection it dwindles at the expense of mainland competitors, and the more quickly if the island site is cramped. Gorée, three miles off Cape Verde, is an islet one end of which stands in cliffs high above the sea, the other being a very small lowland that encloses a tiny but easily defended harbor, protected from all but south winds. It was ideal for shelter, defense, and the early trade in slaves with a mainland rendered savage by slave raids. Today it has been superseded by Dakar, on the tip of Cape Verde. Dakar provides an ample site for the peaceful trade and railroad terminals of today, but requires harbor works. On the opposite side of Africa, Zanzibar retained its dominance of the hinterland trade until the 20th century. It is a large island with adequate harborage, but lies a score miles offshore. It has now lost its business to Dar-es-Salaam and Mombasa, rail terminals with direct connection to the hinterland. Mombasa, incidentally, was itself an onshore island settlement, which was able to retain its prestige by linking itself to the mainland with a bridge.

Where islands are wanting or are unserviceable, peninsulas are often utilized for footholds on unfriendly shores. By erecting a wall or stockade across the neck at the base of a peninsula it can be effectively defended. Jamestown and Boston, early settlements on the Atlantic coast of North America, and most of stations between the Congo and the Cape of Good Hope, are among the many of this type.

With a well defended island or peninsula as a base, penetration of the interior is only a matter of time. Cortes conquered Mexico by effrontery and luck within a few days of his anchorage behind San Juan de Ulloa. Indeed, far from using the island as a base, he deliberately destroyed his ships and operated without a base. This is a unique case. Occupation of the interior from such island sites as Calcutta and Bombay in India, and a string of footholds on the east coast of South America from Georgetown in Demerara to Rio Grande do

Sul in southern Brazil,[1] took years or even decades. In middle Africa four centuries passed before the interior was explored.[2]

## RIVERS AS AVENUES OF PENETRATION

Penetration of the interior is generally facilitated when the island foothold lies at or near the mouth of a navigable river. In North America the St. Lawrence and the Mississippi furnish two ready avenues of entrance to the very heart of the continent, and explorations were followed by fluvial trade routes dotted with stations. Many important interior cities of the continent bear French names because they were founded by these initial traders as posts at critical confluences, narrows, and breaks in navigation on river or lake. It is not mere coincidence that the commercial outlets on these streams, Montreal and New Orleans, occupy island sites. The shorter but navigable streams which empty into the sea between the mouths of these mighty waterways served to open the tidewater and in some cases the higher land beyond. Of them the Hudson and the James were settled from island sites near their mouths.

In parts of the Orient the principal trading contacts with the outside world are still made by way of streams. Because most of the large rivers of that quarter reach the sea through deltas, the initial trading towns typically grew up on islands.

In South America the major streams figure little in opening the continent. All of them rise in difficult country, never very productive and climatically inimical to settlement by Europeans. Exceptions must be made for the lower course of the Paraná and for the affluents of the Lagoa dos Patos, streams instrumental in settling the northern Pampa and the lowland of extreme southern Brazil, respectively. In so far as the rainy, marshy Amazon Basin has been exploited, the river has been the sole artery of communication.

The major African rivers and a number of lesser ones have been intermittently used and abandoned. African exploration was spurred by the desire to discover the sources of the four largest, although the courses of all were paradoxically traced downstream. Political pene-

---

[1] The island stations include Recife, Victoria, Santos, and Florianopolis. Pará, Bahia, and Rio de Janeiro began on well-defined peninsulas.

[2] African insular stations sometime famous are Gorée, Bathurst, Bissau, Conakry, Monrovia, Grand Bassam, Assinie, Kwitta, Whydah, Cotonou, Lagos, Forcados, Akassa, Brass, Bonny, Calabar, Victoria, Chinde, Quelimane, Old Kilwa, and Mombasa. The outstanding peninsular sites are Dakar, Loanda, Lobito, Walvis Bay, Lüderitz Bay, and Capetown.

tration of the continent made rather less use of the rivers than of the overland routes. Early commercial endeavors utilized the streams but were hampered by many interruptions to navigation. A goodly number of these were caused by falls and rapids, due to the fact that nearly every navigable African stream drains an interior structural basin. Outside the rainiest sections long dry seasons parch the land and reduce the rivers to shallows, except for the Nile, fed by large lakes and extensive marshes. Even where the rivers are navigable traffic has dwindled with the construction of competing railroads. A few boat lines connect remote interior points during the wet season. Where boats still monopolize the traffic they persist because the stream basins are marshy or choked with rain forest. The vast, quaking bog of the Bahr-el-Ghazal (White Nile), and deltas of the Niger and Zambesi, have no railroads. In the heavily forested Inner Congo Basin railroads are confined to portages around cataracts.

### GEOPOLITICAL ORGANIZATION OF OVERSEAS POSSESSIONS

Once the hinterland has been articulated with the coast by whatever means, it becomes an integral part of the imperial structure. This is illustrated by the location of administrative centers.

The ruling state develops its trade primarily with reference to its own needs. The coast remains the critical zone of contact between the dependency and the maritime state which is undertaking its development. This fact, added to the inertia of every established site, tends to keep the seat of administration on or near the coast. Very often it remains in the port where the first landhold was made. Indeed, unless there are cogent reasons for removal, it is almost certain to remain there. In the whole colonial world (excluding the British Commonwealth of Nations) there are few inland administrative capitals of dependencies that possess a seacoast. Of them, several lie in the interior to take advantage of the salubrity of high altitude in low latitudes. These include Asmara (Italian East Africa), Nairobi (Kenya), Windhoek (Southwest Africa), and Tanarive (Madagascar). To them may be added summer capitals, such as Simla (India), Myingyan (Burma), Buitenzorg (Netherlands Indies), and Baguio (Philippines). Mexico City and Guatemala City were former highland capitals in Spanish low-latitude domains, and at times Caracas, Bogotá, and Sucré served similarly. Nova Lisboa (Angola) on the railroad and the upland, is designated to take over the administrative functions from Loanda on the coast. The capital of India has recently been transferred from coastal Calcutta to inland Delhi for historical and sentimental reasons, and to take advantage of a somewhat less humid climate. French and Belgian equatorial Africa are administered from opposite sides of Stanley Pool on the Congo, main artery of both possessions. Administrations may be moved from one coastal point to another, although such removals are rare. They usually follow a prime shift in trade routes, chiefly the substitution of railroads for inland waterways. In Africa Dakar superseded St. Louis, Abidjan is replacing Grand Bassam, and Lourenço Marques has succeeded Mozambique. Nearly two centuries ago the capital of Brazil, then a Portuguese colony, was moved from Bahia to Rio de Janeiro for the sake of a more central position as the southern coast and the interior overtook the north coast in population and wealth.

Frequently colonial sub-capitals occupy inland sites convenient to transport connections with the coast or central to dense populations. These are more readily shifted than the older and better entrenched coast capitals. A number of them are new creations of the overseas government, set up for administrative efficiency and to permit the construction of buildings ad libitum, instead of being forced to conform to sites already occupied by indigenous populations.

In overseas conquest and colonization islands have served as stepping stones between the old country and the new. Some of the most valuable of these lie well out at sea, but others cluster not far offshore, and may lie close to the territory of some foreign state. Ancient Hellas used the islands of the Aegean in establishing colonies on the shore of Asia Minor, and the Ionian archipelago in moving into the Italian peninsula. The Norse route to North America made use of the Faeroes, Iceland, and Greenland. The latter, while of continental size, is insular in having only occasional habitable spots along the icy coast. Without the West Indies the exploration and conquest of the American mainlands would have been more difficult than it was.

The colonial empires of today utilize stepping-stone islands for fueling stations, relays for cables, radio stations, and as naval and air bases — critical defense points and links in imperial strategy. The band of United States possessions flung across the Pacific toward the Philippines is keyed upon the Hawaiian group, where stands a major naval station. The recent American claim to two uninhabitable islets is calculated to strengthen the chain. France and Japan have very incomplete chains, and they lie chiefly in the Western Pacific. Great Britain is the chief exemplar of imperial stepping stones. The Mediterranean route to India and the Far East is marked at all its narrows by islands

(Fig. 37): Gibraltar (not physically an island, but because of its tenuous connection with a foreign mainland practically so), Malta, Cyprus, and Aden (another peninsula). Ceylon, Penang, and Singapore carry on the chain of strategic islands to Hong Kong, squarely in the Pacific. Between Singapore and Australia the Netherlands Indies interpose, but eastward from Australia, New Zealand and British South Sea islands go some distance toward bridging the Pacific to Canada. In the South Atlantic the sea route to South Africa is flanked by British Ascension, St. Helena, and Tristan da Cunha. The claims to Antarctica, now significant in connection with whaling, receive support from British control of the Falklands and South Georgia (Fig. 12).

### THE PACIFIC BASIN, AN ISLAND REALM

The character of chains of stepping stones may best be illustrated by the concurrence of national forces in the Pacific. In that realm water is dominant. The Pacific Basin comprises nearly half the ocean surface. The lands which face it make up less than one-sixth of the land surface of the earth, and so emphasize the paramountcy of the water. The Pacific islands, except Japan and New Zealand, are small and scattered in clusters, but most of the archipelagoes lie in the western two-thirds of the basin, between 30° N. and 30° S. (Fig. 6). The eastern third of the Pacific is the earth's most extensive desert, with scarcely an island and deficient even in sea life. The vast oceanic void of the Pacific, seeded sparsely with islets, is the last frontier, excepting the polar icecaps. To it people of European stock came late, to occupy its narrow eastern coasts. Opposite, on its wider western borders, the ancient oriental civilizations had stayed at home. It was only when the restless occidental world projected its unsettling shadow across the great ocean that East and West met face to face. This occurred late in the era of exploration.

In spite of Magellan's transit of the Pacific within a generation of the discoveries of America and Asia, European powers were not attracted to it until their nationals began to exploit its most obvious resource — fisheries. In pursuit of whales New Englanders and others discovered many of the island groups in the 18th and 19th centuries. At about the same time Russian sealers found the swarming breeding

FIG. 6. The Pacific Basin.

Possessions and mandates are not differentiated.
Islands within the dotted areas are administered by the nations indicated: A — Australia; F — France; G B — Great Britain; J — Japan; N — Netherlands; N Z — New Zealand; U S — United States.

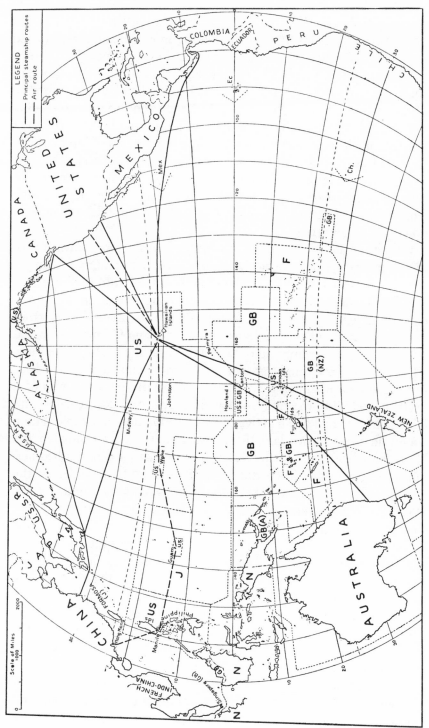

grounds of Alaska. Whales and seals are the farthest ranging of all pelagic creatures, and they are among the most quickly exterminated forms of marine life, whenever their value rises high enough to launch ships in pursuit of them. Efforts to regulate the taking of these animals through internal agreements have gone hand in hand with preemption of the Pacific lands by the Powers. Fisheries of other sorts, including salmon and halibut in the North Pacific, and pearls off the north coast of Australia, have joined whaling and sealing as causes of international friction. In this respect the Pacific is typical of all the oceans. The issue arises wherever profitable fishing can be carried on outside the three-mile limit of national waters, that is to say on all the major fishing banks except those too remote from markets to tempt fishermen from non-riparian countries.

Once the Pacific came to be frequented by fishermen, it was recognized as a new field of exploitation by interested nations. British explorers and settlers established themselves on the last of the large land masses, Australia and New Zealand. This brought them to the threshold of the sea region most heavily studded with islands. The other actively expanding European powers — France and Germany — joined Great Britain in preempting these islands after the mid-19th century. The two rising maritime states of the North Pacific entered the lists, but because of proximity a bit later. First the United States plumped itself squarely into the midst of Pacific affairs. American whalers and China clippers had taken active parts in exploration and exploitation, American missionaries laid the foundation for later claims to the Hawaiian Islands, and finally American imperialism extinguished and inherited Spanish claims within and on the western border of the Pacific. When Germany lost its Pacific possessions as a result of the World War, they were divided, largely on the principle of proximity, among national states exclusively Pacific. Japan, one of the Great Powers since it defeated Russia a decade earlier, received all the German islands north of the Equator, these being the nearest to the island empire. To Australia and New Zealand, as members of the British Commonwealth of Nations, were adjudged respectively German New Guinea and adjacent islands, and German Samoa. These same dominions and Great Britain jointly administer Nauru, especially valued for its phosphate deposits.

The Pacific realm has projected itself into the international sphere with unparalleled speed. Unconsidered and almost unknown a century ago, it is now crisscrossed by lines of transportation and communication. They carry less business than the Atlantic lines, but they are quite as varied. Regular air service across the Pacific began some years earlier than across the Atlantic, apart from the short traverse between Capes Verde and São Roque. The spanning of the large ocean is made possible by the strings of islands which provide regularly spaced landing places for refueling (Fig. 6). In this respect the Pacific has no advantage over the Atlantic, where Bermuda and the Azores might be used as stepping stones. Indeed, the longest unavoidable hop in either ocean is between California and the Hawaiian Islands.[1] But in the Pacific, numerous suitable island landing places were in the hands of a single nation which therefore met no political obstacles in establishing the new route. On mainland Asia, rival European trading stations offered hospitality. Two of the islands on the trans-Pacific route, Midway and Wake, were uninhabited when the United States authorized their use as way stations, and they have to be stocked from a continental base. In contrast, terminals of the Atlantic routes lie under different flags, except Newfoundland and Ireland, and national rivalry has delayed the organization of regular air service. Yet the most serious handicap of the Atlantic as compared to the Pacific is the fact that the Pacific route lies in the comparatively calm atmosphere of the low latitudes, instead of a turbulent area of cyclonic storms such as swirl from North America to Europe.

If all the British territory be considered as politically unified, the Pacific realm is divided among four Great Powers. Of them France alone holds no mainland abutting on the Pacific, except colonial Indo-China. This dependency is effectually cut off from the French islands in the South Pacific by American, British, and even Dutch holdings. Deprived of a continental base, the French islands lie at the mercy of the British Empire, and nearer Australia or New Zealand than any other large land base.

Of the three remaining powers concerned in the Pacific Japan is confined to that ocean. Its interest is therefore undivided. Its oceanic

---

[1] The distances are as follows:

*Trans-Pacific*
San Francisco to Honolulu — 2402 miles.
Honolulu to Midway Island — 1304 miles.
Midway to Wake Island — 1185 miles.
Wake to Guam — 1508 miles.
Guam to Manila — 1589 miles.
Manila to Macao — 716 miles.
Macao to Hong Kong — 43 miles.

*Trans-Atlantic*
Botwood (Newf.) to Foynes (Ireland) — 1995 miles.
New York to Bermuda — 775 miles.
Bermuda to Azores — 2070 miles.
Azores to Lisbon — 1050 miles.

possessions are relatively compact and close to its homeland. Japan's insularity has undoubtedly played a large part in fostering naval power which now ranks along with that of Great Britain and the United States, the two other states vitally concerned in the Pacific Ocean. The ultimate force that can be exerted from the northwestern angle of the Pacific will be determined by the destiny of China's large resources. In so far as Japan succeeds in directing China's resources, they will be used in part to increase Japanese naval power. If China can make itself an independent Great Power, it may or may not see fit to support a powerful navy.

British interests in the Pacific are centered at the northeast (Canadian coast) and opposite at the southwest (Australia, New Zealand, and the oceanic islands). They extend southward along stepping-stone islands to the Antarctic Continent, and they include Hong Kong, almost in the lee of Japanese Formosa and valuable only along with free trade in China. Forming a back-yard connection between Britain's major self-governing dominions, the Pacific is far less important to the British Empire than the Atlantic and Indian Ocean links. Nevertheless the trans-Pacific routes are used in peacetime, and might become critically valuable in wartime as alternatives to the more direct imperial connections. No considerable British naval power has ever been concentrated in the Pacific Ocean. Until the recent completion of the Singapore naval base, capital ships could not refit in British ports anywhere within range of the Pacific. Now it is possible to provide for an effective naval force in the southeastern quadrant of the ocean, with home stations in Australia and New Zealand and advance bases on some of the small islands which have deep harbors. Both the self-governing dominions are preparing to aid in their own defense by supplying war vessels. The enemy they fear is obviously Japan, not far away, and equipped with the third, or perhaps the second navy afloat. The stress laid upon naval strength by the Japanese, coupled with its concentration in the Pacific, makes its navy a threat out of proportion to the slender natural resources of the country and even to its population, large as it is.

The potential naval strength of Great Britain in the southwestern Pacific is unknown but can, if desired, be built up on well-distributed bases, one of which is the strategic key to the Indian Ocean, a sea which in turn is tied to the homeland both through the Mediterranean and around Africa. In the remainder of the Pacific the position of Britain is weak. In the northwest quadrant Japan stands paramount today. Its only possible rivals are China and Soviet Russia, both inland states which have never shown the least aptitude for seagoing. The southwest quadrant is almost literally " the ends of the earth." Devoid of islands, it is traversed by no important trade route, now that sailing vessels have all but disappeared from the oceans. The narrow belt of South America between the Andes and the Pacific produces little or nothing demanded by its vis à vis, New Zealand and the Australian ecumene. On the contrary each of the south Pacific coasts is drawn in an opposite direction into the commercial orbit of Northwest Europe, the one via the Caribbean and Atlantic United States, the other via India and the Mediterranean.

It is in the northeast quadrant, where Canada, the United States, and Mexico-Central America share the coastline, that British power is weakest in comparison to its territorial holdings and its stake in strategy. American and Canadian coastlines may be roughly adjudged as near parity in political utility although the American population on the Pacific slope is twelve times as great. The advantage of local population is greatly enhanced by the fact that, in addition, the United States holds the remaining three strategic trumps in this quadrant.

Near its southeast angle the Panama Canal has been dug to create the only ice-free water gate between the Atlantic and the Pacific north of Cape Horn. It is a precariously narrow and fragile entrance, but so long as it remains open it falls only a little short of bisecting the barrier of land and ice which stretches through the 145 degrees of latitude. This concentration upon Panama contrasts with the four separate seaways linking the Indian and Pacific oceans between 1° N. and 47° S. Lat., even if Singapore is given full allowance as the most important, because the most northerly of them. Lacking the Panama Canal, Britain must rely on the long Canadian route for a British transcursion of the barrier Americas.

The northwest angle of the quadrant is cut by the intersection of the Great Circle route between North America and Asia and the crescent chain of Aleutian Islands, dependencies of Alaska. On one of this chain, Unalaska, Dutch Harbor is suitable for a naval base close to the shortest seaway across the northern Pacific. Without a base on the Aleutians, British dominance of the North Pacific route is impossible.

About a dozen degrees within the southwest angle lie the Hawaiian Islands, belonging to the United States. This group includes the largest one of the mid-Pacific islands, along with several others capable of producing subsistence for a considerable population if necessary. Much of the terrain is rugged and easily fortified, and in Pearl Harbor its owners possess a first-class site for a naval base, on the most populous of the islands, not far from the capital. Inherently the Hawaiian cluster does not differ materially in size or resources from some of the others, notably the Fiji, Solomon, and New Hebrides groups. Its pre-eminence among Pacific islands grows out of its location at the " cross-roads of the Pacific." Great Circle routes from the principal ports of Western Canada to New Zealand and from Panama to Singapore traverse the Hawaiian archipelago, and the most direct sea lanes from Canada to Australia, and from Hong Kong to Cape Horn, pass near it. To enhance its significance much of the passenger traffic between North America (including Canadian ports) and East Asia detours in order to substitute a sunny voyage and a pleasant stop at Honolulu for the foggy and cold route through the northern Pacific. Without Hawaii, Britain cannot aspire to political and naval domination of the northeastern Pacific.

It is largely the springboard of the Hawaiian Islands that gives the United States a strong position in Pacific affairs. The very year which brought the Territory of Hawaii under the American flag by petition, an unrelated series of incidents ended in the military conquest of the Philippine Islands. This archipelago forms a nexus between Japan and mainland Asia to the north, and the East Indies to the south. Its possession brings the United States into the southwestern quadrant of the ocean, already checkered with cross-currents of conflicting national interests. As stepping stones between the Hawaiian and the Philippine archipelagoes, the States holds two islets: isolated Wake Island, and Guam, one of the numerous Ladrones. All the remaining islands along the route between Hawaii and the Philippines were German until the World War transferred them to Japan. So long as they remained in the hands of a European state which had no con-tinental Pacific base, foreign dominion constituted no serious threat to the United States. When they were converted into potential ad-vance bases of a first-rate naval power whose home waters lay only 1500 miles from Guam, an issue between the United States and Japan was joined. After the World War, America transferred its principal naval operations to the Pacific, relying on the Panama Canal (completed just before the war) to maintain ready liason between its Pacific and Atlantic coasts. To base the fleet adequately, naval stations dot the California coast and Pearl Harbor in the Hawaiian group has been equipped as a self-contained unit of defense. Dutch Harbor in the Aleutian Islands and on the North Pacific Great Circle route, is sub-ject to fortification.

In the new arrangements aviation has taken a prominent part. Air bases are subsidiary to naval bases and airplane carriers form units in the battle fleets. Commercial airplanes fly a newly pioneered route which takes off at San Francisco and uses the stepping-stone American islands, including the Philippines, as way stations *en route* to South China.

A branch of the trans-Pacific route may be traced from the Hawaiian group to the very heart of Oceania, via Johnston, Howland, Baker, and the one member of the Samoan Islands which has a harbor of the first class. To shorten the strides between stepping stones to Samoa the American government has laid claim to two uninhabited specks, Canton and Enderbury in the Phoenix group. All these islands lie close to the sea track between Canada and New Zealand. Britain and the United States havé agreed to occupy Canton and Enderbury jointly. Presumably their value will derive from service as air bases.

Closely associated with the use of islands as naval and air bases, is their function as stations for cable and radio transmission. The military value of cables has been considerably lessened by the introduction of powerful radio stations which are of course independent of an uninterrupted chain of islands.

It is not too much to say that the Pacific is the first ocean to precipitate the struggle among the nations for control of an oceanic area. Earlier maritime struggles either concerned enclosed seas or the continental margins of the other oceans. In terms of present and potential resources, well balanced distribution of population, and ease of exchange, the South Pacific has no impressive commercial future, and even the North Pacific is inferior commercially to all the other oceans except the South Atlantic (and of course the Arctic). In spite of its secondary economic rank, the strategic and political importance of the Pacific is indubitable. Two of the three leading navies of the seas are concentrated there and the third is taking steps to augment its Pacific force. The extreme regional contrasts existing on earth come to grips with each other across this ocean. The oldest civilizations face the youngest. The most crushingly overpopulated continent faces the two which have the least dense population in ratio to their resources. A society which scarcely knows machinery, and operates on human drudgery tempered with but a few work animals, faces the most mechanized nations on earth, countries in which human labor receives the highest pay known to history. Civilizations in which stability and the past are revered face the restless and forward-looking civilization whose ferment has stirred the whole world.

It does not necessarily follow that all these antitheses will burst into armed conflict. The Pacific Ocean is so vast that naval engagements are likely to go hard with the aggressor, who must maintain a long line of communications. Except for the mainland of Asia the natural resources in pawn may be insufficient in the aggregate or too little concentrated to make war for them worth the price. It appears that since the World War command of the sea can no longer mean absolute superiority of fighting units on the part of a single nation because no nation can command the sea unless it includes in that command the Pacific Ocean. Nevertheless, it remains true that the navy which can destroy or immobilize an enemy fleet has won its naval war, and the World War appears to have proved that this can be done by any state which can muster and maintain superiority at the theater of action, even though the difference in force is slight.

Whether or not war impends in the Pacific realm, the clash of societies which confront each other across that ocean has produced unstable equilibrium. This is true of all contrasting social and political groups on opposite seashores, but it is rendered especially precarious in the Pacific where the contrast in outlook is accompanied by an approach to parity in political power, at least within the Pacific realm. The balance is rendered more sensitive by the interpenetration of political control among the islands. Are they to serve as stepping stones to increased national might or to impairment of national prestige? The Pacific realm is too recent an international arena to permit a conclusive answer to that question.

### RELICT ISLANDS

In oceans longer subjected to the stresses of international struggles, some islands and coastal footholds, once prized for their strategic value, have ceased to serve as stepping stones to empire. They may bear witness to tentative advances of states no longer waxing, toward goals never reached. Or they may be vestiges of former political greatness, left in their owner's hands when more valuable or more extensive territory (usually on the mainland) has been seized by a new aggressor.

Coastal waters of Europe itself are dotted with islands over which sovereignty is vested in one neighbor, while language and customs bear a deeper-seated affiliation with another. The Aaland Islands occupy the entrance to the Gulf of Bothnia and lie almost equidistant from the entrance to Stockholm inlet and the Gulf of Finland. Although geologically an outlier of Finland, the archipelago is inhabited chiefly by Swedes and was part of Sweden until lost to Russia along with

Finland. When Finland gained independence a secession move-ment on the islands was quelled by giving them autonomy. Another Baltic island, Bornholm, 22 miles from the Swedish coast and 100 from Denmark, has been under Danish commercial influence and political control since Hanseatic times.

The Channel Islands, in sight of the French coast and tucked into the angle formed by the two peninsulas, Brittany and the Cotentin, are British, although their inhabitants speak French, live under local laws rooted in feudalism, and hold their land according to the Norman tenure. They are remnants of the medieval era when the king of Eng-land was also the ruler of Normandy and Brittany. When England lost Normandy the islands were retained and attached to the English crown, as befitted a maritime state. Insular vestiges of Venetian sea-power along the east coast of the Adriatic Sea are retained by Venice's heir, the Kingdom of Italy. Turkey keeps its grip in the Greek-speaking Aegean archipelago only at the entrance of the Dardanelles. Most of the other islands adhere to Greece, its political center of gravity now as always in Aegean waters rather than on either peninsula. Yet mod-ern Greece is a weak state which had to accrete the islands piecemeal, as its own force and international crises afforded opportunities. Be-fore it had a chance to wrest the more remote islands from the slacken-ing hold of the Turkish Sultanate, states far more powerful than either annexed them. Britain seized Cyprus before Greece had succeeded in incorporating Crete. Italy occupied the Dodecanese just before the World War enabled Greece to extend its sovereignty to Aegean islands remaining in Turkish hands.

North and Middle America are screened with island remnants of former mainland colonies of Europe. Until 1898 Spain held Cuba and Puerto Rico, 75 years after losing its last mainland possession. French Martinique and Guadeloupe of the Lesser Antilles are remnants of a Caribbean island empire that included Haiti and a mainland Louisiana comprising almost one-third of the present United States. Jamaica and many lesser islands, notably the Bahamas, only sixty miles off the Florida coast, and the Bermudas, represent the former British North America, most of which was lost in 1783. Even the Dutch have and until 1915 the Danes had Caribbean relics of former wider claims. Two tiny French islands just outside the Gulf of St. Lawrence similarly stand for a once French mainland; in this case the islands were expressly remanded to France as sites for summer fishing operations by Bretons at work on the Grand Banks.

Claims of Danes, Swedes, Dutch, and even Brandenburgers to bits of the Guinea coast existed until recently Some of these points are insular or peninsular sites, easier to hold than mainland areas. In many cases they had never been followed up by effective claims to any part of the interior.

On the coast of India both Portugal and France retain a few stations, once the spearheads of anticipated expansion, now the evidences of accepted defeat. These are not islands, and therefore are exceptional illustrations of the principle of relict sovereignty. Most of the similar footholds (peninsulas in nearly every case) along the coast of China have been seized from remotely situated European powers by nearby Japan. Only the *islands* at the mouth of the Si River remain in European possession.

Few sites of relict sovereignty are critical in current political affairs, although almost any of them might be used as a base for aggression against the nearby mainland. Italy occupied the Dodecanese as a military maneuver in a war with Turkey. The Panama Canal is believed to be vulnerable to an attack based on any of the nearer Caribbean islands which happen to be in the hands of seapowers.

There is a strong tendency for rising mainland powers to possess themselves of relict islands. Puerto Rico and the United States's Virgin Islands (formerly Danish) are clear cases, one bought in at a forced sale subsequent to conquest, the other purchased in the open market. Cuba indicates the same tendency, although it is less apparent. The preoccupation of American statesmen with Cuba for a century before it was delivered from Spain by American arms has been paralleled ever since that event by the often reluctant but always faithful reflection of American policy in Cuba, nominally independent but economically a helpless appendage of its close continental neighbor. Temporary military occupation of Haiti and Santo Domingo adds variety to the modes whereby the United States attempts to control the nearer Caribbean islands, no matter what their legal status. Germany sacrificed large claims in Africa for the tiny speck Heligoland, which happens to be only twenty-eight miles off the mouths of rivers on which lie the two chief German ports. Affirmations by continental powers to special rights in nearby islands are straws in the wind of national forces.

## THE CONCEPT OF THE EXPLOITABLE WORLD

Peripheral, maritime Europe has had a checkered career of success and failure in its expansion across the oceans to lands beyond. Some states have been proved to lack the combination of internal resources, favored location, and flexible government which are the conditions of successful imperialism. In so far as these states retain overseas possessions, they hold them on sufferance of the Great Powers. In most cases, perhaps in all, they hold them because the Powers have thus far been unable to agree upon division of the spoils among themselves.

Without exception the unquestionably successful imperial national states are populous. They possess natural resources at home, notable in quantity and varied in character. They have developed an internal administration flexible enough to recognize the necessity of making considerable concessions to local environment in the lands under their control outside the homeland. Imperial aspirations are no longer confined to states of Western Europe. It is noteworthy that every state which becomes a Great Power or which wishes to consider itself a Great Power adopts an imperialistic program. Thus it comes about that as new states suitably endowed by nature make themselves Great Powers or merely achieve effective political independence, the area available for incorporation in the empires of the Powers shrinks. Still more significant, the natural resources of the remaining area available for colonies are generally minor in comparison to the endowment of the rising national states which emancipate themselves from economic and political dependence, an achievement predicated on possession of the most favored human habitats.

After the Discoveries had disclosed the Orient and the New World to wondering European eyes, all these lands were considered subjects for exploitation by European energy (Fig. 7). Private ventures and official penetration by agencies of the state went hand in hand and supplemented each other. Exploitation of oriental and New World resources has created the interdependent economy based on international trade which characterizes the world of today. The utilization of these resources has entailed social and political responsibilities aptly termed " the white man's burden." From the beginning the urge to turn a profit has been paramount in exploiting the non-European world. Nevertheless other motives have played conspicuous parts on every one of the overseas stages. Missionary zeal ranks high among these motives, including its metamorphosed forms, education and medical service. Curiosity has brought innumerable individuals into the theater as explorers, as students of all the natural and anthropological sciences, and above all, as adventurers. Finally, and increasingly as time goes on, national governments have assumed major roles as political sovereigns and administrators, chiefly if not wholly for the sake of national prestige.

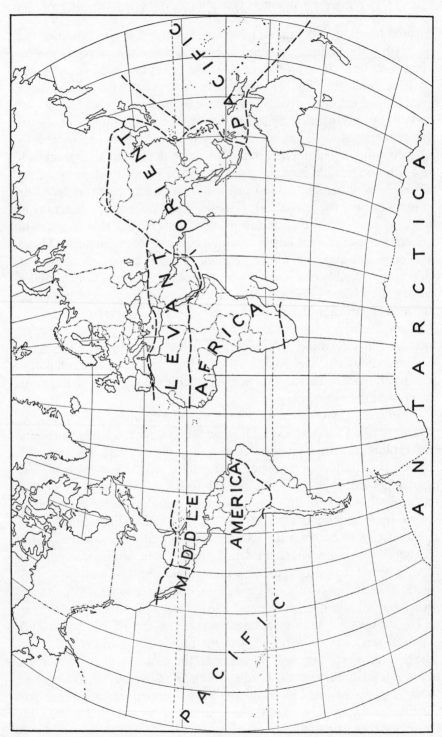

The five centuries since Portuguese mariners pushed hesitantly down the Saharan coast have witnessed cardinal changes in the realms open to exploitation. Exploration has unceasingly opened new areas — the African coast, the Americas, South and East Asia, Inner Asia, Australia, the Pacific Basin, interior Africa, and at last Antarctica. It should be noted that except for the African continent, these discoveries were made in descending order of the value of the natural resources they uncovered. The exploitable world has been subject to varying degrees of political domination by European states. Spheres of influence, protectorates, dependencies, possessions are terms expressing some of these gradations. The political status of exploitable areas is peculiarly unstable. The real test of exploitability is economic subservience rather than political dependence. Cuba, politically independent, is exploitable, whereas British Canada is not.

As one exploitable realm after another has been opened, some areas earlier seized have succeeded in emancipating themselves from European control. These are primarily the regions of the middle latitudes, precisely those regions where Europeans can readily become acclimated. In the New World European settlers established replicas of their homelands which in time reached their political majority and in one way or another cut their leading strings. First in point of time appeared the United States of America, followed by states of South America and the successive members of the British Commonwealth of Nations. Today, most of East Asia has ceased to be exploitable by Europeans, thus completing the roster of middle-latitude areas which have established political, if not legal separatism from Europe, accompanied by practically complete independence of action in economic affairs.

Concurrent with the emancipation of most middle-latitude regions from servitude to Europe has been the wane of certain Western European Powers and the rise of Great Powers outside peripheral Europe. Only Britain and France remain of the truly peripheral Powers, although Germany and Italy in Central Europe have followed the pattern of their western neighbors with such fidelity as to range themselves among the exploiting European states. Three non-European states have risen to first rank in political power. Of them the United States is Europe's ethnic and spiritual offspring. Its political system is that of peripheral Europe as modified in a new world not too unlike the old. Russia has long been coated with a veneer of Western European cul-

FIG. 7. The exploitable world.
The map projection (Van der Grinten's) grossly exaggerates areas toward the poles.

ture, although its present government appears to be in many respects antithetic to the system worked out west of the Adriatic-North Sea line. Russian exploitation has been confined to Inner Asia, where its influence has scarcely been challenged. Russia differs from all the other Great Powers in its immense land area, its few and unsatisfactory contacts with the ocean, and its total lack of overseas colonies. Its significance with respect to the exploitable world is therefore rigorously limited by its location in the interior of Eurasia. Japan, the latest of the non-European Great Powers to assert itself, is as essentially peripheral in location as Great Britain itself. It had only to imitate the political system devised in Western Europe to place itself in the rank of the exploiting states. Many people have believed that China would some day establish itself as another Great Power. Its resources are in its favor, and its population is obviously not incompetent, although it may be excessive. As yet China has been unable to organize itself according to the efficient standards of Western Europe, and is still considered exploitable, particularly by Japan.

The lands in the higher latitudes provide a very meager foundation for human life, and must be exploited from bases in middle latitudes if they are to be utilized at all. Except for Antarctica, where spheres of influence are just now being tentatively claimed, all the circumpolar lands outside Europe are divided among Russia, Canada, the United States, Great Britain, and Denmark. The shares of the three countries last named are relatively small, and Greenland with its icecap promises to be of no greater utility than the ice continent, Antarctica.

There remain then, as areas subject to exploitation, the low latitudes, to which must be added a few extensions beyond the Tropics.

Among low-latitude regions the Orient combines large size and high productivity in amplest measure. Several oriental lands had become the habitats of dense and advanced populations long before Europe heard of them. Then for centuries they were the fabulous sources of luxury goods and of commodities of low-latitude origin. They became the magnet which drew European vessels across the uncharted oceans and one terminus of the first interoceanic trade route. They remain the chief repository of exploitable resources, especially if the word be construed to include the dense populations which can be exploited as markets. All the maritime nations of the world deal with the Orient. Its dense populations and its distinctive craftsmanship have kept it upon a different technological plane from the Occident for many centuries. In East Asia especially, Japan is taking the lead in exploitation. In their several political domains Great Britain, Netherlands, and

France have the advantage. The United States figures importantly because it is the outstanding trading country on the far shore of the Pacific.

After the initial voyage of Columbus, the Americas shot above the European horizon as second only to the Orient as a source of wealth. For a century exploitation was confined chiefly to silver and gold, derived from the low-latitude highlands. Then followed two centuries of occupation of middle-latitude America, both North and South, brought to a close by successful political revolts on the part of virtually the entire mainland south of Canada. Another century has passed, and it is now clear that in the economic sphere the Dominion of Canada has become more truly independent than most of the sovereign states of Middle America. It is not far beside the mark to insist that the part of the Americas which lies within the Tropics, remains effectively a field for European economic exploitation. Were it not for the Monroe Doctrine it would be subjected to political subordination as well. Yet even there, a number of states which possess highland cores are restive, and Mexico at least has gone far to overthrow economic exploitation as well as political direction from abroad. At one time or another, every European state with overseas interests of importance has taken a hand in the Americas. Today the paramount interest in the Caribbean region is that of the United States, now among the exploiting countries. The proximity of a large and well-endowed middle-latitude nation close to a productive segment of the low latitudes creates a reciprocal economy which cannot fail to have political ramifications.

Central Africa is the latest of the extensive low-latitude regions to be subjected to European direction. The political map of that continent is a reasonably accurate representation of colonial force on the earth, except that neither Japan nor the United States has any real stake there.

The remaining areas generally considered to be exploitable are not altogether within the Tropics.

The Pacific realm is a great waste of water, dotted here and there with islands. It is the route from the United States to the Orient and from Japan to Middle America, but its economic value appears to be slight.

From Europe the principal route to the Pacific skirts the Orient and both realms may be reached by two sea lanes. One swings around Africa; the other traverses the Levant, itself the most refractory of all the exploitable areas. The natural resources of the arid Levant are insignificant, and its population is too meager and too scattered to evolve into a self-sustaining unit, as most other middle-latitude regions once exploited have done. Its importance lies in its location as the transit land between Europe on the one hand and all the remaining exploitable fields save Middle America, in the loose but effective psychological coherence of the desert dwellers from the western Sahara to Mongolia, and in the irreconcilability between its nomadic concept of the state as a roving social group unattached to the land and the territorial concept on which European hegemony is founded.

In contrast to the regions facing the sea which European states have considered to be subject to exploitation are the continental heartlands.[1] In most cases the continents have been subdivided among exploiting states along boundaries pushed inland from the coast. Australia is perhaps the neatest example of this practice. There every coast suited to European colonization has become the seat of a colony, leaving the arid heart and the unattractive north coast unsettled, to be administered by the federal government of the continent. In Africa the pattern is much the same but more complicated because of the more complex pattern of natural features. There the heartland possesses considerable value. Part of it makes the farther end of a long extension of British territory thrust from a base on the south coast of the continent. The remainder is the Belgian Congo, a colony with striking correspondence to the form of the Congo River Basin. The heartland of South America is likewise comprised chiefly within a single river valley. Nearly all of it is politically Brazilian territory, although its exploitation remains largely in the hands of Europeans. The legal distinction between the Congo (possessed by a European state) and the Amazon (part of an American sovereignty) should not mask their geopolitical similarity.

In North America and Eurasia the heartlands have escaped the grasp of Western European exploitation. With the insignificant exceptions of southern California and coastal Alaska, no part of English-speaking North America was occupied from a base on the Pacific side. This emphasizes the disparity between active Europe and the small Atlantic on the one hand and passive Asia and the vast Pacific on the other. The heartland of the continent, and the northern three-quarters of the Pacific coast as well, were therefore colonized from the Atlantic seaboard. Because this was settlement colonization from a broad land base and not overseas exploitation from fragmentary coastal stations, the North American ecumene is essentially continental in character and outlook. In this respect it differs profoundly from the peripheral states of Europe and from the British Nations in other continents.

The heartland *par excellence* is that of Eurasia. Larger than the

---

[1] The term is borrowed from H. J. Mackinder: *Democratic Ideals and Reality*. New York: Holt, 1919.

whole of the United States and Canada by one-seventh, Soviet Russia lacks the long ocean frontages which modify the continental outlook of those countries. Instead, its ecumene lies embedded between Arctic wastes and the vast deserts and lofty mountains of central Asia. Its only lookouts to seaward are on the Black Sea, the Gulf of Finland, the White Sea, and the Sea of Japan. All these except the White Sea are cut off from open ocean by one or more formidable powers which stand guard at the outer narrows. Throughout its history, the peoples of the Eurasian heartland have alternately been preoccupied with consolidating their vast and diverse territory, and obsessed with the desire to reach outlets on salt water. Never for a moment have they been free to participate in the overseas endeavors habitual among the states of Western and Central Europe, and even among the self-determining nations of the other continents. Russia's adoption over a period of several centuries of the political paraphernalia of Western Europe hid the deep cleavage in outlook between coastal countries and this heartland. With the establishment of the Soviet Union, Russia declared its independence of peripheral Europe.

The federated organization of the Russian state recognizes the impossibility of creating complete political uniformity among such vast and diverse environments. Its autocratic character may mean only that absolutism, the simplest and most efficient form of government, is required to launch a novel political system. The essential deviation of this system from that of the rest of the occidental world appears to be its emphasis on the group rather than on the individual. It is not clear that this springs from the heartland character of the country, but something of the same tendency appears in Germany and the United States, both of them countries in which the continental outlook notably colors political attitudes.

The vast tracts held to be exploitable, at least in the economic sphere, if not also in the political sense, are varied in nature. Nevertheless, every one is handicapped by environment, or by a lack of balance between natural resources and population density in an interdependent world. The intercommunicating oceans have made neighbors of all the landsmen of the earth. Juxtaposition has enabled some states to exploit others. At the same time it has put into the hands of denizens in all the continents the political tools shaped in Western Europe. Much of the earth today is ruled according to the formula evolved in the coastland states of peripheral Europe.

## CHAPTER FIVE

# The Coastland State and World Power

THE major geopolitical fact of modern times is the conquest of the world by the political system evolved in the coastland states of Western Europe. An area of 1,200,000 square miles required barely 500 years to spread its mode of government over the entire inhabited globe, with its 57,510,000 square miles of land surface. Even if Tibet be eliminated as independent of and untouched by the European mode of government, the ratio is only negligibly reduced. Stated boldly in terms of area, the accomplishment is incredible. To bring it within the bounds of comprehension, it is necessary to inquire into the character of this European area which gave its people such political advantages over regions of utmost diversity: populous lands occupied by stable civilizations no less advanced and presumably by races no less competent; [1] new countries barely scratched by primitive societies; and vast wastes almost impervious to penetration.

Some roots of the Western European system run deep into medieval soil from which the modern occidental world has sprung; a few penetrate the subsoil of classical antiquity. To trace their ramifications is the business of the historian; the geographer, while recognizing their significance, will turn rather to the European habitat to find the foundation on which the dazzling structure of European political hegemony has been reared.

## THE "CONTINENT" OF EUROPE

A map of the world discloses at once that Europe is a continent only by courtesy; in reality it is merely one of four huge peninsulas which

---

[1] Geographers are bound to accept the findings of physical anthropologists, who aver that the physical or intellectual superiority of no race has as yet been demonstrated. (See Hooton, Ernest A.: "Plain Statements about Race," Science, 83 (1936), 511–13). The use of the word "race" to mean linguistic unity or nationality is eschewed throughout this book.

depend from the southerly and westerly margins of Asia. Of the four it is the least set off from the main mass by barriers of mountain and desert, and the least differentiated by contrasts in climate and the resultant vegetation (Fig. 8). It cannot be classed as a continent by any objective geographic test.[1] The name is a heritage of the times when Europeans were ignorant or only vaguely conscious of any part of the earth beyond their own. It serves today as a convenient collective appellation for the group of states which has grown up on this particular peninsula of the Eurasian land mass.

A more careful comparison of the four major Eurasian peninsulas discloses that Europe alone among them is compound — a peninsula composed of lesser peninsulas. Some of the smaller of these, such as Denmark and Brittany, merge without notable break into the land mass from which they jut. Most of the larger ones are more or less cut off on the landward side by mountains which, although ordinarily barriers to human endeavor, have been overpassed at some epochs and to some degree. Of this group the larger Scandinavian Peninsula alone lacks a mountain barrier across its base. Nevertheless, it is the most segregated of all, being virtually an island, through the fact that the long digression by land, rendered difficult in winter by ice and snow and in summer by marsh overlying frozen subsoil, is no line of access. The British Isles throughout much of their history have been quite as close to mainland Europe as has Scandinavia or Iberia.

In emphasizing Europe's ragged outline, it must be borne in mind that peninsular form does not in itself imply close contact with the sea. A coastline may be regular and therefore devoid of harbors; access to the interior may be blocked by mountains, aridity, or other natural barriers; or the fringing sea may interpose heavy surf or shelves and floes of ice. In all these respects Europe scores heavily when compared to Arabia, India, or Indo-China (Fig. 8). In the whole of Europe the only long coastline conspicuously devoid of harbors is the easterly side of Italy, and only the central and somewhat sterile plateau of Spain is difficult of access from the fringing coastal lowlands. Even the Balkan upland, although hard to reach from the seas to the west, is easily penetrated from the east. The Scandinavian Mountains and the Alps are crosshatched by low and gentle passes. No part of the long coastline of Europe is beset by undue storminess, and only the Arctic shore east of the White Sea is impaired by ice blockade.

[1] A. J. Herbertson's wall map, Natural Regions of the World (Oxford: Clarendon Press, 1912), summarizes the identity of Europe and Asia as to natural environment. Francis Delaisi's Les Deux Europes (Paris: Payot, 1929) calls attention to the lack of unity within Europe from the standpoint of economic geography.

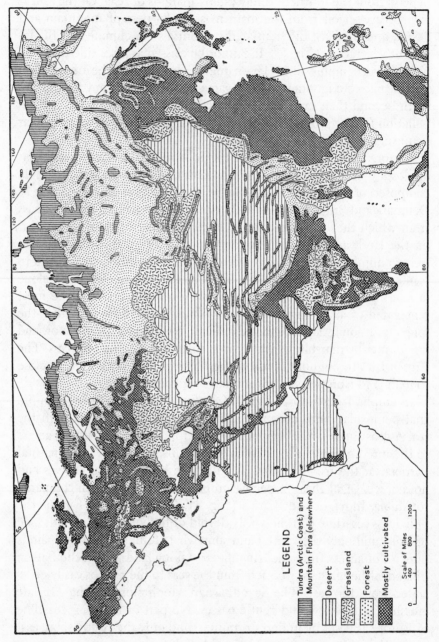

Fig. 8. The Eurasian heartland and its peninsulas. The vegetation is a clue to climate and to landforms.

The mainland of the extreme west of Europe is itself but a somewhat broader peninsula, from which Italy, Iberia, Brittany, and Denmark branch. It is only eastward of a line connecting the head of the Adriatic Sea with the outlet of the Baltic (Fig. 9) that ratio of coastline to area decreases notably, and Eurasia begins to wear a continental air. This

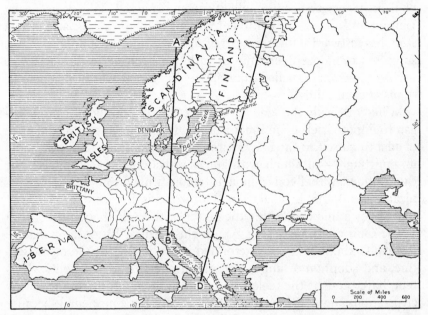

FIG. 9. Europe, showing tripartite and dual subdivisions.

A —————— B Diagrammatic division between Western and East Central Europe.
C —————— D Diagrammatic division between East Central and Eastern Europe.
⊔⊔⊔⊔⊔⊔⊔⊔⊔ Limit of floating ice blocking coastline in winter.

line, which roughly bisects Germany, is critical for the political geography of Europe and the entire earth. West of it navigable rivers lead from the very heart of the lands to the many-harbored coasts, which themselves are snug reentrants of the open ocean, protected from storms and at the same time in easy contact with the high sea. The whole area can maintain contact among its members along two waterways — via the long coasting sea route reaching from Venice to Copenhagen, and via navigable rivers. These are supplemented by easy portages which can be readily grooved with canals. Except for the Mediterranean peninsulas these inland water routes are maintained by evenly distributed rainfall throughout the year. East of the Adriatic-Baltic line navigable streams are farther apart, they fluctuate more widely with the seasons, and they lead to enclosed seas. Moreover, all the rivers and some of the harbors are blocked by ice in the long, cold winter. These lands of inner

Europe have witnessed a history very different from that of peripheral Europe. They were scarcely touched by the civilizing mind of Hellas and the guiding hand of Rome. When Rome's defenses weakened, and new blood streamed into the Empire from the coniferous forests of Central Europe, peripheral Europe was modified, but the essentials of Roman society lived on, albeit metamorphosed. Wooded Central Europe, and all the vast continent, originally forest or grassland, which stretches eastward across the heart of Asia without a notable barrier, was subjected to a dozen centuries of turbulence stirred up by successive waves of migrants expelled from the dry interior of Asia during periods of insufficient rainfall.

When gradually the sedentary civilization of peripheral Europe began to impose itself upon inner Europe, it conquered only at the price of adapting itself to the new environment. Begun early and continued unremittingly — although with many setbacks — in Central Europe the conquest was effective enough to constitute a middle zone recognizably European in character. This zone is bordered on the east roughly by a line connecting the outlet of the Adriatic with the head of the Gulf of Finland (Fig. 9). In this Central European zone the Roman Catholic faith, later reformed in the north, the Germanic culture, and adoption or imposition of peripheral Europe's political system, have brought the region into close affinity with the source of its civilization. Nevertheless, its outlook is basically continental, because its interior position has always set it apart from the periphery of Europe. This outlook has been modified by technological advances of the past century, but not abandoned. Despite steamships, railroads, and airplanes, Central Europe faces up-Baltic and down-Danube. Even today few parts of it are crossed by paved highroads, and none of it has a network of paved byroads.

Still farther east lies the true core of the Eurasian land mass, with a political outlook never attuned to that which prevails in peripheral Europe. This Eastern Europe includes Russia, a country inundated by successive waves of emigrants from the heart of Asia recently enough to give rise to the current saying: " Scratch a Russian and you will find a Tatar "; it embraces Turkey, interloper in Europe from steppes of nomadic Asia. All of it is the heir of Byzantine civilization, particularly as transmitted through the Orthodox church and the Cyrillic alphabet. Some of it has been overlaid for one, two, or six centuries with the desert-born faith of Islam and the concepts implicit in Arabic literature. This is the region where a new political system is being tried, a system rooted in the technology of modern peripheral Europe to be sure, and conceivably better adapted to the world of the machine age than is the national capitalistic state. Whatever the outcome of the experiment, the Soviet mode of government is opposed in basic concepts to that of peripheral Europe, and it is being tried out in an environment fundamentally different.

For the purposes of political geography the Europe of the atlas must be divided, then, into three parts — western or peripheral, central or inner, and eastern or Asiatic. In Western, peripheral, maritime, Europe the national state was born, and from Western Europe it spread — first to Central Europe and later to all parts of the globe.

## THREE DEGREES OF POLITICAL INTEGRATION

Like every other continent, Europe is a compound of natural units. But Western Europe is distinctive in that no one of these units is so large as to be out of scale with its neighbors. Under primitive conditions, economic and political society tends to correspond to natural units. As improved transportation brings peoples into closer contact, they coalesce into somewhat larger entities. In times of accelerated exchange and advanced technology, barriers still more stubborn have been overcome sufficiently to forge states embracing considerable area. Most of these states have as their cores lowlands of moderate size ringed about by barriers (hills or mountains) areas easily discernible on a well-made relief map and traditionally recognized by names in common use, even though they may have lost their political independence. The Po Plain, Andalusia, Aquitaine, the Paris Basin, the English Plain, the Scottish Lowland are some of them. Others are set off by distinct local climates, as Old Castile, New Castile, and Algarve. A few rest upon edaphic conditions: Jutland is bounded on its land side by a waste of sandy plain; Skåne coincides with the part of Sweden well-mantled with glacial deposits; Friesland was originally a group of hillocks rising above a marshy delta; Franconia, one of the few natural units to have lost all semblance of political coherence, is a lowland mainly alluvial, surrounded by low hills, barriers only because of their sterility; Brittany is a granitic hill country of infertile soil. A number of the basins renowned because of their long political history are limestone plains, and their stable soils enhance the utility of their gentle surface and easy access to water transportation. Some of these, and others not underlain by limestone, benefit by a layer of finely divided, fertile, well-drained soil which in all ages since neolithic times has favored agriculture. Such soil is called by the French " limon " a term adopted for use in these pages.

Such a mosaic of habitable units is favorable to political beginnings. A small community assured a livelihood by fertile fields and in a measure protected from outsiders by encircling hills or other barrier boundaries, can and does develop social stability. If, once established but not too firmly fixed in a mold, such a group can coalesce with neighboring units as intercourse grows, the broadening territorial base will support an ever-expanding state.

The feudal society of medieval Europe was admirably suited to the natural setting. Because this system was imprinted with traditions of Imperial Rome, the whole of Western Europe was looked upon as the domain of the Emperor, descendant of the Caesars. Yet, the lord of the manor was in simple fact the boss of a large subsistence farm, operated by a number of families legally attached to the land. As lessee of the farm, the squire owed allegiance and rent to a superior nobleman, commonly a baron or a bishop. His and neighboring manors constituted a naturally marked unit of land, such as a small valley, a fertile pocket of plain surrounded by marsh or forest, an irrigable piedmont slope or floodplain. Innumerable such natural units of the least order of magnitude fostered the feeling of political unity among near neighbors. The common people met on occasional market days under the walls of the baron's castle or the monastery church for chaffering and merrymaking, or they took refuge there when beset by enemies from beyond the borders of their " country." The several squires of the manors fought under their liege lord in defense of their lands or carried war into enemy country.

Hundreds of baronies, bishoprics, viscounties, and abbeys never succeeded in expanding. Indeed, many were subdivided through inheritance or conquest. Others, which occupied the cores of larger arable regions, became renowned agricultural centers. As forests and marshes gave way to fields and pastures, arable units coalesced. The scattered force of small units was superseded by the consolidated strength of large ones. Among others, Wessex, Guienne, Saxony, and The County of Portugal at one time figured importantly in political affairs. If, besides having fertile fields, a district was situated to profit also by trade, it was almost sure to wax politically powerful. Provence and Burgundy, Swabia and Lorraine, Venice and Lombardy, are cases. Even lacking the best soil, a first-class trading location aggrandized its lucky overlord; the counts of Champagne grew rich in one of the poorest agricultural districts of France. Trade stimulated the growth of cities, and in cities manufacturing flourished. Tuscany and Flanders, especially, throve on manufacture, added to trade and farming.

Not a few counties, duchies, archbishoprics, and even republics, of this second order of magnitude enjoyed regal wealth, and their rulers exercised almost regal power — Normandy, Burgundy, Cologne, Saxony, Austria, Venice, Genoa, and Tuscany among them. The heads of these countries lacked one thing needful — the recognition by their peers as kings by divine right. The unquestioned right to rule Europe had been since Roman times vested in the Emperor, heir of the Caesars. The practical effectiveness of imperial power dwindled as the Roman state disintegrated. It disappeared when the rulers could no longer keep the provinces of their empire in constant communication with the capital city. Paved roads sank to pitted and muddy trails punctuated by detours, or were abandoned to grass; fallen bridges ceased to be replaced; marshes reasserted themselves as drainage ditches became clogged. In the dry south aqueducts broke and ran dry, leaving irrigated fields to revert to brush; in the humid north the resurgent forest increasingly separated the communities of a declining population, which as it shrank clustered on the spots best suited to subsistence agriculture. The feudal system was the practical substitute for the defunct Roman government. True, for a few brief years Charlemagne welded a considerable part of Western Europe into a semblance of its former unity. Upon his death this pallid afterglow of Roman glory faded, and feudalism reasserted itself with renewed force. No emperor could hold together a world in which technology and communication had been reduced to primitive terms.

The concept of the *imperium* persisted, notwithstanding. The Universal Church kept alive the unity of Christendom. Feeble trickles of trade held to the routes along which powerful currents of commerce had formerly surged. Yet, when finally the imperial title was revived in the 10th century, it laid claim only to Italy, the eastern fringe of what had been Roman Gaul, and the adjacent country which the Romans had known as German. Within this realm the shadowy authority inherited from Rome helped to prevent any one ruler, no matter how powerful, from achieving domination over the rest. The larger subdivisions of the Atlantic border of the Roman Empire shook off their hoary allegiance and accepted kings as valid representatives of supreme terrestrial authority. Each of them came to be identified with one of the naturally marked units of the first order of magnitude, into which the Atlantic seaboard falls.

Great Britain, cut off from the mainland by sea, ultimately became incorporated under English hegemony. France slowly defined itself as the region lying between the Pyrenees Mountains and the line of the

Alps-Jura-Vosges-Ardennes. Spain welded the whole Iberian Peninsula except the humid lowland of the Atlantic littoral, which became Portugal. Scandinavia, never a part of the Roman Empire, likewise set up for itself, borrowing the political machinery of its neighbors. It was in these kingdoms marginal to the Atlantic Ocean that the European national state was born and nurtured, and from them Europeans set out to discover and conquer the earth. From them Central Europe finally learned how to scrap its vestigial Roman *Imperium* and to substitute national states. Through conquest, example, or imitation, every people under the sun has been dominated or disturbed by this political system.

## EXTENSION OVERSEAS OF PERIPHERAL EUROPE'S POLITICAL POWER

The political system evolved in peripheral Europe was later carried to the ends of the earth by colonization, as in North America, by conquest, as in Africa, and by copying, as in Japan. Nevertheless, all the groundwork was laid by states on the western fringe of Europe. These people undertook voyages overseas, which established contacts, on foreign shores of the most diverse natural environments, with people of every degree of civilization. In the process several European countries created political empires. A number of these empires are small, some were short-lived, others are of recent origin. To analyze the geopolitical structure of the whole colonial world is beyond the scope of this book. The specific incidence of colonialism in the Americas and in Africa appears in other chapters. It will suffice here to consider the British Empire, as illustrating every aspect of imperial political geography.

Colonial movements have eternally been associated with the sea, that enticing avenue to unknown worlds. With the Discoveries, overseas movement stepped up to an order of magnitude hitherto undreamed. At that period the more highly endowed natural units of Western Europe, crystallizing out of feudal chaos into vigorous national states, found the ancient trade routes to the Orient blocked, just when their demand for silks and spices was rapidly mounting. The obstacles were states of nomadic origin in the arid transit land south and east of the Mediterranean Sea. These steppeland folk knew little of the economics of trade, and either forbade it or overtaxed it. The same thing had happened before and had perforce been tolerated. This time Europe was not helpless. Ancient learning had been revived, and recent inventions had emancipated sailors from point-to-point navigation. Closure of the land route east to Asia in the face of increasing traffic directed the attention of maritime interests in the newly organized national states to possible sea routes north and south. Some individuals even held the belief that the Orient might be reached by boldly sailing west across the ocean. All these projects were vitalized by the energy which, so long expended on petty internal strife among tiny states, could now be turned by the newly unified national states to external interests.

Attracted by the expectation of profit and spurred by the political force generated from newly consolidated national resources, maritime ascendency dramatically deserted the enclosed Mediterranean and Baltic seas and settled upon the seafaring states facing the Atlantic Ocean.

Norway and Denmark set their seal upon islands of the northern ocean, but were stopped by the perennial ice of the Arctic from reaching the Orient. Portugal, consolidated by a long struggle for independence from the Moors, carried its war across the Strait of Gibraltar into enemy country. Thereupon, it launched exploration along the West African coast as a natural outlet for its newly released political drive. The fishing banks which continue without break in the cool current that laves Portugal and Morocco and the Sahara provided a school for mariners. In less than a century Portuguese ships reached India and China from the south. The route west, not to the Indies, but to new worlds, was traced under Spanish auspices. Spain followed Portugal in suddenly finding energy directed for centuries against the Moorish invaders, released under a new dispensation of political unification. Yet it appears to have required an extraordinary motive to take up the fantastic challenge of sailing west to reach the east. This motive was supplied by the rivalry between Spain and Portugal, the one section of the Iberian Peninsula which had made good its separatism from Spain.

Every coastal state between the Pyrenees and the Baltic has at some time taken a hand in overseas expansion. The intermediate ones entered the lists later than the countries which lay closest to the unexplored routes to north and south. While the ocean routes were being traced by states which had already emerged from medieval fission, France and Britain were engaged in consolidating their larger refractory territories, and the peoples of the Germanic plain were struggling for independence. One by one, as these units achieved their goal, they became contenders for a share of overseas trade and overseas dependencies.

## The Role of Britain

The most successful of the maritime states has been Great Britain, as attested by its continuous leadership in the colonial field since the beginning of the 17th century and by its dominant position today among the colonial powers. Many of the elements of this success lie within the British Isles.

The British Isles lie very much on the margin of Europe. So long as culture stemmed from the south, and the trunkline of trade connected the Mediterranean region with the mass of the continent north of the mountains, they were outposts on the frontier. Much of the fertile soil was originally covered with forest or marsh, and the only valuable mineral mined in early times was tin, a rich ore easily exported. The islands as a whole and in their larger lowlands, face the mainland, not too far away to see in bright weather from points in southeast England. For this reason the islands cannot entirely escape continental influences. For a millennium they were subjected to conquest after conquest; for another five hundred years, relict bits of mainland remained in the hands of English rulers; and the British sovereignty of the French-speaking Channel Islands today is current evidence of the ancient interdependence. Military conquest was more spectacular, but no more important, than the position of the islands as an overseas frontier country devoted to grazing sheep for the woolen manufacture of Flanders across the Channel. The imposing ruins of Cistercian monasteries, built from the profits of the woolen trade, give some notion of Britain as the Australia of the day.

The Discoveries reoriented Europe. The British Isles found themselves in the front row of the newly enlarged theater of world trade, and and on the main aisle to the commercial foyer of all North Europe. In these respects its position was no better than that of France, and it suffered the handicap of having no direct land routes to the interior. In compensation it had no land borders to defend. Preoccupation with land defense cost France its first colonial empire (Ch. 6) and forced the Netherlands to sacrifice some of its overseas territory and much of its overseas trade.

By fortunate coincidence, England, as the organizing nucleus of the British Isles, succeeded in integrating the southern half of the island of Great Britain just prior to the Discoveries, and was able to attach the northern extension of the great British island (Scotland), at almost the moment it embarked on overseas colonization in earnest. These steps were outward symbols of the inner character of the British state — a loose centralization which permits considerable latitude in local government. In forming such a state nature played a part.

Each of the larger British islands is a patchwork of till-mantled lowlands on sedimentary rocks, set apart by highlands chiefly crystalline

FIG. 10. The basins facing the " Narrow Seas."

and ice-scoured. The English plain at the southeast is the most distinctive of the lowlands. Its climate is the least rainy and its agriculture therefore leans more toward tillage than in moister regions. It faces the continent on two sides: the Paris Basin, core of France, on the south; the Rhenish Lowland, with its commercial possibilities, on the east (Fig. 10). Indeed, the London Basin and Flanders form a structural unit cleft by the Channel of water which traverses the bottom of the depression, and the Thames was a tributary of the Rhine in a not very remote geological past. The whole plain is easy of access from the sea

by way of drowned river mouths, and in every important estuary stands
an island ready to serve invaders as a springboard for conquest of the
mainland. Napoleon was only expressing an age-old fact in current
terms when he said, " Belgium is a pistol pointed at the heart of
England."

Because no other part of the British Isles possesses the combination
of natural conditions here listed, the English Plain takes the lead in
tillage and trade, bears the brunt of conquest from overseas, and holds
the stroke oar whenever an independent Britain faces the mainland.
The territorial and administrative integration of the English Plain was
the political realization of its natural unity.

The successive waves of conquest made England a hybrid of all peoples of peripheral Europe. The Roman occupation was based on northern Gaul, where a crossing of 23 miles at the Channel narrows brought
the galleys to a cove protected from west winds by a cliffed promontory
that marks the end of a long ridge of chalk (Fig. 11). The route inland
for the legions follows a narrow belt of well-drained ground between
this ridge and the tidal marshes which then bordered the Thames as
far up the river as the first suitable ford (Westminster). A shipway for
goods lay in the creeks of the Thames estuary, screened in part by the
islands of Sheppey and Thanet (the latter now attached to the mainland by meadow). To insure the safety of the shipway and of the
Thames crossing, a counterpart of the south shore road was built from
Colchester, the capital of the defeated Britons, to London. It traversed
open, well-drained ground north of the river marshes. The first zone of
conquest was flanked by the fenlands on the northeast, and by hills and
woods northwest, west, and south. From its focus at London the Romans built radial roads which held the English Plain and the surrounding minor lowlands in their net. The north road, skirting the fenland,
led and still leads past the series of small lowlands along the east side of
the island as far as the Scottish Lowland. Northwest across the Mid-
lands a road, branching at Wroxeter near the Severn crossing, led to the
lowlands which lie among the foothills of the Welsh mountains, and
to the great camp at Chester and the Irish Sea. West and southwest
another trunk road forked at Silchester for the Severn estuary and the
south coast lowlands. Laterals crossed these main lines, and many subsidiary roads completed the web.

Many Roman roads carry trunk traffic today, and the Roman pattern (radial roads in each lowland linked by pass routes across intervening uplands) has remained unchanged except for digressions to
serve post-Roman urban sites and a tendency to conform to rugged

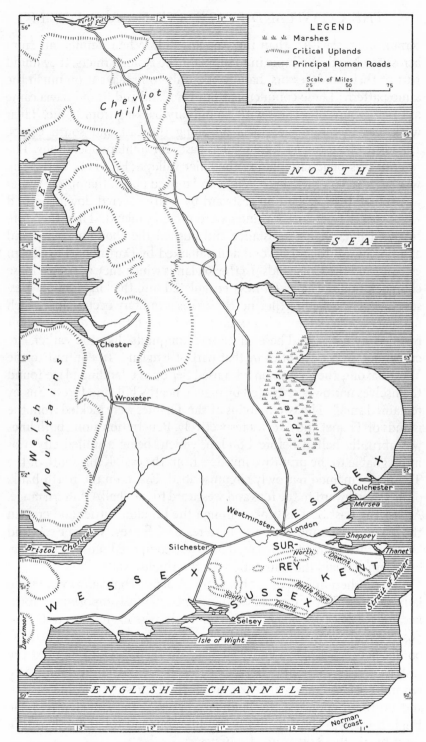

FIG. 11. Penetration of the British Isles from the direction of the European continent.

terrain more slavishly than the Romans did. When immigrants from across the North Sea came in to supplant the Roman rulers, they undid part of their predecessors' handiwork, only to reweave it on much the same pattern. These conquerors from Friesland and Scandinavia came as small groups of settlers with no military backing from home. Their work was therefore piecemeal all along the east and south coasts. Islands in the estuaries were used as bases for military operations. The interior was penetrated along the chief valleys (Fig. 11). The group which started on the Isle of Wight and moved up Southampton Water was cut off from expansion eastward by heath-covered downs beyond which other bodies of kinsmen were moving inland. They therefore followed lines of less resistance and pushed the aborigines westward and northward to and beyond a line marked by Dartmoor, the Severn estuary, and the Cotswolds. In the lowlands which they overran a loose confederation of shares (shires) coagulated into the kingdom of Wessex. Later it pushed farther northward as a military occupation which made its way by subjugating small districts, each from a defense point fortified by a castle. These successive conquests, like the earlier, are embalmed in the counties in that part of England. In contrast to the West Saxons, their kinsmen who used Selsey as a landing place found themselves narrowly restricted by marsh, heathy hill, and forest. Sussex remained small. The two margins of the Thames were tackled from the islands of Thanet and Mersea respectively. Penetration along both lines was abruptly halted before London, which, being a walled city, was impregnable to the primitive invaders from the east. Kent, south of the Thames, remained narrowly circumscribed. Essex, on the north bank, pushed northward to the fens and westward to the chalk Chiltern range. At last the East Saxons broke through the London barrier and crossed the Thames to found their Southern realm — Surrey. When Essex and Wessex then merged their kingdoms they comprised most of the English Plain and laid the foundation for the English state.

The northern lowlands, as far as the Scottish Highlands, were similarly overrun, but remained of minor geopolitical importance. Each became the ancestor of a modern county. In passing, it is interesting to observe that Scots reoccupied the banks of the Forth and forced the border between English and Scots back to the Cheviot range. At the eastern end of these hills Berwick controls the coastal lowland, there ten miles wide. During the span when the Danes overran the eastern and northern counties, the boundary between the Danelaw and the English law was the Thames below London, and for the rest, with a short break, the Roman road to Chester.

The slow integration of the English Plain, interrupted by the Danish invasion, was resumed only to be rushed to completion by the Norman conquest. Like the Roman occupation it was a military operation rather than a folk migration. It was predicated on crossing near the narrows of the Channel, but from a point on the Norman coast. Landing was therefore made on the one bit of well-drained coast separating the marshes which occupy the seafront between the North Downs and the South Downs. For several elective kingdoms of fluctuating size the Norman rulers substituted a single state under a hereditary king. Personal union with the richer parts of France stimulated trade and urban life. The sovereigns supported the cities in order to repress the growing power of the feudal, landed nobility, which waxed independent under a line of non-resident kings. These men extorted the Magna Charta from their sovereign, and in time became strong enough to depose and destroy kings and their heirs. Benefiting from this strife between king and lords, townsmen and small landholders slowly acquired political personality expressed in the House of Commons in Parliament. Finally, the nobility destroyed itself in civil war, leaving the king supreme in power, checked only by Parliament. This gave opportunity for unification of the law courts, some centralization of administration, and political subordination of the church to the state. All these advances in government were made possible by freedom from invasion. This alone made it safe to check royal power in a military age and rendered it unnecessary to subordinate local government to central authority.

As soon as England became unified, it was able to fend off invaders from the continent. Thenceforth, external conflict was confined to English aggression — attempts to subjugate France and non-English portions of the British Isles. This fighting took place beyond the borders of England. The Hundred Years' War determined that England could not subdue any considerable part of the European mainland in the face of rising nationalism there. Armed expeditions into the Welsh upland brought victories, but not allegiance, and the more remote, larger, and wilder Scotland, protected by its mountains and enriched by its lowland, resisted conquest until long after the consolidation of England had been completed. Wales and Scotland joined forces with England only when each gave a line of kings to Great Britain. Each has retained a large degree of autonomy. Ireland, separated from the main island by a tempestuous sea and out of reach of peaceful penetration which helps to make conquests effective, has never been integrated with its English neighbor. The fissure which separated the extreme north from the rest of the island stems from a plantation of Scottish colonists, sent as a military measure, and subsequent emigration of Scots across the narrow North Channel.

England had just emerged from civil war as a moderately centralized state to which Wales was loosely attached as an indication of the political " Great " Britain to come, when the Discoveries opened fresh outlets for the energy newly released by political consolidation. Chief of these were opportunities for overseas commerce, which soon became so profitable that land ceased to be the paramount basis of English wealth. Rich merchants advanced the interests of the urban communities, especially London, the capital and trade center of England and entrepôt for North Sea and Baltic commerce, and Bristol, the English port most favorably situated for colonial traffic. Fishermen putting out of all the little bays about the islands made admirable sailors, both for the merchant marine and for the navy, urged by merchant interests. Farm laborers who were being squeezed off the land by the enclosure of common pastures and by more efficient use of the soil were ready to emigrate to the new continents in the hope of finding a livelihood denied at home. The English Plain redoubled its wealth, based now on harbors as well as fertile fields. Its merchants increased their political power as burghers in Commons, and as active heads of firms which had members of the House of Lords as sleeping partners. A few obtained patents of nobility themselves, generally after purchasing estates and so entering the rank of landlords — the group from which the upper house of Parliament is drawn.

These alterations in the structure of society have since been described as a " Commercial Revolution." A conspicuous aspect of it was a prolonged tussle for political supremacy between the landowners, who had been entrenched for many centuries as the ruling class, and the rising commercial interests, backed by many landowners who were not averse to profiting from new sources of wealth. The issue was joined in a new civil war. All the lesser and poorer lowlands of the British Isles as well as the rugged highlands ranged themselves under the king, who was of Scottish origin, against the English Plain, which dominated Parliament and ruled by its authority. The battles occurred along the Cotswold hills, in the marshes and on the moors of southwest England, and in Ireland. The final flareups, belated aftermaths, came in the Scottish Highlands.

This struggle was jeopardized by an easily frustrated invasion of England by Holland, a leading naval power, but it could not have taken place at all had it not been for the inability of the larger continental landpowers to attack a vigorous state entrenched on an island. Success of the English commercial interests broadened the franchise and converted an absolutism based on land to an oligarchy composed of landowners and merchants who ruled with little regard to their monarch.

During the long civil conflict in the 17th century the home government had been too preoccupied to pay attention to the infant colonies which had been planted overseas just before the war broke out. In consequence the colonists had been able to adapt their institutions to novel environments without interference from stay-at-homes who were ignorant of nature's impositions in the New World. This was one of the chief elements in the success of British colonies when pitted against those of other nations. When civil war was over, colonial trade was fostered by the home government, to the profit of both Britain and its dependencies.

Hardly had the Commercial Revolution been accepted as a fact when the Industrial Revolution once again broadened the economic base of British society and strengthened the British Empire. Small waterpower sites in the upland of central and northern England gave manufacturing its first impetus, but its flowering came with the invention which transplanted the industrial society to a new foundation — coal and iron (Fig. 3). In several of the lesser lowlands of Great Britain, including Scotland and Wales, coal is abundant and useful both for making steam and for smelting iron and firing pottery. Easily worked iron ore on or near the coalfields sufficed until the new industrial life was well established. Ample deposits of high-grade pottery clay lie a bit farther away. At several points coal lies on tidewater and can be used to fill ships outbound for raw materials and foodstuffs, and unable to find a cargo of more valuable but less bulky manufactured goods. Both mines and factories could be manned by a rapidly increasing population, unchecked by wars in defense of its homeland. The overseas dependencies provided raw materials and food, and their markets absorbed some of the surplus manufactures.

At home the political maneuvers of the merchants a century earlier were repeated by mine and factory owners. They attached great merchants and landlords to their cause, saw to it that expanding manufactural boroughs received representation in Commons, and took their place as elements in the political society of the nation. All this without another civil war, however. Expansion occurred nearly everywhere in Great Britain except in the heart of the English Plain, where there was neither water-power, coal, nor iron Thus the new technology redressed the balance within England as between the southeast and the northwest. Scotland and Wales, possessing coal, have followed in the wake of

England, thus completing the economic consolidation of Great Britain, although not its political centralization. Ireland, lacking opportunities for trade and having neither coal nor iron, remained an agricultural province, the rift between it and England ever widening.

The favorable combination of nature at home gave Britain the lead among European states in the race for colonies, and in wealth created by foreign trade. The profound internal alterations in the economic basis of society were gradually matched by an increasing political flexibility. This in turn could be applied to colonial administration in the form of varying degrees of self-government for the dependencies. In the struggle for colonial supremacy which Britain won in the 18th century, the British dependencies effectively aided the mother country by their ability to fight their own battles, whereas the colonies of France, alternately pampered and pinched by paternal government, proved liabilities rather than assets. When Britain, successful in dominating the colonial world, undertook to put its most advanced colonies into an economic straight-jacket, they revolted, and with the aid of France, severed their political ties to the homeland. As a result of this costly lesson, the British Empire within the middle latitudes has in time transformed itself into the British Commonwealth of Nations.

## The Geopolitical Grounding of the British Empire

Politically and legally the several parts of the British Empire present a composite, even confused, structure. Diverse elements, in the evolution of several centuries, have been wrought into a mosaic of complex forms, instead of being welded into a uniform state. Considered from the standpoint of political geography, the picture is less puzzling.

The unparalleled Empire has been possible because the British Isles are unique. They lie close to continental Europe, they face it, and they participate in its economic and political life, but they are separated from the mainland by a belt of water which has thus far rendered them practically immune to invasion so long as the islanders maintain a powerful navy. Relieved by control of home waters from the perennial menace of invading armies, conflicting interests within the state need not accept dictation from autocratic government. Instead they can safely struggle for a political order which permits maximum ingenuity in the utilization of natural endowments. The lowland seats of political force have been large enough and well enough endowed with natural resources to establish unquestioned independence from counterpart political kernels on the adjacent continent, but hardly sufficient to reduce their rivals to dependence (Ch. 6). Trade with the mainland continued after military stalemate had been reached. The islands were already hospitable to the idea of overseas commerce and practiced in the art of trade when the Discoveries found them on the frontier and left them at the front door of Europe.

The Strait of Dover is like the girdle of an hourglass (Fig. 10), and with the " narrow seas " between Brittany and the Zuider Zee makes a double funnel through which pours practically all the seaborne traffic of North Europe. The other outlet of the North Sea lies too far off-side, and the straits between the islands in that quarter are too stormy to attract ships, even from the Baltic region. Of the two shores of the Channel and its double north of the Strait of Dover, the English offers the larger number of natural harbors and fewer shoals. These advantages of the early days have now been largely offset by harbor works and dredging. Nevertheless, the shipping lane has always followed the English shore of the Channel because its numerous high but snub promontories favor point-to-point sailing. These maritime advantages must not be overrated. Both France and the Netherlands built up notable colonial empires in the course of their commercial rivalry with England. The Netherlands had to accept a secondary place among colonial nations primarily because of its small home base, a land which has only grass and gardens as resources of consequence. The inferior Channel coast of France is compensated by harbors on the Bay of Biscay and the Mediterranean. In its unsuccessful struggle with Britain over colonial spoils it was handicapped far less by an unsatisfactory Channel coastline than by the need to defend a long land boundary and by the centralized government which that military necessity helped to produce. Although powerful in war, central authority is incompetent to administer in detail far-flung colonies only vaguely understood by the home government. When war was carried overseas in the 18th century, British colonies, schooled in self-reliance, needed only moderate support from home to offset the superior French war machine fighting far from its base without support from local colonies.

The British advantage in the colonial realm was redoubled when manufacture revolutionized occidental economic society. Britain's abundant coal gave it the lead in manufacturing wares which the dependencies were eager to buy in exchange for raw materials for British factories and food for British workmen. Trade leaped ahead and showered new wealth on commercial England. Small lowlands, hitherto minor producers of wealth, now rose in rank. Coal on tidewater in South Wales, the Tyne Valley, and the Scottish Lowland was fed di-

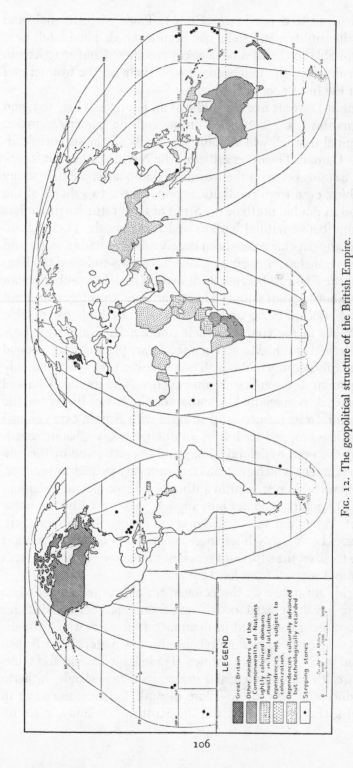

Fig. 12. The geopolitical structure of the British Empire.

The base is the homolosine projection used by courtesy of University of Chicago Press (J. Paul Goode's series of base maps; H. M. Leppard, editor).

LEGEND

Great Britain

Other members of the Commonwealth of Nations

Lightly colonized domans mostly in low latitudes

Dependencies not subject to colonization.

Dependencies culturally advanced but technologically retarded

• Stepping stones

Scale of Miles
0        1500      3000
      750      2250

rectly into ships. Coal in those places and a bit farther inland gave rise to more than half a dozen manufactural districts of the first order of magnitude. These found their outlets by way of ports hitherto insignificant, particularly Glasgow in Scotland and Liverpool in Northwest England, both facing the New World rather than Europe. None of this expansion occurred on the English Plain, which now had to share its traditional leadership with upstart lowlands. Nevertheless, London benefited, both as the capital of a rapidly expanding state and as the economic metropolis entrenched in power by its age and by its position facing the continent.

The British Empire has evolved as an integral part of the unique character of the British Isles. As other nations have developed their commerce, their coal and iron manufacture, and their colonial empires, they have diminished the distance between themselves and Great Britain, so long the leader in world markets and in world affairs. The utilization of electricity and petroleum has jeopardized the economic place of Great Britain, because the British islands possess little water-power and no oil. There is little petroleum in the whole empire, and such water-power as is developed to run mills in the dependencies will still further cut into homeland manufacture. The empire no longer rests upon a physical base either inherently unique or developed beyond effective competition from its rivals. Nevertheless, it remains one of the largest, if not the very largest aggregation of resources and therefore of political power that the world has ever seen. If it should disintegrate, the political evolution which has marked the past millennium will be set in reverse. Its internal structure as related to earth conditions may shed some light on its probable stability.

## The Geopolitical Structure of the British Empire

Stripping aside legal formulae, the British Empire consists of half a dozen types of components (Fig. 12). Unique among them is Great Britain and Northern Ireland, economic dynamo which generated the political system, and which keeps it going. The imperial capital, London, is the proliferation on the identical site of the capital of the Lower Thames Valley. Located at the farthest downstream easy crossing, it stands, by corollary, at the head of ocean navigation. It has by steps become the capital of the English Plain, of all England, of England and Wales, of Great Britain, and of the United Kingdom. In governing this accretion of all the peoples of the British Isles, London has achieved a loose union entirely compatible with the retention of local nationality, so strikingly exemplified in recent Irish history. In the southern four-fifths of Ireland nearly three centuries of enforced political union failed to create harmony, and this unit has been transferred to another category within the British Commonwealth. Lacking the sinews of manufacture, and separated from world trade and from easy contact with great Britain by stormy seas, this part of Ireland has never been brought into the orbit of British life except by armed conquest. Ireland was finally conquered after the church in Great Britain had become Protestant, but before the reform movement had touched the smaller island. The religious schism, itself an expression of Ireland's remoteness from European currents, has intensified the Irish antipathy for Great Britain. Only in the north, where Scotland lies close by, have Scottish coal and Scottish immigrants kept one-fifth of the island attached to the United Kingdom.

Within each community of the United Kingdom a gradually broadening economic base has been accompanied by a widening franchise, until today essentially all adults are entitled to vote for political officers. Less tangible, but equally pertinent, has been a growing flexibility of the political order. This unconsciously evolved to cope with the gradual foliation of society from a simple subsistence agriculture to a compound agricultural-commercial-mining-manufactural basis. It has enabled the government to adapt itself to the many changes which have altered the face of Europe more than once during the course of British history. This has occurred with the minimum of conflict, and quite without recourse to destructive political revolutions which have marred the orderly progression of continental European states. It is this increasing flexibility that has permitted the English Plain to absorb into its political life the complex components of the empire.

### THE SELF-GOVERNING DOMINIONS OF MIDDLE LATITUDES

A part of the expansion of British authority overseas has been the achievement of emigrants from Great Britain who have sought new homes in the New World. This colonization by settlement aims to recreate the old land in the new. At the outset colonists struck out for any and all lands to which Britain laid claim. Very often they moved under the auspices of a chartered company, which furnished part or all of the needed capital. A number of expeditions failed — some because they were ill-equipped, others because they were in advance of their time. In general, however, success of colonization is to be measured by the natural environment of the habitat selected. With few and dubious exceptions settlement colonies have evolved only within the middle latitudes and on low-latitude highlands. Even there small size or meager resources have prevented some dependencies from achieving self-government, the goal of all colonies of transplanted Britishers. The Greek colonies, classic prototypes of those of Britain, were independent of the mother-state from the beginning. Even in the uniform environment of Mediterranean shores, the ancient world did not envisage a colonial empire. In the modern world, overseas settlements were conceived as subject to the mother country, bound to accept direction from " home." It was only the political turmoil within England occasioned by growing commerce during the first century of the British colonies that kept maternal hands off the infant settlements. When once free to turn to colonial problems, Britain undertook a program of dictation and coercion to the end of making the colonies economically reciprocal to the homeland. It was too late! The string of colonies which occupied the most favored environment under the British flag outside Great Britain itself insisted upon self-determination of their internal life. In a century and a half of autonomous existence, they had learned the wisdom of local option — the necessity to pursue a course within the frame of nature as it existed on the Atlantic seaboard of North America, whether or not it suited the interests of men in the British Isles.

The immediate outcome of the refusal of the thirteen colonies to accept British dictation was their independence. In the heat of conflict this appeared to be the only possible alternative to abject subjugation. In winning independence they were aided by the long, cold winters of the northern colonies, the impassable roads of a frontier country after rains, the paucity of bridges, and above all by the handicap which Britain suffered in fighting from a base three thousand miles away. For Great Britain the ulterior outcome of the American Revolution was a chastened attitude toward its remaining middle-latitude colonies. British willingness, thenceforth, to let its settlement colonies go their own course, coupled with natural attachment on the part of the remaining middle-latitude colonies to the homeland from which they had recently sprung, engendered a novel concept in colonial administration. This was the creation of autonomous dominions, with machinery of government duplicating that of the mother country — a locally elected Parliament to govern, and a representative appointed by the king of Great Britain to reign as viceroy. One by one the larger middle-latitude colonies have been transformed into self-governing dominions. To strengthen them and simplify government, those which desired union have been incorporated into federations, each vastly larger in area than the mother country, and equivalent in population to many independent nations.

Recently the aggregation of self-governing dominions, plus Great Britain and Northern Ireland have been denominated " The British Commonwealth of Nations." The appellation is an attempt to fit the facts more precisely than does the term " Empire." All the members of the Commonwealth have almost complete sovereign rights, including coinage, a flag, control over customs as regards other parts of the British Empire as well as the world outside, and several of them appoint and receive diplomatic representatives from independent states. Possibly any one of them could refuse to enter a British war or could undertake a war of its own. It is generally conceded that the transoceanic constituents could withdraw from the British Empire without striking a blow. Nothing binds them but sentimental attachment, the prestige of the kingship, and self-interest.

The Irish Free State is the most recent of the British Commonwealth of Nations. It enjoys the same attributes of sovereignty as the rest, and more, because its voters elect their own titular head of the government instead of accepting a governor appointed by the king. Nevertheless, its location poses the question of its right to secede. Lying between Great Britain and the open Atlantic, its indented coast might be used as an enemy seabase to impair British maritime access to the outside world. It lies less than fifty miles from the larger island at four points, one of which is only 30 miles from the Scottish shore, and so might serve as a base for enemy airplanes or for enemy long range guns. Finally, it makes a land-border with Northern Ireland which would require defense, thus destroying the insularity which has been one of Great Britain's chief military and psychological advantages in all its rivalries with continental European states. The demand of an Irish party for outright independence calls attention to a fundamental difference between it and the self-governing dominions outside Europe. It was not colonized by people from Great Britain.

In one instance a self-governing dominion has relapsed into the status of crown colony from which it sprang. This is Newfoundland, with its appendage, Labrador. The oldest of all British settlement colonies, its meager resources proved insufficient to sustain the burden of self-government, which includes self-financing.

All the self-governing dominions except Ireland and New Zealand are encumbered with vast areas of waste land. These are palliated in spots by mineral deposits, and so long as the governments are not compelled to extend military protection over their desert and tundra, the wastes do not overwhelm the ecumene. Federation has strengthened the governments which are faced with this problem of waste land disproportionate to the ecumene. The Commonwealth of Australia pursues a unified policy of reserving even its tropical territories for settlement by Europeans. The Union of South Africa was able to assume the administration of the adjacent desert because the resources of the colonies were pooled. The Dominion of Canada succeeds while Newfoundland failed.

Each of the dependencies which has attained the status of self-government possesses a core suited to permanent habitation by people of European stock. In British Columbia and much of New Zealand, the cores resemble the British Isles in climate, the aspect of nature most critical in " acclimatization." Southeastern Australia and the Maritime Provinces of Canada experience similar climate, but more subject to extremes of heat and cold. These are accentuated in the core lands of interior Canada. Three colonies, the Cape Colony and West and South Australia, originated in spots of climate akin to the Mediterranean coastlands so much sought by British tourists, while the highland components of the Union of South Africa are not too unlike interior, upland Spain. Of the twenty-one units which, individually or in federation, comprise the six self-governing members of the British Commonwealth of Nations, only two originated in climates not found in Europe. These two began on narrow coastal strips of humid-subtropical climate in Australia and Africa and both promptly expanded into the higher or drier interior. Queensland is the only one in which the ecumene remains primarily in a climate unparalleled anywhere in Europe.

A few of the longer-settled constituents of the British Commonwealth of Nations appear to be approaching a stable population. Most of them are rapidly growing, both by expanding into new lands and by increasing the density of the established ecumene. In this they parallel the other middle-latitude portions of the new worlds opened by the Discoveries, the United States of America and the countries of Latin America beyond the Tropic of Capricorn. It is striking that Great Britain alone, of all the European colonial powers, holds large overseas domains situated in climates familiar to Europeans at home. It is hard to escape the conclusion that centuries of adaptation to changing conditions at home developed a government flexible enough to create the loose association of quasi-independent " nations " which reaches across 320 degrees of longitude and 130 degrees of latitude. Considering the remarkable nature of the achievement, the price — independence of thirteen North American colonies — does not appear excessive.

These members of the British Commonwealth of Nations incorporate the two principal plantations in middle latitudes of rival North European powers. The French occupation of the narrow Saint Lawrence Valley was complete and exclusive when France ceded Quebec to Britain. With the loose unity of the British Isles as a precedent, Canada has become a federation of political regions of which one is French in language and culture although not in its political sympathies. The Boer occupation of South Africa was diffuse and incipient when the British took over the colony from the Netherlands. In general the Boers remained rural while British cities grew up in their midst. This cleavage was accentuated by the exploitation of minerals and the rise of mining cities almost exclusively British. No regional *modus vivendi* as between Boers and British can be devised. The modified Dutch language, Africaans, and the Boer traditions are rallying points for those who desire secession of the Union of South Africa from the British Commonwealth. As in the case of Quebec, the Boers feel even less attachment to the Netherlands than to Great Britain.

Of all the self-governing dominions, only South Africa has a native problem. Elsewhere the aboriginal inhabitants of middle-latitude lands shrank to insignificance before the European onslaught, or retreated before the irresistible tide of migrant settlers hungry for lands like those they had known at home. In South Africa most of the ecumene is owned by European stock, but its occupance is shared by Africans, and in places by Indians, races too vital to eliminate, especially in the less desirable territory, where African occupancy is well-nigh exclusive. European population, including protectorates and mandates, amounts to slightly less than 18 percent of the total.

### LIGHTLY COLONIZED DOMAINS WITHIN THE LOW LATITUDES

This situation is repeated on a smaller scale in Southern Rodesia, where Europeans constitute only 4 percent of the total. There, in a highland resembling that of the Union, but farther from the sea and closer to the Equator, as well as lower in altitude, the handful of Europeans of British origin has obtained responsible self-government, but not the status of a dominion. Southern Rodesia exemplifies the borderline between the British Commonwealth of Nations and the other categories of the British Empire. Politically, it has been granted gradual increase in local autonomy generally accorded by Britain to dependencies which prove equal to the task. Ethnically, it remains a sample of the dependency overwhelmingly native in population, but salted with a small group of permanent European settlers.

Others in this list are Kenya, where bits of highland have attracted settlement under the Equator, and a number of small and scattered dependencies in other parts of the low latitudes (Fig. 12). Most of these are small islands in the trade-wind belt, easy to dominate because of their small size, and not too inimical to European health in the early days of imperial expansion, thanks to their cooling breezes. They were the prize overseas possessions of the British crown in the 18th century, chiefly because they were the sole sources of sugar at that time. Except for Mauritius they lie in the Caribbean Sea or face it. From the beginning the plantations, on which the economic life of nearly all these colonies was founded and still rests, have been owned and operated by people of European extraction and worked by colored races imported from other parts of the low latitudes. They are administered as crown colonies, but in the course of their long history the inhabitants have acquired varying degrees of voice in the government. Usually they elect certain members of the governor's legislative council, although in a few places there is a local elected legislature.

### DEPENDENCIES NOT SUBJECT TO COLONIZATION

Far larger and today more valuable than the scattered low-latitude colonies with permanent European settlements, are the lowland dependencies within the tropics which are conceded to be unsuited to European habitation, except for terms of service lasting a few years (Fig. 12). These constitute the new tropical empire which has superseded the sugar islands as the prime source of many low-latitude raw materials and foodstuffs. Several are extensive mainland holdings, chiefly in Africa. Others occupy segments of the larger East Indian Islands. The rest lie scattered about the Southwestern Pacific, and are small. Virtually all of them have been attached to the Empire in the later decades of imperial expansion, and in competition with the ambitions of France, Germany, and Italy, for raw materials, foodstuffs, and markets. The absence of permanent European colonists is the chief feature distinguishing them from the lightly colonized low-latitude dependencies, which date from the earlier imperial rivalry when Portugal, the Netherlands, and France were Britain's rival contenders for territory in which to trade and plant, and each left deposits of their nationals wherever they went. The determination of British authorities not to open most parts of the new tropical empire to European settlement is based mainly on its insalubrious climate, but partly also on the desire to preserve these regions intact for their respective indigenes.

Some are governed as crown colonies, a larger number are protectorates, a few are mandates under the League of Nations. These varieties of legal status are mainly relict forms which once coincided with fact. Today all three technical forms of control are likely to be inextricably woven into the fabric of a single political unit. Some appear today only in the subordinate rank of local administrative divisions.

A more meaningful distinction than the legal status can be deduced from relations with local authorities. In some cases officers sent out from Britain have supplanted indigenous government, and rule directly, either without or with the advice of local men of standing. In other cases the British authorities operate through locally constituted government, generally the very government which was in operation when the country was brought under British sovereignty. These two modes of government, direct and indirect rule, are ranged in antithesis in dependencies not subject to colonization, in regions where the indigenes are primitive and also in parts of the world where peoples culturally advanced are subjected to European governments (Ch. 11).

### DEPENDENCIES TECHNOLOGICALLY RETARDED BUT CULTURALLY ADVANCED

Dependencies of the types discussed in the two foregoing sections are not confined to the British Empire. Similar colonies make up the bulk of all the colonial empires of the world. Most of them are ruled directly from home. The variety of government permitted in the British possessions exceeds that of any other empire. Here again flexibility is the keynote of administration, and the nature of the rule accords with the nature of the land and people ruled. This is particularly noteworthy in indirect rule, which is scarcely found outside the British sovereignty.

Indirect administration has proved especially useful in handling communities culturally as advanced in some respects as Europe, which technologically are retarded. This has made European political domination possible, but cultural advancement sets up obstacles to smooth administration. Some of these obstacles are cleared away by a flexible system of government which at the same time exerts its force through indirect rule. The British holdings belonging to this category lie in the Near and Middle East (Fig. 12). There centuries of civilization have created units of population very different from Western Europe in most respects, but no less advanced except in two critical fields of endeavor — mechanical and political technology.

British domination of India, together with adjacent Burma and Ceylon, is the most paradoxical single feat in the whole history of imperialism. Great Britain (less than 95,000 square miles), a fragmentary outpost on one of Eurasia's four major peninsular extensions, rules India, another of those peninsulas, almost as large as the whole of Europe west of Russia (1,834,000 square miles compared to 2,104,-000). Great Britain, numbering slightly over 46,000,000 people, rules India's population of almost 325,000,000. Incredible, until the geography beyond these facts is investigated.

Great Britain is the acme of peninsular Europe, which doubles and redoubles the force of its people by extending their resources to the ends of the earth via the seaways. India's long coastline is very little indented save for a few large but very shallow bays. Its best contacts with the sea are tortuous and shifting silt-laden channels of its numerous deltas. So continental is India that in its political geography the sea never figured until European mariners opened the country to the world at large during the age of the Discoveries. Great Britain has been kept in a state of continual political and economic flux — at first by sweeping conquests political in nature and economic in incidence, later by revolutions which thoroughly churned the political as well as the economic society of the whole country. India has lain contemplatively impervious to outside influences. Successive torrents of outsiders pouring over the northwest passes, the only vulnerable land border, have been absorbed into the mass of inert population, after political conquests shortlived and confined to parts of the area. Great Britain is small enough to lie within a single type of climate, and its relief is moderate enough to permit intimate association between lowlanders and highlanders. India runs the gamut of the low-latitude climates, and its wide range and large scale of relief differentiates human life from place to place without favoring segregation into strongly marked regions. Great Britain could hardly fail to coagulate about the English Plain, favored by nature beyond any other part of the islands. India has no natural coreland which through centuries repeatedly assumes the leadership and in time becomes accepted as dominant.

Lacking a nuclear core, the several regions have lost a good part of whatever natural differentiation they may have had. Their outlines have been blurred by overprints of social patterns which neither coincide with, nature nor correspond with each other. Two of these are familiar bases of dissension and division in the occidental world; the third is distinctive in India. Languages are quite as numerous in India as they are in Europe. About a dozen are spoken by at least 9,000,000 people, groups larger than those which use several European languages.

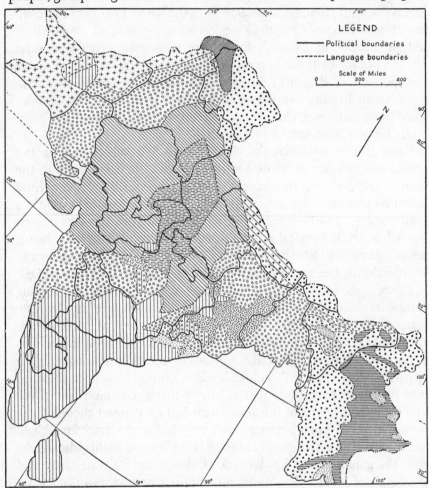

FIG. 13. Languages and governments in India, Burma, and Ceylon.

In view of the evils besetting Europe which are caused by differences in speech, it suffices to remark that as yet language scarcely figures in India as a political weapon. The languages are localized, but their pattern is extremely complex (Fig. 13).

More exacerbating than the use of different languages are religious differences, recalling the religious friction which kept Europe at war for many decades not so long ago. In India, however, the differences are not only sectarian within a single religion, but refer also to the deeper cleavage among the four world religions, each of which has millions of followers. There are even groups of Animists, to complete the diversity. Religion and region rarely correspond even in broad outlines. Burma, never really a part of India except under British rule, is largely Buddhist. The deserts of the Indus and the vicinity of the northwest passes are dominantly Moslem. Thus Islam betrays its intrusion from the steppes and deserts, and discloses its peculiar suitability to arid and semi-arid conditions. Nevertheless, neither of these geographic conclusions can be pushed too hard, because there are adherents of Islam scattered about the Dekkan, and they constitute a majority in the very heart of the rainy floodplains of the Lower Ganges. The distribution of Moslems appears to be intimately connected with local history, particularly the effectiveness of control exerted by conquering Mohammedan invaders from the northwest.

Most of the remaining people are Hindu in religion, although Christians and Animists are scattered among them, either as small groups or as individuals. Religious conflict is generated chiefly as between Hindu and Moslem. The one is a passive faith, the other a fanatically aggressive one. With this basic cause for strife, go countless superficial antitheses which can occasion outbursts, such as the Hindu veneration of animal life, and particularly cattle, as opposed to the Moslem custom of killing pests and eating meat, especially beef.

Religion frequently offers an excuse for conflicts which really stem from the juxtaposition of antithetic social systems. The vast majority of the population is Hindu, but it is unable to exert force commensurate to its numbers because it is divided into castes. These groups and members of all the other religions are segregated into communities which live side by side but have little or no common experience. In occidental society the only comparable phenomena are the communities of colored people and Amerinds in the Western Hemisphere and the Jewish communities in East Central Europe. In the Western World " communities " are strictly localized and yet they create awkward problems. In India they are the warp and woof of all society.

To cap all these unrelated social patterns is the political subdivision (Fig. 13). This in large measure represents the situation at the moment when the British arrived to conquer India in the 18th century. The grouping of local states was temporary, merely a stage in the kaleidoscope of dominations which had been sweeping over India time out of mind. It bears no observable relation to other existing patterns — religious groups, linguistic groups, or natural units — except in detail here and there. The first effect of the British conquest was to stop internal wars and thus to freeze the political units as they happened to stand. Soon afterwards some modifications were made, chiefly by bringing under British administration most of the coastal states and those readily accessible via rivers. Even then the former state boundaries tended to remain the new provincial boundaries, and the units of British administration coincided with the supplanted native states.

It is the fragmentation of the Indian social structure that has permitted British rule. No group — linguistic, religious, community, or political — resents government by the British quite so much as it fears government by other groups of Indians.

As the years have added their experience, British administration has been modified, but it has never lost its essential character — local government to suit local situations. The well-known division between British India and the Native States is but a crude measure of the variety of local government. Sometimes there are holdovers from history. Ceylon, a relatively late addition to the British Empire, has never been attached to Indian government, although it is far less insular than most offshore islands, being like the tip of the peninsula physically, ethnically, economically, and culturally. Even the strait which separates it from the mainland is too shallow to permit the passage of large ships, and a train ferry completes the link in communication afforded by easily constructed causeways on the intervening reefs. Sometimes relict forms are swept away as the need arises. Burma, long treated as a part of British India, has now been separated. This accords with its distinctiveness in ethnic character, in density of population, in economic production, and in religion, as well as its separation from India by a wide band of mountain ranges and low-latitude jungle. Within the Native States, many of which are autocratic in tradition, absolutism is tempered by British pressure, exerted by the British Resident at the court of the Indian ruler.

British authority is moving in the direction of centralization and democracy. The Supreme Government controls posts, customs, and in most cases currency. Native rulers may not send ambassadors or make war, although they can keep limited armies. A movement has been launched to federate all of India. Already the Native States have a Chamber of Princes to consult together on matters of imperial or common concern. Some have legislative councils to advise the ruler. All the provinces of British India are governed with the aid of elective legislatures.

The capital of the Supreme Government was for many decades Calcutta, an ocean port and therefore in close touch with Great Britain, and on the edge of the most densely inhabited part of British India. In summer the European government was accustomed to remove from the humid head of the delta to Simla lying between 6600 and 8000 feet elevation in the footmountains of the Himalayas. Some time ago it was decided to remove the capital to a new site near Delhi, the traditional Mogul capital and more than once the administrative seat of much of India, though never of all. The new location is well inland, suggesting that the government no longer feels the need of protection by men-of-war. It lies in the densely populated Ganges lowland, but well north of the center of population. Its position is near a principal junction of railroads which radiate down the Ganges lowland, up onto the Dekkan, and across the Indus Basin. Lying rather toward the northwest frontier from which all India's invaders have come, except the Europeans, gives it somewhat the semblance of a military capital. The new buildings include one for the legislative assembly, the membership of which is chosen by the provinces of British India. It is contemplated to add to this group representatives of such Native States as care to join the federation. The summer capital (April to October) remains at Simla. No place on the Indian lowland is cool enough at that season to suit administrators from Northwest Europe.

The trend toward centralization looks in the direction of an India which may someday be able to insist on its independence. This is already evident in the growing movements demanding emancipation, movements in which Indians trained in Great Britain are often leaders. This yearning is given material support by the construction of railroads, which permit all but the poorest to move about, and by the democratizing influence of factories, common carriers, newspapers, and the like. As occidental modes of life increase they tend to break down the communities.

At present the prospect of Indian independence is diminished by mutual jealousy of Hindu and Moslem religious groups. British democracy is at the opposite pole from Hindu caste, and lies closer to the traditions of Islam. Nevertheless, the Hindu groups are conscious of their numerical superiority, and endeavor to twist democratic government into domination by total numbers, which in practice would mean domination by the castes, to the exclusion of the outcastes. So long as these internal frictions continue to generate riots, the British rule appears to be both justified and secure. The number of Europeans engaged as political officers has never been large. In the lower brackets British are being superseded by Indians as fast as indigenes can qualify. Political officers sent out from Europe number about 4000. As in other low-latitude dependencies, they work in short terms and retire to the British Isles when their active days are over. Much of the same sort of administration functions in the British territory on the Malay Peninsula. There the aboriginal Malay population is augmented by large numbers of Chinese and some Indians.

The trend toward independence observable in India appears also in the territories now and recently British at the southeast corner of the Mediterranean Sea. This region is partly low-latitude desert and partly steppe of the lower-middle-latitude type, with a coastal fringe of very dry Mediterranean climate. It may be considered as subtropical rather than tropical, and its dryness makes it climatically fit for permanent settlement by British folk. On the other hand aridity restricts its value for production which, except the ribbon of Lower Nile Valley, is negligible. The region does, however, control the Suez Canal and therefore holds a value in the British Empire out of all proportion to its productivity or its population. Great Britain has never claimed sovereignty over any of the territory, but in the form of protectorate, mandate, or special treaty it exercises supervision of the Canal zone and occupies or holds exclusive naval concessions in each of the three ports which can best be used as naval or air bases for its defense or for attack upon it. Egypt, covered by a protectorate for more than a generation, has since the World War been recognized as independent. This is the first instance of an evolution which may eventuate in all the dependencies where long-standing traditions and advanced culture come to find expression in local patriotism. It is reasonable to suppose that were it not for the transcendent military importance of the Suez Canal, the last faint shadow of special British privilege would already have been removed from the sovereignty of Egypt.

## STEPPING STONES

The Suez Canal is one of the knots in the web of empire where the routes which bind its parts are caught together at a point of exceptional and critical strategic character (Fig.12).

The imperial ways include all forms of rapid transportation and communication, and the Empire is so scattered that nearly every trade route and communication line on earth has a British possession along it or at its terminus. Nevertheless, the parts of the Empire are linked by water for all heavy traffic and for most other freight, passengers, and mail. Except for the transcontinental lines across Canada, railroads may be disregarded as major links in the imperial chain of transportation.

Several air routes operate over the land rather than the sea, and airways have become second only to ocean routes in the fabric of empire. In some instances planes skirt the seashore rather than plunge boldly across non-British territory. Elsewhere the sea route is most direct. It therefore happens that the critical districts that must serve as sea bases can often be utilized as air bases too. With the radio in common use the strategic value of telegraph and telephone wires has diminished.

Nearly 65 percent of the land and more than 75 percent of the population controlled by Great Britain face the Indian Ocean or lie just beyond its margins. This includes every self-governing dominion except Canada, and nearly all the leading dependencies in the other categories except Nigeria. Most of the remaining Empire is unequally scattered about the margins of the North Atlantic Ocean. Canada forms a long land link to the Pacific, whence seaways extend to Australia and so complete the encirclement of the globe. Not more than 2,000,000 people inhabit British territory in the Pacific Basin.

## The Indian Ocean Connections

The distribution of the Empire being what it is, the most critical lines of communication are those which tie the Indian Ocean holdings to Great Britain. There are alternative sea routes, a short one through the Mediterranean and Red seas, and a long one which follows the open ocean around the Cape of Good Hope. The very long routes which involve the Pacific Ocean are not in any real sense competitive either in trade or in strategy with the two first named.

So long as the Suez Canal remains open, all constrictions on the inland sea route are vital to British control of that shortcut (Ch. 9). Only a little less so are three points farther east, which control certain vital lanes for shipping. The table on the following page lists the critical passages and the suzerainty of their controlling shores.

It will be observed that the passages in the list which do not give rise to political clash are entirely in the hands of a single power. Those which are objects of concern but not burning questions are shared with some friendly power, preferably a small and weak state. A sea route is no more secure than its least defensible constriction. From this fact springs the potential value to the British Empire of the alternative route via open ocean.

On the African seaway to the Indian Ocean there are no constrictions. The critical points are therefore the convenient stopping places. First in importance among these is the tip of South Africa, where Cape-

## TABLE IV

| Passage | Control Points and Harbors | Suzerainty |
|---|---|---|
| Strait of Gibraltar | Rock of Gibraltar | Great Britain |
| | Southern Pillar of Hercules | Spain |
| | Harbor of Tangier | International Commission |
| Waist of the Mediterranean | Malta | Great Britain |
| | Sicily and Pantelleria | Italy |
| | Tunisia (Bizerta) | France |
| Suez Canal | The Canal Zone | Great Britain |
| | Alexandria | Great Britain |
| | Haifa | Great Britain |
| Strait of Bab-el-Mandeb | Perim Island | Great Britain |
| | Sheikh Saïd | France |
| | Peninsula of Doumeirah | Italy |
| | Aden Harbor | Great Britain |
| Tip of India | Ceylon (Colombo) | Great Britain |
| Strait of Malacca | Singapore Island | Great Britain |
| | Malay Mainland | Great Britain |
| | Sumatra and Offshore Archipelagoes | Netherlands |
| Torres Strait | Australia | Great Britain |
| | New Guinea | Great Britain |
| Bass Strait | Australia (Melbourne) | Great Britain |
| | Tasmania | Great Britain |

town and Durban share the business. The other convenient stations are islands — the Canaries and the Cape Verde group, respectively Spanish and Portuguese, and the three in the South Atlantic, all British. The Canaries and Saint Helena have shown themselves to possess strategic value.

Among all the nodes mentioned, the four which lie between Great Britain and the open Indian Ocean along the Mediterranean and Red seas are the most valuable as links of empire. They are also the only ones seriously threatened by ambitious rivals. The others have not been strengthened by fortifications until recently, when Singapore stands completed as a naval base of the first class.

Like so many other springboards of European conquest, Singapore is a small island, separated from the mainland by a narrow channel (Fig. 14). True to type, it has become the administrative center for all the British possessions in Malaya. Yet its greater significance lies in its control of the strait, nine miles wide, which forms the most direct and easiest sea lane around the southeast corner of the Asiatic land mass. This has made the town, which faces the strait, the active entrepôt for all that quarter. It was not until Japan pushed into the front rank of naval powers that the British government undertook to shape a key to fit the unlocked eastern gate to the Indian Ocean. The essence of the fortifications is a naval base capable of refitting any ship afloat. It has been dredged from the jungly tidal marsh on the landward side of the island. The naval base, the city, and the passage before the island are protected by air bases, and by long-range guns, some of which are emplaced on the islets which stand guard at the narrowest point on the channel.

Based on Singapore a fleet is believed to be competent to operate anywhere in the Indian Ocean, southeastward to New Zealand, and northeastward to China, where Hong Kong is the symbol of British imperial interests. British effectiveness in the China Seas is conditioned by cooperation from the Netherlands and France. The Netherlands shares with Britain the Strait of Singapore, and controls the scarcely wider Sunda Strait, second route around the corner of Asia. It is not to be supposed that the Netherlands government objects to fortifications raised by a power which has left the Netherlands Indies intact for more than a century. France has given formal support to an advance line of defense toward Japan: first, in announcing improvement of its small naval base at Cam Ranh at the easternmost extension of bulging Indo-China; second, by declaring its right to the Paracel Islands; and third, by joining Great Britain in declaring that occupation of the island of Hainan by a foreign power would be considered an unfriendly act.[1]

Airways to and within the Indian Ocean realm are regularly flown (Fig. 2). As yet stops must be so close together that some landings are dependent on the goodwill of foreign nations. This is particularly true of France, crossed by all the lines on their way to the Eastern Mediterranean. The Italian peninsula lies on the direct route, and Malta is the first base controlled by Britain. In Egypt the relations are close but not altogether assured. There three lines diverge. The principal air lane traverses the British mandates Palestine and Trans-Jordan, and the former mandate Iraq. The British island Bahrein in the Persian Gulf provides a stepping stone on the way to India, whence the route to Singapore lies over India, Burma, and Malaya. The crossing to Australia has to make use of Java, a possession of the Netherlands.

To permit longer operating range, to take advantage of the natural landing place furnished by water surfaces, and to fly as much as possible over the *mare liberum* and by so much reduce dependence on foreign governments, flying boats are now being used on the Mediterranean and Indian Ocean routes. A Red Sea route alternative to the Nile has been charted to emancipate from Egypt the connections with the Egyptian Sudan and Aden. Even in British territory coast routes are preferred to inland routes which do not follow rivers, as in East Africa.

## Imperial Connections in Atlantic and Pacific

The position of Great Britain is far less strong in the Atlantic and Pacific oceans than in the Indian Ocean. Naval bases are far apart, and the airline hops are too long to be based on British soil as yet, although faster planes may remedy this fault. Several of the most important constrictions or stepping stones on the routes are in foreign hands.

The seaways to Canada and the Caribbean are direct and little trammelled by actual or potential foreign bases. British Bermuda lies some distance off the routes. The Portuguese Azores are near the Great Circle between the English Channel and the Caribbean. So long as Portugal remains weak and an ally of Britain, this is no disadvantage to the Empire.

In the South Atlantic the Falkland Islands (also claimed by Argentina) proved of worth as a naval base during the World War, and they and their somewhat distant neighbors serve as stepping stones for Ant-

---

[1] Shortly thereafter Japan nullified the second and third of these formalities by annexing the Paracel Islands and landing a force on Hainan as a military measure.

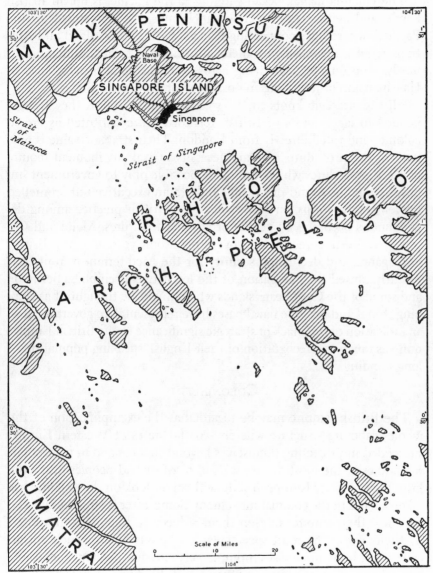

FIG. 14. Singapore in its setting.

arctic exploration and possible British claims to parts of the Antarctic Continent.

The Panama Canal, ocean gateway to the Pacific, is not in British hands, and neither are the Hawaiian Islands, the " crossroads of the Pacific," where lines connecting Canada with New Zealand and Australia require a base even for merchant shipping, to say nothing of war needs. The only regular flying across the Pacific also makes use of Hawaiian and other islands in possession of the United States.

All the strategic knots in the web of empire, unless they be embedded in larger units of British territory, are constituted as crown colonies and ruled directly from London. Their strategic value is warrant for this procedure. Military necessity may at any moment require political procedures which are legally possible only to government imposed from above and practicable only to an executive untrammelled by democratic forms. In accordance with British practice among dependencies occupied by people of advanced cultures, Malta and Cyprus were given representative government some years ago. Anti-British propaganda and decreasing security for the Mediterranean route has recently caused the abrogation of the legislative assemblies. Bermuda and some of the Caribbean islands which might be thought of as stepping stones and possible naval bases have representative government — an indication of their lack of strategic significance to the British Empire quite as much as a recognition of their English-speaking population of long standing.

## COLONIALISM

The British Empire may be regarded as the exemplification of the whole elaborate structure whereby coastal states of Western Europe succeeded in projecting themselves beyond the seas and in incorporating bodies of the most diverse sorts of territory and peoples into a political unity. Every European state with an outlook on the Atlantic has taken a hand in the colonial movement. Some, after temporary success, have lost their empires or seen them reduced to fragments unwanted by their rivals. The most spectacular of these is Spain, which got an early start, built up a vast empire largely through precious metals extracted from its dominions, and then lost its holdings when less ephemeral resources than gold and silver strengthened the colonies while more fortunately located states in northern Europe seized the carrying trade. Denmark and Sweden lost their footing because of their slender homeland bases. France, in the 18th century, and Germany, in the 20th, were deprived of theirs by military conquest. In each case the losing side received little aid from its colonies, partly because the home government had followed a policy of close supervision which had deprived the colonials of self-reliance.

Throughout the world the art of managing colones is still in the experimental stage. Each of the states which controls a colonial empire has set up machinery of government differing from the others. Most of the parts of this machinery have been sent out from home, and therefore resemble the political mechanism of the ruling country, especially in middle-latitude dominions. In the pitiless low-latitude environment, where most of the present-day colonies lie, those parts which won't work have been discarded, and others better calculated to aid in sustaining the white man's burden have been fabricated on the spot. The Netherlands, Belgium, the United States, and Portugal all have their different colonial machines, each operating in a relatively circumscribed overseas area. The effectiveness of these machines varies with the worth and the handicaps of the colonial region, but it also tends to conform to the resources and political experience of the ruling nation. Portugal, poverty-stricken and " colony-poor," has done little to develop its possessions beyond crude extraction of their most accessible resources. The United States and Belgium, manufactural nations of great wealth, although of very different magnitude, have disclosed their inexperience in colonial administration by making mistakes which they constantly endeavor to correct. The Netherlands, prosperous and versed in overseas possessions, is carrying out an original, unified, and apparently successful development of its one important colonial dependency.

More significant than any of these are the records of the two outstanding colonizing powers, Great Britain and France. Their colonial experiments have been carried out on a front extending from the Caribbean to the China Sea, and in every type of low-latitude lowland environment. They have learned to deal with each local situation more or less according to its needs. In one way with South Asia, possessing a highly organized and ancient material and spiritual culture; in quite another with the more primitive folk of jungle and bush. In Africa these two powers control adjacent and almost identical regions — areas which present a matchless laboratory of colonial machines in operation (Ch. 11).

Colonial administration is the ". white man's burden," a picturesque phrase often quoted jocosely, even by those who are helping to bear it. Taken seriously, it defines neatly the political sway of the Western European system of government over most of the world inhabited by people of darker skins. The white men who shoulder this burden are attempting to integrate all the continents into one economic and cultural ensemble. More precisely, they are applying the political forms and methods of Western Europe to lands with other and often antithetic political traditions. These lands comprise the Orient, the Levant, and all the low-latitude lowlands.

In such of these lands as are in the middle latitudes local tradition is powerful, deriving from and reinforced by middle-latitude energy which has frustrated European benevolence and interference. Japan, by imitating the forms and practices of European government, although perhaps not quite grasping its spirit, and China, by its bulk refractory to European control, have escaped into a political world of their own. This world, compounded of occidental and oriental elements, is already beyond the lifting power of the white man, and he is being forced to drop the oriental part of his burden. The Levant, except that part of the Mediterranean coast which faces western Europe, is likewise rejecting the proffer of assistance, apart from borrowing the habiliments of occidental polity. There Turkey leads the way, followed by Iran, Iraq, Arabia, and Egypt.

By this self-elimination the white man's burden is being reduced to the low latitudes. Even within the tropics many highlands have demonstrated their power to set up political housekeeping for themselves and have rejected the European as a bearer of political responsibility for their welfare. Thus the load is being resolved into the governing of peoples indigenous to low-latitude lowlands, to the end that they may be brought within the economic and cultural orbit of the Occident.

## CHAPTER SIX

# France, Archetype of the Occidental National State

NO two states, even those which share in common a peripheral location on the western margin of Europe, are alike in all aspects of their natural environment. Partly for this reason the details of their political pattern and structure differ also. Of the nations of Western Europe, France is most representative, and may be considered the archetype of the group. It stands at the apex of the Eurasian triangle (Fig. 15), and each of the three broad physical divisions of Europe — northern plain, central mountains, and Mediterranean coastland — extends into France. This entanglement with its landward neighbors makes its strong national unity more significant than that of countries more effectively insulated from Central and Eastern Europe. Its area ranks it first among the peripheral states (Germany and Poland being larger), but its population sets it below Britain, Germany, and Italy. Nevertheless, its ecumene is virtually coextensive with its area, so that it lacks the empty districts that so often mislead the earnest student of the political map. As one of the Great Powers, it is a political unit of first magnitude, and it incorporates a fair sampling of components of both the second and third magnitude. Alone among European states it includes large areas of both Mediterranean and North European landscape. No other, except Spain, occupies frontage on both the Atlantic Ocean and the Mediterranean Sea.

## The Alternation of Division and Union

Two opposed areal forces have been constantly at work in shaping the French state, and their concurrence is the key to its political geography. The compact territory north of the Pyrenees and west of the Alps-Jura-Vosges-Ardennes tends to become politically unified (Fig.

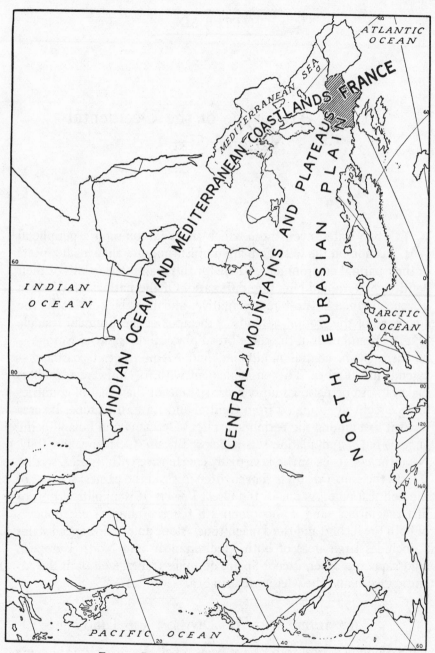

FIG. 15. France, the apex of the Eurasian triangle.

16). No less does each of the major river basins — Rhône, Garonne, Loire, Seine, and Moselle-Meuse — tend to assert its independence. The degree of unity varies with the strength of the political organization current at any period. There have been in historic times three alternations between schism and union.

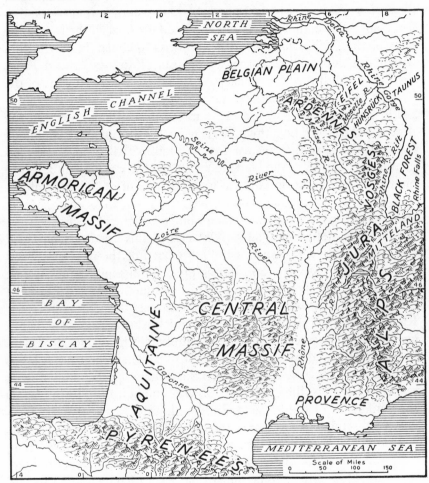

FIG. 16. The physical components of France.
Each type of country continues across the eastern boundary.

*Division.* One of the first Roman annexations outside the Italian Peninsula was the Mediterranean seacoast between the Maritime Alps and the Pyrenees, including the inseparable valley of the Lower Rhône. Known as " The Province," this territory was the prototype of Roman administration outside Italy. Seventy-five years later Caesar found non-Mediterranean Gaul divided into three parts: Aquitaine (the basin of the Garonne), the Seine-Loire Basin, and the Belgian Plain (physically partly in the Rhine drainage, but politically often linked to France).

*Union.* As Roman territory Gaul continued to be administered in three units, with varying boundaries but with unchanging cores. In time the line between the new acquisition and The Province faded to the status of interprovincial boundary. The eastern border of the unified Gaul followed the crescent of the Western Alps all the way to the Falls of the Rhine, and included the Swiss Mittelland and the Jura Mountains, with all the passageways opening off to the eastward. From the Rhine Falls the stream itself was made the eastern boundary of the Empire. It was in no sense a barrier, but simply the most patent north-south marker in the low and easily traversable hill-land between the Alps and the North Sea. It could easily be announced and maintained as the military frontier against tribes disseminated through the German forests. At times the land along the left bank was organized into military provinces, at times it was incorporated into Gaul. Several fortress towns were constructed on the left bank, and two of them, Mainz and Cologne, were sites of permanent bridges, each with a fortified garrison at its eastern end. The weakest part of this line is a steep-sided and flat-floored valley between the great bend of the river near Basel and the gorge where it breaks through the Taunus, just below Mainz. This fertile Rift Valley, formed by the foundering of a strip of the earth's crust, is the western border of a deep reentrant between Upper Rhine and Upper Danube, the rest of which is rugged country that in enemy hands threatened the Roman frontiers. The conquest of Gaul had been followed by seizure of the Alps and their foreland as far as the Danube. Less than a century later the Romans built a series of walls and trenches from the great bend of the Danube to the Rhine below the confluence of the Moselle. Besides eliminating the dangerous reentrant this move incorporated the Black Forest which dominates the eastern side of the Rift Valley, and the fertile Neckar and Lower Main valleys. Although intended to be an advance base for further military operations, this proved to be the last outpost of Roman power toward Germany. After two hundred years it was abandoned; traces of the earthworks can still be seen.

*Division.* As the legions were withdrawn from the Rhine boundary by a relaxing Roman power, successive tribes of Germans penetrated Gaul. Major concentrations of power conformed roughly to the major river basins. Visigoths occupied Aquitaine, Burgundians the Rhône Basin, Alamanni pushed into the Rhine Rift Valley (without deserting their center in the hill country to the eastward), and Franks controlled the Seine Basin from a triple base along the Rhine — in the Main-Rhine confluence, on the North European Plain between the Rhine gorge and its delta, and on the fertile spots (limon soils) amid the marshes and sandy heaths of the Rhine delta itself. The Loire Basin lay divided between Visigothic and Frankish power. Caesar had noted some such division lines between Gaulish tribes as those of the Germanic invaders, and it was to reappear chronically for a thousand years after Roman unity broke down.

*Union.* Charlemagne, a Frankish ruler, welded the units together, along with much German and Italian territory. For decades after his death, the western triad of basins remained unified, but the Rhône-Rhine Depression was severed from the Frankish (*i.e.,* French) territories.

*Division.* While in theory the unity of the western basins has never since Charlemagne been abandoned, in practice the country fell into feudalization so complete that effective political units were of the second or even the third order of magnitude, rather than the first. Only slowly did Aquitaine reassert its coherence. It was some centuries before the Inner Paris Basin was able to harmonize political and natural unity by conquering Normandy from the Norman dukes, and thus occupying the whole of the Seine Basin. The unity of the lands along the Loire is largely nullified by passage of the stream through three major landform regions, the middle one being the politically powerful " Paris Basin." The Loire Basin remained divided among a number of counties until each bit was absorbed by the French monarchy. (This dissection is visible in the map of French administrative provinces until the Revolution of 1789.)

*Union.* Slowly, under the French kings centered in the Paris Basin nearly all Roman Gaul, including The Province, now known as Provence, was knit into the French state of today.[1] The exception is the eastern borderland north of the Alps, where the river boundary failed to hold, once military force on opposite banks became equal.

## INTERNAL PATTERN

France presents an irregular checkerboard of high and low land (Fig. 16). The Central, Armorican, and Vosges-Ardennes massifs, all hill

---

[1] Wherever territories held under feudal tenure are discussed, a realm or lesser domain is assumed to comprise only the lands actually being administered by the lord, *i.e.,* the demesne. While the moral ascendancy and the practical advantages of suzerainty are recognized, especially in the case of kings and emperors, geographic reality more nearly coincides with domain lands not allotted to quasi-independent vassals.

lands rather than mountain lands, interspace with the lowland river basins. The lowlands, fertile farmed areas and foci of trade, have been the traditional centers of political integration, especially those with a single nuclear core. The lower and wider basins face different seas, and provide a diversity of outlook for their inhabitants. The Rhône, debouching into the calm Mediterranean with its connections to the Orient, belongs to a world very unlike that of Garonne and Loire, leading to the tempestuous Bay of Biscay and the open Atlantic, or that of the Seine and Rhine, turned toward the semi-enclosed waters of north Europe. But if each basin faces outward, it has postern doors leading to its neighbors. Exchange of surplus between the moderately contrasting products of the several lowlands, and transfer of goods from overseas, have always maintained trade tracks across the intervening highlands along the lines most easily traversed. The highlands, beyond the sphere of these trade routes, have ever been refuge areas in times of stress. Armorica is the last stand of Celts; the Central Massif is the home of the Albigensian protest against the Roman Church. As usual in highlands, these rugged and infertile hills produce more children than food, and the outflow of surplus population sometimes jeopardizes the political balance of the lowlands to which they move.

## THE RHÔNE BASIN AND ITS CONNECTIONS

The Lower Rhône Basin and the adjacent coastland between the Alps and the Pyrenees is the only Mediterranean part of France. Because of its special climate it supplies the whole country with *vin ordinaire* from its extensive vineyards, and with early fruits and vegetables from its truck gardens. For the same reason the coast along the base of the Alps has become the leading pleasure resort of the country.

Its principal political significance, however, lies in its character as a focus of routes. One must travel eastward to the Dardanelles to find another breach in the mountain wall so deep and wide as the cleft which is described by the Rhône and its tributaries (Fig. 17). The lower Rhône and its extension the Saône form the stem of a Y. The easterly fork, passing through the gap between Jura and Vosges, finds itself in the valley of the Rhine, an easily navigated stream all the way to its mouth. The westerly fork, which divides into several alternative routes, makes contact across ranges of hills readily passable in times

Fig. 17. The connections between Mediterranean France and the north European plain. Principal routes are suggested by the towns and rivers named.

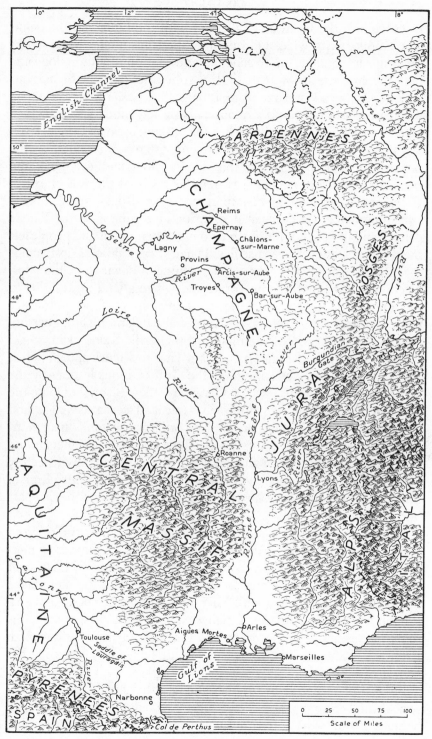

of peace into the headwater valleys of both the Loire and the Seine. The Rhône, swift, wide, and running fullest in summer when fed by melting Alpine snow, is a treacherous stream, tumultuous in flood and beset by sandbars at low water. Of its tributaries only the Saône, meandering across a lacustrine plain, is navigable. Easier to descend than to breast, the waterway is arduous at best, and much less used than land routes which parallel the streams, although canals connect several of the upper branches with adjacent systems. Marseilles, on the pouch-shaped harbor nearest the deltaic outlet of the Rhône, and freed by a west-setting coastal current from fluvial silt, was already a Greek commercial colony of importance in pre-Roman days. Its relative importance has never abated. Arles, at the head of the Rhône delta, stands on the last bit of high ground. There goods and people left the river to cross over to Marseilles. The next critical point upstream is the site of Lyons, where the Rhône, plunging down from the Alps, meets the north-south Saône route, and where a land route leads to Roanne and the northwest. Lyons does duty also as principal transfer point for the trade which takes the several overland forks higher upstream, besides being the metropolis of the fertile Saône plain.

Secondary to the Rhône passway but vital to French integration is the route from the western end of the Gulf of Lions leading by the easy Saddle of Lauragais into the Garonne Valley. Below Toulouse the Garonne, although rather swift, is navigable, and a canal as well as land routes link it to the Mediterranean. Narbonne was Rome's direct point of contact with Aquitaine. Its site, on a tongue of slightly higher ground projecting into the lagoon-and-bar coast, was the least unsatisfactory landing place on that section of coast. Continued silting since Roman times, and the use of large ships render it valueless as a commercial port in the present day.

As though it were not enough to be the focus of routes leading from all the other river basins of France, the Rhône lowland makes connection with Spain through the Col de Perthus, the only easy traverse of the Pyrenees except that around the Atlantic end of the mountains. Similarly it makes contact with Italy by means of the coast route. Although today both railroad and highway follow the coast eastward, this route has always been narrow and in times of war it is easily closed. Even the road-conscious Romans made little use of it, preferring the seaway or Alpine passes.

Because of its high value for trade and its rather slight importance for agriculture before the days of fast and refrigerated transportation, and because a long narrow territory is hard to defend, the Rhône route early became a bone of contention between the masters of the Paris Basin and the masters of the Rhine. The coastal lowland to the west of the river was riven from the valley proper, and fairly early fell into the hands of the French kings, although piecemeal. When St. Louis wished to outfit for a Crusade in the mid-13th century, he possessed no natural harbor on the Mediterranean and so built Aigues Mortes among the lagoons at the west edge of the Rhône delta. The critical ports did not become French until late — Marseilles in 1481 and Narbonne in 1507. Until then the part of Provence east of the Rhône had been as closely linked with Germany as with France; at times it was considered a part of the Holy Roman (German) Empire. In reality it was an integral part of Burgundy, a name that symbolizes the repeated attempts to express territorially and politically the trade value of the Rhône-Rhine Depression. It would be a miracle if such a state, a long ribbon with few naturally marked boundaries and still fewer suitable for effective military defense, could hold its own against the cupidity of states more powerfully based. In the end the Rhône half of Burgundy fell to France, partly because the distant German base lay beyond a mountain rampart, whereas the French center was separated from it only by hill country.[1]

## AQUITAINE, AN INTEGER OF FRANCE

The broad lowland facing the Bay of Biscay is a region of fertile alluvial plains and gentle hills, basking in a climate which combines Mediterranean and North European features. In range and yield of crops it leads among agricultural regions of France, if not all Western Europe. Here, if anywhere, one might suppose, a powerful state ought to arise in the day when agriculture was the paramount basis of economic life. Instead, during the whole of the middle ages it lay divided between the power centered at Bordeaux and the power centered at Toulouse, finally to be ingested piecemeal by the French Kingdom.

The easy route from the Mediterranean across the Saddle of Lauragais descends in nearly a straight line to the great bend of the Garonne. At this strategic site astride the route, tapping a number of other productive valleys which penetrate both the Pyrenees and the Central Massif, and in the midst of a fertile, rolling plain, stands Toulouse. The Garonne, a powerful and swift stream, can be navigated from this point, although the canal which comes over the saddle from Narbonne now continues almost to the estuary. This route, however valuable lo-

---

[1] Additional proof of the French kings' advantage is presented on pp. 160-4.

cally, has never held the major economic and strategic value inherent in the Rhône-Rhine Depression, and the Counts of Toulouse lost their autonomy earlier than any other leading power of the Midi.[1]

Even without the aid of Toulouse and the Middle Garonne Basin, the plain of which Bordeaux is the metropolis for some centuries threatened the unity of the region we know today as France. This occurred, however, during the three centuries when Aquitaine was ruled by the lord of the Lower Loire and the Lower Seine, who at the same time was King of England. Aquitaine by itself, although large, is not so broad a base for political power as it appears on a relief map. A wide swath of country reaching from the Garonne estuary almost to the Pyrenees along the coast is sand dune, sandy plain, and marsh, of no agricultural value (The Landes). Another considerable region of marsh south of the Loire (The Vendée), while serving to carry the barrier of the Poitou hills to the coast, further reduces the arable acreage. Because of the regular shoreline of sand dunes both north and south of the Garonne, harbors are few, Bordeaux, sixty miles up the estuary, being by all odds the most satisfactory port in the whole region. The political connection with England favored trade in wine, but the Bay of Biscay, because of its storminess, has always been a terror to sailors. Bordeaux benefited, long after its incorporation in France, from the creation of overseas colonies; still later the advent of large steamships mitigated the dangers of navigation in the Bay. This advantageous readjustment of its economic geography came too late to aid in the struggle for political independence.

Neither of the major powers of the Aquitanian lowland succeeded in annexing the fringe of small feudal holdings entrenched on the flank of the Pyrenees, each of which incorporated piedmont grain fields and marshy lowland pastures with mountain valleys and pastures on the watersheds, and were neither truly French nor truly Spanish. The French kings had to await the 17th century before defining the Pyrenees boundary line.

### THE MIDI VS. THE NORTH

The Midi at length was subordinated to the power of the French north, despite strong factors favoring its independence. It had been more thoroughly Romanized than the North, and remained less affected by subsequent Germanic invaders, who promptly lost them-

---

[1] The French use this term loosely to mean the whole South, from the Alps to the Bay of Biscay.

selves in the culture they conquered. It retained the Roman Law with little modification; even in such details of administration as the Salt Tax it maintained individuality until the Revolution of 1789. It spoke a well-differentiated romance tongue known as Provençal. Its products continued to be Mediterranean produce — wheat, wine, nuts, olives.

Some of these very distinctions proved to be weaknesses which permitted the conquest. The agricultural wealth, especially the wine, incited the cupidity of the less favored northern neighbors. The easy routes of access made familiar by movements of traders, and the wealth inherent in controlling the trade itself, further urged conquest. No one district within the Midi was clearly favored beyond all the others as the center of political force. The Mediterranean lowland, cleft shortly after the death of Charlemagne, never regained unity. The Biscay lowland likewise split in two.

The Rhône Basin appeared at one time on the point of making good its independence. Its rulers even bore the title of king, and their realm was held in fief, not to France, but to the remote and weak German Emperor. As the trans-European trade via the Seine Basin increased, the French influence in the Rhône waxed, until capped by annexation.

## THE SUBDIVIDED LOIRE BASIN

The Loire and its tributaries, fed mainly by the sporadic but often heavy rains of the Central Massif, is the least satisfactory for navigation of all the major French river systems. Alternately a raging torrent and an expanse of shallow water underlain by inconstant sandbars, it carries today less traffic than any of the others, although during the middle ages it was used for want of any better road. Until the unexplored Atlantic was converted into a seaway the Middle and Lower Loire, like the Garonne, linked only local units and had no part in the world trade which traversed Europe in a north-south direction (Figs. 16 and 17). One short segment of the stream, between the great bend at Orléans and the junction of the Cher at Tours, could be utilized in the great lowland route between the Basins of the Seine and the Garonne. Above Orléans, the Loire and its long tributary, the Allier, serve as routes between the Rhône and Paris basins, alternative to routes via the Upper Seine system. Its fragmentary character is the key to the political geography of the Loire Basin. None of its landward boundaries are definitive. Hence political units tend to be small, resting upon agricultural productivity of a tributary valley, or the market value of a confluence, or a defense point on which a walled castle might be built.

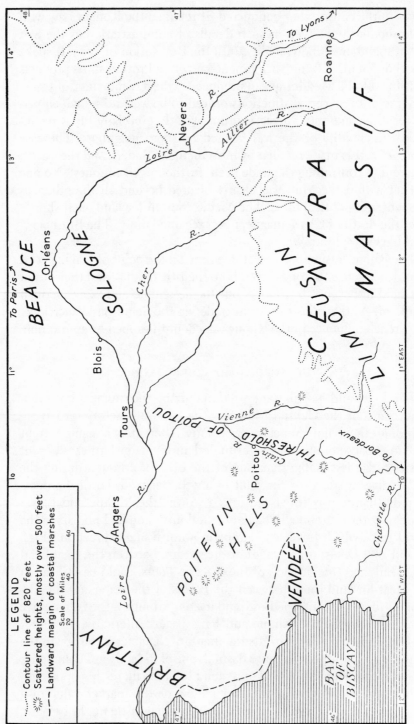

FIG. 18. The Loire valley as a border zone.

LEGEND

....... Contour line of 820 feet

☀ Scattered heights, mostly over 500 feet

— — Landward margin of coastal marshes

Scale of Miles
0    20    40    60

The feudal cleavage which divided uniform Aquitaine between Bordeaux and Toulouse, chopped the Loire Basin into more than a dozen small autonomies — including such famous names as Bourbon, Nevers, Orléans, Berry, Blois, Touraine, Poitou, Maine, Anjou, Vendôme, and Brittany (Fig. 18). Such a pattern confutes the superficial unity of the Basin, and proclaims the region a zone of transition. This is further attested by comparing the political with the geological map. The lower reaches are part of granitic, as well as of ethnic, Brittany; the great bend encroaches upon the saucer-like Paris Basin; while the upper course lies within the Central Massif. Most of the Loire lowland is so easily linked with the Seine Basin that the deflection of many small political units into the orbit of Paris need occasion no surprise.

The real barrier lies somewhat south of the Loire, where the Central Massif reaches northwestward by way of the Limousin and the Gâtine. This barrier is prolonged to the seacoast by the amphibious, southern Vendée, but between the numerous defense points of the Gâtine and the rugged Limousin Plateau lies the wide open gate beneath the walls of Poitiers — the " Threshold of Poitou." From the beginning of the 6th century the struggle between the rulers of the Paris Basin and the rulers of Aquitaine waged almost unceasingly across this doorsill. Because of this enmity the northerners permitted the Saracens to overrun the Midi a century later. Only when the Moorish army had crossed the threshold and was preparing to conquer North Europe, did Franks and Aquitainians join forces to defeat their common enemy, at some point not far north of the site of Poitiers.[1] As soon as the flight of the Moors across the Pyrenees removed the external danger, the internal struggle for possession of the precious passway reopened. The lords of Poitou made themselves masters of Aquitaine and by the middle-12th century the whole domain had been married into the hands of the king of England, who already possessed the northwest of France, from Poitou to beyond the mouth of the Seine. Poitiers was the key to the vital connection between northern and southern holdings of the king of England; it was no less the wedge with which the king of France might split the power of his overweening vassal. For three centuries the struggle went on. Long after the English kings definitively lost Normandy to France they clung to Aquitaine. Whenever they held the Threshold they kept possession of all the lowland. Whenever they lost the Threshold to the French king, their power shrank to a mere strip along the coast. When the French waxed strong enough to occupy it perma-

[1] Perhaps near the confluence of the Clain, the little stream above which Poitiers stands, and the larger Vienne.

nently, ultimate evacuation by the English of Bordeaux and so of France was inevitable. France could not be unified without possession of the Threshold, and the most serious threat unification ever faced was the accumulation of the lands north and south of Poitiers in the hand of the kings of England.[1]

## THE SEINE BASIN AND UNIFICATION

The Seine and its tributaries provide the most useful system of waterways in France. Except in their extreme headwaters, their gradients are gentle. Fed mainly by the uniform and moderate rains of the North, they carry enough water at all seasons to support laden boats. High water interferes with navigation once every few years for a short time in spring. Nearly every one of the larger tributaries makes easy and close contact with one of the other major river systems of the country (Fig. 16). Only the Garonne lies too remote. In time half a dozen canals were dug across the low watersheds, and the traffic in the masterstream and its connections toward the northeast remains large — one of the few active inland waterways in these days of rail- and motor-roads.

The river basin is elliptical, but all the principal tributaries lie in its eastern hemicycle (Fig. 19). More striking still, a crow flight of less than one hundred miles over the middle course of the river passes the confluence of every one of these larger streams. In the midst of this convergence of waterways islands half fill the stream. Partially protected by their natural moat, the islands provide defensible ground for any people forced to take refuge there. As they need to expand, rough terrain close to the river on the left bank provides a more vulnerable, but still defensible site. The marshy plain on the right bank promises much room for further extension of city. In addition to the river highway, an overland route crossing dry plateaus north and south of the Seine, descends to the river at this point by way of the Bièvre Valley and the Pass of La Chapelle. The river crossing is facilitated by the islands, which simplify the problem of bridge building, as soon as bridges might be desired, by dividing the wide stream into two narrow ones. This central location is, of course, the site of Paris (Fig. 20). Caesar found a Gallic tribe entrenched upon the fortress island. The peace which he and his successors enforced permitted the Roman town to

---

[1] The Battle of Poitiers, fought nearly 100 years before the final overthrow of English power in France, was only one of a series which covered a period of 950 years, and by no means the most significant, in spite of its spectacular character and its renown in history. It was, in fact, the last marked success of the British arms on this critical ground. Its site was in the passway, seven miles southeast of Poitiers.

expand to the hill of the left bank. The age of turbulence which followed saw the city reduced to the confines of its easily defended nucleus, the Île de la Cité. From this nucleus began the political expansion which created France. The Cité provided protection in times of stress for the surrounding farmlands, which in turn supported it by

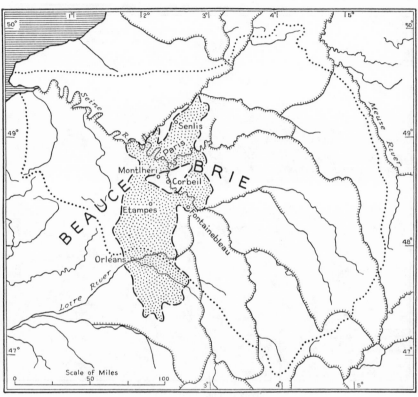

FIG. 19. The Seine Basin and surroundings.

The Île de France is stippled. The Seine Basin is outlined with dots. Feathered streams are navigable.

their husbandry. It served also as capital for a still wider area of surrounding plain.

The region intimately affiliated with Paris during the middle ages was known as the Île de France. Not of course an island surrounded by water, but a political island, surrounded by Norman, Burgundian, English, and other unfriendly powers. Yet in some sense it was and still is a physical island as well. The Seine Basin derives its circular shape from a series of underlying rock strata which dip gently toward a center at the site of Paris (Fig. 21). Where edges of these strata are exposed at the surface they have been worn away unevenly. Each stratum of resistant rock, protecting softer layers beneath, has thus come to form a concentric, although not continuous, ring of hills, sloping gently toward the Paris center, but presenting a steep and broken declivity on the out-facing flank. From the edge, as the English descriptively call the crest of this sort of ridge, the gentle slope behind hardly appears to

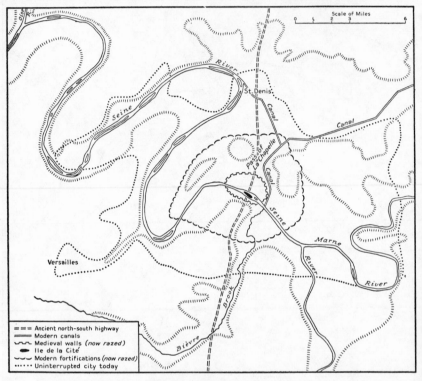

FIG. 20. The site of Paris.

The high ground immediately south and west of the city rises gently, whereas that to the north and east is precipitous and loftier.

be a hill, whereas the lowland in front lies spread out at the feet like a map. Where there are several resistant strata, as in the case of the country surrounding Paris, an outspread lowland such as this represents the surface of the next lower resistant member of the series, and in turn rises gently to an edge overlooking another lowland. It may be compared to a nest of saucers of very thick china. In the Paris Basin the concentric rings of hills disappear altogether at the south, and they are not clearcut at the west. In contrast, the easterly hemicycle is marked off at intervals by no less than seven conspicuous edges. Repeating them once more the Vosges Mountains, although quite different in structure, present a pseudoform, in that the slope toward Paris is relatively gentle, whereas the east face is a steep fault-scarp, at the base of which the Rhine Rift Valley, some 1500 feet below, appears as another flat.

The Inner Paris Basin came into its own with the reconstitution of Europe which is associated with the folk migrations of Germanic tribes. For the Romans it had always lain a little offside. When the Franks, after making their way along the narrows of the North European Plain, reached the northern tabular uplands of the Paris Basin, they destroyed the last vestiges of Roman power near Soissons. In a few years they had traversed the inviting overland route which crosses the Seine at Paris, and had defeated the Visigoths near Tours (i.e., on the Threshold of Poitou, Fig. 18). Whereupon the natural focus of the newly won region, Paris, was made the official capital. Its functions must have been few, since the court moved with the king, and the Frankish kings lived a migratory life. Later, this land fell to vassals of the king, who removed his capital to Laon, superb defense point at the northern apex of the Inner Paris Basin.

## THE ANCIENT ÎLE DE FRANCE

The Île de France in its beginnings was merely a group of feudal units which owed allegiance to the Frankish Emperors, and later to their successors, the French kings. Several of its rivals were larger and some were wealthier. But its focal position helped its rulers to obtain for themselves the royal crown, at first intermittently, alternating with the line of Charlemagne, afterwards by right of inheritance. This honor, although an asset in the end, was often a handicap in days of feudal ascendancy, since it awakened the jealousy of powerful vassals who were equals, sometimes superiors, of their master in every material power, and incited them to pit their combined strength against their hapless sovereign.

The territory of the Île fluctuated in the manner of feudal units, which had notoriously fluid boundaries, but throughout its early period its strategic axis was the hundred-mile course of the Seine within which that river receives the waters of all its chief tributaries. Downstream, the Oise marked the political boundary. The heart of political France is the pair of limestone uplands which flank the Seine.

On the left bank, i.e., mainly to the southward of Paris, Beauce reaches a long arm toward Orléans. Beauce is high, dry, and treeless. Its few streams are sharply trenched, and the ground-water table lies well

below the surface of the level upland. Fortunately the pervious limestone is mantled with limon soil, retentive of moisture. This soil, ab-
sorbing a fair share of the well distributed rains, somewhat reduces the
rapidity of runoff and makes the district just moist enough for wheat.
The most extensive area of high physical uniformity in all the country
west of the Rhine and the Alps, it has been occupied by farmers ever
since neolithic man began to practice crude agriculture.[1] East and west
it is flanked by country more broken, dotted with lakelets, largely
wooded, and progressively infertile, a sort of terrain which the French
designate as gâtine, i.e., waste. So characteristic is this of the land immediately east of Beauce that it goes by the name of Gâtinais. To the
west, the fertile plain gradually gives way to spots of gâtine, and finally
to the Hills of Perche. These constitute the inmost edge of the Paris
Basin on this side, but an ill-marked one. Moreover, the alignment is
concave outward, and so spoils the circular form which elsewhere
characterizes the rims of the saucers. Between these less favored lands,
the smooth Beauce runs unbroken except by minor, narrow valleys to
the Loire, where that river encroaches upon the Paris Basin. Without
interruption from the beginning of the 7th century, Paris controlled
the eastern half of Beauce. For good measure, it incorporated the Loire
valley itself in the vicinity of Orléans, a strategic town both because it
lies on the outside of the great bend of the river, and because there
an island facilitates bridging the unruly current. The Île de France
found a suitable southern boundary in the lake-dotted Sologne, immediately south of the Loire. There, wet clay soils, useless for fields, kept
the population sparse and poor, and so provided a reasonably satisfactory zone for a stable boundary.

In the heart of Beauce lay the strength of the Dukes of France in
the first century of their rule as kings. They lived mainly at Orléans,
sometimes at Étampes, halfway between Orléans and Paris, more
rarely at Senlis to the north of Paris (Fig. 19). The first of the long

[1] See Map Illustrating the Occupation of the Soil, in Vidal de la Blache, Paul:
*Tableau de la Géographie de la France*, opposite p. 54. Paris: Hachette, 1911.

FIG. 21. The easterly side of the Paris Basin.

C — Charleville; Ch — Châlons-sur-Marne; D — Dijon; É — Épernay; Él — Épinal;
L — Langres; Ln — Laon; M — Metz; N — Nancy; O — Orléans; R — Reims; S —
Soissons; St — Strasbourg; T — Toul; Th — Thionville; Tr — Troyes; V — Verdun.

The part played by the edges in the military strategy of the World War is dealt with
by Douglas W. Johnson in two books: *Topography and Strategy in the War* (Holt,
1917), and *Battlefields of the World War*; American Geographical Society Research
Series No. 3 (Oxford University Press, 1921). These volumes contain numerous dia-
grams of parts of the area. The map here presented draws upon these and other sources,
checked by studies made by the author in the field.

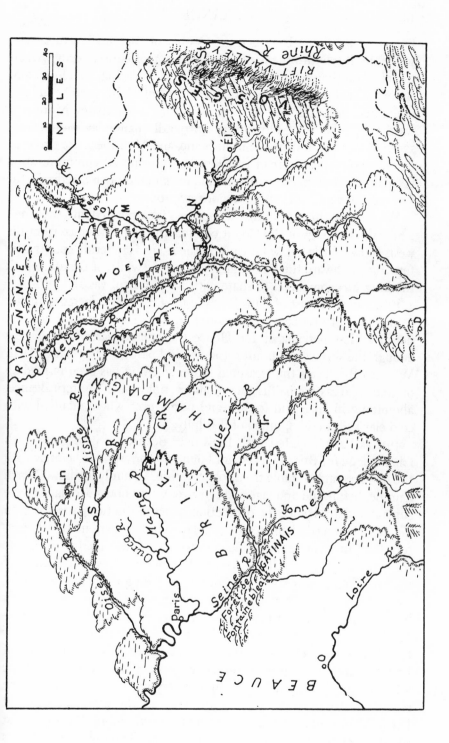

line of French kings bestowed the County of Paris upon a vassal, and soon after it fell into the hands of the Bishop of Paris, already well entrenched on the eastern half of the Île de la Cité (Fig. 20). For a long time the mainland bridgeheads were controlled by vassals, and the king rarely risked himself to these dangerous subordinates. More awkward still, a block of territory in unfriendly hands lay immediately south of Paris. In it Corbeil on the Seine, and Montlhéri, the strongest defense point on the road to Étampes, interrupted communication between the two major parts of the king's demesne and reduced the commercial value of both his major trade routes.

When once this seat of disaffection was incorporated into the king's lands, the holdings of the Count of Blois threatened France from the west. Blois, a little below Orléans on the Loire, is in fertile country, extending northward the full length and half the width of Beauce, which the king was compelled to share with his powerful vassal.

East and southeast of Paris lies Brie (Fig. 21), to a degree a smaller counterpart of Beauce. Its cavernous limestone is underlain at no great depth by less pervious strata. Hence the ground-water table is near enough the surface to permit meadows and pastures, as well as wheat. Western Brie bears the treasured limon soil, and has been farmed *ab origine*. The eastern half is a wet country, not unlike Western Beauce, abounding in lakes and forests, and nearly everywhere mantled with cold clay soil. Besides, much of it is hilly.

Just as Paris disputed with Blois over Beauce, so it disputed with Champagne for Brie. The ancient boundary corresponded closely with the line separating arable from forested Brie. In rainly medieval North Europe, before tile drainage and fertilizer were known, wet lands were superabundant. Hence the distinction between the two parts was even more pronounced than it seems today. This appears in the derogatory term implying a miserable country, which was used to designate the east — La Brie Pouilleuse. But had it not been for the feebleness of the early French kings and the potency of their great vassals of Champagne, the boundary might easily have been pushed out to include both halves of Brie, which is encircled on the south and east by a stiff military barrier: none other than the innermost of the concentric edges of the Paris Basin. This, sometimes known as the Cliff of the Isle of France, stands on an average more than 300 feet above the Champagne lowland, and has figured critically in every military campaign of the region's history, usually to the advantage of the power centered at Paris. Champagne of the middle ages ranked among the wealthiest countries of north Europe — not from its sparkling wine, which was not invented until the 18th century, but from trans-European trade which, after leaving the Saône Plain, followed the wide and easily traversed lowland east of the edge, before forking, in Champagne, westward toward Paris and the Lower Seine and northward toward the corridor of the Belgian lowland (Fig. 17). On these lines the Romans had maintained their chief roads in the region, and medieval trade followed the same routes. So long as the master of this lucrative and growing but vulnerable resource (trade) was able, he would prefer to keep his overlord at the safe distance of western Brie, rather than to have his hostile castles overlooking the main trade route itself.

The remaining bit of immemorial French royal domain lies to the north of Paris, between the Marne and Oise tributaries of the Seine. This region is reminiscent of Brie, although the range of its relief is greater and dissection is more pronounced. It is divided into a drier and more arable west and a wetter, more rugged, and more wooded east. And the political boundary remained for a long period to accentuate this contrast in the terrain. The principal streams, beginning with the Marne, have carved flat and marshy valleys scores of feet below the upland levels. Because most of them flow west, each forms a military barrier of a sort, available equally to an invader of the Basin and to its defender. Between the Ourcq and the Oise rivers a ridge of sandstone, deeply wooded as such ridges almost invariably are, parallels these river defenses more than 300 feet above the plain, and helps to outline the ancient confines of the Île de France.

### THE NUCLEUS OF THE LARGER FRANCE

Even in its earliest period the kingdom of France foreshadowed its nuclear quality. The location of Paris, although by no means central in the France of today, combines two of the salient characters of a capital. First, it is focal. Its site is a crossing of land and water routes. Its location is near the foregathering of a wide circle of navigable streams with their easy portage connections. Its arable surroundings, the region most easily incorporated and defended as well as most necessary to its livelihood, reached modestly outward to west, north, and east, but extended far to the south, in the direction of the bulk of the territory which it was one day to fashion into France. Besides being focal, it stands as near as a focal capital may to the weak eastern frontier. More specifically, it looks northeast down the broad corridor north of the Ardennes, where, between tumbled hills and boggy plain, the roads from the continental interior of Eurasia lie open.

Although the early Île de France fell short of the first prime military barrier provided by nature, and its later territorial growth has only crudely conformed to the several concentric rims of the Basin, yet the terrain furnished a succession of domiciles for the growing state. Each one could serve for a habitation until it was outgrown — until the concepts and methods of governance had become powerful and flexible enough to embrace successfully the next adjacent terrain and its inhabitants.

In this territorial and national expansion there was no sharp break in principle from the simple procedure current in the darkest ages, of joining three or four manors into a single unit. Because of its natural grouping of tiny environmental units into clusters, and the equally natural assemblage of those clusters into regions, and of the regions into combinations having reciprocal resources, Western Europe is the best conceivable incubator for the national state. And nowhere else in Western Europe is regionalism at once so diverse and so neat, as at the convergence of all the great avenues of Eurasian culture, in the blend of highland and lowland, of North Europe and South, which goes by the name of France. The instrument of political union in that area, the Île de France, is not an accident, but the favored core of the Paris Basin and of concentrically larger zones which it was able gradually to dominate.

The Paris Basin possesses the virtue of moderation. It is neither tiny nor huge; its soil varies from moderately fertile to moderately infertile; its mineral wealth consists of the commonplace rocks, sands and clays; its streams, although navigable, cannot float large boats; it lies adjacent to, but not squarely athwart the major routes of commerce, either by land or by sea. Above all, its successive naturally marked military barriers give repeated pause to the enemy, but must be defended if he is to be repulsed; and the successive naturally marked political boundaries serve only to give an expanding state necessary breathing spells, because beyond each one lies the enticing vision of the next promised land.

The most natural direction of French expansion would appear to be downstream. Disregarding meanders it is only about 150 miles by way of the Seine Valley from the ancient boundary of the Île de France at the confluence of the Oise, to the open sea; the navigable Seine invites trade, and trade is a powerful incentive to political union. The configuration of the land along the lower river is much the same as in the Île de France. Scattered along the upland on both sides of the Seine, and bordering the Norman coast, are notable districts of limon soil. For a time the coastal zone, penetrated by navigable valleys, traced by sea-roving Saxons and Northmen, was more strongly Germanized than the Île de France, and always the proximity of the sea gave to Normans an interest in fishing and seaborne trade not shared by its inland neighbor. When the duke of Normandy, vassal of France, became king of England and so peer of France, latent enmity flared up. For a time Normandy was a pawn between the two realms; then adjacence, increasing trade, and a common language, all brought to popular attention by intermittent enforced union with France, laid the kindling of national union which was ignited by the flaming patriotism of Joan of Arc. Once Normans had come to feel themselves compatriots of the French, these two major components of the Seine Basin welded themselves into a firm political union.

To bring under the aegis of the Île de France the farspread territories of Aquitaine was a task more slowly accomplished. The separate and often hostile feudal units in the Middle Loire Basin had first to be linked permanently to France. Then came the long struggle with the south (the Midi) — less Germanized, speaking Provencal (almost another language), remote in thought and feeling from Paris, and ardently supporting its allegiance to its local lords, one of whom was also king of England. The religious protest, precursor of the Protestant Reformation, which broke out in the County of Toulouse, was at the same time a symbol of the Midi's resistance to domination from the North, and the excuse for the king to prosecute to bitter success his conquest of that hotbed of heresy. When the Protestant Reformation did at last irrepressibly embroil Europe, it was in the Midi that the Huguenots were powerful, and gave to the local leaders encouragement to rebel against their Parisian king.

Incorporation of the Midi within the French state means much more than conquest of territory and the elimination of dangerous rival overlords. Until the levelling Revolution of 1789, the Midi retained many of its individual customs and laws — vestiges of its long-standing independence.[1] It can scarcely be doubted that if the French state had not recognized and compromised with these regional traditions, there would have been incessant friction and frequent revolts. During the centuries between the conquest of the Midi and the regimentation of France by the Revolutionary and Napoleonic governments, many of the sharp distinctions between the regions blurred, although lesser

---

[1] It kept its Roman, written, law, quite at variance with the feudal, " customary," law of all the north. Its salt-tax, as an example of many similar distinctions, was generally lower than in the north, in Aquitaine strikingly so: 6 sous in Poitou for the quantity which paid 60 in adjacent Touraine.

ones, traditions and practices which do no violence to national unity, persist even today.

The Rhône-Saône Basin was attached to France bit by bit, some of it at about the time of the conquest of Aquitaine, the rest much later. As a major line of trans-European trade, with branches leading both northeast down the Rhine and northwest into the Paris Basin, its control vitally concerned the rising powers of the north — increasingly so as trade multiplied. Its lowland arable core is small, and its disproportionate length lies broken into separate basins, connected but tenuously by the waterway. Numerous easy routes east and west emphasize its character as a corridor with many doors. Little wonder that it has rarely been politically unified, and never for long until the last fragment was incorporated into the French national state near the end of its era of territorial expansion.

## THE PARIS BASIN AND EASTWARD

The expansion of the Île de France toward the northwest, west, and south was delayed long enough to permit the necessary ingestion of each " country " before a new advance was made. In this way, the regions inhabited by peoples closest akin in origin, traditions, and language to the denizens of the Inner Paris Basin, and therefore most easily assimilated, became integral parts of France. The distinctions which they retained were relict expressions of their regionality, and those which they lost were sacrificed in the interests of prosperity engendered by political union — wealth based on reciprocal use of diverse regional resources. Despite interruptions and repulses, the nuclear Île de France had multiplied its area manyfold by the time English rule in Normandy and Aquitaine collapsed. With exclusion of the English, it incorporated most of the lands southwest of a line projected from the Mediterranean base of the Maritime Alps through Paris to the Channel. The only recalcitrant exception was the peninsula of Brittany, where infertile crystalline hills had provided a refuge for harassed Celts ever since, a thousand years before, they had been rammed into this bit of farthest western Europe by Germanic tribes.[1]

Northeastward from this line the Île de France protruded, but still the boundary stood little more than 100 miles from the gates of Paris in its maximum reach northeast, and well under 200 miles to the southeast. So slight an advance in this quarter relative to the large increments

[1] Even in the 20th century the people of Lower Brittany are not fully reconciled to France, and demand a measure of autonomy. Thus do culture and environment join in separatism.

of territory west and southward suggests either lack of incentive to conquest or powerful opposing forces. The shape of the bulge, when applied to a physical map, is seen to correspond closely to the drainage pattern of the Seine system and the concentric edges of the Paris Basin (Fig. 21).

The first severe tussle of the lords of Paris with their antean enemies to the eastward, who appear to derive inexhaustible energy from contact with central Europe, centered upon Champagne.

Some 60 miles south of the city the Inner Paris Basin is separated from fertile Beauce and sodden Gâtinais by an expanse of sandy plain which has been deeply wooded from time immemorial and today goes by the name, Forest of Fontainebleau. There the Seine breaks through the innermost edge on its way to Paris. Inconspicuous to the west where it fades into the level Beauce, the Cliff of the Isle of France begins immediately east of the Seine whence it sweeps in an almost perfect semicircle 220 miles to La Fère, northwest of Laon. Below the edge lies a plain so lightly etched by the few rivers which cross it, so nearly unbroken by remnants of superior strata, and so uniformly underlain by porous limestone that its dry, featureless surface makes it by turns the favored highway for commerce and the inevitable theater for clashing armies. This is the Champagne Pouilleuse, the " miserable openland," sparsely peopled and good only for grazing sheep and growing pinewood.

The least unproductive section lies immediately southeast of Brie. For about 75 miles the Seine flows at the base of the edge which limits Brie, and which there stands 330 feet above the river valley, its even crest only slightly nicked here and there by a short tributary or by unequal erosion. The gently sloping surface of the lowland rises 800 feet in 50 miles to the next edge, which, like its neighbor to the north. stands about 300 feet above the succeeding lowland. Between the peat-covered valley of the Seine and the sandy, wooded crest of the second edge, plain is succeeded by gentle hills. Trenching the height and crossing the whole width of the backslope, the Yonne River makes an easy route from the hills overlooking the Saône plain all the way to its confluence with the Seine, not far above Fontainebleau. This route the Romans knew and utilized, and today it is traversed by the main line of railway between Paris and the Rhône Basin. Firmly entrenched in western Brie on the Cliff of the Isle, and commanding the easy sortie made by the Seine, the French kings won this part of the Champagne as the first of their possessions eastward of the nuclear Île de France.

Control of the remaining Champagne Pouilleuse was long delayed.

The 125 miles of the east-facing innermost escarpment between the Aube-Seine confluence and the Aisne River, although appearing little broken when viewed from below, is cut through to the level of the Champagne by four streams and rather deeply notched by another, now vanished. He who can defend these passes can dominate the Champagne; and conversely, he who can take the passes holds the key to Paris. Although transected by valleys, this segment of the escarpment is higher on the average than the sections to the south and the north of it. It culminates dramatically in the massive bastion which pushes out into the plain between the Marne and the Vesle rivers — the Mountain of Reims. Near its outer end this promontory rises 550 feet above the adjacent plain. In the reentrant to the south Épernay crowds into a cranny of the escarpment, safely above the marshy floodplain of the Marne. At the northern foot of its mountain Reims spreads out beside the Vesle, in a vestibule of lowland screened from the open plain by a unique group of outlying hills.

Forty or fifty miles to the eastward the porous limestone of the Champagne Pouilleuse rises to form the second concentric edge, but, north of the Seine, reaching only about 150 feet above the narrow lowland beyond. This plain, in sharp contrast to its western neighbor, is mantled with clay holding numerous lakes and marshes and insuring the greenest of summer landscapes. Thus it has earned the sobriquet La Champagne Humide, the " wet openland." In spite of low relief, its marshy surface interferes with movement, and its only fertile parts are the alluvial valleys. Each principal stream, where it crosses the edge, has given rise to a combined market and defense town — Rethel on the Aisne, Vitry-le François on the Marne, Troyes on the Seine, and Joigny on the Yonne.

East of Champagne, as will be seen (pp. 160–2), the country becomes increasingly difficult for north-south movement until the Rhine Valley is reached. Hence the significance of the terrain of the Counts of Champagne lay in its utility as a highway of trade (Fig. 17).

Where the Seine cuts through the second edge, Troyes gathers into a node all the highways from the east and south. No less than three separate routes to the Saône Plain meet there, and the easiest, although not the most direct, road between Paris and the upper Rhine and its western tributaries leaves the Seine Valley at Troyes. On this road grew up a chain of fairs which shifted about but together maintained a year round emporium patronized by merchants from all Europe. Two of these were in Troyes itself. Two others held at Provins, the metropolis of Eastern Brie, and on the route which led almost to the gates of

Paris before leaving the territory of Champagne. The remaining two were at the confines of the country — one at Lagny, on the threshold of the Ile de France, located at a narrows favorable for crossing the marshy Marne Valley on the way from Champagne to Paris; the other at Bar-sur-Aube, which guards a principal water-gate through the fourth *edge*, in the eastern precincts of the count's holdings.

Northward from Troyes the great trade route to the North European Plain and England takes its way obliquely across the dry Champagne by way of Arcis-sur-Aube, Châlons-sur-Marne, and Reims. From Reims roads fork to the narrows of the Channel, to the Lower Rhine, and to the Lower Seine. From Châlons the Marne Valley leads to Épernay and Paris. Fairs less famous and prolonged, but well attended, were held at the four principal nodal sites on this route — Arcis, Châlons, Epernay, and Reims. All the Champagne fairs were protected by special legislation, administered by a corps of magistrates whose sole business it was. Roads were protected so far as possible from bandits, and canal building was undertaken to improve navigation on the Seine.

Waxing wealthy on trade in a land mostly too dry or too wet to farm, the lords of Champagne held territory outside Champagne and Brie from which they derived their title. Eastward these holdings reached into the Meuse Valley and crossed the line between the Kingdom of France and the Empire of the Germans. In the west for a time they included Blois, with half of Beauce, and Touraine, thus controlling the route to Aquitaine. Faced on the east with wealth flowing along busy trade routes, and on the west with wealth skimmed from fertile fields, the kings of France appeared to be no match for their powerful vassals of Champagne. In the long run the weakness of scattered holdings appeared, when the western fiefs were lost to Champagne. Seventy years later a lucky marriage brought to the French king Champagne itself, together with the eastern part of the Inner Paris Basin.

Either from a desire to deflect the trade to Paris, or because any agrarian state notoriously misunderstands the requirements of commerce, the new ruler forbade Flemish merchants to attend the fairs of Champagne. Although this was a staggering blow, the fairs continued to function for more than three centuries. A part of what the Champagne lost, the Île de France gained, and in time it came to foster trade as sedulously as its rival had done. By adding commerce to agriculture as a second mainstay of its people, the constitution of the French monarchy proved itself supple enough to continue to grow and to thrive in a radically changing political atmosphere.

It is oddly perverse that the vital addition to France of Champagne and its bordering edges was accomplished without battles, for the Dry Champagne is the age-old theater of war no less than of trade. For the Romans it served a triple purpose: highway to the Channel at its narrowest crossing, base line for the frontier garrisons along the Rhine; and main trade route between the Mediterranean and the north. When Roman Gaul was being shattered by armed populations wedging in from the east, many of the sledgehammer blows fell in this critical zone. On its open, dry flat Attila deployed his horde of horsemen from the grassland of eastern Europe, in making his final bid for control of western Europe, and was defeated.[1]

Toward the end of the middle ages, in the long continued assaults upon France that awoke in the French a sense of nationality, and thus transformed a feudal territory into a national state, the Champagne battleground was again chosen, first by the English, then by the Burgundians and their successor, the Hapsburg Emperor. Three centuries more and Napoleon lost his imperial crown on these same fields. The latest chapter was written only the other day, in repeated battles between August 1914 and October 1918, the first and last of which were the two most decisive on the western front and therefore the turning points of the whole World War.

In all these battles the strategy has been similar. To enter Paris from the east, an army must control the escarpment of the Inner Basin. To obtain this control has always involved fighting on the Champagne lowland. Although Paris often has been threatened and occasionally taken, its possession of the strategic interior position coupled with its admirable natural defenses, have given it an advantage which in the long run of history has made it repeatedly the political core of the western apex of the Eurasian triangle.

Physically and historically the north-facing segment of the Inner Edge and its apron of dry lowland is intimately linked with that part which looks eastward. Politically it has a special niche which requires separate treatment.

Barely 50 miles of high ground marks the last stand of the edge between the Aisne and the Oise. All the north part of the Inner Basin is carved into blocks by the several right-bank branches of the Oise. Each block maintains its standard elevation of about 300 feet above the valleys. To dislodge an army posted above these marshy river trenches is a herculean task. As the World War proved, possession of one or more

[1] The battle of the Catalaunian Plains, commonly known as the Battle of Châlons; some authorities believe it occurred near the hamlet of La Cheppe, a few miles northeast of Châlons and on the edge of the great maneuvers field laid out by Napoleon III, others favor a site north of Troyes. In either case the terrain must have been the same.

of these outlying military barriers does not necessarily devolve control of the Inner Basin, because either the south or the north margin of each block may be fortified for defense. At the salient where the trend of the edge alters from north-south to east-west, stands the Chemin des Dames, a ridge 15 miles long and half as broad. To the west is the larger and less steeply cliffed Forêt de St. Gobain. In the stream-carved depression between them stand two eminences, small and flat-topped — true mesas. The one in advance, a lone sentinel on the plain, is crowned by the most conspicuous defense-point city in the whole Paris Basin. This is Laon, fortress and capital of the Frankish kings when Paris was vassal territory. From Laon they directed the struggle for supremacy which was at last won by the upstart island in the Seine with its nodal location. Physical outliers of the Inner Paris Basin, Laon and its neighboring heights became part of the royal domain — political and defensive outposts of the Île de France. Between the two lay fiefs of independent vassals, entrenched in the hilliest part of the Inner Basin. Long before they were added to the royal domain, the French kings had pushed their holdings northward along the less broken sandy lowland bordering the Oise River, as far as Noyon and its protective screen of mesas. From them — most northwesterly outposts of the Cliff of the Isle of France — and from the disjoined heights of Laon, lies spread the plain of North Europe, a lowland generally below 600 feet elevation which from the Pyrenees sweeps unbroken and ever broadening until it becomes the vast expanse of Russia.

## THE RHINE BASIN AND BUFFER POLITICS

Eastward along this narrow part of the plain the Romans pressed their advantage over the Gauls (Fig. 22). From the northeast came the Franks, pushing outward from the Rhineland of their origin without losing contact with it, thereby assimilating the Latin culture to their own without destroying either. Wars fought on this plain, rather than in the American or Asiatic colonies, determined the allocation of the 18th century colonial empire among the maritime states of Western Europe. A little south of Brussels, in the transition zone between Germanic and Romanic speech, is Waterloo, where the French ambition to dominate the Lower Rhine was abruptly checked in a single battle. A hundred years later, a hundred miles to westward, in the same transition belt, the German ambition to destroy French power was slowly mired in four years of muddy trench warfare which pivoted on the low ridge of Messines. No wonder this part of the Plain between the low limestone hills northwest of Laon and the Rhine Valley where it is flattest and where it narrows to a corridor 125 miles wide, has been called " the cockpit of Europe." It has been a battleground throughout history, at times for years without interruption.

It is not only in the strategy of battles that the region has been significant to a degree unwarranted by its size. Much of it is closely dotted with farm villages, among which sprawl numerous large cities. The

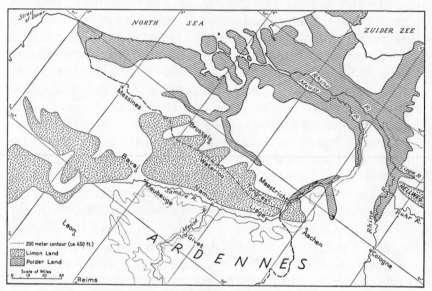

FIG. 22. The narrows of the north European plain.
The zone of coastal sanddunes is too narrow to be shown on this scale.

population for some 800 years has been the densest in Europe, persisting in its lead throughout all the changes of agricultural, commercial, and industrial revolutions. This points to a unique combination of favoring circumstances — arable soil, a major crossroads for trade, and raw materials for manufacturing.

The coast is fringed by a band of sand dunes, rarely more than three miles wide, and averaging no more than one. Because the surface soil is dry, while potable water may be had anywhere by digging a shallow hole, this line can be used as a routeway. Because the surface is pitted and the sand makes heavy going, it is rarely so used. The dunes fend the sea from a considerable expanse of river-borne alluvium and clay soil which lies below or not far above high tide. With the aid of dikes along the rivers and innumerable drainage canals which crisscross the almost literally flat plain, this wet land has been converted into farms intensively worked and highly productive. This Flemish region was the first district of Europe to emerge from the crude farm system of the middle ages, and ever since it has been a rich larder for townsfolk of the vicinity and for invading armies. As a passway, however, it is handicapped by muddy roads, numerous bridges across the lesser waterways, and unbridged main streams.

South of the polders which have been reclaimed from the outer delta of Meuse and Rhine, stretch sandy heaths, largely wooded even today and scantily settled. Near the western tip of the Ardennes, such a forest touched the hill country until the later middle ages. Elsewhere a belt of fertile limon soil lies between this heathland and the rugged, forested Ardennes. Almost straight, gentle in gradients, free from heavy forest and sodden marsh, this has been the traditional passway along this narrows in the plain of North Europe. At its eastern end it focuses on Cologne, the major crossing of the Rhine between the gorge and the delta of that stream. In the west it branches to the Strait of Dover, to the Lower Seine Valley, and to the Paris Basin. A main Roman road traversed the woodland about Bavai, in order to follow the open belt via Tongres, crossing the Meuse at Maastricht, and passing through Aachen. This broad highway is supplemented by an alternative route, the narrow but smooth road of the valleys of the Sambre and its master-stream the Meuse, a nearly straight trench cut into the Ardennes near their northern margin, past the fortress towns Maubeuge and Namur, to Liége, and thence across a spur of hills to Cologne.

As farms replaced forest and marsh, the region traversed by these routes was breathed upon by all the currents of trade and politics stirring in Western Europe, and it became the first seat of manufacturing north of the Mediterranean coastlands. A list of the towns of Flanders is a catalog of textiles — named from the place of their origin. Manufactures, besides creating new wealth, increased trade and stirred the farmers to make their acres yield more abundantly. Grown rich, the cities excited the cupidity of all the princes of Europe. When the Industrial Revolution altered the meaning of *manufacturing*, the district was found to lie upon excellent coal. Thereby it kept its lead among manufacturing regions of the world. Long bandied about by vicissitudes of war and politics, the Low Countries have occasionally been united, more usually divided. Profiting from their border location, they have been able to establish independence of their larger neighbors.

For the past hundred years most of the strategic corridor has belonged to the Belgian monarchy, leaving the ends in the hands of two major powers. Independence in the Low Countries, and particularly

Belgium, rests upon a stalemate between their powerful neighbors — a stalemate which has been maintained by the third interested power, England, whenever either of the belligerents domiciled at the ends of the Flemish corridor threatens to overthrow the balance.

The complementary nature of the Inner Paris Basin and the concentric Champagne has been established. East of the Wet Champagne the serried belts of lowland rising to an edge overlooking the next lowland are repeated. They are, however, less neatly arranged than their counterparts to the west, partly because they are less continuous and less uniform, partly because among them lies the watershed between the Seine and the Rhine basins. All this country has traditionally been quasi-independent of either the Paris Basin or the German lowlands. Frequently during the feudal age a local lord effectively unified a territory part of which he held (according to feudal law) from the king of France and part from the emperor of Germany. An irrepressible urge to create a long narrow country covering the Rhône-Rhine trade route, with this hill-land as its core, has repeatedly been quenched by the rival claims of the Rhône-Champagne route, supported by the well-manned natural defenses of the Paris Basin. It has been easier to shatter the longitudinal trading state, sprawling along its highway of commerce and open to attack on both sides, than to bring the many bits into which it breaks into cohesive union with either neighbor. Most of the area is now grafted into France, but scars of the prolonged struggle still appear in autonomous Luxemburg and in the repeated transfer of Alsace and Lorraine between France and Germany, to say nothing of the Low Countries and Switzerland.

At the north, four of the edges (Argonne to Côtes de Moselle) converge in the vicinity of the Charleville just south of the Ardennes Massif (Fig. 21). Between the two uplands lies a hilly east-west route which traverses Luxemburg and extreme southern Belgium, and enters the valley of the Meuse near Sedan, where that stream flows along the north face of the clustered escarpments. From the Champagne to the Rhine the Romans maintained a main road along this passageway, and routes follow it today, somewhat interrupted by its division among four nations. Southward from this convergence the Argonne, less than 70 miles long, extends its narrow but forbidding, sandy, and forested bulk. In that distance it is trenched to the level of the adjacent plain in several places. The great route from northern Lorraine to Paris proceeds through one of these notches rather than digressing about the south end of the range only 10 miles away. No bar to passage in peacetime, the Argonne can become a formidable barrier to armies if only

the notches are adequately guarded. The next edge (the fourth, count-
ing from Paris) is low and the adjacent lowland is inconspicuously set
off from it. Unlike the Argonne, it extends well round into the southeast quadrant of the Basin. Because of its insignificance as a surface feature, no first-flight trading towns have grown up along it, although it has
served the exigencies of military commanders more than once. In its
northern half, it forms the watershed between Seine and Rhine basins.
Its southerly extension is crossed by several tributaries of the Seine.

If this edge is the least noteworthy of the series, the next one to the
east (the fifth from Paris), ranks with the Cliff of the Isle of France.
From the north, where it leaves its easterly neighbors, it swings in a
wide semicircle and transgresses into the basin of the Loire River. To
the south it forms no notable feature of the landscape, but to the north
it rises to a great rampart. The Meuse, tributary to the Rhine, crosses it
twice in a deeply entrenched valley, and eastward of the river the edge,
called here the Côtes de Meuse, stands 500 feet above the Woevre, a
plain as flat and as wide as the Champagne Pouilleuse, but mantled
with clay, and therefore lake-studded, marshy, and verdant. Midway the
edge is traversed by the main east-west route. Below, where this route
crosses the Meuse, lies Verdun. Southwestward from the trench
through which the Meuse passes behind its Côtes, the elevation of
the edge diminishes to 300 feet or less, its eminence not always clearly
distinguishable from the other hills in that generally rather rugged
region.

The next (sixth) edge closely duplicates its neighbor. Swinging
sharply southward, 800 feet high at the bend near Thionville, it likewise becomes entangled with a river, the Moselle this, which flows at its
base, now east and now west of the ridge, for nearly 100 miles. There
the heights rise 500 feet above the lowland, which, about as wide as
the Woevre, is rolling country and easy to traverse. Where the Moselle
first crosses the edge, the city of Nancy guards a double door made by
Moselle and Meurthe. Inside, on the sharp bend, and screened by outliers of the Côtes de Meuse, lies Toul on the road between Strasbourg
and the Seine Valley. Fifty miles north, where the Moselle again cuts
the Côtes, Metz is guardian city. Verdun, Toul, Nancy, Metz — these
strategic sites on the complex pattern of ridge and river are leads in
the drama of life as played in this borderland between Western and
Central Europe.

Southward the edge continues its well-marked course. Langres, standing squarely on a conspicuously abrupt crest, is close to the headwaters of the Marne and its route from Paris. Dijon, ancient capital of

Burgundy, lies on the Saône Plain at the base of the bluff, where a stream has cut an easy route through the *edge*, here called the Côte d'Or, to the headwaters of the Yonne. Farther south the *edge* merges into the steep eastern face of the Central Massif.

Eastward from the Côtes de Moselle, beyond Metz and Nancy, lies a vale a few miles wide, crossed by the Moselle and its tributaries and largely in fields, although patched with forest where the soils are wet and heavy. This dip slope rises to a seventh *edge*, more irregular than any of those farther west, and cut by the streams into segments known by different names. Tongues and outliers of the heights project eastward between the valleys, forming natural bastions for mounting defenses, and permitting their defenders to rake the intervening vales along which the routes pass. One mass, the Côtes de Delme halfway between Metz and Nancy, is higher than the rest because it retains a cap of the strata which crown the Moselle *edge*. It rises steeply on both east and west flanks. In 1871 the German boundary was drawn to include this height, to serve as a defensive screen for Metz.

Beyond the seventh *edge* the country is rolling, characterized by minor ridges and deeply entrenched streams, and covered with clay and sand soils. This is the Plain of Lorraine, rising not too steeply to the Vosges Mountains, a mass of crystalline rocks, deeply dissected and covered with dense spruce forest. The eastern face of the Vosges marks a fault line, which from the east appears as a formidable mountain wall, reaching a maximum of 2100 feet elevation above the flat floor of the Rhine Valley. Toward the north end a defile permits road, canal, and main railroad to cross to Strasbourg. Still farther north the Gate of Lorraine, a rolling upland between the Vosges and the Ardennes, opens into the fertile heart of Germany, where the lower end of the Rhine Rift Valley spreads eastward into the confluence area of Main and Rhine. By this broad, open way German armies invaded France in 1870 and 1914. At the south, the Vosges drop abruptly to the Burgundian Gate, an almost level passway between the upper end of the Rhine Rift Valley and the Saône Plain. It is the natural highway of trade from the Mediterranean to Central Europe. It was the inviting door which led the Romans to the country of the Germans, and which a few centuries later led the first German invaders into Roman Gaul — the Alemanni, a tribe which in the French tongue designates all Germans today.

From this corner of the Saône Plain Lorraine can be reached by way of alternative routes through the rugged Monts Faucilles. These routes converge upon Épinal, where the Moselle enters the Lorraine Plain.

## The Eastern Boundary of France Today

The Vosges constitute the last outpost of France on the east. Across the Rift Valley of the Rhine their counterpart, the Black Forest, presents a forbidding face to the west. For a short time the Romans controlled the whole Rift Valley and the mountains between which it lies, and the several " middle kingdoms " of the Rhône-Rhine trade route have forged but never permanently welded the two highlands into political unity. Today, with France and Germany centered well to the west and east, the Rift Valley is a borderland, not a coreland. It is untenable so long as an unfriendly power controls the heights immediately above. Alsace therefore goes with the Vosges and Baden with the Black Forest. The outlines of those two historic units faithfully portray their military strategy, and the marshy banks of the Rhine constitute the most clearly marked boundary in the whole zone. Contrarily, the river itself is a bond to those who occupy the adjacent lowlands and use its easily navigated current. Here, as nearly everywhere east of Paris, trade and war function in opposition on the same terrain.

The eastern boundary of France is unstable. It has always marked the zone in which concurrent forces have at the moment reached stalemate. During the feudal period the minute subdivision of landholdings, and the complex and often shadowy political connection between vassal territory and the king's domain, made a zonal boundary fitting and functional. For centuries the border was in constant flux. As communication became swifter and more regular, a linear and permanent boundary became the goal. Traders desired it to guarantee minimum cost and annoyance in crossing from country to country. Kings in remote Paris no longer had to depend on the initiative of competent and often disloyal vassals to protect their borders, but could dispatch and maintain armies of their own along the frontier. Civil administration was extended to include the whole state, and became more and more centralized. Feudal quasi-sovereignties were suppressed into provinces. Improvements in geodesy made it possible to survey linear boundaries accurately, demarcation along the east side of France being the first line completed pursuant to the general readjustment of boundaries after Napoleon's downfall in 1815. (The linear boundary had been accepted in principle a century earlier.)

While the political line has succeeded the political zone, permanency has not supplanted flux. In the whole broad band of the boundary zone there is no belt so inhospitable as to be unpeopled.

Even the mountains and hills modify the distribution of population surprisingly little. Rather, they are features significant primarily in military maneuvers, secondarily in the pattern of routes. The unprejudiced foreigner cannot point to a place where nature has unmistakably marked a boundary, and the gateways between the principal mountain masses are zones of such gradual human transition that the boundary arbitrarily cleaves linguistic units, cuts towns off from their trade territory, and describes lines most of which are historical accidents. At the south base of the Alps, along the Mediterranean coast, France has pushed eastward into Italian-speaking settlements. North of the Alps, where the Rhône Vale marks the transition between Alps and Jura, a long tongue of French speech belongs to Switzerland. The political boundary near the west end of Lake Geneva, severs the city Geneva from much of its natural trade territory. An attempt to solve the problem has created free zones for trade, but the solution is only partial and attempts are frequently made to move the economic boundary eastward to coincide with the political line. Between the Jura and the Vosges the Burgundian Gate marks the border between French and German speech, and all of lowland Alsace, alternately French and German in government, has remained for centuries Germanic in language. Between Vosges and Ardennes jumbled terrain goes hand-in-hand with mingled languages. The Saar Basin lies squarely in the Lorraine Gate. A plebiscite in 1935 ranged that district conclusively with Germany, after a decade and a half of special administration for the economic benefit of France. In general the German language overlaps the present political border, just as French overlapped the border between 1871 and 1918. The hilly lane which leads westward from the Lorraine Gate between the converging edges of the Paris Basin and the crystalline Ardennes Massif, is occupied by French-speaking people except in its eastern end. From this point to the North Sea the interlacing of linguistic borders (German, French, and Flemish) with political boundaries (Luxemburg, Belgium, and France) traces an intricate pattern. Over an airline distance of 60 miles the Franco-Belgian boundary cuts through the midst of French-speaking people in order to follow high ground along the southern margin of the Ardennes. Where the Meuse furrows its deep trench through the massif, the Wedge of Givet pierces the side of Belgium, its point resting on an abrupt hill, military guardian of French interests. The length of the wedge crudely measures the age-old flux of political and ecclesiastical suzerainty along the whole front in dispute between the powers of the edges and those of the coastal lowland. The plain between the Ardennes and the sea, least defined of all the eastern gates of France, is crossed by a political line which enters Flemish country near the coast.

## THE UNITY OF FRANCE

National unity burns as vigorously in France as in any other country, thanks to the long continued effort necessary to combine a number of distinct regions and to achieve and maintain an eastern boundary which the terrain made possible but never inevitable. The unitary form of government and the highly centralized administration of the state are concomitants of this tireless striving for territorial cohesion. Only in outer Celtic Brittany and in borderland Germanic Alsace are there groups which demand autonomy.

The part played by the nuclear Paris Basin in the long struggle to weld the lowlands into a single state has been crowned by a radial pattern of communication lines which is both the expression and the symbol of Paris as the hub of France.

It would be flying in the face of the long view of history to assert that French solidarity, forged of diverse regions, is invincible. It may be safe to expect that it will endure so long as the emotion of patriotism is identified with that group of physical units which we call France, and so long as the area wields the power to maintain its independence of potential enemies.

## CHAPTER SEVEN

# A Conflict of Maritime and Interior Interests—Germany

THE German state of the present age is the antithesis of France. Instead of being centralized and unitary by tradition it was federal in law until 1919 and in practice until the Nazi régime of 1933.[1] Modern Germany dates from 1870, almost exactly a millennium after Charlemagne's empire was dissected in such a way as to leave the outline of modern France on the political map. It germinated on land which lay outside European civilization at that remote date. The contemporary German Reich is so far from coincident with the German language or the Germanic nationalities, that five [2] independent states use German or cognate tongues as official languages, apart from the usual zonal language boundaries of Germany itself.

The political history of Germanic Europe traces confusing disintegration paralleled by surprising unification. The mundane base on which these contrasting forces evolved has two salient characteristics. First, it is a region of crossroads: a crude gridiron of waterways, including both rivers and marginal seas, accentuated by the arrangement of hill-lands and valleys (Fig. 23). Second, it is merely a piece of a larger Central Europe, in which neither barrier boundaries nor internal environment set a decisive mold for plastic statecraft.

## URDEUTSCHLAND

The forging of modern Germany from the resilient core called Prussia is but the latest phase of a millennial struggle to consolidate the

[1] It is easy to abolish by law a long-standing mode of government, but traditional practices of a people tend to reassert themselves. This was admitted in France when Napoleon recognized the irrepressible unity and centralization of the state and abandoned the diffusion of power which had been one of the accomplished objectives of the French Revolution.

[2] Switzerland, Luxemburg, Flemish Belgium, the Netherlands, and Slovakia.

habitable basins of Central Europe. The foundation of the modern edifice must be sought in the strip of country which borders the Rhine. Although today almost the western outpost of Germany, the Rhine is in sober fact precisely what is claimed for it by romantiç poetry and legend — the fatherland of Germany.

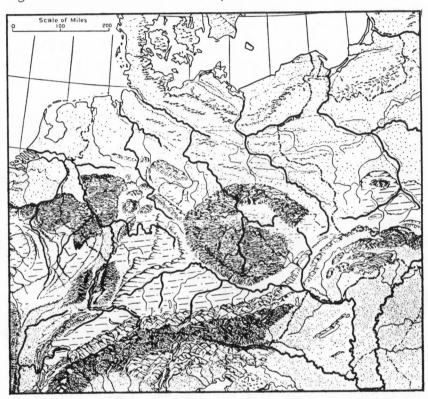

FIG. 23. Germany as a piece of central Europe.

Modified from A. K. Lobeck's " Physiographic Diagram of Europe." Courtesy of the cartographer and the Geographical Press.

Ancient Germany, " Urdeutschland," long since vanished, grew up in the border zone shared by Roman provincials and German tribes. Roman rule reached the Rhine-Danube line and for a time incorporated trans-fluvial lands between the mouth of the Moselle and the great bend of the Danube, besides waging wars of conquest as far east as the Lower Elbe. Resident Germans subjected to Rome and tribesmen who were permitted to settle within the Empire were followed by migrant tribes which took lands without permission. In the end Germanic languages prevailed westward to the Jura-Vosges-Ardennes zone of barriers to communication, while Germanic tribes became sedentary and Romanized, and reestablished the " Roman " Empire in a hardly recognizable medieval version.

The Empire, as reconstituted by Frankish Germans, had its nucleus in the Rhineland. It made effective claim to the Atlantic margin of continental Europe as far as the Pyrenees, excepting hilly, granitic, Celtic Brittany. Southward it overspread the Alps to include two-thirds of Italy and Rome itself. To the east the frontier lay in the zone which marked the limit of German occupation (approximated in Fig. 9). From the head of the Adriatic Sea to the gorge of the Danube River the break between Western, Latin Rome and Eastern, Hellenic Rome corresponded with waterless (karst) coast ranges and with the rugged eastern Alps, bordered by grassland plains. This barrier zone the Holy Roman Empire inherited as its boundary. North of the Danube the new power advanced beyond the line of effective Roman occupation, its assured boundary being the Bohemian Forest and the projection thereof northwestward along ranges and marshes to the North Sea. Like its classical prototype, it laid claim to all the country as far east as the line of the Elbe-Saale.

In all Europe there is no more critical zone of demarcation than this which runs from the Adriatic to the eastern shore of the North Sea (Fig. 9). Along it lie the frayed boundaries between South Slavs and Italians, between Hungarians and Germans and West Slavs. In it both Austria and Prussia took root, states which between them have dominated Germany for more than six centuries.

In the last half of the 9th century the Empire relinquished the major part of France and set itself up as a tripartite realm consisting of Germany, Burgundy, and Italy (Fig. 24). Burgurdy was essentially the Rhône-Saône trough, together with the vital connections toward the Rhine — the Burgundian Gate, the Upper Rhône, and the (Swiss) Mittelland. Gradually it faded from the political scene, the major part of it being absorbed by France, the remainder by Switzerland. Italy was tenuously held for about 500 years, but only by repeated military expeditions, no less than 37 being of major scope, and by continual expenditure of money. Both Burgundy and Italy were in fact foreign holdings and the Holy Roman Emperor was really the elected king of the Germans. The Germanic character of his administration is indicated

FIG. 24. Empire and Stem Duchies in medieval Germany.
——————— Boundary of the Empire.
–.–.–.–  The non-German areas within the Empire
– – – – –  The Germanic Stem Duchies
.........  Sub-units of Saxony

Scale of Miles
0    50    100    150

FRISIA

LOWER LORRAINE

UPPER LORRAINE

SAXONY

THUR-INGIA

FRANCONIA

Cologne

Coblenz

Frankfurt

Mainz

Trier

Worms

SWABIA

BAVARIA

BURGUNDY

ITALY

by the fact that the chancelleries of his three realms were German archbishoprics — Mainz for Germany, Trier for Burgundy, and Cologne
for Italy. Even after Burgundy and Italy were lost, the Imperial title
was tenaciously retained, a fact of profound geopolitical significance,
both as an indication of geographic reciprocity among the three realms
and as a force in the territorial disintegration of Germany.

While German rulers were reaching out for imperial dominion,
they were in fact the heads of a group of territorial units of the second
order of magnitude. Each was historically a tribal seat, politically a
duchy within the German Kingdom, and physically a segment of river
basin and its surrounding and segregating hills (Figs. 23 and 24).

## LOTHARINGIA

Along the western border lay Lotharingia, which early separated into
two parts. Upper Lotharingia is the Moselle Basin, to which is appended the Meuse Valley above its gorge in the Ardennes. It occupies
that part of the Paris Basin which drains into the Rhine (Ch. 6), and
on its borders are the passes through the Monts Faucilles, the Lorraine
Gate, and the Rhine Gorge with the important station Coblenz.

Lower Lotharingia is the Lower Meuse region, controlling all the elements of the east-west routeways both in the margin of the Ardennes
and on the lowland between the hills and the marshes, and focusing
upon the crossing of those routes with the Rhineway between its gorge
and the head of its delta (Fig. 22). The earliest capital of the emperor-
kings was at Aachen, and thither the German kings invariably went to
be crowned. The floodplain of the Rhine in this district lies between
terraces. Xanten and Neusz, citadels founded by the Romans, stand on
outliers of the lowest of the left-bank terraces, where the floodplain is
merging into delta. Wesel, on the right bank at the mouth of the Lippe,
is a later foundation, serving similarly to protect and profit from trade.
Cologne, also a Roman foundation on the left bank, has always been
the principal crossing place of this segment of the Rhine, despite its
location at the base of rugged hills which rise sharply on the east and
force routes to choose between steep gradients and long detours. To
offset this disadvantage of approach the crossing itself is unmatched.
Here the river flows in a trench only 2300 feet wide, and bordering it
the lower terrace stands safe above floods on both sides. Along here
also the gradient of the stream flattens, making this the bulk-breaking
point for boats. Until modern times Cologne was the leading seaport
of the Rhine. During the ages of insecurity, the city walls were built on

the banks of ravines which made the terrace site a peninsula. Because the river is too wide to shoot across with bow and arrow, the western was the only vulnerable side of the city.

All the western areas of Lotharingia were lost to Germany in the long struggle between the Paris Basin and the successive states of the Rhineland (Ch. 6). The Rhineland and its approaches remained German in speech and in political affiliation. In the internal disintegration which paralleled the displacement of the boundary, the remnants of Lotharingia remained within the Empire, either autonomous or as fiefs of other German rulers.

## SWABIA

The Upper Rhine is ancient Swabia (Figs. 23 and 24). On a physical map its most conspicuous feature is the Rhine Rift Valley, but its most significant geopolitical area is the transit land between the Rift Valley and the passes of the central Alps — Great St. Bernard, St. Gotthard, Septimer, and Splügen — and connections with the Inn Valley and Brenner Pass (Fig. 25). By way of these routes Germany and Italy were interlocked, and for about 400 years, until the late 13th century, the emperors allowed Germany to break down into petty states while they poured German wealth and lives through these passes in the vain effort to hold the " Roman " part of their empire and control the valuable trade between their reciprocal realms.

The nucleus of Swabia is the Lake of Constance. Its borders are fertile, limon-covered terraces, and it lies among trade routes. To its eastern end the Rhine brings six pass routes from Italy. At Augsburg, a border Swabian town, this route converges upon an alternative coming over from the Brenner Pass. Augsburg has usually fallen to the master of one or the other of these routes. The routes west of Lake Constance are even more important. From Ulm, head of navigation on the Danube, a route to the Rhône Basin crosses the Rhine a little below the lake; splitting on the point of the Jura, one fork follows the Rhine to its elbow and passes through the Burgundian Gate to the Saône Plain, the other traverses the Mittelland to Lake Geneva and the Rhône River. Near the confluence of Aar and Rhine this route leaves Swabian territory for that of Burgundy, a kingdom usually independent of the Empire. Just short of the border it crosses the most important of Swabian routes — a knot of several lines connecting the Rhine Rift Valley with Italy by way of different passes.

The ultimate failure of the German (Swabian) emperors in Italy

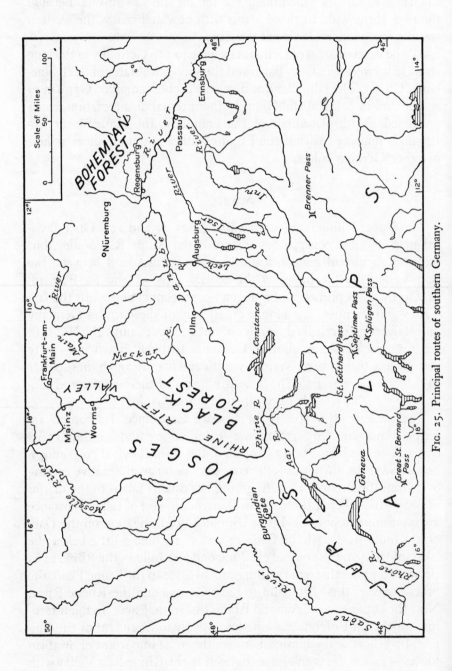

FIG. 25. Principal routes of southern Germany.

Scale of Miles

BOHEMIAN FOREST

Regensburg
Ennsburg
Passau
River
River
River
Inn
Brenner Pass
Nüremburg
Isar
Augsburg
Lech
Danube River
Ulm
Neckar R.
L. Constance
Septimer Pass
Splügen Pass
Frankfurt-am-Main
Main
BLACK FOREST
RHINE RIFT VALLEY
St. Gotthard Pass
Mainz
Worms
Rhine R.
VOSGES
Aar R.
Great St. Bernard Pass
Moselle River
Burgundian Gate
L. Geneva
JURA
Rhône R.
Saône
ALPS

was marked by the birth of the Swiss Confederation astride these routes and nourished by their traffic. When Swabia, never in control of the Mittelland, was shorn of all its southern border, and the Augsburg route as well, it became merely a borderland itself, an outpost of Urdeutschland and the Empire.

## FRANCONIA

Northward from Swabia the Rift Valley continues, but between lower hills — the Lorraine Gate on the west, the Odenwald on the east (Figs. 23 and 24). The northern end of the great rift, deserted by the Rhine, is drained by the Lower Main. That broad lowland is Franconia, the heart of Urdeutschland. Upon it converge routes from every other part. The Rift Valley and the Neckar provide two highways into Swabia. The Lorraine Gate and the Moselle riverway stand open to Upper Lotharingia, the Rhine Gorge is a narrow but much used artery to Lower Lotharingia. The Main leads east to Bavaria, and alternative vales in minor fault rifts carry routes north to Saxony. These roads diverge in the midst of the lowland, where the way from the south along the east side of the Rift Valley crosses the Main River. There stands Frankfurt, the Ford of the Franks. On the Rhine, opposite the mouth of the Main and only a dozen miles by river above the head of its gorge, is Mainz, center of Roman power in the Upper Rhine region, and the chief German stronghold of the Church throughout the middle ages. Worms, farther upstream where the Rift Valley broadens into the Franconian Basin and near the confluence of the Neckar, has situation akin to Mainz but far less strategic.

The centrality of Franconia suggests it as the natural nucleus of a larger Germany. Instead, it broke up more completely than any other unit of Urdeutschland, leaving not even a vestigial successor to carry on its name. Unlike Paris, Frankfurt has been afforded no political advantage by its surrounding hills. On the contrary, the several separate blocks of hill-land, tumbled and relatively infertile, either set up as separate states or were annexed by jealous rivals. The small, fertile lowland, crisscrossed by routes, and therefore highly vulnerable, was itself chopped to pieces, leaving Frankfurt an independent Free City, but isolated from the area of which it is the natural center. The fate of Franconia illustrates the weakness of a transit land in an age of continual fighting. Repeatedly overrun by armies, its trade suffers and its valuable routes and sites are the prey of rival political forces. In such times centrality is a less desirable quality in a capital than a strong location not far from a military frontier, so that it may serve as a stronghold for defense and a base for operations beyond the border. In France the political center of gravity shifted from central Orléans to Paris close to the frontier, as soon as the northeastern Paris Basin became a prime political objective and military theater. So in Germany the capital, first at Aachen on the inner frontier of Lotharingia, later became peripatetic among the duchies which lay on the south and east borders of Urdeutschland, and finally migrated beyond its eastern limit in order to remain close to the frontier. Seldom did it tarry long within Franconia, the central German state.

## SAXONY

Swabia, Franconia, and the two Lotharingias occupied most of the Rhineland. The rest, deltaic Frisia, was an appendage of Saxony (Figs. 23 and 24). Until after 1100, when the Frisians gradually learned how to drain their polders, they lived on scattered bits of slightly higher ground standing in an expanse of marsh, or at the edges of heaths and forests characteristic of sandy deposits left by continental ice sheets. Isolation, poverty, and natural defense, all concomitants of their unreclaimed delta, made these folk in practice independent, since the place would not repay the cost of subjugation. Out of this meager environment grew, in later centuries, The Netherlands.

Marsh and sandy heath extend eastward from Frisia all along the lowland fronting the North and Baltic seas. Southward the marshy basin of the Ems River pushes past the west end of the Teutoberger Forest[1] almost to the forested margins of the marshy Lippe Valley (Fig. 26). South of the sinuous, entrenched Ruhr River hills rise sharply 500 feet, to culminate in the Westerwald. Between the Ruhr and the Lippe lies the Hellweg (the Clearway), a belt of chalky soil, partly overlaid by loess.[2] On it runs the ancient highway of the North European Plain, continuation of the piedmont route along the northern foot of the Ardennes (Ch. 6 and Fig. 22). That route, after crossing

---

[1] " Forest " is the term applied to many of the ranges and hill-lands of the line of geologically ancient mountains which separates High Germany from Low Germany. The designation tellingly suggests that the dense forest cover, rather than the height or steepness of these uplands, was the feature which most impressed the denizens of the district.

[2] By "loess" (French equivalent, limon) no technical meaning is implied. The word, said to have been originally applied to the soil of the western margin of the Rhine Rift Valley, is used to designate the fertile, fine grained soil, believed to have been wind laid, which in the wet climate of Europe is well drained. Originally it was either grassed or covered with light woodland, easily removed by primitive settlers.

the Meuse at Maastricht and touching the old Carolingian capital at Aachen, climbs 150 feet over the Vorgebirge and drops 250 feet to the Rhine Valley and Cologne. Immediately east of Cologne the Wester-wald bars progress, and although routes through it have existed at least since Hansa times, the ancient passway leads northward, seeking the

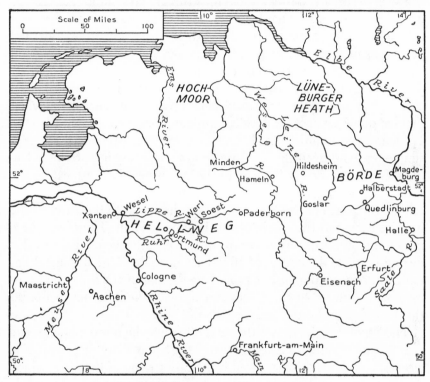

FIG. 26. The east-west route of northern Germany.

Hellweg. The climb to a ridge some 500 feet above the valleys of Rhine and Ruhr, and the crossing of the deeply entrenched Ruhr, appear to have been compensated by the open straight path along the Hellweg. Long before the discovery of coal in the vicinity, cities dotted this open plain: Dortmund, terminal of the crossover from Cologne, and an Imperial city; Werl, seat of the early local rulers; Soest, the central town of the fertile belt. Paderborn, bishop's seat near the eastern end of the Hellweg, stands at a forking of routes, one southward through Hesse to Frankfurt-am-Main via vales eroded in soft sediments, the other eastward, between the Teutoburger Forest and the Egge Range, into the valley of the Weser.

East of the Weser, masses of hills, *en echelon* with the Teutoburger

Forest, culminate in the Harz Mountains, where the higher levels stand more than 2000 feet above the sea. The grain of all the rugged country bisected by the Weser runs northwest-southeast. Every range has its steeper slope to the northeast, and below it a marshy valley. Beyond the front ranges, the plain extends for miles. This terrain is reminiscent of the eastern Paris Basin, although its ribs are crystalline rock instead of sediments of varying hardness and its steep slopes are faultline scarps instead of resistant strata. Like the Paris Basin, it constitutes a natural defense against people living on the plain beyond. The rugged land and the marshes it encloses constitute the Saxon folk-fortress,[1] and its marshy outer boundary marks the confines of Urdeutschland (Fig. 24). The high ground earliest occupied lacks fertility, but the marshes when drained prove productive. Besides farmland, the region possesses, in the Harz, mineral wealth —gold, silver, and copper — easily worked in a simple age, and until the late middle ages the most important in Europe. Goslar, nestled at the base of the massif near its north extremity, is the medieval mining metropolis, and now and again a political capital. To the south of the Harz, Thuringia lies open to the basin of the Middle Elbe and the whole North European Plain. Therefore, these mountains stand out as a bastion in the Elbe lowlands. Behind this jutting bastion, the border of effectively occupied Urdeutschland lies under an almost straight line projecting the axis of the Bohemian Forest northwestward to the North Sea through the Thuringian Forest, the Teutoburger Forest, and the bogs of Frisia.

The Saxon folk-fortress is the catapult from which was launched the great push of Germans eastward across the Slavic Plain (Fig. 27). The weakest spot in its defensive wall is the easterly end of the Harz, which drops gently to a plain unhampered by marshes, and toward the Saale River open, loessial, and fertile. As early as Charlemagne Germans moved across this plain to establish at Halle an outpost of defense and a contact for trade and evangelization. On islands in the braided river salt springs (hall is Celtic for salt) furnished the primary inducement for a settlement. It grew into a fortified trading town, and was by exception on the far bank of the stream in order to take advantage of slightly higher ground close to the salt works.

A hundred and thirty years later a bridgehead fortress was established in Magdeburg on the left bank of the Lower Elbe at its great bend. Nearby were salt pits, and westward toward Brunswick stretches an

[1] " Folk-fortress " refers to a region easy to defend because of its nature, in this case a forested and rugged hill-land, utilized by its isolated inhabitants as a nuclear core of government.

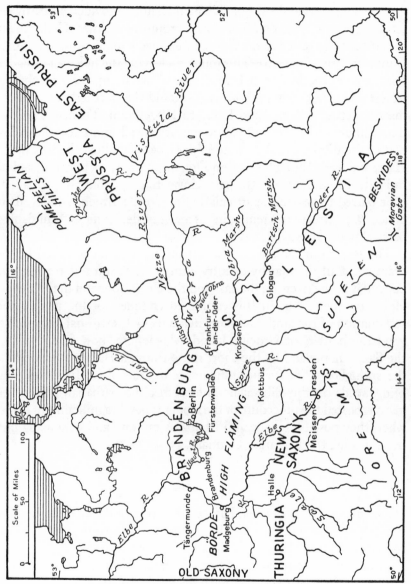

FIG. 27. The region of the Saxon conquests.

expanse of limon soils known as the Börde, attractive to landlords and peasants alike. At Magdeburg the stream could be crossed on firm ground, and an island west of the main channel provided an easily defended site for a citadel. The town promptly eclipsed Halle in importance, because it lies on the main east-west highway of the North European Plain (Fig. 26). This route, on leaving the hills east of Paderborn, crosses the Weser at Hameln, between the tips of Teutoburger Forest and Wesergebirge, and passes round the northerly ends of the massifs between Weser and Leine to Hildesheim. Thence it follows discontinuous blocks of limon through Brunswick and across the widest part of the Börde. Another route from Hildesheim hugs the base of the Harz, and leads through Quedlinburg, often used as a political capital, to Halle. From this route the parallel way to Magdeburg was for a long time barred by marshes, particularly the Grosses Bruch, a valley abandoned by its stream but remaining as a wet swale, far more formidable a barrier than a river.

The leap from the hills to the Elbe-Saale line was followed by the draining of all the marshy country within the Saxon folk-fortress and beyond it to the rivers on the east and the Hochmoor and the Lüneberg Heath on the north. In this combined conquest of the people and reclamation of the land, Germany made its first territorial advance beyond the borders of Urdeutschland. Magdeburg, now firmly knit to the Saxon homeland by the short route through Halberstadt, became the springboard for further plunges across the plain. In staking out bridgeheads on the Elbe-Saale line against the barbarian Slavs, Germans repeated the procedure of the Romans nearly a millennium earlier when they posed Cologne and Mainz as military and colonizing outposts against the barbarian Germans.

## BAVARIA

Saxony, the Weser power, has a counterpart in Bavaria, the Danube power (Figs. 23 and 24). Neither belongs to the Rhine, yet both are rooted in Rhenish tributaries. Each looks toward the east.

Bavaria is the Cinderella of the sisterhood of stem duchies. Mountainous in the south and the north, its intermediate plain is cursed by infertile soil (largely glacial gravels and sands), and burdened with forest interspersed with patches and belts of marsh. Here and there, as in a zone between the great northern bend of the Danube and the mouth of the Isar, fertile soil affords a livelihood to a farming population, and an overland east-west route, alternative to the waterway.

Like Swabia, Bavaria is linked to Italy. Instead of having several Alpine passes, all high, Bavaria has only one, but that one, the Brenner, the most favorable in all the Alps (Fig. 25). Easy in gradient on both approaches, its crest is only 4470 feet above the sea. It connects the Lower Po Plain and Venice with the Franconian plexus of Germany. One route passes through the heart of Bavaria along the line of the Upper Isar and across to Regensburg, an ancient Roman outpost at the northernmost bend of the Danube. From Regensburg the route lies across undulating country to Nüremberg, on a tributary of the Main and at the northwest corner of the Duchy. An alternative reaches Nüremberg by way of the Lech and Augsburg. Augsburg was preferred to Regensburg, particularly in the earlier centuries, because it was the largest market in South Germany. From it Ulm could be reached as readily as Nüremberg, and it tapped not only the Brenner, but also the Septimer and nearby passes. This gave it greater variety and volume of business than Regensburg, on the wooded eastern frontier of Urdeutschland.

Down Danube the Bavarian Plain gives place suddenly to hill-land through which the Danube forces its way swiftly in a series of gorges. The first of these begins at Passau, which had been a Roman fortress at the Inn confluence. With its citadel on the high ground between the streams, Passau combines defense with trade on and crossing the rivers. Just below it is the traditional political boundary of Bavaria, and so of Urdeutschland. Not only the Middle Danube Basin, but also the Alpine passes leading into it, lie outside the area traditionally German.

At about the time the Saxons were founding Halle, Bavaria reoccupied, as an outpost and a trading post with the barbarians, another Roman fort town, Ennsburg, at the next important confluence below Passau. A hundred years later both these strongholds fell before the advancing horde of Magyars, who overran all Danubian Bavaria and were not thrown back until they had reached the open plain under the southern walls of Augsburg. (Battle of Lechfeld, 955.) After this reverse, the Bavarian dukes undertook to guard all the easy approaches to their lands which the Danube and its tributaries push into the eastern Alps. Carrying out this plan involved the Bavarians in a push eastward not unlike the movement of Saxons in the north. Thus the two non-Rhenish powers of Urdeutschland began an expansion which completed its cycle only with the founding of the present German state in the mid-19th century, culminating in the merger of Austria in Germany in 1938.

## DISSOLUTION OF URDEUTSCHLAND

For 400 years after France and Germany finally separated in the mid-9th century, Urdeutschland was the leading country of Europe. It exerted a vague authority over the border lands of Lotharingia and Burgundy, and it dominated the politics and much of the trade of Italy. Its emperor was the titular lay head of Christendom, counterpart to the pope in the spiritual sphere. Yet while France and other Western European states were being pieced together slowly and with many setbacks, Urdeutschland disintegrated. The six duchies split into more than 300 fragments ranging from individual cities and single castles, to districts comprising some 50,000 square miles. This is in harmony with the structure of feudal government, and integration appears to be exceptional in an age of small-scale, subsistence economy. Whenever trade creates common interests over a considerable area, efforts at political integration follow, as with the Hansa of North Germany subsequent to the dissolution of Urdeutschland. In the 19th century, each step in the unification of Germany marked a swift recrudescence in trade and manufacturing, and several of the political amalgamations were heralded by customs unions, organized for the purpose of abolishing paralyzing tariffs.

In an age when commerce was far less important everywhere than agriculture, its relatively high value in Urdeutschland contributed to the disintegration into petty political units. Every landholder levied tolls on routes passing through his domain, and bitter competition for rich centers raged between lay lords, church lords, and the townsfolk themselves. The principal foci of trade, such as the Rhine Trough and the line between Lake Constance and the Middle Weser, became the most thoroughly dissected districts. The absence of naturally marked external boundaries no doubt favored disintegration. Constant attention to a weak military frontier seriously interferes with internal progress. Furthermore, fighting is more destructive to trade than to agriculture, because at worst the land remains, while goods in transit are the most vulnerable of chattels.

On the west, German frontier problems are the obverse of those of France (Ch. 6). On the east, the temptation to expand over land of the less advanced Slavs was constant and irresistible, except where the Bohemian Forest and the Ore Mountains project a forbidding wedge of wooded ranges between inviting lowlands. Southward, trade incited continued interference in Italy, and the imperial title lent to this activity legal propriety. To strengthen themselves for the Italian wars, nearly all the emperors granted particularist privileges in Germany. The support of petty vassals was rewarded with practical independence, growing commercial cities were given charters which made them " Imperial " or " Free," and the demesne of the emperors was prodigally squandered in return for armies and ready money.

The internal physical structure of Urdeutschland is inimical to unity. The tribes did not set in the mold of stem duchies because of tribal coherence, but because each group settled down in a core of arable lowland separated from its neighbors by wooded hills, marshy lowlands, or sandy heaths and forests. Yet none of these barrier zones of wasteland was permanent. Forest, the chief enemy of medieval Germans, was enthusiastically cut off, leaving hills or sand plains easily traversed. Marshes were drained, converting traffic barriers into fields or even valley highways. As unpeopled belts narrowed, it was found that no duchy had superior natural military protection against the others comparable to the advantage of the Paris Basin in France. Each one lay athwart major trade routes which originated and terminated outside Germany, and so was subject to the weakness that afflicted the Champagne or the Rhône Basin. Not one possessed clear superiority of power based on either agricultural or commercial resources.

As long as the duchies counted in the welter of German politics, they tended to pair off, because no one of them could ever hope to be supreme. Burgundy and Lotharingia faded from the scene early, leaving the two Rhine duchies, Swabia and Franconia, to stand off the Danube and Elbe powers, Bavaria and Saxony. This political linking seems to correspond to the rival trade routes which terminate in Italy and the North European Plain. Its objective was to obtain the coveted title of emperor, an office to which any of the dukes might legally be elected. The balance was so nice, and so easily overset, that no one ducal line succeeded in retaining the imperial title for long. Just as in France, possession of the supreme office tended to league all rivals against the king-emperor. Unlike the French kingship, the office remained elective because none of the evenly matched duchies could tolerate the idea of its being made hereditary in a rival house. So it moved from one to another, and by the mid-13th century became a luxury so expensive that none of the petty units into which Urdeutschland had by that time been split could afford it. After it had gone begging for two decades, it was bid in by Austria, an upstart unit of Germany which had grown up in the rough school of border marches established outside Urdeutschland in the Middle Danube Basin.

## CONQUEST GERMANY [1]

The feudal mode of defending border territory often began with military conquest, followed by the establishment of a subject district, called a march (*i.e.*, border), ruled by a vassal whose business it was to hold his lands against the neighboring enemy. Only a strong man could succeed with such an assignment, and he had to be conceded special privileges, among them a large, standing armed force. He and his troops usually got plenty of practice in warfare. His resolute character, his military experience, and his situation on the confines of the state to which he owed allegiance, all fostered a spirit of complete independence in an age when liege loyalty was much prated but little practised. The history of feudal marches is largely the history of revolts, and many of them were successful.

### AUSTRIA

The East March of Bavaria at the end of 200 years of existence became the Duchy of Austria within the Holy Roman Empire, on an equal footing with Bavaria, its creator (Figs. 23 and 24). Profiting on the increasing trade which passed along the Danube, and on that which moved between Italy and North Europe across the great breach between the Alps proper and their extension in the Balkan Peninsula, Austria annexed the remaining marches set up by Bavaria along its eastern border and became the chief resource of its rulers, the Hapsburgs from Swabia. Not only did Austria eclipse its mother state, but it also seized Bavaria's lucrative Brenner Pass and diverted much of its trade to Augsburg and the Swabian holdings of its rulers. The Duke of Austria came to be regularly elected emperor, and under the aegis of that title, Austrian power dominated Germany until the 19th century. The geopolitical structure of Austria is a distinct story, because its relations to Germany make only half of it. It is adumbrated in Chapter 8, particularly with reference to the significance of Vienna.

### THE MARCHES OF THE NORTHERN PLAIN

For present-day Germany the expansion across the North European Plain is more immediately significant than the expansion down Danube (Figs. 23 and 27). In the process of throwing out advance

[1] This term is used in antithesis to "Urdeutschland," to characterize the territory now in eastern Germany conquered by Germans from Slavs, beginning with the 12th century.

bases along the Elbe-Saale line, Thuringia was staked out as a march. This basin is cut off from Franconia by the wooded range known as the Thuringian Forest and lies open to the east. It is intimately related to the eastern part of the Saxon folk-fortress because both are drained by the Saale River. As the country of the Middle Elbe was brought under German sway, Thuringia became a transit land between it and the Middle Rhine by way of the natural passway through the barrier ranges (at the north end of the Thuringian Forest) below the walls of Eisenach. Other routes from the north and the south, converging at Erfurt, increased in importance as Germans pushed eastward. Thuringia became a leading trade focus and, like its forerunners farther west, disintegrated into a patchwork of little autonomous territories.

With the bridgeheads, Halle and Magdeburg, securely established (although only after successive colonies had been destroyed by resentful Slavs), the German push toward the east gathered momentum. Several marches, under different names and with shifting boundaries, were planted in the Elbe Basin from the Ore Mountains northward. All but one of them occupied the country directly east of Halle.

On both sides of the Saale, and eastward to the Elbe, discontinuous blocks of limon soil attracted agricultural settlers. In the Ore Mountains silver and other metals rivalling in value those of the Harz were discovered, and drew many miners from the older Saxon workings. Meissen, and Dresden 15 miles upstream and 300 years younger, occupy the critical place where the Elbe breaks through the Ore Mountains from Bohemia. One or the other has always been the political center of this region.

Beyond the Elbe the country is far less propitious. Except for limon soils in the pocket of Silesia, all the land to and beyond the Oder is a region of low moraines, sand-plains, and disordered drainage, its forest and marsh unrelieved by lightly wooded openings on fertile soil. The country merges without notable topographic break into the Oder Basin, yet it remains cut off from it. Between steep mountains on the south and wide marshes on the north, heavily forested sand-plains complete the barrier to German movement and create a refuge for Slavs. To this day forest and heath cover most of the Upper Spree Basin, where Wendish, a dialect akin to Polish, is everyday speech. Early overland routes avoided marshes and converged upon stream crossings where the floodplain is narrowest. Thus road and river formed a braided pattern. The sole east-west roads of consequence converged upon Kottbus, where the Spree can be crossed below the forest country and above its expansion into wide marshes. From Magdeburg one of these routes traverses the High Fläming, the belt of high ground between the Spree marshes and the Elbe Valley; the other is the road from Halle, more direct, but handicapped by the crossings of three marshy valleys. Eastward from Kottbus the route forks: to Glogau, the anteroom to Silesia, and to Krossen and the Lower Oder Valley. Both these terminals lie on the main Brandenburg-Silesia route (p. 187).

The trans-Elbe settlements were made under the " new law," also called " Magdeburg " or " Halle " law. In its territorial aspects this law appears to have originated in the polders of the Rhine Delta, where dikes blocked off the land in rectangles, which thus became the natural units for peasant holdings. As men of the Rhine Delta moved eastward to drain marshes, they generally farmed their polders as freemen. Land which did not require drainage came to be distributed in blocks of similar shape, comprising from 20 to 60 acres each. This was a notable departure from the usual arrangement under feudal tenure, in which the plowland of each peasant was scattered over the countryside in narrow strips. Landlords held correspondingly large and unified estates, much of which was likely to be heath, forest, and unreclaimed marsh. Because most of the land is infertile and the summers are cool in this part of Germany, stock raising and tillage of the extensive type fitted the environment, and subdivision of the holdings took place slowly or not at all. The " new law " helped to keep them intact, and thus suited the circumstances, because the land values remained low and a large holding was required to make a suitable living. The peasants, however, were either brought in from " old law " Germany as serfs or sank to that status as time passed and back rents accumulated, proof that the " new law " was essentially feudal, however modified the pattern it traced on the land.

As older Saxony disintegrated under the " old law," several of the marches were consolidated into a new Saxony. Its margraves inherited the Saxon right of helping to elect the emperors. In time marginal territory was lost, but the nucleus, including most of the richer resources, became a kingdom which remained autonomous within Germany until the Nazi revolution of 1933.

## BRANDENBURG

Among the marches set up on the Saxon frontier, the North March has played an even more conspicuous role than has new Saxony (Figs.

23 and 27). It is rooted in a narrow strip of arable land on the west side of the Elbe, a few miles below Magdeburg, and an early capital was Tängermunde, situated in the comparative safety of the left bank. However, the North March grew to its political majority on land beyond the Elbe.

As farming country this terrain is unpropitious, its core being low, east-west trending moraines rising out of a dump of glacial sand. Between the higher ridges the sluggish Spree and Havel, and a series of lakes, trace the route of more vigorous drainage during a geological age preceding the invasion of the continental ice sheet. This line continues the great highway of the Plain from Magdeburg on the bend of the Elbe to the Valley of the Oder. The waterways could be navigated and centuries later were easily canalized, but the most used early routes followed the high ground on either side. From the crossing of the Elbe at Magdeburg, the route plunges through forest and across heath to the lower bend of the Havel. There stands Brandenburg, onetime capital from which the whole political unit later took its historic name. Thence alternative routes avoid wet ground so far as possible, to converge upon the Spree just above its confluence with the Havel. There two towns grew up, on sandy, dry sites above each bank. When it became desirable to locate the capital of the military march closer to the advancing frontier, one of them, Berlin, was utilized. After two centuries, the site was rededicated as capital when the margrave built a castle on an island between the rival towns, dominated them both, and so laid the foundation for modern Berlin.

Political expansion eastward continued, and the local bishopric followed it as far as the Oder, but finally came to rest at Fürstenwalde, halfway between Berlin and the Oder, where the main route southeast discharges local offshoots through a break in the hills. The political capital remained at Berlin, the true route focus of the district.

At the longitude of Berlin the North European Plain is no wider than along the Rhine axis. Southeastward the Sudetes-Beskides-Carpathians and northeastward the Baltic Coast diverge so rapidly as to double the width of the Plain at the longitude of Warsaw. Routes spread fanwise from Berlin to tap this widening lowland.

Almost due east one line makes for Küstrin, on dry ground above the confluence of Warta and Oder. The Warta and its tributary the Netze occupy a broad exit trough excavated by glacial waters and the pre-glacial Vistula. Navigable for small craft, a portage of only 15 miles separates them from the Lower Brahe which lies in the same trough and leads to the elbow of the Vistula, whence that river carries the waterway to the Baltic. An ancient overland highway parallels the waterway, traversing the high ground north of the valley. These routes conduct to Prussia and all the Baltic coast conquered for German culture by the Teutonic Knights in the centuries following the close of the Crusades. Continued movement along them Germanized the routeway, making a " bridge " of German settlement and culture between Brandenburg and East Prussia.

Southeastward from Berlin an overland route crosses the Oder at Frankfurt. The town stands on high ground west of the river, opposite a belt of floodplain only about two miles wide, the narrowest in all this part of the stream's course. Once across the barrier river, the route forks. One branch ascends the Oder Basin, taking shortcuts from great bend to great bend of the looping stream. From Upper Silesia, a continuation of this route passes through the Moravian Gate, a breach between Sudetes and Beskides, and traverses Moravia to the Danube and Vienna. Fertile Lower Silesia became Germanized, in town and in country; the less arable farmlands of Upper Silesia were left to the Slavs, while Germans formed the majority in most towns there.

The second highway from Frankfurt-an-der-Oder leads east, yet only 60 miles away touches the point of a wedge of country from which the Germans never dislodged the Poles. This district, largely a plain of limon soils, originally lightly wooded, and suited to agriculture, early became a Polish center. That a block of lowland plain, drained by the Warta into the Oder and directly in the jaws of the pincers made by the advancing German frontier, should have resisted Germanization, is an admirable illustration of the barrier character of marshes. The fertile limon lands connect to eastward with the Vistula Basin across a threshold of sandy moraine which segregates the ancient core of Poland from its present capital. On the other sides the fertile district is bordered with marshy vales. Those which carry streams, like the Warta and the Netze, have few crossing places and are avoided even today by roads. Others, boggy swales deserted by flowing water, formed the most impassable barriers in this part of Europe until bridged by long causeways. On the north the Netze, and particularly the unnavigable Warta, establish a double barricade. On the south a like pair of barriers makes a still more effective protection. The Bartsch Marsh forms the clearcut east boundary of Lower Silesia. Behind it a series of marshy lakes and intervening bogs, the Obra Marsh, forms a second hindrance to movement. Bending abruptly northward, the Obra Marsh continues its barrier to its confluence with the Warta. Parallel to it, at from two to twelve miles to the westward, a swale, the Faule-

Obra, runs north from the marshy floodplain of the Oder and makes connection by lakes with the lower Obra itself, thus completing the double line of barriers on that side.

Because the way due east from Berlin was barred, the two routes, one northeast across the German bridge to the Lower Vistula, the other southeast up the Oder, dominated the geopolitical strategy of Brandenburg until modern engineering bridged the marsh barriers and laid the main road and railroad directly across Poland to Warsaw and the east.

Other routes focusing on Berlin were less important in the beginning but have been increasingly used. They are the two which run north to the Baltic and south to Saxony and the Czech folk-fortress. The north road, reaching out to the lower Oder, became important with the flowering of Baltic Sea trade in Hansa times. The south road, to Dresden, Bohemia, and Vienna, is alternative to the Silesian route through the Moravian Gate; it came into its own with the railroad age. Increasing use of these routes enhanced the focal situation of Berlin. When the sluggish stream system of the plain was canalized into navigable waterways, Berlin, midway between Elbe and Oder, was the natural nexus.

As trade grew and the marshes were drained to make farmland, the margrave of Brandenburg was able to elevate himself to the rank of Elector, an office shared by seven potentates of the Empire.

While Brandenburg was intermittently and with numerous setbacks pushing the German frontier eastward along the inland route, another group of Germans had been forcing Slavic power back from the Baltic coast. These men, the Crusading Order of the Teutonic Knights, turned from the Holy Land to Christianize the Baltic pagans. They established feudal holdings along the coastal lowland as far as the Gulf of Finland. Germans became landlords while the population they conquered became serfs. Where rivers laid lines of contact to the interior, frontier trade throve, attracting German merchants. In most parts of the realm Teutonization did not go deep, but on either side of the Lower Vistula the inhabitants were displaced wholly or in part by German colonists. East of the river a small tribe of Slavs was pushed southward into the rugged moraine which there parallels the coast, and was replaced on the coastal lowland of East Prussia by settlement wholly Germanic. The moraine has remained a military barrier which neither Germans on the north nor Poles on the south have ever been able to break down. West of the river another group of Slavs was similarly forced into the hill-land of Pomerelia. These hills trend north-south,

bar expansion eastward of Germans of the Pomeranian coast; and leave
the Vistula Valley wide open from the coast to central Poland. This
north-south corridor, known as West Prussia, therefore came to be a
mixture of Germans and Poles, with Poles predominant everywhere
except in the narrow Germanic bridge along the Netze-Brahe-Vistula
route.

During the 16th century the realm of the Teutonic Knights broke
up. Most of it was seized by Poland, Russia, and Sweden. Germanic
East Prussia fell to a branch of the ruling house of Brandenburg, which
incorporated it with the older state half a century later.

At this period of the early 17th century, when Brandenburg was
reaching its eastern limit, it also acquired territories to the westward.
Although small and widely scattered, most of these lands controlled
important points or districts on the ancient Saxon route to the east.
Magdeburg, Halberstadt, and Goslar gave Brandenburg an uninterrupted backtrack to the tip of the Harz Mountains (Fig. 26). Other
significant bits of ancient Saxony which came into Brandenburg hands
were Minden — at the crossing of the Weser immediately north of
the Wesergebirge, which had superseded the fords in the hilly country when the marshland was drained — and a part of the Hellweg. Still
farther west the Rhine Valley just above the delta, including the confluence of the Lippe and the ancient Roman stronghold Xanten,
rounded out Brandenburg interests across the whole of North Germany.

At a casual glance, this piecemeal country appears no different from
any other tattered heir of feudal Germany. Beneath the surface it was
unique in two respects. It was ruled by a family which had a compact
to alienate no lands and to pass the inheritance by primogeniture.
These legal advantages, innovations in Germany, enabled the country
to amalgamate whatever territory its members inherited. It acquired
territory on every German river along the important east-west route
which lies inland from the infertile and marshy coastal zone; thus it
combined the social and political coherence of being an exclusively
North German state with the economic advantage of tapping the trade
of South Germany, Bohemia, and Poland.

By the mid-18th century Prussia was the largest all-German state.
At the beginning of that century the Elector of Brandenburg had
achieved the title of " King in Prussia," a district which lay outside the
Empire. Thus he achieved a distinction shared among German rulers

only by the Austrian duke's kingship in Hungary. Toward the end of the century Brandenburg and East Prussia were physically united by annexation of West Prussia, including the Netze routeway. A few years later, more Polish territory between East Prussia and Upper Silesia was seized, its marsh guardians having been destroyed by drainage.

The overturn of Germany by the Napoleonic wars and their aftermath proved a blessing to Prussia, although in disguise. All its holdings west of the Elbe were conquered by Napoleon and consolidated into a few large political units along with scores of petty units which never had belonged to Prussia. Serfdom was abolished in these new states and manorial land tenure was superseded by outright ownership by individuals. The Empire was dissolved, leaving Prussia on a legal level with Austria. In the settlement after Waterloo, Prussia got back more territory in the west than it had lost. The state extended from East Prussia and Upper Silesia to the Rhine, broken only along the Leine. Some of the new land was compensation for losses of Polish territory — none of which was retained except adjacent West Prussia and the fertile district beyond the marshes. Even this subtraction was an advantage, because Prussia, now six-sevenths German, had no important interests outside Germany. Under the new constitution Prussia and Austria shared the hegemony of the new German Confederation, but Austria divided its attention between Germany and its non-German possessions in the Middle Danube, Italy, and the Low Countries. In a very real sense, Napoleon laid the foundation for the German Reich of today.

When Germany settled down after Napoleon's disappearance from Europe, it was still afflicted by internal subdivision and jealousy. Each autonomous state within the German Confederation had its own coinage, measurements, and posts, and set up tariffs at its boundaries. Yet the worst abuses had been abolished. More than 300 political units had been reduced to 39. The Industrial Revolution was in process of transforming the coal basins of the Rhineland — the Rhineland was mainly Prussian — and Prussia was in a position to take the lead in economic and political reform. A customs union initiated in 1834 under Prussian leadership paved the way for political union. This could not be accomplished in the presence of Austria, leader in imperial Germany for more than 500 years, and now politically stronger than ever by virtue of the presidency of the new German Confederation.

Prussia, however, had grown to be a military match for its ancient enemy, even when Austria was allied with the lesser German states, whose rulers almost always opposed the strongest German power. A short and decisive war was fought on Bohemian soil not far from the Moravian Gate, a repetition on slightly different ground of the military strategy of a century earlier, when Prussia had seized Upper Silesia from Austria and marched into the Moravian passway. Austria was ousted from the Confederation, and Prussia took, as spoils of war, four autonomous states. One of these lay between its Elbe and its Weser-Rhine territories; the others made a Prussian corridor of the Weser route to the Main River and gave access along the Main to the Rhine. The twenty-one remaining autonomies north of the Main joined the new North German Confederation, which put foreign affairs and the army, as well as tariffs, under the control of the President of the Confederation, who was by terms of the constitution the king of Prussia. The German states south of the Main, excepting Austria, were already joined with the confederation of the north by a customs union. Soon their fear of French aggression threw them into the arms of the new Germany. Then the North German Confederation became the German Empire, in which Bavaria, the largest unit after Prussia, retained a degree of autonomy. This was swept away by the constitution of a republic at the close of the World War. At that time provision was made for the union of small States, and Thuringia reconstituted itself, reducing the component units of the Empire from 25 to 18.

The Nazi government of the Third Reich has proposed to abandon all the ancient subdivisions, redistricting the country into about a dozen administrative units. If adopted, the new system will blur the contrasts between the traditional districts. The basic regionalism of Germany may thus become modified. Up to the present two principal lines of cleavage persist. One, between south and north, has been conspicuous especially during the 19th century. It appears in the struggle between Austria and Prussia, in dialect, in religion (with important exceptions), and in the constriction of German-speaking people between the Lorraine Gate and the wedge of the Czech folk-fortress. It rests on the eternal distinction between hill-land and plain, reinforced by different external relations.

The other, between west and east, is not so obvious, but it has been for a century even more critical. This is nothing less than the modern expression of the ancient cleavage between Urdeutschland or " old law " Germany and Conquest or " new law " Germany, separated by the line of the Elbe. Austria, facing down Danube, never asserted control over its mother-state, Bavaria, and gradually evolved as a typical south-German State. After some decades of independence from the German nation, it is now an integral and subordinate section of the

Reich, very like neighboring Bavaria in temper and character. East of the Elbe the predominance of sandy or ill-drained soil has made stock-raising a dominant business. For that region the mode of landholding originally set up in Conquest Germany is well suited — large estates, worked in large units. Untouched by Napoleon and the ideas engendered in the French Revolution, this region has remained the stronghold of *junkertum* — a medieval agricultural system, conservative protestantism, and reactionary politics. Even its ports face the backwater of the Baltic. Only Berlin, a manufactural hive induced by natural and political nodality, feels the strong economic and social currents set up by the Industrial Revolution.

West of the Elbe lies modern Germany. The commerce of the ports on the streams which empty into the open North Sea, the trade which pulsates north-south and east-west along all the ancient routes, the heavy manufacturing associated with the coal fields of the Ruhr and Saar basins (both tributary to the Rhine), and the light manufacturing widespread in all the hill country — these combine to put it in the front rank of industrial states, while careful farming keeps it high in the list of agricultural countries. Napoleonic interference set this " old law " Germany ahead of the " new law " east, by sweeping away many medieval inequalities there, while leaving Brandenburg-Prussia much as it had been. Customs union and political consolidation of the 19th century benefited it far more than it did the east, which was already unified, and had less stake in trade. To Urdeutschland in the narrow sense are added new Saxony, with its lignite, metals, and teeming farms and factories, and the lower Elbe with Hamburg, chief seaport of Germany, near its mouth.

The manufactural region of the Elbe follows upstream across the Ore Mountains into Bohemia, and together with adjacent Moravia and Upper Silesia, carries the mode of and outlook of life characteristic of western Germany to its eastern boundary. Moreover, the larger part of this region is foreign to Germany by language, tradition, and sentiment, even though incorporated within the German state. Its weight in the balance between west and east is bound to be considerable, although as yet incalculable.

By the 20th century (and long before the annexation of Bohemia-Moravia) the west furnished a high proportion of the taxes with which to run the Reich. Owing to the political constitution, however, Prussia remained the controlling element in the state. And in Prussia the conservative east dominated the progressive west, partly because the legislative districts had not been reallotted with the rise of manufacturing and consequent growth of cities, and partly because the political capital was embedded in the forests of the east, and the executive, a landholder and the titular chief of the *junkers*, had many prerogatives. In effect the immense power of a highly industrialized state was wielded by a small group of landlords essentially medieval in outlook. Such a situation is dangerous. A people engaged in commerce and manufacturing, both vulnerable activities, is less inclined to war than an agricultural group, because the land suffers less in warfare than any other form of property. Nowhere in Europe was the lag between progressive economic life and stagnant political forms so great as in the Germany of the years preceding the World War. This is to say that Germany, alone among the national states of the west, had not yet obliterated the ancient cleavage between Western and Eastern Europe, a fission intensified by the Industrial Revolution.

Put in other words, the cleavage between peripheral Europe, with its outlook on the sea and its minerals which serve as the basis for manufacturing as well as mining, and interior Europe, still dependent to a high degree on the sole resource of the soil, passes through Germany (Fig. 9).

It is not, however, exactly the same line as that which separated Urdeutschland from Conquest Germany for so many centuries. That line, determined by the relative safety of the hills and by easily farmed light soils, was blurred with the first attempts of the Saxons to expand over the fertile plains bordering the Elbe. It was further shifted with drainage of marshlands on the plain. Yet both these moves merely extended the primary resource of the soil. The critical shift in the line came with the development of overseas trade. Then the Elbe Valley, leading to the open North Sea, began to swing within the orbit of peripheral Europe. This tendency was solidly buttressed in the 19th century by the utilization of lignite in that part of the Elbe designated as the Kingdom of Saxony, and by associated new uses for the long-known minerals of the Ore Mountains which form the southern boundary of this Kingdom. There one of the densest populations in Europe keeps industry humming. The new line between peripheral and interior Germany is today marked by the Elbe, or more precisely by the infertile or marshy regions immediately to the east of it. The dualism of Germany remains.

## CHAPTER EIGHT

# East Central Europe Exemplified in its Capitals

BETWEEN peripheral Western Europe and continental Russia lies a broad belt of states collectively described as East Central Europe. Its eastern boundary does not deviate much from a line projected from the Bosporus through the head of the Gulf of Finland. Its western margin is more irregular; it approximates the Adriatic and Baltic seas and a line connecting them (Fig. 9). This belt, scarcely three-fifths as large as Western Europe and with considerably less than half the population, is apportioned among an even larger number of nationalities (14 as against 12). More than half of them were newly created sovereignties at the close of the World War; none except Turkey is much more than a century old. Every one has had its boundaries radically revised within the past quarter century; further revisions are in process. Already two of the sovereignties, Czechoslovakia and Albania, have been suppressed and their lands divided among their neighbors.

## AN AREA GEOPOLITICALLY IMMATURE

These evidences of political immaturity are consistent with the ethnic instability of the area. Long after folk migrations had ceased in Western Europe, the central parts of the continent continued to be overrun by migrants from Eastern Europe and from Asia who ascended the Danube Valley, or were gathered into the funnel-like plain of North Europe (Fig. 15). To arrest the successive waves of invasion Germanic West Central Europe thrust itself into the two breaches south and north of the Czech folk-fortress and created the march states, Austria and Prussia, which have recently amalgamated in the German Reich (Ch. 7.). The diverse groups of immigrants brought with them a variety of languages and dialects, some of which attached themselves to the different natural units in which the roving conquerors gradually settled down. In this evolution Central Europe was only repeating the earlier history of Western Europe. There is evidence that in time the core areas blessed with superior resources might have imposed their dialects upon surrounding peoples, just as occurred in the larger states of Western Europe. This would have reduced the number of self-conscious groups and improved the correlation between political boundaries and nature-made barriers. Two circumstances thwarted this evolution, making stable political boundaries difficult to achieve.

Few Central European lowlands stand out as natural nuclei for political organization, and fewer still are protected by natural barriers affording military advantage. In these respects Germany is the prototype, not France or Britain or the peninsulas of Western Europe. Even where barrier boundaries exist, the budding nations of this central area were repeatedly subjected to conquest by more powerful neighboring states. Whether the conquerors were Asiatic Turks, Germans from the West, or Russians from Eastern Europe, the effect of their imposed rule was to fan the flames of local patriotism. While fanatical and enduring national feeling was thus being created, subordination of nationalities to the larger state left them without well-defined boundaries, such as normally develop by friction between independent neighbors. Whenever the throttling hand of the conquerors has been lifted, the damped fires of national aspirations burst spontaneously into boundary wars. These have been embittered by the broad zones of linguistic intermixture fostered by centuries of administration superposed upon neighboring groups without reference to their individualities.

At the end of the World War, internal disintegration of Russia, and defeat of Germany, Austria, and Turkey temporarily paralyzed all the states which had imposed their rule upon East Central Europe. The opportunity was seized to constitute the area into national states. Of the possible bases for such a reorganization only two were utilized. Linguistic coherence was the announced objective. To the degree that language coincided with nationality, it was a realizable ideal for the core areas of the several linguistic units. But to draw satisfactory boundaries on this basis alone was impossible because of broad bands of linguistic interpenetration along all the language frontiers. The substitution of a political *line* for a social *zone* necessitates arbitrary decision. At the close of four years of intensive warfare the temper of the judges (*viz.*, the victorious Great Powers) was such as to render impartial decision difficult. It is not surprising, therefore, that while the corelands of all the new and revised states were based on language, the boundaries were drawn so as to deprive the vanquished of any debatable spoils. It thus turned out that each of the new, unstable states was sovereign over strips of territory along its borders that are claimed by defeated neighbors. To make matters worse, each of these contested areas includes enough inhabitants whose nationalistic sympathies reach across the border, to form a political party which unceasingly agitates for secession.

The boundaries of East Central Europe are indubitably fragile lines. They lack the bulwark of economic convenience, because they have ruthlessly severed areas intimately linked by railroads and roads. In many cases rural districts have been cut off from their market centers, some mining camps have been broken apart, and in at least one instance a large city (Katowice) has been cut in two by a national boundary. The economic structure of society is usually more responsive to variations in resources and terrain than is its linguistic structure. Disregard of economic convenience is often a symptom of refusal to accept the guidance of a passive but incontrovertible force — the regional coherence of natural phenomena. To separate underground mine workings from their pitheads by a national boundary is possible, but it compels a rearrangement of the physical and financial handling of the mine. In time the inhabitants of a boundary zone discover means to minimize the awkwardness of a boundary which controverts nature.

Even if the boundaries are unstable it does not necessarily follow that the core areas of East Central Europe should not have been made the nuclei of national states. The vitality of a political unit is to be measured by its core rather than by its boundaries. This is exemplified in the central feature of government, the capital. Although every Central European capital of today and the recent past not long since had its power enhanced, and a few former capitals have been shorn of their functions as seats of government, the vitality of certain places as political centers may be accepted as a gauge of geopolitical forces in a region of debatable political boundaries.

The fixed capital of the national state of today is an outgrowth of the efficient communication and transport systems of the modern world. In simpler societies the rulers are wont to move about within their domains, in part to administer justice, but chiefly to permit the ruler's court to live off the country. Yet even a minor chief in any sedentary society possesses a preferred abode. Choice may be compounded of personal preference, convenience to routes, and military necessity. In the long run strategic superiority or commercial convenience, or more probably concurrence of the two forces, confines the locus of the capital to a relatively small area, and not infrequently to a specific site where battle or trade can be effectively directed because of natural advantages. As the capital becomes associated with a particular place, the affections of the ruler and his subjects make it an epitome of the national life, in which their history and traditions are enshrined. With the coming of modern overland lines of transportation the capital becomes increasingly the traffic focus of the country, even though it be located offside for military reasons. Its symbolic authority is buttressed by increasing size and wealth which accompany multiplication of administrative business and concentration of trade and industry at the political center.

The capitals of East Central Europe illustrate every type of national center. Taken together with certain sites no longer used as capitals, they represent most of the stages in the rise and decline of political seats. They incarnate the corelands that have evolved as nationalities far more pointedly than do the national boundaries.

CAPITALS OF THE NORTH EUROPEAN PLAIN

One of the essential contrasts between Western and Central Europe is the width of the northern plain. From the Pyrenees to the Sudetes the lowland is a belt nowhere much more than 200 miles wide and nowhere much less. Its climate, its river-borne commerce, and its outlook are coastal. A little east of Berlin the Baltic shoreline swings northeast and then due north, while the mountain masses of interior Europe trend southeast and then south. Somewhere in Eastern Germany the east-bound traveler becomes conscious that he has left peripheral Europe and is well into the Eurasian continent. The plain extends indefinitely without the minor alternations in terrain and land-use which lend to Western Europe the charm of infinite variety. The streams lie far apart, the climate is continental. This is the section of Europe where the occupations and the language of the inhabitants partake of the uniformity of their countryside, but where no large independent state has succeeded in persisting unmodified for more than two or three generations.

The heavily glaciated eastern coast of the Baltic Sea, in spite of its physical unity, is divided into four states (Fig. 28). Their population ranges from a little more than a million to three times that number. Only Finland exceeds the area of Portugal, one of the smallest states of Western Europe, and its ecumene is little larger than those of the

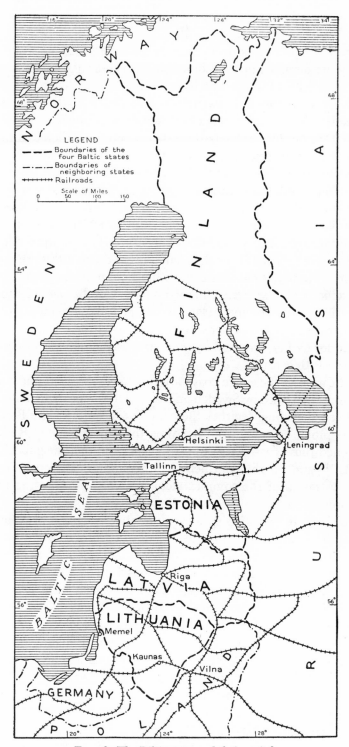

FIG. 28. The Baltic states and their capitals.

others. They are economically the coastal outlets for land-locked Russia, but are deprived of their hinterland because they are cultural outposts of Western Europe, and have received their religion and civilization from Germany and Sweden by way of the Baltic. Hence their national aspirations are foreign to those of the inlanders — people who received the heritage of the past overland from the Hellenic world. The coast has been historically the base of cultural diffusion, and it remains today the line of commercial contact with the world at large. Three of the four capitals are coastal cities, the principal ports of their respective countries. Riga, capital of Latvia, stands eight miles up the Dvina River, accessible to the Hansa ships which traded there during the middle ages, but protected in a measure from piratical raids. Today, it maintains itself through an anteport at the mouth of the stream. Tallinn, Estonia, began as a Danish foothold on a crag of the escarpment which rises above the Gulf of Finland. Combining defense point and harbor, it too became a Hansa town. Helsinki, the modern capital of Finland, succeeded earlier seats of administration chiefly because of its superior harbor, screened by protecting islands. It was insignificant until the 19th century.

Unification of the entire coast, attempted by the Teutonic Knights, and more than once by Sweden and Russia, has repeatedly failed after shortlived shackling. Neither the commercial unity of the Baltic Sea nor the profits accruing from handling the export trade of Russia has reconciled these coastal folk to each other or to their neighbors across the Baltic and on the continental hinterland. Their separatism is a neat illustration of the complex elements which go into the making of nationalities.

The Finns and the Ests speak agglutinative languages of Asiatic origin, wholly unlike the phonetic tongues of Europe. Many of them bear certain ethnic resemblances to Mongoloid peoples of the Arctic fringe of Eurasia. Finland was continuously under the Swedish influence from the mid-12th century, and Estonia has been Danish and Swedish for long periods, interrupted by a prolonged Germanization under the Teutonic Knights. Both countries accepted the Lutheran version of reformed Christianity. Both are predominantly outlets for products of the boreal coniferous forest. Despite all these similarities they are cleft by the Gulf of Finland, and Estonia possesses a value as an ice-free outlet for Leningrad. This has subjected it to longer and heavier Russian impress than Finland.

Latvia and Lithuania constitute another pair of ethnic and linguistic kinsmen. They are separated neither by a dividing sea nor by relations to totally distinct hinterlands. Their feeling of mutual foreignness rises entirely from their divergent histories, although the variance has environmental roots. Latvia, deeply indented by the Gulf of Riga, was alternately subjected to Teutonic Knights and German bishops for four centuries, followed by shorter vassalage of parts of the area to Sweden, Denmark, Poland, and Russia, before finally being annexed by Russia *in toto*. More than half the population is Lutheran, a quarter is Roman Catholic, and a considerable number is Orthodox.

Lithuania, in contrast to its three neighbors, is more than 80 percent Roman Catholic. Moreover, its coastline is short and cannot boast a single harbor. When Lithuania was constituted a state at the close of the World War, Memel, a Prussian, Protestant port city lying on the German frontier, was attached to it to serve as an outlet, but was given semi-autonomous status. Little wonder that it was reclaimed by Germany as that country resumed its traditional push toward the east two decades later. Harborless Lithuania proper, a country of forests, heaths, and marshes, has scarcely been scratched by intruders from the Baltic. The inhabitants turned their backs on the inhospitable coast and made their capital at Vilna, an inland route focus in disordered moraine country. Military expansion along natural routes in sparsely settled country made Lithuania a large state during the high middle ages, and led to Poland, the country of the Vistula Basin. In the mid-14th century the two realms were joined in a personal union under the Lithuanian ruler. Two centuries later this was cemented into a legislative union. In time Polish culture dominated the Lithuanian, even in Vilna, which had ceased to be the capital upon the establishment of personal union with Poland.

In the 90 years after 1721 Russia succeeded in annexing the entire Baltic coast north of Prussian Memel, thus for the first time in history giving free play to the economic reciprocity of coast and hinterland. Riga, near the mouth of the Dvina, became the natural outlet for the bulky forest products which constitute the chief resource of the region, and other river and seacoast towns throve to the measure of their situations. More recently railroads have been built to facilitate trade to and from the interior, and ports lacking river connections have been thereby given a share of the trade. These lines, built to serve business and to conform to terrain, but without reference to local politics, have since been overlaid by supplementary national lines which pay little attention to either nature or an interdependent economic society. Postwar construction has thus commenced to remake the unit system into national nets.

The disintegration of Russia under the hammer blows of the World War was the opportunity for fourfold nationality to arise along the Baltic coast. The three states which are truly littoral adopted as capitals their principal ports. Lithuania occupied its historical capital, Vilna, only to be ousted by a Russian army. This force was in turn ejected by Polish troops, which have ever since occupied Vilna and its district as a Polish center of long standing, although not a capital city. Lithuania has been compelled to make shift with Kaunas as capital. This city, like Vilna, is an inland route focus but with a shorter reach. Nationalistic but weak Lithuania has been forced to give way to. Poland. For two decades the disputed boundary between the two states was closed. In 1938 Poland took advantage of Germany's preoccupation with annexation of Austria to compel Lithuania to accept the military line as the political boundary and to open it to peaceable intercourse.

The capitals of all the Baltic countries are new as seats of national states, and therefore lack the prestige which attaches to sites traditionally associated with national history. This suggests that the extreme division along lines of nationality realized by the treaties which closed the World War may have been in crucial respects unsound. Only five years after the peace, the two middle states, Estonia and Latvia, took the first steps toward a customs union in an effort to modify the evils attending sovereignty based on rampant national feeling in disregard of economic stability. A federation of Poland and Lithuania might benefit both nations. Lithuania would thereby gain a hinterland and strong military backing. Poland might construct a port as adequate as its recent creation at the end of the narrow Polish Corridor between two parts of Germany, and far less vulnerable from the military standpoint. Indeed such a union was envisaged by the Powers when the German port of Memel was awarded to Lithuania. Latvia and Estonia formerly derived much of their wealth from the transit trade to and from the heart of Russia. If and when Russian surpluses accrue once more, transit trade will demand some degree of reciprocity.

The Polish capital, Warsaw, is more centrally located than most of its contemporaries (Fig. 29). It was made the capital of resurrected Poland at the close of the World War because of its history as the capital of the former Kingdom of Poland for more than two centuries before its partition. It had first become the capital of the Kingdom of Poland because of its central and neutral position in an expanding state.

Poland, although merely a segment of the extensive plain of North Europe, is subdivided into districts of superior fertility by belts of sand, marsh, or other wasteland barriers. The area occupied by Polish-speaking people appears to have been too large to be politically unified during the middle ages, or perhaps no one fertile kernel was large

FIG. 29. The components and the capitals of Poland.

enough to dominate its neighbors, all being subject to repeated ravaging by Tatars from the east.

The original center of the Polish nationality is " Great Poland," the lake region plus the adjacent fertile plain traversed by the Warta (Ch. 7). Gniezno, among the lakes, is in name and in fact the " nest " that cradled Poland. There the Roman Church established a diocese as early as the 9th century, and Kruzvica somewhat to the eastward was the first Polish capital. Later, secular power moved to Poznań, in the center of a fertile district blessed with limon soils, and situated on a low terrace above the Warta River, where the stream could be crossed easily by way of an island. A century ago the head of the Polish Church migrated to Poznań, although the cathedral remains at Gniezno.

The Upper Vistula domain, styled Little Poland, is an unglaciated region of limon-covered hills, the most fertile land occupied by Poles. The lords of Little Poland claimed hegemony among their rivals and styled themselves " Duke of all the Polands." Their capital, Cracow, lies in an acute bend of the Vistula, where a high bluff serves to defend the town at its base and to control traffic along the river. This riverway connects the Polish Plain with both Silesia and the Danube Valley, and so leads to the threshold of the Moravian Gate. Enriched by agriculture and trade, and secure in their defense point, the rulers of Little Poland succeeded in annexing Great Poland — the district about Poznań. Cracow thereby became the capital in a sense hitherto unrealized, and for two centuries was the center of Polish political life.

As German expansion gathered force, the loosely organized state of Poland lost Silesia, on its southwest border, to Austria and Prussia. It then turned its attention northeastward across the plain. The semi-independent Polish principality of Masovia occupied the Middle Vistula Basin. There, in the center of a fertile plain similar to that of Poznań, stands Warsaw on a terrace more than 100 feet above the river, which there occupies a relatively narrow valley not too difficult to cross. Above the town tributaries from the southwest, and below it tributaries from the northeast make it a center of navigation. Its growing trade brought to it the government of the principality. Beyond it Lithuania became a field for Polish economic exploitation. In the mid-16th century the heiress to the Polish crown married the Grand Duke of Lithuania, thus joining the two environmentally uniform but linguistically distinct states in personal union. As a compromise between the conflicting claims of the traditional capitals of Cracow and Vilna, both well offside in the new territorial unit, Warsaw was made the capital. This function it retained until the combined Lithuania-Poland was partitioned among Russia, Prussia, and Austria in the later years of the 18th century. The partition attached the Poles to three nations at three different economic levels. Russian Poland stayed about as it was, Austrian Poland advanced slowly, and Prussian Poland became one of the most efficiently used districts in Europe. The distinction may be obliterated in time, but today, after two decades of unity (achieved in the World War), the partition boundaries stand out as clearly on the cultural landscape as if they were marked by high walls.

For the reconstituted Poland of today Warsaw is the most suitable capital, being a chief port on the arterial river of the country at the crossing of the main east-west railroad line of north Europe. Although it has historic associations it lacks the prestige of great age. This belongs to Cracow; its historic castle enshrines deceased rulers and patriots and embodies the life of medieval Poland. The castle is in process of rehabilitation, so that visiting Poles may see it as the outward symbol of Poland's past prowess. It may be that Poland clings tenaciously to the former Lithuanian capital, Vilna, to make it impossible for Lithuanians to sublimate their past in the fashion of Cracow.

## CAPITALS OF THE MIDDLE DANUBE AREA

The jumble of plains, hill-lands, and mountain ranges between the eastern Alps and the eastern crescent of the Carpathians shelters a variety of languages and nationalities unparalleled elsewhere on the European continent. The diverse terrain has helped to isolate the inhabitants and limit their community of feeling to small groups (Fig. 30). At the same time the Danube cuts a broad path on the longest axis of the area, and connects it with the outside world, both upstream and downstream. This route has been used by wave after wave of migrants from Eastern Europe and from Asia, by organized armies of Western Europe since Roman times, and by traders and merchants in every period of peace. The patchwork of states which occupy the region today manifests this confused environmental and historical background.

The easiest and perhaps the most ancient route connecting the plain of North Central Europe and the Middle Danube lands lies between the complex massifs which surround Bohemia and the long crescent of the Carpathian ranges. This is the Moravian Gate, a pass scarcely more than 1000 feet above the sea and the width of a river valley. A low saddle separates a headwater of the Oder from a tributary of the Morava (March), a Danube affluent from the north.[1] Along these corridor valleys and through the gap runs a prehistoric route since traversed by every successive type of overland way. Probably it was the chief track followed by Baltic amber on its way to the Mediterranean World of antiquity. Folk migrations and armies have surged over the pass in both directions time out of mind. The approaches, Moravia and Silesia, are corridor lands, disputed for centuries between Germans and Slavs. Silesia, where Germans predominate, was cleft by the treaties which

[1] Not to be confused with the Morava of Yugoslavia, which enters the Danube from the south, a few miles below Belgrad.

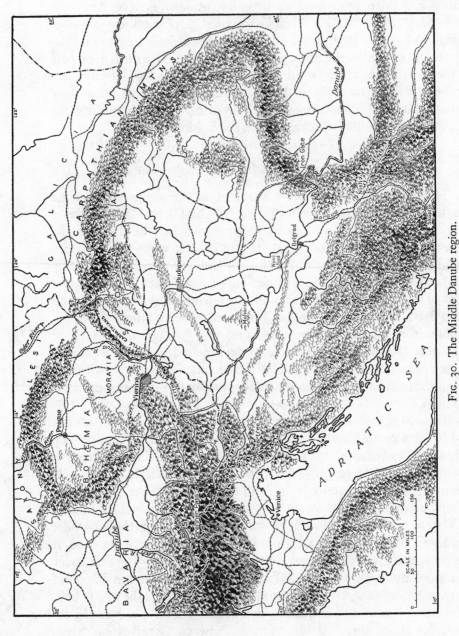

Fig. 30. The Middle Danube region.

A modification of a map published by the author in the *Journal of Geography* 34 (1935), 134. Reproduced by permission.

concluded the World War, giving to Slavic Poland the lowland route which leads northeastward. Moravia, where Slavs are in the majority, is dotted with German settlements, solid wedges at the north and south. This settlement exemplifies Moravia's historic role as transit land between the two German march states, Austria and Prussia. Moravia itself came into existence as a march, its frontiers being ethnic to north and south, and cultural to the east. Although politically independent for brief periods, the median position of Moravia has generally hitched it to one or another of its neighbors — occasionally Silesia, rarely Poland, frequently Austria, today Germany. Through all its temporary attachments, its fate has steadfastly been linked with that of its western neighbor, Bohemia, with which it forms a linguistic unit.

Bohemia today is the spearhead of the Slavic world in Western Europe. Almost surrounded by Germans, it is tenuously tied to the Slavic world by way of Moravia. It projects 250 miles into the side of German Europe and is separated from its massive western neighbor by a belt of hill-land. The more rugged sections are still forested, but in places the land is farmed right over the crests. Within the ring of bounding heights are districts as lofty, steep, and wooded as the least cultivated border blocks. In the northwest, and in part in the southwest, where two parallel lines of hills contrive a double line of barriers, the basins between are occupied by a population solidly German-speaking. Until 1938 the linguistic boundary therefore lay a few miles to the east of the political boundary, one of the oldest in all Europe. This paradox is resolved in the light of history.

Bohemia remains as the last souvenir of the medieval time when Slavs occupied all Europe east of the line traced by the Elbe-Saale, the Bohemian Forest, and the Styrian Alps (Ch. 7). When German pressure slowly forced Slavic sovereignty down Danube and back across the northern plain, it was unable to dislodge the Bohemians from their folk-fortress. A tumbled country, surrounded on all sides by upthrust blocks of mountains, it was at that time heavily forested. It constitutes the drainage basin of the Upper Elbe River, but the tortuous exit of that stream through the surrounding hills permitted no accompanying land route until the railroad era. Even today no road follows the valley. The easiest natural outlet of the Bohemian Basin lies through a pass in the Bohemian-Moravian highlands, and this has been the line of contact most fruitful of political results. Bohemia's first political affiliation has been with Slavs of the Morava Valley, its second with the Germans seated on the Danube at the mouth of the Morava. Before it developed close connections with either, the Bohemian folk lived isolated in their wooded basin, slowly acquiring the unity which has survived centuries of German influence.

The segregating force of the border hills was not reinforced by the presence of an unmistakable locus for a capital. Prague, which appears never to have had its position disputed, is central in the basin, but its river is not navigable, and gorges above and below the city make the site difficult of access for overland routes. Its initial advantage appears to have been two steep-sided remnants of terrace, 150 feet above the river and almost severed from the upland by tributary valleys. These defense points, on opposite banks of the river and less than two miles apart, came to be united politically. Whereupon the ruler cut through a sill of hard rock which caused frequent inundations of a broad flood-plain overlooked by the two heights, and so opened the lowland to settlement. There the commercial and later the manufactural city has evolved, while its political functions have continued to be associated with the defense points, particularly the Hradshin, across the river from the business quarters.

With gradual extension of territory until it incorporated the entire basin, Prague remained the capital, being sufficiently central. At the same time its political leadership was not jeopardized by excessive commercial prosperity, because the great highroads passed around this aloof and rugged highland. When the military force of the Bohemian folk-fortress was able to dominate the Moravian Gate trade route, the combined state throve. This is a close parallel to the union of the stronghold Île de France with the Champagne trade route (Ch. 6). Unlike the French counterpart, further growth of the Czech state was halted by the ethnic and linguistic barriers which closely hem it in. For a time it controlled the sandy plain of Lausitz beyond the Sudetes Mountains, but even this meager and sparsely peopled land was soon absorbed by kindred Germanic states which lay on the same side of the mountains.

From the 12th century, Bohemia was sometimes ruled jointly with Austria, and in the early 16th century the two countries were embraced in a personal union. Thenceforth for four centuries Bohemia-Moravia was embroiled in every German issue and in every Middle Danube issue. Prague sank to the level of a seat of provincial administration.

When the World War redrew the map of Central Europe along linguistic and ethnic lines, the Czechs, all but cut off from the other Slavs at the Moravian Gate, were compounded with their eastern Slavic neighbors to make the Czechoslovak state. These adjunct peoples, Slovaks and Ruthenes, tail off to the vanishing point between the Carpathian barrier range and the Hungarian and Rumanian occupiers of the central Danube lowland. The Carpathian Slavs had never before been united politically with their western neighbors, and although the Slovak tongue is a near kin of the Czech, Ruthenians speak a language more closely allied to that of Slavs resident in Poland across the Carpathians, and in the Ukraine, Russia. The ungainly length and extreme narrowness of the new state, coupled with absence of naturally marked barriers east of Bohemia except for the Carpathians, has emphasized the linguistic divisions, the border minorities, and the lack of a common history. Taken together, these conditions made the Czechoslovak Republic established at the close of the World War, one of the least coherent states in Europe. Whatever consolidation it achieved was the work of Bohemia-Moravia, a highly unified nationality fortunate in the possession of coal and other raw materials as bases for an energetic industrial society. As capital, the historic Bohemian center was chosen, in spite of its position within 50 miles of the northeastern frontier and more than 500 from the eastern end of the country. Although not selected as an advance military capital, it lies on the side of its strongest and most aggressive neighbor.

The weakness of the state has been made apparent to the whole world by the events since September, 1938. The predominantly German population between the two lines of hills that border Bohemia and in the approaches to the Moravian Gate has overset the sole boundary in East Central Europe that has persisted more than 25 years. In the first move, much of the barrier margin of the Czech folk-fortress was transferred to Germany. In the wake of German aggression Polish forces occupied territory in Silesia inhabited largely by Polish people, and Hungarians pushed their frontier into Slovakia. Then Germany absorbed Bohemia-Moravia outright and established a " protectorate " over Slovakia. Hungary then occupied Ruthenia.

These moves illustrate the insecure situation in East Central Europe arising from the narrow outlook of the treaties which closed the World War. The authors of these documents were preoccupied with politics and failed to take sufficient account of geography. Most, if not all the new states of this part of Europe are too small to function effectively in a world integrated by modern communication. Czechoslovakia proved additionally weak because of its long, narrow shape, broken up by rugged terrain and lying athwart a major lowland thoroughfare. The principle of linguistic unity, according to which these states were constructed, is a powerful force in the hands of strong aggressors but a weak defense of small peoples, particularly where, as in Central Europe, no clean-cut boundary lines between languages exist. As always among states, those which hold valuable natural resources can keep them from covetous neighbors only if they possess the necessary might. By subdividing East Central Europe into small units, many of them lacking the combination of natural conditions needed to carry on independently, the World War merely set the stage for rearrangements of boundaries in such a way as to aggrandize the strongest states in or adjacent to the region. Czechoslovakia, by the first aggressive move on the part of Germany shorn of its natural defenses and much of its wealth, almost bisected on the line of the Moravian Gate, its capital only 30 miles from the new frontier of its strongest neighbor, was easy prey for that neighbor. Prague, once again demoted to be the administrative center of a province, nevertheless remains the capital of the Czech nationality. Moreover, it remains a viable political kernel, regardless of its legal status.

Except for the somewhat isolated basin of Bohemia, a relief map of the Middle Danube area makes its central plain appear to be its only possible nucleus (Fig. 30). Yet the political map discloses this plain as divided among four nations, two of which have their capital cities along its margins. No capital — indeed no large city — has ever stood in the center of the lowland. On the contrary, for long periods the plain has been ruled from capitals beyond its borders.

The absence of a centrally situated capital ceases to mystify when it is realized that much of this region is marshy and other large districts are sandy, and that the only natural defense points are islands among the braided river channels — the most elevated of them being subject to inundation. Political control of such a region must be achieved by closing its gates to invaders. Decisive battles to determine which power shall hold the plain and its gates have been fought on the plain itself. Two are recorded by history, and both took place at Mohács, a narrow passway between the Danube River and the Alpine foreland, almost exactly midway along the stream's course across the plain. On the first occasion the north-moving Turks annihilated the Hungarian army on Mohács field. On the second the south-marching Austrian army decisively defeated the Turks. That this route should have been invariably followed by armies is due to the marshiness of the central plain north and east of the river, a more formidable barrier then than now, when drainage and diking have greatly reduced the area of morass.

The principal gates to the plain are the clefts made by the Danube in its entrance and exit. The exit is made through such a vise-like gorge that it is called the " Iron Gate." Turbulent water churning between bare cliffs makes it a terror to navigation, and an interruption to passage along the riverbank. The Romans bridged the stream and slung a road along the cliff face. Today the impeding rocks have been blasted away and a road and a railroad follow the north bank. During the rest of time, men have taken alternative routes around the obstruction, through passes some miles north or south of the river. The Danube enters its middle plain by a longer but not impassable gorge, avoided by railroads in favor of the gentle upland, but used by travelers in boats and over the road.

Budapest and Belgrad, the two capitals of the plain, are intimately related to these two lines of ingress and egress. Both occupy easily defended sites on the Danube waterway where rugged fingers of the hill-land extend farthest into the plain. Each has been alternately the spearhead of a drive into the plain from the hills behind, and the last bulwark of the plain against a push from the opposite direction. Both have changed hands many times in their militaristic history.

Of the two, Budapest has the closer physical and historic association with the plain. Its site is partly on the plain, and it is the gateway through which have poured the civilizing influences of the West. It is a dual city, each part performing its distinct function and until half a century ago preserving a separate corporate existence.

Buda is the defense point generally preferred to possible alternatives in the district where the Danube emerges from its last gorge onto its central plain (Fig. 30). The gorge itself is marked by the sharp swerve of the stream course from east to south. At its head stands Esztergom, an easily defended site, once the capital of the Hungarians, and today the seat of their archbishop. Well articulated with the small basin above the gorge, it is somewhat cut off from the large plain below, river traffic, especially that coming upstream, being impeded by the swift current. Below the gorge continue bluffs and hills along the right bank for a score of miles. The last outliers crest 770 feet above the stream, which flows in a single channel hardly more than 3000 feet wide, instead of braiding among islands as is the rule for its course across the plain (Fig. 31). Immediately above and below the bluffs large islands have at times served for defense, utilizing the river and floodplain marshes as barriers. The initial foothold of Magyar tribesmen in the vicinity appears to have been the downstream island. Behind the upstream island the Romans established their frontier trading town and armed camp on a narrow ribbon of lowland, at the outlet of an easy overland route from the west. The flat land for the camp, the road for the legions, the screening island in front, and hot springs on the spot made an ideal site for the Romans, who depended on well-equipped infantry to overawe the primitive tribes of the plain beyond the river. When Roman power flagged and active, nomadic plainsmen pushed in from the Lower Danube and even Asia, the valley town was destroyed. The next known settlement was a defensive position on the hills at Old Buda adjacent to the Roman ruins. Later the center was moved to the higher crags of modern Buda. After the mid-14th century the Hungarian ruler generally made the place the capital of his kingdom, which included all the plain to the line of the Sava-Danube, and the surrounding hill-land. After the Turks inundated the whole plain in a single wave of conquest, they were held at bay for fifteen years before the stronghold of Buda. When finally they conquered the fortress they made it their administrative outpost and military headquarters throughout the 140 years they occupied the plain. When dislodged from Buda by Austrian forces they lost the entire lowland which it controls, i.e., to the Sava-Danube line. Thereafter Hungary was ruled under personal union with its Austrian liberators. Buda remained the capital but was not often visited by its Viennese king except on the occasion of his coronation in the ancient church. In the 19th century it submerged its political functions and identity in the greater capital city, Budapest.

Pest does not share the antiquity of the Roman ancestor of Buda. It grew up in the middle ages as a trading post for the plainsmen on the riverbank opposite the defense point. Built on a floodplain to serve as a port for down-river traffic and as a ferry port for the overland routes which strike the river at Buda, it has often been flooded. Having no defense from the extensive open plain except its stockade, it has often been sacked. In time Hungary came to be imbedded in the body of the Austro-Hungarian state and invasions of Pest ceased. After a severe flood a little more than a century ago, the streets were raised to a new level and dikes were built to protect the town. Thereupon it forged rapidly ahead of Buda, profiting from its position as a trans-fluvial distributing and collecting point on a large plain, and having a flat site with unlimited room for expansion. In the mid-19th century, when Hungary was placed on a political parity with Austria, Pest became the seat of the Hungarian Parliament, Law Courts, and administrative offices. Steamships have facilitated up-river traffic on the swift stream, suspension bridges cross the wide and deep river, and the roads are supplemented by railroads which use the ancient Roman pass and also swing around south of the Buda hills.

Budapest today expresses its several political functions more clearly than do most capitals. In Buda, the medieval defense point on the

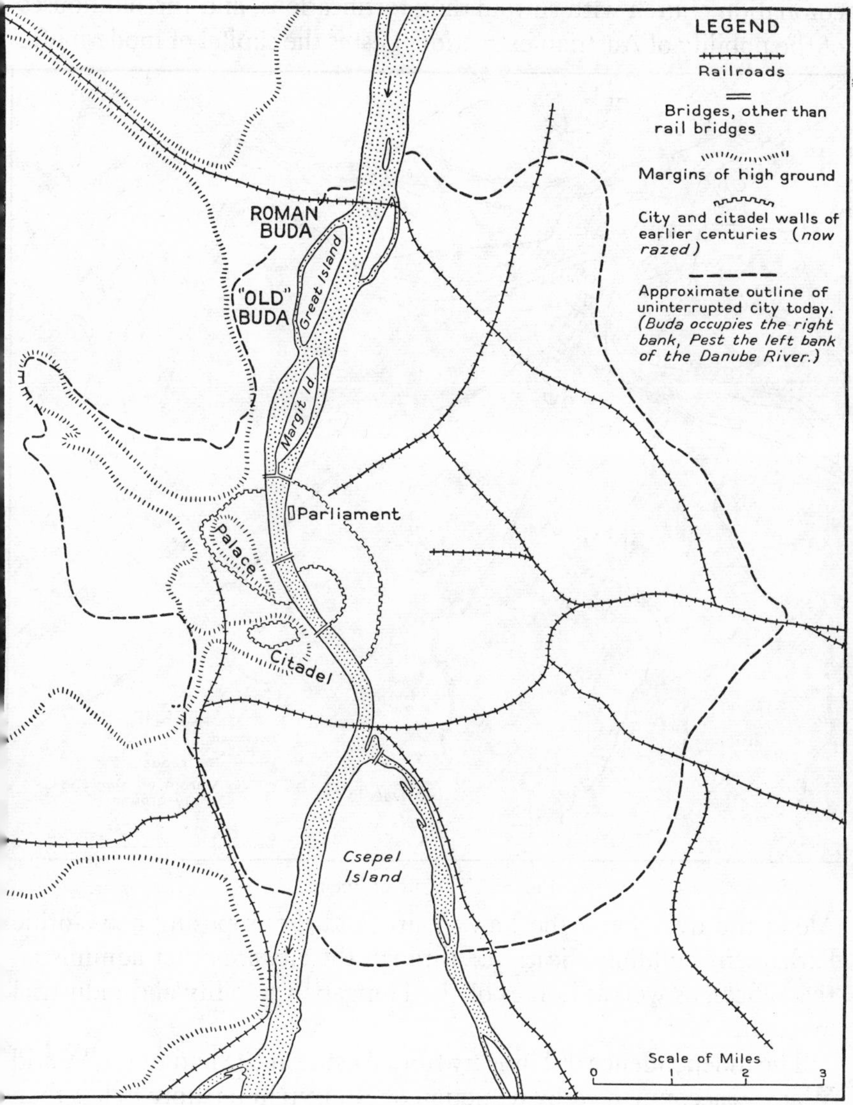
LEGEND
Railroads
Bridges, other than rail bridges
Margins of high ground
City and citadel walls of earlier centuries (*now razed*)
Approximate outline of uninterrupted city today. (*Buda occupies the right bank, Pest the left bank of the Danube River.*)
ROMAN BUDA
"OLD" BUDA
Great Island
Margit Id
Parliament
Palace
Citadel
Csepel Island
Scale of Miles
0
1
2
3

FIG. 31. The site of Budapest.

highest cliff overlooking the river, is crowned by an ancient fort, rebuilt by each successive conqueror of the place. On a lower hill are the
royal preserves: the vast 18th-century royal palace, the 14th-century
coronation church with surrounding fortifications, and the old houses
of the nobility of Austrian extraction. Pest is the capital of modern life.

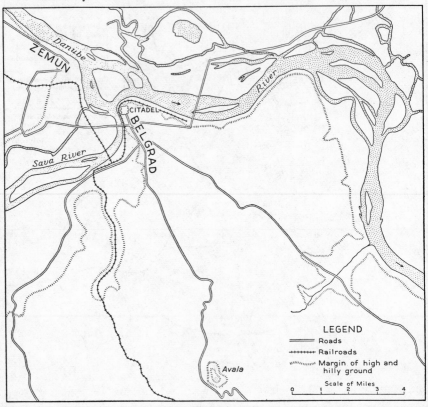

Fɪɢ. 32. The site of Belgrad.

Along the river stand the Law Courts and the imposing neo-Gothic
Parliament buildings. Scattered through the city are other administrative offices, as well as homes of the Hungarian nobility and industrial
magnates.

    The independence of Hungary from Austria at the end of the World
War was accompanied by reduction of Hungarian territory to less than
a third and its population to less than half. As a result the political
functions of the capital have been fully enfranchised, but at the same
time the area administered is much reduced. It has been somewhat
increased in 1938–39 by increments of territory at the expense of
Slovakia and Ruthenia. This is in line with the urge to unity between
plain and adjacent hill-land, implicit in the natural environment.

Belgrad is to some extent the counterpart or alternative to Budapest. Yet its relations to the Middle Danube Plain have generally been confined to the southern fringe and even there its periods of domination over any considerable area have been short.

The fortress occupies the first high ground which rises sharply above the Danube upstream from the tangle of hills and bluffs that mark the Iron Gate (Fig. 30). This is a cliff 150 feet above the river which terminates a long spur of the Serbian hills, rising between two tributaries of the Danube — the trench of the Morava to the east and the broad floodplain of the Sava system to the west (Fig. 32). This spur is the conspicuous landmark of all the country around, particularly its culminating peak, 1525 feet above the plain and less than ten miles from the Danube. The much lower terminal cliff bears an ancient fort, latest in a long succession which may have begun even before the first recorded fortification, a Celtic work of the 3rd century B.C. Every state which has aspired to control the plain has fought for possession of this fortress. Many of them have won it, because the cliff, although an obvious stronghold, is not impregnable. Rather has it been the football between forces from the northwest and forces from the southeast, both focused upon Belgrad by the confluent streams: the Danube descending across the plain from the north, and bending eastward under Belgrad to plunge through the Iron Gate; the Sava skirting the plain from the west to join its masterstream under the walls of the city; the Morava, which enters the Danube 20 miles downstream, and with its headwaters ramifies to the heart of the Balkan Peninsula and thence, over easy saddles, to the Aegean Sea and the Bosporus. Some notion of Belgrad's military desirability and defensive weakness is recorded in the names of its successive masters.

Celts — 3rd century B.C.
Romans — 29 B.C.
Barbarians (Huns, Sarmatians, Goths, Gepids) alternating with Byzantines — 4th to 6th centuries A.D.
Byzantines — mid-6th century
Franks (Charlemagne) — end of 8th century
Byzantines — early 9th century
Bulgarians — late 9th century
Byzantines — early 11th century
Hungarians — 1124
Serbs — 1185
Hungarians — 1427

Turks — 1521
Austrians — 1688
Turks — 1739
Austrians — 1789
Turks — 1792
Serbs — 1807
Turks — 1813
Serbs — 1834, except for a Turkish garrison in the citadel
Serbs in possession of the citadel — 1867
Austrians — 1915
Yugoslavs — 1919

From the foregoing chronology it will appear that Belgrad has functioned in two distinct realms. At times it has been an outpost of a remote capital, a pawn in the game of the great powers of the era. At other times it has been a bulwark of local liberties. It is noteworthy that it has rarely served as capital of a sovereign state, although it is always the administrative center of a considerable province. The only state which has made it its capital is Serbia, once briefly during the medieval Serb Empire, and again in the Serb kingdom which arose in the 19th century and today goes by the name Yugoslavia.

The core of the Serb nationality is the basin of the Morava, but this rugged hill country is devoid of barrier boundaries. Clear evidence of the absence of naturally marked boundaries appears in the distribution of the Serb language. Westward it is spoken all the way to the Dalmatian coast. In its cognate form, Croatian, it occupies the basin of the Sava and finds its boundary along the Drava River. Opposite Belgrad and the mouth of the Morava it was carried onto the Hungarian Plain by Serbs seeking to escape Turkish domination. It is one of several languages spoken in the Vardar Basin, linguistically the most mixed area in the Balkan Peninsula. Today Yugoslavia roughly corresponds to the maximum extension of the Serbian tongue. In the expanding states, past and present, the shifting center of gravity has generally been indicated by the location of the capital.

The first Serbian state grew up about a nucleus in the heart of the hill-land, at Rashka on a tributary of the Morava, in the mid-12th century (Fig. 30). From the coreland of the Serb people expansion in all directions is almost equally easy, and no clearly defined limits are reached short of the sea. The boundaries of any Serb state therefore are set by the resistance neighboring forces can interpose. These neighbors are the powers which control the Adriatic Sea, the Middle Danube Plain, the Bulgarian basins, and the coast between Vardar and Bosporus. The hill folk of Rashka found the times propitious. Venice and Hungary were embroiled in conflict, and unable to prevent the Serbs from incorporating all the country between their center and the Adriatic coast and also downstream to Belgrad and the Danube. The Byzantine Empire was decadent and helpless to prevent Serb expansion along the line of the Vardar to the Aegean. Only the Bulgar power put up effective resistance, and before the middle of the 14th century it had been defeated in the Struma Valley and reduced to vassalage, although not annexed to the Serb state. The long axis of Serbia now followed the Morava-Vardar line, and further expansion at the expense of Byzantium made the south the active frontier. In recognition of this, the capital was removed to Skoplje, on the Upper Vardar where the Morava trench and the route from Rashka converge. At the same time an autonomous Serbian state church was set up with its headquarters in one of the two largest of the fertile karst basins near the center of the realm.

Further territorial gains were checked by the rise of a new power on the Aegean coast. Ottoman Turks first crossed to Europe at the Dardanelles. Within a generation they had made military conquests of the lowlands which flank the Rhodope Mountains and had planted outposts on the Lower Vardar and at the critical confluence of the Morava where stands Nish. Before the end of the century which saw its apogee, the medieval Serb state had been shattered by defeat on the plain of Kossovo, a large karst basin located midway between the old and new capitals. Kossovo brought all of Serbia under the Turkish yoke except the extreme north, where Belgrad was made the capital of the independent remnant, but not for long. As a principal stronghold on the Hungarian frontier, it became a bone of contention between Hungarians and Turks, the two rivals for control of the Middle Danube Basin, and fell first to the one then to the other. After its occupation by the Turks only five years elapsed before the entire Hungarian Plain was overrun, including Novi Sad, a defense point fifty miles up the Danube where the stream is commanded by an isolated range of high hills, and Pest, under the very guns of Buda.

The real significance of Belgrad as a capital is discovered in the unwinding of the cords which the Turks threw across Southeastern Europe. Just as Hungary had held the fortress to ward off conquest of the plain, so Austro-Hungarian forces under the direction of their joint monarch seized the position as an advance base to guarantee their reconquest of the lowland. In the early 18th century Austrians occupied not only the city but also its hinterland in the Lower Morava Basin to a line which fell short of the strategic route center at Nish. Territorially, this was essentially a reconstitution of the last remnant of the medieval Serb state. Near the beginning of the 19th century this same unit asserted its national independence and occupied Belgrad, then lost the whole of the city to the Turks, and finally regained the commercial section but not the citadel. Step by step the Serb nation shook off Turkish suzerainty and expanded its territory. These changes were accompanied by the emancipation of the Turkish quarter of Belgrad. At no time since 1800 has this place been questioned as the core and capital of the Serb nation, although for decades it lay on the Serb frontier, and today remains far offside, especially with reference to the western districts of Yugoslavia.

In spite of the acceptance of Belgrad as capital of the modern Yugoslav kingdom, its physical fitness is questionable from the geopolitical standpoint (Fig. 32). Its value as a defense point remains, although the citadel as now constructed has no military value. It is a trade center of some pretension, being at the confluence of two navigable streams. The port and commercial city are on the Sava, a few yards above the confluence with the swifter masterstream. The marshy floodplains of both streams were worthless until reclamation on a large scale was undertaken by the Yugoslav government a few years ago. Owing to inundation and to political separation no city has ever occupied the plain opposite the defense point. Today land for railroad yards, factories, and an international fair ground is being developed in the angle between the two streams, and a power plant and warehouses face the Danube below the citadel. All the land across the Danube is open and marshy. Until the recent construction of a railroad bridge within sight of the city there was no link between the two sides of the river. The Sava is crossed by a railroad bridge (pre-war), and by a road bridge (post-war). These connections call attention to the fact that Belgrad lies at a strategic point on the route between Central and Southeastern Europe. There the overland line diverges from the Danube to reach the Bosporus and make connection with Asia, by way of the Morava Valley and the Bulgarian basins. The political functions of Belgrad are scattered along the narrow ridge which forms the backbone of a somewhat hilly city. Residential districts cling to the slopes or dot the ridge in its long extension south from the center. It must be concluded that the site is uncomfortably constrained to be the capital of a large state, and that the location is international in character, rather than hub of the nation.

Belgrad is kernel of a single group, the Serbs, in a mixed population. Although with negligible exceptions it has been on the border between opposed political or social units ever since Roman times, until 1920 it was rarely adjacent to or part of the territory of Croats, Slovenes, Bosnians, Montenegrins, or Macedonians. All these districts are now incorporated in Yugoslavia, yet their inhabitants are in one or more ways distinct from the Serbs. Their capital is a backward Levantine fort and a small-town capital of a little nation of farmers, suddenly made to do duty as the head of a large and diverse state, much of which looks back upon centuries of cultural and political attachment to the world of Western Europe.

The weakness of Belgrad as a capital is accentuated by the numerous and incessant shifts in political boundaries within the region ruled to-day from that place. Some of these changes can be ascribed to political immaturity, but they all bear out the lack of naturally marked borders.

On the north the boundary embraces parts of the Middle Danube Plain never before joined to the Balkan hill-land except under the loose autonomy of Turkish rule. On the west the transit lands between the Middle Danube and the Adriatic were never under orders from Belgrad or any other Serb center until after the World War. Farther south, the Dalmatian coast is, politically, one of the most refractory regions on earth. The indented and island-studded coastline is a narrow but indestructibly maritime zone which every Adriatic power feels it must dominate. The mountains which rise abruptly from the sea, present obstacles to communication with the hinterland, both because they are high and rugged, and because their karst surface provides only scattered and scant spots capable of nurturing prosperity. The mountaineers, although only a few miles from salt water, have in every age been landsmen, and the conflict between interior and maritime interests is irrepressible. To the southeast the Yugoslav boundary cuts off the Lower Vardar Valley and the sea. Here the contrast between inland and coastal people is sharpened by the political line. The concession to Yugoslavia of a free port in Greek Thessalonike recognizes the urge of an inland state to use an easy and age-old valley route for trade.

Like Poland, Yugoslavia needs time to harmonize its various peoples and forge into reciprocity its varied resources. Continuous striving, led by Croats, for decentralization of the government, intermittently produces schemes for federalizing the state. Such plans have thus far failed of fruition, because a new nation, internally subdivided by nature and beset by potential enemies on all sides, can be held together most readily by a unitary government in its most absolute form. Today, the capital, symbol of the state, is an exclusively Serbian place. No center of government could be less hospitable to the principle of federation.

The capitals of the Middle Danube can be understood only in conjunction with Vienna. Although no longer the capital of an independent state, Vienna's position is such that the Middle Danube region is bound to reckon with the state which controls it (Fig. 30). That this state is Germany accords with the facts that Austria was founded as an extension of the medieval German state and that for centuries Germany recognized the ruler of Austria as its overlord. The roles of Austria as a leading German state and of Vienna as the first capital of the German world are transformed into the humbler stations of a province and a provincial frontier city of Germany, but the stage remains the same.

Vienna has a dual function by virtue of its peerless location and site. It is a leading city of Germany; it is a potential capital of the whole Middle Danube region.

Between the mighty Alps and the lesser bastion of low mountains which protects Bohemia, the Danube, major routeway since prehistoric times, furrows its way from its upper course in the hills of Bavarian Germany to its less turbulent but still powerful meandering across the Hungarian Plain. Although the stream is navigable, in places it fills its gorge and to this day forces the road onto the upland. On leaving the hills it traverses an anteroom of lowland before breaking through the gate where the Little Carpathians and the Leitha Range stand like sentinels. Northward from this anteroom the Morava (March) Valley opens routes to the Elbe, Oder, and Vistula — lines to the North Sea and the Baltic; southward alternative passes through the high but much broken Alps lead to the Adriatic gulf of the Mediterranean. At the crossing of these east-west and north-south routes, the Romans found it worth while to establish a military and commercial post, Carnuntum, opposite the mouth of the Morava and inside the military curtain of the Leitha. There wet lowlands and high-perched defense points provide an indifferent site for a trade, which gravitated to a Roman foundation some 35 miles up the Danube on the site of a Celtic settlement. Europe has never since been without its Vienna.

Touching one of the outer strands of the Danube, which traces a braided pattern across the flat and fertile, but frequently flooded Vienna Basin, the city has been able to profit from water-borne trade without being inundated by the stream itself or by floods of barbaric horsemen who periodically have broken through the Leitha gate and made their way toward central and western Europe. Defended by the hills which lie at its back, Vienna, by stalwart resistance to these hordes, has repeatedly earned the thanks of Western European civilization.

For several centuries after its establishment Austria, as a military outpost of Bavaria, found full scope for its powers in fending off interloping swarms of Asiatics. As late as 1683 Turks unsuccessfully stormed the walls of Vienna. In the intervals of peace, operations of merchants were binding all the neighboring country to the natural hub, Vienna,

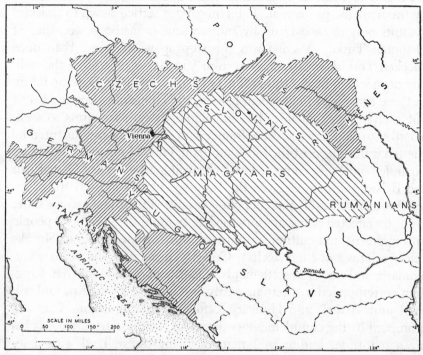

FIG. 33. Pre-war Austria-Hungary in its matrix of diverse peoples. Boundaries of adjacent states are shown. Hungarian territory is lightly ruled; Austrian territory is heavily shaded. This map was published by the author in the *Journal of Geography* 34 (1935), 137. Reproduced by permission.

and step by step the flag followed trade. This was frontier trade, always lucrative.

Moravia, gateway to the north, led conquering Austrian arms into both lowlands to which the Gate gives access — Silesia and Galician Poland. To protect this route it was necessary to dominate the Czech folk-fortress. The Bohemian bastion is relatively weak on the southeast and from Vienna trade, backed by military force, enmeshed the partly Germanized Czechs in the Austrian state (Fig. 33). Southward the long, easy route around the end of the Alps leads to the Vienna Basin, as do also all the Alpine passes as far west as the Brenner. Gradually the city on the Danube came to dominate these routes and pushed its sway down the Italian slope of the Alps and across Slovenia to the head of the Adriatic Sea. These conquered peoples were so distinct in language and culture from their German rulers that they resisted assimilation beyond incorporation into a single political unit.

The Hungarian Plain is the heart of the Middle Danube region. The Roman foundation Vienna had been refounded as the capital of a German March in an effort to block invasions of the Upper Danube by the nomadic plainsmen. The Hungarians settled down to peaceful pursuits only to be overrun by another semi-nomadic power, that of Ottoman Turkey. Vienna was the stopgap which more than once checked Turkish expansion, and from Vienna was organized the military push which finally thrust the Turks back from the Danube Basin. In these centuries of checkered history, the Hungarians became a unit not merely unassimilable, but invincible to Austrian arms as well. Thanks to a military tradition, founded on nomadism and nurtured by guerilla warfare against the long dominant Turk, Hungary's boundaries expanded until they coincided with the well-marked ring of Carpathian and Balkan mountains. Even the Danube entered and left the country through defiles in the encircling heights. Like the Austrian state, Hungary effected political unity too late to mold the peripheral people into linguistic and cultural uniformity, but included blocs of Slovaks (close relatives of the Czechs), Croats (kinsmen of the Serbs), Rumanians, and scattered settlements of Germans. The Hungarian Kingdom corresponded to a terrene entity, but was not a linguistic and cultural unit. Austria and Hungary formed a working union. This was prompted by the complementary nature of their resources, Austria being a maritime, trading and manufacturing transit land with dairy products the chief rural output, and Hungary an inland producer of feed- and food-grain and of livestock for slaughter.

In creating a state of the Middle Danube region Vienna realized its destiny in the realm of economic geography. The lowland basin is sharply set off from the plain of North Europe by the steep, forested Carpathians, and definitely although much less effectively by the wooded hills which link the Carpathians to the Upper Danube — a trade divide stretching from the boundary between Austria and older Germany to the Iron Gate (Figs. 30 and 33). On the north only in Polish Galicia did Austria transgress the naturally marked border of an exclusive Middle Danube state. Nature has less pointedly demarked the southerly border of the basin. The urge toward salt water which every state feels and few have failed to satisfy, can be argued as a reasonable explanation for inclusion of the passes of the eastern Alps in a Middle Danube state. Eastward from the Adriatic, such a state must find its limit somewhere in the Balkans. If the Austro-Hungarian monarchy did not there coincide with the ideal boundary, it must be admitted that the ideal is difficult to determine, even judged by landforms or language alone.

Measured by resources Austria-Hungary as a dual monarchy was powerful and well balanced. The Hungarian Plain served as larder (grain and meat); the Carpathian and Balkan hill-lands provided forest products, including hogs, and here and there metals; these productive Hungarian lands lay in the clasp of Austria.

To the north the coal, iron, and petroleum of Bohemia, Moravia, Silesia, and Galicia furnished the sinews of manufacture; to the south Austria had access to the sea. The two claws of this curious geopolitical animal had for a body German Austria. Its plexus is the trade ganglion, Vienna, through which all parts of the empire were integrated and by means of which each profited from political connection with the others.

But however well balanced its economic geography, no national state can be assured of long-lived success without a satisfactory correlation of its political geography. There must be a combination of customs, tradition, language, and history sufficiently uniform to create that intangible emotional unity — nationality. A common nationality the Austro-Hungarian Empire lacked. The state was triply weak: its technical organization was dual, a scheme which fostered friction and provided a standing invitation to disruption; each of the two parts held in unwilling embrace three or four inimical peoples, every one of which ardently longed for independence or political affiliation with cognate peoples outside the state; Austria itself, head and heart of the monarchy, remained German and subject to the powerful attraction of political Germany, expressed through the culture and history which Austrians share with the whole German folk.

As a result of events in the German world, Austria, long a Middle Danube power, was forced to step out of German politics in the mid-19th century. From this moment Vienna was devoted exclusively to its Middle Danube empire, sound enough as an economico-geographic entity. Only the passage of long time and probably also the substitution of free federation of the several nationalities for the dual monarchy could hope to achieve political stability in the Middle Danube Basin. Instead, the World War intervened, weakening the economic structure of the area and widening its political fissures into chasms. By the peace treaties the region was rearranged in rough accordance with nationality — excepting only Austria itself which, deprived of its business

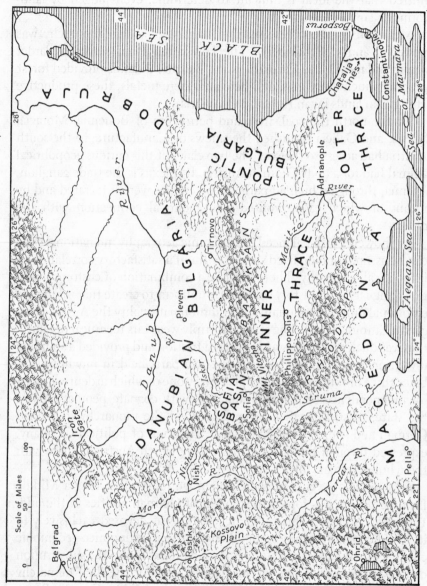

Fig. 34. Bulgaria, geopolitical core of the Balkan Peninsula, and its connections.

of heading a powerful Middle Danube state, was for two decades denied its alternative destiny, union with Germany.[1] Little wonder that post-war Austria was bowed down by economic depression and upheaved by political strife!

The ancient and ineluctable route focus, Vienna, is now returned to Germany, thus completing the dismemberment of the Middle Danube Basin along linguistic lines. It is not to be supposed that by reattachment to the body of Germany, Vienna will cease to function as a participant in the economic life of the great lowland which it faces. The political implications of the dual function vested by nature in the Vienna Basin have not been set at rest by the Anschluss.

### CAPITALS OF EXTREME SOUTHEASTERN EUROPE

The kernel of political force in the interior Balkans is Sofia (Fig. 34). It is recurrently, and oftener than any other place, the capital of the heartlands of the peninsula. Its own immediate vicinity is strikingly unified, and at the same time reaches out in all directions through easy passes to achieve dominion over adjacent valleys, basins, and even coastal lowlands. In these respects it parallels Vienna, although its operations are confined to a smaller and less productive area.

The Sofia Basin is about 80 miles long and half as wide, rather flat with sluggish streams meandering across it to find an exit through the northern rim to the Danube, and the volcanic mass of Vitosha standing guard on its southerly side. It is formed by the knot of mountains where the diminishing north-south ranges associated with the Dinaric and Albanian Alps give way to the east-west Balkan and Rhodope ranges. Through the broad crests of these mountains easy passes lead in all directions; northward down the Isker Valley outlet to the lowland of the Lower Danube; eastward across alternative passes to the Maritza Basin and the Bosporus; southward along the Struma Valley to the Macedonian Plain and the Aegean Sea; westward by way of the Nishava Valley to the Morava-Vardar line, reached at Nish. The Sofia Basin is a fertile land, but inferior to a number of other units of the central Balkans both in fertility and in size. Its value derives primarily from its nodal position which has made it a trade center and a seat of political power.

Sofia occupies the inevitable site of the metropolis of the basin. It is

---

[1] A third possibility was continuation of Austria as a small, independent state, maintained by mutual jealousy of powerful neighbors. The mountainous section lends itself to this device (witness Switzerland), but the route-plexus at Vienna belongs to the larger political world.

not far from the center. Lying on the alluvial apron of Mt. Vitosha, it is free from the marshiness of the river floodplains. A gentle but defensible hill rises close by a copious flow of hot springs. The residence of the ruler has generally occupied the hill or one of its slopes, and a long succession of state-controlled bathing establishments has been fixed by the springs of hot water in the valley at its foot. Nothing of the Roman baths remains, but a Turkish mosque formerly attached to the springs, stands beside the modern municipal " Turkish " bathhouse.

So long as Rome city remained the center of the Roman state, Sofia was a minor administrative center and a pleasant stop on the new north road connecting Durazzo with Byzantium via Nish (Fig. 35). When Byzantium, renamed Constantinople, was elevated to be capital of the Roman Empire, the Sofia Basin became an advance base against barbarian hordes and the key to the western Balkan Peninsula. Thenceforth the nodal connections of the district have been apparent in its repeated transfer from one administrative unit to another. As an unforested, flat-floored basin it resembles its neighbor basins to the east rather than the hill country to the west, and the basins have always been easier to conquer than the more rugged lands. This resulted in differentiation in racial stock with every increment from the outside, a process begun long before the dawn of history. For the same reason the basins have generally been administered differently from the hill-land. The Sofia Basin, as a military stronghold at the threshold of the hills, has partaken of the life of both halves of the Balkan Peninsula.

In the Byzantian era it was generally the westernmost political district of Thrace, administered from the Bosporus. At the same time its ecclesiastical affiliation was customarily with the Morava Valley and country to the north or west of it. Sometimes the metropolitan city lay as far west as the Albanian lakes. After the Turks overswept the peninsula they permitted the hilly west more liberty than the basins of the east. West of the Morava, native landowners retained some of the soil and the native Orthodox church became the rallying ground of patriotic emotion. In the basins the land was worked by Christians for Turkish overlords and the church was subordinated to the Greek patriarch, resident, like the lay ruler, in Constantinople. This strict régime extended to include the Morava-Vardar line, which could be held from the Sofia Basin and the Macedonian lowland.

In the ceaseless wars waged upon peoples infiltering from beyond the Danube, Sofia was pillaged by nomads, settled by sedentary Slavs, and fought over by Turks, Russians, Rumanians, Serbs, and Hungarians.

The alternation of rule is approximated below:

ca. 100 A.D. — Roman foundation
447          — burned by the Huns
809          — capital of Bulgarian Empire
1018         — captured by Byzantium and made a frontier
                fortress
1186         — captured by Bulgarians
1382         — captured by Turks
1443         — occupied by Hungarians and retaken by Turks
1878         — made capital of the modern Bulgarian king-
                dom

During almost exactly two-thirds of its known history, the Sofia Basin has been governed from the Bosporus, being utilized as a node of routes and an advance base against Danubian and trans-Danubian lands. Its remaining years have been passed as a unit of an independent Bulgarian state, very often the core unit with the city as capital of the country.

Any vigorous power seated on the Dardanelles and Bosporus operates against the Bulgarian lands from a base at Adrianople, on a hill which rises conspicuously above the often flooded confluence of the Maritza and two of its tributaries (Fig. 34). This spot is the ligature between the several basins which combine to form Bulgaria and the long swells of large but gentle hills which comprise Outer Thrace.

Northward a valley route gives access to the coastal lowland of the Black Sea, a region sometimes called Pontic Bulgaria. Southward the Lower Maritza leads to the Macedonian Plain and ultimately up the Struma Valley toward Sofia. Westward the route which ascends the Maritza traverses Inner Thrace and passes its metropolis and stronghold, Philippopolis, the city founded by Macedonian Philip to dominate this part of his expanding empire. The strategic value of Philippopolis derives from flat-topped, cliffed hills which jut from the plain a few rods from the river. On and among them lies the city, controlling the stream. From Inner Thrace alternative routes lead by easy stages to the Sofia Basin, which, because of its pinnacle position, enclosed character, and small size, is far stronger, in the military sense, than its larger and richer neighbor.

The north road which the Roman Emperor Trajan built through the Balkan country traverses Thrace, and Trajan's successor capitalized the strategic value of the hill at the Maritza confluence by occupying it and giving it his name — Hadrianopolis. Roman rule refused to treat Bulgaria as a political entity, and the resultant dissidence between the political and ecclesiastical administrative units hampered the growth of a Bulgarian state. Turkish rule permitted the practice of all religions, but the Orthodox Church, no less than the Turkish state, was administered from Constantinople. The policy of the head of the church, himself a Greek, was Hellenization of all Orthodox believers, and the ecclesiastical administrative unit in which Bulgaria lay spread far beyond its borders. Both these facts militated against the Bulgarian realization of individuality.

Yet in spite of handicaps, three separate Bulgarian states have thrown off the yoke of Constantinople and have given expression to the reciprocal political character of a specific group of physical units in the eastern part of the Balkan Peninsula. Two of these states originated in the middle ages, the other is of recent origin. All three illustrate the infirmity of barrier boundaries within the Balkan area.

The nuclear core of Bulgaria is neither the Sofia Basin nor Inner Thrace, but the strip of lowland between the Danube and the Balkan range. Below the Iron Gate the Danube is two-fifths to three-quarters of a mile wide, and its north bank affords few crossing places and is the most persistent of all boundaries to the Bulgarian area. It has never been transgressed, ethnically or even politically, from Roman times to the present day, except when a superpower has clamped all southeastern Europe in its mighty grasp. Even at such periods the two sides of the river have been separately administered. The capital of the Bulgarian coreland is Tirnovo, near the confluence of routes: southward over the Balkan mountains to Inner Thrace and eastward over lower hills to the Black Sea coast. The Balkan range disappears in this coastal lowland, Pontic Bulgaria, which in turn connects with Inner Thrace, by way of a range of low hills. Beyond, to the northeast, stands the sterile, low plateau Dobruja, the transit land over which mongoloid Bulgars and other and larger elements of the Bulgarian population, chiefly Slavic, appear to have entered the Balkan Peninsula.

From a base in Pontic and Danubian Bulgaria (to which Dobruja was attached), the Bulgarians crossed the Balkans and took the Sofia Basin at the beginning of the 9th century. In doing this they established a pattern of political expansion which has been repeated more than once. They also achieved a political combination of great coherence and expansive force. To the cradle of their state, protected by naturally marked frontiers and lying off the main highways, they welded the Sofia Basin, a node of trade and a position conducive to expansion, and made its metropolis their capital. In little more than a century the Bulgarian Empire incorporated Inner Thrace, the Struma Valley as far as the Macedonian Plain, the Morava Basin except for the Serb coreland about Rashka, the Upper Vardar, and all the karstic hill-land about the lakes where Serbs, Albanians, Greeks, and Bulgarians mingle in an association even more complex than their landforms. At its apogee, the state reached across the Balkan Peninsula from the mouth of the Danube to Durazzo at the outlet of the Adriatic.

The boundaries of the Bulgarian church were made to coincide with those of the state, and its head was emancipated from Constantinople just as was the ruler of the country. Both precedents were thereafter cited as reasons for Bulgarian independence, but the church proved to be a more effective rallying round than the state.

Awkward communication in this large, mountainous area was a source of inherent weakness, while lack of naturally marked barrier boundaries invited onslaughts from enemies. The state split along the line of the late-Roman administrative division, leaving the Sofia Basin in the western half, on the frontier, and bereft of its position as capital. This destroyed the geopolitical coherence of the area. The eastern part, with its capital retracted to Tirnovo, was soon reconquered piecemeal by the Byzantines. In the west the capital migrated about the hill-land, always becoming more excentric, until it reached Ohrid. The strength of this unit was the Sofia Basin, which, thanks to its military vitality, held out nearly half a century. When it fell the western units disintegrated under blows from Serbs, Hungarians, and Byzantines. All but the Lower Morava Valley was reincorporated like the eastern half, into the Byzantine Empire.

A century and a half after the débâcle, a new Bulgarian state grew up in the mold of its predecessor. Working from a capital at Tirnovo in the coreland, it extended eastward to Pontic Bulgaria and Dobruja, and westward into the Sofia Basin and thence to Inner Thrace, the Morava and Vardar, and the Struma. The new state sealed its independence from Byzantium by a victory at Adrianople, only to meet reverses from the north and west. Recurrent incursions of Tatar nomads from South Russia weakened the regions along the Danube. A Serb state rose in the west, pushed the Bulgarian régime out of the Morava and Vardar basins, and seized the Upper Struma Valley.

Not long after these reverses, the state was obliterated by the Turks. Within a few years of their arrival on the European side of the Dardanelles the Turks had overrun Inner Thrace, a dominion which they confirmed by a victory over the Serb forces near the gateway to that region, twenty miles west of Adrianople. In another decade they took Sofia, which, although not the Bulgarian capital, was the military key to both the Morava Valley and Danubian Bulgaria. After overwhelming the Serb resistance in the Morava, the Turks turned to the Danubian coreland of Bulgaria, which they quickly mastered. Less than half a century after they first set foot on European soil, all the strictly Bulgarian lands and, save for the Morava below Nish, all the lands Bulgarian states had ever ruled were in Turkish hands.

Just as Bulgaria was the first of the Balkan states to succumb to Turkey, so it was the last to emerge from the centuries of eclipse. As in the middle ages both support of and impetus to Bulgarian moves came from the northeast. Already all the peoples which had been overrun by the Turks and which lay farther from the Bosporus had asserted their autonomy, when Russia stepped in as champion of Slavs and of Orthodox Christianity. In 1870 the Bulgarian demand for a church administered by Bulgar and not Greek clergy was granted by Turkey under Russian pressure. A few years later Russian support took shape in an armed invasion of Turkish Bulgaria, which swiftly forced the Turkish army back from Dobruja but became stalled before the fortified town of Pleven in Danubian Bulgaria. When, with Rumanian aid, this fortified town was reduced by siege, the armies swept through the passes to effect a junction with Serb forces between Sofia and Nish, to overrun Inner Thrace, and to seize Adrianople. These quick successes forced Turkey to relinquish the struggle. The plan of the Russian government to reconstitute Bulgaria at once as the major political unit of the Balkan Peninsula was thwarted by the jealousy of other European Powers — Austria-Hungary, eager to complete its reconquest of the Middle Danube lands and hopeful of succeeding to domination in the Balkan Peninsula beyond; and Great Britain, fearful of Russian influence so close to the Bosporus. Instead, the integration of Bulgaria has followed its customary piecework pattern, with slight variations.

The Danubian coreland and the adjacent half of Pontic Bulgaria were constituted as an autonomous principality, and to them was added the Sofia Basin. This made it possible to settle on Sofia as capital of the new and almost sovereign state. Sofia was selected instead of Tirnovo, which had superior claims on historical grounds, because of its strategic position on routes leading to lands occupied by Bulgarians but left in Turkish hands. Among these the chief was Inner Thrace to which was added the southern half of Pontic Bulgaria. This province was to remain under Turkish military occupation but was granted administrative autonomy with a Christian governor. Dobruja, inhabited by a mixture of Bulgarians, Turks, and Rumanians, was handed to Rumania as compensation for its efforts in ousting Turkey from Bulgaria proper. If this did violence to Bulgarian history and sentiment, it gave Rumania its first and even today its only harbor on the Black Sea.

The separation of Inner Thrace from a unified Bulgaria constituted of the coreland plus the Sofia Basin lasted less than a decade. A revolution at Philippopolis, the Thracian capital, ended in union. It also brought a Serb army into the Sofia Basin along the ancient route from Nish, the confluence city which had been attached to Serbia by the very settlement that had rejuvenated Bulgaria. It was as if the Serb government recognized its military weakness in the presence of a Bulgarian state compounded of its four traditional inner components. True to history, the Bulgarians repelled the invasion and were once again on the way to the Morava Valley when Austria-Hungary intervened and forced the restoration of the *status quo ante bellum.*

A generation later successive wars which culminated in the World War again demonstrated the inherent military strength of the Bulgarian area and the fear this strength awakens in the surrounding governments. The first of these wars was fought by an alliance of Bulgaria, Serbia, Montenegro, and Greece against Turkey. Pushing down the Struma and the Maritza, Bulgarian armies seized the Aegean coastal lowland between the two rivers. Moving eastward they took all Outer Thrace, including Adrianople, as far as the Chatalja Lines. This is a natural barrier of hillcrests, shallow lakes, and marshes which crosses the Thracian peninsula some 30 miles from Istanbul (Constantinople). It had been strongly fortified a generation earlier in anticipation of the Russian onslaught and now proved its worth in its first test. In the meantime, Serb and Greek armies had overrun the Vardar and the Western Macedonian hills — a region which Bulgaria had staked out for itself by prolonged propaganda.

No sooner had peace been established, with Turkey deprived of its ancient advance base, Adrianople, and restricted to little more than the seacoast of the Bosporus and Dardanelles, than the victors began to quarrel over the spoils. This developed into a war in which Bulgaria took the offensive, but was promptly defeated by a combination of Greece, Serbia, Rumania, and Turkey. Turkey regained Adrianople. Rumania sheared off an additional slice of Dobruja, a section not needed for access to the coast, and not Rumanian in population.

Serbia and Greece divided Macedonia and the Vardar country. Bulgaria's sole increments of territory after the two wars were the upper Struma Valley, a district generally joined to the Sofia Basin, and an arbitrary corridor to the Aegean in the vicinity of the Maritza.

The Balkan conflicts were almost immediately swallowed up in the larger struggle of the powers. This time Bulgaria and Turkey sided with Germany and Austria-Hungary, chiefly because Serbia, Greece, and Rumania were among the Allies. For a time during hostilities, Bulgaria achieved its goal of a reconstituted medieval empire. It held all the territory from mid-Dobruja to Ohrid, and from a point below Nish to Adrianople. In addition it extended to the Aegean between the Maritza and the Kora Su rivers. With defeat once more and peace, Bulgaria was shorn of most of its gains of the preceding years. It was shut out from the Aegean coast by Greece, and lost to Serbia parcels of land having military value all along its western margin.

The territory which has repeatedly constituted itself as Bulgaria is the most coherent part of the Balkan Peninsula. The four central components — Danubian and Pontic Bulgaria, the Sofia Basin, and Inner Thrace — constitute an entity with greater political vitality than most other states of East Central Europe. No state which has for its core the straits between the Aegean and Black seas can maintain itself without controlling this inner mosaic of Bulgarian lands (Ch. 9). Conversely, however, no Bulgarian state has ever succeeded in annexing the coast of The Straits, and rarely their advance base, Adrianople. The principal territorial ambition of Bulgaria today is to obtain frontage on the Aegean Sea, despite the fact that no Bulgarian state has ever held Aegean seacoast except for a few months during an interval in the recent Balkan wars. The student of political geography cannot fail to be impressed with the coherence of Bulgaria in contrast to the disjunction of Yugoslavia. The fact that as constituted today, Bulgaria has only 42 percent of the area and 48 percent of the population of its western neighbor, needs to be associated with the schisms which cleave the larger state and the repeated conquest of territory all along the Morava-Vardar line by the state which rests its military force on Sofia.

The remaining capitals of extreme southeastern Europe lack the geopolitical significance of Sofia, except Istanbul, which belongs to the larger realm of world affairs and is discussed in Chapter 9.

Athens, capital of modern Greece, has everything in its favor and no real rival. It is the chief port in a state which consists of islands and peninsular coastal lowlands. It lies near the crossing of all the more important seaways in the Greek world, and so occupies the most central

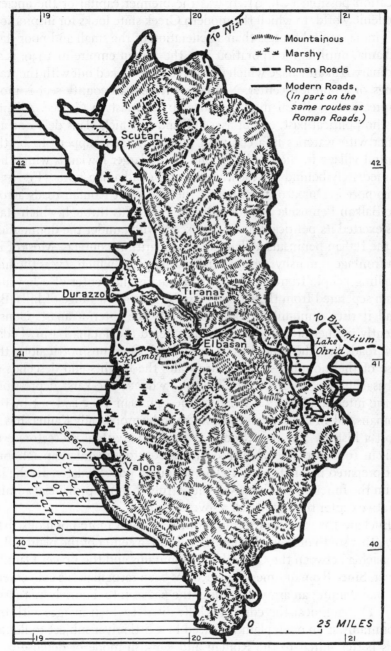

Legend on map:
- Mountainous
- Marshy
- Roman Roads
- Modern Roads, (*in part on the same routes as Roman Roads.*)

To Nish

Scutari

Durazzo

Tirana

Elbasan

To Byzantium

Lake Ohrid

Skhumbi

Saseno I.

Strait of Otranto

Valona

0    25 MILES

FIG. 35. Albania. Base by courtesy of E. A. Ackerman.

location possible (Ch. 9). It was the premier capital of the ancient Hellenic world, to which the modern Greek state looks for inspiration.

Tirana, capital for less than a generation of the small and poor state Albania, until its incorporation into the Italian empire in 1939, is an ordinary Balkan village which is slowly being decked out with the trappings of a political center. Nearly any American county seat is more impressively political in appearance. In contrast to Greece, Albania has no political past, except as a hill-land in which clans defy one another with warcries in a common tongue. Tirana happens to be the central village in the particular one of the larger lowlands which lies immediately behind the most useful of the Albanian ports (Fig. 35). This port is Durazzo, terminus of the two great Roman roads across the Balkan Peninsula and for a decade the nexus through which Italy has exerted its political influence. Except when under the domination of the Italian peninsula, Albania has no maritime contacts. Most of its sea frontage is marshy and malarial coastal plain, which severs the hill-dwelling people from the Adriatic. Tirana is the center of a lowland basin separated from the coastal plain by only a low range of hills. Behind it rises a mountain wall which sets the interior apart. Consequently neither of the Roman roads entered the Tirana Basin. Today new roads link the capital to its hinterland. One runs north along the base of the mountains. The other scales the heights and descends at Elbasan to the valley of the Shkumbi, whence the karst depressions of the interior lakes are reached by the Egnatian Way laid out by the Romans. Of all the capitals in East Central Europe, only Kaunas has so short a history. The reduction of Albania to a virtual protectorate of Italy in 1928 insured it against seizure by covetous mainland neighbors, but prepared it for the easy Italian conquest a decade later. In the interim the function of Tirana was more truly that of a provincial administrative center than capital of a sovereign state.

Bucharest is capital of a state both larger and more populous than any other south of Poland. Traditionally it is a center of the plain called Walachia between the Carpathian Mountains and the Lower Danube River. Since Roman times the place has been recognized as convenient for maintaining an army defending the passes into Transylvania (Fig. 36). The site, near the edge of a hilly district which merges with the mountains, is an open plain traversed by a little river subject to floods. It is better suited to the Roman and Turkish mode of defense by a standing army, than to the typical medieval dependence on a natural stronghold. Under Turkish rule it came to be used as a convenient ecclesiastical and lay administrative center for the Walachian Plain, as well as a military camp to guard the passes to Transylvania, which was enemy territory except for a century and three-quarters, and remained restive and unruly even then  Bucharest was already the seat of an autonomous Rumanian church when Walachia achieved political au-tonomy and made it an autonomous capital.

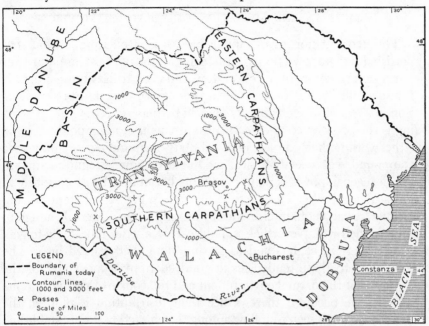

FIG. 36. Rumania, a combination of folk-fortress and surrounding plains.

Successive accessions of territory have left Bucharest far offside in a state which today incorporates the southwestern segment of the open plain of east Europe, the Transylvanian hill- and mountain-land, the eastern margin of the Middle Danube Plain, and Dobruja. Yet no other locus in the country is superior. It is not far from the external angle of the Eastern and Southern Carpathians. This puts it in the border zone between the plains which make up the two nuclei of pres-ent-day Rumania. Bucharest's location southwest of the angle is for-tunate. Because the Eastern Carpathians are more compact than the Southern, nearly all the frequented passes to Transylvania and the Mid-dle Danube Plain lie west of the longitude of the city. The one most used of all leads to the Braşov Basin and like most of the others clings generally to the gentle slopes instead of following through a river val-ley. The one stream cutting through the mountains had to await the railroad before its trough was utilized for a route. The one territorial accession close to Bucharest is Dobruja, where the country's only salt-water port has been constructed, at a point far enough from the Danube delta to be free from silt. No other densely populated part of the country lies so close to this fast-growing port as the district about the capital.

## CAPITALS AND MIGRATION OF POLITICAL POWER

The frequent shifting of capitals in East Central Europe which has persisted into our own time is an evidence of the political immaturity of the region in comparison to Western and even to Eastern Europe. It is also an illustration of the difficulties attendant on territorial unification in a region where naturally marked barriers are few. Quite as striking is the persistence of certain sites in playing leading political roles, either within their immediately tributary surroundings or in an area compounded of several physical and linguistic units. Prognostication in political geography is perhaps even more hazardous than forecasting in physical geography. This is especially true in regions where local conditions are subject to interference by outside forces powerful enough to impose their will. Nevertheless, political force tends repeatedly to generate at certain centers and to expand along well-marked lines. The only clues to these tendencies are derived from a knowledge of the character of the natural environment and the course of political events which have occurred there. Once their distribution is plotted, the march of time is seen to follow among the charted paths of established alternative possibilities, rather than to break new trails.

## CHAPTER NINE

# The Mediterranean Realm

NO other part of the world has occupied the forefront of political attention so consistently and so long as the Mediterranean Sea and its coasts. The eventful and intricate history of more than three millennia in this area is traced upon a simple geopolitical pattern. This is the eternal tension between landpower and seapower in a region where, more than elsewhere on the earth, they rest upon a natural environment equally favorable to each.

The complex group of gulfs and straits which make up the Mediterranean Sea joins forces with the circumferent mountains and deserts to create a notable degree of environmental unity within the basin (Fig. 37). This is accentuated by the pattern of economic life, repeated with minor variations throughout the area. Yet the whole region has been politically unified but once, and partial unifications have generally proved unstable. This paradox has no simple explanation. Similar units of terrain scattered along both coasts over some 50° of longitude have tended to develop, not as economic and political complements, but as rival trading states. With the exception of the Italian Peninsula, no one subdivision of the marginal lands has ever possessed the natural resources, the location, the size, and the climate — in short, the geographic stature — needed to dominate the many disseminated land units within the region. Even if able to cope with rivals within the area, local powers, including Rome itself, have always been overthrown by outsiders who have forced their way into the basin through one or another of the many breaches in its border barriers. These outside forces have not only overturned established governments; they have brought in extraneous modes of life which have differentiated the peoples of the Mediterranean for long periods and thereby greatly increased the difficulties of political unification. The contrast between those coasts occupied by Moslems from the deserts and those occupied by Christians from humid Europe illustrates this cleavage, espe-

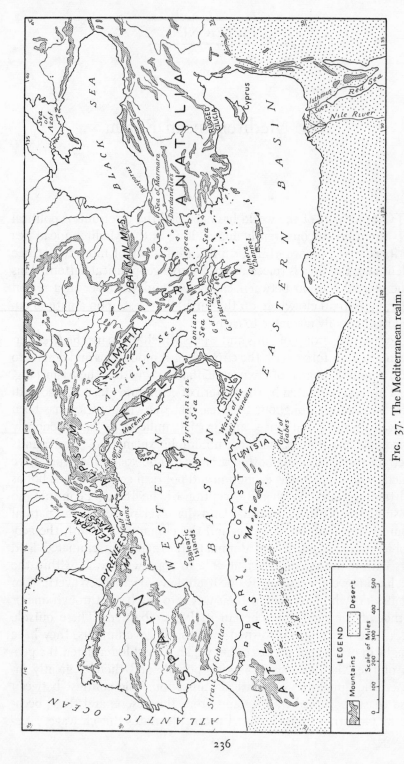

Fig. 37. The Mediterranean realm.

The base is modified from J. Paul Goode's series of base maps (H. M. Leppard, editor), and is used by courtesy of University of Chicago Press.

cially where it rent apart firmly welded units such as the Graeco-Roman Aegean and the lands bordering the narrows which divide its Eastern and Western basins, the so-called " Waist " of the Mediterranean.

Whatever the political conditions in the Mediterranean World, the region has consistently ranked high in geopolitical significance. From the dawn of history (which appears to have been cradled in the Nile oasis, that unique adjunct of the Mediterranean), until the oceanic Discoveries of the 15th century, the lands bordering the Middle Sea occupied the center of world affairs. There the political system of Western Europe was born. There raged the battles between the political ideals bred in the maritime atmosphere of the Mediterranean and the concepts brought in by landpowers from desert, steppe, and forest. There the tenuous and indirect contact with the independent civilization of the Orient persisted from classical antiquity, and finally became the incentive of the Discoveries made by way of the Occident.

The sea voyages which closed the 15th century relegated the Mediterranean to a secondary place in world affairs, by diverting trade between Europe and the Orient to the ocean-way. Its prestige as a political forum was restored by steam navigation, which rendered the Red Sea readily passable for the first time in history and warranted the construction of a sea-going canal through the Isthmus of Suez. The canal short-circuited the circum-African route and converted the Mediterranean from a pouch to a gut, traversed by ships of all nations.

As a persistent theater of world-shaking politics the Mediterranean Sea, with its coasts and surrounding barriers, has no peers. The issues may change in detail, but they remain the same in outline: dominance of narrows and control of smaller or larger bays and basins; rights of free navigation and struggles of maritime states against encroaching landpowers.

### TYPES OF MEDITERRANEAN COASTS

A cursory glance at any large-scale relief map will show that the Mediterranean coast differs in physical character from place to place. Its political complexion is no less varied, because some sorts of coastline have fostered maritime occupance, others have repelled it, and still others both favor and discourage.

The characteristic Mediterranean state is a small country in which the unique Mediterranean system of agriculture supports and is dominated by trade, supplemented in many cases by fishing or extracting minerals. Its chief embodiments have grown up on indented coasts

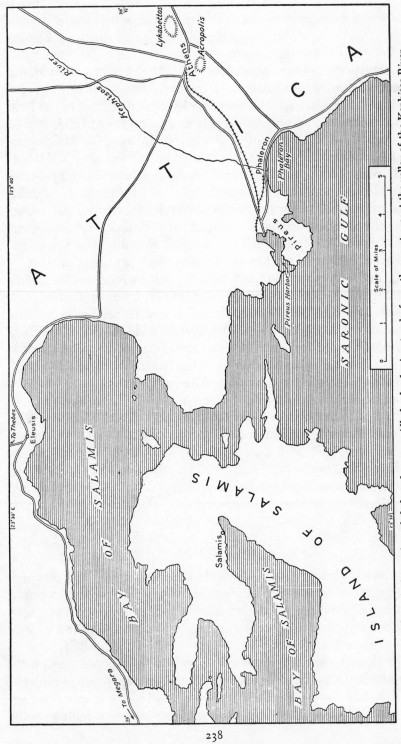

FIG. 38. Athens in its setting of sheltered waters. All the lands rise steeply from the coast except the valley of the Kephisos River.

where partly drowned ridges or low mountain ranges embrace well sheltered harbors, behind each of which a valley of arable alluvial soils rises to the surrounding upland, where livestock grazes. Such coasts almost surround the Aegean, which occupies a basin caused by the foundering of land masses between Greece and Anatolia. Much like them are the shin and toe of Italy, the east end of the Atlas range, and Sicily between. On a smaller scale the shores of the Strait of Gibraltar duplicate the favorable conditions. The eastern Pyrenees, and the Riviera where the Alps drop into the sea, furnish the requisite coast but with interior valleys rather too small and mountains too vast to match the harbors.

The beginnings of most states on all these indented coasts have been confined to a single harbor with its supporting hinterland. Those which are further favored by nature have exceeded their narrow origins. A conspicuous example of this group is Athens. Although drier and hotter than the ideal, the chief city of the Attic lowland possesses a cliff-faced acropolis, its flat top 512 feet above the plain, easily defended and rarely conquered. Atop this mesa and later at its base, the city could grow, immune to piratical attacks (Fig. 38). Four miles away its harbor, the Pireus, takes the pouch form typical of these coasts and, easily enclosed between walls, made a haven for war vessels and merchant ships relatively safe from human enemies as well as storms. Until late Hellenic times, and again from the early middle ages until the 18th century, foreign merchant ships hesitated to enter pouch harbors, fearing them as potential traps. To them Athens offered the open roadstead Phaleron, even nearer the Acropolis than Pireus, where the small rowed boats of antiquity could be beached and the deeper draft sailing craft could be anchored, but whence they could quickly flee if necessary. The advantage of the double harbor persists to this day, when all commercial shipping gratefully utilizes the facilities of the Pireus, equipped with wharves and warehouses. However, it is somewhat small for the volume of its trade, and Phaleron is now utilized as the ordinary anchorage of the Greek navy.

At an early date Athens was able to subordinate its next neighbor, Eleusis, and much later it advanced into the Saronic Gulf, where islands both screen the mainland and serve as stepping stones to the outer sea. Finally it capped its empire by dominating numerous Aegean islands, stepping stones to Marmara cities, including those which control The Straits, a term commonly applied to the two ribbons Dardanelles and Bosporus. In this progression Athens exemplifies the rise of typical Mediterranean maritime states. Rhodes, Corinth, Carthage,

Syracuse, Marseilles, Genoa, Constantinople, Naples, and many lesser states are its geopolitical doublets, differing only in detail.

Not every Mediterranean city-state of the first rank has benefited from location on a coast of drowned transverse ridges. Phoenician Tyre and Sidon and the later Antioch waxed powerful at the base of emer-

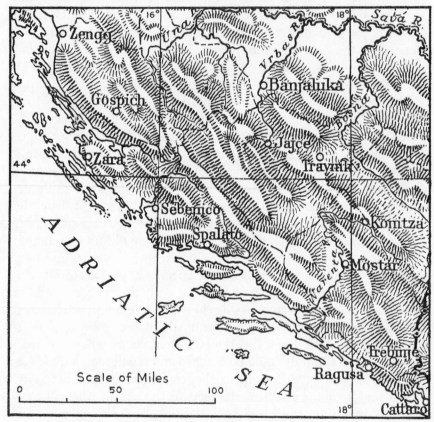

Courtesy of the American Geographical Society, New York.

Fig. 39. A typical pirate coast — Dalmatia, on the eastern shore of the Adriatic Sea.

The southwest corner of the map touches the coast of Italy. The watershed lies close to the sea; Slavic placenames of the interior contrast sharply with Italian names of the coast towns.

gent mountains which parallel the coast and provide neither commodious harbors nor sufficient farm country. Their political power rested on their location at the only possible havens near the end of the great overland trade route to the Persian Gulf. It is noteworthy that all the states along this coast have been shortlived. Like Palestine's Haifa today, their ports are significant as nerve-ends of Levantine landpower, in connection with which the east coast of the Mediterranean Sea will be more fully discussed (pp. 261 ff.).

Where ranges of mountains parallel to the coast have been partly drowned, the coastal waters form labyrinths of inlets and canals among peninsulas and islands. These waters may be shallow or deep, but their steep shores are likely to lack commodious landing facilities, and access to the hinterland is difficult. The mountain flank, exposed to the sea, bears forests, including conifers, and these, aside from fisheries, are the only resource upon which the inhabitants can rely. With ample wood for shipbuilding and dependent upon fishing for a livelihood, the people of such coasts have from time immemorial been proficient in the arts of navigation, and have undertaken to supplement their meager resources by raiding the shipping of more favored folk. Classic corsair coasts are Dalmatia (Fig. 39), Barbary, and two faces of Anatolia — most of the north coast, and on the south, Rugged Cilicia. Denizens of these coasts, possessing no commercial stake to make them dread war, have recurrently damaged the shipping of maritime states so heavily as to force them, rivals though they were, to organize into political leagues powerful enough to cope with privateering. Such leagues have characterized Mediterranean politics from Minoan times to the 19th century, when the national state superseded the traditional city-state as the dominant form of political organization. Either alone or with allies, ancient Rhodes and Athens, medieval Venice and Genoa, modern France and Britain have by turns undertaken the extirpation of Mediterranean pirates, but until a generation ago, only Rome succeeded. Today pirate coasts have lost their advantages. Lacking iron and coal, their inhabitants cannot build or run steel steamships. Even if they had modern fighting ships, many of the hideouts would be too shallow to accommodate them. Merchantmen, relatively independent of winds and currents, can avoid many pirate lairs and can often outsail marauders, while fast warships can track them down.

Procedures akin to those of pirates can exist today only during wars. In the World War five out of the thirteen million tons of neutral and allied shipping destroyed, went to the bottom of Mediterranean waters. A little of this is credited to exploits of two German cruisers which used the Dardenelles as a base for their forays. But these ships were soon bottled up, in contrast to the submarines which continued depredations throughout the war, haunting the Adriatic and Ionian seas, the Cythera Channel, and other spots beloved of pirates from the beginning. Until the submarine shall have been brought under the sanctions of international law, its potential damage is incalculable. Within the year leading powers have agreed that submarines must abide by the rules for taking prizes. As this would reduce their power to almost nothing, the effectiveness of this sanction is in doubt. Since it was promulgated, an unidentified submarine has threatened shipping in and near the entrance of the Dardanelles, and others have sunk merchantmen in the Western Basin. These depredations appear to have been incidental to the Spanish civil war. In a war among the nations, states penned within the Mediterranean might try to break a strangling blockade, facilitated by the narrows, by means of submarine attacks, facilitated by the ragged coasts long utilized by corsairs.

In contrast to the two sorts of indented coast are long reaches of harborless lowlands which afford no effective contact with the sea, except for fishermen who beach their boats in the scattered roadsteads, or seek haven among deltaic lagoons (Fig. 37). If such a coast lacks a fertile hinterland, as does Africa from the Gulf of Gabes to the Nile, it remains negligible in world affairs. If the littoral is productive as along eastern Spain and eastern Italy, the inhabitants may become prosperous farmers, unconcerned with maritime life.

Coasts which are not only harborless, but also low-lying, repel mariners. There shoal waters and paucity of landmarks make navigation difficult, even dangerous. Many coastal plains in process of slow emergence from the sea are sandy wastes, or are grown up to scrub pines. In places, the waves and currents build low sandbars offshore. On them dunes heap themselves in endlessly changing patterns. Behind lie shallow lagoons and marshes watered by sluggish streams, haunts of malarial mosquitoes which at times have driven the population to the hills, leaving the lowland deserted. On the west side of the Italian peninsula, the ruins of Hellenic Paestum, medieval Ninfa, and towns of the Maremma attest this desolation. Every Mediterranean coastal plain has shared this untoward experience, as have also many deltas. Deltas are numerous in this sea of slight tides and marked indentations. Even more strikingly than coastal plains of emergence, deltas present featureless, amphibious faces to the sea. Offshore waters are not only shallow, but also treacherous, because active sedimentation rapidly alters the contour of the sea floor. Despite these handicaps, their fertile soils, extensive fluvial plains, and ready access to hinterland larger than common in the Mediterranean world, have made deltas the sites of important ports. These have most generally been founded by vigorous states able to afford the construction of artificial harbors and to protect the port cities without benefit of a defense point provided by nature.

Few deltaic coasts can support a port more royally than the Po Delta (Fig. 40). Besides being the outlet for the large, mountain-bordered river basin, it is in a position to handle trade across the easy passes of the Tuscan Apennines and the perennial exchange between Mediterranean and North Europe across the Brenner and other passes of the Eastern Alps. The mighty Po and several smaller streams dump their sediment into a south-moving shore current. Sites north of the river are therefore less subject to siltation than sites south of it, and except for the minor trans-Apennine trade, are more closely articulated to the hinterland. Antedating Roman times, Spina on the natural levee of a distributary, was the outlet for trans-Apennine Etruscans. It was succeeded by Atria, founded by 520 B.C. on a similar site on the Tartarus River, halfway between Po and Adige. After the Roman conquest, Aquileia was built (181 B.C.) four miles from the lagoons, up the navigable Aquilo, to render it safe from Dalmatian pirates. It served the combined purpose of an outlet for the northern Po Plain and an outpost toward the passes which nick the mountain wall near the head of the Adriatic Sea. When, later, Rome had vanquished the pirates of the Dalmatian coast, Trieste, in a mountain-girt gulf immediately east of the delta and at the foot of the Peartree Pass, replaced Aquileia, suffering from a shallowing fluvial harbor, as the ultimate choice of Rome for its chief Adriatic port of commerce. Ravenna, built on piling among lagoons near the southern margin of the delta, was the chief Roman naval base in the Adriatic, being less exposed to land enemies than Trieste. After the north was overrun by barbarians from beyond the passes, Ravenna remained the port for so much of the delta as the Roman Empire managed to retain. Rapid sedimentation destroyed its harbor by the close of the middle ages and it now stands among marshes six miles from the sea. Venice, originally an insular refuge of delta dwellers driven from their mainland homes by barbarian tribes spilling down over the Alps, survived to inherit the commerce of both the Lower Po Plain and north central Europe. Located on islands within a lagoon free from rapid sedimentation, Venice has been able to maintain in its outer harbor a depth of water adequate for ocean ships of each succeeding age. The current, concentrated by jetties, has scoured its bar to 24 feet, from its natural depth of eight feet, and dredging keeps the channel deep enough for any ships which ply in the Adriatic. Nevertheless, Trieste, since 1919 once again subject to Rome, is already pressing.Venice for first rank among Italian ports in the Adriatic. All the other Po Delta ports, even if not destroyed by men, have lost their trade because their fluvial or lagoon harbors

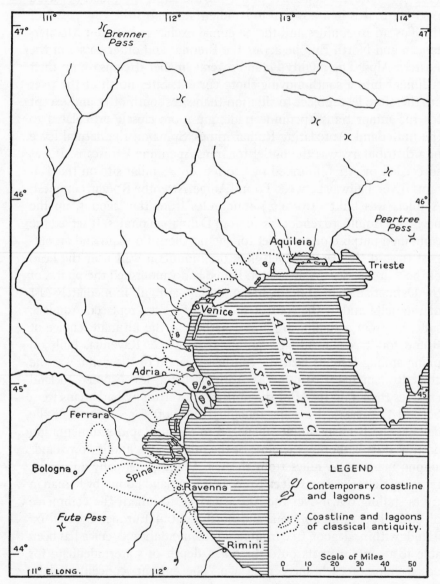

FIG. 40. The Po Delta, its successive ports, and its passroute connections.

have silted and the seaward-growing face of the delta has left them as inland towns.

Other delta ports have had a like experience. Narbonne, founded as the maritime capital of Rome's first province beyond Italy, has been, since the 14th century or earlier, stranded on the malarial marshes of the Aude. Ostia, port of ancient Rome, although relocated and linked to the sea by a canal, was superseded in classical times by Civitavecchia, offside the zone of rapid sedimentation. Today Ostia is an archaeological site more than two miles from open water. Aigues Mortes, model Crusader's port on the outer Rhône Delta, is the outstanding example of an unrestored medieval city because its inhabitants, fewer today than in the middle ages, have never found it necessary to rebuild. Pisa, two miles up the Arno in Roman times, now lies seven miles inland. In that case the silting of the harbor was accelerated by a skillfully planned jetty built at the behest of rival Genoa in 1284. But even if it had not been subjected to political vindictiveness, the port of Pisa was doomed. Already in the 10th century the city was four miles from the river mouth, and its abandonment for Leghorn took place at the beginning of the 15th. Valencia, facing the fate of these earlier sacrifices to the growth of deltas, has built a port a few miles downstream from the city. The delta ports along the northern coast of the Black Sea have had a checkered history, less because of their unstable sites than because of military vicissitudes. Located as they are on the vast open plain of Eastern Europe, they follow the fortunes of landpower, and are only tenuously Mediterranean.

Two, and only two, Mediterranean delta ports have maintained themselves through the centuries. Both lie at the delta margin, on the side from which the shore current sets. Alexandria's harbor is formed by a low limestone ridge which stands as a string of islands and reefs a mile off the sandy and marshy western margin of the Nile Delta — a unique feature of the coastal fringe of that productive oasis. In founding the city, Alexander the Great tied the longest island to the mainland with a causeway, thus forming the double harbor so prized by the ancient Mediterranean navigators. Sedimentation has vitiated the eastern harbor and widened the causeway to a half mile. A modern breakwater thrusts the line of the original sheltering island westward and forms a capacious and deep harbor west of the causeway. Marseilles originated on a pouch-shaped harbor set into the limestone hills which border the Rhône Delta on the east and mark the beginning of the Riviera. It not only profits from the trade of a large inland plain and a major breach in the mountain barrier, but also enjoys the site features of the true maritime foundation — pouch harbor, roadstead, island screen, and defense point.

Articulation of sea and land is a critical item in the political structure of the Mediterranean World. The closeness of the jointure is determined by the character of the coastline. Yet, like all aspects of natural environment, the utility of any particular stretch of coast varies with changing technology and with political requirements. In times when ships are small, as in early antiquity and again in the middle ages, indentations fine in scale could serve as ports on coasts unapproachable by the larger Roman ships, and quite harborless in the eyes of the modern mariner. Such are small, shallow rivermouths as on south coast Sicily, and the partial shelter afforded by short promontories as at Tarragona, Sète, and the ports of Elis. In compensation, peoples who can afford to build and sail large vessels can muster funds to provide harbors for their accommodations at points where the trade warrants by building jetties to increase the accommodation of natural indentations. The aboriginal pouch harbor of Marseilles is now used for fishing boats only, while commercial vessels dock in capacious basins constructed in the open Mediterranean. Genoa is following the same evolution. Some vessels use the inner Golden Horn at Istanbul, and to permit their entrance swing bridges still ride on pontoons, but the principal wharves are along the wide mouth of the Horn where the current prevented anchorage of small ships of earlier ages, and where steamships of today must berth with their prows pointing up-Bosporus. The natural harbor at Trieste is reserved for coastwise shipping, while the larger ships are protected by a breakwater across the mouth of the more open, outer harbor. Recently Great Britain has made a sheltered port of Haifa's open roadstead in order to tap resources of the Levant, while the better located, natural harbor of Alexandretta lies fallow, a bone of contention between France and Turkey. Some natural harbors, formerly adequate, have had to be abandoned in favor of man-made shelters. Phoenician Palermo stood on a point between two narrow bays. By Arab times one of these had been nearly filled by silt, while the other was made a powerful naval base. Today both are dry land, but the wide sweep of the roadstead offers some shelter, and breakwaters have been constructed to form a harbor adequate to accommodate modern traffic.

Less common than supplemental inclosure is excavation in shoal water. A number of ports have thus been improved, and some constructed de novo, by states possessing ill-favored coastlines. Most conspicuous of this group are delta ports. Ancient Rome excavated the harbors of Ostia and Narbonne. In the 13th century the king of France built Aigues Mortes amid the Rhône lagoons, because the natural and traditional port, Marseilles, was in other hands. Port Saïd is a by-product of the Suez Canal.

## MEDITERRANEAN ALCOVES AND VESTIBULES

Even more striking than the varied coastlines, is the separation of Mediterranean waters into bays and basins by narrows varying in width from a few hundred yards to a hundred miles. The pouch shape commonly found in harbors is duplicated on larger scales in the Gulf of Corinth, the Adriatic Sea, the Sea of Azof, and the Black Sea (Fig. 37). In fact the Mediterranean in toto is a gigantic pouch depending from the Atlantic Ocean. The narrow opening to each of these waters has persistently been a focus of political ambitions, because the state in control of the mouth of a purse is in a position to exploit the resources of the purse itself. Each of the narrows is approached by a vestibule. Domination of their shores and of any islands endowed with harbors has been only less vital than control of the narrows themselves. The Gulf of Patras, with Cefalonia, the Ionian Sea with Corfu, the Sea of Marmara, and the waters off Crimea and Trafalgar are storied with struggles.

Less obviously, but to much the same end, the larger basins that are not culs de sac, are approached through narrows and in some cases through island-studded vestibules. The Sea of Marmara is entered by way of the Dardanelles, with the islands Tenedos and Lemnos as outer warders. The Aegean has three separate entrances — the narrow channel opposite Rhodes and the two wide ones flanking Crete — each with island guardians: Rhodes, Astropalaia, Crete, and Cythera. The Tyrrhenian Sea, although open at four points, can be effectively closed by any state which controls its three marginal islands, coupled with Elba in the northern entrance. The two principal divisions of the Mediterranean itself, the Eastern and the Western basins, are separated by the narrows between Tunisia and Sicily, in which lie Pantelleria and Malta.

The Red Sea carries out the pattern of the Mediterranean and the opening of the Suez Canal made it a dependent body of water. The Strait of Bab-el-Mandeb is partly blocked by Perim, and other islands lie within and without the narrows.

From earliest times, each maritime state has forcibly closed its land-locked home port to foreigners. Those which were able to forge ahead of rival neighbors, thanks to favorable home environment such as Athens had, have always undertaken to extend their political sway over the whole of the bay, gulf, or sea into which their harbor opened. The superior advantage is likely to be location at a crossing of sea lanes, as at Athens, or at the inner end of a long bay, where contact is made with land routes, as at Venice. At first the claims were modest. For example, the Aegean was recognized as three seas, and even such open gulfs as those of Lions and Gabes and the Egyptian Sea were looked upon as physical entities and to some degree political preserves of riparian states. In pressing their claims, so far as their puissance permitted, many such states were aided by the conformation of their pouch-like or island-screened home seas. These could be dominated by naval prowess. Bestriding the outlets and excluding outsiders by war and treaty, one maritime state after another vindicated its claim to open water hardly to be classified as " enclosed." Minoan rulers of Crete appear to have established hegemony over the southern Aegean. Phoenicians made the term " a Tyrian sea " synonymous with any body of water controlled by a state. Athens at the height of its power claimed dominion over Aegean waters and by conquest and treaty prohibited or restricted the passage of foreign vessels. Carthage set treaty limits to Roman shipping; then Rome turned the tables, and surpassed the loftiest aspirations of all its forerunners, by dominating the whole Mediterranean, which Romans for three centuries justifiably looked upon as mare nostrum. The last obstacles to Roman supremacy were pirates, who could be put down only by seawide, permanent policing. From the last decades of the republic until the weakening empire abandoned its vigilance, corsairs rarely appeared and were promptly subjugated.

As Roman vigor flagged, local powers reasserted dominance over the more segregated waters. Pirates once more harried shipping until it was almost driven from the sea. Centuries later, rising maritime states of the Ligurian, Tyrrhenian, Adriatic, and Aegean seas once again levied tolls upon foreign shipping or excluded it from their home waters. The popes, as rulers of Rome, excommunicated pirates who passed through adjacent waters of the Tyrrhenian Sea — mare ecclesiae. As in classical antiquity, treaties gave legal sanction to these prerogatives. Of all the claimants, Venice was the most successful. It established its " seignory of the Adriatic " (also described as a realm and an empire) by extending its sway over nearly the whole east coast, including Valona on the Strait of Otranto, the so-called " Gibraltar of the Adriatic," and Corfu, the guardian of the vestibule to that sea.

Even the Holy Roman Empire and Spain recognized the Venetian claim, which was symbolized in the annual ceremony of espousal. The Doge, attended by the diplomatic corps, was rowed out to the open Adriatic in the state barge. There he cast a ring into the water, saying: " We espouse thee, O Sea, in sign of a real and perpetual union." Venice succeeded in closing also the Corinthian Gulf and The Straits, although both later fell into the hands of the Turkish landpower, which in turn prohibited Christian shipping.

With the discovery of an ocean route to the Orient, new ideals of the rights of navigation slowly supplanted the concepts fostered in the enclosed waters of the Mediterranean. From the end of the 15th century until the opening of the Suez Canal in 1869 maritime life in the Mediterranean sank into ever deepening eclipse. Toward the end of the 18th century the once domineering states of north Italy issued edicts which, in asserting their sovereignty over waters to the distance of a cannon shot from their shores, implicitly abandoned claims to waters beyond, even in enclosed seas such as the Adriatic and the Tyrrhenian.

Yet, however modest the claims, narrow waters have always been close to the heart of Mediterranean politics. The state which controls one of them controls the traffic of the inner sea to which it leads, whatever the legal status of the farther shores. Moreover, most narrows are crossroads of shipping, because important sea lanes tend to skirt coasts and to traverse open stretches of water at their narrowest point. Because of the distribution of islands this is to some extent true even today, especially in the Aegean, but less so than when sailed and rowed ships took every advantage of winds and currents. Until the compass and rudder came into common use in the 14th century, ships did not customarily venture beyond sight of land.

### LANDPOWER IN THE MEDITERRANEAN WORLD

In spite of the importance of narrows to maritime states, the right of seapower to control them has been frequently disputed by landpower, which views them as barriers to expansion, annoying ferries on the march of empire. The mightiest struggles in Mediterranean history have been generated by the cross purposes of landpower and seapower at narrows.

## The Strait of Gibraltar

The only natural water entrance to Mediterranean seas in historic times has been the western gateway, a bit less than eight miles wide

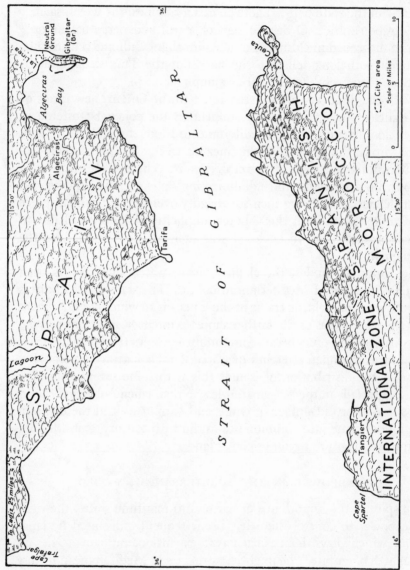

FIG. 41. The Strait of Gibraltar.

(Fig. 41). To the ancient world it gave upon an ocean not unknown, but known to be full of dangers — immense waves and raging storms, parching heat to southward, sodden cold to the north, and out to sea terrors unguessed. The long inner vestibule between the rugged Rif and the soaring Sierra Nevada ends dramatically in the two towering peninsulas which stand, doorposts, just inside the narrow gate itself. Hercules, perhaps the personification of very early seagoing peoples, gave his name to these " Pillars," and by extension to the whole narrows. This name symbolizes the attitude of the classical Mediterranean man, to whom his sea was the world. Behind the Pillars, reaching from the desert to the Pyrenees, rise masses of mountain and plateau which, by their geology and climate, and their consequent landforms, vegetation, and utilization are two parts of a physical unity, a dual base for landpower. Carthage unified them politically, and when bereft of seapower and unable to make a naval attack upon the rising Roman state, ferried its army from Africa to Europe. Rome seized and held these Carthaginian colonies with its victorious legions. As Roman power waned, wandering Vandals moved as conquerers from Europe to Africa, ferrying across the narrowest part of the strait. They were succeeded by Saracens making their swift way in the reverse direction. The Moors for centuries validated the saying " Africa begins at the Pyrenees," and levied toll upon such foreign ships as dared to pass through the strait. Their ejection from Europe synchronized with the flowering of Iberian seapower and for a time Spain held the north coast and Portugal the south. The adjacence of Spain told to its advantage, and Portugal lost its African footing to its land-minded neighbor.

With the discoveries of continents beyond the Mediterranean fringe and ocean ways tributary thereto, the entrance to the Mediterranean was faced about to the west, and the Sea itself became a mere spur of the great ocean trade routes. For the first time the water route became paramount in political importance over the water gate. This is signalized in the name by which we refer to it, " The Strait of Gibraltar." As the name further shows, the northern Pillar is the key to the strait, although its significance can be appraised only in view of other strategic spots bordering the narrows. Control of the strait is vested in four harbors which vary greatly in strategic value. They stand at corners of a quadrilateral: the two Pillars, Gibraltar and Ceuta, inside the Strait, and two pilasters, Tarifa and Tangier, outside.

Tarifa lies at the base of a low cliffed headland which marks the narrowest part of the strait. Its harbor was made by tying an island to the mainland with a causeway. Being small and ill-sheltered, it has had little subsequent political significance, and although in Spanish hands since the 14th century, its Moorish fortifications have never been remodeled.

Ceuta was the last place on the African continent to fall to the advancing Moors, and Portugal wrested it from their retreating descendants three-quarters of a century before their eviction from Europe. The site is a cliffed headland 636 feet high, which marks the end of the lofty African shore of the strait. The harbor lies open to the strong east winds. Spain, which took over the place (along with Portugal) in the 16th century, has held it ever since. From the mid-19th century the Spanish holding has been extended eastward along the Rif mountains in the face of bitter opposition from the tribesmen. They had been pacified scarcely a decade when civil war was launched through Spain from Ceuta as a base, with many Moors taking part in the new advance cross the strait. In the hands of a power of major rank, Ceuta might be made a leading point of defense for the strait. The harbor can be sheltered, and bases for land and seaplanes are feasible. It has been repeatedly suggested that Great Britain might do well to exchange Ceuta and its immediate hinterland for the narrow confines of Gibraltar, but British public opinion clings to " The Rock " as the symbol of British power overseas. By treaty between Spain, France, and Britain, Spanish Morocco may not be fortified.

Twenty-three miles west of the narrows lies Tangier, the only other strategic site on the African side of the strait. Its harbor, an amphitheater in the hills, with one long side open to the sea, is unfortunately open also to north winds sweeping in from the open Atlantic. A submarine platform extends the westerly point of the haven and breaks the worst of the waves, and there fishermen and other small ships have taken refuge for three millennia at least. Only recently has an adequate jetty been built on this platform to protect ships of moderate size, and not many can be accommodated at a time. The site of the town is the hilly front face of the rugged country which makes northern Morocco, and it affords no protection against enemies from the land; indeed, it is Morocco's only accessible northern port. Hence as a site for defense of the strait, Tangier suffers certain disadvantages: it is offside the narrows, it is incapable of defense from the landward side, and it provides inadequate anchorage for warships and little land suitable for an airplane base. Occupied since Roman times, Tangier figured prominently in the reorientation of trade routes and the renaissance of the Christian Iberian states. Seized from the Moors by Portugal, the state most interested in the route around Africa, it fell to Spain, was regained by Portugal, given to England, and abandoned to the Moors — all in the space of two centuries. A little later the trading nations of western Europe established consulates there, a practice which was followed by Belgium, Germany, and Italy, as they in turn aspired to trade either to Africa or through the strait, and felt obliged to keep a finger on the pulse of commerce in that vicinity. Tangier, the only port on the strait not under a European flag, was the logical place for assuring their interests. From this practice developed the International Zone, as a compromise solution of vexatious political rivalries. The zone extends inland about ten miles. Although technically remaining under Moorish sovereignty, Spain, France, Germany, and Britain at first shared responsibility for administration; Germany fell out during the World War, and in 1928 Italy was added on an equality with Britain, after making a show of force in the harbor to demand inclusion. The present arrangement is supported by treaties, but more cogently by a stalemate of conflicting interests of the signatory states. Tangier has been called the " lock to which Gibraltar is the key." Britain, as the leading seapower interested in keeping the strait open to trade, is determined to prevent the whole south coast from falling to Spain, which might then be in a position to close the narrows. Italy finds the arrangement a convenient way of publicizing its vital interest in the marine outlet from the Mediterranean. Spain never ceases to hope for control of Tangier, the port best combining suitable harbor and access to interior Morocco. France, as overlord of most of Morocco, is interested in an all-land route from the home country. This would require tunnelling beneath the strait, a proposal which is periodically revived. Such a boring would not cross the narrowest water. Its logical African terminus would be the International Zone, to connect with the ancient, easy trade route south. Such a tunnel would benefit Spain quite as much as France.

The fourth point of the quadrilateral, and generally accounted its touchstone, is Gibraltar, the northern Pillar of Hercules. On the south coast of the strait, the 3000-foot mountains which soar above the narrowest part, diminish to a fifth that elevation to make the peninsula of Ceuta. The north coast is much less lofty (most of it under 1000 feet) and rises as arable hills interspersed with low bluffs. Its climax is the very end, 15 miles east of the narrows. There a limestone rock stands nearly 1400 feet above the water. The steeply dipping east face presents bare rock ranging from 300 to 1000 feet high, skirted by detritus standing at an angle of 30–40°. At its northern end a sand-bar, averaging some ten feet above the water, ties it to the mainland

and completes the well-protected harbor at the western foot of the rock. On this side vertical cliffs stand guard over steep slopes of detritus, to which clings the town of 20,000 people — garrison, purveyor to the armed forces, and free port of call for traders and tourists. The bay is rather too large to be a snug harbor, but it is open only to rare storms from the south, and breakwaters have made an inner haven affording complete protection. In compensation the largest navy can find fair shelter in the bay. More and more Gibraltar is becoming a refueling and revictualling point for naval vessels exclusively. If the town is not wholly naval, the rock itself emphatically is nothing else.

Galleries connecting gun emplacements, stores, and underground quarters honeycomb the landward side and make it impregnable against any challenge from the ocean. Until recently no gun from the mainland could shell the stronghold across the five-mile width of the bay. Today it is within easy range, not only of the coast, but also of the heights of the mainland across the bay. Most naval authorities agree that Gibraltar harbor might be rendered untenable by batteries on Spanish soil. Even if an artificial harbor were constructed east of the rock, it might still be shelled. Moreover, there is no space on British territory for landing planes, and a seaplane base would be as vulnerable to land attack as any other part of the harbor. It is these changes in the technology of warfare which have suggested an exchange of Gibraltar for Ceuta. So long as Spain remains weak and friendly to Great Britain, so long as Ceuta remains unfortified and Tangier neutralized, the fortress of Gibraltar remains the key to the strait. But it is by no means certain that this status will persist. Gibraltar was seized by its present master at the beginning of the 18th century as a foothold in that part of the world to protect British trade moving from Europe to the Orient around the Cape of Good Hope. Later it played a part as a naval base for thwarting French ambitions in the eastern Mediterranean whence a potential shortcut to the Orient could be brought into being by combining water and land routes. Only when the Suez Canal was completed did Gibraltar's major function become that of watchdog of the strait.

Other places within the zone of the strait figure little in its strategy. The lowlying Island of Alboran, 135 miles east of the narrows and in the middle of the exit from the inner vestibule to the larger sea, is vitiated by its lack of water, vegetation, and harbor. Cadiz, 55 miles from the narrows on the Atlantic coast of Spain, combines a commodious and sheltered harbor with easy access to the Guadalquivir Basin. It has given southern Spain an Atlantic outlet, thus emancipating the country from dependence upon the master of the strait — Portuguese, Moroccan, or British. It has not played the critical role of outer warder characteristic of ports similarly situated with respect to gulfs and seas within the Mediterranean.

The narrow entrance to the Mediterranean has never ceased to be a cross current of maritime and terrene interest. The similarity and continentality of the two sides has facilitated unified political control, now from the south, now from the north. Nevertheless, despite repeated unification, to go back no farther than the seven centuries of Moorish domination in Iberia and continuous Iberian occupation of strategic points in Africa for five, the strait remains a mordant cleft between cultures. Today its prime significance is as a waterway — a through route for world trade and colonial government and an exit for Mediterranean peoples.

## " The Straits "

Nowhere on earth have landpower and seapower struggled more intensely or more often than at the double narrows Dardanelles and Bosporus which mark the ends of the Sea of Marmara (Fig. 42). The Black Sea, farther inland and farther north than other Mediterranean waters, is less Mediterranean than continental in climate and crops. This distinction is accentuated by its transgression of the mountain bounds which everywhere else flank the northern margin of the Mediterranean, so that it lies open to the vast plain of northeast Europe. Contrast in natural conditions has vigorously stimulated trade between the greater basin and the lesser from early times, reinforced in the past half century by the mineral wealth, especially petroleum, of the country beyond. Water-borne commerce through The Straits is easy today, apart from careful navigation required in all constricted waters. In the days of sail and oar the strong outward setting currents of both Bosporus (2–4 miles per hour) and the Dardanelles (5 miles an hour at maximum) made the passage more difficult, especially when complicated by adverse wind. No matter what the type of ship, its progress can always be arrested from settlements at critical points along the shores of the riverlike narrows. It therefore becomes the object of maritime states to dominate all these points.

Maritime objectives have often been thwarted by land forces because both the Bosporus and the Dardanelles are so narrow that they can quickly be crossed with boats or by pontoon bridges. The immediate shores of the whole Marmara region, although hilly in places, nowhere interpose obstruction to overland movements, and on both

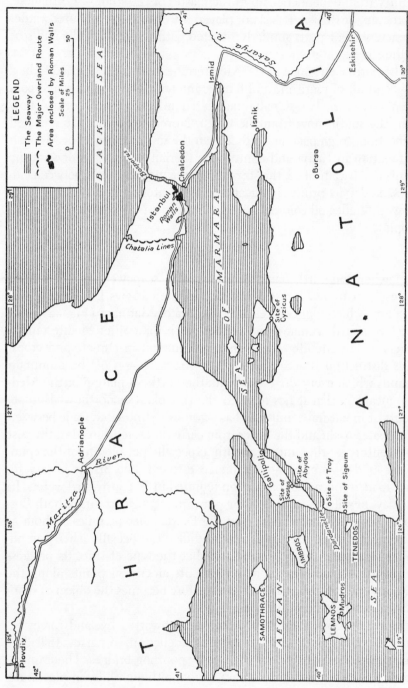

FIG. 42. The crossing of land routes between Europe and Asia with the waterway between the Mediterranean and Black seas.

coasts easy routes from the interior deploy. In Anatolia ancient tracks traverse the upland both north and south of the central steppe, to converge upon Eskisehir (Old Fort), as do modern roads and railroads. The road avoids the gorge of the lower Sakarya River (although the railroad follows it) and makes its way to Bursa on the lowland, thence diverging to the two straits. In Thrace several routes which cross the tangled ranges of the Balkan Peninsula converge upon Adrianople. From there the main lines of communication run to the Bosporus. The route to the Dardanelles has been secondary except when the Bosporus crossing has been debarred. However, the route from the Dardanelles into Macedonia along the north shore of the Aegean has figured prominently as a highway for armies.

Antedating historical record, conflicting issues between seapower and landpower appear in the veiled language of traditional poetry and the sherds of archeology. Troy, rebuilt several times on the same site, owes its persistence to the common practice of portaging between a port in the shelter of the island Tenedos, and the Dardanelles. This was done to avoid north winds and the outflowing current at the entrance. In its heyday Troy, three miles inland on the tip of a flat-topped spur around which the land route passed, controlled also the Gallipoli Peninsula north of the strait, and commanded the trade through the waterway. It is easy to believe that as Hellenes increasingly sought the Black Sea, they came into prolonged conflict with the tribute-taking Trojans, whose city they must have rejoiced to destroy. Hellenic domination of the Dardanelles paved the way for colonies of several Aegean city-states. Some, like Cyzicus on a peninsular double harbor in the Marmara Sea, profited from the tuna runs and from trade with the interior. Others were founded to trans-ship goods and control navigation through the narrows. One of these was Sigeum at the entrance to the Dardanelles. During the World War Turkish batteries stood within a mile of the ancient site to fend off the British effort to force the strait. Abydos and Sestos stand a mile apart on opposite sides of the narrowest part of the Dardanelles (4430 feet) where baffling eddies impede navigation, and Chalcedon and Byzantium, at the Marmara entrance to the Bosporus, which is less than a mile wide, combined the functions, being at once guardians of the narrows and emporia of trade. All these sites except Cyzicus are occupied today, and one or another of them has figured in every major conflict of the region throughout historic time.

The weakness of seapower in The Straits has always been the vulnerable location of the maritime bases, open as they are to extensive land masses behind them. A case in point is the conflict between Hellas and Persia. With the integration of Persian landpower on the Anatolian plateau, the Hellenic sea route was threatened by a push into Thrace and Macedonia. The Persians crossed both straits, and maintained a pontoon bridge across the Dardanelles at the narrows. From this vantage the army marched to Athens, before being forced to retreat by loss of a naval battle off the Athenian coast. The Hellenes followed up their victory by sailing to The Straits to regain control of the sea lane. This done, they dedicated to the gods the shore cables of the Persians' bridge. Athens, by alliances with all the strategically placed cities on the route, was then able, for a time, to control the grain trade of the Black Sea.

Some centuries after the Persian rout, Macedonia, European in origin and Hellenic in culture, nevertheless threatened the Greek world because it was geographically a landpower which bestrode the Dardanelles in the attempt, successful though shortlived, to unify the Balkan and Anatolian peninsulas. Once again a pontoon bridge linked the shores. The center of political gravity in the Macedonian state was the region of the Vardar River; there stood its capital, Pella. Thence it pushed, not only across the Dardanelles, but also across the Rhodope Mountains into the Maritza Basin, where an outpost fort and mart, Plovdiv (Philippopolis), was built on and among the easily fortified mesas which have ever since been the bulwark of its defense. This was the first step in thrusting Mediterranean government into Balkan territory beyond the immediate hinterland, a move which shifted the geopolitical center of gravity from the Dardanelles to the Bosporus.

The second step was taken by Rome. Although by origin a landpower, the Roman state made itself amphibious, and in the eastern Mediterranean inherited the economic system of the Hellenes, including an important grain supply from the Black Sea. As a terrene support in maintaining the sea lane, Rome built the Egnatian Way from Durazzo near the outlet of the Adriatic across the heart of what had been Macedonia and on to Byzantium at the mouth of the Bosporus. When this road proved vulnerable from the north, a new road was constructed from Aquileia at the head of the Adriatic along what has come to be considered the core of the Balkan Peninsula, viz., the Sava Valley to Belgrad on the Danube, thence up the Morava to Nish, across the passes to Sofia and Plovdiv, thence to the sharp bend of the Maritza where the Romans founded Adrianople (Hadrianopolis) on a knoll at the confluence of three streams, the valleys of which provide easy land routes. Thence the road continues across the ridge-and-valley country of Outer Thrace to Byzantium. By thus utilizing the mechanics of landpower, Rome protected the seaway through The Straits from land enemies of the eastern and central European plains. South of The Straits Asiatic landpower was kept at bay by almost constant fighting. For some centuries Anatolia was safely Roman, but the lowlands beyond were embraced within the Empire only intermittently.

Removal of the Roman capital to Byzantium, renamed Constantinople, signalized the weakening of Roman landpower and its continued dependence upon commerce. The new capital could ordinarily obtain grain from the Black Sea and from Egypt, but in case of emergency could fall back on the immediate hinterland, Thrace. Minerals and lumber could come from the nearby Anatolian coast of the Black Sea. With the advance into the Upper Balkan Peninsula, the Bosporus superseded the Dardanelles as the principal crossing, because it lies in the direct line of the new route from Adrianople to Anatolia.

Behind Adrianople as an advance base, the tip of the peninsula is protected by the range of steep and easily fortified hills known as the Chatalja Lines, parallel to and some 30 miles west of the Bosporus (Fig. 42). This range is structurally the end of Asia Minor, the Bosporus being a drowned valley, which itself bars the way of intruders from Asia Minor. Outlying defenses on that side are Ismid and Isnik, in the dissected country near the base of the interior plateau. By fortunate coincidence the only harbor in the vicinity suitable for a large port is the drowned river valley (ria) called the Golden Horn, six and a half miles long, which debouches at the very threshold of the Bosporus. At its mouth stands a hill well suited to fortification. Behind the city, traversing the base of the tongue of land between the Sea of Marmara and the Golden Horn, the Romans built the prodigious walls which can be seen today, in places almost intact.

For about a millennium Constantinople maintained itself as the guardian of The Straits. Although its landward boundaries fluctuated violently with the surgings of Slavs from the northwest and Turks from the southeast, it maintained its hegemony in The Straits so long as it controlled the Aegean approaches to the narrows and a modicum of Balkan hinterland and Black Sea coast. In the mid-14th century the Turks pushed across the Dardanelles by way of the Abydos narrows which had so often been used, and held united the Anatolian and Balkan peninsulas in a grip which is not yet broken. The military strength of Constantinople against landpower is measured by the century which elapsed before the Turks captured it from the rear, by successively taking Adrianople, the Chatalja Lines, and the city walls.

Firmly astride The Straits, Turkey asserted the right to close them to all vessels of all nations at all times. This right is easy to enforce, because the ribbons of water are at the mercy of gunfire from the shores, even the earliest weapons having had adequate range. Turkish dominion on The Straits has been contested chiefly by Russia. As the rising Black Sea power, demanding an exit to the ocean, Russia compelled Turkey to relax its closure as regards merchant vessels as early as 1774, and warships passed through the Dardanelles 25 years later. The general adoption of three nautical miles from shore as the territorial limit of riparian states could not affect either the Dardanelles or the Bosporus, which are well under six miles in width. In line with the general rule for straits, successive treaties have been signed giving special privileges to signatory powers. For two centuries the renaissance of Christian states and their emancipation from Turkish control presaged the disappearance of Turkey from the European side of the narrows. This trend was checked by the World War.

The coalition in 1914 of the Central Powers — Germany, Austria-Hungary, Bulgaria, and Turkey — was, from the standpoint of The Straits, a mighty recrudescence of landpower. To break it down and reestablish contact between the Western European belligerents and their Russian ally, maritime Great Britain and France undertook to open the waterway. Using the island harbor of Mudros on warder Lemnos as a base, British forces were landed on the outer side of Gallipoli Peninsula and a French brigade on the Anatolian mainland near ancient Sigeum. A bitter campaign failed to take any major defenses of the Dardanelles, and Russia remained bottled within the Black Sea. The treaty settlement which closed the war, dictated by the frustrated maritime allies, demilitarized the whole length of the narrow waters for the first time in history. At the same time it provided for exchange of populations, so that Gallipoli and all of Outer Thrace, including Adrianople, are now settled almost exclusively by Turks, and even Constantinople has lost much of its Greek population. A treaty is a weak stay against the will of a united people to control its own territory. To prevent Turkey's denouncing its treaty obligations, leading signatory powers agreed to permit remilitarization of The Straits, only thirteen years after they were declared open to free navigation. Except when Turkey is at war, merchant vessels and even small warships may pass through, but submarines are excluded and air lanes are strictly defined. As long as Soviet Russia continues to look chiefly inward and minimizes external contacts, The Straits hold little political significance. Turkey permits trade through the narrows, although not on terms wholly acceptable to maritime nations. Capital warships are excluded. For the moment Russia and the powers of Western Europe are satisfied with that status. Constantinople, now renamed Istanbul, remains the outstanding commercial metropolis of the waterway, and it retains much of its international political significance despite the removal of the Turkish capital to Ankara in the Anatolian core of the country. The diplomatic and consular representatives of foreign governments continue to reside in Istanbul, and the President of the Republic has his summer home there.

The Straits have been for long periods subject to landpower, seapower being dominant only when continental forces have been disorganized or subjected to a maritime state. The third alternative, a small state centered upon the Sea of Marmara, has always failed after a brief existence. When the Macedonian Empire fell apart, one of the succession states extended across The Straits, including the Aegean third of Anatolia, and Thrace and beyond. The establishment of its capital on the north coast of the Sea of Marmara indicates that body of water as its core area. This state was overthrown by Anatolian landpower. When the feeble Byzantine Empire fell to Venetian seapower the maritime state which was set up controlled little more than Constantinople and the seaway. After half a century it gave way before the lords of adjacent Anatolia, who conquered Constantinople from their base at Ismid, with the aid of a Genoese naval force. This revived Roman Empire in turn fell piecemeal to the Turks. Its doom was ordained by the Turkish conquest of Adrianople. At the end of the World War an attempt was made to set up a neutral Government of The Straits, but it quickly succumbed to Turkish arms. It seems clear that no state which lacks the hinterlands can hope to maintain itself against a vigorous landpower working from either a Balkan or an Anatolian interior base.

## The Mediterranean Nexus with the Orient

At its eastern end the Mediterranean makes contact with the Orient, which, from prehistoric times to the end of the middle ages, was the fabulous source of goods ranging from exotic products of the low latitudes to prized handwork of civilizations different from those of the Mediterranean world. Discovery of an ocean route to the Orient transmuted that legendary area from fable to fact, and increased its trade with Europe. For 350 subsequent years most of this trade deserted the Mediterranean, and by 1830 places so far east as Constantinople were receiving Java coffee and other oriental goods via the Strait of Gibral-

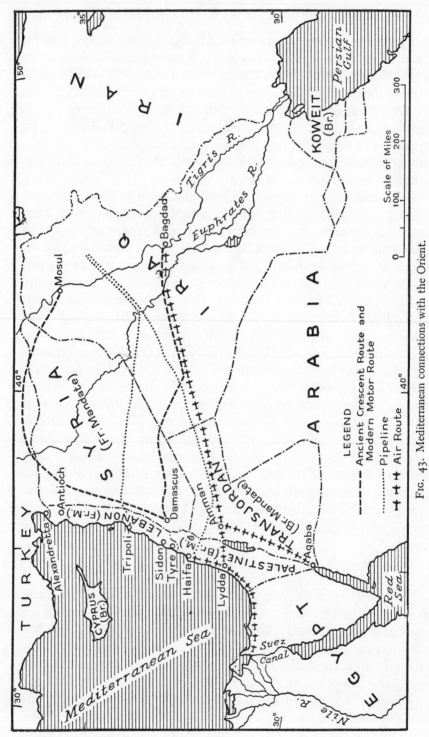

Fig. 43. Mediterranean connections with the Orient.

tar. Events of the past six decades have reestablished the oldest of world trade routes to a rank among the leading three in traffic carried. Of these events the first and by far the most important was the construction of a canal for seagoing steamships through the Isthmus of Suez. Others have been the building of a railway from the Bosporus to the lower Tigris and the Persian Gulf, the running of regular motorbusses across the Levantine desert to Mesopotamia, the flying of airlanes radiating from the southeast corner of the Mediterranean Sea, and laying of pipelines for bringing petroleum from Iraq to the Levantine coast (Fig. 43).

Until modern technology made possible these five modes of transport, there were but two practical routes between the Mediterranean and lands to the eastward. One the caravan trail swinging in a crescent between the mountains of Anatolia and the desert of Arabia, the other the Nile-Red Sea waterway. Until almost our own day the overland route carried most of the traffic. It nourished all the successive political powers of the Levantine coast — Phoenician cities, Hellenistic and Roman Antioch, and the only Crusaders' feudal states which were in any degree successful. Although this route has often languished, its vitality is remarkable in view of its geopolitical handicaps. It is a long route across open country niggardly of both water and food; from both sides it is subject to raids by half-starved, unfixed peoples of the desert and the hills. The wealth moving along it is bound to be coveted by every considerable land force in the vicinity. As proof of this it has been dominated by each of the Mesopotamian powers of antiquity, by Egypt, by nomads of the Arabian desert, and by denizens of Anatolia. As long as it remained the preferred route to the east, its successive masters were able to collect handsome tribute from its merchants. At times these masters, pastoral nomads ignorant of the functioning of trade, regulated it so unwisely that traffic suffered temporary eclipse, only to revive when legal restrictions were relaxed.

The arrival of one of these peoples, the Osmanli Turks, synchronized roughly with political and technological advances in Western Europe which included the birth of national states, the use in navigation of compass, fixed rudder, and sextant, and the revival of classical learning. This time, thanks to these advances in the arts and sciences, the oriental trade found an avenue of escape from nomadic impositions by circumnavigating Africa. The fall of the crescent caravan route dragged down the city states of the whole Mediterranean region, a decline which lasted until two generations ago.

Today modifications of the ancient overland route are growing in economic and political significance as partial or potential rivals of the waterways to the Indies. The rail and air lines which terminate at Constantinople are exemplifications of the goal of landpower which would fain extend its territory from central Europe to India. Before the World War this was boldly championed as " Pan-Germanism," and the Eurasian alliance under German hegemony which fought that war represented the recurrent urge of landpower to unite, not only the two sides of The Straits, but vast hinterlands as well. The motor routes, airlanes, and pipelines connect the Levantine coast with Mesopotamia by shortcuts across the desert rather than by slavish adherence to the ancient crescent route (Fig. 43). This represents the diminution of dependence upon a favoring natural environment made possible by the advanced technology of the day, and these lines of transport may be considered as legitimate successors of the caravans of other days, which followed the longer, but climatically less hazardous, crescent route. They are in the hands of the British and the French, who between them divide most of the Levantine littoral since the close of the World War, by virtue of mandates from the League of Nations.

Each of these powers has built a pipeline to bring Iraq petroleum to the Mediterranean coast. By breakwaters, Britain has created at Haifa a petroleum and general port which ranks high in tonnage among all Mediterranean ports. The French outlet at Tripoli has increased its trade, although the harbor needs to have its island shelter improved by a breakwater. In peacetime this is the most accessible petroleum for both merchantmen and naval vessels of the controlling states, but the supply might be cut off in case of a war involving the Mediterranean. The military value of the pipelines is affected by the terms of the mandates, which prohibit fortifications at the outlet harbors.

The motor routes more or less parallel the pipelines. Their function is to carry passengers and mail to Bagdad, the commercial node of Mesopotamia, whence routes lead on to Persia, and to sea at the head of the Persian Gulf. Within their restricted sphere these motor routes are commercial competitors of the Bagdad Railway. By offering a shorter land haul they appeal to travelers, who find overland journeys in the Near East uncomfortable at best. Politically the motor transport sponsored by maritime Britain and France is calculated to offset the rail transport sponsored by Central European interests; i.e., seapower arrayed against landpower.

The air route operated by the French connects Tripoli with Bagdad, and supplements the motor route. The British system of airways performs a double function. At Lydda, lines from Haifa and the north end of the Suez Canal combine for the flight across the desert to Bagdad, the airway center of the Near East. These airways are both commercial and strategic, because they connect with the British Isles and with India, thus forming critical midway stations on the British Empire's main line of rapid transport. The principal air bases are Lydda in the mandate of Palestine, and Amman, capital of mandated Trans-Jordan. An alternative route from Egypt avoids Palestine by using the naval base Aqaba, at the head of the Red Sea Gulf of that name, instead of Lydda. This point lies, significantly, just within Trans-Jordan, a political entity newly created at the close of the World War, and curiously shaped to accommodate as much as possible of the desert route of the British pipeline, as well as a sea and sky base on the Red Sea.

If the strategy of maritime powers were not apparent in the boundaries of Trans-Jordan, it would be evident in the swift flux of politics in all the territory along the landways to the Orient. The region traversed by the routes from the Levantine Mediterranean Coast to Mesopotamia was conquered from Turkey in the World War and divided into five mandates: Lebanon on the coast and Syria behind it were handed to France; Palestine (likewise on the coast), Trans-Jordan, and Iraq to Britain. In all these areas chronic strife between nomadic and sedentary populations has given the mandatory powers much trouble. This recurrently crystallizes as riots fanned by religious fanaticism, because the nomads are Moslem whereas many of the settled peoples are Jewish or Christian, especially in the coastal mandates. In Palestine the issue has been exacerbated by the Zionist plan to make there a homeland for Jews from Europe. This project has been favored by the British government as calculated to thrust a spearhead of sedentary European civilization into the Moslem Levant, with its unstable, nomadic society. After two decades the enmity between these two groups is so acute that proposals have been made to segregate Jews and Arabs in separate districts within a territory already too small and too unproductive to make a political unit suited to the large-scale operations of the contemporary world.

Another solution proposed is relinquishment of the mandates. In 1932 Britain did formally give up its mandate over Iraq, although this appears to have made little tangible difference in its status, since the petroleum and other resources of the new state are still in the hands of companies owned and managed in Britain and other European countries.

France ceded Alexandretta to Turkey in 1939, and will surrender perhaps its mandates over Syria and Lebanon at some later date. On the coast Britain has vital interests which have dictated pacification by force rather than evacuation. The difference between French and British action betokens Britain's vital concern for the overland routes in this part of the world. In addition, it points to the special British interest in the route to the Red Sea by way of Egypt. This has always been alternative to the overland routes eastward, and today it lies within easy flying distance of both Palestine and Trans-Jordan.

In ancient times the shortcut from the Mediterranean to the Red Sea did not follow across the low sanddunes of the Isthmus of Suez. Rather it crossed the 150 miles of desert between the Nile and the Red Sea, taking off at times from the great bend near Thebes, and at times from one of the easterly distributaries on the delta. To avoid the long caravan trek (from five to eleven days at the Great Bend), canals from the delta to the Gulf of Suez were early projected and one was constructed in 1900 B.C., followed by no less than six others up to 650 A.D. They were generally failures because adverse winds in the Gulf of Suez, complicated by coral reefs and powerful currents, made the route dangerous for vessels propelled by oars or sails. It was not until the advent of steamships that the upper Red Sea ceased to thwart mariners. The contemporary Suez Canal was dug in response to the change in navigation, being completed in 1869. Construction of a ditch straight across the low-lying Isthmus, through sandy desert and shallow lakes, was not difficult, but maintenance requires constant dredging. At the Mediterranean entrance the littoral current carries silt from the Nile eastward, and this has necessitated repeated extensions of the west side of the canal by a jetty. Since the canal was started, the shoreline along the jetty has advanced nearly 3000 feet. All this work is amply rewarded, however, by the stream of shipping which pays toll in order to benefit from the shortcut.

Because the Suez Canal is dug through Egyptian territory, and the canal is the main carrier between Europe and the Middle and Far East, Egypt is even more critical in the politics of this region than are the nearby mandates. Although the construction of the canal was bitterly opposed in Britain, it had been completed only half a dozen years when the British government bought a majority of the stock in the company in order to control it. This was followed by the establishment of a British protectorate over Egypt itself in 1882, as a means of keeping the peace. Assumption, between 1878 and 1898, of sovereignty over the Egyptian Sudan put into British hands potential control of the Nile water, essential to the oasis agriculture upon which Egypt subsists. Under British commercial stimulation and political guidance, Egypt rapidly emerged as a prosperous region, and a generation of Egyptian leaders grew up with leisure and training which enabled them to cogitate upon and demand social and political opportunities to match the improving economic condition. Chief of these was insistence upon political independence.

In 1921 the British government agreed to abandon its protectorate on condition that the interests of foreigners settled in Egypt and the safety of the canal remain under British protection. The changes effected altered the form of government, but British troops remained and British air bases continued to cover the country. Friction likewise continued, with the result that the Anglo-Egyptian Sudan was divorced from Egypt and the British government renounced its obligation to restrict the diversion of Nile water for irrigation in the Sudan. This threat to the very existence of Egypt was in substantiation of an official pronouncement that Britain would in no degree relax its hold on the canal.

The tide of nationalism continued to rise, and fifteen years after the protectorate was lifted, a treaty provided for abandonment of all British air bases except along the canal, and for withdrawal of permanent troops to the same zone. In return Egypt grants naval privileges in Alexandria harbor and the right of Britain to move troops to any part of Egypt if invasion threatens. These successive adjustments disclose a sincere effort to grant the fullest possible autonomy compatible with undiminished British domination of the canal route. This does not mean, however, that British control of the canal is unrestricted.

The Convention of Constantinople signed in 1888 by Great Britain and other powers (although not by Egypt), provided that the Suez Canal is to be kept open without discrimination in peace and war to merchantmen and to naval vessels of all nations. No permanent fortifications are permitted along it and no power shall blockade either entrance. This agreement has been lived up to, although British forces possess the physical power to close the canal at any time. The right-of-way is generally given to petroleum tankers, followed in order by warships, passenger mail ships, and freighters.

At the Suez Canal and along the overland routes between it and the mountains of Anatolia, the maritime interests of the Mediterranean have always struck athwart the continental interests of peoples of desert and steppe who are either nomadic or confined to the inland view of desert-bound oases. Ancient Egypt remained an inland state until its seaward barrier of marshy outer delta was penetrated by Hellenic mariners. One after another, the unfixed land tribesmen have overrun the trade routes and either destroyed or mulcted the traffic. The issues in Syria, Palestine, Iraq, and Egypt express the current phase of this unending struggle for control of this crossroads of landpower and seapower where dry, barren Africa and West Asia are slit by a wet scratch linking the humid, productive Orient with Europe.

## The Waist

No more startling geopolitical paradox exists than the issues between landpower and seapower which are recurrently generated at the Waist of the Mediterranean (Fig. 44). The physical structure of the area is so balanced that either the maritime or the continental outlook is possible to denizens of either shore. Nevertheless, the projecting coast of Africa has usually turned seaward in its prosperous periods, whereas whenever the peninsula of Italy has been united, it has derived its force and shaped its course from a base inland.

Of the two water connections between the two major basins of the Mediterranean, the Strait of Messina, only two miles wide, is likely to be controlled by a state which occupies both its shores. Between Cape Bon and the southwest end of Sicily lie eighty miles of water, a belt so wide that it cannot be closed by a landpower, even though on clear days the mountains of the far shore may be discerned. Its strategy therefore must be based on seapower, quite in contrast to that of the other principal Mediterranean narrows (considered in the foregoing pages). The periods of history when both shores have been controlled by a single power are few, but exclusive domination of the Waist has invariably been associated with hegemony throughout a large part or all of the Mediterranean World.

Although the Phoenicians knew the value of the Waist, and took pains to possess the south coast of Sicily, and even the small channel islands, Malta and Pantelleria, the first major crisis of record was consequent upon the rise of ancient Carthage as mistress of the Western Basin. Situated on a small but well-sheltered double harbor, Carthage faced the narrows. Pent in the narrow zone between sea and desert, it was really an insular seapower, despite location on the African continent. It was nourished by the frontier trade of the Western Basin, for which it acted as middleman in dealing with the longer established societies of the Eastern Basin. From Phoenicia Carthage inherited the island of Malta. Because of its location east of the narrows and its well protected harbor, Malta is the traditional key to the channel. By making itself sovereign over the commodious harbors at the west end of

Sicily and the landing stages in river mouths of the south coast, Carthage completed its control of the Waist, except for the passage through the swift currents of the Strait of Messina. For many decades this was kept open by the Hellenic trading cities of east Sicily, especially Syracuse, which had great naval strength because of a well-shel-

Fig. 44. The Waist of the Mediterranean.

tered double harbor protected by high ground. These cities traded in the Tyrrhenian Sea, but Carthaginian vessels sank any ship they found in the open Western Basin, all of which they defined as territorial waters. By treaty foreign ships were expressly forbidden to pass west of Cape Bon, Sardinia, and Corsica. Only the mariners from Marseilles succeeded in defying this prohibition. This they did by arming all their merchantmen, which became in appearance and performance privateers, not averse to preying upon Carthaginian shipping when opportunity arose.

Among the West Mediterranean states excluded by Carthage from waters beyond the Tyrrhenian Sea was Rome,[1] the rising landpower

---

[1] By treaties of 509, 348, and 306 B.C.

of the fertile, harborless heart of Central Italy. In the course of its peninsular, overland expansion, Rome absorbed the Hellenic maritime city-states which had grown up on the numerous harbors dotting the Italian coast from the Bay of Naples to the Gulf of Taranto. Inheriting their trade, Rome also inherited their feud with Carthage. The issue was joined over control of Sicily, which would carry with it the right of passage into the Western Basin.

Rome learned to use seapower only by severe effort. Utilizing the ships of the subject and allied maritime cities, the first foothold on Sicily was seized by ferrying infantrymen across the narrow Strait of Messina. When Carthage challenged this initial transgression, the Romans destroyed the Carthaginian naval force by a novel mode of warfare essentially military, rather than naval. While the ships were held in a viselike embrace, Roman infantrymen swarmed across the gunwales and fought what amounted to land engagements on the enemy vessels. Their success gave to Rome Sicily and undisputed access to the Western Basin with its large potential trade and maritime obligations.

At this time Rome established Brindisi on the one excellent natural harbor of east-coast Italy as a defiance to the Adriatic pirates, a move followed up by seizure of Valona, Durazzo, and Corfu, the other strategic points of the Lower Adriatic. Thus was laid the foundation for Roman aggression in the Adriatic, the Gulf of Corinth, and finally in the Aegean Sea.

These conquests once made, the Romans turned again to their landsman's preoccupation with crops and armies. They allowed their fleet to deteriorate, not once, but thrice, before they learned that eternal vigilance is the price of hegemony in Mediterranean waters. Twice more they were compelled to fight Carthage, recurrent struggles which ended only with treaty stipulation that the city be razed and rebuilt on a site ten miles inland as a symbol and a living example of its forfeiture of maritime power.

Conflicts in the Eastern Basin somewhat paralleled those in the West, until Corinth, mistress of the trade across the Isthmus of Corinth, was conquered in the very year which saw Carthage plowed under. After destroying its principal maritime rivals, Rome let its navy dwindle until the city was brought to the verge of starvation by piratical marauders who drove Roman grain ships off the sea except in the dead of winter, a season considered by the ancients so dangerous to navigation that they embarked only on exceptional occasions. Not until two centuries after its first steps toward naval power did Rome establish a permanent sea-police. Then, for the first time, all the Mediterranean sea lanes were cleared of enemies to peaceful shipping.

Once become truly amphibian, Rome maintained itself for four centuries as the mistress of *mare nostrum*, as Roman citizens delighted to call the Mediterranean. In achieving this unequaled feat, Rome was aided by its central position, first within the Tyrrhenian area, then in the whole Mediterranean. Other advantages included *matériel* for a fleet — lumber and spars from the Italian mountains and iron from the island of Elba. Chief of all, it possessed, in the lower Tiber region, a larger and more productive land base than any rival. This was extended by territorial accretions as the roads and the legions devolved the length of the peninsula and overflowed upon the Po Plain. Lacking suitable harbors on the coast adjacent to the city, Rome established its principal naval base at Misenum on the Bay of Naples, near the leading passenger port of the country. In maintaining the navy, as well as the army, the resources of Italy told heavily against all enemies. When it came to the devastation of warfare itself, the fields and flocks of the Roman landpower proved to be far less vulnerable than ships and cities, the principal resources of its Carthaginian, Hellenic, and corsair enemies.

As the Roman power waned, the Waist reasserted its role as a critical zone. Wandering Germanic tribesmen forced their way into western Sicily from Africa, to be overthrown by the remnant of Rome seated at Byzantium. Now become an Aegean power, Eastern Rome, like its Hellenic predecessors, based its naval and military operations against the Western Mediterranean on the east Sicilian coast. Indeed, Syracuse held on as the last urban relic of antiquity in the west, until it was engulfed by a wave of Saracens which had earlier swept across the Waist from Tunisia to western Sicily. In the heyday of Saracen power, Tunisia and Sicily were united and traffic through the Waist was subject to closure. Because this occurred during the lowest ebb of Mediterranean trade, it did not affect much shipping, but it marked a degree and distribution of domination in the western Mediterranean closely corresponding to that of Carthage a millennium earlier. After two centuries Sicily was wrested from the Moslems by Normans, who, like their successors, the Aragonese, approached from the west and made Palermo their marine and political center. From this time until the mid-19th century, Sicily and southern, maritime Italy were customarily unified, as their name, Two Sicilies, indicates. The insular character of the lower Italian peninsula is borne out by its successive occupation by Hellenes and Normans, alike sea-rovers.

The long enduring union of Sicily with adjacent Italy clove Europe from Africa through the Waist, which became thenceforth not merely a political line, but also the division between Christian and Moslem societies, separated by such a social breach that for centuries piratical raids and crusades were the only forms of intercourse between them. This condition persisted so long and so late that it remains one of the basic elements in current political geography of the Mediterranean. We have seen how it figures in control of The Straits, disturbs political suzerainty along the Levantine Coast and produces international arrangements at the Strait of Gibraltar. It is no less critical at the Waist. There the Moslems of French Tunisia and Italian Libya are alternately wooed and incited to hostility by interests which desire to bring about changes in the political status at the narrows.

The present pattern of forces there and elsewhere in the Mediterranean World is the product of the 19th century. There, as elsewhere, the power of Islam has given way before European might, and there as at Gibraltar, the opening of the Suez Canal placed a premium upon control of both coasts unequaled since the days of Carthage and Rome. As in the earlier case, the political force of the Italian Peninsula has become the dominating factor. This force rests on landpower today as in ancient Rome. Once more, the landpower of central Italy has assimilated to itself the maritime interests of South Italy and the Tyrrhenian islands adjacent to the Waist.

So long as the Italian flag did not fly on the North African coast, control of the Waist could be disputed among the powers with naval bases adjacent to the narrows. Of these states Italy's center of organized force has lain farthest away until recently, having been centered at the major naval base Taranto. Britain since 1814 has been sovereign over the mid-channel island Malta. Although 140 miles east of the narrows, it is blessed with a well-sheltered and commodious harbor (Valetta), handicapped only by a narrow entrance somewhat risky for large vessels in bad weather. Except when threatened in Northwest Europe, Britain has made Malta its chief overseas naval base ever since the Suez Canal was opened. France, after occupying Tunisia in 1881, improved the harbor of Bizerta, 150 miles from the west tip of Sicily, and raised it to the rank of its principal African naval base.

When Italy, since 1870 a reunited landpower, seized Libya in 1912 and thereby completed the European conquest of the North African coast, it threw a chain of Italian terrene interest and influence athwart the Waist, hitherto an open highway guaranteed by the interests of Great Britain and France in the route to the Levant and the Orient, and buttressed by British Malta and French Bizerta. With the extinction of relict separatism in Italy by the Fascist government, Libya has been closely attached to the peninsula. Tripoli and Tobruk are auxiliary naval bases, and a military road has been built the length of the colony, parallel to the coast. Italian emigration, considerable throughout the Moslem Mediterranean world, has brought the Italian population of Tunisia almost to the number of the French inhabitants, and Italian propaganda makes no secret of the government's desire to undermine French authority and to supplant the French flag.

The submarine and the airplane have furthered Italian designs. Three advance naval bases have been constructed: at the promontory-sheltered harbor of Cagliari in southeastern Sardinia, at Trapani in western Sicily, a neolithic site which the Carthaginians fortified, and at Augusta, a promontory harbor midway on the Sicilian east coast. Air bases at Taormina and elsewhere supplement the naval footholds and extend a line of force from the central Italian naval base, Gaeta at the southern margin of the Latin plain, to Tripoli. It is proposed to complete the chain by fortifying the island of Pantelleria, almost in the narrows, and nearer Africa than Sicily (44 as against 64 miles). This island, although used by the Phoenicians, has not figured in modern strategy because it has no adequate harbor and lacks a proper water supply. These deficiencies can be remedied by engineering technique and outlay of capital.

As a result of these preparations both Britain and France have recognized the threat to their bases, and are withdrawing to safer distance. France has announced the construction of a new base at Mers-el-Kebir on the harbor of Oran, 650 miles west of Bizerta. Britain has arranged with Egypt to have special provisions for its fleet in the harbor of Alexandria, 950 miles east of Malta. Indeed, the Malta fleet withdrew to Alexandria during the bitterness occasioned by the Italian conquest of Ethiopia in 1935–36. At the same time representative government in Malta, which had been used as a mouthpiece of Italian interests, was suppressed and the island reverted to the status of crown colony, which subjects it to the direct authority of the British executive.

In the swift realignment of force at the Waist which has taken place since Italy has reasserted itself as a vigorous landpower and claimed for itself the heritage of ancient Rome, the focus is Tunisia. The stage is set for a renewed reiteration of " Cartago delenda est," but it would be hazardous to reason that the upshot must be a repetition of ancient history. The geopolitical structure of the Mediterranean World itself is different from that of antiquity, and the contemporary setting of the Mediterranean area among the six continents and the seven seas introduces external influences of unmeasured strength.

## THE PATTERN OF FORCE IN THE CONTEMPORARY MEDITERRANEAN

The concurrence of political force established with the opening of the Suez Canal in the Mediterranean area has been upset by the consolidation of its central peninsula, coupled with novel weapons (long-range guns, submarines, airplanes). Several minor states are makeweights in the balance of power, Russia is a potential element of unguessed strength, and France is a major Mediterranean power. Nevertheless, Italy and Britain are the real protagonists of opposed viewpoints of maritime rights within the Mediterranean. Although not strictly correct in the legalistic sense, this is geopolitically nothing less than a revival of the ancient doctrine of a *mare liberum* versus a *mare clausum*. The concept of a sea politically and physically closed to foreign vessels took form in the pouch harbors, enclosed bays, and narrow straits of Mediterranean waters in the earliest times, and was relinquished reluctantly only during the period of Mediterranean eclipse after the Discoveries of the 15th century diverted trade to the open oceans. There the absurdity and impossibility of claiming the right of closure became the foundation of the doctrine of the free sea, a dogma applied subsequently to the larger Mediterranean bays and seas. Even then the ease with which physically enclosed waters may be converted into political preserves, kept most Mediterranean states from wholeheartedly adopting three miles seaward as the limit of their territorial waters.

Greece accepted the three-mile limit only in 1869; Turkey claimed a five-mile zone in its war with Italy in 1911; Spain consistently but unsuccessfully has stood for a six-mile belt; France at times assumed the right to station warships beyond the limit; Russia probably has never relinquished its demand for a twelve-mile zone. Most important of all, Italy is positive in denying a limitation to three miles. During the World War it maintained the right to enforce neutrality in a six-mile zone, and its customs law operates to about the same distance (ten kilometers). In 1922 Italy recommended a ten-mile limit for belligerent airplanes. In 1927 it denied the right of international law to enforce a three-mile limitation. Italians talk about *Mare Nostro* and point out that no other Great Power lacks frontage on the open ocean. At the same time they observe that for Britain the inland sea is only a "shortcut" to the colonies. This has aroused unofficial Britons to insist upon the Mediterranean as a "vital route" of empire; and even officials point out that it is an "arterial way."

This phrasemaking calls attention to the profound alteration of Mediterranean conditions occasioned by the Suez Canal, which at last converted the Middle Sea from a commercial backwater to a thoroughfare of ocean traffic. During the sag in significance of the Mediterranean between 1498 and 1869, all Britain's holdings had been confined to the Western Basin. Tangier (1662–84) and Gibraltar (1704) were successive bases for operations in the adjacent Atlantic. Minorca (1708–56), Malta (1800), and Corfu (1815–64) — three islands with well-sheltered natural harbors — were occupied to check French moves toward the Levant, i.e., toward the combination sea-and-land shortcuts to India. When the Suez Canal, opened in spite of British opposition (1869), reestablished the Mediterranean as a major theater of world politics, only Gibraltar and Malta remained in British hands. Control of the Canal Company (1875) a protectorate over Egypt (1882), and the assumption of sovereignty over the Egyptian Sudan (1878–98), Aden (1839), Perim (1857), Somaliland (1884), Socotra (1876), and Cyprus (1878) were acts calculated to guarantee British domination of the newly created Mediterranean strait, and to assure uncontested use of the seaway to India and Australia.

The shipway was uncontested until Italy, consolidated for the first time since the Roman Empire at almost the moment the Suez Canal was opened for traffic, began to assert its demands for leadership in the Mediterranean. By virtue of Sicily and Sardinia, Italian control of the Tyrrhenian Sea is complete except for the north entrance (52 miles wide), where France holds Corsica. In the Adriatic the people of the peninsula are making the third major effort recorded by history to establish complete domination. Since the World War Italy has been sovereign over the only part of the Dalmatian coast which is well articulated with the hinterland, including the chief commercial ports and the naval base of the pre-war Austro-Hungarian monarchy, several strategic islands, and one bit of mainland on the Yugoslav coast. Yugoslavia agrees to forbid its ports to foreign states in wartime; Italian fishermen hold the right to ply their trade in Yugoslav territorial waters; Italian factories, manned by Italian workmen, may be built to a line 30 miles inland. The territorial integrity of Albania was upheld for a time by Italian diplomacy, except that Italy has long been sovereign of the island Saseno in the mouth of Valona Harbor at the Strait of Otranto (Fig. 35), besides holding treaty rights to a piece of land in the harbor of Durazzo, Albania's only real port, and a seafront of 30 miles between the Shkumbi and Arzen rivers. In return for loans, Italy handles Albanian shipping, builds Albanian roads, mints Albanian money, pumps Albanian petroleum, and officers the Albanian army. After a decade of economic dependence upon Italy, political annexation by Italy amounted to nothing more than deposition of the Albanian king.

The only check to Italian aspirations in the Adriatic sphere lies in the Ionian Islands of Greece. In 1923 Britain refused to permit Italy to seize Corfu. One further potential check remains in Britain's treaty right to use Argostolion on Cefalonia as a naval base.

Imposition of Italian hegemony in the adjacent seas may be reckoned either as the effort of an alert householder to bar the gates to his exposed demesne, or as the first steps toward political domination of the whole Mediterranean. Peninsular Italy is vulnerable from the sea, because the only continuous rail lines lie close to the two coasts, and all the major cities except Florence stand within range of battleship guns (including the political capital). From maintaining outer defenses of the Tyrrhenian Sea to closure of the Waist of the Mediterranean is physically but a step, whereas politically it involves dislodgement of France from Tunisia and withdrawal of Britain from Malta.

In the Western Basin Italy has no effective holdings. Insistence upon having a voice in the international councils at Tangier was followed by intervention in the Spanish Civil War of 1936–39, thus insuring a part in the settlement. This is a twofold threat to Britain. Spain alone occupies defensible sites on both sides of the Strait of Gibraltar. Modern guns have put the harbor of Gibraltar at the mercy of the Spanish heights across Algeciras Bay. Italy is likewise concerned in the future of the Balearic Islands. The strategic harbor of Port Mahon at the west end of the chain is within striking distance of both north-south and east-west trade in the Western Basin — lanes of vital import to France as well as to Britain.

In the Eastern Basin Italian interests have territorial foundations and economic superstructures (Fig. 45). Many Italian citizens live and engage in business in all principal ports. In the Aegean the government is busy making strategic capital of the Dodecanese, thirteen [1] islands which fringe the coast of southwest Anatolia. Four of the islands (Rhodes, Leros, Stampalia, and Castellorizo) possess deep and roomy harbors suitable for naval bases, of which two are under construction. Rhodes is being equipped as a strategic and commercial port, in the

1 Italy has added one to the twelve which gave the archipelago its name.

hope of reviving its recurrent former glories: when as a prominent Hellenic state it formulated the earliest law of the sea; when as ally of Rome it aided Roman aspirations in the Aegean; when, as seat of the Knights of St. John, it held out as rearguard outpost of Christendom against the Turkish onslaught. From the Dodecanese, Italy can prob-

Fɪɢ. 45. The geopolitical status in the Aegean region.

ably control the 18-mile wide strait between Rhodes and the mainland and the wider and more used sea lane between Rhodes and Crete.

To counter Italy's strong position in the Aegean, Britain has done no more than to obtain from Greece the right to utilize certain harbors as naval bases. From the long pocket of Suda Bay in northwest Crete it is possible to dominate the Cythera Channel, alternative entrance to the Aegean. From the roomy Gulf of Volo with its narrow entrance, the major basin of the Aegean can be policed. From the commodious harbor of Mudros on Lemnos a watchful eye can be kept on The Straits. This and other islands were used by British forces during the World War.

The Straits are wholly Turkish. and since 1936 have been remilitarized by consent of the interested Great Powers. Turkey, a landpower, is thereby able to pen the fleet of Russia, a far greater landpower, in the Black Sea. For the moment The Straits are relatively insignificant in Mediterranean politics. Meanwhile the Aegean forecourt, with its islands and peninsulas, affords a superb board for the game of strategic chess between Britain and Italy.

In the vicinity of Suez, Italy has no foothold to counter British Haifa and Alexandria. Tobruk, on the African mainland due south of Crete, has been fortified, and the military road along the coast of Italian North Africa is considered to be a weapon pointing toward Egypt. The Italian government has lately bought into the semi-official British company which exploits the Iraq oil fields. Near the Strait of Bab-el-Mandeb (at the southern end of the Red Sea) the Italian colonies Eretria (1885) and Somali (1899) have been capped by Doumeirah, fifteen miles from British Perim, ceded by France at the beginning of 1935. Seizure of Ethiopia has at last given Italy's African Empire a territory having natural resources of value, in contrast to the almost exclusively political significance of all the earlier holdings. This real stake beyond Suez weakens Italy's position as proponent of the closed sea, unless Italy can dislodge Britain from the Canal.

Great Britain, besides consolidating its forces at both ends of the Red Sea, has turned its attention to Cyprus. Long ago occupied as a possible outer guard of the canal, this island has been lying politically fallow. It possesses one feasible harbor, now being doubled in capacity, and air bases are proposed for both the coast and the interior plateau. Crown colony administration has lately been substituted for representative government. Clearly the British intend to maintain the Mediterranean waters as free seas, an objective dictated by the pattern of the British Empire in relation to the Middle Sea.

Just as surely, Italy would like to exert special authority in those waters. All interested parties have taken official cognizance of possible political closure of Mediterranean waters in case of war and interference with complete freedom of passage in peacetime. To be sure the legality of a limit to territorial waters has not been expressly challenged, and sanctions reinforced by nearly three centuries of international usage have weight in the balancing of forces. Nevertheless, legal sanctions always tend to conform to the stresses of political power. Italy, no less than its predecessors on the central Mediterranean peninsula, is unmistakably interested in political closure of the circumscribed waters which have always fostered the concept of mare nostrum.

Indeed, there is no aspect of Mediterranean affairs today unimpeachably novel. Every current problem has arisen before. Paramount among them all is the issue between seapower and landpower.

## CHAPTER TEN

# Geopolitical Structures in Italy

IT is natural for the Italian state to aspire toward Mediterranean hegemony. The whole region south of the arc of the Alps is now unified for the first time since Roman days, and the temptation to emulate the expansion of the Roman state is strong. The practicability of such a course is determined by the concurrence of the innate force of Italy and the forces of other interests in the Mediterranean realm. The distribution of all these forces has been sketched (Ch. 9). Those in opposition to Italy are powerful and some have their bases beyond the Mediterranean. The inherent force of Italy is as yet unmeasured. Italian unity is some 70 years old. Its only prototype (the Roman state) endured, after unifying Italy, less than 500 years. That the remaining 2500 years of Italian history have seen the area subdivided, often minutely, suggests a serious weakness in geopolitical structure not apparent from the map.

Whether united or divided, Italy remains " a geographical expression," because its boundaries are obvious — the sea and the Alps. To reach them has been the objective of every strong Italian power. A survey of the means whereby unification was accomplished, once by Rome, now by " Italy," will disclose reasons for the more usual discrepancy between the naturally marked and the politically realized boundaries.

The heart of the lands south of the Alps is the Apennine Peninsula, or peninsular Italy (Fig. 46). It is a characteristic Mediterranean region of mountains of moderate height and basins of no considerable size. It is separated from the Po Plain by a single range of mountains cresting just over 5000 feet and sectioned by narrow and rather high passes (ca. 2500 feet). It faces the Western Mediterranean because all the larger plains and every high-grade natural harbor except Brindisi lie on that side. Much of the emergent and narrow coastal plain of the east shore is fertile and populous, but lacks easy contact with the sea except for tiny vessels. It lies at the mercy of maritime denizens of the indented opposite coast. This shore, rising abruptly to a mountain watershed, has been described as " the fourth wall of Italy."

Intimately associated with the peninsular mainland are the islands to westward which complete a right triangle surrounding the Tyrrhenian Sea. Like the peninsula, the islands bear all the earmarks of Mediterranean nature. They are occupied by linguistic groups akin to the neighboring coasts of Italy.

Between the Apennines and the Alps spreads the Po Plain, far more extensive and flatter than any basin farther south. Its climate is continental rather than Mediterranean, it is well watered by Alpine streams, and it is a transit land between Mediterranean Europe and the north. The Alps, though high (crests ca. 15,000 feet), are trenched by numerous passes at elevations of from 4000 to 8000 feet. They spread fanwise through the crescent of ranges to all parts of northwest and north central Europe. The Alps have been a barrier at all seasons, and particularly in winter, but a barrier transgressed by both commerce and politics, even in the snowiest time of year. The existence of Switzerland as a country occupying basins of Rhine, Rhône, and Po watersheds, is proof enough of the incompleteness of the barrier.

The first state to unify Italy began midway along the west side of the peninsula and expanded in all directions. Until late in Roman history the Po Plain was considered non-Italian territory. The second state to unify Italy began in the Upper Po Plain and moved southeastward. Rome achieved unification under the form of a republic frequently interrupted by dictatorships. Italy of today took form under a constitutional monarchy, but at the first serious crisis representative government was superseded by a dictatorship. Both the parallels and the divergencies between the two Italian unifications emphasize the variety of political evolution possible in an area lacking an outstanding geopolitical nucleus. A comparison of ancient Rome with modern Italy, and of both with the political units dominant during the long periods of disunity, discloses the blocks with which Italian political edifices are constructed.

### ROMAN UNITY

Most of the political units which existed in Italy at the dawn of history, many of which have since then repeatedly announced their political integrity, are inland areas. The coast is ill supplied with harbors, except in a few short reaches. Much of the coastal plain has always been marshy and therefore unsuitable for habitation.

Fig. 46. The Italian Peninsula and adjacent lands, showing the principal physical features that underlie their political character.

The most isolated of all the inland units of the peninsula lies among the southern Apennines (Fig. 46). Originally forested, this somewhat dissected upland culminates in the Sila, a crystalline plateau 3300–3900 feet above the sea, in the " toe of the boot." Secure in their fastnesses, and having no interest in or contact with the sea, the aboriginal mountain tribesmen, chief of which were the Samnites, were conquered by Rome only after many unsuccessful attempts.

The Po Plain is in many ways the antithesis of the southern upland. It is cut off from the peninsula by a well-defined range of mountains, and mountains surround it except on the east, where the river deposits take the form of a delta, uninhabitable without comprehensive drainage works. This region was never thought of by the Romans as part of Italy, although they finally occupied it, when their political technique improved sufficiently to assimilate so large a plain.

The central Apennines divide into two chains, each of which is cleft by streams flowing to the adjacent coast. The moderately fertile central basins are interconnected and adjoin the Samnite highlands by a broad but rugged watershed. The heart of this naturally defended region is the Sabine folk-fortress, a trapezoid lying east of the center of the peninsula between the highest of the Apennines, the Gran Sasso and the Maiella, and the Sabine Mountains, visible from Rome (Fig. 47). The easiest route from sea to sea across the center of the peninsula runs through the heart of the Sabine country, by way of its capital, Rieti. A more direct alternative route joins the first just within the eastern margin of the district, in order to utilize the Pescara Valley to pass through the high Apennines and descend to the Adriatic. On a mountain flank high above this strategic junction a powerful alliance of hill peoples made its capital in a final rebellion against Roman power. In order to have access to the Adriatic Sea and to insure its own safety, every Tiber power should control the Sabine folk-fortress. When not linked to Rome it typically coheres with the Samnite hill-land to the south. The difficulty of amalgamating rugged interior with coastal lowland is seen in the bitter war between the hill people and Rome nearly seven centuries after the founding of the city.

The northern Apennines consist of a single range, swinging in a bow from the Sabine frontier to the Gulf of Genoa. Between them and the Tyrrhenian Sea lies a broken volcanic hill-land, and volcanic masses continue southward to Vesuvius. Whether of limestone or lava, the lower slopes of the mountains are gentle, fertile, and farmed. Along their whole length villages and even small cities early grew up on defense points in the foothills of the Apennines and on dissected

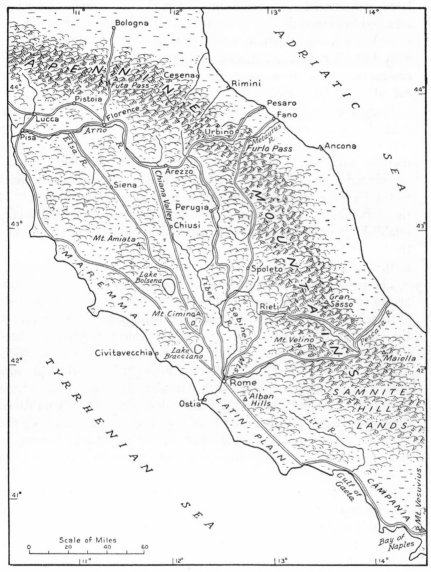

FIG. 47. The geopolitical framework of central Italy.

283

volcanic remnants. North of the Lower Tiber, in the gentle hill-land anciently called Etruria, today Tuscany, these separate but not isolated communities appear to have been akin in origin, and when attacked from outside, readily formed loose alliances of city-states. Although some groups may have arrived from overseas, most Etruscans early lost effective contact with maritime life. Their shore, a wide coastal plain fringed by bars, dunes, and lagoons, discourages access except at the larger river mouths.

Along the inner margin of Tuscany the Tiber river system penetrates deeply, giving to the metropolis of its lower course a line of easy access to and across the Northern Apennines. The main stream can be used by small boats at some seasons. A tributary valley, partially abandoned in an earlier geological epoch, makes an easy roadway direct to the Upper Arno. Hill roads follow high ground on either side of the Tiber itself. Lines of economic and political force perennially establish themselves along these alternative routes, making it relatively easy for Rome to dominate inner Tuscany, the part belonging to the Apennines.

The western section, consisting of hills mainly volcanic in origin, and of coastal lowland, is divided by nature into east-west bands. Two of these barriers are mountain masses, one culminating in Mt. Cimino, the other in Mt. Amiata. The third is the Arno floodplain. In three leaps Rome expanded across this country to the crest of the Apennines. The first pushed the frontier to the rugged hills, then presumably covered with forest, marked by Mt. Cimino, some 35 miles from the city. The second reached the marshy floodplain of the Arno River, difficult to cross and requiring causeways and bridges to insure the communications of an invading army. The third attained the mountains, and put at Rome's disposal several passes to the central Po Plain.

Southward from the Lower Tiber the double chain of the Apennines occupies most of the peninsula's width, and the coastal lowland is only here and there interrupted by hill masses, mostly of volcanic origin. Along this lowland the Romans found their easiest line of expansion, and marked it with their first paved road, the Appian Way. It is separated into two halves by a barrier of hills running to the coast. The northern unit, the marsh-fringed Latin Plain, was Rome's first considerable conquest. Beyond the narrow barrier of hills the Campania, somewhat smaller but more fertile, is punctuated by Mt. Vesuvius, supposed by the early inhabitants to be extinct, like its neighbors to the north. A little to the south the coastal corridor is abruptly blocked by a lofty spur of the Apennines, which juts into the sea as a long peninsula and forces the Appian Way inland. In this vicinity Rome made its first contact with maritime city states of Hellenic foundation, there because of the harbors provided by the ragged coast.

Only four considerable reaches of Italian shoreline are favorable to vigorous maritime life (Fig. 46). Three of these Hellenic colonists occupied before the rise of Rome. The Eastern Mediterranean Basin makes its readiest contact with Italy at the "heel of the boot" — a small, lowlying peninsula that can be dominated from bases on its harbors. Taranto, well sheltered, was the earliest Greek city in Italy. It is supplemented by Brindisi, an island-screened harbor better located for trade but subject to strong winds which at times sweep down the Adriatic, and by minor cities on the Gulf of Taranto. The second Hellenic coast is eastern Sicily, where landing places range from the double harbor of Syracuse, considered ideal by the ancients, to numerous roadsteads in the lee of promontories. Less enduring were trading posts on the other shores of Sicily and on the other Tyrrhenian islands. The third coast occupied by Greek colonies faces the gulfs of Salerno and Naples, at the south end of the Campania. No Hellenic city was established on the Ligurian Gulf, the remaining strip of Italian coastline favorable to maritime flowering.

The three centers of Hellenic life faced outward, and lived by carrying on coasting trade in the Tyrrhenian and Adriatic Seas. They also did a small frontier business with the tribesmen of the interior, and built ships of lumber brought down from mountain forests. Only at the north end did their settlements come into direct contact with any considerable inland area. The Gulf of Naples is the only wide-open sea gate to the Tyrrhenian lowland, although it lies at the south end of the long series of coastal plains which extend in front of the hill-lands of the Samnites, Sabines, and Tuscans. Both the southern and the northern reentrants of the gulf have access to the lowland alongside Mt. Vesuvius. The northern bays, being better protected from stormy winds and closer to the large lowland, developed the more vigorous commercial life. In many respects their commercial cities have been the ports of Rome ever since they were absorbed by the military city of the Tiber.

In this diverse region called Italy — paradoxically a land-minded peninsula with scattered and narrow fringes of marine interests — Rome was implanted. The city-state rose to greatness on its median location, repeated in every order of magnitude, up to the limits of the ancient world. It is on the middle peninsula of the Mediterranean

Sea. It lies about central along the length of the peninsula. It has a middling situation in the volcanic hill-land that comprises the largest and most productive region south of the Po Plain. It lies at the focus of trade routes — up and down the coast, across central Italy to the Adriatic, and up the Tiber Valley and beyond, to the Po Plain (Fig. 46). Protected from pirates by being 18 miles up the Tiber Valley, it was at the beginning a seaport (Fig. 47). When ships outgrew the Tiber, the city constructed successive harbors in the constantly silt-ing mouth of the river. In still narrower terms, it is central on an agricultural plain of modest size (85 by 25 miles maximum dimensions), which, with surrounding hills, provides characteristic Mediterranean arable and grazing land for an energetic rural community.

In spite of conspicuous nodality in terms of natural environment, early Rome was not a political center. The value of the site was apparently recognized by all the surrounding peoples, who strove for its possession and for centuries nullified each other's efforts to capitalize its inherent values. Latins may have occupied the southernmost of the famed seven hills. Etruscan remains have been found on the Palatine Hill, and the Sabines spilled down the Tiber Valley from their inland fastness, as far as the Quirinal, where they built a fortress. Legends have it that men from overseas pushed into the district, fought the Sabines and seized their women, and set their citadel on the defense point provided by the Capitoline Hill. Originally on the left bank, Rome early reached across the Tiber for a hold on the hills which rise opposite the settlement. The boundary against the Etruscans long lay just beyond the bridgehead protected by the Janiculum Hill. The wooden bridge which spanned the Tiber was chopped down in war-time to make the turbulent river a line of defense, as the legend of Horatius suggests.

Rome's reputation as " the eternal city " is founded on its defensible site and a location that never lost its utility as a trade center throughout centuries of economic evolution. At first the city can have been little more than a market town for a small agricultural district; then it grew into a trading focus for central Italy, a mart for the Tyrrhenian Sea, and finally an emporium for the whole Mediterranean. Its site is the place where the Tiber breaks through a ridge of volcanic origin. The ridge is lower than but continuous with the Alban Hills to the south and the lake-filled craters to the north. The celebrated seven hills are in fact left-bank remnants of the ridge carved by the Tiber in crossing it. All stand at about the same elevation: 125–130 feet above the floodplain. Three of them, the Aventine, the Pala-

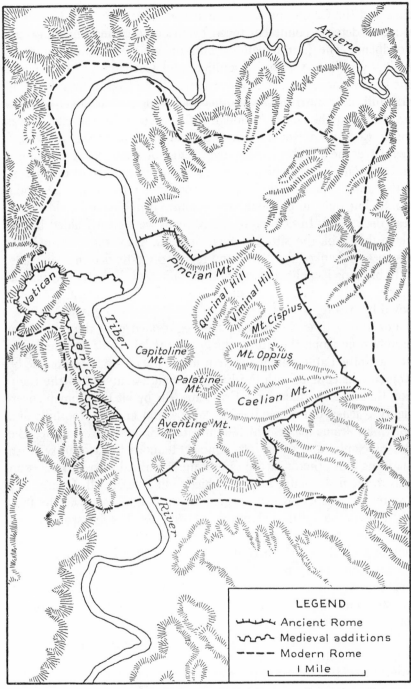

Vatican

Janiculum

Tiber

Pincian Mt.

Quirinal Hill

Viminal Hill

Mt. Cispius

Capitoline Mt.

Mt. Oppius

Palatine Mt.

Caelian Mt.

Aventine Mt.

River

Aniene R.

LEGEND

〰〰 Ancient Rome

〰〰 Medieval additions

- - - - Modern Rome

⊢——— 1 Mile ———⊣

Fɪɢ. 48. Rome and its environs.

tine, and the Capitoline, are isolated and steep-sided heights — their value as defense points enhanced by the original marshiness of the floodplain. The four remaining hills on which ancient Rome was built — Quirinal, Viminal, Esquiline, and Caelian — are tongues of the high ground, projecting into the flat floor of the valley. The Pincian hill, next upstream, is another such tongue, but larger and less severed from the ridge. Although today covered by the city, it was under gardens in Roman times. Similar massive projections stand guard over the right bank of the river. Chief of these are the Janiculum and the Vatican hills, the former being used as an outpost defense by early Rome. The advantages of this focal point for trade were undeniable, but only an energetic and resolute people could hold it and reap the reward. In holding it, the Romans were greatly aided by the defensibility of the site. As their strength grew they drained the marshes, embanked the Tiber, and repeatedly extended the city walls.

In bringing its political sway to the confines of the naturally marked borders of Italy, Rome met and solved each of the critical problems posed by nature.

For a long time the Roman state controlled only the city and a narrow zone along the Tiber, chiefly on the left bank. Its identification with the Latin Plain is apparent in the use of the Latin tongue by Romans. Its contact with the Etruscan country survives in the tradition that its early rulers were Etruscans. Bit by bit the Roman sovereignty reached out along the coastal lowland and the foothills and outlying volcanic masses which dominate it. Southward it touched the Bay of Naples and came into contact, tenuous for a century, with maritime cities there. At the same time it pushed across the Tuscan hills to the first notable heights, which culminate in Mt. Cimino. By a system of alliances Roman hegemony was established over the folk-fortresses of the central and southern Apennines. The first strides across the mountains toward the Po Plain preceded the complete subjugation of both the southern Hellenic coast and the Tuscan hill-land.

The spearhead of penetration lay along the Tiber (Fig. 47). The stream itself was more or less used for trade in the early days, and it was supplemented by the Flaminian Way, which follows high ground some miles east of the river.

From valleys tributary to the Tiber, several passes lead across the Apennines to the narrow lowland along the Adriatic Sea. The primary Roman road reaches the coast at Fano by way of the Furlo Pass, where an early emperor built a tunnel for it, and the Metaurus River, in the valley of which a Roman victory against Carthaginian invaders sealed the doom of Carthage as a rival of Rome. At Fano the highway transforms itself into a coast road. Rimini remained for nearly four centuries Rome's frontier fortress, with lines of communication via alternative passes. The Rubicon is one of the tiny streams a little north of the town, not far from the lagoons which then occupied the flank of the Po Delta as far inland as Ferrara. From Rimini two roads fork. One was built on the offshore bar to Ravenna (Figs. 40 and 49). The other runs the length of the plain at the foot of the Apennines. Roman conquest of the plain was launched from the transmontane base between the Apennines, the Adriatic, and the Po lagoons. As it advanced it was supported by passes leading from the Arno Valley. It was not completed until the Romans had become sea-minded enough to operate against the upper end of the Po Basin through passes based on the Gulf of Genoa. Centuries later, when invading barbarians came sweeping down upon the plain through the eastern Alpine passes, the wedge of land south of the Po Delta long remained a Roman outpost of defense, attested by Ravenna's importance in late Roman history.

The principal political significance of the Po Plain arises from its contact with the world beyond the Alps. Until the folk migrations which marked the demise of the Roman state, no power in North Europe could cope with the combined Alpine barrier and Roman military prowess. The weakest spot in the Italian land border is the head of the Adriatic Sea. There the Alps break down to a karst plateau less than 3000 feet high and approached by valleys the heads of which are separated by only thirty miles of rather level upland. This passway provides the shortest and least elevated transit from Mediterranean sea level to interior lowland to be found between the Dardanelles and the Rhône. As soon as the Po Plain had been conquered, Rome made its base for defense of this partly open gate at Aquileia, at the exact head of the Adriatic Sea. Situated in a marshy district four miles upstream to gain partial protection against pirates, its port has long since been rendered useless by silting. Its successors have been Venice and Trieste. The radial passes which traverse the western and central Alps converge on some point in the Middle Po Plain. No one spot is singled out by nature, and rival cities have striven for supremacy. Milan has been more generally successful than any other place.

Rome's Mediterranean interests reached out chiefly through the maritime coasts which had seen the planting of Hellenic settlements. The springboard to the Eastern Basin is the " heel of the boot." Control of the Waist was then as now linked through Sicily to " Africa," as the Romans knew what is today called Tunisia (Ch. 9).

### FUTILE ATTEMPTS AT REINTEGRATION

Disintegration of the Roman Empire extended to Italy itself, which was scarcely less disrupted than the outlying territories. Throughout the long succeeding ages when Italy lay dismembered, its northern half disclosed almost continuous connections with landpower, while its southern half developed maritime contacts. This characterization can be asseverated in spite of the seagoing cities of the north and the land-minded tribesmen of the southern mountains.

The boundary between the north and the south has shifted from time to time, as boundaries usually do in periods of political flux. On the Tyrrhenian slope it has clung close to the southern end of the Latin Plain, marked by outlying hills behind the Gulf of Gaeta, and including most of the Liri Valley (Fig. 47). During the early centuries of disintegration the line usually continued directly across the peninsula, leaving the Sabine folk-fortress with the north. With the rise of a unified Kingdom of Two Sicilies, comprising the island and the lower part of the peninsula, this critical crossing of the central Apennines was annexed to the south.

Several forces contributed to the differentiation between the north and the south. Many of the folk migrations of different Germanic tribes reached their objective in Italy. Naturally most of these moved across the Alps and left a thinning trace of their blood all the way from the northern Po Plain to the Lower Tiber and even beyond. One group only came to rest in southern Italy, which it reached by way of Spain, North Africa, and Sicily, i.e., overseas. Its contribution to South Italian blood and society must have been slight indeed. Much later seagoing Normans added increments of north European blood to the south, particularly Sicily.

The chaos of the folk migrations was succeeded by similar but more specifically political invasions.

A rejuvenated Eastern Roman Empire endeavored to expand to the Western Mediterranean Basin, particularly to the Italian coast. Byzantine generals repeated the landing of Hellenes 1300 years earlier on the east coast of Sicily. From that foothold they seized, and held briefly, all the maritime sections of coast on the mainland and on the Tyrrhenian islands. Later, Moslems operating from a base on the African side of the Mediterranean Waist, conquered the islands but gained no footing on the peninsula. They were soon thrown back upon Tunisia by Normans, free-lance traders and seagoing adventurers from North Europe. They wrested Sicily from the Moslems, added the peninsular coastlands occupied much earlier by Hellenes, and laid a light rein on the hill folk of the mountainous interior. The foundation of Norman political power, balanced between Sicily and South Italy, was not altered in essence until the unification of all Italy in the 19th century. On it was reared a succession of states originating from and at times subordinate to overseas powers. The region is linked to Iberia by way of the Balearic stepping-stone islands. Several of its conquerors have come from northeastern Spain.

The Moslem conquest of North Africa, by cutting off the south rim of the Mediterranean, deprived Southern Italy of its central position. This handicap reinforced the innate paucity of its resources. It remained a relatively minor factor in the geopolitical structure of divided Italy in spite of its large size, except for occasional flares of economic prosperity. The modest and fleeting fame of its leading cities, Palermo, Amalfi, and Naples, compared to the refulgent renown of contemporary Venice, Genoa, or even Pisa, is a measure of its maritime power. Needless to say it never developed an inland city to compare with Florence, Milan, and half a dozen lesser city-states of the Po Plain and the Tuscan hills.

Political invasions of North Italy were more numerous, more prolonged, and fraught with greater political weight than those of the south. This was natural because the economic stakes were far higher. As Islam closed in on Europe from the southwest and the southeast, only the central section of the Mediterranean coast, from the Pyrenees to the Dalmatian mountains, remained open to trade. Except for the Rhône Valley, the dwindling stream of commerce between Mediterranean and North Europe, and between the Orient and the Occident, was concentrated on North Italy. Economic values of the trade routes became intertwined with political ideals that accentuated intercourse across the Alps and prolonged Italian disruption for centuries.

While Moslems were pushing their way into Europe, the first North European state to master Italy as far as the south end of the Latin Plain and the Central Apennines, drove its sway across the Alps. Under the spell of Charlemagne, this state revived the waning tradition of the Roman Empire. It established its capital in Rome itself, although the strength of the state was derived from North Europe, all of which had been heavily de-Romanized by the folk migrations, and some of which had never been within the Roman realm. Established in an age when most Roman roads had sunk into the mud, when economic pursuits were largely confined to subsistence farming and household crafts, when linguistic divergence was already well marked, Charlemagne's state was fantastically out of harmony with reality. That it soon clove in rough accord with linguistic lines was to be expected. That for a millennium after it had vanished, Central Europeans maintained the fiction of unity, and that for four centuries they strove valiantly to give expression to that fictitious unity in effective political terms, is a tribute to the pertinacity of the human mind, at least when its political objective is reinforced by tempting economic prospects. Until the middle of the 13th century, the imperial successors to Charlemagne's Roman crown worked ceaselessly to subjugate Italy. Because Rome was their prime political objective, the papal rulers of Rome relentlessly fought them back. Little by little the vigor of imperial incursions waned. Repeatedly the aspirants to world empire wasted German wealth and German blood (their only real power being derived from Germany) in fruitless efforts to conquer a country where the summers are hot and pestilential, and the winters bar the routes of access with deep snow. When the emperors finally abandoned the hopeless struggle, they were replaced, after a short interim, by rising national states beyond the Alps and across the northern gulfs of the Mediterranean. For five centuries these foreign interlopers pitted the leading Italian powers against each other or annexed them outright, supported rebellions on the part of restive subject districts, and fought some of their own major wars on Italian soil. Not until the 19th century had more than half elapsed did Italy achieve its second political unification.

Long before Charlemagne seized the crown of the Roman Empire, Rome itself had come under the temporal sway of its bishop, none other than the primate of Latin Christendom, who claimed spiritual authority over all the lands of the revived Roman Empire. The territory temporally ruled by the Papacy was gradually extended, more or less in the pattern set by pagan Rome (Fig. 48). By Charlemagne's time it included the whole Latin Plain, and Tuscany as far north as the heights culminating in Mt. Amiata. Thenceforth, regardless of imperial claims, the States of the Church continued to grow, but only in one direction — up the Tiber and across the Apennines to the southeastern corner of the Po Plain.

The steps in expansion are marked by strictures in the route. Spoleto guards the pass between two Tiber tributaries followed by the Flaminian Way and its medieval successor in preference to the marshy valley of the Tiber itself. Spoleto stubbornly eluded the papal grasp, being by turns capital of a state comprising the ancient Sabine folk-fortress of the Central Apennines, an outpost of Lombard power reaching southward from the Po Plain, and a border city of Tuscany. It did not finally become part of the States of the Church until the mid-14th century. Meantime papal connections to the north were maintained by the alternative route past Perugia, perched on its defense point nearly a thousand feet above the Tiber. Although not annexed to the Papal States until the mid-16th century, as an independent city-state it was traditionally friendly to the papal cause. The narrow Furlo Pass across the Apennines proved an easily blocked route under medieval conditions of warfare, which gave the advantage to defense. However, five alternative pass routes lead across the Northern Apennines to the coast between Ancona and Rimini. The one most used in the middle ages debouched upon Pésaro. By the early 16th century the Papacy possessed an uninterrupted strip of territory which cut Italy in two along a north-south line from the Latin Plain to the mouth of the Po. Ravenna was the real objective of papal expansion. Because of its defensibility among the marshes, it succeeded Rome as the capital of the declining Western Roman Empire. This position it retained under the revived Byzantine authority in Italy, even being made ecclesiastically independent of the pope. By its military strength, its location, and its tradition, it was the natural Italian base of operations for later Holy Roman emperors against the popes. When they gave it up to the Papacy, the imperial cause in Italy was seriously handicapped. By slow accretions lasting over a period of a thousand years, the Papacy acquired a modest temporal domain, occupying the border zone betwen south and north Italy.

During this period dozens of small political units north and west of the States of the Church made an endlessly changing patchwork of alliances and conquests. Not one succeeded in achieving more than moderate size until the 19th century. The fatal fissility of the area inheres in the broken character of its terrain and the lack of a center clearly marked by nature for dominance. Its inherent weakness is accentuated by easy interference from outside, both by way of numerous and well-travelled passes through the Alps and by alternative sea routes from Spain, France, and the non-Italian side of the Adriatic. In the long struggle between medieval emperors and popes and in the succeeding clashes among national states, the North Italian sovereignties were pawns. At the same time they were torn by feuds with each other, generated by local conditions of a complex terrain which gave the leadership to no single political nucleus.

Wars of general European interest, thus superposed on conflicts of local origin and significance, create a confusing tangle of political events in which the Italian city-states appear to change sides with no real reason. As long as emperors were opposing popes, each wooed or intimidated the cities. The emperor's favors included charters of political independence — grants of broad autonomy. Under them the towns having favorable locations for trade and crafts grew into thriving mercantile cities. This wealth the invading imperial troops freely requisitioned when pressed by necessity. Traffic in pilgrims and financing of papal undertakings caused more than one town to prosper. Others, even the proudest, quailed at threat of a papal interdict, with its probable train of proletarian uprisings. More than one deserted the imperial cause when placed beyond the pale of religious comforts. When national rivalries succeeded the imperial-papal controversy, the states of Tuscany and the Po Plain continued to be overrun by foreign armies. This further delayed the slow process of political unification. Yet, although masked by larger European affairs, a degree of unification was occurring, similar to the earlier amalgamations of kindred territory in Iberia, France, Britain, and eastern Germany. Little by little, Florence, Milan, and Venice annexed sufficient territory to rank along with the States of the Church and Two Sicilies as the five chief powers of Italy.

While the States of the Church were slowly being amassed along the east side of the Tiber, the Tuscan country west of the river was embroiled in a confused struggle in which the ideal of Tuscan unity, the local patriotism of the individual city-states and their immediate vicinities, and the titanic wrestling of emperors and popes, all played important parts.

During Roman days the main roads through Tuscany followed low ground so far as possible (Fig. 47). One skirted the coast. Another led across the hills to Chiusi, thence the length of the flat-floored, drained Chiana Valley and into the Arno Valley by a low threshold over which the upper course of the stream once contributed its waters to the Tiber. At Florence the road forked: to the right across the Futa Pass to the Po Plain at Bologna; to the left down the Arno Valley to Lucca and the coast road. With reversion of the land to a state of nature, accompanying Roman political decline and consequent abandonment of artificial drainage, the coastal route became marshy and malarial, and that part of the inland route in the Chiana Valley had to be abandoned for higher ground. Of the two alternative highroads one lies a little west of the Tiber Valley and passes through Perugia and Arezzo. The other tends to follow the crests of the volcanic hill country — past Mounts Cimino and Amiata and the hilltop route-focus marked by Siena. Thence one road leads down the tributary Elsa Valley to the Lower Arno, Lucca and Pisa, and northwest Italy. Others cut across the hill-land to the Middle Arno, Florence and Pistoia, and north and northeast Italy.

These Tuscan roads were the alternative routes followed by successive emperors on their way to coronation at Rome. Because most imperial visits were made at the head of Germanic armies, the pope customarily exerted his utmost power to keep the northerners out of Rome, and even out of Tuscany. When he failed, the Tuscan cities had to take sides. To gain their own ends they frequently shifted from one to the other. Sometimes their adherence was determined by the relative strength of the two claimants to lordship over Western Christendom. It might quite as well originate in local politics.

In the welter of little wars among the rising cities of Tuscany, five early vanquished their lesser neighbors and thenceforth became pitted in the final matches for hegemony. Arezzo and Siena lie in productive hill country, one on either highroad between the Arno and the Lower Tiber. Lucca and Florence, both on the Arno lowland, command the principal roads between that basin and the Po Plain. Pisa, a seaport originally on the Arno near its mouth, was the natural outlet for all the hill-land of northern Tuscany.

In the earlier centuries of the long struggle, the hill-towns, Arezzo and Siena, possessed military advantages over the others, particularly Florence and Pisa. Their strategic sites restricted their economic scope, however, and in time each was forced to assume the defensive against lowland Florence, which finally conquered them.

Forcing its way downstream, Florence, as an interior metropolis with a growing trade, increasingly coveted the maritime business of Pisa. When finally Pisa succumbed, its function as a seaport had nearly played out. Silting of the river mouth and correlative building of coastal sandbars were Pisa's natural enemies. They were greatly aided by human enemies from a jealous, competing, maritime state. Genoa, after defeating Pisa in a naval battle near the end of the 13th century, decreed the construction of a jetty at the Arno mouth diabolically calculated to hasten the building of the bar.

Lucca, somewhat apart in its encircling hills, escaped Florentine domination until almost the moment of Italian unification under other than Tuscan auspices. Long before that event it had ceased to figure as an aspirant to hegemony in Tuscany.

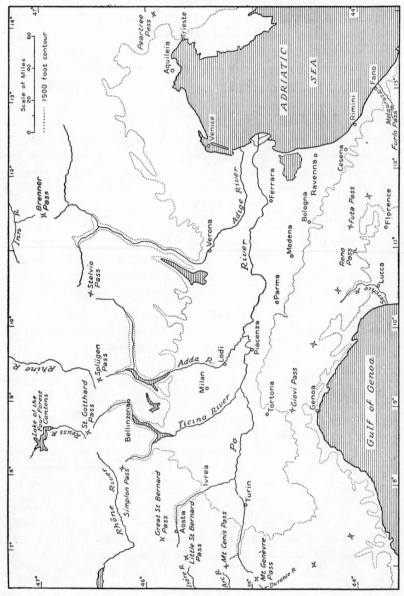

FIG. 49. The Po Plain and its connections.

Florence, by reconstituting the duchy of Tuscany, made itself the most central powerful state in Italy except the States of the Church. Its nodal situation was improved by redraining the Chiana Marsh, thus preparing the way for reconstitution of the lowland route to Rome. The advantage of its central position was not buttressed by a sufficient aggregation of natural resources to make Tuscany notably richer or more powerful than certain of its contemporaries. Moreover, it lies too close to Rome to escape interference from the temporal interests of the Papacy. The intrigues of the emperors were superseded by meddling on the part of French kings. Finally, during the crystallization of Italian national feeling, it survived merely as an appendage of the Austrian royal house.

In all the fighting, whether between papal and imperial forces, or among the national and dynastic powers of Spain, France, and Austria, the Po Plain has been the chief battlefield. It is the highroad between Germany and the Italian Peninsula, and no less between the Rhône Basin and the Middle Danube.

The political pattern of the Po Plain is closely associated with passes through the Alps and the Apennines (Fig. 49). It is the tendency of the Apennines to create cities at the outlets to passes along their northern base. With the breakdown of effective superior authority, each city tended to develop as a state. In time those at the east end were absorbed in the States of the Church, including two important passes. One of these leads to Cesena and Ravenna, the other to Bologna. The latter, the Futa, had been the track for an early Roman road, and today, along with its near neighbor, the Reno, carries the chief rail connection between the Po Plain and peninsular Italy. These passes diverge from the Arno Valley, as do others which cross to city-states farther west that retained their independence until merged into a unified Italy. Beyond Lucca the passes are based on the seacoast. The chief of them leads from Genoa to Tortona, whence routes diverge to Turin, Milan, and Piacenza. Until the 18th century Tortona was politically associated with Milan; since then with Turin.

The leading states of the Po Plain grew up on the Alpine slope, because through the passes of the Alps moved the rich prize of trade and the dire threat of political conquest. As the Alpine passes fall into three groups, differentiated by their character and their articulation with North Europe, so the Alpine alluvial apron is divided among three principal groups of city-states. Embroiled in bitter rivalry among themselves, the cities at the mouths of the numerous passes were likely to be subordinated to city-states farther out on the plain. These cities served fertile reaches of surrounding plain, acted as distribution and collection points for goods crisscrossing the basin, and above all, gathered into their streets the trade of alternative mountain pass routes which focus upon them.

In the whole crescent of the Alps the lowest and easiest, albeit the longest, lie in the east. Because they leave the gate to Italy half unbarred, and because the folk migrations surged westward from East Central Europe, they were the routes most used by invading peoples as soon as Roman legions no longer forbade entrance. Venice was founded as a refuge for Romans driven before the invaders. Among them were citizens of Aquileia, the Roman military outpost set to guard the low saddle at the east end of the Alps.

Many bars off the Po mouth and islands within its deltaic lagoons were occupied much as was Venice, but the settlement on Rialto had the most favorable location for maritime pursuits, on which the refugees had to depend for a living. It faces the most navigable opening between the bars, called significantly enough, the " Gate through the Beach," and south-setting currents deposit most of the silt of the delta-building streams farther south. This situation at the least unfavorable spot of the delta enabled the town to build its corporate fortune on trade. It fell heir to the business between the Eastern Roman Empire and northeastern Italy. In time the trade routes were extended at both ends — to the Levant and North Central Europe.

In this process the lagoon island gradually extended its control over considerable adjacent mainland. Venetian eyes early turned landward to find a suitable supply of fresh water in the streams which debouch into the lagoon. It was found possible to retard the rate of silting in the Venetian waterways by diverting certain of these streams. With the tranquilizing of Italy and the rise of transalpine trade, Venetian interests were drawn farther inland. Verona, at the outlet of the low and easy Brenner Pass, chief route to the Upper Danube Basin, was firmly allied to Venice at an early day, although not formally annexed until the beginning of the 15th century. Medieval Venice also became the successor to classical Aquileia as guardian of the routes across the passes to the Sava Valley and the Middle Danube Plain. Separated from the Apennine slope by the broad marshes of the Lower Po, it held lands south of the river only briefly. Its main avenue of conquest lay to westward on the piedmont plain of the Alps, until finally it took for its boundary the Adda River, only sixteen miles east of Milan.

With decline in transalpine trade after the opening of ocean routes to the Orient, Venice became impoverished. Its aspiration to hegemony over Italy had to be relinquished, and finally it was annexed to Austria. Control of the head of the Adriatic is at least as valuable to the Middle Danube region as to Italy. The location, at any given period, of the political boundary between Italian and Slavo-Germanic states in that quarter is a crude measure of their relative political strength. Venice, the least Italian of Italian states, and in the 19th century the one most effectively subjected to foreign power, was manifestly out of the running as standard bearer in unification of Italy, so long as it remained annexed to a transalpine state. It is more than a striking coincidence that the Austrian ruler of Venetia wore also the crown of the Holy Roman Emperor. The interests of Germany in Italy are perpetual, and nowhere are they so easily converted into political domination as where the Alpine barrier is weakest.

The half-dozen principal passes of the Central Alps converge upon the block of terrain between two Po tributaries, the Ticino and the Adda. Within this area no single spot is notably favored. During the early middle ages Milan and Lodi contested for the trade of the passes, until Lodi was destroyed by its rival. When, later, it was rebuilt on a new site at the Adda crossing, it had lost its opportunity, and Milan has remained the undisputed metropolis of the region. Routes impinge upon it, not only from beyond the Central Alps, but also from Turin, at the outlet of the Western Alps; from Tortona at the northern mouth of the Giovi Pass and from Genoa at its opposite end; and from Piacenza, at the ancient and still principal crossing of the Po. Thence leads the road along the base of the Apennines on which are strung all the cities guarding the passes over into peninsular Italy.

Milan took a leading part in North Italian affairs and in its heyday its domain reached from the crest of the Apennines to the high range of the Alps, where its boundary was marked by the Simplon, Splügen, and Stelvio passes and by the narrows at Bellinzona, outpost of the St. Gotthard. Even Bologna, at the north end of the Futa Pass, and Verona and other cities below the Brenner, were briefly under Milanese control, during the interim between invasions of the Holy Roman emperors and invasions of French kings and Austrian archdukes. Beset on either hand by rival cities of the Po Plain, Milanese territory shrank. Then it lay alternately under the pall of French and Austrian armies, for which its lands were the chief battlegrounds. Thereby it was disqualified to lead the way to Italian unification.

Through the Western Alps two pairs of passes converge upon two focal points in the Upper Po Basin. The southerly pair, leading respectively from the Durance and the Isère valleys, debouch immediately upon Turin. The two northerly, lying on opposite flanks of the Mt. Blanc mass, originate, one in the Valais (Upper Rhône), the other in the Isère. Joining at Aosta, still in the mountains, they reach the plain at Ivrea. Thence the route across the plain is directed by rugged terrain to Turin. In this way Turin is made the undisputed center of the Upper Po Plain, the region which has come to be known as Piedmont. By virtue of the passes, a mountain state which originated north of the Alps gained control of Piedmont. Bit by bit the center of its political interest shifted across the mountains. It expanded eastward at the expense of Milanese territory. Under the cover of Napoleonic arms it reached the Ticino River, only a score of miles west of Milan, and incorporated Genoa on the Mediterranean and, briefly, Parma midway along the Apennine side of the Po Plain.

As a part of France, Piedmont was no more fitted to unify Italy than was Austrian Venice. With the fall of Napoleon, it regained its independence without losing much of its Napoleonic heritage, thanks to which it was, after Two Sicilies, the largest state in Italy. It was far better situated than its southern rival to take advantage of the technological advances of the succeeding decades. With Genoa for a port, a new manufacturing center based on water power from the Alps rising in Turin, and its territory the outlet for several of the busiest Alpine passes, Piedmont was easily the most progressive Italian state. Moreover, all the others were under Austrian influence, except perhaps the papal lands, which lay athwart the peninsula, a political barrier to Italian unity. On its part, Piedmont suffered by standing in the shadow of its French connections, still close because of adjacence and the ancestral holdings of the royal house on the French side of the Alps.

## UNIFICATION OF ITALY

The steps in Italian unification are startlingly reminiscent of the age-old interference of outside forces, including the Papacy, complicated by internal disturbances. The single but momentous difference was the outcome — unity instead of disruption. The geography of Europe had not changed between the mid-18th and the mid-19th centuries, but in the political world the insidious ferment of the French Revolution carried to Italy by Napoleon's conquests, had at last awakened the sense of national patriotism among Italian-speaking folk.

The ground-swell of Italian aspiration to national unity broke as a mighty wave in the northwest and swiftly inundated the whole country. The first step was taken by Piedmont in an attack upon adjacent Austria on the plains of Milanese Lombardy. Because Piedmont was allied with French forces in this war, the clash had the semblance of another chapter in the ancient history of Austro-French rivalry for control of Italy. Instead, it unleashed spontaneous uprisings everywhere. The French government, aghast at the explosive force of nationalism, withdrew at the end of a summer campaign which altered the political map to the extent of transferring the central Po Plain from Austria to Piedmont. Patriotism, once unleashed, refused to down and looked to Piedmont for continued leadership. As the price of French acquiescence in recognizing its annexation of the entire Po Plain except Venetia, Piedmont relinquished to France all its lands beyond the Alps. Retraction of its territory to lands unequivocally Italian cleared the Piedmont government of any suspicion of subordination to France, and adherence of Central Italy followed.

The next year a Piedmontese subject assembled volunteers to aid the rebels in Two Sicilies. His small army sailed from Genoa to island Sicily and thence to the nearby mainland, and once again effected a conquest of maritime South Italy from an overseas base. Thus in the course of two summer campaigns most of the Italian-speaking people of Europe were merged with Piedmont into " Italy." The exceptions were the Austrian holdings in the northeast, and the Patrimony of St. Peter, essentially the ancient papal lands between the Central Apennines and the sea, reaching from the south end of the Latin Plain to the heights of Mt. Amiata.

Rounding out the unified Italian state was incidental to events in those transalpine nations which so long had kept Italy disunified. Austria was compelled to cede Venetia to the new Italian state as a result of its defeat by Prussia, with which Piedmont was allied. This war was a stage in the unification of Germany, being accomplished simultaneously with Italian integration. The Patrimony of St. Peter was annexed to Italy in a succeeding stage of German unification, when French troops were withdrawn from Rome to fight along the Rhine. After that there remained of unredeemed Italian-speaking territory only the outlets to certain Alpine passes and a fringe of islands on the Dalmatian coast. Except for a bit of Switzerland below the St. Gotthard, these fell to Italy as spoils of the World War, in which German states were leagued against France, to which Italy once more adhered.

The capitals of Italy have been three. For five years after Piedmont began its territorial accretions, government continued to be administered from Turin, long the capital of the nuclear Kingdom of Piedmont-Sardinia. Then Florence was made the seat of administration. In fundamental respects it is the most central of the illustrious political cities of the nation. It is situated not far from the areal center, both north-south and east-west. The denser population north of the city offsets the larger area to the south of it. It is a nexus of main routes of transportation, including the main trans-Apennine links. It lies in a small basin among the hills, a location utterly characteristic of peninsular Italy, but only sixty miles from the extensive Po Plain. It is one of three first-rank inland Italian cities, the others being Turin and Milan, both far from central, and traditionally subject to invasion across the Alps.

Despite all the practical advantages of Florence as a national capital for the Italian state, the government was transferred to Rome as soon as that city came under Italian sovereignty. Rome had not been able to avail itself of the currents of life stemming from the Industrial Revolution because it lacks minerals, power, and access to the sea. Its location is central only for peninsular Italy, and the economic core of Italy had moved to the Po Plain with the ever-increasing magnitude of economic operations. Even in agriculture the Roman vicinity suffered by comparison with most other parts of Italy. Its undrained coastal lowland, marshy and malarial, was fit only for summer grazing. Its hills were denuded of trees and deprived of the fertile topsoil which lent them value in classical times. Although not a seaport nowadays, it lies well within the range of heavy guns such as battleships carry. Its glory as the capital of secular empire had long been eclipsed by its effulgence as the seat of Roman Catholic Christendom. The pope still lived at Rome and implacably refused to accept the loss of temporal power forced upon him by Italian arms. All these disadvantages were deemed outweighed by Rome's unique position as the one-time capital of the world. By making it the capital of contemporary Italy, Italian nationalism was confounded with Roman supremacy.

Italian territorial unity was achieved under a temperate constitutional monarchy. Its material integration seemed to be moderately successful until its first crucial test, the World War. The effort then put forth disclosed the state as dangerously weak. The existing government, without being legally modified, was superseded in fact by a dictatorship. This procedure, much like the practice of ancient Rome, led the way to economic and social unification, to match the political unity accomplished two generations earlier. The issue of church and state has been settled by setting up a tiny sovereign " Vatican State" on the left bank of the Tiber (Fig. 48). There the pope is ruler. The rest of Rome is the Italian capital, in which medieval, papal centuries are being rapidly obliterated by the exhumation of remains of ancient secular Rome. The population of the capital city has already surpassed that of the economic metropolis, Milan, and has spread over a large area surrounding the congested quarters of earlier epochs; this although Rome has few factories and no considerable trade. The marshes of the coastal lowland are being drained by the state, and settled with farmers who irrigate and intensively till the reclaimed land. Once again paved roads, as well as railroads, are being built to lead to Rome.

## CHAPTER ELEVEN

# Africa, an Exploitable Continent

WHILE the Mediterranean region from time immemorial has been playing its chameleon role as stimulus to coastal trading powers and magnet to inland military forces, the southern boundary of that region has remained the Sahara, the "Great Desert" — except for the polar icecaps the most formidable and persistent barrier on earth.

## THE SAHARA BARRIER

The Mediterranean fringe of Africa (Fig. 50) has been the seat of some of the earth's most ancient civilizations, societies which succeeded so brilliantly that they passed their enlightenment throughout Europe and beyond, to the "new" continents — North and South America and Australia. Yet to all these more accessible areas the impenetrable bulk of Africa lay unknown and unknowing, except in the most fragmentary way. Throughout history, and again today, whenever the Mediterranean coastlands of the African continent have been drawn into the orbit of Mediterranean life, geopolitical Africa unquestionably begins at the Sahara. When the Moslem power from desert Arabia spread westward on the heels of the camel, North Africa ceased for centuries to belong to the European, Mediterranean world, but it did not draw appreciably closer to trans-Saharan Africa, which remained a world apart — Black Africa.

To be sure, goods and tales occasionally percolated across the barrier from earliest times. Presumably they moved in both directions, but because Black Africa has always been content to keep to itself, only those moving northward tantalized human curiosity to any purpose. Some think that legends of the lost Atlantis may refer to elevated parts of West Africa at a time (for which geologic evidence exists) when the lower-lying lands were submerged beneath shallow seas. Certainly Carthage penetrated to the oases which fringe the southern base of the Atlas, and even as far as Fezzan, the most accessible of the interior oases. At that period oxen and horses were used for transport, and a few goods moved between the Libyan coast and the Sudan, by short stages from one independent group to another.

In Egypt the Nileway was a standing challenge to exploration and explanation, because the Nile water, sole foundation of Egyptian life, obviously came from somewhere. Yet even there the barriers proved insuperable. The desert country traversed by the Nile as it leaps rapids after rapids in its sinuous, gorge-bound course above

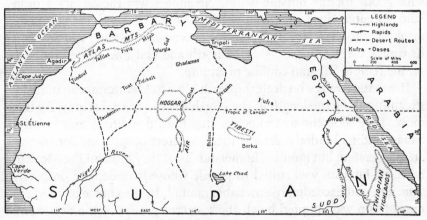

FIG. 50. The Sahara barrier.

Wadi-Halfa, the cliff-like scarp of the Ethiopian highland, the impenetrable tangle of vegetation (sudd) blocking the White Nile in its marshy expanses — all combined to keep communication near the vanishing point. Only by way of the Red Sea did the Egyptian world of antiquity reach beyond these barriers to find the gold of Ophir (perhaps Rhodesia or some other part of East Africa).

Through the long life of the Western Roman Empire, its unquestioned southern boundary remained the Sahara — a lifeless waste inhabited in only a few spots and there by peaceable Negroes whose lack of mobile transport chained them to their respective oases. Then the camel was introduced from Egypt, where it had been used for several centuries. This revolutionized the central and western Sahara by instituting trans-Saharan camel caravan routes, populating some oases for the first time, and in oases already occupied gradually substituting white Africans from the north for the aboriginal black Africans. The political structure of the region altered with the new economic and social status introduced by the redoubled range (i.e., increased speed) of transportation. Many oases became way stations on caravan routes laid out to obtain salt, antimony, ostrich plumes, and the few other products of the desert. Occasional camel trains traversed the three or four trans-Saharan routes. All this was negligible, however, compared to the rise of nomadic tribes, sustained by herds of camels, which could subsist for a part of the year on the scattered herbage of the steppes of the interior highlands, and along the wadis which carry off their rare but torrential desert rains. Rendered mobile by their camels, these intruders made themselves lords of the oases as well as the steppe and levied repeated tribute on every passing caravan laden with goods for the outside world. No longer was the Sahara a dead land, valuable alone as a fixed political boundary zone. It became an insoluble problem for the Byzantine successor of Rome, which, from its capital on the Bosporus, faced north and east and turned its back on the remote Saharan confine of empire.

It was the Arabs who dealt the death blow to Mediterranean unity by streaming along the length of the North African coastal steppe. By this move, they took the first effective step toward political unity of the Sahara and its borderlands. For them, a desert people, the Sahara was an exaggerated, but familiar, homeland. To it they brought the Moslem faith, its fatalism well suited to people whose lives depend on barely sufficient and exceedingly unreliable rainfall. In the course of a millennium Islam was adopted by all the scattered groups of the desert and by nearly all of the more numerous peoples of the Sudan, which may be thought of as low-latitude steppe, and hence not too unlike the desert to accept desert ways. Again and again large areas of the central and western Sudan have been integrated into short-lived states, each of which has been created with reference to control of one or more of the lucrative Saharan trade routes. The capitals of several of these states lay along the plane of contact between the Sudan and the Sahara, especially where the great bend of the Niger thrusts a loop of navigable water into the desert itself (Fig. 51).

The distribution of these states and the routes and resources they controlled makes a fascinating story of the political geography of the past. Some of them existed at the time of the European conquest of the Sudan, and formed the groundwork on which was built " indirect rule," that useful and significant method of current colonial administration (pp. 384 ff.). This conquest, however, was based on the nearby sea, and not on remote North Africa, and had to wait fifteen centuries after the camel had reached the western Sahara. As long as the only feasible route to the Sudan lay through Saharan wastes, that threshold remained so formidable a barrier that it was crossed only a few times a year, despite the enduring penetration of the Moslem faith, and the political unities which grew out of religious uniformity. Until almost the end of the 18th century interior Black Africa remained unknown to the people of Europe, except in the guise of fantastic yarns. The Sahara itself, however vexing it may be to sedentary peoples

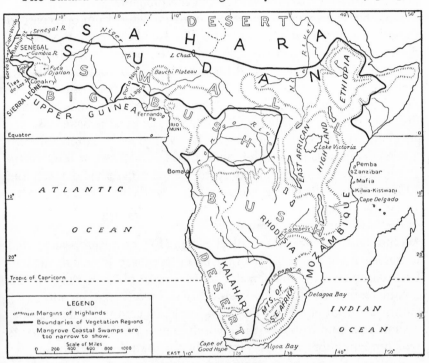

FIG. 51. Black Africa.

along its borders, has never successfully unified itself. Resources are so meager and so uniform that no basis for commercial reciprocity within the desert exists, apart from the commensal life imposed by nomads of the highlands upon circumjacent oasis farmers. The vast unpeopled spaces prevent cohesion between dispersed social groups; indeed, the result is to engender hostile rivalry for domination of the caravan trails, the only place where they are likely to meet. Because of its scanty resources and unreliable production, the Sahara has perennially been a region of dispersal. This produces the settlements of desert folk in Barbary and the intermittent filtration of Saharans into the Sudan. On both margins of the desert the extruded people long remain distinct. Some play political roles, notably the Fulani, many of whom live as nomadic cattle-herders commensally with sedentary Negro farmers, while others have made themselves masters of Sudanese populations.

## THE BARRIER COAST

If the Sahara has cut Black Africa off from the shortest line of contact with Mediterranean civilizations, combinations of natural barriers have made access from the sea scarcely less difficult.

No other continent stretches an unbroken desert from one coast to the other across its greatest breadth. The Red Sea route athwart this desert, although known from ancient times, never ceased to plague mariners compelled to depend on the wind for propulsion (Ch. 9). The Saharan west coast is without a satisfactory harbor from Agadir to Port Étienne, places nearly 10° of latitude apart. For an even longer distance, from Cape Juby to Cape Verde, the coast is waterless, and generally fringed with sanddunes. The average daily temperature increases as one sails toward the south. Little wonder that it took Portuguese mariners a quarter century to pass the desert and reach the " Green Cape," even with the aid of the most skilled of Italian navigators, the advice of foremost European geographers, and the patronage of the Portuguese royal family.

Once fairly on the coast of Black Africa (Fig. 51), Europeans found it scarcely more accessible than the desert approach, although the natural resistance varies in character from place to place. Because of this invulnerability Africa has remained the Dark (i.e., self-contained) Continent until our own time. As a whole, its compact bulk presents a short coastline to the outside world, devoid of major embayments which might afford easy penetration by sea toward the center.[1]

In detail, the coastal margins are repellent, especially to Europeans. Along all of Guinea, hard-won footholds were repeatedly given up in despair. The coast earned the sinister sobriquet " White Man's Grave." The first of the barriers met by inquisitive seafarers are the tornadoes, sudden and violent, at the beginnings and ends of the rainy periods. These enhance the danger from the treacherous currents and the still more treacherous submerged rocks along the coast. Even where there are no hidden reefs there is the eternal surf, passable only in small boats and at the risk of drowning. Most of the streams cannot be entered even by small seagoing ships, because the surf maintains shallow, shifting bars across their mouths. The Gambia alone opens an easy water

---

[1] The ratio of coastline to area of the several continents is as follows:
Africa — 1 mile to 1420 square miles.
South America — 1 mile to 689 square miles.
Australia — 1 mile to 534 square miles.
Asia }
Europe } Eurasia — 1 mile to 763 square miles.
              1 mile to 289 square miles.
North America — 1 mile to 407 square miles.

route into the land, and it leads to a sandy, semi-arid country. The only other ready harbors are Sierra Leone and the Congo estuary, locked by mountains which block easy movement inland, and the sandspit harbors south of the Congo, lacking articulation with natural lines of ingress.

Once through the barriers interposed by the ocean, intrepid pioneers found themselves pent in by the appalling verdure of the rain forest, a forest partly amphibious, growing out of lagoon and delta as well as terra firma. A forest in which even the farms look like more jungle. In it lurked human enemies, their black faces indistinguishable in the forest gloom, equipped with spears and poisoned arrows. But more destructive than all these patent enemies were the unrecognized water-borne destroyers — dysentery in the drinking water; malaria, black-water fever, yellow fever, and sleeping sickness hatching on the surface of stagnant pools or in the undergrowth along the streams.

The east coast is hardly more accessible than the west side. In the north forbidding desert warns off prospective settlers. South of the Equator mangrove swamps line much of the shore, and only the deltaic Zambesi affords lines of penetration, shallow and shifting.

In spite of these obstacles, trade, the siren, kept luring to their doom Portuguese, Spanish, Dutch, French, British, even Danes and Brandenburgers. This trade was the most lucrative ever known, as sinister as the dank forest itself, because along with gold, ivory, and pepper grains, its chief item was slaves. For many years the captains dropped anchor where best they might, be it outside the surf or within one of the rivers where the bar permitted, and traded with natives who came on board. By limiting the size of the group admitted and by administering prompt and terrible retribution for any show of insubordination on the part of the visitors, the ships' crews warded off their human enemies. By staying on the water they reduced somewhat the number of insect visitants. But this sort of desultory trade was tantalizing. The next step was to moor hulks of dismantled sailing vessels at favored points to which natives might come to chaffer at their own convenience and repeatedly. The " captain " of the hulk still carried on the business, and in much the same fashion as his intermittent predecessor, the captain of the sailing vessel. When visited by a ship from the outside world, he transferred his collection of African goods and restocked with gewgaws, cotton cloths, squarefaced bottles of gin, cowrie shells, and manillas.[1]

[1] Manillas are copper bars of varying sizes, bent into the shape of a horseshoe, which superseded cowrie shells from India as a medium of exchange and are still so used in remote villages. From their form they are believed to be descendants of copper rivets taken from hulls which broke up on the coast, but from early time they were made for the trade in English foundries.

From anchored hulks to trading stations on the shore was an inevitable step. By this time European ships were plying regularly to India, and footholds were precariously established all the way from desert on the west to desert on the east. These stations were generally walled compounds housing the European traders and their African servants, and serving as transit warehouses for trade goods, including slaves. The passions engendered by slaving, both in the native societies and among the competing nationals of European states, made terra firma a danger zone for those who profited from the trade. Many of these early land stations were appropriately called castles, for they were built of bricks or stones brought to the coast as ballast and in form resembled medieval European castles, complete to crenellations, moats, and drawbridges. But their dungeons housed slaves awaiting shipment overseas, instead of prisoners of war. Other stations, less ambitious, consisted of simple but strong walled compounds to enclose the stores and the slave prisons.

Even those strongholds which proved exempt by virtue of their stout architecture from successful attacks by men, suffered unabated the onslaughts of insects and bacteria. Although the cause of the persistent coast scourges was undetermined until the turn of the 20th century, men early recognized their association with low and wet sites. For this reason, as well as for defense, wind-swept promontories were prized. Such are the wave-cut cliffs along Gold Coast and southeast Africa, and the sandy spits formed by the strong current which sets northward from the Cape of Good Hope to near the Congo mouth. The sandspits also afford shelter from the southwest, the direction from which most storms approach that coast. Behind the promontories lie open roadsteads in which surf and storms are slightly diminished. This is especially true of the several cases where wave-cut, undersea platforms mark the roots of vanished cliffs and break the force of the waves.

Slightly less convenient for trade, but more easily occupied and defended, were rugged offshore islands. Unfortunately, the smooth African coastline provides few such islands. Gorée, three miles out but in the lee of Cape Verde, Conakry (before it was tied to the mainland by a causeway) and the other volcanic îles de Los which splay out from a narrow peninsula on an otherwise swampy foreshore, a group of islets off Rio Muni, Mozambique, with its coral islets two miles out at the mouth of a shallow bay, and Kilwa-Kissiwani just offshore with a reef-protected harbor, are the only ones ideally located. Fernando Po, Zanzibar, Pemba, and Mafia, 20 miles or more at sea, are too remote to be serviceable as native trading stations, although Zanzibar and Fernando Po have been entrepôts. Nevertheless, these islands, as well as those closer in, provided favorable seats for the establishment of political power. At times the island ports have been capitals of vaguely defined but occasionally extensive authority on the mainland coast vis à vis. The Spanish held their islands in the Gulf of Guinea a century before they made good their claim to Rio Muni on the mainland, and insular Fernando Po remains the seat of administration for mainland, as well as islands. Control of Senegal accompanied the transfer from hand to hand of Gorée, and the island was one of the two foci from which effective French occupation of the mainland spread after the mid-19th century. More than once Mozambique has been the only bit of territory retained by Portugal in East Africa, and from it as a nucleus has grown the present colony, often called Mozambique in unconscious tribute to its origin. As early as the 10th century emigrant Arabs were in control of the islands and mainland coast of equatorial East Africa. Their capital was Kilwa-Kissiwani, near the south end of their long strip of coast, but enjoying insular protection and adjacence to the mainland. Arab rule was rejuvenated in the early 18th century with the island of Zanzibar as the seat of government, and rose to the rank of an independent state for a generation in mid-19th century. An Arab proverb has it that " When you play on the flute at Zanzibar, all Africa as far as the lakes dances." The claim of the Sultan of Zanzibar to suzerainty on the mainland was not extinguished until European powers began to partition the continent in earnest toward the end of the 19th century.

In time several of these prized insular springboards became relict properties of states which had lost their claims to the adjacent mainland. Zanzibar (with Pemba), although under British guidance, is to this day ruled by its hereditary Sultan; it was not transferred from the British Foreign Office to the Colonial Office until a quarter century after the mainland had been handed over to Italy, Britain, and Germany. On the west coast, the îles de Los remained British 60 years after the mainland became incontestably French. Portugal retained its hold on Fernando Po more than a century after it had lost all its nearby mainland settlements.

Conspicuous as has been the part played by offshore islands in the geopolitical evolution of Africa, they have been superseded by settlements more closely articulated to the mainland. These include the cliffed promontories and sandspits already mentioned. Yet on the whole the most lucrative trading sites have been at the mouths of large rivers, and most of them debouch either through mangrove fringed deltas or into lagoons behind sandbars. Islands of the delta mosaics and bars between ocean and lagoon were therefore commonly utilized for stations in spite of their unhealthfulness. Many of them have been abandoned at times, and some permanently, but others have hung on in the face of the heavy odds. The swampy islands at the mouth of the Geba remained in Portuguese hands when trade rivals took all its other West African territory. The capital of Portuguese Guinea is today on one of these islets. A succession of stations on islands fringing the Niger and Zambesi deltas has bloomed and withered with the alternation of channels carrying sufficient water to sweep the bar. Bars between quiet lagoon and boisterous ocean furnish sandy and lightly forested sites for trading posts, most of which lie opposite the mouths of small streams which are navigable for canoes. With rare exceptions trading stations on delta islands and bars have assumed no political functions, perhaps because their ephemeral nature has been recognized.

The river-mouth posts which have the advantage of easily navigated estuaries are few. Chief among them is the Congo. There Boma, the most accessible harbor in the estuary, was the seat of administration until a decade ago. In the Gambia Bathurst, on an island seven miles upstream, remains the political capital of the colony.

Whether the administration was centered on an offshore island, on a comparatively healthful promontory or spit, or on a sandbar or deltaic fragment, the interior remained effectually hidden from the short-term traders and officials who tenuously occupied the coast.

For three centuries Africa remained for Europeans a long line of land that must be circumnavigated in order to reach the Orient and its wealth — a line punctuated with precarious footings where ship's companies could replenish their water supply and perhaps obtain a few fresh provisions to vary the monotonous ship fare and combat scurvy. (The Portuguese have left informing traces of this practice en route to and from their chief Indian possession, Goa, in the names of two bays — Algoa and Delagoa.) Wherever they could, these way stations built up trade in African products as well. Goods were brought down from the secretive interior on foot, either in headloads of about 60 pounds each, or as consignments of slaves.

In the course of 350 years of European wars and as incidents in the rise to nationhood of successive European states, this long line of African coast changed hands many times. To study the kaleidoscope of political suzerainty would serve only to bring out a few facts of geographic significance, which may better be stated at once.

1. Each European state with colonial ambitions has tried to satisfy those ambitions on the African coast.

2. States like Sweden, Denmark, and Brandenburg, crippled by weak home bases, have long since given up the struggle and retired from the field.

3. Portugal, Spain, and Holland, once mighty colonial powers but handicapped by paucity of resources at home, have seen the magnificent ribbons of their onetime claims reduced to scattered patches. (The Dutch influence, indeed, is confined to the political attitudes of the Boers, long under British rule.)

4. Before interior Africa became known to the outside world, nearly all the most lucrative strips of coast had fallen into the hands of either Britain or France.

5. While claims to the coast were still vague and boundaries were undetermined, the newly consolidated national states of Europe — Germany, Belgium, and Italy — made demands for slices of the colonial melon.

Except in the far south, most of the African coast south of the Sahara is fringed with " big bush." This is the dense, tall forest of the lands of unending heat and rain, supplemented along much of the coast by mangrove swamp, an amphibious zone affording neither anchorage nor landing place. Powerful oceanic currents and heavy surf pick up silt brought out by streams, pile it across their mouths, and so render the rivers useless as natural harbors. Currents and waves have turned long reaches of the coast into harborless beaches and bars. Here and there a sandspit encloses a small bit of quiet water, and in a few places the extraordinarily regular land line is broached by a structural indentation of larger size, affording uneasy anchorage but lacking ready contact with the interior. Natural access to the interior is confined to streams, the ideal havens for disease-bearing mosquitoes and flies. Except for the streams of Upper Guinea, and the Zambesi River, all tumble off the central plateau a few miles from the coast, and are therefore useless as avenues for penetration of the interior. When it is remembered that to these natural difficulties, the Europeans added the bitterness of constant pillaging for slaves, it is not surprising that exploration of the interior was long delayed.

The natives of the big bush themselves were not accustomed to traverse the narrow but overmastering band of verdure which stretched between the sea and the more open interior. Slaves and other produce were obtained by coastal tribes, who acted as middlemen, from groups farther inland, who raided their neighbors for slaves, or bartered for goods which changed hands several times in moving across the big bush. Each of these tribes occupied only a small part of the land to which it laid claim. Insulated from its neighbors by the all-encompassing forest, it lived chiefly by shifting its crudely cultivated plots every two or three years onto the virgin soil of the tall forest. It developed its own language, its own customs. Except for salt and fish, it required little from the outside world. The sea, the lagoons, the lakes, and the streams were used rather for warpaths than for trade routes. This separatism is enhanced by the ideal quality of the big bush as a refuge area for peoples driven out of more vulnerable homes in open country. The African big bush contains great diversity of physical types, from pygmies to true Negroes. Yet, regardless of their social origin, the tribes of the big bush follow the simple and disparate mode of life exacted by the extreme environment in which they find themselves. Thus they gave the Europeans who managed to seize bits of the coastline no native organization which could be impressed into the service of opening up the interior.

### THE STUBBORN INTERIOR

Equatorial rains carry the big bush across the Inner Congo Basin, and are largely responsible for making it the last of the large African river basins to be explored and opened to occupation by European traders and governments (Fig. 51).

In the southwestern part of the continent deserts and mountains discouraged penetration, although the barrier is by no means so awkward as the Sahara. The parched zone extends only halfway across the continent, lying as a patch along the west coast. Also unlike the Sahara, it is not a center of dispersion. Instead it is a refuge area for some of the most primitive tribes of Africa. These people still subsist by collecting and gathering nature's store, and never offered a serious threat to European encroachment. Nevertheless, their country is so unproductive that it presented a knotty problem to Europeans who might wish to traverse it. This problem was solved first by small groups of Boers who turned nomads in order to survive.

Between the deserts, north and south, and the big bush of the Congo are the vast reaches of " small bush " which make up the bulk of Black Africa. This is country beaten by torrential downpours during a season of rains lasting from two to six months, followed by unremitting drouth during the rest of the year. Coarse grasses spring up green with the rains and turn yellow and harsh during the drouth. In places the grassy savanna presents long vistas unbroken by trees except along water-courses. More commonly it is studded with trees, mostly low, some of them thorny. They may be either scattered about, to give the impression of a park, or knotted in clumps and thickets. The character of the vegetation varies broadly with rainfall. Locally it is much affected by altitude, by slope, by exposure to wind and sun, by ground water, and possibly by soil. Big game abounds in most of this country, consisting as it does of open grassy plains alternating with bush which affords every degree of cover and varied herbage as well. Here, as elsewhere in Black Africa, the indigenes have adapted their life to an exigent natural environment. In the driest small bush may be found nomads who subsist entirely on their herds of humped cattle, fat-tailed sheep, or short-legged goats. Throughout much of the Sudan, and in places on the East African Highland, tribes of nomads pasture their animals on the range during the green season, and by arrangement with sedentary inhabitants of the country turn them onto stubble fields during the drouth. These settled peoples take advantage of high elevations, slopes facing the rains, a high water table, or friable soil, to farm such of the land as will yield a living to the tiller of the soil. In most places shifting cultivation is practiced, but on especially favored locations crops can be and are grown year after year.

Lacking the protection afforded to wet-land farmers by the big bush, these cultivators in the small bush have learned to maintain their independence of the nomads by building mud-walled cities or thorn-enclosed villages, and by maintaining fighting forces. In many tribes nearly the whole adult male population is enrolled in the army, the farm work being left to the women and children. The tribes compelled to shift their farms every few years have remained small. Each group requires territory enough to accommodate several removals to fresh soils. The large tracts of fallow land segregate the tribe from neighboring groups, who are known only as potential enemies. Had all of the small bush been inhabited by such small, wide-spaced tribes, Europeans would have found the inhabitants easier to subjugate than has proved to be the case.

Where nature has been generous, the small bush has seen the rise of indigenous states which could muster considerable military and political strength. Sedentary farming tribes have sometimes found themselves close enough together to form alliances. More commonly the most favored or the most capable have been able to conquer weaker neighbors. The small bush may be easily traversed in all directions during the dry season. This gives to a strong military force scope for conquest. At the same time, there are very few naturally marked frontiers within the small bush. Hence it is difficult to maintain a military state with stable boundaries. Over the centuries large political units of the African small bush have recurrently risen and fallen, coalesced and subdivided. Presumably no two have ever had exactly the same boundaries, and rarely has any one site become the political capital of more than a single state, although it may go on through the centuries as a commercial center of some importance. Yet repeatedly one or another powerful group has wielded formidable military force. Cultural conformity has marched with political unification. In a number of cases unity of culture has supplemented uniformity of nature in laying the foundation for a rising state. This has been conspicuously true of Islam, wherever it has gone, and probably also of Ethiopian Christianity. Indeed, most students of African history accept the premise that the powerful indigenous states were organized by outsiders, chiefly Moslems from the Sahara or Arabia. This can be proved for certain empires which grew up in the Western Sudan at the end of the 18th century, and it may account for the fighting qualities of the 19th century "Fuzzie-Wuzzies" of the eastern Sudan. However, it is not proved that earlier Sudanese states of equal scope may not have been of Black African origin. The highly organized kingdoms of the hilly country west and south of Lake Victoria (Fig. 51), and the vigorous Zulu tribes which for a century gave pause to the settlement of South Africa were neither Mohammedan nor Christian. The one thing certain is the fact that every well-organized state in Black Africa sprang out of favorable natural conditions.

The leading native states of the East African Highland occupied the best spots of that entire region. Contrary to common belief, much of the high country, especially in Tanganyika and Northern Rhodesia, is limited by drouth to nomadic occupance. In contrast, the major highland of Ethiopia receives rain over a long enough period to assure the growth of crops as well as forage for stock. Much of it is high enough to stand well within the temperate high-altitude climates which have been so significant a factor in the geopolitical character of Latin America (Ch. 13). Finally, it is set apart from the rest of Africa by precipitous escarpments. On the seaward side, presumptively accessible to outsiders, the isolation is enhanced by a band of exceptionally torrid desert. Internal unity and isolation from the outside world have combined to give Ethiopia a political organization more effective than that of other parts of Black Africa. Quite likely this has been true for some thousands of years. The states of the high and hilly country between

Lake Victoria and the Western Rift Valley (outlined by the line of long, narrow lakes), have benefited chiefly by favorable distribution of rains falling on arable slopes in an altitude conducive to vigorous health. Less sharply cut off from the outside world than Ethiopia, they have created three or four political (tribal) units, none of which has been able to dominate the others.

The warlike inhabitants of the South African Highland occupied the best country on the continent — country of every climatic gradation from humid subtropical to semi-arid. Much of it lies outside the zone of the tsetse fly and even malaria is absent at the highest levels. Moreover the natural vegetation provides pasturage more nourishing than that of the low-latitude savannas. When these tribes were faced by Europeans making their way inland from the Cape of Good Hope, they had not yet completely settled the productive High Veld. Actually they were in process of pushing the earlier inhabitants off the better lands. The impetus of their drive against Hottentot and Bushman may have given them extra power when they turned against Boer and Britisher. In any event, they worked from a productive base, a fulcrum which gave maximum leverage to their human force.

The dozen or more recorded states which at one time or another waxed powerful in the Sudan are not related to any such obvious advantages of the natural environment as have been listed for those of eastern Africa. Yet advantages they had. Notwithstanding its superficial uniformity, the Sudan is a varied region in which arable tracts alternate with dense bush or reaches of sand. Although the reasons for the distinction are not fully understood, it seems likely that arable land is associated with high level of the ground water table. Where the arable tracts are large enough to support a considerable population, powerful tribes have thrived. Some of these, aided by a considerable degree of isolation, have forged for themselves mighty military names without actually becoming states of the first rank. This is notably true of the groups occupying the dry margin of the Sudan between Lake Chad and the Nile. Others, located between Lake Chad and the Senegal River, have made themselves major African powers. Generally they have accomplished this by establishing political domination over a number of arable tracts and the matrix of grazing country in which the farmland is set. Most, if not all of them controlled one or more trade routes into or across the Sahara and into the big bush.

Although refuge districts are not so common in the small bush as in the rain forest, they do exist. Most characteristic are small and isolated highlands, such as the Bauchi Plateau of Nigeria, the Futa

Djallon of French Guinea, one or two spots in East Africa, and Basuto-land in South Africa. Either too high or too low to possess a climate superior to that of surrounding lands they also lack favorable soil. Their one value is their isolation. This derives from the precipitous and wooded slopes and escarpments which set each highland off from surrounding country. Steep, wooded hills make awkward, if not impassable, barriers for the tribes of horsemen who from early times have been the agents of political integration in most parts of the small bush. Because the tribes which take refuge in regions so ill-favored by nature are usually too weak and poverty-stricken to endanger the encompassing powers, they have generally been let alone. Minor types of refuges include marshy expanses and secluded valleys.

It has long been the practice of harried Africans to withdraw into thickets and into the edge of the big bush, to escape temporary persecution. Formerly, and until the present time in Ethiopia, the object was to escape enslavement, or impressment as gatherers of rubber and other forest products. The same trick has often been played upon the tax-collector, who might enter a village in perfect repair and with warm hearths but containing not a vestige of movable property.

Slavery is endemic in Black Africa, and widely practised by most, if not all tribes. Nevertheless, it rose to critical levels only with the evolution of powerful states which could turn their military forces from conquests in which enslavement was incidental, to forays for the purpose of seizing slaves. Slave-raiding presumably resulted in the creation of special refuge areas before the appearance of Europeans south of the Sahara.

Bushmen who now carry on their primitive life by collecting such meager products as the Kalahari Desert affords, appear to have been driven from better land by the onrush of Hottentots and Bantu from the northeast. The Hottentots themselves had been driven into the dry southwest of the continent before the earliest European settlers arrived there. Both these peoples, weak at best, were shattered by being forced into the most barren part of the continent south of the Sahara, and proved amenable to the demands of the Boer settlers, even when they were enslaved.

A much farther-reaching movement in pursuit of refuge occurred in several places along the inner margin of the big bush, particularly in Upper Guinea. After the Sudanese empires had readily forced their rule upon unsheltered peoples of the small bush, some took refuge in the big bush rather than submit, thus depopulating considerable areas along the southern margin of the Sudan. This incited the powerful rulers of the north to encourage slave raids into the big bush, from which they drew a steady stream of human chattels, not only for their own use, but also for shipment to Barbary, Egypt, Arabia, and the whole Mohammedan world. As a defense against these raids a number of tribes in the edge of the big bush defended themselves in compact cities, each surrounded by a ring of gardens, the whole protected by a mud wall. This, identical with the system of defense in vogue among the Sudanese empires, went hand in hand with a political solidarity rare in the big bush. After Europeans arrived on the Guinea coast and instigated slave raids to supply labor for American plantations, these same tribes found themselves beset from the south as well as from the north. This only stiffened their resistance, and perhaps lifted their military organization to new peaks. Much later, after the sea-borne slave trade of the Occident had been abolished, this line of powerful military states for some time blocked the movement of European armies from the coast to the Sudan, by engaging in repeated wars against all comers, particularly the British and French. The size of colonies shown on a present-day political map of this part of Africa is partly a result of the military refuges established in the landward edge of the big bush. However, a remark of one of the bravest of the warring chieftains points to the basic cause of his success. He said: " The bush is stronger than the cannon of the white men."

## THE PATTERNS OF VEGETATION AND INDIGENOUS LIFE

He was wrong, as events of the succeeding decades proved, but for four centuries before his time ( the 1860s) the white men's cannon had blazed away in vain efforts to penetrate the unyielding borders of low-latitude Africa. When Europeans finally did crash through the shell which had so long resisted their best efforts, they found an indigenous society affected only here and there by influences from beyond Black Africa.

This society conformed with striking fidelity to the pattern of natural vegetation. Its great subdivisions were the desert, the big bush, and the small bush.

In the deserts widely spaced hamlets of farmers hugged the oases from which they drew their sustenance. In the Sahara, these sedentary groups were politically subservient to neighboring nomads whose homes were the highland steppes. In the deserts of the southwest backward tribes found refuge from the onslaught of more vigorous peoples, and in the parts verging toward steppe, Bushmen collected such a living as nature provided. The political role of African deserts has been negative, except as the Sahara permitted trickles of Moslem culture to reach the Sudan.

The big bush was scarcely more populous than the least arid districts within the deserts. Except for the dense populations recently impacted in inner Guinea, the denizens of the deep forest lived in small and discrete tribes, each largely self-sustaining on a simple diet derived from forest, garden, and stream or sea. Each looked upon its neighbors, known to exist beyond a wide belt of virgin timber and cutover jungle, as enemies, or as a possible source of slaves (to use or to sell). The big bush, abetted by terrors of rugged terrain, disease-laden insects, and human hate, long delayed penetration to the interior by outsiders, whether from the Indian Ocean or the Atlantic.

Much of Africa belongs to the category of small bush — the most varied and on the whole the most productive of the vegetation realms of the continent, and including the major highlands as well as much lowland. There modest resources permitted the evolution of political organizations more advanced than those of desert or big bush. The absence of barriers brought neighboring tribes into close contact. Easy communication made conquest an obvious objective, and stimulated the rise of military states, organized either to expand by force or to resist the expansion of ruthless neighbors. Because the small bush varies in character from place to place, regions favored by nature saw a succession of powerful states which dominated surrounding regions less easily defended or too poor in resources to match the military strength of their conquerors. Stories of the prowess of the more conspicuous inland states reached the outside world, which had no real measure of their force, and was by turns awed and tantalized by the tales.

## PRELIMINARY CHALLENGES BY THE OUTSIDE WORLD

### From the South

As the Portuguese were the first permanent European occupiers of the coast, so they were the first to establish themselves inland. Missionaries settled in the Upper Zambesi Basin in the 16th century, and both churchmen and traders entered Ethiopia at about the same time. These intrepid pioneers were beset by the exceptional odds of the environment of interior Africa, and they could obtain no effective support from the little European state from which they came. Portugal was already losing parts of its empire — disproportionately extensive for a mother country small in area and population and cursed with niggardly soil. Nearly all its holdings north of the Congo River fell into the greedy clutches of maritime rivals during the 16th and 17th centuries. Deprived of support from home, the Portuguese settlements were withdrawn, and inner Africa relapsed into its age-old invulnerability, leaving no trace save for a few bridges spanning Ethiopian torrents — links in forgotten highways, that continue to perform their function even today.

It should occasion no surprise to learn that the first effective settlements beyond the immediate coast were those at the southern end of the continent, beyond the Tropic of Capricorn. Every principal type of climate found in the lower middle latitudes is represented there, including plateaus standing 5000 feet above the sea. Four or five structural roadsteads permit anchorage, and neither the foreshore nor the coastal lowland is clogged with vegetation. The southwest tip (Fig. 52) has the dry summers and the rainy winters characteristic of the Mediterranean world. It is entirely suited to settlement by Europeans, especially to south Europeans. Why the Portuguese engaged in the Indian trade overlooked it, remains a puzzle.

When Dutch traders made it a way-station to India in the middle of the 17th century, they found the local indigenes neither unfriendly nor strong. The immediate hinterland of the Cape Peninsula is a belt of sterile, flat lowland, but behind it lies a small district well suited to Mediterranean agriculture. The favored zone is narrow, however, and gives way to dissected plateau, scarred by ravines filled with impenetrable scrub and forest, and crowned by desert and semi-desert. In spite of obstacles placed in the way of farming by nature and by the trade-minded Dutch East India Company, which ruled the settlement, many colonists gradually moved eastward and became known as Boers, i.e., farmers, to distinguish them from the citizens of Capetown. Pent between desert on the north and warlike Bantu tribesmen on the east, and faced with many problems of acclimatization, pests, and novel farm practices, the Boers moved inland very slowly. By the end of the 18th century they had pushed cultivation to its limit — the escarpment which rises to the Little Karroo. Beyond, semi-nomadic Boers had reduced the Hottentots to servitude and had extended their livestock ranches as far as the Great Fish River and the Sneuwbergen. There they lived in virtual political independence. Most of this country is suitable only for grazing, and the carrying capacity is low. Hence the dispersed ranches and the feudal and patriarchal character of a society formed of white owners and enslaved colored workers.

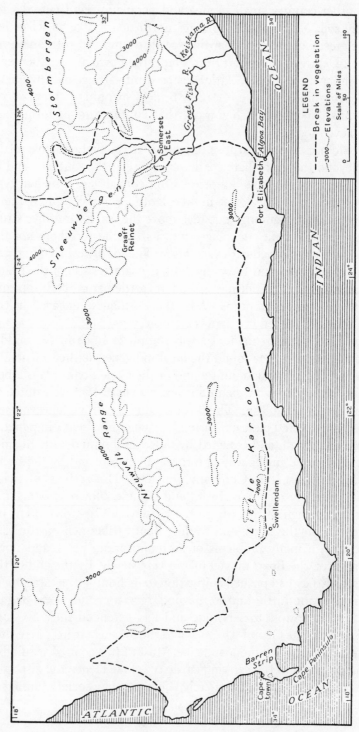

Fig. 52. The Cape region of South Africa.

As an incident of the Napoleonic Wars, the British came into possession of Dutch South Africa. The new masters enforced the Great Fish River boundary against the encroaching Bantu, whose eagerness to move westwards had been whetted by the decimation of Hottentot inhabitants through smallpox epidemics. They even settled a few thousand military colonists in and about Port Elizabeth to fend off the Bantu. On the whole these colonists suffered more severely from the trials of farming in a new country than from Bantu enemies, although in 1834 tribesmen laid waste the country west of the agreed boundary as far as a line from Algoa Bay to Somerset East. When the enraged colonists, British and Boer, drove the intruders back east to the Keiskama River, the home government restored to the Bantu the newly seized territory and even some land in the Fish River basin long occupied by Boers.

This proved to be the final straw in the list of Boer grievances against the British government. Others had been the grant of civil rights to Hottentots, the quartering of Hottentot regiments on the Boers, administration of the law courts exclusively in English, and abolition of slavery with inadequate compensation to their owners — the process to begin at the end of this very year 1834 and to be completed in four years. Thereupon many groups of Boers, both ranchers and sedentary farmers of the Cape region, determined to move into the wilderness where they might maintain their independence of European authority. This movement, known as the Great Trek, commenced in 1835. It initiated the European occupance of nearly all the highland of South Africa suited to permanent settlement by white people. The pioneers numbered less than 8000 and they suffered desperate hardships. At least one group disappeared without trace, others are known to have been killed by the natives whom they intended to displace. Still others died by malaria or lost their cattle, their only source of livelihood, by tsetse fly infection when they tried to cross the deeply incised Limpopo Valley to reach the highland of Rhodesia. By mid-century the tenacity of the pioneers had assured their success, although both they and the succeeding generation had still to wage several wars with the Bantu. These energetic indigenes naturally resisted being deprived of their best lands, and were not readily enslaved, as the Hottentots had been. In this stubborn conflict, the Boers were unintentionally aided by British settlements on the humid subtropical coast of the continent. The first foothold there was gained a decade before the Great Trek began, and more than one bloody encounter occurred between Boer and British pioneers on that productive and desired lowland, before their boundary was established along the crest of the Drakensberg. For both white groups, however, the threat from the indigenes was more serious than their own feud. The most serious of all the Bantu wars broke out in 1850, in the form of an uprising of tribes trying to regain possession of the High Veld. They were joined by the black military police of eastern Cape Colony, and by many Hottentots. The quelling of this revolt established the white man in possession of strategic nuclei of territory in each of the principal natural units of the continent south of the Limpopo River — the Mediterranean corner, the humid subtropical lowland, the Low Veld, and the High Veld (Figs. 52 and 55).

Even the southwest desert was brought into the South African orbit to the full extent of its known value. Between 1843 and 1866 the British annexed guano-covered islands off the coast of Great Namaqualand, and a few years later, Walvis Bay, the only safe natural harbor on the desert coast.

## From the East

Since the mid-17th century, Arabs of Oman had been contesting the east coast of Africa with the Portuguese. Using the offshore island Zanzibar as a base (Fig. 51), the Arabian traders soon succeeded in pushing the Portuguese south of Cape Delgado (today the northern boundary of Portuguese East Africa). The most lasting result of the Arabian activity was the conversion of many east coast Africans to Islam. In a sense Portuguese interests were reestablished on the strip of coast from which its European traders had been expelled, when numbers of native merchants from Goa, the Portuguese trading station on the west coast of India, settled on Zanzibar. In 1832 the ruler of Oman transferred his court to Zanzibar and began an active trade on the mainland, for which the island city is admirably located to serve as entrepôt. By the middle of the century these traders had established a modest business with folk of the East African Highland. In the 1860s the tie between Oman and Zanzibar was severed and the opening of the Suez Canal placed the east coast of Africa on a new plane of interest to the commercial nations of Europe. French, British, and German citizens entered the newly opened trade sphere, and initiated events which led to political steps by their governments.

## From the West and North

The second third of the 19th century, which saw the founding of stable settlements in East, and especially in South Africa, proved less auspicious for Europeans interested in the west coast, between the deserts.

Nothing occurred to encourage European settlement more effective than the traditional practice of " sitting down in the country " until retirement, or more often death, brought in fresh recruits as short-lived replacements. On the contrary, business waned. By this time the pepper grains of the Grain Coast (Fig. 51) were supplanted by a supply from India; the placer mines of the Gold Coast had been worked out and the elephants of the Ivory Coast had been exterminated, as is the fate of uncontrolled extractive industry. Even the slave trade, backbone of west coast business, had been given the *coup de grâce* by an awakening humanitarianism in Western Europe and was languishing.

Beginning with Denmark in 1803, every European trading nation and most of the states of the Americas had legally abolished the overseas trade in slaves by 1836. Violations of the laws were continuous, however, because the business was profitable if on one voyage in three a slave ship escaped capture by the patrols. Effective abolition of the trade awaited abolition of the institution of slavery. This was begun by Great Britain within its dominions in 1838, followed by other European states. Nevertheless the trade persisted because slavery continued to be legal in several American countries, notably the United States, Cuba, and Brazil. As late as 1861 Great Britain took over Lagos, in the heart of the Slave Coast, as the headquarters of its anti-slaver patrol. With emancipation in the United States in 1863 and in Cuba in 1870 overseas shipments of slaves rapidly dwindled. Clearly west coast Africa was on the down grade. Disheartened Danes and Dutch sold out their West African holdings to the British. Once-flourishing trading posts began to be reclaimed by the swiftly growing bush. The British and the French governments held on to their principal stations partly through inertia, and partly to thwart any recrudescence of the slave trade, while smuggling of slaves to Brazil kept Portuguese interests in Angola alive.

Meanwhile Europeans had been shocked to learn that the slave trade continued to flourish in the Moslem world, fed by a constant transfer of Negroes from Guinea across the Sahara to Barbary, and from the East African Highland to the Red Sea coast and thence to the Mohammedan Levant. These revelations were made by men who plunged into the heart of unknown Africa to explore it, beginning with the late 18th century.

Specifically nearly every expedition had for its objective the search for the headwaters of one of the major African rivers. The hydrography of Africa is unusual, and quite outside the experience of European geographers of those times (Fig. 53). Crudely stated, the continent consists of half a dozen vast structural basins. Each of these saucer-like depressions might be expected to retain the runoff from its whole area. Most of the desert basins do absorb all of the light rainfall they

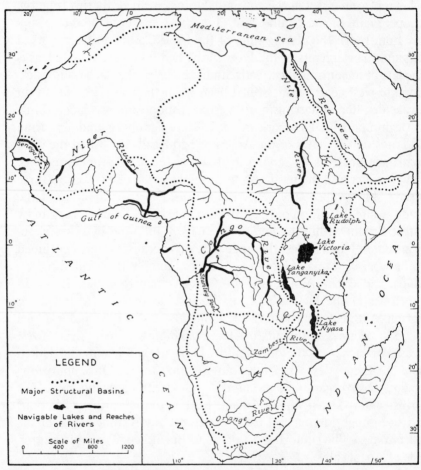

FIG. 53. African hydrographic basins and navigable reaches of the rivers.

receive. The saltpans and marshes along the northern margin of the southwest desert are striking proofs of this, as are Lake Chad and the frayed lower ends of many lesser stream systems in the Sahara. The braided course and numerous lakes of the Niger just above Timbuctu, the extensive marsh of the Nile above the Sobat confluence, and the lakes on the Zambesi above Victoria Falls, are in like case, except that coastal streams have tapped them and carried off their waters to the sea. There is evidence that the Inner Congo Basin, the bottom of that vast structural depression, was a huge lake until drained by the stream which plunges over the escarpment of the plateau below Stanley Pool. All the great rivers which have succeeded in draining large sectors of the structural basins, and a number of lesser streams, such as the Orange, which serve smaller segments in the same way, are beset by falls and rapids as they make their arduous way through the basin edges. In this critical zone their valleys are deep gorges, hardly more suitable as routes for roads and railroads than are the streams themselves as waterways. Below the gorges, in every case but the Congo, the major rivers find their way into the sea through tortuous delta channels, and except for the Nile their lowest courses are walled with rain forest and mangrove swamp.

When interest in interior Africa rose high enough to instigate exploration on the part of individual Europeans, it naturally focused on finding the sources of the great rivers which had mystified the learned world and yet stubbornly resisted exploration upstream from their mouths. In every instance the headwaters were first reached by expeditions overland from some point on the coast affording readier access to the interior than the river valleys themselves; e.g., the Upper Niger was discovered after a Saharan crossing. The earliest of these venturesome expeditions was undertaken before 1800, but so difficult was the country that more than half a century elapsed before the Niger, the Nile, and the Zambesi gave up their secrets. The unity of each stream system was proved by following it downstream to its mouth. The final scene in the drama of illuminating the Dark Continent took place in the Congo in the 1860s and early 1870s, with the widely publicized explorations of Livingstone and Stanley.

By 1870 a generation of white people had grown up with at least a casual interest in Africa, thanks to reports of successive explorations which had penetrated to the core of the continent from every side. Ardent groups of abolitionists fanned the growing sentiment which was actively opposed to Negro slavery in any part of the world. At this very time stable European colonization in extra-tropical South Africa became assured, and the Suez route to East Africa, hitherto the most remote part of the continent, turned the attention of the maritime world to the trading establishments which Indians and Arabians had founded on that coast. The big bush on the west side of the continent had been proved less invulnerable than had been thought, by the discovery that long reaches of river in both the Niger and Congo systems are navigable for light-draft steamships, as well as for canoes (Fig. 53).

When, by 1876, the river patterns had been traced, the stage was set for exploitation on the part of Europeans of the whole of the African continent, as distinct from the narrow band of coastline hitherto constituting the zone of European occupation. Religious fervor, both in the guise of Christian missions and as humanitarianism advocating abolition of slavery, was one powerful incentive to increased participation in African affairs. The desire of the maritime states of Europe to extend their colonial holdings was another. In part this was a political sentiment. It was also a response to the need for increased raw materials in a Europe fast industrializing itself and making itself purveyor of manufactured goods to the world at large. Raw materials and foodstuffs needed by manufactural populations cannot be obtained with assurance in regions of unstable or unsympathetic government, and no device for insuring an acquiescent administration surpasses outright political control.

With its opening to world trade, Africa proved itself a reservoir of several commodities required by the swift march of manufacturing. At the outset these consisted mainly of forest products and minerals, extractive in character, which lay ready to hand. Subsequently some of them, indigenous vegetable products, as well as other useful commodities not native to Africa, have come to be produced on a commercial scale either on plantations or native farms. Others have all but disappeared from the exports of the continent. Each played its part in inviting European traders into Africa, and on their heels came European governments intent upon protecting the interests of their nationals. Once established in force, none of the European states which interested itself in Africa at this period has voluntarily withdrawn. The economic penetration in search of trade goods, and the missionary penetration in search of souls to save, translated themselves into the political partition of the continent among the maritime powers of Europe.

### THE POLITICAL SCRAMBLE FOR AFRICAN RESOURCES

The rearrangement of European interests in Africa from scattered and vaguely defined toeholds along 13,000 miles of coast to carefully surveyed and delimited blocks of territory comprising the whole vast mass of the continent, was initiated by France and Great Britain in a treaty of 1857 which defined what amounted to respective spheres of influence along the Guinea coast. Thenceforth European diplomacy has ceaselessly tried to minimize the friction generated by the swiftly advancing territorial claims of the seven states which have taken part in the partition. That burning African issues have not flamed into European war is a tribute to the spirit of compromise, and perhaps also to a recognition, often belated, that the white man's safety in Africa consists in maintaining a united front in the presence of the black. Only twice have redistributions of African territory resulted from war. Both were incidental to greater issues — one the question of Boer or British supremacy in South Africa, the other the World War.

The revised estimate of the value of African resources which accompanied and followed the opening of the interior to trade was based only partially on discoveries, such as diamonds, gold, tin, copper, and finally coal, manganese, and chromium. It lay quite as much in new uses of well-known products which inventions of the time were incorporating into the world's everyday life. These included products native to the bush — rubber, palm oil, shea butter, ostrich plumes, kapok — and the American immigrant, cacao. Other commodities, increasingly in demand, could be successfully produced, either with native or imported stock or by developing hybrids in which the superior quality of more favored regions is blended with native resistance to African plagues. The more important of these are hides and skins, peanuts, cotton, coffee, bananas, sisal, and ginger. Every part of Black Africa has profited to some extent by the overseas market for these goods and lesser items. The shift in the commodities of West African trade illustrates the commercial revolution associated with the political partition of the continent. Of the old leaders, pepper grains, ivory, gold, and slaves, only gold now figures among the exports, and it is produced from vein mines instead of placers.

## THE CONGO THE TOUCHSTONE OF THE CHANGE

Revaluation of the longtime exploited coastal zone coincided with the swift and dramatic opening of the interior. The two decades 1854–1873 were marked by the first complete reconnaissance of all the major river basins. The two mainsprings of this culmination of the previous two generations of painful, piecemeal penetration were missionary, anti-slavery zeal, and human curiosity. Trade did not figure in the interests of the explorers, much less the desire of governments for new colonies. The reports of active slave trading throughout the continent encouraged redoubled missionary effort and disposed liberal governments in Great Britain to take steps to check transportation of slaves overland as well as overseas. At the same time the explorers' reports that inner Africa possessed unfathomed natural resources tempted trading interests to investigate the commercial opportunities.

The Congo, the last great African basin to be traversed by venturesome white men, was the first to be exploited. This is no paradox, because the big bush extends far inland only in the inner Congo Basin, and the big bush offers extractable commodities more numerous and more obvious than those of the small bush. Here was a fresh source of ivory, by this time all but exhausted in the coastal forests. Here grows the oil palm, the chief reason for the rejuvenation of trade on the West African coast just then taking place. Here might develop a big lumber trade. Above all, here was rubber, on the threshold of the most rapidly rising demand in its meteoric history (Ch. 3).

Scarcely had news of the Congo discoveries reached Europe when people of varied interests from several European countries undertook a more thorough exploration, having in mind scientific study as well as the possibility of developing new trade. They organized as the "International Association of the Congo." Capital was supplied by citizens of countries long in the African trade (an Englishman was the first president), and also from countries which were taking shape during the 19th century. Among them were the Belgians, with the king at their head. The intellectual interests of the association were soon buried under the commercial opportunities for extracting rubber and other forest products. Frontier trade generally needs protection by government, and the business of the association was no exception to the rule. It was natural that this protection should be lent by the chief political figure in the active group, the king of the Belgians. To the consternation of many people in Europe who had supported African exploration from humanitarian motives, it was divulged after some years that ivory and rubber in the Congo were being gathered by indigenes forced to labor under conditions as bad as or worse than slavery. Righteous indignation spread and in time took effect in the form of political restraint upon unregulated exploitation by individual nations, of the Congo and much of the rest of Middle Africa as well (between the Sahara and the Zambesi, see Fig. 51). A decade after its inception, the sphere of the International Association of the Congo was transformed into the Conventional Basin of the Congo, established by international conference of interested governments.

This creation was an incident in the general exploitation of the African continent which followed on the heels of the Congo venture, and which in a single human generation reshaped the map and reoriented the lives of the inhabitants. The instruments of this geographic revolution have been economic and social intrusions, such as mines, railroads, harbor works, detribalization, European education, and sanitation. The direction of it has been in the main political.

## Reshaping the Map of Africa

The political map of Africa today is the product of diplomatic chess among the colonial powers, a game played on European council tables since the 1880s by men who never saw Africa. Yet it would be wrong to conclude that natural environment has had nothing to do with the partition of the continent. Each colony is based on occupation of or claim to some strip of coast by colonizing states in their successive bids for overseas dominion during the four centuries preceding the mad scramble for territory precipitated by the exploitation of the Congo. The inducement of natural resources, the repulsion of natural obstacles, and the vicissitudes of statecraft within colonizing countries of widely diverse nature have been the forces at work reshaping the map of Africa.

Prior to the partition of the continent Portugal, Spain, Great Britain, France, Belgium, Germany, and Italy had claims to patches and strips of coastline. On the basis of these claims, spheres of influence were outlined by diplomats whenever rival claims became threatening. Then traders, miners, missionaries, government agents, sometimes backed or led by small armed forces, pushed inland until they made contact with similar groups under the rival flag. The diplomats, accepting the line of contact as a colonial boundary, or adopting some other boundary in consideration of concessions elsewhere on the globe, then sent out commissions to mark the line, and it thereafter appears in the atlases.

Only in rare cases have boundaries between tribes been adopted as demarcations between European colonies. Because tribal boundaries have resulted from centuries of human occupance they may be presumed to have more reality than the lines of accidental clash between rivals racing to seize the maximum territory. Tribes which are severed by a colonial boundary suffer social disintegration, and in many cases economic loss. Some of them have shown a tendency to gravitate to one side or the other of the line in order to save their integrity. Especial difficulties arise when a line bisects the pasture ground of nomadic groups. These folk are accustomed to moving freely within the limits of their domain, and have no concept of land as a possession beyond the right to use the forage it produces and the waterholes it

contains. They can ill brook restriction to one side of a line to them
not only mythical but even nonsensical. Wise administrators have
generally solved the problem by allowing them the freedom of movement they have traditionally enjoyed. The sponsors of colonial boundaries have little regard for the more delicate nuances of the landscape,

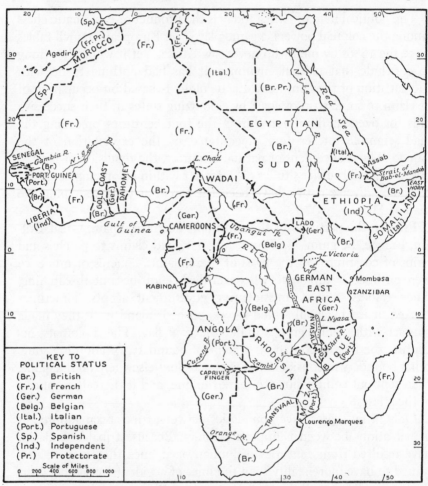

FIG. 54. Pre-war political holdings in Black Africa.

quite possibly because they have never seen it. Nevertheless, the location of every one of the boundaries has been indirectly affected by
the natural environment.

Because each colonial nucleus was a strip of coast on which economic and political penetration of the interior was based, numerous
boundary lines run inland more or less at right angles to the coastline
from which they start (Fig. 54). These lines cross the successive cli-

matic and vegetational zones which dominate the natural scene, and with few exceptions they override the inequalities of terrain as well. Few of the African mountains are prohibitive barriers to penetration, and except in Barbary, high plateaus are areas of attraction to Europeans because there the unremitting heat invariably met on the low-latitude lowlands is modified. On the landward side, some domains are cut off a short distance inland, while others penetrate to the core of the continent. This has occurred because the speed and effectiveness of the rivals in the race for territory is conditioned in large part by the natural obstacles they must surmount and the natural avenues for movement of which they can take advantage. In West Africa the British were impeded by the difficulties of the big bush which lay behind their principal coastal bases, while the French could make their way rapidly across the small bush from its articulation with the sea in Senegal and could even utilize the navigable Senegal and Upper Niger rivers during the wet season when overland movement is hampered by soft ground (Fig. 53). The French lost no time in fruitless attempts to move inland from their own footholds in the big bush, because their coastal reaches south of Conakry were vitiated by the absence of harbors or even roadsteads. In Central Africa radial navigation on the wide Congo River and its affluents focuses at Stanley Pool and aided little Belgium in effective occupation of the most immediately productive part of the vast Congo Basin, from a sliver of coast at the estuary to which its claim was dubious. In South Africa the Portuguese, and subsequently the Germans, were unable to make effective their ambition to join their east and west coast colonies in the face of easy expansion by the British along the backbone of the African upland, from an extra-tropical base at the southern tip of the continent.

All the newly drawn boundaries were imposed arbitrarily on African tribes. Many groups were thereby cut in two, with consequent difficulties of administration for their new masters. For the European miners, traders, and missionaries admitted to the interior by the promise of a stable government, the lines were antecedent to settlement. In most places they remain so, because occupance of interior Africa by Europeans is far from complete, and not half a dozen white settlements stand near political borders. A number of slight alterations in the boundaries have been made without ruffling the tenor of life among Europeans resident in Africa.

The first inroads into the interior were made, not by a country traditionally in the African trade, but by Belgium, one of the upstart states of the 19th century. The partition of the continent was forced upon reluctant nations of maritime Europe by another new nation. Germany, unified at last in 1870, possesses a large share of the mineral resources on which modern industrial society is based. It has, besides, adequate ports for foreign trade on the North Sea, a not too secluded arm of the world ocean, and was already making a bid for a share in overseas business, not excepting the African coast. German explorers had taken a notable part in discovering interior Africa. Germans were interested in the International Association of the Congo. In 1884 Germany astonished the world by sending agents to occupy all of the desert coast between the Cunene and Orange rivers not yet claimed by Great Britain, to seize a bit of inhospitable frontage to which claims were shadowy, between British Gold Coast and French Dahomey, and to impose a protectorate over Cameroons, occupied by British missionaries but disclaimed by the British government a few years earlier. At the same time the German government proposed a conference of interested nations to consider African questions, including the parlous exploitation of the Congo by an " international company."

The conference convened in Berlin toward the end of 1884 and rose early in 1885. It accepted the prospective partition of Africa among the new maritime states, Germany, Belgium, and Italy, as well as the traditional African powers, and agreed that annexations of territory must not be made in advance of due notice to other powers, and that occupation must be effective. They initiated for a vast area comprising the bulk of tropical Africa, the most comprehensive international control attempted prior to the creation of the League of Nations. Thereupon commenced the wild scramble for territory, the operation and geography of which has been sketched above. By the turn of the century very little of Africa remained unclaimed by some European power. France and Great Britain had taken advantage of their early start and their position as leading maritime powers to obtain the largest holdings. Mutual jealousy among the greater states maintained weak Portugal as a large African power. Germany by exerting its new-found political strength obtained even larger holdings. The Congo was soon to be taken over by the Belgian state. Italy, frustrated in a war against the highland Ethiopians, had succeeded only in obtaining barren deserts between its real objective and the sea. Spain was confirmed in its relatively unimportant claims. Only two territories remained outside the European pale: Ethiopia, a highland fastness of warlike chieftains, further protected by the mutual jealousy of Italy, France, and Britain; and Liberia, tacitly admitted to be under the suzerainty of the United States of America.

## DIRECTIVES OF POLICY

The geopolitical trends underlying the accessions of territory appear to have included diverse and sometimes conflicting objectives:

1. maximum territory;
2. access to river basins;
3. free navigation on the streams;
4. unified holdings;
5. avoidance of war;
6. regulation of trade in slaves firearms, and alcohol.

1. Each state tried to obtain the maximum territory possible, regardless of its known value. This ambition often has its reward when some despised district is discovered to contain unguessed wealth or when some resource suddenly appreciates due to technological advances. There is evidence that Great Britain was an exception to this practice and at most times strove only for areas containing considerable natural resources.

2. Each state pressed to gain for each of its holdings access to as many of the major hydrographic systems as possible, even when access had to be purchased at the sacrifice of claims elsewhere (Fig. 54). To meet this demand Britain extended to Leopold's Congo Free State privileges in the district of Lado on the Upper Nile, and to Germany " Caprivi's Finger," linking the district of German Southwest Africa to the Zambesi. France made over to Germany tongue-like extensions of German Cameroons to Lake Chad and to the Ubangi (a Congo affluent). The latter cession cut French Equatorial Africa in two and was the price of German abandonment of claims to Morocco. The projection of British Nyasaland to a navigable outlet on the Shiré explains the southern tip of that territory, and France was similarly given the uppermost port on the Gambia River. The same urge led to the expansion of French Equatorial Africa to the Congo, and of German East Africa to the Rift Valley lakes, although the shape of these two units on the map is not so fantastic as the curious outlines first noted. An obverse case is found on the lower Congo, where the need of Leopold's Congo State for an outlet to the sea led to the separation of Kabinda from the rest of Portuguese West Africa. In most cases the dearly bought bits of territory were never used. Every one of them, except the Congo estuary, the Shiré, and the Gambia, is separated from the sea by impassable falls and rapids, and the ports on the Shiré and Gambia at the respective heads of navigation can be reached by ships only at high water.

Roads and railroads have superseded or forestalled river navigation wherever trade has risen to levels that might warrant improvement of the waterways. Belgium gave up its administration of Lado soon after taking over the Congo, and Germany lost all its painfully acquired " strips " by the World War, along with the colonies to which they were appended.

3. That the riverways were looked upon as vital is further attested by the recurrent efforts to open the major streams freely to the flags of all nations. It was the drafting of a treaty in which Great Britain proposed to recognize Portuguese claims to control of the Congo estuary, which occasioned the Berlin Conference of 1884–85. That international gathering made navigation of the Congo and the Niger one of its principal agenda, and declared both rivers free even in time of war to all merchant ships, including the use of railroads built to get around impediments to navigation. A few years later the Zambesi system and the major affluents of Lake Chad were similarly opened to all comers, and France was permitted free use of the Gambia, and given the right to establish trading stations on the Niger Delta near its mouth. Subsequently some of these arrangements were modified, chiefly in the direction of permitting suzerain states to levy customs duties for revenue. At the close of the World War the privileges were restricted to members of the League of Nations and signatories of the Treaty of St. Germain. Methods of commercial exploitation adopted in some of the territories have tended to nullify these carefully drawn rules for safeguarding free trade. A treaty right to use a waterway is of little value to foreign nations if their nationals are effectively excluded from doing business along its banks.

4. Each state worked hard to weld into single units its scattered coastal holdings. This could be done only by gaining control of vast areas of hinterland. The outcome was affected by several factors. Of these the relative accessibility of the back country to the rival states is the most obviously geographic. Others included the backing given by the home governments, and their bargaining position. The democratic governments of the 19th-century European nations blew now hot, now cold on overseas expansion. It is of record that the British government refused to take over administration of Cameroons, Mombasa, the whole mainland coast belonging to Zanzibar, Katanga, Durban, and Orange Free State, after Britishers on the ground had made all arrangements for the transfers. In some cases a government made concessions in Africa in exchange for an advantage in some other part of the world. Germany abandoned its claims to Zanzibar to obtain the

island of Heligoland in the German Ocean. Britain sacrificed the hinterland of the Gambia River (the one natural line of ingress to West Africa, which gave a whip hand over French Guinea), the off-shore Îles de Los, and some Nigerian territory, in return for French fishing rights on the Newfoundland coast. France contributed gener-ously to German Cameroons in return for the quashing of German claims to the port of Agadir, Morocco. The Netherlands withdrew from South Africa entirely, as part of a complex agreement which in-cluded also Southeast Asia and the Guianas of South America. Time has proved some of these concessions wise, others mistaken.

The outstanding ambitions of the several powers for African terri-tory were six in number. During the period of partition Italy set up claims along the desert coast of the East Horn and hoped to consoli-date them by means of Ethiopia. Leopold wished to extend his Congo State from the mouth of the Congo to the upper waters of the Nile. France desired to control a broad east-west band from the Gulf of Guinea to the Red Sea. Portugal hoped to unite its east- and west-coast holdings across Rhodesia. Germany also aspired to Rhodesia as a link between German Southwest and German East Africa. Most ambi-tious of all, and cutting athwart all the other (east-west) schemes, was the Cape-to-Cairo project of Great Britain. As might be expected from so formidable and complex a rivalry, the partition ended in a stalemate in which each contestant attained a part of its objective and none was entirely successful.

The government of the Belgian Congo abandoned its effort to ob-tain a footing on the Nile. In the Congo estuary it contented itself with the right bank and one landing place on the left bank near the base of the Livingstone Falls. As a seaport this was somewhat awk-ward because of eddying currents, yet because on Stanley Pool at the head of the falls Belgium controls only the left bank, its railroad portage around the falls must lie on that side of the river. After the World War, in order to obtain 3 square kilometers of land necessary for reconstructing the railroad to standard South African gauge, Bel-gium ceded to Portugal 3000 square kilometers of interior territory, land on the Angola border of the Congo about to be opened to ex-ploitation by construction of the Benguella Railroad through Portu-guese and Belgian territory.

France was unable to realize its dream in the eastern third of Africa's northern subcontinent, but in the west was eminently successful. It abandoned to Britain its claims to Egypt in return for a free hand in Morocco. A brush in the Egyptian Sudan which nearly precipitated war was resolved when France agreed to withdraw from the Nile Basin and instead to take Wadai, the innermost Sudan. This district remains today the part of Africa most remote from the outside world. In West Africa French agents and troops based on the Senegal coast, moved swiftly inland along the open Sudan and made contact with French settlements in the big bush that alternated with the British holdings there. France consolidated a huge block of territory and left the four British territories, the two German holdings, and the insignificant Portuguese Guinea and Liberia discrete units.

Portugal has remained an African colonial power because the Great Powers have never been able to agree as to the disposition of the territorial spoils in case of partition. At one time France and Germany would have been willing to see the two Portuguese lands south of the Equator coalesce, in order to forestall the northward march of British domination. When the boundaries were drawn, both Angola and Mozambique were allotted surprisingly large shares of the interior, as well as all the harbors on 10° of west coast and 16° of east coast. This gave to Portugal a whip hand in the shipping of goods to and from the small bush of Africa all the way from the inner Congo Basin to the Vaal River (Fig. 52). For a time the Zambesi River and the short wagon road connecting the Transvaal Rand with Lourenço Marques, the only practical routes, were controlled by Portugal. The governments of the interior, British in the one case, Boer in the other, made treaties exempting most transit goods from taxation by Portuguese authorities. Subsequently the construction of railroads roughly paralleling these east-coast routes, their extension to the very heart of the interior, and a railroad from this core to the west coast through Angola, have made Portuguese ports the most direct outlets for a large percentage of the minerals of the continent, as well as for products of farm and range.

Portuguese suzerainty of these strategic lands has not been openly questioned. All the inland territories tributary to Portuguese outlets, except the southern Congo, are British and the railroads without exception have been ventures of British capital. Britain has been Portugal's commercial ally since the early days of the port-wine traffic, and this sentimental bond and long habit of cooperation undoubtedly minimizes the awkwardness of the unfortunately placed boundary lines. Belgium, being like Portugal a small state, is not disposed to suggest territorial changes in Portuguese Africa, lest the example be used against itself. Nevertheless, the possession by a weak state of the direct outlets for valuable natural resources being exploited by powerful interests, is geopolitically unstable, the more so because Portugal has found itself unable to develop the resources of its large and potentially valuable territories.

Germany entered the field too late to obtain coastal footholds of high value, with the exception of Cameroons. In every case the hinterlands of its dominions bristle with natural obstacles to rapid penetration. These handicaps, accentuated by mistakes made by inexperienced administrators, somewhat impaired the vigor of the German colonial movement. On the west coast Germany had to be content with frail, ribbon extensions to the nearest major streams and lakes, and to abandon its somewhat fantastic claim to a Nile outlet for Cameroons. In its East African enterprise it was able to thrust a compact chunk of territory inland to the boundary of the Belgian Congo. This appeared to block the dream of an all-British string of possessions from the Cape to the mouth of the Nile.

When the partition was complete the British holdings held first rank, as to both size and resources. This was true, even though they were hemmed in by Portuguese coasts and cut into separate units by French, Belgian, and German annexations. Britain fared best in the rivalry for the great basins which had figured so conspicuously in the opening of the interior. The British flag flew over the best of the Niger Basin, much of the long Nile Basin, and a generous segment of the Zambesi. It even reached the uppermost waters of the Congo and shared with France and Germany the shores of Lake Chad. Only in the case of lakes Victoria and Nyasa did its boundaries lie in navigable water, so often a bone of contention, and it controlled the mouth of every considerable stream in which it had large interests, except the Zambesi.

Of all the contenders for African territory in the partition, Italy alone failed. Italy was the least maritime of them, lacking the long tradition of the west European states and the active commerce of Belgium and Germany. Its home base was superior to Portugal, but inferior to the others, probably even to Belgium, because it lacked the coal and iron on which 19th-century nations founded their empires of manufacturing and commerce. Italy was politically unified the very year that saw German unity achieved, and had no more a colonial tradition than did Germany. It did not even display an interest in Libya, immediately across the Mediterranean, until German interests founded a chartered company in Austria to develop that barren land. Italy's real interests in Africa began on the east coast, with the opening of the Suez Canal, an event bound to reorient the Mediterranean world (Ch. 9). A foothold at Assab, just within the Strait of Bab-el-Mandeb, predated the break-up of the Sultanate of Zanzibar. When mainland East African coasts were being claimed as one of the first moves toward the continent's partition, Italy was allowed a sphere of influence along the Somali coast (Fig. 56). At the same time Britain consolidated its position at the southern entrance of the Red Sea, and France obtained a strategic piece of territory fronting on Bab-el-Mandeb, as a part of its far-reaching plan for an empire stretching across widest Africa. Thus Britain, France, and Italy occupied positions of about equal strength at the southern outlet of the Red Sea. All three coveted Ethiopia, a highland of great natural promise, but also a formidable natural folk-fortress, protected by precipitous cliffs that mark the edge of a rift valley and girt by forbidding deserts on the seaward sides. Italy undertook its conquest, was repulsed, and in time joined Britain and France in guaranteeing the independence of the Ethiopian Empire. A generation later a greatly strengthened Italy bought off France, whose interests in this part of Africa had been declining, and achieved the postponed conquest of the highland and the welding of Italian holdings in Black Africa into a single although not easily articulated block.

5. The states which succeeded in obtaining large territories have generally preferred to make concessions to the rising colonial powers rather than fight over Africa. Most of the international conferences of the three decades before the outbreak of the international war in 1914, were called for the purpose of dealing with African problems, and many bilateral treaties supplemented the agreements of the conferences.

6. A corollary of the foregoing is the international character of certain perennial African problems. The slave trade depended upon well-organized states of the small bush or the coast to bring a steady stream of labor from the inner big bush, or from weak tribes anywhere. The extractive industries and plantations of the low latitudes have depended for labor on the local supply, supplemented in many cases by drafts from populous districts not too far away. Both these movements of labor have cut athwart the boundary lines of dependencies and require international control. The terrifying epidemic diseases of Africa — yellow fever, sleeping sickness, malaria — know no political confines, although they are intimately related to natural conditions. Finally, alcohol and firearms, imported into Africa through European agents, are scourges transcending colonial boundaries. Possessed of modern weapons, populous African states might defy their European

overlords. Possessed of alcohol, African labor degenerates, African trade suffers, and African morale goes to pot.

A desire to stop the overseas slave trade brought about the first international action — embodied in the form of treaties undertaking joint action against the practice and granting bases for anti-slaver patrols. The Conference of 1884–85 was called in part to prevent slave trading in the Congo Basin. In altered form, as forced labor used to gather rubber, Leopold's Congo remained the subject of international investigation until its administration was cleaned up when the Belgian government took over. In the meantime international conferences discussed liquor, firearms, and sleeping sickness, as well as forced labor, and all have continued to be objects of international regulation. Growing humanitarianism in Europe has consistently championed the amelioration of African life, and has forced governments to take action. Gradually the economic wisdom of this course has appeared. The most valuable African resource is human labor — Africa being the only important reservoir of manpower outside Java and India that has proved able to perform hard manual labor in low-latitude lowlands. Epidemic disease depletes local supplies of this labor, excessive indulgence in alcohol makes it worthless, and possession of rifles might jeopardize the white man's authority over it. The rising importance of foodstuffs and raw materials from the low latitudes and the economic development of much of Africa are bound up with the well-being of Negro labor.

## STRATEGY OF CONQUEST

The underlying directives of policy in the scramble for African territory have been a curious blend of high-minded humanitarianism and crass exploitation. A uniform political procedure has been the vehicle which has carried the European economic order into Africa from the west, south, and east coasts.

Discovery of the coast was largely the work of Portuguese officials, who drew on the national exchequer to keep the work going in the face of discouragingly meager results. Trade was undertaken by private companies chartered by one or another European government for the purpose. In the absence of direct European government, these early companies found that they could trade only if they administered government to Africans among whom they settled, as well as to their European employees. Missionaries who came out looked to the chartered companies for protection. As penetration inland extended the area served by missionaries or by traders, the companies were compelled to extend the range of their political functions. Very often this outran the wildest dreams of the home governments, which sometimes refused to give backing to the territorial advances of their nationals.

Abuses crept into the administration of many of the chartered companies. In South Africa the Dutch East India Company tried to keep under its thumb the farmers whom it had brought out to supply Capetown with locally grown food, and forbade them to push beyond the lowland fringe of the Cape region. This prohibition could not be enforced in a region of middle-latitude climate in which the pioneers could keep their health. In the central African big bush the few Europeans could easily be kept within bounds during their ephemeral stays, but the companies regularly succumbed to the temptation to exploit ruthlessly the scattered tribes. These peoples were too ill organized to resist, whether they lived under company rule or were victims of company thirst for slaves or other natural resources. As wave after wave of humanitarianism swept over Western Europe, the companies had to choose between reform and relinquishing their charters. The scandal which grew out of rubber gathering in Leopold's Congo was better publicized than its predecessors, but both in the shameful exploitation of the forest inhabitants and in the ultimate acceptance by the Belgian government of responsibility for administration, it was typical. In the small bush the chartered companies and in South Africa the bands of pioneers roused the opposition of organized native states. The usual procedure of chartered companies and pioneer bands was to treat with chieftains for land. To Europeans this meant ownership, to Africans usufruct. This variance in the concept of property almost invariably led to friction and the warriors of the native chiefs, although ill armed, were sometimes able to overpower the company forces or pioneers by sheer numbers. European supremacy in the black world was seen to be endangered by defeats on the field of battle, and in the big bush direct administration by European governments superseded company administration.

The form of control varies. In general the original foothold on the coast, perhaps no more than an island or a narrow band of mainland, is technically a colony of the claimant state. The hinterland was originally conceived as a sphere of influence, agreed upon among the rival governments. So much of this sphere as might be converted into a protectorate of the African inhabitants was so converted during the two decades of the great scramble. In this procedure can be traced the insistence upon benevolent governance by enlightened European publics. At the same time it permits economic exploitation untrammelled by the interference of foreign governments.

The economic functions of some chartered companies have continued long after their political functions were shorn away, whereas other charters have been cancelled. Major undertakings which require large blocks of capital, such as railroads, mines, forest industries, and plantations, are commonly organized as stock companies. In practice the distinction between some of them and the governments of the districts in which they are paramount, is hazy. As a rule private business and political administration tend to differentiate as a region develops and both the economic and social structure of life becomes increasingly complex.

The military conquest of Africa was accomplished with remarkably little warfare. In places missionaries peacefully entered and lived in a district some years before traders found their way thither. In the big bush armed conflicts were scattered and sporadic, as might be expected from the character of the contacts between European and African. No large engagements occurred there.

The deserts were the last areas to be conquered, excepting the Ethiopian highland. Almost void of the resources desired by private industry, their waterless empty spaces could not easily be dominated by European infantry or even cavalry. This was equally true in the face of resolute resistance by inured nomads mounted on fast camels in the Sahara, and in pursuit of ever-retreating bands of primitive tribesmen in the southwest deserts. After most of the rest of the continent had been " pacified," home governments undertook the conquest of the deserts. In the end those of the southwest were subordinated to German and British rule by aid of railroads which skirt and cross portions of them. French and Italians pushed rails into the northern edge of the Sahara, but they depend chiefly upon organized regiments mounted on camels, officered by Europeans, and manned by desert men who accept government pay in lieu of the loot of caravans and extortion from oasis dwellers.

It is the small bush which has been the scene of bitter and lengthy conflicts between European and African, for it is in the small bush that African states of considerable extent developed formidable military power. For some centuries before the advent of Europeans, these states had been waging wars against each other. This is attested by the few extant documents, but more vividly by the cities and villages of the Sudan, uniformly surrounded by high mud walls and in many cases further protected by dry moats and hedges of thornbush. In the southern half of the continent stockaded villages are ubiquitous, everywhere protected by mud or stone walls, piling, or thornbush. In the Sudan native physical vigor had been reinforced by horses, firearms, and a mode of building which originated in trans-Saharan lands bathed in the stream of Mediterranean culture. In the southern part of the continent the Europeans intercepted a powerful folk migration of Bantu which, progressing south- and southwestward, was victoriously driving before it the Hottentots and Bushmen.

SOUTH AFRICA

Extra-tropical South Africa saw the earliest effective European occupation on the continent. A full generation before the Conference of 1884–85 opened the rest of Africa, the Bantu migration had been stopped and nuclei of European settlement marked each natural region which could assure provender and health for permanent settlers. The brunt of the thrust against the oncoming Bantu had been borne by the Boers, farmers and ranchers of Netherlands and of Huguenot extraction, whose ancestors had come in to grow food for the traders of Capetown. Their ambition to carve out of the wilderness subsistence farms to be worked by Africans, brought them into perennial strife with the Bantu, who resented both the loss of their lands and the threat of enslavement. The pioneering Boers received no countenance from the Dutch East India Company, and by the end of the 18th century had at least two settlements openly independent of the authorities at Capetown — one at Swellendam toward the eastern end of the arable lowland tip of the continent, the other at Graaf-Reinet, well inland in the Central Karroo (Fig. 52). At this juncture Capetown and the rest of Netherlands Africa was transferred to the British crown. A quarter century later British settlements on the two best-sheltered remaining harbors of the narrow seaboard of South Africa extended trading interests right around the coast. These interests looked to their hinterland as the source of exportable products and as markets. The self-sustaining Boers on their vast but inefficient ranches wanted few outside products, had no surplus to sell, and asked only to be let alone. Thus the feud between trading company and Boer was perpetuated; it was even exacerbated by differences of language and tradition. When the modest agricultural resources of the High Veld were found to be supplemented by incredible mineral wealth, the static, pastoral life of the Boers was irretrievably shattered by the dynamic urge to exploit the fabulous new riches on the part of British South Africans and Europeans.

In the calmer days before diamonds and gold were discovered, critical conflicts occurred both between European and African and between Boer and Briton, but they were localized.

One zone of friction was the front of the Bantu migration southwestward, which was opposed by Boers moving eastward. As early as 1778 the Great Fish River was declared the boundary, but for three-quarters of a century the actual line fluctuated from a line running north from Algoa Bay (to Somerset East) to the line of the Great Kei River. After 1820 the Boers were aided in maintaining this front by British settlements on and immediately behind Algoa Bay. Most of the land between the two extreme positions of the Bantu front was settled by British colonists. In the zone of contention the Bantu population remains to this day notably denser than in the areas to the westward. East of the Great Kei boundary are large areas reserved to native use. These occupy all the land between the sea and the tip of native Basutoland, and separate the Europeans of the Cape Province from those of Natal.

A second area of prolonged strife is the hinterland of the port of Durban (Fig. 55). Durban harbor is one of the three easiest points d'appui on the South African coast, the Capetown district and Algoa Bay being the others. Its occupation by British parties followed on the heels of the settlements at Algoa Bay. Behind the narrow coastal lowland successive dissected terraces rise like gigantic steps to the high mountains 100–150 miles inland which mark the eastern border of the South African Plateau (High Veld). British settlements had not begun to climb these steps when Boer pioneers of the Great Trek spilled over the crest of the Drakensberg. They found much of the terraced foreland, or " Middle Veld," partially depopulated by warfare among the Bantu, and quickly spread their scattered settlements over the country south of the Tugela River, establishing their local capital, Pieter-Maritzburg, on the Middle Veld but directly behind Durban and only 70 miles up the trail. These pioneer Boers, inured to privations, were not deterred when the Bantu massacred their first outposts; on the contrary they retorted by destroying the kraal and forces of the chief who had instigated the massacre. Conflict with the British settlements vanquished them, however. They besieged Durban, and on being repulsed most of them withdrew to the High Veld. The British colony of Natal was then declared to extend on the north to the Tugela and Buffalo rivers, a boundary naturally marked not only

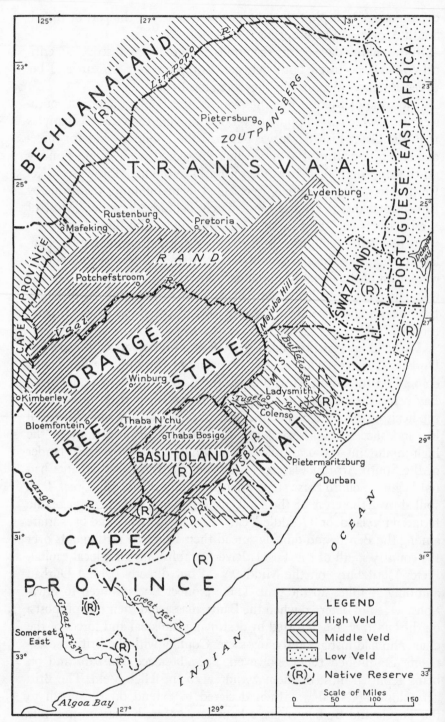

FIG. 55. Southeastern Africa.

346

by the streams but also by the tangled vegetation of their valleys. Beyond this line lay Bantu country, the higher levels of which were afterward occupied by Boers. Today the lowlands north of the Tugela include large native reserves. Subsequently whenever Boer and British struggled for supremacy in South Africa, the triangle between the Upper Tugela and Buffalo rivers and the Drakensberg was the scene of severe fighting. The last dangerous irruption of Bantu was the Zulu uprising of 1879 within and beyond the northern border of Natal. This followed close upon British annexation of the Boer Transvaal state and furnished an opportunity for the Boers to regain their independence. This they did in battles which culminated about Majuba Hill, a mountain of the Drakensberg range which overlooks the principal pass between Natal and the Transvaal. Thirty years later, in the final war between British and Boer this strategic pass was again the scene of fighting. In this war Ladysmith, on a high terrace below the Drakensberg and at the junction of routes connecting Durban with both the Orange Free State and the Transvaal, was one of the chief objectives. Critical action took place both near the town and some miles below it, at the crossing of the Tugela River.

Although much fighting took place along the approaches to the plateau, both in Cape Province and in Natal, the ultimate issues at stake were two: the natural resources of the High Veld, particularly its immense mineral wealth; and the disposition of its African inhabitants. The High Veld is the most productive farmland in all Africa and shares with the Cape lowland the distinction of being the most healthful part of Black Africa for people of European extraction. When the pioneers of the Great Trek reached the highland they found it almost depopulated as a result of tribal wars. Their settlement at Winburg in the heart of the best farm country became the political nucleus of the Orange Free State, the first stable Boer republic. In establishing themselves on the open grassy plain, the pioneers relied for defense upon the isolated, abrupt mountain Thaba N'chu, where they left their women and children while driving Bantu enemies beyond the Vaal River. Half a century later this same stronghold was an important element in the British control of the Free State and its capital. Other and similar sharp elevations, ranging from hillocks to mountains have played leading roles in struggles for possession of the country, especially in the guerilla warfare which was the avowed procedure of the Boers during the last two years of the South African War.

In establishing themselves on the level High Veld, where nearly all the land bears excellent natural pasturage, the Boers relentlessly took possession of all the land. This left the helpless remnants of the African population the bitter choice of becoming slaves on the Boer estates or taking refuge in less desirable districts. Such country flanked the rich grasslands which the Boers had seized. To the east the South African highland culminates in a rugged watershed area. Thither groups of Basuto had fled during the tribal turbulence that began shortly before the Boers' arrival. There many others went to escape enslavement by the white men. Their principal defense point was the flat-topped mountain Thaba Bosigo, which three different European forces found impregnable. At last the British government, not averse to reducing Boer territory, and openly opposed to Boer methods of dealing with the natives, established a protectorate over the mountain refuge occupied by the Basuto. To the west of the Orange Free State lies the desert, adopted as a refuge by the Bechuana. A part of this was annexed to Cape Province as a means of holding for Great Britain the Kimberley diamond district. When the land scramble of 1885 was launched, a British Protectorate was thrown over most of the remainder of the desert and much land besides. This was a check to expansion of the independent Boer republic beyond the Vaal, and it served equally well as a buffer against the new German protectorate over Southwest Africa and provided a narrow route along a corridor of steppe from the Cape Colony to the highland of Rhodesia.

The Transvaal settlements, the offshoots of the Orange Free State, organized spontaneously as four semi-independent units centered respectively at Potchefstroom just across the Vaal, Rustenburg on the northern margin of the High Veld, Lydenburg in the lee of the Drakensberg, and Zoutpansberg in the mountainous extension of the highland far to the north. Segregation came naturally to people scattered widely on huge landholdings, patriarchal in their social structure, self-sustaining in a region of uniform production, and feeling no need for political reciprocity. They early obtained independence from the parent state and thenceforth resisted reabsorption. An attempt to amalgamate the four Transvaal units with the capital at Potchefstroom in the southwest failed because 'all the remote eastern settlements opposed it. Union was accomplished by setting up a compromise capital at Pretoria, between three of the four original political centers. Zoutpansberg — still remote, almost surrounded by Low Veld which was proving unsuited for Europeans and was going back into the hands of Africans, and poorer than the others because of rough terrain — remained a center of opposition to the authorities at Pretoria.

Nearly two decades after the union the Republic was so rent by dissension that it was helpless to resist annexation to Great Britain proclaimed at Pretoria. Subordination to a foreign power was spurned in a revolt which succeeded in winning the first battle of Majuba Hill. Nevertheless, the Transvaal was shorn of part of its Middle Veld and the British government reserved the right to supervise the foreign affairs of the rest of the landlocked state. This unstable arrangement was rendered still more precarious when gold brought the first heavy British immigration into Boer territory. The conservative Boers disliked any interference with their way of life, which was based on the Old Testament and therefore suited a semi-nomadic, pastoral society. The foreigners found the Boer government an obstacle to rapid exploitation of the mineral wealth. British interests which had already laid the foundation for British domination of Rhodesia and for a corridor of approach thereto along the steppe on the Transvaal frontier, were pushing a railroad line along that corridor. This route hugged the political boundary and came to be used by its backers as a line of communications for smuggling arms into the Rand gold mining district. Finally, from a base on the railroad at Mafeking, due west of the Rand, an armed force invaded the Transvaal. Although it was unauthorized and a failure, the raid proved to the Boers, not only that they were ringed about and could no longer escape into the wilderness, but also that in the presence of gold their independence at home was in jeopardy. In their fury against the intrusive foreigners all the schisms within the Transvaal were forgotten and to cap the climax the two Boer republics were fused into unity for the first time. They joined forces to fight the changes they could no longer escape. It is not surprising that they promptly seized Kimberley and Mafeking, the two thorns along their vulnerable west side, and that these became principal foci in the fighting.

Their defeat and the consequent transfer to a single sovereignty of the four important South African centers of European settlement, synchronized with the great push into interior Africa from the west and east. Because of the age, density, and permanence of the South African settlements, this promptly became the side from which the most active and effective expansion took place. In spite of the distance, the core of the continent was first provided with an overseas outlet by way of South Africa.

## EAST AFRICA

At the two ends of the Sudan the conquest of the African states was not seriously complicated by struggles among the European invaders, as was the case in South Africa. No part of the small bush of north-central Africa extends beyond the Tropic. Ethiopia and a few isolated islands of high ground in east central Africa do afford possible sites for permanent European settlement, but even today their suitability remains to be proved. Moreover, they are inaccessible from the coast. Nowhere north of the Zambesi had European settlement amounted to more than the usual short-term tours of duty by traders and mission-aries at widely separated stations, when the conference of 1884–85 started the race for effective political domination of the interior. In this race British, French, Germans, Italians, and Belgians repeatedly made contact along hotly disputed border zones. With remarkable restraint they refrained from fighting on such occasions, even when the leaders had armed forces at their backs. A few times Belgian and British or British and Italian detachments attempted cooperative oper-ations, although not very successfully. This attitude is probably a tribute to the inexorable bush rather than to brotherly love. Low-latitude Africa promptly teaches European intruders that they can prosper, if at all, only by presenting a united front.

In the northeastern part of the continent Great Britain's interests were in the ascendant some years before the Conference convened. This part of the continent lies on the border between Black Africa and the Moslem world, and the well-organized states of the Ethiopian Highlands and the Middle Nile drew a constant stream of slaves from the Upper Nile and Congo basins. Some they kept, more they funneled down the Nile or across the Red Sea from the ancient Sudanese port, Suakin (Fig. 56). The British antipathy against dealing in human beings was focused on this region by the opening of the Suez Canal in 1869. Almost immediately the British government found itself in-volved in the administration of lands bordering the Red Sea. A British governor was installed in the turbulent eastern Sudan, with the assent of Egypt, which had claimed that vast area for half a century without controlling territory much beyond the seaports. British rule, far more effective, at once incurred the enmity of all groups which had been profiting from the slave trade. At the beginning of the 1880s a fanatical Moslem raised the banner of holy war against the infidel intruders. His seat was Omdurman at the confluence of the two main branches of the Nile. The military leader of the revolt was a slave dealer of Suakin. The crusade swiftly flamed across a thousand miles of small bush. One British force was purposely misled into a waterless area and cut to pieces. Another was besieged at Khartum, in the fork of the White and Blue Nile, and was destroyed before reinforcements reached the town

by way of the Nile Valley. Thereupon the British evacuated the Middle
Nile. Ironically, this reverse occurred while the Conference of Berlin
was planning the partition of Africa.

The fortunes of aggressive European states continued to sink in
northeast Africa. A decade after British withdrawal from the Middle

FIG. 56. Northeastern Africa.

Nile, Italy, struggling to consolidate its desert frontages near the
Eastern Horn of the continent, was decisively defeated at the north
end of the Ethiopian Highland. For a time Italian forces in Eretria
were forced back to the port towns.

This reverse was a signal for the renewal of British activity in the
Sudan. Even before the destruction of its forces there, Britain had
declared a protectorate over Egypt, and slowly had brought to life an
orderly native government. That country could now serve as a base for
the reconquest of the Nilotic Sudan.

Men on the ground early recognized that railroads would be a price-

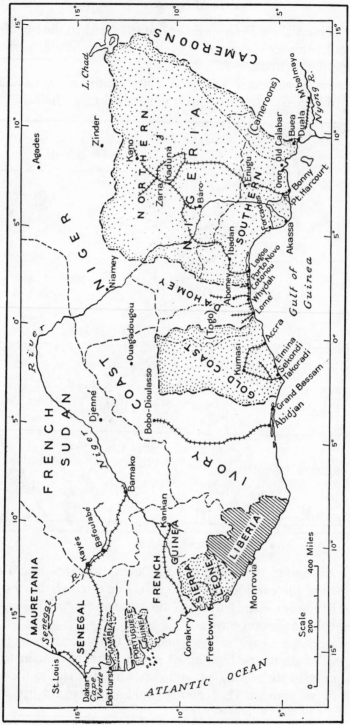

Fig. 57. West Africa.

French territory is left white; other European colonies are stippled; independent areas are shaded.

A modification of a map published by the author in Geographic Aspects of International Relations; The Harris Foundation Lectures of the University of Chicago, 1937, Charles C. Colby, editor, p. 138. Reproduced by courtesy of the University of Chicago Press.

less aid in subduing the region. In the first attempt a line was started from Suakin but abandoned after the *débâcle* at the beginning of 1885. The military conquest was made by way of the Nile route during the last years of the century. The long reaches of navigable water favor this line of ingress, but they are interrupted by series of rapids, each some tens of miles in length. To expedite the movement of troops, a railroad was swiftly pushed from the foot of the rapids which marks the confines of Egypt, across the desert and then along the chord of the great arc described by the stream. When the line had reached the Atbara, leaving only one rapid between the railhead and Omdurman, the attack upon the Sudan was started in earnest. The following year saw the fall of Omdurman, the capital of the revolt. Seats of disaffection remained in areas of hill country, and the new century had dawned before the last of the guerillas had been taken in the hills south of Suakin. As an incident in the reopening of the Nile the British ran across a French force encamped on the site of an ancient African capital at Fashoda, near the upper end of the navigable White Nile. The detachment had come overland from the western Sudan with the hope of establishing a French claim to the whole Sudan. Instead of fighting, the rivals submitted their claims to settlement by Anglo-French diplomacy. The " Fashoda Incident " is the classic example of military restraint of European adversaries in the presence of mighty and threatening Africa.

Before the end of the century the diplomats had agreed to leave the Nile country to Britain while France was allowed a free hand in the central Sudan. Thereupon the British and Egyptian governments set up joint rule over the " Anglo-Egyptian " Sudan. A few years later France and Britain ironed out the remaining wrinkle in their relations over northwest Africa by ceding their rights in Egypt and Morocco respectively.

Thus it turned out that in northeast Africa, just as in South Africa, effective bases for penetration of the continent were established at the turn of the 20th century.

WEST AFRICA

The contenders for the western and central Sudan after the Conference of 1884–85 had thrown down the political bars, were Britain, France, and Germany. On the inner margin of the big bush (Fig. 57) they met resistance from African states which had derived political coherence and large size as a heritage of the slave trade. Some of them had organized for the purpose of slave raiding and had enriched them-selves on its profits. Others had been impacted into dense settlements, their towns defended by mud walls, in an effort to escape enslavement. Although slave trading had virtually disappeared on the high seas, it persisted toward the Sudan. Europeans entered the domains of these native states with the avowed intention of abolishing the Sudanese slave trade as well as to establish trade in other commodities. This stirred the hostility of all the predatory tribes, some of which had already defeated European troops. The Ashanti in the hinterland of Gold Coast were the stoutest of these tribes, and were not conquered until after the end of the century. Their capitulation paved the way for a railroad and the danger of insurrection was among the reasons urging its construction. Of all the British coastal possessions, Nigeria provided the best natural routes to the inner big bush and to the Sudan. This had given it preeminence as a base for slave raiding. In the mid-19th century, efforts to stamp out the overseas slave trade brought about British occupation of a belt of coast in the vicinity of Lagos as the base for a naval patrol. Fifty years passed before British control of the entire delta coast was made effective. Meanwhile British traders had been operating on the navigable Lower Niger under a royal charter and in time the home government, pursuant to the arrangements of the Conference of 1884–85, declared a sphere of influence almost co-incident with the trade territory of the company. By its charter the company exercised political as well as economic supervision. Its pro-cedure was to push operations inland by making trade agreements with chiefs there. Its commitments ultimately entailed a topheavy load of political administration. Toward the end of the century the British government began to fear French encroachments, and felt it advisable to take over the political aspects of penetration. This was done at the opening of the new century, leaving to the Niger Company its eco-nomic pursuits. Within three years the legendary walled cities of the country between Lake Chad and the Middle Niger opened their gates, after a feeble show of resistance, to a small force of coast Africans officered by Britishers.

The earliest French steps into the interior followed the open way, in part via navigable rivers, up the Senegal and down the Upper and Middle Niger. As in the case of the British, the advance guard met de-termined resistance, but during the years of fiercest international com-petition, French troops moved rapidly the length of the Sudan to Lake Chad. Meantime the British were struggling to make headway through the big bush from their bases on Gold Coast and the Lower Niger.

They could not employ Sierra Leone as a military base because mountains there accentuate difficulties of the bush. Gambia, where the wide-mouthed river gave the British access to the small bush unequaled by any French line of ingress, had been rendered useless by treaties which gave to France the entire river basin except for a strip ten kilometers (ca. six miles) wide along each bank to a point just below the head of navigation.

The successful military occupation by the French of vast territory in the Sudan was partial fulfillment of a grandiose scheme for the acquisition of half the continent. Tunisia had been added to France's North African dominions shortly before the scramble began. Its hinterland, along with Algeria, established a claim to the western Sahara. However, no military aid from Barbary could reach the small French forces operating in the Sudan. The rapid and dangerous extension of military investment along more than 30° of longitude from the base at Cape Verde had to rely for support on the four French footholds on the coast of the Gulf of Guinea. One of these, Ivory Coast, had been occupied at the outset of the race, chiefly for this purpose. The French conquest was complete by 1900, the very year the British occupied the Sudanese portions of Gold Coast and Nigeria.

## Assimilation of the Conquests

The conversion of spheres of influence to defined colonies is but the initial step in the real business of reshaping the map of Africa. There remains the problem of pacifying and governing the newly acquired populations, the necessity for effectively piercing the armorlike border of the continent by lines of communication and routes of transportation, the utilization of novel resources and the creation of markets for goods of European origin.

### THE STRATEGY OF RAILROADS

In the clear light of subsequent events some of the territorial objectives for which rival governments bitterly contested appear hardly worth the effort. This is due in part to the shift in values from one locale to another as an early established extractive industry has waned and been succeeded by a freshly discovered resource, or as extraction has been superseded by a more stable pursuit, generally agriculture. It is due in part to the construction of railroads, which have displaced the rivers as the basic fabric of transportation throughout the continent.

The pattern of rails, and in a minor and subsidiary measure of roads also, has evolved through concurrence of several forces. Chief of these are the presence at specific inland points of valuable resources which require transportation to the coast, and the location of natural harbors or of roadsteads which can be converted into harbors at moderate cost. The exact routes chosen take account of terrain — particularly hilly or mountainous country, marsh or swamp, and wide rivers. Some early railroads supplemented river transportation and the course they follow can be explained only by that fact. Some, built originally to ship a resource located not far from the coast, have been extended when other valuable commodities have been discovered farther inland, but not necessarily on a prolongation of the original axis. Embracing and circumscribing all these conditioning natural features is the fixed frame of political boundaries. Each dependency is forced to build and maintain its separate outlets for its resources. As a rule the railroads are constructed and operated by the local administration. In some instances construction has been undertaken by some chartered company which has the concession to mineral, forestal, or other natural resources in the interior. Such companies are usually hardly distinguishable from the local government, and in a number of cases have disposed of their railroad properties to the public authorities. The few lines in private hands are mainly spurs to mines, and many of them carry nothing but their own freight and passengers. Even in the Union of South Africa, where the rail system is most mature, not more than 5 percent of all the mileage is in private hands.

Until after 1900 there were few established routes other than the navigable waterways, outside extreme South Africa. In the years between 1885 and the turn of the century the nations engaged in the African land-grab had been engrossed in establishing spheres of influence, converting them into dependencies actually occupied, and agreeing upon definitive boundaries for their newly-won dominions. This was quite enough, and moreover, it was fortunate for the peace of the continent that transportation had to wait until the political boundaries had been marked on the ground. Either consciously or intuitively, the governments recognized that friction along borders is minimized when the lines are clearly defined. Nearly every boundary was demarked close upon agreement as to its general location. This was done in spite of the difficulties faced by boundary commissions in the primeval bush. These included, in one place or another, heat, sodden soil, almost impenetrable vegetation, marsh, desert, lack of drinking water, and inimical Africans. As a result of this swift conversion of vague claims to accurately bounded dependencies, most of the political boundaries of European holdings were established antecedent to their development as overseas possessions. Hence the railroads and roads subsequently constructed have conformed to the established political arrangements with minimum stress. The current pattern of railroad lines, although palpably unfinished, measures economic forces, confined within a rigid political framework, and conforming to the distribution of natural resources and environmental obstacles and facilities.

## IN WEST AFRICA

In West Africa regular trans-Saharan routes comprise three motorways (Fig. 57) which are traversed at intervals of several weeks during the cooler season, if the traffic warrants and the weather favors. These are subsidized by the governments whose territory is traversed and only serve to emphasize the persistence of the Sahara as a barrier to movement. Practically, West Africa is accessible only from the seacoast.

In each dependency (except Gambia and Portuguese Guinea, which are scarcely more than strips of river bank), a railroad line pierces the big bush from a base on the least unfavorable roadstead. Some of them find their inland terminals on navigable water. M'balmayo is such a terminal on the Nyong. Passengers and freight on the Senegal and French Guinea railroads can be transferred to the other line via the Upper Niger — during the wet season. Other rail lines originally took off at the head of wet-season navigation to traverse riverless tracts of small bush. Kayes on the Senegal and Baro on the Niger were once railroad termini, but for the sake of maintaining service to the coast the year round, these inland lines have been extended to the sea, and navigation on the rivers has been diminished or abandoned.

Several routes terminate in or pass through commercial and political capitals of African states important at the time of European conquest. Such lines can pick up business in an established market and facilitate administration in possible foci of political disaffection. In order from west to east, these towns and cities include Bafoulabé, Kankan, Kumasi, Abomey, Ibadan, Zaria, and Kano. A number of other equally significant capitals are not served by rails, but all are reached by extensions from the railheads in the form of motor roads which are passable at all seasons. Such roads are cheaply constructed in the small bush, and are now being built in the big bush as well, but at higher cost, especially for maintenance.

The few branch railroads have been built to serve local districts of special value, generally mines or plantations. Scarcely any of them maintain regular passenger service. Only two of the dozen original European colonies have rail termini at more than one port. In Gold Coast the first line was projected inland from Sekondi, an open roadstead in the lee of a long promontory. Its terminal is Kumasi, the interior metropolis, reached by way of gold fields being opened soon after 1900. Two decades later a second line was finally built to connect Kumasi with Accra, the seat of European administration on a relatively dry and healthful bit of coast, rather than to move the capital to the rail terminal in the rain-drenched vicinity of Sekondi. The infant railroad " system " of Nigeria likewise owes its origin to valuable minerals. After the railroad had been built from the head of navigation on the Niger to Kano, the principal inland metropolis, interests engaged in extracting tin from placers on the plateau east of the line built a narrow-gauge connection down to Zaria. When, during the World War, shortage of ships led to the mining of coal at Enugu to supply West African needs, a line was built from the mines to Port Harcourt on a navigable mouth of the Niger. Finally, transshipment of tin was obviated by closing the gap between tin and coal with a line of the usual British African gauge, also extended to join the original railroad at Kaduna.

## IN EAST AFRICA

East African railroads between the Sahara and the Eastern Horn of the continent, present a pattern similar to that of West Africa (Fig. 56). British, Italian, and French dependencies have a railroad terminal apiece on the Red Sea, and today these carry most of the external business of that quarter of the continent. All of them were commenced near the beginning of the century, but difficulties of terrain retarded construction on the French and Italian projects.

The British line from the Red Sea to the Nile has justified its construction parallel to the ancient caravan route, but it had to await completion of a railroad in the Sudanese section of the Nile Valley. This was undertaken as a military measure and reached the first serious obstacle, the Atbara tributary river, before the conquest of the towns at the confluence of the Blue and White Nile. Rails were pushed to this strategic center just before the new century opened. The combination rail-and-river route is handicapped by four transshipments between Khartum and ocean steamers. (Four, instead of three, because the South African gauge gives way to European standard gauge at Luxor.)

The nearness of a functioning port on the Red Sea at Suakin impelled the construction of a line connecting with the valley rails at the confluence of the Atbara. Suakin harbor proved too small and a new outlet was found at Port Sudan. Scarcely more than a decade after the first line reached Khartum, an extension was thrust westward along the axis of the Sudan to the first principal center of population beyond the Nile. Both trade and administration thereby benefited. Since the interruption caused by the World War, the incipient system has ramified to tap and interconnect all the leading production districts north of the extensive marshes of the upper Sudan. Even that region and the Upper Nile have been put in regular communication with the coast by river steamer. To accomplish this a channel had to be cut and maintained through the tangle of marsh vegetation (sudd) which clogs the Nile in the great marsh that represents one of the major structural basins of the African continent. This was not accomplished until political stability underwrote regular and systematic attack on the encroaching plant life.

Farther south, railroads have been retarded by desert, by the precipitous face of a high plateau, and in Ethiopia by the continuance of African administration a full generation after the rest of the area had been taken over by European governments. From a nearby French port a line finished in 1915 takes advantage of the Rift Valley to ascend to the Ethiopian capital. The comparable but much shorter Italian line rises to nearly the same elevation (ca. 8000 feet). The conquest of Ethiopia by Italy appears to have resulted in partial reorientation of the highland toward the Italian port, accomplished by new roads articulated to the rail line already in operation.

## IN THE SOUTHERN SUBCONTINENT

The railroad pattern of Africa south of the Sudan and Ethiopia presents the triumph of the direct route over political obstacles, and the superiority of continouous rails over waterways on which navigation is interrupted.

In the less elevated highland south of Ethiopia, British interests were inherited from trade relations with Zanzibar and from explorations and missionary ventures in the basin of the Upper Nile (Fig. 51). For a time it was expected that this region would empty its trade, as it does its water, into the Nile, especially in view of the stiff climb required to reach it from the Indian Ocean. After the Middle Nile had been closed to Europeans by the crusade of the 1880s, a railroad line was undertaken from Mombasa, the most suitable seaport under British control, construction being begun in the year the military railroad of the Sudan was launched from the foot of the Second Cataract (Fig. 58). Its objective was Lake Victoria, which was attained just about the time the Nile was cleared of sudd. This gives the region two outlets, but all business except a negligible tourist trade uses the short line to the east coast in preference to the long Nile route with its transshipments.

Mineral deposits have been the successive lodestones which have drawn railroads step by step from south, east, and north to the core of the southern half of the continent. There, in the mineralized Katanga district of the southernmost Congo, is the meeting place of a thin web of lines which, with their connections via inland waterways, reach the coast at a dozen points between the two intersections of the coastline with the Equator.

The discovery in the early 1870s of the unmatched diamond deposits at Kimberley and other places in the vicinity of the Orange-Vaal confluence first pulled a railroad line from Capetown up the steps of the plateau face. It was 1881 before Cape Colony's gauge was standardized at 3' 6" and the line came to be actively pushed from the base of the highland, where its terminal had rested for two decades. Once on the plateau, the rails skirt the desert instead of bisecting the farmlands, settled much earlier but self-sustaining, in contrast to the new mining camps which required facile contact with their overseas market, and the source of machinery, and of much food. By coincidence Kimberley was reached in 1885, the very year which initiated the scramble among the powers for central Africa. The new terminal had two coastal outlets, a line from Port Elizabeth having been constructed while the Capetown route was being projected inland.

Completion of the two lines from ports in the Cape Province to Kimberley coincided with the first important discoveries of gold in the country beyond the Vaal River. These culminated in the Rand in 1886. The gold camps needed railroad transportation even more urgently than the diamond districts. There ensued a race to serve this new and more remote mining country. The Cape Province sent a branch from its Port Elizabeth-Kimberley line through the heart of the arable High Veld and in 1892 reached Johannesburg, coeval with the Rand goldfield and already its metropolis. Later the port of East London was made an additional rail terminal for the South African system. Natal Province pushed a railroad from its port, Durban. Owing to stiffer gradients, this line did not attain its goal until 1895. Meanwhile the Boer government of the Transvaal, annoyed at being in economic

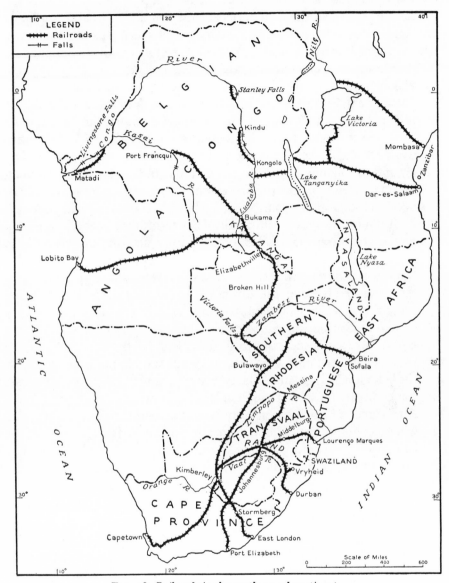

FIG. 58. Railroads in the southern subcontinent.

The line of the Congo River, where thickened, indicates a navigable reach of the stream.

bondage to the hated British, completed in 1894 a line of rails to Lourenço Marques, at the same time the nearest port and the best natural harbor among all the rival outlets of the Rand. Thus nature and politics combined to pierce the boundary barrier which separates the Transvaal from Portuguese East Africa. Coal to run the diamond and gold mines and the railroads themselves, is supplied from fields through which the railroads were built in their progress from coast to mine. (Stormberg Valley on the East London line, Vryheid and Newcastle in Natal, and Middelburg on the Lourenço Marques line.)

The next magnet for rails was Southern Rhodesia, where old native workings of gold were rediscovered in 1864. Lines extending to Kimberley and to Johannesburg both pointed toward Rhodesia. The Kimberley line was selected for the first extension, in spite of bordering desert, because the proposed route could be built in country already governed by Britain instead of in unfriendly Boer territory. The work was commenced before any railroad had tapped Johannesburg, and reached the coreland of Southern Rhodesia at Bulawayo only five years after the Rand was linked to the sea. Thence it was consistently pushed along the watershed between the Zambesi and the coastal streams, partly because this was promising country, and partly to minimize costs of construction. During the same years a line was being built inland from Beira, chosen as a successor to historic Sofala as the most suitable site for a port on the gulf which marks the closest approach of the sea to the Rhodesian highland. The rail route through Southern Rhodesia was completed just after the Boer War had unified extra-tropical South Africa under British sovereignty, and during the short span of years when economic penetration into interior Africa from all coasts was being vigorously initiated. In every sense Southern Rhodesia is transitional between the middle and the low latitudes. Although within the tropics, its elevation modifies the climate and gives it some bits of High Veld akin to the much larger plateau south of the Limpopo River. Suitable for permanent settlement by Europeans, these spots are islands in a sea of typical low-latitude lowland, which beyond the Zambesi spreads unrelieved to the northern Sahara. It is therefore more than coincidence that by 1900 Europeans had advanced farther inland in this region than elsewhere in Black Africa, and that two rail lines were in operation, one following the long highland route from middle-latitude seacoasts, the other traversing the short route to the nearest coast. This duplication in Southern Rhodesia of the railroad pattern of the Transvaal emphasizes the urge for direct outlets to ocean harbors, even across barriers of swampy plain, steep gradients, and political disconformity. As the railroad progressed the scattered gold mines of this region were reopened and the second major mineral deposit — chromic iron ore — was tapped, but only at two points rather than along its axis, which lies east of the line.

The stretch of rails which connects Northern with Southern Rho- desia was undertaken to open the more remote province, but without particular expectation of tapping mineral wealth. From Bulawayo it aimed at Victoria Falls, a scenic wonder of the first magnitude. En route it crosses the coalfield which parallels the Zambesi for many miles. Useful at once to drive locomotives, this coal has since been shipped as far north as the Belgian Congo to serve mines. However, this valuable mineral resource would apparently be traversed by any line crossing the stream between Victoria Falls and the final rapids. From Victoria Falls the rails turn abruptly northeastward toward the narrow waist of British territory between southeasternmost Belgian Congo and northwestern Portuguese Africa. At Broken Hill the line opened rich deposits of zinc and lead. There it remained for some years, until it was deflected from its original course (into northeastern Rhodesia) by the further exploitation of the mineralized core of central Africa. This continues without marked interruption from Broken Hill to its culmination in Katanga, and includes deposits of vanadium, manganese, iron, gold, and silver. Just south of the political boundary are productive copper mines, counterparts of those north of the border. A little prior to the World War the line was extended into Katanga, giving that district its first all-rail outlets to the sea. Of the alternative ports, Beira obtains the bulk of the business, being the nearest.

In Katanga, one of the largest sources of copper on earth, are found also tin, uranium, gold, iron, and coal, as well as cobalt in the form of a byproduct of copper mining. These riches, coupled with location in the center of the southern lobe of Africa, have instigated the construction of several lines of transport other than the system of South Africa, to which the Rhodesian line hitched it.

The mineralized districts lie in the unnavigable headwaters of the Congo Basin, but below the confluence marked by the town of Bukama the river becomes navigable, although there are three considerable interruptions, due to rapids and falls, between Bukama and the estuary.

As part of the general move inland in Africa after 1900, a company was formed to build a railroad from the major navigable reach of the Congo to the Nile. With the discovery of copper in Katanga, this purpose was abandoned in favor of two rail portages around the Stanley

Falls and the rapids which beset the stream between Kongolo and Kindu. These, with the recently relocated line around the Livingstone Falls on the Lower Congo, were envisioned as making a feasible outlet for Katanga entirely through Belgian territory. They were completed the very year the Rhodesian line crossed the Congo border. Alternative outlets to the Congo estuary and to Beira facilitated the rapid expansion of mining stimulated by the World War. This in turn warranted maximum use of available outlets, and in the last year of the war rails ran the length of the mineralized zone to the head of navigation on the Congo system. Increasing freight in turn encouraged the completion of other routes into Katanga which had been projected as independent items in the attack on interior Africa, and from opposite sides of the continent.

While the Rhodesian railroad was crossing the Zambesi and the portage line around Stanley Falls was being built, the government of German East Africa undertook a line from Dar-es-Salaam, the colony's most capacious natural harbor, to Lake Tanganyika. This line crosses much sterile country and must depend for traffic on the lake region. It was finished just as the World War broke out, and was supplemented a year later by a Belgian line from Lake Tanganyika to the navigable Lualaba. This combination of rail and water routes gives access to Katanga, but it is unused, being as awkward as the break-bulk route via the Congo and having its ocean terminal on the same remote coast as Beira, the end of an existing all-rail route. The line was warranted only by political emulation.

A bit before the launching of the German line, British capitalists interested in Katanga mines obtained a concession from the Portuguese government to construct a railroad from Lobito Bay, one of the sandspit harbors on the Angolan coast, by way of the ancient overland watershed trail between the Congo and Zambesi headstreams. It was difficult to obtain the concession, and subsequently obstacles were repeatedly thrust in the way of construction of the route, by interests in other outlets of Katanga, chiefly German. After the World War had eliminated German opposition and fostered cooperation between Britain and Belgium, construction moved more rapidly. The line was completed in 1931 and immediately began to assert its superiority over all its competitors, as providing the shortest route to Europe, and at the same time involving only one transshipment between the mining district and the European port.

After the Angolan line had been begun, a second all-Belgian route was projected in the form of railroad from Katanga to Matadi on the

Congo Estuary. It was completed as far as Port Francqui, near the head of navigation on the Kasai, a little before the Angolan line was opened. This line involves three transshipments, and neither before nor since the completion of its all-rail rival has it carried heavy freight, despite its unified political character.

Thanks mainly to mineral deposits of the first order of magnitude, a light net of railroad lines enmeshed the massive bulk of Black Africa in exactly half a century. In addition a large percentage of the branch lines run to mineralized districts which are able to pay for their construction.

Several of the lines cross political borders in obedience to the paramountcy of direct access over boundary obstacles. Others have been built without economic justification out of emulation among European governments. Still others circumvent unfriendly political territory by traversing country inferior in resources or fretted with handicaps of terrain. The roundabout route and heavy gradients on the line from Johannesburg to Lourenço Marques expresses the unwillingness of its Boer backers to follow the ancient and comparatively easy trail through British Swaziland. The direction of this trail is pointed out by the alternative rails from the port which stub against the Swazi boundary. This line, built by Portuguese interests, has never been completed across British territory because of the fear that it will cut the throat of the established railroad. The semi-desert route of the main line into Southern Rhodesia was chosen to avoid what was at the time Boer territory. Afterwards copper drew the Transvaal rails to Messina on the Rhodesian border, and gold pulled a feeler southward from the Rhodesian main line. A bridge and an easy connection about 100 miles long would expedite traffic along the axis of the most productive part of South Africa, but might hurt the established line. The connection can now be made, but only by changing to motor vehicles.

### COMMUNICATIONS BETWEEN THE CAPE AND CAIRO

An overland, all-British route linking the north coast and the south tip of Africa along the Nile Valley and the highland of East and South Africa, was first proposed in 1876 by Edwin Arnold, an English writer who had gained a colonial viewpoint through residence in India. The Suez Canal had recently been opened, but Egypt had not yet been declared a protectorate. Along the East African coast Aden was the only British possession north of the Tugela River in Natal (although Zanzibar was under British influence). In interior Africa Britain's farthest north was a questionable claim to Kimberley, which had just then leaped into prominence as a diamond-bearing district. The concept has been fostered by at least three of British Africa's greatest empire builders. The Cape-to-Cairo idea has been commonly accepted to mean a railroad running wholly through territory incontestably British and uninterrupted by transshipments. Such a railroad has never been an imminent geographic likelihood. Perhaps its proponents intended it primarily as a means to kindle British enthusiasm over territory which would have an axis extending the full length of the continent.

The whole history of African exploitation has followed the pattern of penetration from points all along the coast. Therefore a land route paralleling the ocean waterway is unlikely to get much transcontinental traffic, however serviceable certain sections of it may be for local carriage. If such a railroad were built, most freight would continue to flow to the nearby ports, to be placed on the cheaper and not much slower sea route. Most passengers would continue to prefer the comfort and relative coolness of an ocean passage to the heat, dust, insects, and monotonous scenery of the long land journey. The high cost of constructing and maintaining a railroad from the Cape to Cairo will be profitable only in case the volume of local traffic here and there is able to pay for the long mileage which can attract little business. The lakes of the Rift Valleys and the navigable reaches of the Nile are ready-to-hand alternatives to railroads over hundreds of miles of the route, but transshipment of cargo and even transfer of passengers is fatal to through business. The mere lack of rail connection across the Zambesi, to link Nyasaland to the port of Beira, so cut off the settlements at the southern end of Lake Nyasa that a railroad bridge (said to be the longest on earth) has been constructed to validate the rest of the system. It may therefore be presumed that until continuous rails on the same gauge connect the tip of South Africa with the mouth of the Nile, the Cape-to-Cairo scheme will remain a vision. On the political side the hope of an all-British route appeared to be shattered when the boundary between German and Belgian possessions was drawn through the Western Rift Valley. As an alternative, Britain obtained an option on a route which would traverse these latitudes in Belgian territory. When the World War furnished a pretext for depriving Germany of its colonies, the all-British route became once more politically possible, because most of German East Africa was allocated to Great Britain. Hardly had Britain obtained a clean political sweep the length of East Africa when discontent in Egypt led it to relinquish its protectorate over that country. With the passing years Britain has limited its control to the Suez Canal Zone, thereby alienating one of the termini of a Cape-to-Cairo railroad. At the same time the Nilotic Sudan has been brought under closer British administration, and the principal gaps in an all-rail route lie in that dependency. The fact is that in two decades no move has been made to realize the dream, the only new rail line in the acquired territory being a connection between the existing east-west line and Lake Victoria — a branch constructed to obtain additional local traffic clearing through the nearby port of Dar-es-Salaam.

If the Cape-to-Cairo connection be conceived in broader terms than continuous rails, routes of a sort do exist. It is now possible for determined tourists to make the journey overland by combining rail, motor road, lake ship, and river steamer. In the feverish search for new worlds to traverse for the fun of it, this has become one of the few long journeys which still provide discomfort and distinctive scenes, if not adventure. Of more practical significance is the air route, regularly flown, carrying mail, passengers, and express. Recently the British government has undertaken to forward by plane all letters addressed to imperial postoffices on this route, without extra charge. This is a new and significant extension of the geopolitical principle of a flat rate for personal communications long ago established within the national boundaries of occidental states. Its proved usefulness in coordinating sections within a country promises to justify the extension of the plan to the larger and more scattered area of the British Empire. As an airway, the Cape-to-Cairo route has already become an important link in imperial articulation.

## GOVERNANCE

After centuries of confinement to the coast, European rule swiftly marched inland from bases on the west, south, and east, and in a few instances from the north. At the opening of the 20th century the major outline of colonial holdings was sketched and many of the boundaries were delimited. Railroads promptly followed occupation. When the World War rudely checked the extension of routes, the basic structure of internal transportation had already been traced. Since the war some of the projects have been completed, and motor roads and airways have come to supplement the railroads, which remain the backbone of political administration as well as economic exploitation.

In the beginning each dependency was segregated from its neighbors under the same or other flags by belts of bush lacking effective means of transport. This remains true today of many units in the political mosaic. With few exceptions such barrier belts do not coincide with naturally marked boundaries, of which there are few in Africa. Some of them betoken commercial immaturity and await the extension of routes which can be financed only as business warrants them. Others reflect reluctance on the part of the holding nations to establish points of ready contact, lest they become points of political friction.

In most instances, whether a barrier belt persists or not, the boundaries between dependencies strike across the grain of nature. In Africa the texture of the natural environment is coarse but pronounced, and indigenous life has become attuned to it. In its broad lines big bush, small bush, and desert, modified by altitude, hilliness, and ground water level constitute the environmental texture of African life. The natural conditions are restated in the mode of agricultural occupance — shifting cultivation, nomadic herding, irrigation agriculture, with spots of sedentary tillage scattered through both types of bush, as well as the desert. They reappear again in the social structure — communal, clustered tribes in the big bush, large groups aggregated into common cultures in the small bush, commensal communities in the desert. Finally they express themselves in political organization — respectively small, independent entities, wide-flung absolutisms, and nomadism dominating scattered sedentary groups. Cross-hatching this pattern with political and economic units based on coastal frontage, imposed by Europeans, has cut most of the geo-aboriginal structures into segments and has joined many of them in combinations novel alike to Africans and Europeans.

Granting that European administration of colonies has varied through the centuries, the diversity of aims and methods today in force among the several nations amounts to laboratory experimentation in colonial governance, in several different and sharply antithetic types of regions. In Africa the antithesis appears in its largest terms as between middle latitudes and low latitudes. In the one Europeans can live permanently without suffering impairment of health from climate and climate-bred diseases. In the other the European must vigilantly and tirelessly struggle to keep in health, and at the end of a few years' sojourn, he must seek refreshment beyond the Tropics.[1] It therefore becomes advisable to consider governance by Europeans separately for the low-latitude and for the middle-latitude parts of the continent, and to include the Barbary Coast of the Mediterranean Sea, as well as Black Africa.

---

[1] Above certain altitudes within the tropics Europeans can apparently live and reproduce. Small groups have remained in the Middle American highlands for four centuries. No such tests have been made in Africa, where the issue remains controversial.

## GOVERNANCE IN MIDDLE-LATITUDE AFRICA

Africa, the continent balanced on the Equator, reaches into the lower middle latitudes at north and at south. France and Italy possess, on the Barbary coast, an environment almost the counterpart of the opposite European shore. Britain, in South Africa, has territory running the gamut of lower-middle-latitude climates. Both ends of the continent are suited to European settlement. Both have large populations of European origin. Nevertheless, these populations make up only a small fraction of the total inhabitants — $\frac{1}{7}$ in the Union of South Africa and Southern Rhodesia, and $\frac{1}{12}$ in Barbary. The masses in both are descendants of the ancient inhabitants. The Europeans sit in the seats of the mighty, having organized the external relations of their holdings to fit into an expanded European world. Both France and Britain, and perhaps also Italy, envision for these lands the ideal of autonomy within the greater (imperial) commonwealth.

In Barbary there is some degree of integration with the political system of the dominant country across the Mediterranean. The portion of Algeria north of the Atlas Mountains has been under French rule for a century (Fig. 50). In one sense it is part of France, comprising three of the 90 departments of that country. Each is represented in the French Senate and Chamber of Deputies. Nevertheless, the integration is incomplete. There is a governor appointed from France, and a separate budget. This budget is acted upon by locally elected delegates who are chosen in two divisions, French and African, a concession to the age-old differences in the societies of the two shores of the Mediterranean. These special political arrangements are officially viewed as temporary expedients. The way is open for Africans to become French citizens. Those of Jewish faith became so long since. Moslems must give up polygamy and other tenets of their religion in order to take advantage of this provision; thus far few have done so. Tunisia and Morocco are protectorates, the one seized just prior to the international scramble for Africa, the other after its close. It is tacitly assumed that they will successively follow Algeria until all Barbary is assimilated to France. At present they are administered from Paris. Distinct judicial systems interpret the laws, courts for Moslems being staffed by native authorities, while courts for Europeans are under French judges. In Morocco a third system handles·cases under Jewish law. Likewise in coastal Libya, where Italian rule was scarcely undertaken until after the World War, native and European administration operate side by side. The indigenes of Barbary are urged to learn the French or Italian language, to accept the ideals of Latin culture, and to fit themselves to become French or Italian citizens in the fullest degree. Because these people are offshoots of the white race, this objective seems not too fantastic, in spite of their Moslem or Jewish faith and the unremitting example of nomadic life set by the adjacent desert. Evidence of progress is clear if Algeria, in a measure part of France, be compared with Morocco, a mere protectorate in which French authority was until lately limited by Britain's right to maintain special courts for British subjects.

In South Africa the European populations have passed through several degrees of dependence and autonomy, ranging from colonies to independent sovereignties. The period of the African partition was marked by rapid exploitation of the mineral wealth of the highlands in the south. Economic emulation led to war between the (two) British dominions and the (two) Boer sovereign states, which together constituted the country south of the Limpopo and Orange rivers. Peace, which synchronized with the end of the partitioning of low-latitude Africa, was followed by the substitution of a single self-governing dominion for the two pairs of rivals. As a member of the British Commonwealth of Nations, the Union of South Africa manages its internal affairs, and presumably could declare itself independent of Great Britain if it chose. Scattered among the constituent territories of the Union are three British protectorates over native reserves, not subject to Union authority. Adjacent is the former German Southwest Africa, held under mandate from the League of Nations by the Union government. These four units occupy country either unsuited to permanent European settlement, or handicapped by ruggedness or by desert climate. Within the Union are smaller native reserves, governed by the constituent members of the federation. Except for a small colored representation in the Cape Province, the Union franchise is exclusively in the hands of people of European extraction. Neither the indigenes nor dark-skinned immigrants, who stem chiefly from India, are contemplated as future citizens. Nowhere else is the color bar raised so rigidly as in parts of South Africa, where the white population is large, but still a small fraction of the colored.

North of the Limpopo River, and extending to the Zambesi, Europeans staked out a new " white man's country " as part of the African partition. It has followed in the steps of the earlier settlements to the southward, except that its European population is homogeneous and fought no war. It was made a self-governing dominion after the World War. In its native reserves, native councils may be chosen to advise

he governor. Because the area suited to permanent European settlement is small, it seems destined to remain more akin to low-latitude
Africa than to the extra-tropical southern end of the continent.

In the two middle-latitude extremes of Africa, then, the colonial machines of France, Italy, and Britain have been organized to achieve a
single purpose — growth out of leading strings and into political maturity. But how different the results! Barbary is to constitute a supplementary France or Italy; the southern boundary of Europe is to be
moved from the Mediterranean to the Sahara. French citizenry has
already been augmented by Africans who live in the European manner.
In contrast South Africa may or may not remain within the British
Empire. Presumably it will do so for commercial advantages, if not
from sentimental attachment. In any event the body politic is to retain
its pure white complexion. Neither in Britain nor in South Africa is it
contemplated that the dark-skinned shall become politically Britons.

In these antitheses can be descried conditions of natural environment. Barbary lies close to France and Italy; South Africa is remote
from the British Isles. Barbary is climatically, and therefore in its production, the double of the Mediterranean Europe; sun-scorched, pastoral South Africa with its store of precious metals is a world apart from
cool, moist Britain, devoted to manufacturing and commerce based
on the mining of coal and iron. The Berber, the Arab, the Moor, " barbarian " though he be, is after all a Mediterranean, as is the Italian or
the Provençal Frenchman; the Hottentot, the Bantu, the Hindu is
racially and traditionally totally at variance with the South African
immigrant from the British Isles or the Netherlands. Divergent national traditions also figure. Since the 10th century France has absorbed
into the French community every increment of territory added to the
original kernel of the state; in contrast the British Empire is an aggregate of relict nationalities, never fully assimilated. Today France and
Italy are determined not to fall behind in the race to maintain population, i.e., war matériel, whereas Britain continues to lay emphasis on
trade figures and to disregard statistics on population.

Closely related to the Mediterranean coastland colonies of France
and Italy is the vast hinterland of desert. Bisected by the Tropic of
Cancer, the Sahara might be permanently settled by Europeans because of its dry climate, were its meager resources not already strained
to sustain the indigenous population. Great Britain, France, and Italy
have succeeded in making it a safe transit land for the few people and
goods that traverse it. Neither economic expansion nor population increase of moment can be anticipated, except for Egypt.

Egypt, unique oasis nourished from the core of Africa, never knew where Nile water came from until the 19th century. It was always a world apart, and today it gives increasing evidence of its distinction from the remainder of the continent. If it were not for the especial political value of the Suez Canal, the few remaining vestiges of control imposed by Great Britain would be abandoned (Ch. 9). It is the only state on the continent which has been able to enforce recognition of its independence upon the European Powers. To this end the natural environment has contributed. Like other oases it is cut off from the world by desert barriers, but it is unique in having an outlet at either end to facilitate external trade. As in other oases its population is engaged almost exclusively in irrigation agriculture, but the arable acreage is so large that it supports 14,000,000 people, instead of a few hundred. Because a uniform way of life begets political solidarity, and because a low-latitude oasis has little in common with Europe, it has been possible to create a national movement opposed to foreign control. The eternal threat to indigenous government in Egypt is the ribbon shape of the ecumene, with consequent danger of revolt at the end farthest from the seat of government. The capitals of independent ancient Egypt were alternately at the head of the delta and at the bend of the stream from which overland routes took off for the Red Sea. Today telegraphic communication and rail and air transportation reduce the handicap of a long, narrow country. Moreover, since antiquity the delta has become the overwhelmingly dominant part of the country, thanks to extension of the irrigated area and the diversion of through traffic from the Lower Nile to the Red Sea.

## GOVERNANCE IN LOW-LATITUDE AFRICA

In low-latitude Africa — the country of the big bush and the country of the small bush — the pattern being etched by Europeans upon the indigenous geographic structure is novel. There alone on earth is found the combination of (1) tropical conditions admittedly irredeemable for permanent European settlement and (2) a large indigenous population primitive in its culture but vital enough to persist and even to prosper under the sway of European administration and exploitation. The European order has been imposed so recently that it could profit from lessons learned in the other low-latitude continents. Nowhere else have half a dozen different nations seized simultaneously upon arbitrary slices of regions uniform in natural environment and in cultural occupance, thus creating an experimental laboratory of governance.

The initial device for dealing with lands discovered by maritime Europeans was the chartered trading company, and Africa has seen a long succession of these firms. Ostensibly created to exploit all or specified natural resources of a particular overseas coast, and sometimes its hinterland, each of these companies found itself involved in much more than trade. No matter how small its concession, the company had some bit of land to serve as a base of operations. In primitive Africa, the Europeans sent out had not only to engage in trade, but also to govern themselves and their African servants. In the mind of the western European, government is inseparable from territory. When increasing opportunities to do business drew an enterprise inland, the company's political functions kept pace.

In the partition of interior Africa, some of these companies became the vehicles by which the national spheres of influence were converted into effective occupation. They made treaties with native chiefs and subsequently sent their armies in to insure the execution of these agreements. They launched the construction of railroads and impressed indigenous labor to build them. They cooperated with missionaries, consular officers of their home governments, and official political agents, to the end of increasing the African holdings of the nation to which they owed their charter. With few exceptions this merger of business and government became onerous to the companies, which were likely to discover that the cost of government exceeded the profits of business. It became vexatious to the home governments, which either considered the companies lax in extending their territorial holdings or conversely were embarrassed when boundaries were pushed so far as to raise the threat of an international war. During the first decade of the 20th century nearly all the chartered companies relinquished their political functions to their respective governments, and the last of them will soon follow suit.

As substitutes for government by chartered trading company, the several legatee governments have initiated a variety of administrative schemes.

In many cases a legal distinction between a narrow zone or small block on the coast and the hinterland has been inherited from the past. A coastal foothold, long subjected to European influence, is likely to be termed a " colony," and in some instances it has privileges not accorded to the back country. Residents of the ancient French possessions in the vicinity of Cape Verde possess the franchise and a considerable measure of self-government. They are represented in the French Chamber by a Deputy. All the rest of French Africa is divided into colonies for administrative purposes; most of these trace back to early coastal footholds, but internal administrative distinctions have been swept away by the orderly French, except in mandated districts obtained at the close of the World War. Spain differentiates between its long-occupied islands and Rio Muni on the mainland, even yet unoccupied. In Portuguese East Africa a chartered trading company retains political administration of Sofala, its ancient center, and a considerable area in the vicinity, whereas the remainder is administered by Portugal. As might be expected, the British possessions exhibit the most general differentiation between coast and interior. In West Africa each dependency comprises a small colony on the coast and a large protectorate made up of land acquired much later. In East Africa the same distinction holds with the titles reversed. There the coast of Kenya and the islands offshore are organized as " protectorates " under the Sultan of Zanzibar, whereas the interior of Kenya is denominated a colony. Farther inland, however, Uganda and Nyasaland are protectorates, in the fashion of West Africa. All these distinctions in British colonies are relict forms illustrative of the region's historical geography rather than significant items in its contemporary geopolitical structure. Belgian, German, and Italian administrations have uniformly treated their dependencies as units, regardless of their past, which in no case was associated with these countries until the latter part of the 19th century.

Both in the early coastal trading and in the later opening of the interior, the chartered companies of whatever nation displayed initiative and aggressiveness. Apart from a few mission stations which became nuclei of political units, every colony and protectorate in low-latitude Africa owes its origin to traders, most of whom were sent out by companies.

So long as slaves remained the chief commodity of trade, the companies were inclined to treat the continent as a human game preserve. They therefore opposed road building and restricted exports to slaves and other commodities, such as ivory and placer gold, which the Africans themselves could extract in small quantity and bring to the exporting stations on the coast. Even when an awakening public conscience in some of the home states undertook to suppress the slave trade, the companies adhered to the ethical standard of the early modern age in which they were rooted, and refused to heed the signs of the times. Therefore when illegal slave trading became unprofitable as well, upon the general abolition of slavery, the companies abruptly lost their business.

It was only gradually that other African resources were recognized as suitable substitutes for slaves. These were less mobile than human beings, bulkier than ivory, and could be had in profitable quantity only at the price of organizing their production and their transportation to the coast. When this was undertaken, it was, like the earlier exploitation, the work of chartered companies, which now reversed the earlier policy and took the lead in opening the interior. To do this they obtained concessions to vast areas in which they were given economic monopoly and also a free hand in administration. This made it easy to extort from the inhabitants the heavy labor needed to obtain the rubber, palm oil, ivory, and other products in quantities sufficient to yield rich profits to the stockholders. Most of the commodities in demand at this time were products of the big bush, where, except for a few rivers, all transport was confined to human porterage. This increased the demand for labor, in an environment sparsely settled, and resulted in virtual enslavement in many areas.

No colonial nation was entirely guiltless, but the Congo Basin exemplified the conditions more conspicuously than any other area. Unexplored until the 1870s, its exploitation was then organized under a private trading company which for a generation had no national status and therefore even less responsibility than the rest. Toward the end of the 19th century the outcry against brutality rose to such a pitch in the civilized world that the Congo administration was forced to take cognizance of it. In the end it relinquished its political functions to a European state, Belgium, which engaged to shoulder the responsibility for the welfare of the Congo natives. During this period the other nations of north Europe with African colonies were coming to the conclusion that political authority vested in trading companies was a firebrand. As rival traders of different nationality approached each other in the African hinterland, the home governments realized that clashes out there and perhaps war in Europe could be averted only if they took over the political functions of the somewhat irresponsible chartered companies. In one district after another, the governments, forced to assume responsibility, had to create overnight effective administrations in an area several times the size of the combined home countries. The army was the initial instrument of the new order, but it could be only a temporary expedient. A civil administration was needed to control industry and trade, and to deal with indigenous populations. The long process of assimilation and integration of indigenous African life with European exploitation and guidance has varied with the local conditions in Africa and with the policy and vigor of the European nations involved.

## THE SECONDARY COLONIAL SYSTEM

Spanish colonies are restricted to Africa, but for all that are negligible (Fig. 54). Until after it proclaimed itself a republic, Spain took almost no cognizance of its holdings.

Portugal, a small country poor in resources and vexed by political turmoil for the past generation, has been the last to abandon the system of chartered companies having political functions. Its African dependencies, disproportionately large and rich compared to the size and wealth of the homeland, were extended to their present confines by mutual jealousy among the Great Powers, and have been preserved intact by the same force. Effective government is confined to the main routes and centers. The mode of government is direct administration by a governor and assistants sent out from Portugal. A feature of Portuguese colonies unique in Black Africa is the existence of considerable groups of mixed European and African parentage who are recognized as belonging to the European population.

German colonies were expunged by the World War, but the effect of thirty years of German control persists. No other nation put so much energy into its African colonies, including experimental study of tropical agriculture. The objective was to produce goods needed by Germany or salable on world markets. The procedure was to establish subsidized trading companies, mining companies, forest companies, plantations, and transportation companies. Their activities were directed in considerable measure by political expediency. At first the indigenes were administered directly, with the benefit of the ruling country in mind. On plantations especially, toll of life was heavy among the workers, and to keep their enterprises going colonial governors resorted to forced labor, undistinguishable from slavery. Partly because of harsh methods, and partly because the Germans were inexperienced in colonial administration, they made mistakes which plunged them into costly native wars in three of their four colonies. Being serious students of colonial governance, they profited from their errors, and came to recognize that diversity of nature is matched by different modes of indigenous life. Thereupon they usually recognized the authority of the scattered native chiefs in the big bush, and in the more advanced societies of the small bush governed through the established forms, so long as the African rulers conformed to the requirements of the commissioners sent out from Germany. Today, after a quarter century, the solid German stamp remains imprinted on the landscape in every center of German activity. Nowhere else in low-latitude Africa are structures so substantial, railroads so far in excess of current demands, or plantations so numerous.

Italian Africa comprised little but desert until the conquest of Ethiopia in 1936. It is too early to foresee all the steps in the assimilation of the Ethiopian highland. The whole East African territory under the Italian flag has been assembled into a single colony. Its administration is in the hands of men sent out from Italy, but there is a small advisory council on which a few Ethiopian chiefs sit. Absolute governments have been customary in Ethiopia, and the legal system is far more elaborate than the tribal simplicity of most of Black Africa. Such a political society can be either an aid or a deterrent to its conquerors. It has been announced that Italian farmers, as well as traders and missionaries, are to take part in the occupation of the highland. This implies settlement colonization. If successful, the planting of permanent European settlers will take Ethiopia out of the category of its low-latitude surroundings and range it alongside Barbary and South Africa. Its people inherit traditions and physical traits not unlike those of Barbary indigenes. Its natural environment is similar to some of the highlands of Middle America where European societies have lived for several centuries. Its future as an extension of Italy is favored by these circumstances. The cloud veiling a roseate future is the relation between colored indigenes and white colonists. It can hardly be imagined that Ethiopia will see the invention of any *modus vivendi* not heretofore tried on equally favorable ground, or that the " color question " will be any less vexatious to both sides than it is in every other place where the two groups occupy the same region as permanent settlers.

When the Belgian government took over administration of the Congo Free State, it inherited the system of chartered companies in its most egregious form. Vast domains in the interior had been assigned by Leopold's government as concessions. Ostensibly they were to be exploited for their extractable forest products or minerals, but as these were obtainable only through the labor of the inhabitants, the companies subjected the unfortunate people to " forced labor " which amounted to slavery. In this region, technically under international jurisdiction and actually subjected to occasional supervision by international conferences and treaties, the companies represented capital from various European nations. Belgians were the heaviest stockholders and the position of the Belgian king as head of the Free State made the exploitation increasingly a Belgian enterprise. When public outcry against the abuses practiced by many of the companies compelled the European powers to insist upon responsible political authority as a substitute for the dubious practices of the Free State, the dominance of Belgian interests and the mutual jealousy of the Great African Powers (at that time Great Britain, France, and Germany) settled the authority upon Belgium. A tiny country and therefore in spite of high density less populous than the other nations which have led in African exploitation, Belgium rates with them in being devoted to manufacturing and to trade in excess of local consumption, and therefore having colonial leanings. In consequence, under Belgian administration the Congo has been tapped by railroads, mines and forests have been consistently developed, and plantation agriculture has been widely attempted.

In taking over the Congo, the Belgian government restricted the chartered companies to their economic functions, although several of them operate on so vast a scale that they exert great political influence, both locally and in Belgium. This appears in governmental encouragement of plantations, in spite of the official declaration that the indigenes have first claim upon the soil, and in governmental toleration of devices to " persuade " Africans to work for the companies, devices which amount to compulsions. The administrative structure is centralized, and the administrative units take no account of tribal distributions. Centralized authority over so large and diverse an area is bound to be faulty. Recognition of this has brought about delegation of some authority to the governors of the four Provinces into which the colony is divided. Unfortunately these do not closely correspond to either natural or ethnic regions. A densely populated district beyond the lakes was mandated to Belgium at the close of the World War in partial payment for German destructiveness in the home country and with an eye to supplying labor to the mines of sparsely populated Katanga (Southern Congo). This district is governed through its native chiefs. Therein Belgium is obeying the terms of the mandate and also following the practice of Germany which, after trying direct rule of the industrious and advanced lakes section of its East African colony, substituted administration through the African social and political structure. Throughout the original area of the Belgian domain Africans are frequently found in minor posts, but they are civil servants within the European system of government rather than representatives of their tribes. In this practice, as well as in the centralization of authority, Belgium has patterned after France. Where the basic plan of administration has been modified, British models have generally been followed. (The two standard systems are discussed in the following section).

## THE TWO PRIMARY COLONIAL SYSTEMS

The antiquated mode of government current in Portuguese colonies, the composite arrangements in the Belgian Congo, the evolution of administrative methods in the former German colonies, and the Italian proposals for occupying Ethiopia, suggest the existence of a wide range of political practice in low-latitude Africa, based on contrasts in the natural environment and on diverse objectives of the governing nations. Disregarding variants, the systems of colonial administration in vogue in Africa are two, direct rule and indirect rule. They are exemplified by the two leading African powers. Without exception France imposes direct rule upon its colonies, exerted through a governor and his subordinates. In British holdings practice varies, but the ideal set up is indirect rule, *i.e.*, government which leaves the African political structure untouched, except for supervision by British political officers, organized, not to supersede the indigenous government, but to parallel and supplement it.

Direct rule is, in the European view, simple and logical — and French. Except for Madagascar, French Africa lies in one vast block, however effectively the parts may be separated by obstacles to transportation. Originating as eight separate units, each based on a distinct strip of coast, the partition of interior Africa linked the French colonies and protectorates first along the line of the Sudan and finally in the Sahara. Vestiges of all these initial holdings remain. Tunisia and Morocco retain the legal status of protectorates. The Algerian coast has become partially assimilated to France, although the hinterland, extending halfway across the Sahara, is a separate colony and belongs geopolitically to France's vast non-Mediterranean holdings. All the remainder of French Africa is governed in two units (cf. Fig. 54). French Equatorial Africa has expanded from the Gabun coast a little north of the Congo estuary, inland to the Congo above the Livingstone Falls, and northward the length of the Lake Chad drainage and beyond to the Tibesti massif, the very heart of the Sahara. To this immense territory the World War added most of German Cameroons. The domain is organized into four sub-colonies. French West Africa is a composite of all the coastal colonies from Cape Arguin (Mauretania) to Dahomey, each of which retains its name and functions as a sub-colony. To them have been added the remaining Sudanese and Saharan territory under French control, including two inland sub-colonies, and the French mandate to German Togo. Each of the two major subdivisions is ruled by a governor-general. Subordinate to him is a governor for each colony, who directs a hierarchy of officials in the administration of the territorial subdivisions of the sub-colony.

All responsible officials directly engaged in administering government are Europeans except the men immediately in control of the smallest units — the villages together with dependent lands surrounding them. These African heads of villages are chosen for their usefulness to French authorities, not for their traditional position in their own world, and they are civil servants of France. European administrators are moved, as a policy, from colony to colony. They do not learn African tongues; on the contrary every effort is made to teach the indigenes French, so that they may imbibe French traditions and in time become French citizens.

Every native adult male is subject to five years in the French army. This is not a special organization, but integral with the levies of France. Two years of the service is spent in France itself, or else in French North Africa. At present not all the young men are drafted, since there are more than can be used. The administrators list those who seem likely to make the best soldiers, and these are taken on probation, the best of them being retained. It is intended that these forces shall be used wherever French armies are required. Like the civil administrators the officers, both commissioned and non-commissioned, are Europeans and divide their service between homeland and several of the overseas colonies. French is the language of the army.

The more or less technical staff services of the administration are engaged in creating a colony-wide system of education, improving agriculture, building towns and routes, and maintaining the all-important medical and sanitary activities of this dangerous country. The organizing heads and technical experts are Europeans, and so are most of those who perform routine duties, such as the jobs of postal clerks, railway ticket collectors, garage mechanics, cooks, and waiters. A good many clerks are women. This practice appears to violate the spirit of French colonial policy, which undertakes to integrate the colonies with the home country in the fullest possible degree. It may be only a temporary expedient, in force until the new generation of Africans emerges from the French schools, from which great things are anticipated.

Business falls within the purview of the government. What shall be produced for export, both on French plantations and on native holdings, is strongly influenced, if not dictated, by the authorities. Trading companies chartered outside of France are not barred, but French organizations have political advantages, despite international agreements insuring unrestricted trade. Only the most powerful British firms have branches in French territory, and there remains but a single German company in Lomé, the capital of former German Togoland. A British banking firm widely ramified in West Africa has withdrawn from French territory, as being a place where transaction of business by foreigners is unduly onerous. Shipping lines under the French flag facilitate French business. Plantations are fostered by the government, although they are not as yet extensive. They presumably will be concentrated in the forest zone, where most plantation crops flourish. Few agricultural concessions have been granted in the small bush, probably because private capital sees no sure return on investments there. Banana plantations lead, and recently special banana ships have been built to carry the output to France. Coffee, pineapples, and sisal are other plantation crops less widely grown.

In view of the immense areas of both West and Equatorial Africa, and the lack of rail connections among their parts, the degree of centralized authority is extrordinary. The railroads, although their physical interconnection is a dream of the future, are administered, or at least financed, as a unit. Schools, public works, medical and agricultural services — all are supervised from the two respective capitals. These capitals lie at the extremities of their colonies, being located handy to Europe rather than to the expanses of interior Africa which they rule.

The effort to spread a uniform mode of life over regions sharply contrasted as to natural environment and indigenous life does not apply to every detail. For example, the architecture adopted for French settlements varies. In the big bush the current European style prevails; in the small bush, a modified Levantine style is in vogue. Nevertheless, in the fundamentals uniformity is enforced so far as possible.

To the African, direct rule means disruption of his traditional tribal organization. The local man whom the French recognize as tribal chief may have no standing among the people beyond the authority he wields as agent of France. Possibly the new system will prevail in the course of time and the tribal tradition will remold itself to the imposed pattern. Quite as possibly the old organization is driven under cover, the real authority being passed on in the traditional line, unknown to the European administrators. A further dislocation of tradition comes with the substitution of ownership of land for usufruct of land. Abuses arising from ill-advised grants of concessions have generally accompanied direct rule. They are, however, to be associated with early phases of exploitation, rather than with any system of government. This is clearly pictured in French Africa, where concessions increase in number and size from west to east, *i.e.*, from the more thoroughly developed areas to those only recently opened up. More general in its effects than concessions (which are localized and limited in time) is the imposition of the European concept of land tenure upon French Africa. This substitutes private, individual ownership of land for tribal rights to the use of land, and destroys the correlated structure of African economic and social life. Lesser effects of the uniform application of direct rule are numerous. One which illustrates both lack of sympathy with regional diversity and the ideal of government for the benefit of the home country is the law governing alcohol. The critical importance of such a law is suggested by the fact that control of the liquor trade in Africa has been the subject of more than one international conference. In French territory whiskey and other foreign hard liquors are prohibited, but brandy, rum, and other French products may be sold, even in Moslem territory where their use is opposed by the Africans on religious grounds.

To the European, direct rule means maximum uniformity of living and working conditions. Albeit the quarters inhabited vary in architecture, life in all of them is patterned as closely as possible on that in France. Many of them approximate French provincial towns, within the limits prescribed by the small and shifting social group. There is at least one hotel, the center of the public social life. Its dining room is the club of the unmarried residents and of visitors from other parts of the colony. Its café is the gathering place of the whole community as the day's heat resolves into the soft tropical night. It provides a room or garden large enough for weekly movies and dances. In the larger places, some differentiation of function is already apparent in the business quarter, lending the aspect of a small European city. A fine church of European design rises high above each town, even though all the indigenous population may attend the little mosques tucked away in obscure streets, or worship at fetish shrines on the forest roadsides or in little openings off the village bypaths. Although most of the jobs are held by men, the community is not predominantly masculine, because men bring out their wives and children for the duration of their own stay, and the term (tour, in local parlance) is rather long. Government employees alternate two years in the colony with six months at home. For traders three years, at least on the first tour, is the rule, followed by four months at home. Young men coming out to engage in trade are exempt from military service, a fact which helps to explain their willingness to undertake such lengthy tours. Missionaries, including nuns, remain for indefinite periods. This distinctively European life is closely surrounded by African society. With scarcely an exception the European quarters are merely segregated districts in the towns. Even in brand new places now being made-to-order, such as Bobo-Dioulasso (Fig. 57), the indigenes live all around the French town, from which they are separated only by the width of a street. Abidjan, the new capital of Ivory Coast, is an exception. There the two indigenous towns are separated from the European center, in the one case by a lagoon, in the other by a wide belt of woodland.

The French envision a Black Africa increasingly integrated with French possessions north of the Sahara, and with France itself. They propose to do all they can to enthrone French language and culture throughout the area they control. The administration is organized as a clean-cut hierarchy in which the army, the missions, and even the business houses are more or less veiled agencies of the political officers.

In this system appear the traditional French reliance upon uniformity, logical order, implicit faith in the practices of the homeland, and devotion to the army. Indeed, the military aspect of the African colonies is itself held to be ample justification for direct rule. Stated crudely, France looks upon Africa as a reservoir of man-power for military defense of the state. All other values, either of French rule to Africans or of French exploitation of African natural resources and markets, are subordinate to military necessity. This suffices to explain the emphasis on coordination of all parts of the colonial dependency, even if orderliness were less important to the French than it is.

The attempt to impose a uniform pattern of administration upon natural environments ranging from big bush to desert and upon peoples ranging from scattered forest dwellers and wandering nomads to large and coherent sedentary organizations, implies a refusal to accept the conditioning forces of nature. In few places on earth has nature been so coercive to indigenous life as in Middle Africa. It remains to be seen whether the advanced occidental technology introduced by France can notably modify its force.

Direct rule begs the question of relations between the European governing class and the African subjects of government. In spite of efforts to make Africans into people of French culture, there is no evidence that the government has in mind racial intermixture, or entertains a hope that Europeans can reside permanently anywhere south of the Sahara. Perhaps in social intercourse the color line is less sharply drawn than in British territory, but persons of mixed blood are not accepted as members of the European communities.

In contrast to the French procedure, indirect rule, increasingly favored by the British government, is complex, devious, accidental — and British. British holdings in low-latitude Africa extend to its farthest confines. Until the World War they were divided into eight blocks by territory belonging to other nations, and six distinct areal units remain (Fig. 54). Some bits of coast have been under British supervision since the 17th century, but long lines of shore and nearly all the hinterland fell to Britain in the swift course of the partition at the end of the 19th. Much of this territory was staked out informally by chartered trading companies, by missionaries, and by government agents who probably exceeded their instructions. Missionaries, especially, lived for years where there was no semblance of European government. The flag followed these pioneers in order to protect British subjects and property. The scramble for territory precipitated by the rising maritime states of Europe forced Britain to choose between " effective occupation " and withdrawal. Government had to be devised overnight to regulate exploitation and trade and at the same time to satisfy the demands of the important fraction of the British body politic which would support African penetration only to the end of crushing the slave-trade.

In the big bush decades of direct, if haphazard, rule had created small, semi-Europeanized districts immediately surrounding the ports and had occasioned some dislocation of African life in a more extensive area. The denizens of the deep forest are scattered and shy, and their primitive tribal organization, articulated with shifting cultivation, lay beyond the ken of most colonial administrators until very recently. On the coast stood the first established British centers, and the only ones in direct contact with home. Direct rule was naturally extended along the coasts and their immediate hinterlands. No other mode of governing primitive " savages " was conceived of. Occupation progressed slowly there and bit by bit the separate tribes were absorbed into the only system of colonial administration then known.

In the small bush conquest proved unexpectedly easy. Perhaps in part for this reason, and because public opinion at home was not unanimously in favor of extending the empire, the men who conquered the small bush with colored regiments recruited from older African dependencies, were faced by the need to create a civil administration but with no personnel for manning it. Either by accident or design the British claims included some of the densest and most advanced populations in interior Africa. In the hinterland of the east coast the region of the Great Lakes was occupied by large tribes of industrious farmers who supported a dense settlement on the fertile soil of their hillsides, and had evolved the most advanced political organization in Bantu Africa. In the Sudanese hinterland of the Lower Niger lay the most populous of the Moslem theocracies of Negro Africa, states which had dominated much of the Sudan during the century preceding the entry of British troops.

These populous and advanced groups might have exerted greater resistance to interference from outside than the less populous areas staked out in the small bush by France, Germany, and Belgium. They became instead the proving ground of a new form of colonial administration.

Making a virtue of necessity, perhaps with native states of India in mind as precedents, two British viceroys, first in Uganda, soon after in Nigeria, undertook to rule through the legal forms and the personnel already in existence. By scattering the few available British political officers to reside at or near the courts of the established African rulers to " advise " them in administering their respective territories, British supervision was promptly installed at minimum expense to the home government and with minimum interference in local life. During the first years detachments of troops were required to enforce the advice of the residents. Now and then a recalcitrant African ruler has had to be deposed. In such cases successors are selected by the tribe in accordance with local practice. Within a surprisingly short time, armed forces were reduced and turned to the job of defense against invasion. Their place has been taken by an African constabulary under British supervision, and a small band of British political officers attached to each residency. This European administration is distinct from the " Native Administration." Very soon after indirect rule was inaugurated in the Sudan and on the lakes highland, similar arrangements began to be applied to the native reserves of South Africa which had come under direct British protection. These districts, although by origin refuge areas, possess climates and tribal organizations which favored the reasoned adoption of a scheme which had been evolved through exigency in tropical Africa.

Indirect rule was so readily accepted by the African rank and file because it promoted their well-being without outraging their traditions. It was accepted by the indigenous ruling caste because it maintained them in ease and considerable power, which they deemed preferable to the deposition which their own code led them to expect after military conquest. The new advisors insisted on only three reforms: intertribal warfare must cease, slave trading must be abolished, and taxation must be equitable. Domestic slavery, an integral part of Moslem life, was not forbidden in the Sudan, although it must in time cease if the prohibition against trade in slaves be strictly enforced.

The arrangement, entered into as an emergency device, has worked so well that it has gradually been extended. Germans adopted something like it for the populous tribes of the lakes region adjacent to the site of the original experiment, and the Belgians have maintained it for the tribes of this area which they took over. Almost everywhere in British low-latitude Africa it has been substituted for direct rule — even in the big bush.

Indirect rule as the norm for low-latitude Africa is predicated on the tested belief that the country is utterly unfit for permanent European settlement. The few Europeans in the area, aside from political officers (including army officers), are either traders and shippers, mining operators, or missionaries. No others are encouraged, and no one who offered himself as a permanent settler on the land would be admitted. These few Europeans stay in the country only for short terms or " tours." For some years in British West Africa this period was 12 months out followed by 6 months at home, and retirement at the end of 18 years. With the improvement in housing, sanitation, communication, and other amenities, life has become less taxing both physically and psychologically. The tour is now 18 months long, followed by 18 weeks at home, with retirement at the age of fifty. Some trading corporations insist on a slightly longer tour for their employees, but it does not deviate much from the rule for government men. Missionaries, who find it harder to get money and who are supposed to possess a devotion to their cause lacking in the more worldly professions, frequently stay in the country much longer. But all go home from time to time, and all leave the country on retirement. Only lately have wives been coming out to join their husbands, and they are likely to stay for even shorter periods than their men do. Children are practically never seen, the only exceptions being those of missionaries.

The number of political officers engaged in administration does not change much from year to year. It may be presumed that the total will always remain small. They cooperate as far as possible with the local authority. The younger men constantly tour the country. They sit as one-man courts, where they listen to complaints of indigenes who feel themselves constrained by their local government. They keep a watchful eye on everything, to the end of preventing trouble. As far as possible they harmonize their own administrative districts with the native tribal territories. The army is voluntary and intended for use in Africa only. Its commissioned officers are Europeans, seconded for tours totalling six years' service; all the rest are indigenes. (At first non-commissioned officers were also Europeans, but all are being replaced by men from the ranks.)

Technical services are organized with European personnel, but as fast as possible are turned over to the local government, perhaps with the loan of a technical advisor or two. The intent is to make the indigenous government increasingly responsible for every branch of administration, but forever subject to the veto of British authority. The technical staffs are constantly engaged in training Africans to carry on their work, and the openings for Europeans in the manual tasks, even such as locomotive engineers, garage mechanics, and draftsmen, will apparently diminish, as local men become adequately trained for the work. There is at least one Native Administration which has a land survey, including the making and printing of maps, staffed exclusively by Africans. In supervisory technical posts Europeans appear likely to remain indefinitely. Whenever there is a new technical job to be undertaken, such as the construction of a waterworks for a city, or the building of a harbor or a railway bridge, it has to be planned and executed by men brought in from Europe, there being no higher training schools in Africa. Just now, European agricultural experts are increasing in number, as the opportunities for developing new crops are being pushed. The medical staff is the most vital of all, since without careful medical attention the death-rate among Europeans would exact an exorbitant price for colonial profits. The doctors in the government hospitals and even the supervising nurses are Europeans, whether the patients are white or colored.

Just what does the British white man get for carrying this African burden? Most directly, there are jobs for the whole hierarchy of government — better paid jobs than at home for the same degrees of responsibility. The danger of disease and the inconvenience of living a life with family ties more or less in abeyance are held to warrant this higher rate of pay. Since each colony or protectorate pays for its own administration, British as well as native, these administrative posts furnish jobs to British nationals who otherwise would have to find support in the overcrowded motherland. The total number of persons thus employed is not large, however, even when the technical staffs are counted in.

The prime objective of the British in their overseas holdings is trade. Although they freely permit nationals of any country to participate in trade and transportation throughout their African dependencies, British firms take the lion's share. No political obstacles handicap foreigners aside from the inevitable handicaps associated with the phrase, " Trade follows the flag." This means that banking and transportation, organized on national lines, inevitably favor those whose connections in Europe are under the same flag. It also means that personal relations facilitate business most readily when all parties belong to the same nation. These include use of the same mother tongue, confidence which everyone tends to feel in fellow-citizens as opposed to foreigners, and the conscious or unconscious preference of officials for their own nationals in dozens of small but telling ways. The possession of dependencies in which trade thrives furnishes many jobs to. British nationals. First of all the agencies of transport — whether private enterprises such as shipping firms or public undertakings like most of the railroads — employ many Europeans, some of them in the homeland. Then there are the trading firms engaged in buying the African surpluses and selling European wares to Africans. With few exceptions, this merchandizing is undifferentiated. Each firm buys every commodity the country has to sell and markets to the remotest villages the cotton cloth, crockery, enamelled ware, gewgaws, and the hundred and one other European wares seen in every native market.

The considerable number of Europeans engaged in buying local produce and running stores constitute the most obvious but not the only communities which earn their living by grace of a government that helps trade to establish itself and to flourish. Each of the firms has a large staff in the home country. The copper, tin, zinc, vanadium, gold, and silver, the palm oil, cacao, peanuts, cotton, skins, and other products of mine, farm, range, and forest which move to the occidental world are the basis of important manufacturing industries there. The manufacture of the European wares purchased by Africans helps to run the wheels of giant industry in Western Europe, and even in the United States.

A cardinal feature of indirect rule is its guarantee that the African system of land tenure will not be molested. This does not apply to mineral wealth, and the mining companies employ a modest number of Europeans in technical and administrative posts. In agriculture the self-denying ordinance precludes plantations, and limits cash crops to the few which respond to somewhat careless handling, but it does not eliminate the European. One by one crops and livestock — products suited to African methods of production and demanded in the world market — have been fostered, and in some cases introduced by government or private agencies. Agricultural experiment stations manned by

Europeans continue to import plant and animal stock from other continents for testing under African conditions. Trained men are sent out to show grazers how to flay a goat and dry the skin free from holes and clean of flesh. Other experts distribute high-grade seed of cotton or peanuts, or instruct the farmers how far apart to plant their cacao trees and how much shade to give them. Demonstration farms raise crops and animals of high quality, as examples of what can be done. When the indigenous farmer brings in his skins, his cacao beans, his peanuts, or his cotton, government inspectors grade them for quality, seal them, and stamp them with the official mark. In order to introduce a new farm product government agents wheedle the trading firms to buy the first few years' crops to their temporary loss, with the hope of ultimate gain as the industry becomes established and the quality improves. This is accomplished by persuasion, without political compulsion. Likewise there is no administrative direction as to what crops the indigenous farmer shall plant or what stock the grazer shall raise.

It is fair to ask what advantages the African gets from this paternal government imposed from outside. Benefits which accrue from the abolition of tribal warfare and slave raiding may properly head the list. Ending the slave raids has diminished domestic slavery by cutting down the source of supply. Nevertheless, many slaves from the pre-European days are still alive. Moreover, it is difficult to prevent people selling themselves or their children in a continent where slavery has been a universal custom time out of mind. However, that practice is uncommon except in times of famine, and with improved transportation no district is too isolated to receive food from outside in case of shortage. In general a single uniform poll tax fixed annually in advance has been substituted for the numerous and unpredictable taxes formerly levied. Tax farming has been abolished along with arbitrary taxation.

The work formerly done by slaves of African masters is now paid for with wages. In addition, the Europeans provide many jobs. Unskilled laborers may become porters on docks, in railway yards, and in the compounds of the trading companies. Many men support their families by acting as servants in European homes. Others are miners. The routine details of both European and native administrations and tending store for the companies are entirely in the hands of clerks who have learned to read and write, either English or one of the African languages. A few, more highly trained, have entered the professions or publish newspapers in the larger cities. Finally, many farmers now raise and sell crops and stock in the markets newly created or greatly expanded by European enterprise.

As it works out, indirect rule operates within the frames set by nature. No effort is made to spread laws or procedures of government uniformly over areas of diverse environment and tradition. For example, Christian missions are encouraged among pagan tribes, and alcoholic liquors are sold there under certain restrictions. But in the Moslem sections missions are excluded unless expressly invited by the native administration, and the sale of alcohol is taboo, in conformity to Moslem law. Every British political officer is required to master at least one African language, and he spends his official life in the region he knows. In the areas where indirect rule was adopted from the moment of conquest, few Africans know English. Those regions centered in the more productive districts of the small bush were already culturally unified when the British came. They were operating under legal systems cognate to those of Islam, and administered by ruling chiefs, who, as in every primitive government, were autocrats. There indirect rule through the established forms and personnel was a natural innovation.

In the big bush and in some niggardly regions in the small bush which had become refuges of harassed tribes, indirect rule did not present itself as a solution of a pressing problem. The primitive tribesmen generally found in these environments practice a communal mode of life, the legal sanctions of which are so foreign to the European habit of thought that only painstaking and sympathetic study can elucidate them. Such study is no mean task, because it must be undertaken for hundreds of small groups scattered about the forest or in rocky fastnesses of hill and plateau, and speaking different languages. Minute subdivision made imposition of direct rule the easiest consequence of outright conquest. Moreover, many of these people, made shy by centuries of slave raiding, shielded their real leaders from British recognition. This gave opportunity for self-seeking individuals to curry favor with the new rulers, although very often these men had no authority beyond what the British could impose. Finally, the coastal colonies had been subject to direct rule for generations, and there detribalization is far advanced or complete. In such places no local rulers exist.

As the success of indirect rule has become assured in the colonies of its origin (Uganda and Northern Nigeria), and the political officers have come to know the languages and political forms of the small tribes, attempts are being made to extend indirect rule over all of British Africa outside the self-governing dominions. Patient study of the local societies is bringing to the fore the chiefs who have been recognized by the people as their rightful rulers throughout the period of direct administration. A few of the indigenous states which had organized to prosecute or to forfend slave raiding are large enough and well organized enough to become autonomous merely by reconstitution of the native ruler. In general, however, no unity of people exists over an area large enough to constitute a province. There indirect rule must be created by gradually bringing tribes together and aiding them to create a native government. Since the effort to accomplish this dates back only a few years, the venture is still in the experimental stage. Presumably the interchange among tribes brought about by cheap fares on the railroads, by the migration of servants with their employers, and by movement to towns where British trade has created jobs, will slowly efface the sharper distinctions among the small tribes, and permit an increasing application of indirect rule.

A feature of British latter-day rule in Africa is the construction of European settlements apart from the African villages and towns. This is an expression of the type of administration which undertakes to govern with the minimum of interference with existing machinery. So far as possible British seats of government are located at a distance from the capitals of native administration, and in towns built by the British. For Uganda the British government is installed at Entebbe, whereas the native seat is on a hill near Kampala, the chief commercial metropolis (Fig. 54). The protectorates of South Africa are likewise administered from marginal points which happen to lie on railroads or in one case a motor road. (Maseru in Basutoland; Mafeking actually in Cape Province, for Bechuanaland; Mbabane in Swaziland.) In Nigeria two entirely new capitals have been planted at conveniently central locations on railroads to house the two sub-administrations of the dependency. Alongside the ancient walled capitals of the Sudan and the inner big bush, British garden communities have been built, separated from the Native Administrations by distances varying from half a mile to four or five miles. Attached to each of these European settlements (which are economic as well as political centers) is a village for Africans from districts outside, generally from the coast towns, who are employed by the Europeans in government, in business, and as household servants. Even in the old coastal settlements, the British have generally striven to separate the European and African quarters, on grounds of sanitation as well as political expediency.

Emphasis on the harmony between indirect rule and natural environment should not mask the trends toward unification apparent in the British dependencies. The army and the currency have been amalgamated to some extent. For these purposes the four West African dependencies are unified, and likewise East Africa, except for Northern Rhodesia, which has its own defense force and uses British currency. The protectorates use currency of the adjacent Union of South Africa.

The British are in low-latitude Africa, it appears, for the sake of trade. Even this they will share with anyone else who cares to make his venture. To this end there must be stable government, but one which requires the least possible alteration of African society, compatible with economic interdependence throughout the world or at least within the British Empire. In the areas where indirect rule prevails the British authorities have obtained leaseholds at convenient points to serve as *pieds à terre* for Europeans. These are organized as "townships" under British law. Elsewhere Europeans can lease ground even for mineral rights only by application to the highest African authority.

In the highland of East Africa, debatable ground for permanent European settlement, administration varies from one dependency to another. Kenya is under direct rule. There steps in the direction of indirect rule are sops to public opinion and are largely inoperative. This should occasion no surprise, for there is a possibility that considerable sections of highland in Kenya can be settled permanently by Europeans, and men on the ground resent self-denying regulations which will minimize or prevent such settlement. In regions believed to be rich in mineral deposits it is hard to establish indirect rule. Powerful economic interests fear that land reserved to Africans will belatedly prove to be really valuable. This appears in the government of Northern Rhodesia, and in recent sacrifice of pledged reserves in Kenya where gold has been unexpectedly discovered.

The two experiments, French and British, have not yet had time to prove their relative worth, since neither is more than a generation old, even in the spots where it has been longest established. Low-latitude Africa is undoubtedly one of the most significant geopolitical laboratories on earth. There, in the region most inimical in all the world to European occupation, two different methods of carrying the white man's burden are being tried out side by side. By the end of the century it may be possible to see which of them is the more successful. Perhaps both will be equally thriving, or both by that time may have failed utterly to solve the burning problem of occidental civilization — the problem of dealing with the low latitudes, particularly the regions where the climate is adverse to white people and favorable to the vital indigenous populations. Nowhere else can this issue be given so throughgoing a test as in Middle Africa.

## FORCES OPERATIVE ON ALL AFRICAN GOVERNANCE

All the distinctive arrangements made by the several powers for the handling of their African possessions interact with conditions of nature, ethnic habits, and economic incentives and bid fair to be considerably modified thereby.

The common practice of disposing of African territory over council tables in European capitals has created arbitrary boundary lines which have become or are likely to become axes of stress. A defenseless country, Portugal, is sovereign over direct coastal outlets of some of the richest British and Belgian holdings. Unable to find the capital to develop routes across its colonies, Portugal hesitates to permit foreign capital to undertake the job, lest economic development end in political control. Already some mineral deposits of first magnitude are known to lie on both sides of certain political boundaries. Any one of them may become a bone of contention. The colonial boundaries cut off some tribes from their natural outlets. Populous tribes west and north of Lake Victoria can deal readily with the outside world only through Kenya or Tanganyika. Those within British territory meet some obstacles, and those under Belgian rule are pretty well cut off from the east coast. Tribes under French rule between Nigeria and the desert must market their skins and peanuts through British territory. One of the chief African resources continues to be its labor. This is often required for mining, extraction from the forest, or intensive plantation farming in areas where the local supply is small. The migration from populous districts of large numbers of able-bodied workmen for a season or for a period lasting from two to five years is common. Many of these migrations involve the crossing of colonial boundary lines and require treaty arrangements among the European states concerned. These become subjects for frequent disputes. Notable migrations are: peanut harvesters from Senegal to Gambia; cacao workers from Ivory Coast to Gold Coast; Ruanda and Urundi men to Katanga; Mozambique labor to the mines of Transvaal and the Rhodesias (Fig. 54).

Some tribes, cleft by the new boundaries, reassemble on one side of the line. In West Africa some border zones in French territory appear to have been vacated and adjacent British land overpopulated, because the French exact more from the Africans than do the British. In the days of forced labor in the Congo Basin many people lost themselves in the bush; they may or may not have crossed political frontiers.

No matter what the mode of administration, European initiative is reorienting African life and even altering some of its fundamental concepts, such as the tenure of land.

The cessation of slave raiding and tribal wars and the introduction of sanitation have doubled the population in many parts of the continent. The construction of ports has turned Africa inside out with respect to markets, and railroads have favored some inland points at the expense of others, besides substituting a rigid pattern of transport for the fluid trails of the indigenes. New markets, improved transportation, and the introduction of improved stock and new plants have combined to modify the system of agriculture and the tenure of agricultural land. The traditional shifting cultivation, in which fields are abandoned every few years, is being replaced in many places by tree crops which remain on the land for many years, or by rotation which permits planting of annual crops on the same land for an indefinite period of years. With continuous use of the land, the concept of ownership replaces that of usufruct, whether the European government presses the change or not. Moreover, the African delights to travel on trains and trucks whether he is on his way to a job or merely tripping. Little by little even the dwellers in the remotest bush are thus brought into contact with other parts of the continent, if not of the world. This is bound to smooth off the contrasting attitudes bred by centuries of isolation.

All the facets of life burnished by the profound changes sketched above, accord with the pattern of European intervention in the Orient, allowing for differences in the natural environment, the density of the population, and the character of the people. It is quite possible that Africans, like orientals, will in time grow restive under European rule of whatever sort, and compel the modification of European objectives, be they trade, armed men, low-latitude products, or merely prestige.

## CHAPTER TWELVE

# Geopolitical Antithesis in the Americas

AN arresting political paradox is the contrast between the empires created on the two American continents by Spain and Britain. Spain, fanatically unified by prolonged warfare against a common Moorish foe, for three centuries after expelling the enemy in 1492 turned its integrating forces upon overseas possessions. The colonial empire was treated as a unit, administered by a hierarchy of officials who were as closely supervised from home as the slow communication of the times permitted. At the end it stood powerless to prevent each of the small and feeble regional groups of mainland colonials from severing individually the frail bonds which held it to the mother country and to the other colonial nuclei. Mainland Spanish America has split into sixteen independent nations, to say nothing of that South America which never was Spanish — Brazil and the relict colonies of three European states.

Britain, the European cradle of individual liberty and of local self-government, permitted more than a dozen separate and antipathetic groups of subjects to set up, in North America, overseas principalities, theocracies, and trading settlements. Beginning with the most diverse aims, they continued to be governed as individuals, in so far as any attention was paid to them by the homeland. In two and a half centuries these colonies, expanding over the whole of the habitable continent, had fused into two strong governments, which also incorporate settlements originated by Spaniards, Dutch, Swedes, and French. One of the two still belongs to the British Empire.

From these eventualities one might conclude that *laissez faire* in government leads to political unity, and enforced unification to disruption. And so it does, wherever the governing power is remote from the governed area. Without doubt the people on the ground know better their political needs and how to satisfy them than can any group of rulers living in a different environment. It was the clumsy attempts of George III's government to yoke together groups of colonies under a single governor appointed by the crown, to direct in detail and from England the administrative acts of this governor, and to impose uniform laws on a strip of country extending through fifteen degrees of latitude, which stiffened into united revolt the thirteen discrete and jealous North American colonies. So long as Spain fought to hold its Empire, adjacent provinces stood shoulder to shoulder in their Wars of Liberation.

Beyond this, the rule does not hold. The North American colonies, having made good their revolt, did not relapse into the anarchic individuality which they had fought to preserve, whereas the defensive unions of Latin American provinces promptly fell apart into fragments corresponding roughly to administrative divisions of Imperial days. Furthermore, the division of Anglo-America between the United States and Canada is wholly different in geopolitical origin from the division of Ibero-America between Portuguese Brazil and the sixteen Spanish republics, despite the superficial similarity presented by a map. A closer analysis of the American scene will disclose differences of natural environment that vitally conditioned the political contrasts in the two continents.

## IBERIA AND AMERICA

The discovery of other continents by Europeans is a shining thread in the fabric of the national state. As considerable blocks of European territory became fused by patriotic emotion into political units embracing considerable natural resources, the new nations found themselves freed from the necessity to guard long frontiers of scattered territory. The energy thus released sought new channels which soon led beyond the confines of Europe. Desire to spread the benefits of Christianity, expectation of wealth from new trade, and lust for adventure were motives mixed in varying proportions in the outpouring of the vigorous young states. Minor practical advantages, such as the clearance of jails and the payment of royal debts, were not passed over.

Of all the new countries of Europe, Portugal first felt the stimulus to seek overseas outlets for its pent energies. Isolated by the Pyrenees, along with Spain, from European concerns, Portugal is set apart from its larger neighbor by a sterile zone on which it turns its back, by prevailing moist lowland in contrast to the dry Spanish Plateau, and by a smiling sea which it faces. The niggardly soil of even the most favored lowlands early encouraged the inhabitants to seek additional food in the sea, and numerous shallow coves provide landing places for the tiny boats of the longshore fishermen. Later, catches from nearby waters were augmented by excursions along the coast of Mauretania beyond the Mediterranean entrance, and by summer voyages to the Iceland cod banks, and even to the Grand Banks (Fig. 59).

The turbulence of ethnic commingling which kept most of Europe seething for a millennium, subsided early in Portugal, far offside the main currents of folk migration. The inhabitants of this small and compact land were early welded into social and political unity by six and a half centuries of struggle with the alien Moslem civilization imposed on them by Moorish invaders from North Africa. This foreign society they had extirpated by the middle of the 13th century, 250 years before neighboring Spain was emancipated. Portuguese leaders, looking for new worlds to conquer, eagerly pushed across the Mediterranean narrows, to harry the Moors on their home ground. A beginning was made by seizing the southern Pillar of Hercules early in the 15th century. But an attack from the sea along a wide front, upon mountainous country like Morocco is one of the most hazardous of tactics, and almost sure to fail. It was therefore superseded by a vague scheme to work down the African coast and take the Moors in the rear. The knowledge which Portuguese fishermen had of this coast stopped at Cape Bojador (26° N.), where the baffling " Bulging Cape " projecting from the long littoral of the Sahara, a shoreline at once harborless and unredeemed desert. It took nearly two decades of persistent effort to overcome this hazard, but in seven years more the Sahara had been by-passed, and the first blacks were brought back from the Sudan, precursors of the millions of African slaves with which the Portuguese built their American Empire.[1]

During these years the plan to conquer the Moors lost itself in the hope of finding a seaway to India, but the discouraging turn of the coast southward at Cameroons Mountain slowed the progress of exploration, and it was not until the end of the century (1499) that Vasco da Gama triumphantly returned to Lisbon with a shipload of eagerly desired goods from India. The glory of that voyage, the appropriate crowning of a century of consistent effort, has been dimmed by the effulgence which history has shed upon the exploit of Columbus eight years earlier. Nevertheless, by way of the sea route it pioneered, the fabulous Orient was hitched to the practical Occident, and the

---

[1] This first phase of African coasting was the project of Prince Henry the Navigator, from 1415 to his death in 1460. By then Cape Palmas (4° N.) had been rounded, and the way to India appeared to stretch eastward.

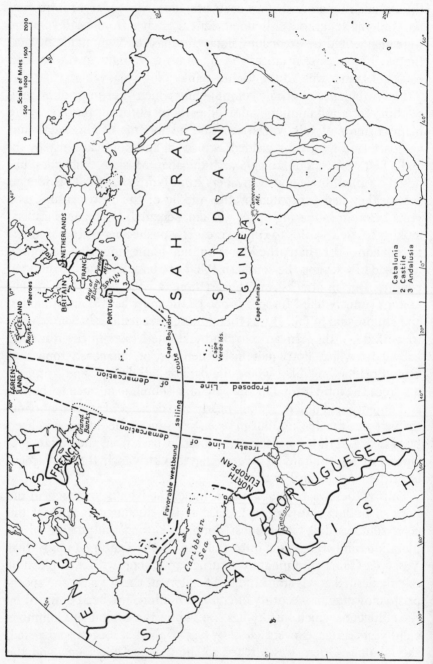

FIG. 59. The Atlantic Ocean in relation to the Discoveries.

The base used is a modification of Robert B. Hall's outline map, published by John Wiley & Sons, Inc.

Atlantic national state, Portugal, swiftly eclipsed the city-states of the Mediterranean World which for centuries had thriven on the trickle of oriental goods filtering through the deserts of Western Asia. Venice, wealthiest of Italian city-states, received the news of the all-sea route to the Orient with public mourning, well recognizing the inevitable eclipse of its own costly and complicated land-and-sea tradeway in competition with the single lading from India to Europe around Africa.

While the Portuguese were slowly unrolling the map of coastal Africa, the Spanish were repeating the experience of their little neighbor in forging a nation. In a region larger and far more varied than Portugal, half a dozen little realms, based on sheltering fastnesses of the humid Pyrenees and Cantabrian Mountains, were coalescing into a national state, as they emerged shoulder to shoulder upon the interlocked expanses of the semi-arid central plateau. Political unification kept pace with territorial advance against the Moors — along the narrow strip of irrigated, east-facing, Mediterranean lowland, and into the broader valleys of Andalusia which look toward the open Atlantic. Its final step, the union of lowland Aragon (or Catalonia, as it is called today), with Castile, the central plateau, ushered in the concerted push which dislodged the Moors from their last stronghold, in the Sierra Nevada of the southeast.

The entry of Spain as a colonizing power in the Americas is less obvious than that of Portugal, but it is also less accidental. Except for fisheries of hardy Basques along the stormy Biscay coast, Spain of the 15th century had no maritime interests. Aloft on its semi-arid plateau the business was grazing, grain, and gold. The east and south coasts have their harbors, but these had been footholds for conquerors from overseas rather than outlets for teeming trade. Only coastal Catalonia in the far northeast, and the extreme southwestern corner of Andalusia have better than mediocre connections with the sea. The whole coastal fringe is cut off from the heart of the nation by rugged mountains or steep escarpments.

The Spain which discovered America was just emerging victorious from centuries of combat against a common enemy, the Moors. In that struggle the Christian kingdoms which had grown up independently in the northern mountains of the Iberian Peninsula had sacrificed their political separatism. The Spanish state of the time of Columbus was the most unified in Europe, except Portugal.

Prime for the conquest of new worlds, Spain was acutely and jealously aware of neighbor Portugal's ventures toward the Orient via the

African coast. Into this setting came Columbus, fresh from the maritime atmosphere of Portugal, with his mad notion of reaching the Orient by sailing in the opposite direction. It may have been woman's intuition that prompted Queen Isabella to support the scheme, or it may have been jealousy of the rival state which shares with Spain the Iberian Peninsula. Whatever the cause, the first result may be seen in the gold brought back by Columbus, preserved for centuries in the treasury of Toledo's cathedral.

The expulsion of the Moors from Spain with its release from internal preoccupation, fixed the date of Columbus's voyage. When he returned early in 1493 with proof that he had reached land to the westward, his royal Spanish sponsors hastened to obtain documents which would guarantee to Spain a division of the spoils for which Portugal had so long been straining, by halving the non-Christian world into two spheres of influence. The line of demarcation as first promulgated was to run 100 leagues (ca. 500 miles) west of the Cape Verde Islands. A year later Spain and Portugal negotiated a treaty which transferred the base line of partition 170 leagues farther west, at the instance of the Portuguese. The reason for this shift is unknown. Its effect was to throw into the Portuguese sphere of influence the eastern triangle of South America — all the land east of a meridian running near the mouth of the Amazon. Some students believe that Portuguese mariners had already discovered land in this quarter. Others think that Spain was glad to make the change because completion of the Great Circle promised to include the Spice Islands, or Moluccas, within the Spanish sphere, according to maps available, which later proved faulty and left the coveted islands to Portugal.

The major effect of the Line of Demarcation was to divert Portuguese energy into colonization of Brazil, after the existence of that land was disclosed. Today Brazil, rather than the Orient, is the monument to Portuguese enterprise, while the rest of Latin America is the contribution of Spain.

## Northwest Europe and America

The Atlantic-facing countries of far north Europe may have fostered expeditions which preceded Columbus to the New World, and they were no less active in pioneering a route to the Orient along the North Coast of the Eurasian land mass than were the Portuguese to the south. Nature nullified both attempts. Ice-packs make the Northeast Passage useless, even today. Exploration westward by way of stepping stones, Faeroes, Iceland, and Greenland, produced no permanent settlement southwest of Greenland, and so was sterile.

Atlantic America north of the Caribbean was destined to be seized and occupied by those nations of Northwest Europe — Britain and France, with a minor contribution from the Dutch — that evolved in a less forbidding environment than that of Scandinavia. These countries lagged far behind their neighbors to south and to north in taking a hand in overseas migration. It is true that they sent out a few early explorers, and that freebooters preyed on the Atlantic commerce of Spain and Portugal. But a full century elapsed before they succeeded in founding permanent settlements.

The very wealth and environmental diversity of the northwest corner of Europe retarded political consolidation. The notable freedom of Britain from invasion after the 11th century eventuated in an advanced order of government noteworthy for its flexibility (Ch. 5), but in the process of evolution preoccupied the islanders with home affairs. France, the most populous and diverse state in Western Europe, required time to correlate its complementary but contrasting parts. Moreover, a portion of its energy was perennially drained off to the east for protection of its land border on that side (Ch. 6). The Netherlands, relatively small, played a minor role in American settlement.

When once these states were able to participate in overseas settlement, they found themselves superbly equipped for the adventure. Their location is enhanced by numerous well-sheltered harbors accessible from the hinterland. Their climate and vegetation are similar in kind to those met on the opposite shore of the Atlantic, although less extreme. The energy saved in internal consolidation released men and money for adventures beyond the national boundaries. In Britain the agricultural revolution which synchronized with political unification threw many men out of jobs. Thereby a reservoir of potential emigrants was created, because Britain, little troubled by foreign wars, could not absorb its surplus population in the army. France, consuming generation after generation of men in fighting to preserve its eastern boundary, had few potential emigrants. At the same time its highly centralized government could marshal its resources for the business of exploiting the new continents, more effectively than could England, embroiled in civil war and embarrassed by constitutional crises.

As in the case of Spain and Portugal, the adventurers who left these countries for America constituted only part of the total colonial enterprise of France, Britain, and the Netherlands, which touched all the continents outside of Europe. Nevertheless, the American part stands today as the most enduring aspect of the expansion which followed upon the Discoveries. Promptly the Netherlands was eliminated from middle-latitude North America, and later France was forced out, leaving little more than Quebec as a testimonial of two centuries of colonial effort. In a very real sense, North America today is a British outgrowth, in contrast to the Iberian stamp upon nearly all the country south of the Gulf of Mexico.

## CHAPTER THIRTEEN

# Latin America

## SWIFT ENVELOPMENT OF THE CONTINENT

FACED with the job of occupying new continents, Portugal, a nation of less than a million people, and Spain, with not many more than six million, enveloped the whole of South America and the tropical part of North America almost at one move.

From the outset the coast was the critical line along which Portuguese America was organized. Numerous deep and well-protected harbors afforded footholds which could be easily defended, while the open sea provided the only possible link between the settlements — tiny clearings carved out of the rain forest of a sodden coastal plain. The steep mountains behind, choked with the still denser forest of the zone bathed in clouds, interposed a barrier to movement inland. But more important, the rainy Portuguese coast of Brazil proved to be the complement to the rainy Portuguese coast of Africa (Fig. 59). The first recorded Portuguese landfall in South America was made by an expedition en route to India, which, in sailing too far west, touched Brazil instead of Africa. For a generation desultory voyages and offhand settlements were largely made by ships engaged in the oriental trade, which normally utilized West African ports as way stations. Then fear of losing Brazil to rival European powers stirred the government to found permanent settlements. A beginning on an admirably protected water not far from the site of Santos was eclipsed by settlements farther north, where sugarcane throve better. This, the first plantation crop to create a rapidly mounting market in Europe, found suitable natural conditions on the Brazilian coast, but suffered from lack of labor. The indigenes, forest dwellers whose patches of crops were attended by the women, would work on plantations only after they had been Christianized, and the missionaries succeeded in abolishing Indian slavery among their converts. On the coast of Africa disease had prevented

403

the establishment of plantations (Ch. 11), but the Negroes were known to be tractable when enslaved, and the missionaries to the Indians considered Negroes to be " natural slaves." From this arose the transfer of thousands of Negroes from their home to the nearest part of the South American mainland, and the secure foundation of Brazil

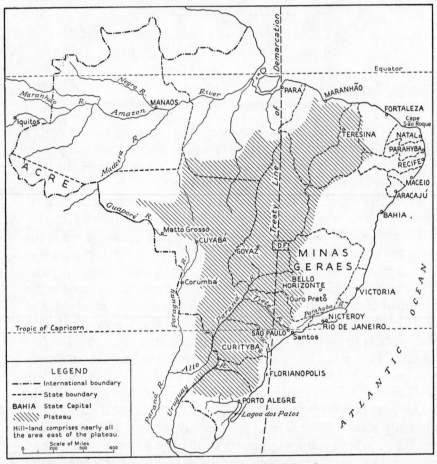

FIG. 60. Portuguese settlement of Brazil.

on slave-operated lowland plantations, mainly on the coast reaching some ten degrees in either direction from Cape São Roque (Fig. 60).

The interior of Brazil, at first only a recruiting ground for slaves and soon abandoned, was explored by men from the southern coastal settlements. There the mountains rise out of the sea, and invite investigation as potential sources of mineral wealth. The plateau, less rugged, higher and farther from the Equator than the hill-land of the north, is easier to traverse and less oppressively hot and moist than the coastland first occupied. Despite these advantages, for a century and a half after the first coastal settlement no profitable basis for occupying the interior could be found. Then gold was discovered in the central part of the highland. The gold rush, followed a generation later by the discovery of diamonds, directly and indirectly stimulated settlement to sweep inland far beyond the Line of Demarcation, and southward to the confines of the high land.

Spain, endowed by papal sanction with the princely remainder of both Americas, began by occupying the Caribbean islands, to which the northeast tradewinds had brought Columbus in 1492. This is the part of the New World most easily reached by any sailing vessel westbound from Spain (Fig. 59). The islands, small enough to be conquered readily and colonized one by one, made excellent advance bases for exploration and settlement on the mainland, where vast area, deep forests, high mountains, wide deserts, and powerful Indian states redoubled the odds against the Europeans. From this insular base, little bands of Spaniards penetrated all the principal regions of tropical America, and beyond. With astonishing celerity they enveloped all of coastal South America west of Spain's treaty line and reached well into what is now the United States (Fig. 61).

The dense rain forest of the Isthmus of Panamá was crossed in 1513; resistance of the powerful Aztec state on the lofty Mexican plateau was overpowered in 1521; the dissected Central American highland was overrun during the next four years; the Peruvian coastal desert and the prodigious Andean wall were surmounted and the Inca power destroyed in 1532 and 1533, the whole plateau being conquered by 1535; the complex terrain of the northern Andes succumbed in the four years following the first success on the Puna; [1] the Central Valley of Chile was occupied in 1541 from the base on the Puna; the first permanent settlement in the lowland of the Plata, in 1538 at Asunción, now the heart of Paraguay, was fostered, although not begun, from the Puna. All the nuclear cores of the future Spanish American nations except the Plata estuary had been occupied in the incredibly short space of 25 years, and from the two major highland bases, Mexico and Peru. The Plata estuary, along with southern Chile, was to the Spaniards the least attractive part of South America, and the hardest to wrest from the hostile natives. Not until 1580 was a permanent settlement established at Buenos Aires, and Montevideo, the germ of Uruguay, was not founded until 1726. But all middle-latitude South

---

[1] Puna is used in these pages to include all the central highland of the Andes; Altiplano is the more restricted intermontane plateau of Peru and Bolivia.

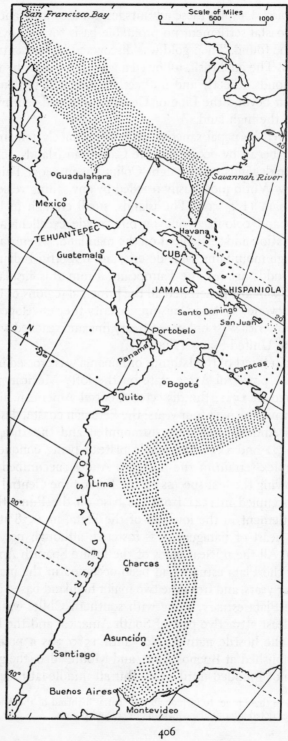

FIG. 61. Spanish occupation of the Americas. The stippled bands represent zones of dispute between the Spanish settlers and their neighbors. The Caribbean islands comprised another such zone.

Labels on map: San Francisco Bay, Guadalajara, Mexico, TEHUANTEPEC, Guatemala, Savannah River, Havana, CUBA, JAMAICA, HISPANIOLA, Santo Domingo, San Juan, Portobelo, Panama, Caracas, Bogotá, Quito, COASTAL DESERT, Lima, Charcas, Asunción, Santiago, Buenos Aires, Montevideo

Scale of Miles 0 500 1000

America had been explored during the first years, as well as much of North America to a line connecting the Savannah Rivermouth on the Atlantic with San Francisco Bay on the Pacific.

## COLONIAL SPANISH AMERICA

The initial broadside attack could not be followed everywhere by immediate and permanent settlement; emigrants from Spain were too few. Instead it concentrated itself in a few channels and thus gained both force and direction. Of these channels the chief led to the two major plateaus of the continents — the Mexican Triangle and the Puna of the Central Andes. For this reason, and also perhaps because the home government was ignorant of the wide range of natural conditions of the Americas, and quite possibly unable to apperceive the vast scale of the American landscape as compared to the southwestern peninsula of Europe, Spain undertook to administer its new possessions with the minimum of subdivision.

From the outset it was obvious that North and South America were so separated, and their approaches so far apart that they would have to be governed separately. To that end two " kingdoms " were set up, each administered by a viceroy. Because gold and silver were the chief resources desired by Spain, and because the easily unified high plateaus of Mexico and Peru were the two chief producers of precious metals, the Spanish colonial viceroyalties were built, literally as well as legally, upon the foundations of Indian empires which Cortes and Pizarro found in these two regions.

Despite their formidable inaccessibility, these plateaus irrisistibly drew the Spaniards, because, as seats of the two most advanced civilizations in the New World, they yielded immediate returns in accumulated gold and silver, and the metal in evidence was an earnest of more to be had for the mining. Mineral wealth, particularly the precious metals, has frequently been a powerful magnet for trade, and sometimes for considerable folk-migrations. Perhaps Spaniards, familiar with metal mining from earliest times, were exceptionally attuned to the siren call. Discovery of stores of precious metals was facilitated by Amerind workings.

The difficulties of reaching and holding the highlands, great though they were, were minimized for the Spanish conquerors by similarity to their homeland. The Mexican and Andean plateaus are not too unlike the Spanish central plateau. All three consist of basins separated by ranges of mountains; all three are arid and dusty much of the year, but subject to torrential rains at times; all three are diurnally intemperate, cold, starfilled nights alternating with blazing heat in the unveiled sun; all three are treeless, and their villages are uncompromising masses of blind walls; all three are short of drinking water, which is found only at the rare points where perennial rivulets trickle or purl from mountain valleys, soon to lose themselves in the thirsty soil of the plateau or rarely to flow sluggishly between mud-brown banks or through wide marshes; all three are more suited to grazing animals than to raising crops, although grain and vegetables grow in favored places. Most of the mountains of the American highlands, bare and dry, or clothed lightly in grass and shrub, differ from Spain's mainly in their much greater height. The effects of higher altitudes are partially offset by lower latitude. Even the irrigated coastal desert of Peru has its counterpart in the irrigated Levant of Mediterranean Spain. The one problem wholly new to the intruders was posed by the strips of heavily forested, swampy coastal lowlands — the Isthmus of Panamá and the Vera Cruz coastal plain, the latter reinforced by the cloud forest of the mountain face.

The Atlantic (Gulf of Mexico) gate to the Mexican highland is an offshore island which gives a modicum of protection for debarkation (Fig. 62). From the mainland opposite, now the city of Vera Cruz, the route of the conquerors lies across the coastal plain, to two alternative routes up the escarpment, one to the north the other to the south of Mt. Orizaba's great bulk. Both these routes were in common use by the Indians, and the invading band led by Cortes needed only guides, not trailbreakers, to lead them to the plateau. Once on the upland both routes continue into the " Valley of Mexico," where the Aztec power was enthroned. From this basin passways across the surrounding mountains were in common use, reaching all the other basins of the triangular high plateau. Southward lies the route to the nearest Pacific port, Acapulco; there the Spaniards found a less arduous approach to the interior than from the Gulf side because it is more gentle and less densely forested. For two centuries Spain designated Acapulco as the sole landing port for the China trade, and the silks and other luxury goods moving between the mother country and its oriental outpost, the Philippine Islands, were compelled to move up and over the Mexican highland rather than across the isthmuses — Panamá or Tehuantepéc (Fig. 61).

To reach Peru from Europe necessitated transshipment at both coasts of Panamá. Three routes were used to cross this barrier, but the two which connect Portobelo on the Atlantic to Old and New Panamá respectively were successively the important ones. The conquerors of the Puna of Peru used for a military base the Inca settlement at the southern extremity of the Gulf of Guayaquil (Fig. 63), in the narrow zone of transition between rain forest and desert, and they penetrated inland with the support of irrigated oases in the desert to the southward. The route of the conquerors was the desert and highland trail made by the Incas to hold their scattered domains; like all the roads of the region, it led to Cuzco, the Inca capital, in a high but easily irrigated upper valley of the Amazon system.

Half a dozen years sufficed to drain these Indian societies, both Mexican and Peruvian, of their accumulated wealth. Then the sources of gold and silver were unremittingly sought, and mines began yielding a steady return, thanks to Spanish experience with metal mining and the forced labor of the indigenes. That some of the most productive mines lay in the most difficult sort of terrain was no serious obstacle. That the highland-bred Amerinds could perform certain sorts of physical work at high altitudes was a providence; although even the native-born, used to the altitude, could not stand many years of labor in the mines, and the death rate was high. The two imperial Indian capitals, converted at the outset into administrative arms of imperial Spain, received progressive embellishment, as the gold and silver interiors of their churches testify. Even the small towns built miracles of lavish display — especially the mining towns, such as Guanajuato and Taxco in Mexico. Yet the treasure left in the country was nothing to the treasure that flowed to Spain over the routes of the conquerors.

## THE TWO MAJOR HIGHLANDS

In launching their first attacks upon the two chief seats of Indian power, the freebooting conquerors were seeking spoils. Spoils they gained in abundance, and in addition they found themselves heirs of political power in the whole mountainous country of western Latin America. Aztec and Inca had but fulfilled the destiny of their highland homes — political unity of bracing uplands that rise above enervating tropical lowland. Even the revolts of subject tribes, which weakened their rulers and threw invaluable armed forces into allegiance with the Spanish invaders, are common phenomena in mountainous terrain, where isolated valleys and basins often nurture intense community spirit. The Spanish monarch, in organizing the administration of his overseas possessions, wittingly or unwittingly conformed to the pattern of nature by setting up the Viceroyalty of Mexico and the Viceroyalty of Peru as the framework of colonial administration.

Almost at the outset the complexity of nature began to assert itself in difficulties of administering all parts of the vast American realm from two centers, Mexico City and Lima. In consequence a hierarchy of administrative provinces evolved under the supreme authority of the viceroys. Each subdivision of the civil power was matched by a subdivision of the ecclesiastical power, in theory. In practice the boundaries of the two sorts of provinces often failed to coincide. Sometimes, especially in the case of remote or strategic areas, a minor territory was governed with as great a degree of independence as provinces of more exalted rank. The legal origins of these inharmonious division lines came to be a fruitful source of authorities to cite in the case of subsequent boundary disputes between the states which succeeded the Spanish colonies. Complexities arising from multiform administration were vexed by changes of boundary lines at frequent intervals. As a result every boundary dispute which has arisen in Latin America has spawned many printed volumes of legalistic arguments, to say nothing of evidence in unpublished state papers.

Engrossing as it is to trace in detail the history of any one of these boundaries, the mass of evidence generally obscures the geopolitical foundation on which it is piled. As a background for understanding the origin of many of the present-day independent republics, it will suffice to record the colonial administrative units which came to exercise a large measure of autonomy, or which, because of being shifted repeatedly from one authority to another, acquired a sense of separatism from both. The earliest territorial subdivision (into *audiencias*) foreshadows the gradual shaping of the political map of South America. Of all these early subdivisions only Guadalajara failed to become the nucleus of an independent state. Of the independent states of today, Paraguay, Uruguay, and four of the six Central American republics are missing. The extra-tropical lowland centers of Chile and Argentina were late foundations.

TABLE 5. EARLY AUDIENCIAS

| In North America: | | In South America: | |
|---|---|---|---|
| Santo Domingo | 1526 | Lima | 1542 |
| Mexico | 1527 | Bogotá | 1549 |
| Panamá | 1535 | Charcas | 1559 |
| Guatemala | 1543 | Quito | 1563 |
| Guadalajara | 1548 | Santiago | 1609 |
| | | Buenos Aires | 1661 |

Almost at once these coordinate administrative subdivisions began to assert their separatism from each other and some exerted increasing political weight. The audiencias were subordinated to viceroyalties, and between the two stood captaincies-general, some of them more, others less subject to the viceregal authority. The hierarchy of these circumscriptions illustrates the actual position of different core areas in the evolution of colonial administration (Fig. 61).

TABLE 6. LATER ADMINISTRATIVE UNITS

In North America:
    The Viceroyalty of Mexico ................ 1542
        The Captaincy-general of Guatemala .... ca. 1550
        The Captaincy-general of Cuba .......... 1777
        The Audiencia of Panamá ............... 1535 (suppressed 1751)
In South America:
    The Viceroyalty of Peru .................. 1542
        The Captaincy-general of Chile .......... 1778
        The Audiencia of Charcas .............. 1559–1778, 1810
        The Audiencia of Quito ............... 1563–1739, 1806

    The Viceroyalty of New Granada .......... 1717–1723, 1739
        The Captaincy-general of Venezuela ....... 1731–1740, 1777
        The Audiencia of Quito ............... 1739–1806

    The Viceroyalty of the Plata .............. 1776
        The Audiencia of Charcas .............. 1778–1810

It will be seen that one or two units were extinguished only to be reestablished. Others, notably the border units Quito and Charcas, were shifted back and forth between neighboring viceroyalties. During colonial times the highlands of Central America remained under a single administration, and the settlements along the Portuguese border, Paraguay and Uruguay, both repeatedly overrun from Brazil, were obviously not suitable centers of administration.

## Mexico

As indicated in the foregoing lists, all the Spanish holdings north of the Isthmus of Panamá were subordinate to the government seated at Mexico City. The core of this viceregal domain is the triangular highland (Fig. 62), lying between the eastern and western ranges which converge and culminate in the great volcanic node where Ixtaccihuatl sleeps and Popocatepetl smokes, and the increasingly arid and broken country which today is traversed by the Mexican-United States boundary. Lying mostly within the low latitudes, its elevation, some 8000 feet

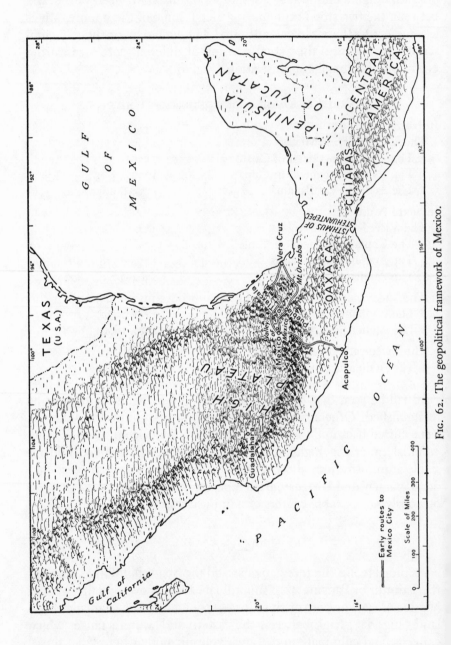

FIG. 62. The geopolitical framework of Mexico.

in the south sinking to 4000 or 5000 in the north, lifts it out of the persistent, moist heat which is the curse that all humid tropical low-lands, during the periods of rain, lay upon Europeans and their prog-eny. This cool, sometimes cold, sunny highland can be made to yield crops of grain and vegetables, and it had been the base of successive indigenous empires, whose domain reached down for the supplemen-tary products of adjacent lowlands. How much more suitable it ought to prove for Europeans, who died of mysterious diseases in the un-wonted humid heat of the Caribbean lowlands, but who could thrive on the highland! They, moreover, could supplement the native agricul-ture by the addition of wheat and barley, and transform it by plowing and hauling with horses and mules, and by introducing the grazing of cattle, sheep, and goats on lands heretofore serving only to feed turkeys.

Within the highland triangle a number of basins lead into each other by way of the streams which drain them. Trails built by the Indians across ranges of no great height tie to their fellows the more isolated basins. Yet any of these units may become a focus for political disaffec-tion, as Cortes found to his salvation and Montezuma to his destruc-tion. Such revolts, down to the one which is only now resolving itself, have always ended in reconstitution of the whole plateau as a unit, al-though its political complexion may be altered by the reforms de-manded by the rebels.

Beyond the plateau the ties are weaker. To the north distance and desert make the farther highlands doubtful terrain. To strengthen this side, a failing Spanish authority in the 18th century sent its mission-aries and dons northward, to extend Spanish rule. They made settle-ments along the Pacific coast with its Mediterranean climate to the edge of the towering redwood forests north of San Francisco Bay. They penetrated the mountains and plateaus of the Southern Rockies to the barrier Grand Canyon. On the Gulf slope they planted their frontier in the humid zone which gives place to aridity in south central Texas.

Despite this effort the rising power of the United States detached the humid plains of Texas, equable, dry-subtropical California, and all the land between, to a line south of the low saddle between the Rockies and the Sierra Madre Occidental. This corridor is the nature-made connect-ing link between California and humid eastern North America (Ch. 15). Even since this retraction of the boundary, the two coasts of the Gulf of California, segregated by mountains and deserts from the core of Mexico, are endemic seats of political disaffection.

The narrow strips of coast at the base of the highland triangle tend to adhere to any power capable of dominating the highland, particularly when, as in the modern era, the ports stand a chance to profit from overseas trade. The highland of Oaxaca, similar in character to the triangle, is linked to its larger neighbor by routes easy as mountain highways are reckoned. The Isthmus of Tehuantepéc, low and choked with rain forest, marks the first line of weakness toward the south. It does not constitute a clearcut break, but rather a zone of cleavage, that continually reappears in the political pattern in some form or other. Today the districts beyond the Isthmus which still belong to the Mexican state are always ripe for revolt. The mainland known as Central America fell away from immediate administration by the Mexican viceroy shortly after his office was established. The Caribbean islands were semi-independent of Mexico from the beginning.

## Peru

The Isthmus of Panamá was the northern limit of the Viceroyalty of Peru, which embraced all of Spanish South America (Fig. 61). Vast as this area is, the physical unity of much of it, and that the very part which interested the Spanish, is well marked. It is the unity of a large, nuclear highland, much of it a plateau-like intermont basin descriptively called the Altiplano (High Plain). It is separated from the sea by a narrow strip of utterly barren desert, and its long axis is projected in both directions to the extremities of the continent by continuous mountain ranges and their associated foothills and intermontane basins. The Amerinds, although handicapped by having only llamas for beasts of burden and foottrails for roads, unified the whole central highland and its extensions northward to include the Basin of Quito, and southward to beyond Cuyo, that final widening of the Andes before they narrow to a single range at 30° S. The Incas held the narrow apron of coastal desert, as well.

The Spaniards promptly duplicated the political pattern of their precursors. To the lands of the Inca Empire they added fringing lowlands. By way of the hinterland of the plateau, where it is penetrated by headwaters of the Paraná drainage, they descended toward the Plata estuary. They pushed into basins and valleys of Central Chile and the Northern Andes. As invaders from the sea, they established footholds along all their Caribbean and Pacific seaboard. The need to maintain unbroken communication with the mother country led them to transfer the political capital from Cuzco in the highland to Lima on the coastal desert (Fig. 63). Two years after taking the Inca capital, the Spaniards made a shortcut to the site of Lima which they developed

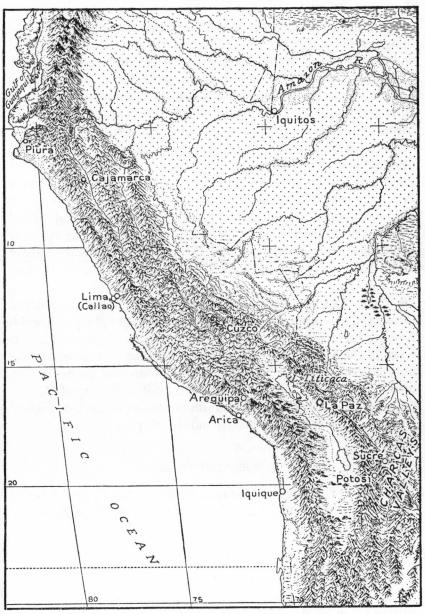

FIG. 63. Principal geopolitical points in Peru.

as the coastal outlet for both the desert and the.Puna. At the outlet to one of the few routes to the upland, the stream which has cut the trail brings considerable water to the alluvial piedmont plain where gentle and even slopes lie athirst for irrigation. Here the city was laid out. Eight miles across the plain a gravelly, low peninsula reaches out toward two island hills. These together ward off the worst of the surf which beats in from the southwest, and make the least unsatisfactory natural harbor on the whole smooth line of coast which skirts the high plateau.

Although for political convenience in administering an overseas colony, the capital was brought to the coast, the material basis of the viceroyalty continued to be the resources of the highland. Like Mexico, Peru has an upland core not too difficult to unify politically. Beyond it administration becomes increasingly difficult. The highland consists of a long chain of interconnected plateaus and basins running from the dissected mountain mass south of the Gulf of Guayaquil to about 27° S. Lat., where the ranges that border the Altiplano on the east fade out. These twenty degrees of latitude almost exactly coincide with the Pacific coast desert, which tends strongly to follow the political fortunes of the adjacent plateau. The remaining periphery of Spanish America appears to have been subjected to the Viceroyalty of Peru because of the intense preoccupation of the home government in the mineralized highland. It consists of humid lowlands, of low mountains, or of high and narrow ranges. Lying north, east, and south of the central core, these diverse regions fall into a number of distinct political units, each possessing a distinctive individuality.

THE SUBORDINATE AREAS

As events turned out, the Peruvian periphery, like Central America and the Caribbean islands, soon broke away to some degree from the central authority.

## Central America

Between the isthmuses of Tehuantepéc and Panamá stands an upland which symbolizes its unity in the name Central America, and its separatism in the subdivision into several independent political units (Fig. 61). As elsewhere in rainy, low-latitude, Spanish-America, the centers of political power lie on the highlands, wherever the terrain offers a choice between high and low altitudes. Lowlands between the uplands and the sea, some of them productive plantation districts, are linked with the highlands to form units economically reciprocal and politically inseparable. The distance from sea to sea is short, ranging between ports from 150 to 300 miles, whereas the highland axis is a thousand miles long. Cross ranges, rising no higher above their base than those which lightly mark off the associated valleys of the Mexican Plateau, in Central America raise barriers scarcely traversed, because a highland in direct reach of the sea has no need of contact with neighboring and competitive highlands. Until the advent of regular air service, the only customary connection between any two of the Central American highlands was a railroad calculated to provide an Atlantic outlet via Guatemala for El Salvador, the one state which has no Atlantic seaboard. The Maya civilization had flourished on the northern flank of this highland cluster, but had never succeeded in dominating the upland itself. Other societies dwelt on the shores of Lake Nicaragua. The discrete nature of the terrain found expression at the very outset of Spanish occupation, in fighting over division of land among the *conquistadores* who had gone to seize it both from Mexico and directly by sea. Seen from overseas as a minor and not very rich appendage of the Mexican Plateau, Spain attached it to the Mexican Viceroyalty. But the awkwardness of administering this difficult country from a remote center led to tacit separation, recognized later as a captaincy-general. Its seat of government was fixed at Guatemala on the northernmost of the highlands. There a considerable plateau at about 6000 feet elevation affords an invaluable cool, wind-swept site for a European center of power. It stands close above the fertile lower slopes of a volcanic range which there descends to the Pacific coast, and is almost as easily reached from the less productive Europe-facing eastern seaboard. Commanding the most considerable aggregation of resources in Central America, Guatemala is handicapped as the political capital of the whole area by its offside location. To the remote and weak highland units southward the comparative wealth of Guatemala was the cause of suspicion.

## Caribbean Islands

The Caribbean islands furnished Spain's earliest base against the mainland and remained its last foothold on American soil — long after the mainland had won its independence. It was easy to take them from their aboriginal inhabitants, who could not flee to fastnesses beyond the reach of pursuit. Once seized, it was easy to develop their latent possibilities as sources of plantation crops. Their strategic and their economic possibilities combined to make them valuable to Spain and alluring to other nations. They early became catspaws in the struggles over colonies and thrones which raged among the adolescent nationalities of Europe, and most of the Lesser Antilles fell into Dutch, French, British, and Danish hands. Jamaica and half of Hispaniola followed suit, and all became excellent bases for harrying Spanish shipping. Sugar (and rum) ranked first among the exports of all the islands, and Jamaica at about the time of the American Revolution was rated as Britain's number one colony. Spain began its colonization of the New World by using Hispaniola as its outfitting base, perhaps because it was about equally near the Isthmus and the entrance to the Gulf of Mexico. A bit later Santo Domingo became the port at which the ships gathered from all mainland ports to await convoy to Spain.

Hispaniola was supplanted by Cuba, and Havana succeeded Santo Domingo as the naval base of Spanish power in the Caribbean. Cuba was the foundation on which rested Spanish control of Florida and Louisiana. Neither the islands nor this subtropical mainland produced notable financial returns, and in time incurred regular deficits in the royal treasury; but their control made certain that the Gulf of Mexico could be kept a closed sea locked by the key of Havana. In view of the fact that Mexico customarily poured into the royal coffers six times as much as Peru, or thrice as much as all Spain's other overseas possessions combined, the importance of dominating the Gulf is self-evident. The critical and distinct role of the islands in the political structure of Spanish America was recognized in time by making them a captaincy-general, centered at Santo Domingo and largely independent of the Mexican viceroyalty.

When the mainland made good its revolt against the mother country, the remaining Spanish islands were too small to throw off the weight of naval force concentrated upon them. Only Hispaniola became independent. There, division of power between France and Spain had long before entangled the government with the French Revolution and produced an independent Negro state.[1] The Spanish half of the island later set up a separate government, independent of both its French rival and of Spain. All the remaining force of Spain was devoted to retaining the strategic centers, Havana (Cuba), and San Juan on Puerto Rico, which guarded the passages between the Greater Antilles. By this time all the mainland bordering the Gulf of Mexico on the north had been absorbed by the United States. The strategic and economic value of Cuba to this rising power was patent. For years public men had been

---

[1] An epidemic of yellow fever so decimated the European forces that the ill-equipped revolutionists won their freedom. Although this is an unusually striking case, tropical diseases have played an important part in the political evolution of the Americas.

expressing the belief that in time Cuba would be irresistibly deflected into the political orbit of its mainland neighbor. It was not, however, until Cuban sugar had come to be dominated by financial investments of citizens of the United States that that power undertook a war against Spain to guarantee Cuban independence (Ch. 3).

## The Isthmus

The Isthmus of Panamá belongs geologically to Central America, historically to South America, and geopolitically to the Caribbean. Its paramount and almost its only function is to serve as the crossing place for trade between Atlantic and Pacific points. Except for the politically imposed movement of Philippine trade across the Mexican Plateau, no other crossing place has ever been utilized except perhaps sporadically or in an emergency. This total disregard of thoroughfares which on the map appear likely competitors, such as the Isthmus of Tehuantepéc, the lake and riverway across Nicaragua, and the linked valleys of the Atrato and San Juan in northwestern Colombia, denotes peerless superiority. Not that the fever-infested rain forest of Panamá is ideal; it is the least objectionable. It is narrower than the others, it is lower than any except the line of lakes in Nicaragua,[1] and it is the most direct connection between the North Atlantic Ocean and West Coast South America.

Slightly different routes across the low divide have been followed, all converging on Panamá, Old or New. Pack trails made Portobelo the Atlantic terminus, railroad and canal have preferred Cristobal. Until the discovery of the mosquito's relation to malaria and yellow fever the Isthmus towns shared the disability of all settlements in the rainy low latitudes. Population of European origin remained at a minimum. Between the annual 40-day fairs at Portobelo, the town was dead. Spain made little attempt to defend this vital link of empire against pirates — the environment defended itself effectually against all Europeans alike. The base of military and naval operations protecting the Isthmian route was the fortress of Cartagena, across the Gulf of Darien from Portobelo. There the recurrent dry season may have given European occupation an advantage in the era before modern sanitary science.

## South America's Northwest Triangle

The northwest triangle of South America (Fig. 64), based roughly on a line drawn from 5° N. on the Atlantic coast to 5° S. on the Pacific,

[1] Panamá, 290 feet; Tehuantepéc, 735 feet; Nicaragua, 153 feet.

is a region in which opposed conditions of natural environment have permitted the tracing of alternative political patterns, each leaving its marks on the geopolitical landscape.

Slightly north of the Equator the ranges of the Andes are buried and masked by volcanos and their debris. The terrain is further complicated

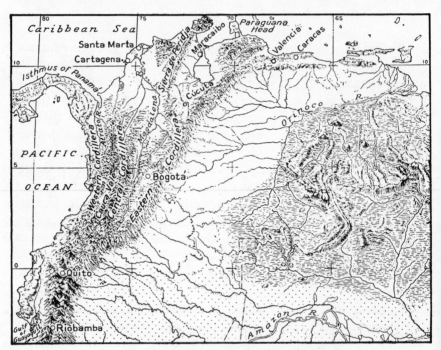

FIG. 64. The northwest triangle of South America.

by dissection transverse to the trend of the chain. To the north the troughs and crests resume their sway, spreading fanwise as three ranges which lose themselves in the Caribbean, or in a coastal plain compounded of marsh, delta, and lakes, which has only recently been reclaimed from that sea by nature. Between the ranges broad vales of varying altitude lend further diversity to the triangle.

A narrow strip of the Caribbean coast, fanned by perennial tradewinds and rainless during part of the year, gives a foothold for European penetration. Settlements making contact with the chief river system are the oldest in the region: Santa Marta, starting point for slave raids, and Cartagena. on an easily defended deep-water harbor, later linked by canal to the Magdalena River above its delta. Farther inland the Caribbean lowland makes an effective barrier even today, except for the access afforded by the streams — navigable although beset by bars. No railroad has ever pushed across this flat to the interior vales and plateaus.

From the marshy valley of the Atrato at the base of the Isthmus of Panamá rain forest spreads unbroken over the low and short coastal range, to continue its tangle of verdure along the Pacific lowland and the seaward face of the much higher Western Cordillera — the westernmost of the three diverging ranges. Although overtopping 10,000 feet only near its ends, this range is steep-sided and its few passes crest above 5000 feet. Mountain and forest oppose a double wall against movement between the Pacific Coast and the interior lowlands.

The Central (and main) Cordillera is covered with forest to elevations approaching 13,000 feet at maximum. Above the long line of green rise snowcapped volcanoes, and in it are lightly etched four or five passes, the most used of which lies at 11,880 feet. In spite of its height and continuity, this range is a slightly less formidable barrier to movement than the combination of range and rain forest along the Pacific. At its northern end it descends and broadens into a plateau standing at about 8500 feet.

The easternmost range, lower and broader than its neighbor, embraces a number of intermontane basins, 8000 to 9000 feet high. These intercommunicate, as do the basins of the Mexican Plateau. Of them Bogotá is the largest. A productive plain of modest size, the Savanna (grassland) of Bogotá lies in the bracing zone favored by European settlers in low-latitude America and called by them the *tierra fria*. Below it the whole gamut of mountain slope climates reaches to the zone of unceasing heat, the *tierra caliente* of the Magdalena Valley. The river is navigable from Hondo, not many miles downstream from the base of the Bogotá Basin, to the sandbars which impede its deltaic mouth. Along its course this waterway serves all the basins in the Eastern Cordillera and also the plateau at the north end of the central range. In the Eastern Cordillera itself an overland route leads from basin to basin to the Caribbean, and turns to follow the coast along the range which rears its uneven heights almost to the delta of the Orinoco.

More detached than any of the basins bordering the Magdalena is the Cauca Vale, between the Central Cordillera and the Pacific range. Lying for most of its length at about 3000 feet, in the plane of contact between *tierra caliente* and *tierra templada*,[1] its fertility and habitability are boxed between mountains west, east, and south, and at the north by a gorge even more impassable than the encompassing moun-

[1] The zone of equable, mild climate between lowland heat and highland cold.

tains. Through the Cauca Vale and passes which give access to it, lies the only feasible route between the long Magdalena thoroughfare and the mountain mass from which the three ranges of the Northern Andes diverge. Its productivity and its utility as a routeway links it, tenuously at times, with the Magdalena Valley and the Bogotá Basin. Southward from the head of the Cauca Vale a mountainous but passable route continues into the high vales and bordering snowcapped ranges and peaks, which form the Andes between the tumbled mountainous masses that mark the north and the south boundaries of the modern state of Ecuador.

The Spanish broke into this complex region almost simultaneously at all its vulnerable points. Landing behind the headland Paraguana at one of the Caribbean termini of the Eastern Cordillera, a group made its way overland; another took boats up the Magdalena River, and a third penetrated from Peru through the vales and across the dissected masses into the Cauca transit land. All converged upon the natural nucleus of the area, the Bogotá Basin, where a Spanish settlement was set up eleven years after the first landings on Caribbean and Pacific shores.[1]

The strikingly focal quality of the Bogotá Basin had already been capitalized by the Indians, who had established there the political center of a state which was paramount over the more backward Indians of much of the neighboring mountain and valley country. They did not hold the remote Cauca Vale, which had been unified by a distinct group of indigenes.

That Bogotá could readily have been approached from the Caribbean both overland and by river is obvious; the expedition from the Pacific side needs explanation. There the rain forest is continuous from the Isthmus of Panamá to the southerly shore of the Gulf of Guayaquil, and the Spaniards, after an ineffectual attempt to land on this repellent coast, finally made their contact in the zone where thickets give way to desert. There, at Tumbez, the Inca power had an outpost, and Inca trails ran both southward toward Cuzco, the capital, and northward toward Quito. Metropolis of the most productive of a communicating series of intermontane basins, the Quito upland was separated but not utterly cut off from the seat of the Inca state by rugged terrain, traversed by a highland road. It was a recent acquisition, imperfectly welded into the Empire. Remote outlier, and rather less accessible by the highland road than from the Gulf of Guayaquil, it fell readily into the hands

[1] This disregards the earliest occupation of the South American mainland at Cumaná near the eastern end of the Venezuelan Highland. It was temporary and played no significant part in the political geography of northwestern South America.

of the European invaders. Once in the Basin of Quito the route to the Cauca Vale lay open, and the *conquistadores* lost no time in following it.

When explored, the northwest triangle of the continent was found to have disappointingly little silver and gold. At the same time the dazzling metallic wealth of Peru blinded Spanish eyes to the many products of the varied country to the north, and the whole vast region was placed under the administration of the Peruvian viceroy. Within a decade remoteness and the individual character of its parts had begun to find expression in the setting up of local governments, each exercising considerable independence of Peru. Earliest of these was Bogotá, which increased its autonomy until, after 150 years, it was elevated into a viceroyalty called New Granada, holding its authority directly from the Spanish king. In the successive steps in the coming of age of New Granada, remoteness from Peru, reinforced by slow communication over difficult mountain trails, found a powerful ally in the natural debouchments of the region toward the Caribbean. Small workings for gold in the Lower Cauca Valley made it worthwhile to turn the nearest port, Cartagena, into a fortress where ships from home might take anchorage secure from pirates. The riverway of the Magdalena, for all its tedious heat, exerted powerful cohesive force upon all the adjacent high basins which used it as their principal thoroughfare. The new political organization merely recognized an existing economic reciprocity, the major elements in which were the interior, represented by Bogotá, and the Caribbean coast, represented by Cartagena.

If the outlet of the great Magdalena system caused all the upper waters and adjacent highlands to face the Caribbean, so much more was the territory to the eastward along the Spanish Main oriented toward the sea. The coastal upland, although high in places, drops down into basins — Maracaibo, Valencia, and Caracas — each only a few miles from sea and harbor. As if to emphasize this orientation, the pastoral Orinoco lowland, although behind the mountains, is easily reached from the several intermontane basins, and near the eastern end of the range opens widely to the sea. Although properly four or five regions, rather than one, the meager finds of mineral wealth caused the whole area to be lumped as a unit subsidiary to Bogotá, and at the same time allowed it a high degree of autonomy. This found expression in a captaincy-general, called Venezuela. Its accepted western boundary came to be, not the lofty continuation of the Eastern Cordillera, with settlements; instead it is the lower but barren Sierra de Perija. No ideal line of demarcation exists, as is attested by the fact that today the high-

land about Cúcuta, west of the boundary between Venezuela and
Colombia, but cut off from the rest of Colombia by a mountain rim,
finds its commercial outlet down-valley to and through Lake Maracaibo, east of the line. The Maracaibo Basin, semi-arid, infertile, and
miasmic, has suddenly vaulted into world affairs by producing fantastic
wealth in petroleum during the past fifteen years. Its metropolis, the
port at the shallow narrows where lake meets gulf, is now the second
city in the country, having overhauled Valencia, supported only by the
modest products of fertile farms.

Venezuela is today less a geopolitical unit than ever. Its federal constitution recognizes the extreme decentralization natural to a territory
in which each part has its metropolis and its seaport, with no counterweight of adequate intercommunication.

Between the head of the Cauca Vale and the deeply dissected
plateau where passes lower than 7500 feet connect the coast with the
Upper Marañon Valley lies a classic borderland. Its incomplete incorporation in the Inca Empire has been mentioned, and its subsequent
subordination to Peru under Spanish rule. Only a quarter of a century
after its conquest, all the mountain sector, including the dissected mass
at its northern end, was granted considerable autonomy under the
authority of colonies already established. This was followed by prolonged tossing of the borderland back and forth between Peru and New
Granada, within each of which it retained a high degree of autonomy.
During this play of forces, the natural articulation of coast and hinterland exerted an increasing influence. For a time the arid oasis of Piura
south of the Gulf of Guayaquil and the rain forest north of the Gulf
were linked to each other, sometimes administered by Peru, sometimes by Quito. Ultimately, however, the humid coast north of the
Gulf, with its port twenty miles upstream on the first bit of well-drained
ground on the deltaic Guayas River, adhered to Quito, while the desert
south of the Gulf remained with Peru. No such clear-cut separation
exists on the highland, especially where the well-defined intermont
basins give way, both at the north and at the south, to tumbled and
dissected mountains. In places the heights lie snowy, unbroken, and
inaccessible; elsewhere they are trenched well into the *tierra caliente*
where swift streams carve their courses through a sun-baked yellow
landscape, and the valleys, slits of intense heat, are usable only where
irrigable. Since the routes must perforce cross the divides and descend
into the valleys of these streams, no obvious boundary line exists in
either barrier zone. It is not surprising that both the Spanish colony and
the independent state which have successively occupied the intermont
basins have been almost continuously embroiled in boundary disputes.

For a century three states have divided the territory of New Granada, in spite of vigorous efforts, for a time successful, to convert the vice-royalty into a single independent country. Each has for its heart one of the major divisions of highland to which both Amerinds and Spaniards conformed. The breakup may be viewed as the triumph of the sea as against the land in a region where overland communication is difficult and even more costly than articulation between highland interior and forested coast. In the world as a whole the sea may be the great element of union; but in this corner of South America, where it is divided by the Isthmus and where separate highlands lie closer (in time if not in distance) to adequate harbors than to each other, a tradition of unity has been vanquished by the dismembering attraction of the ocean.

## SOUTHERN SOUTH AMERICA

The middle-latitude parts of the continent held little interest for either the Spanish monarchy or the Spanish colonials. The first surge of exploration had sent expeditions southward from the Peruvian Puna the full length of the easily traversed Altiplano, and far beyond, into the diversified country of the southern Andes and the monotonous plains of the Paraná river system.

In about 22° S. Lat. the character of the highland subtly changes, although the general altitude remains about the same (12,000 feet). The unbroken surface of the wide Altiplano gives way to a tangle of mountain chains, nodes, and isolated peaks, a section of the Puna generally called Atacama (Fig. 65). Rainless, swept by bitterly cold winds, baked by untempered sun, this inhospitable highland is traversed by routes which lead to the lower lands on the flanks of the southern Andes. On the east side of the Puna de Atacama itself, and continuing southward through some fifteen degrees of latitude, a number of intermont basins and of valleys opening to the east lie at low enough elevations to yield many middle-latitude crops wherever they can be irrigated, and receive enough rain to subsist hardy animals. Across the Puna, and more especially farther south, through the few high passes which incise the 20,000-foot wall of the main Cordillera, lie routes to the lowland of Chile.

All this high dry country had been subjected to the Incas who, at first keeping to their accustomed habitats, highland and desert, at length pushed beyond them into the Central Chilean Basin with its dry-subtropical climate. Forests were unfamiliar to the Incas, and it is not surprising that their rule failed to penetrate the wooded part of the basin, the margin of which then lay not far from the Maule River.

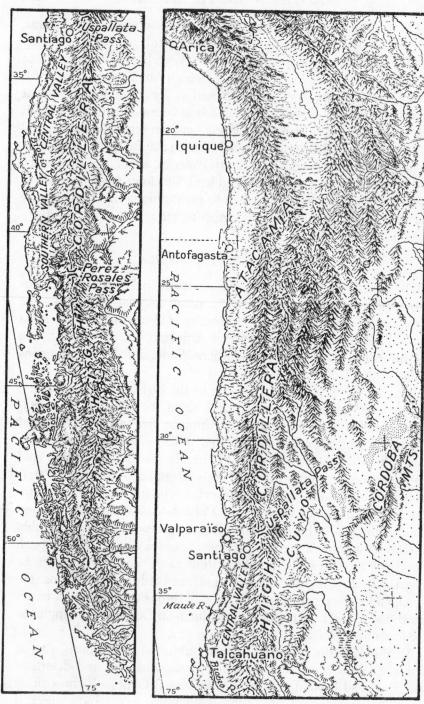

Fig. 65. Chile.

426

Following the roads of the Incas during the first years of their conquest, plodded Spaniards insatiable for precious metals. To such seekers the country proved disappointingly barren. Yet the Central Valley of Chile must have presented a home-like landscape to an Andalusian, just as Cuyo, the piedmont on the east side of the cordillera must have seemed another Castile to men from the Spanish Plateau. Once discovered, neither region was abandoned. Accustomed to the Mediterranean climate, the Spaniards pushed settlement to its limit at the mouth of the river Bio-Bio, a line only one basin south of the Inca frontier. Beyond, the cool climate and dense vegetation harbored a tribe of hard-fighting Indians who destroyed every incipient attempt at settlement and stubbornly resisted European encroachments until half a century ago.

Small in size and scanty in contributions to the home country, the remoteness of the Chilean Valley from Peru by the overland route and its poverty in precious metals caused it to be left to itself. The political individuality of Chile was early recognized, and it was finally elevated to a captaincy-general largely independent, much as was Venezuela. To Chile was attached Cuyo, a collective name for the irrigated oases immediately across the narrow cordillera, a district bounded to the east and south by extensive saltpans and by irreclaimable desert.

The valleys to the north of Cuyo, where the Puna de Atacama and the Altiplano fray out into the lowland, remained attached to the government of the plateau. Some of their rivers contribute to the Paraná drainage. Others, although losing themselves in an extensive saltpan, lead toward the low mountains of Córdoba, remotest outlier of the Andean highland. These the Incas had never occupied, but the Spaniards promptly established themselves there on a basis of irrigation and grazing. Forts in the hills along all the eastern outliers of the Andes provided defenses easily held against plains Indians.

From the Pilcomayo River northward the east-facing Andean valleys are cloud-filled and receive a quota of rain (Fig. 63). Lying in the tierra templada, they yield varied crops, while the broad mountain spurs between them furnish excellent grass pasture for animals. On that side a wide band of wooded foothills today marks the edge of settlement, just as it once marked the limit of Inca power. Eastward stretches the Chaco — a flat country of coarse grasses, broken here and there by thickets of small thorny trees, and in places by expanses of scattered trees dotted about as in a park. Throughout most of the year waterless and parched, much of the Chaco is inundated during the rainy season. The few sluggish rivers which cross it are not navigable.

The traditional capital of this southeast border of the Altiplano is Sucré, in one of the open valleys some 3000 feet below the level of the Altiplano, and on a route between Potosí, the most celebrated silver mining camp of all Peru, and the Plata lowland (Fig. 63). This combination of high plateau, yielding the much desired silver, and valleys moist or dry, producing grain and draft animals for the mining camps, was the base from which were launched the first successful settlements on the extensive plain tributary to the Plata (Fig. 66).

The Plata estuary, inviting as it seems today, lies very far from the main routes of colonial Spanish trade. Besides, it is beyond the long coast of Brazil, which the Portuguese jealously guarded. They undertook to push their settlement to the very banks of the Plata estuary itself. Its western shore furnishes no snug haven, and no natural defense point where a handful of Europeans might hold their ground in the midst of enemy Indians. Exploration of the Paraná preceded the conquest of Peru, and the earliest attempt to occupy the site of Buenos Aires was contemporaneous with Pizzaro's exploit. It was as lamentable a failure as the founding of Peru was a spectacular success. The plains, devoid of domestic animals, yielded barely sufficient food to the wretched hunting tribes which thinly occupied it. The infant Spanish settlement could neither find food enough for itself, nor compel the fugitive Indians to supply the lack.

Retreating up-river, the would-be settlers finally found a foothold in wooded country at the lakelike junction of two streams, where the Indians practiced crude tillage and because of their sedentary habits could be forced to supply the invaders. There arose Asunción, first permanent settlement on the Plata lowlands. From there the pioneer settlers made contact with the Altiplano, and became attached to the government of the Altiplano.

The next generation pushed downstream and established a line of forts all the way to the Plata estuary. There they reestablished Buenos Aires in the face of resistance of the Indians, still irreconcilable, and now increased in number and strengthened in power, thanks to the descendants of strayed Spanish cattle and horses. These animals provided the indigenes no less than the invaders with the necessary instruments of getting a decent living on an open grassland. They also supplied the means of fighting the Spaniards on horseback, instead of fleeing on foot, as their fathers had done.

During their infancy, all the down-river settlements required military support from Asunción and the highland core of Spanish authority. Political subordination to the older and richer Altiplano was therefore

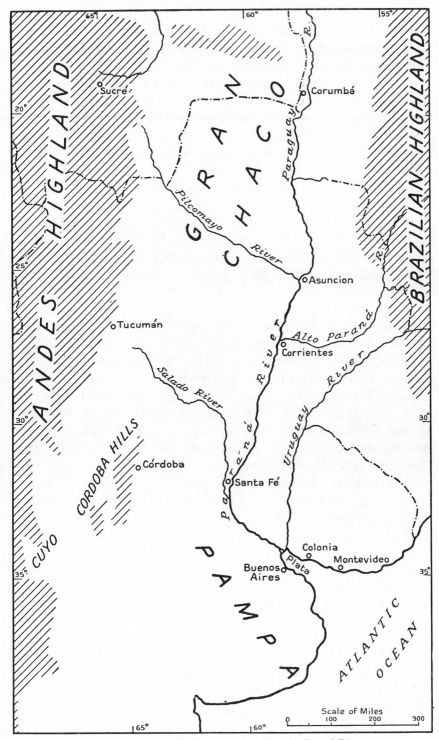

FIG. 66. The zone of settlements related to the Paraná River.

429

sound strategy. That this political attachment was retained long after the settlements were fairly established is perhaps the most extraordinary case on record of economic inversion by political means.

The Plata colony long remained the stepchild of the Spanish régime. It could show no gold nor any minerals. Its products, grain and livestock, duplicated Spanish production, and in those pre-factory days there was no world market for meat and wheat. For decades all traffic between the mother country and the Plata was legally required to move by way of the inland plain, the Altiplano, the coastal desert, the Pacific Ocean, and the Isthmus of Panamá, and unrestricted trade between Buenos Aires and Spain was not permitted until the end of the 18th century. This incredible attempt to reverse the natural current of trade demonstrates how intensely Spain concentrated on precious minerals in its colonial venture. The effects were to retard the development of the lowland, to create a smugglers' paradise, and to instil an attitude of law-breaking and revolt.

From time to time increasing measures of autonomy were granted, in the vain hope of coping with the smugglers, until at last Buenos Aires became the capital of the fourth viceroyalty in America. To it were attached all the river settlements and also the basins and valleys of the eastern Andes. Cuyo was detached from Chile, a recognition of the divisive force of the mountain barrier, as compared to the unity of grass-covered plains. The more northerly valleys, leading directly up to the Altiplano, could not so logically be separated, and the whole government of Charcas, long the master, now became subordinate to the new Viceroyalty of the Plata.

The shift did not affect the whole Puna. It had early proved too extensive to administer from a single center and the southern section was implemented with administrative machinery at about the time Bogotá and Quito were similarly recognized. In this region of soaring peaks and profound gorges, the division line crosses the Altiplano, the sole extensive plain (Fig. 63). Moreover, it traverses Lake Titicaca, its shining waters dotted with boats of fishermen and traders whose little farms cling to the steep slopes that rise abruptly from the water's edge. In spite of the local economic bond it creates, the lake has stubbornly persisted as a political barrier. The ancient society of the southern Altiplano used it as a military frontier, behind which it conserved its language and its customs, if not its independence, in the teeth of the advancing Inca power. With slight interruption since, the roadless waste of water has been cleft by some sort of administrative boundary, in this country where communication adhered strictly to overland trails for man and llama until the day of railroads.

The combination of plateau and valley which constituted the double core of this unit of Charcas, has been described (pp. 427–8). In addition it included the part of the coastal desert immediately adjacent — a region of slight value in the period when most trade moved north and south, with Lima and the Plata as its termini. On the south the desert associated with Charcas is naturally delimited by the extension, toward the coast, of saltpans and high mountains along the northern margin of Atacama; in time the political boundary came to coincide with this natural mark although for a century overland trade routes toward Chile took it well southward into the Atacama Desert. On the north the boundary is less well-marked; there the political line shifted between extremes a little short of the sites of Arequipa and Iquique.

## Independent Spanish America

In the political arrangements of colonial Spain sketched above, the nuclei of the independent republics which succeeded Spanish authority are visible.

## Mexico

The republic of Mexico corresponds areally with its Spanish predecessor, except for its northern and southern borders (Fig. 62). On the north the United States of America seized all the humid fringe and part of the desert which sets a limit to the Mexican ecumene. On the south Mexico early lost the highland of Central America as a field of direct administration. Indeed the revolt from Spain brought back to the Mexican political fold the north flank of that highland, the province of Chiapas. The lowlands of Yucatan and the Isthmus of Tehuantepéc, marginal and not densely populated, adhere likewise to the Mexican core. That core, the highland which saw the first continental conquest by Spanish arms, retained its political integrity through the centuries. The western end of the upland, somewhat separated from the main highland by deeply incised gorges, and having its own direct access to salt water on the Pacific, promised for a time to set up a separate administration with Guadalajara as its nucleus. The unimportance of the Pacific in the Spanish colonial scheme, the relatively small tributary region, and the powerful hand of the viceroy in Mexico City combined to submerge these aspirations toward autonomy centered at Guadalajara.

## Guatemala and Its Neighbors

As Spanish authority waned and Mexico cast off allegiance to the
mother country, the captaincy-general of Guatemala stood loyal (Fig.
67). Whereupon the face of the plateau which opens on to the Isthmus
of Tehuantepéc allied itself with Revolutionary Mexico. To prevent

FIG. 67. Sovereignties of Central America.

defection of the highland blocks to the south, Guatemala, shorn of its
northern border, established a succession government independent of
both Spain and Mexico. Although this was a federal union, the government seated at Guatemala evoked jealousy and misunderstanding in
the smaller highlands, cut off by mountains and distance from the
capital. Shortly the union broke into five states. Repeated attempts
at reunion, even in attenuated form of a joint court of arbitration, have
failed, either because all five could not be brought to join, or because
members would not accept the decisions of the central body.

El Salvador is the Pacific slope of the crescent of high mountains
that almost severs the Guatemalan plateau from the appended territory which it was given to administer in 1543. Equally difficult terrain
is politically unified in a dozen places in tropical America. But El
Salvador, being on the Pacific side, has a climatic régime of alternating
wet and dry seasons which has made intensive agriculture possible, and
with it a population denser than elsewhere in Central America and
with a larger European infusion than in Guatemala. Its very smallness

made possible the effective political organization which led the revolt against Guatemalan suzerainty following the war of independence. Possessing no back country of untamed wilderness, its landward boundary is the line between dense and sparse settlement that roughly corresponds with the sharp rise of the dividing ranges.

Nicaragua has for its core the lacustrine plains of about 1200 feet elevation which distinguish this section of the varied Central American upland. Like El Salvador, this ecumene lies on the Pacific side of the highest ranges, and so has the benefit of a marked dry season. However, the country possesses also an Atlantic frontage, and because of the lakes, it is potentially valuable as the route of an interoceanic canal. Separated from Guatemala by the forested mountains of Honduras and having El Salvador as a first line of defense, Nicaragua was able to make good its independence.

Most of Honduras is rugged mountain, fringed by the widest coastal swamp on the rainy Atlantic side of Central America. Although the country has only a peephole on the Pacific (Gulf of Fonseca) its capital is on that side — a city lacking rail connection with either coast. This wild terrain is the physical barrier which supported the revolt against Guatemala.

Costa Rica, smallest of the Central American countries, is ideally perched on a broken upland of moderate elevation. Its core lies in the lower levels of the *tierra templada*. Its coastal strips are narrow and therefore not serious handicaps to external movement. It reaches out to lay hold upon the lacustrine plains of Nicaragua, but the small Costa Rican section plays no significant role in the country's life. The cleavage between Costa Rica and Nicaragua is not evident in the natural landscape; it seems to derive chiefly from the distinct connections with the outside world, and in the fact that Indians in Costa Rica were exterminated more generally than in Nicaragua, leaving the country with the highest percentage of white population in all low-latitude America.

## Panamá

When the day of separation from Spain arrived, traditional connection with Cartagena led the small population of the Isthmus of Panamá to declare for union with its neighbor to the south. But Colombia, having frontage on both oceans, needs the Isthmian transit route less than any other part of the Western Hemisphere except Central America and Mexico. Political unification of Pacific and Atlantic North America brought in its wake the Panamá railroad. The growing ocean commerce of the 19th century focused international attention on the possibility of an interoceanic canal. The successful cutting was made only after medical and sanitary science had eliminated malaria, blackwater fever, and yellow fever, proof that the most obstinate opponent to canal building was the mosquito.

As in the case of Suez, the other interoceanic canal, the changing political arrangements respecting Panamá emphasize its dual geography — a district of considerable interest to all the world but of special importance to the leading power in America. So long as its function was to join Peru to Spain it remained subordinate to the Peruvian viceroyalty. While the Americas were occupied by a number of weak independent states, Panamá remained a little-esteemed appendage of the adjacent mainland unit. When the United States stepped on to the international scene as a world power with colonial stakes in both Caribbean and Pacific, its interest in the possible canal links between the two seaboards became paramount. Its leasing of the Canal Zone and construction of the costly seaway followed immediately. Detachment of the province of Panamá from Colombia, and its elevation to independent status, was a by-product of canal construction. That Panamanian politics have ever since depended upon the United States policy in the Canal Zone is incontrovertible. Many think that the United States tacitly admitted its culpability in the revolution of 1902 by paying outraged Colombia $25,000,000 a score of years later. Notwithstanding its paramount position, the nation which owns the Canal recognizes the interests of the other American states and of the world at large. Panamá is legally independent, not a colony of the United States. Tolls are equal to all users of the Canal, no matter what their nationality.

So long as seaborne trade remains important, the Isthmus will never be allowed to revert to the isolation which was its lot before the conquest of Peru. Today it is the principal strategic spot in the Caribbean realm, and therefore the leading focus of international concern.

## The Successors of New Granada

The most complex terrain in Spanish America was governed by Spain as New Granada. Although this region fought for its political independence as a unit, it promptly fell apart into the succession states Colombia, Venezuela, and Ecuador (Fig. 64).

Even today Colombia, the heartland of New Granada, is physically one of the less unified countries of Latin America. Rails have attached the major highlands bordering the Magdalena to the water highway, but they have also deflected the Cúcuta basin to neighboring Venezuela. Rails have bound the Cauca Vale to the Pacific Ocean, and that unhealthful coast is punctured by a modern port which diverts business formerly attached to the Magdalena waterway. It still is necessary to take to the road or the trail to gain Bogotá from the Cauca. Everywhere except in the rain forest, the automobile road is an invaluable adjunct to the railroad, and forges tenuous links between lines which have failed to surmount mountain barriers. Still more promising is connection by air. As everywhere in low-latitude America, local airplane service has unified the scattered inhabitants to a degree undreamed of a few years ago. No major block of settled Colombian country is now more than a day from any other. Who shall say that New Granada might not have perpetuated its colonial boundaries if its declaration of independence had postdated the gas engine? For half a century after Venezuela and Ecuador went their separate ways Colombia was organized as a federal state, the component States corresponding to the several semi-isolated blocks in which the major groups of population live. The half century since has been lived out under a unitary constitution. Improved transportation should make unitary government increasingly adapted to the country.

Venezuela comprises the several spots of dense population which mark the more habitable basins facing the Caribbean Sea east of the range which bounds the Magdalena lowland. The basins vary from sea level to 2600 feet elevation, and each has its separate line of access. That the nation has not disintegrated may be rooted in part in its possession of the broad Orinoco Basin, a unified habitat of sparse population directly accessible to all the populous centers. Railroads are confined to the coastal zone, and the Orinoco riverway parallels the seaboard. Recently automobile roads, particularly a route joining the coastal basins, have for the first time placed the several districts in quick communication with each other. The abundance of petroleum about Lake Maracaibo, the most remote, but today the richest of the centers, favors the use of motor roads.

The Ecuador of today has for its core a platform 7500 to 9000 feet high, from the eastern and western borders of which continuous series of snowy volcanoes soar to more than double the elevation of the intervening chain of basins. These basins, of which Quito is the largest and most productive, are separated from each other by gentle but tremendous swells, the piedmont slopes of the volcanoes. Although easily traversed because of their even gradients, these sills rise into the zone of the páramo — cold, bleak, rain-swept, and foggy expanses of black soil, little more than raw humus, which produces harsh herbage. The páramos to this day remain devoid of habitations, except where road work has induced temporary shelters. On their margins the wrecks of abandoned homes testify to the incapacity of man to cope with even their least savage sections. In spite of interruptions, the whole long intermont belt is a unit. Its parts were linked by a fortified Inca road to the imperial capital at Cuzco, just as today automobiles between Quito and Riobamba bump over the remains of a military road which dates from Spanish times. Not that any sort of road exists between the intermont highland and Peru. All the dissected country about the international border is difficult to reach from any side, and no road other than an untravelled mountain trail crosses the boundary. A considerable chunk of high ground here is still in dispute between the two countries.

The other partner in the Ecuador team is the coastal zone, a rainy lowland abounding in fertile alluvium washed down from the volcanic heights, and the source of all the country's export goods. The port, Guayaquil, long notorious for fever, but now brought inside the pale of safely habitable cities by sanitation, is far more active than the highland capital. The combination of cool highland and hot coast has its counterparts in every tropical American state. In Ecuador the antithesis between their interests — the self-subsisting, political integrity of the interior in contrast with the interdependent, outward facing, coastal lowland — constitutes a perennial threat of political rupture which sometimes expresses itself in upheaval. Ordinarily, however, the dissonance is drowned in blatant expressions of nationalism. The country even keeps its own time, based on the longitude of Quito, and about 20 minutes off standard time.

While the northwest triangle of the continent was separating from Peru and breaking up into three political blocks, their distinctive highland nuclei drawn ever farther apart by the pull of the sea, a strikingly parallel cleavage was appearing in the lands to the south of the Peruvian center of political power.

## CHILE

Chile is clearly set off from its trans-Andean neighbors by unoccupied mountains, whatever may be the difficulties of marking the boundary in detail, and has for its nuclear core the Central Valley — the region of dry-subtropical climate (Fig. 65). Its series of sunny, intercommunicating valleys between the high cordillera and the coast range is bounded on the north by desert and on the south by humid forest country. Above this Central Valley the Andean wall towers to its greatest heights. Passes are few, and the most direct links to Cuyo, beyond the mountain wall, debouch near the center of the chain of basins. In the largest of the basins stands Santiago, nourished by irrigation water from a glacier-fed stream, and capital of the country from the moment of its seizure by Spain. From the Central Valley settlers gradually occupied irrigable bits of streamside scattered along the desert immediately to northward. This movement took them well beyond the naturally marked barrier along the southern border of the Desert of Atacama. In the south, when finally the Indian resistance was broken and the forests had been converted into pastures, the Southern Valley became a junior partner in the economic and political life of the country. The fiord coast at the extreme south — even today unpopulated wilderness of evergreen forest — is merely the tail of the snakelike form which the map of Chile resembles.

This expansion along 1700 miles of ribbon between mountains and ocean took place in the shelter of the heights, which barred the overland routes from Peru. The landform barrier is accentuated by climate: on the north by parching desert alternately blazing and bitter; on the east by long winters of deep snow and unexpected summer freshets that sweep away the streambed trails. A region so far from the center of political power must be self-reliant or perish. Chile is schooled by experience in this doctrine, and is not by accident one of the first of the Spanish continental colonies to have maintained its independence of the mother country. The strategy of its successful revolt, however, is the strategy primarily of the sea and only secondarily of the mountains.

Until the completion recently of a railroad which links all the interior basins, the sea has been the only facile route between the major divisions — northern deserts, Central Valley, and Southern Valley. The two chief points of contact with the sea are critically related to the Central Valley. One marks its southern extremity, where the deeply entrenched Biobio provides a water-level route through the Coast Range close to the commodious and easily fortified harbor of Talcahuano. The other is Valparaíso. Besides facing the most spacious and best protected of the open roadsteads which serve for harbors between Talcahuano and Guayaquil, it is, with one exception, the port nearest the capital. Within ten miles of it rivers furrow a route of relatively easy gradients all the way from the coast to the most usable Andean pass, by way of the productive Central Valley.

The hinterland of these major ports and also the many lesser road-steads lies open to invasion by enemy sea power, unless the government assumes naval contròl of the coast. Politically, it is fortunate for Chilean unity that its coast fronts the most extensive desert on the globe — the untenanted waste of the South Pacific. No enemy need be feared from that quarter, nor any serious threat from barren Patagonia beyond the stormy waters of Cape Horn.

By means of seapower Chilean independence was assured in two moves. First the harbors of Talcahuano and Valparaíso were seized by the rebellious Chileans, who then transported an army to the coast of Peru, invested the port of Lima (Callao) from a base on islands close to the shore, and occupied the ancient capital itself. Thereupon Spain acknowledged Chilean independence as the price of Lima's evacuation. Two generations later, after Chile had used the sea lane to encroach upon the segment of coastal desert that had been traditionally the appendage of either Peru or Charcas, Chilean seapower converted *de facto* occupation into *de jure* possession in a struggle aptly termed " The War of the Pacific." This war repeated the seizure of Lima, in addition to maintaining a supply line from the Central Valley to the scattered ports in the disputed zone of desert. Today Chile supports the largest navy in the South Pacific, about equal to that of Brazil, a state ten times as populous. Argentina has twice as many capital ships and enlists nearly a third more men, but in ratio to population the Chilean force outranks this competitor also.

In spite of its unparalleled disproportion of length to breadth, Chile is not a federal state. Its beginnings from a single and unquestioned nucleus, the coherence of its early settlements, coincidence of the ecumene with the central third of the ribbon, ceaseless Indian fighting, and an intensifying offensive against neighboring states, have all favored a unitary constitution.

### NATIONS ON THE PLATA

In antithesis to Chile, the coast of Argentina has been an insignificant geopolitical feature of the country. Few harbors, semi-arid or arid climate, and the absence of a single navigable stream south of the Plata have combined to concentrate the life of the country upon that estuary and along the ample streams which contribute their waters to its brown flood (Fig. 66). All the critical centers of the plains border the Paraná river system. Asunción, at the transfer point from large river boats to small; Corientes, focus of three waterways; Santa Fé, head of ocean navigation and ancient point of contact with the highland settlements of the northwest; Rosario, heir of Santa Fé in the era of railroads and steamships; Buenos Aires, the commercial metropolis, on a bit of ground above the waters which inundate much of the western shore of the estuary whenever high tide and east winds join forces to hold back the outpouring fresh water; and finally, Montevideo on its steep-sided peninsula, its capacious harbor overlooked by the fortress mount toward which the city faces.

The unity of the lands linked by the stream system, and the long lead of Buenos Aires over the other centers which its focal position made possible, were the bases of the powerful and persistent struggle for a unitary state during, and long after, the declaration of independence from Spain. Opposed stood the interior highlands, separate units having interests distinct from each other and from the river settlements. To them were added protests of the district of Asunción, separated from the lower river by miles of wooded shore and swampy hinterland, and of the Eastern Shore (the land beyond the estuary) differentiated from the Argentine heart of the Pampa by alternating Spanish and Portuguese régimes. In the long run the highland basins won their demand for federation and remained with the estuary, their only outlet to the world after the arbitrary impositions of Spain were released and the roundabout route via Peru and Panamá was abandoned. The highland and the lowland are increasingly finding that their products are reciprocal, and that union aids both. The Argentine state has always been federal, and its components exercise a considerable measure of local self-government. The railroad has enabled Argentina to cast a close net of communication lines across the flat, grassy Pampa, and to weld the western basins firmly to the capital. No other city in the Americas, not even Chicago, is more conspicuously the center of a radial pattern of rails than Buenos Aires, thanks to the flatness of the terrain and the paucity of streams in all the country south and west of the Paraná River. The economic predominance of the Pampa and the focusing of its overland routes upon Buenos Aires favor centralization of government. Thus changing technology of communication has reopened the issue between unitary and federal interests.

Although isolated and self-subsistent, the people of the district about Asunción felt the insurgency all along the Paraná riverway, and ejected the local Spanish authorities. At first the rebels consented to join Buenos Aires in a federation and were accepted on that basis. While the down-river settlements were still embroiled in their attempt to impose a unitary state, the Asunción district set up independently as Paraguay. A generation later a conflict was precipitated by a dispute over the boundary between Paraguay and Brazil. The Portuguese had sporadically occupied parts of Paraguay during the colonial era, but were regularly thrown back by Spanish forces. This time both Argentina and Uruguay leagued with Brazil, and the Paraguayan population was almost exterminated. In the end the balance of power between the Brazilian highland and the Plata lowland maintained the independence of Paraguay. A state which owes its existence to isolation, it faces dispute and warfare on each border as soon as time changes that margin of the country from an unpopulated wilderness to a promising source of wealth.

Uruguay, the " Eastern Border," with its nucleus at Montevideo, the strategic key to the estuary, was not relinquished by the Plata government without a stubborn struggle. Since in the end the federal plan was accepted by Buenos Aires, the separation of Uruguay from the rest of the Plata territory would seem to have been unnecessary. Its full significance appears only in the light of the geopolitical story of Brazil. Close connection between the settlements on the two sides of the Plata is traditional. Although it requires some ten hours for a small steamer to run between Buenos Aires and Montevideo, there are numerous other and closer connections across narrower parts of the dividing stream, and frequent and well-patronized service attests the economic unity of the two shores. Uruguay, in today's view of the world routes of communication, stands on the way between the Argentine Pampa and the rest of the world.

In the early years of Spanish occupation of the Plata, this route was legally taboo, and was used only by smugglers. In the contraband trade English vessels took a leading part, supported by repeated Portuguese penetration of all the country as far as the Uruguay River and the Plata itself, from bases along the Brazilian coast and on the Brazilian Highland. Colonia, a Portuguese settlement directly opposite Buenos Aires, long threatened the political unity and even the linguistic affinity of the Plata settlements. Montevideo, the seed of Uruguay, was founded late (in 1726), as a Spanish outpost against Brazilian encroachment. The long-standing friendship between England and Portugal in Europe stood Brazil in good stead in the New World. Not until Great Britain became engrossed in its attempt to quell its revolting North American colonies did Spain effectually check Portuguese aggression. The creation of the Viceroyalty of the Plata at that juncture was intended to solidify the Spanish settlements along the

Paraná and, by enlarging the scope of east-coast trade, to render smuggling unprofitable.

In the wars for independence Uruguay, like all the other peripheral settlements, espoused the federalist cause against Buenos Aires. In the conflict it was once more overrun by its Portuguese neighbors. A few years later Argentina supported a rebellion on the Eastern Shore and drove the Brazilians north. Once more Great Britain intervened, this time to foster a peace treaty which recognized Uruguay's independence of Spain, Portugal, and Argentina — all three. The degree of connection with the older Plata settlement is embodied in the official name, La Banda Oriental del Uruguay. Its subsequent economic history has paralleled that of pastoral parts of Argentina, because it produces meat products almost exclusively on its grassy and none too fertile plain. Its law has tended to perpetuate vast landholdings which can operate effectively only as livestock ranches. A minor expression of its independence is its standard of time, one half-hour faster than "Atlantic time," which Argentina uses. It has remained provincial to Argentina in two respects: its business, both exporting and local retail trade, is intimately linked with Argentine firms; its rocky coast and salt-water beaches have been made a summer resort for people from the fresh-water and flat shoreline of the western side of the estuary.

The boundary with Brazil, while not the limit of cattle rearing, does mark the limit of exclusive dependence on animals. The sharp distinction in economic life today characteristic of the international boundary appears to have developed from a difference in land systems rather than from coincidence between political and environmental frontiers. Nevertheless the boundary lies in a zone of climatic transition, where semiarid, middle-latitude conditions give way to a humid, subtropical régime.

Paraguay and Uruguay are not the only offshoots of the Confederation of the Plata. The third state to arise from the disintegrating territories of southern colonial Peru is Bolivia, the successor to Charcas.

## The Heartland of Spanish South America

Under colonial administration, Charcas was never dignified by a government more exalted than an *audiencia*. Like a number of other *audiencias* this territory might have lost its individuality in a superior authority had it not been traditionally associated with both the Altiplano and the lowlands of the Plata (Figs. 63 and 66). After exerting authority over the river settlements for two centuries, it was during the generation preceding the revolutions legally subordinated to the Viceroyalty of the Plata. As in all the other states peripheral to Peru, revolt seethed in Charcas, taking advantage of its ancient and numerous traditions of separatism. Campaigns directed against Peru by the rebellious Confederation of the Plata were fought in territory belonging to Charcas. Nevertheless, the military force of Spain, firmly entrenched on the Peruvian Puna, defeated all local military uprisings and repelled invasions from the disaffected Plata. It was only after the Spanish power in South America had been destroyed by the armies from New Granada that Charcas was able to assert its independence. Then its leaders took the step of declaring for separation from both the viceroyalties to which it had been attached. Thus it came about that a mere *audiencia* was converted into a national state — a state which adopted the name Bolivia.

Independence could not alter the geopolitical character of Bolivia as the plexus of the continent, vulnerable from every side because of the fantastic contrasts of natural environment within its borders and because of the defenseless quality of those borders. Piecemeal its boundaries have been nibbled away by greedy neighbors (Ch. 14). A unitary state in form, in fact it is a loose bundle of regions, the strongest of which seizes the reins of government and holds them as long as it can. The legal capital (Sucré), central, traditional, and equipped with appropriate buildings, stands unused while government is exercised illegally but permanently from makeshift quarters in a frigid city (La Paz) slung inconveniently in the precipitous bed of a ravine far below the bleakest part of the Altiplano, near the political frontier. A land whose products must be exported to have value, Bolivia possesses no seacoast, nor even a river port. Located " on the roof of the world," its geopolitical edifice has no secure foundation.

Peru, first among South American regions to succumb to the Spanish *conquistadores*, was last to assert its independence. As the seat of Spanish authority in South America, it lay more centrally under the weight of colonial militarism than any other part of the realm. As the administrative fountainhead, it received more political plums than its neighbors, and its interests reciprocated those of the mother country.

The political combination of highland and lowland, so generally the basis for political unity (or duality) in tropical America, applies to Peru as well. Its highland is the major part of the Puna, including the northern Altiplano. Its lowland is coastal desert, a continuation of that which lies below the Bolivian highland. But the Peruvian section is not a dreary, streamless waste dropped down between the main Cordillera and the Coast Range; rather it is a piedmont skirting the massive front of the high plateau, and across it a number of streams carry water available for irrigation. The Indians preceded the Spanish in irrigating some ten such valleys. Each of these formed a ready-made sea base for military operations against the interior when Europeans first came sailing along the coast. A few of these valleys are nature-made routes up to the Puna. Of them all, Lima best suited the requirements of the invading Spaniards, because it best combined sheltered harbor, large irrigable area, and the terminus of a route up country. In addition it is foggy and cool two-thirds of the year, a mitigating blessing on that scorched coast. The larger and more productive part of the Puna is more naturally approached from some port farther south, however, and the Quito highland, as well as the coastal deserts, are all much more easily tapped directly from harbors north and south of Lima. Isolated by desert and mountain, the geopolitical function of the Peruvian capital resembles that of an offshore island base for controlling discrete holdings.

Just as expansion of the Spanish colonial empire had moved outward from Peru as a center, so destruction of that empire closed in upon Peru from the periphery. When the army of the Plata was thrown back from Charcas by the royal army based on the Puna, it joined forces with the naval power of Chile and moving northward by sea took Lima. When the army of Venezuela had gathered momentum in its course through the several regions of New Granada, and had infected with rebellion the highland of Quito and the lowland of Guayaquil, its leaders, partly through Lima and partly by way of the back country, organized the revolt which fought for and won the Peruvian Puna, and thereby brought to an end the Spanish power.

Republican Peru reproduces with fidelity the pattern of colonial Peru. Lima remains the quasi-insular capital and the head of the nation. The constitution is unitary, in spite of the scattered and diverse regions which make up the state, because no one of them possesses resources sufficient to challenge the supremacy of Lima. This supremacy is partly traditional, but for half a century the rich mining region of the immediate hinterland has been tied to the capital by a railroad. This route is now extended to the Amazon lowland as a motor road, the first highway connecting coastal desert, Puna, and Amazon rain forests in any of the four Andean countries which might profit by such a thoroughfare (Ch. 14). The airplane is a boon to Lima, because it knits the several provinces more closely to the capital than has before been possible.

PORTUGUESE AMERICA

The 65,000,000 mainland Americans for whom Spanish is the official language find themselves distributed among 16 republics, of which the most populous counts 16,500,000 inhabitants. Persistent factors in bringing about this diffraction are the broken terrain of much of the country, including lofty mountains and miasmic tropical lowlands, its extension through a full quadrant of latitude, with the wide range of climate implied, and its long coastline, facing four seas. The specific political subdivision which holds today is not the only possible arrangement, although it conforms with remarkable fidelity to previous political patterns in the same area The details of the present geopolitical structures have arisen from the interplay of environment and event which has been sketched in the preceding pages.

In striking contrast with Spanish America, the Portuguese part is a single political unit — Brazil (Fig. 60). One of the largest countries on earth (Table I, p. 11), its area, comprising almost half of Ibero-America, contains two-fifths of its total population (42,000,000).

Certain of the conditions which made this unity possible spring to the eye from the map. The country is a squarish block, it faces only one ocean, it contains no extreme highlands. Countering these advantages are: extension through nearly forty degress of latitude, accentuated by coincidence of highest latitude with high altitude; the vast extent of rain forest, including almost the entire coastal lowland; and the difficulty of overland movement as compared to easy communication by sea.

The country does in fact fall into two major parts — the Amazon lowland, and the coastal lowland with its associated high hinterland. The sole nexus between the two is the part of the coastal lowland which is also the Amazon outlet. The Amazon Basin resolves into a system of river highways, easily navigable by ocean-going vessels for a considerable distance,[1] and usable by lesser craft to falls and rapids in the far interior. This well-articulated and ready-made system of routes touches nearly all the settlements. These are thinly strung along the rivers because the interstream areas of the central part of the basin are inundated much of the year, and the higher surrounding levels are grasslands devoid of water for long spells. The first comers to the outlet of the Amazon were readily able to spread a wide-meshed net of

---

[1] The Amazon can be followed at low water by ocean steamships of 14 feet draft to Iquitos, 2000 miles inland, and nearly 500 miles farther at high water by large river ships.

administration over nearly the whole basin. It is a curious accident of history that the treaty whereby Portugal and Spain divided the earth should have placed the southernmost and most navigable mouth of this river system just inside the Portuguese sphere. From this base Jesuit missionaries operated as the chief agents of conquest, and it is reasonable to suppose that had they been Spanish instead of Portuguese, their work would have brought the whole vast, sparsely settled basin to the Spanish domain. Instead, Spanish American countries hold only its westernmost fringe, into which Spanish explorers early worked their way from the Andes. As the boundary stands, it marks critical reaches of the numerous tributary streams — a wide marsh traversed by a grass-choked stream; a falls or rapids, reinforced by close-pressing rain forest, and so halting navigation; or a critical confluence where Spanish and Portuguese moved to a stalemate.. Between these points of reference the boundary runs arbitrarily cross country, most often in straight lines (Ch. 14).

As yet the Amazon Basin has been only an adjunct to Brazil, although during about two decades at the height of the rubber gathering, it was a lucrative appendage. The populous Brazil which provides the base for political power has always been the coast southward from the Amazon mouths, together with its hinterland, ever expanding along the western frontier of settlement. Local parlance recognizes this in referring to the coast on either side of Cape São Roque as " The Northeast." To " The Northeast " are counterposed " The South," meaning the block of land south of the Tropic of Capricorn, and the country between north and south, which bears no distinctive appellation, but which it is convenient to call " The Center." These three areas are the main components of the country's geopolitical structure. They express the adaptation to natural conditions of the arbitrary political pattern originally imposed on the region by officials in Lisbon.

The Brazilian coastline is punctuated at rather wide intervals by well sheltered harbors, thus affording footholds at many points. To encourage settlement the home government allotted to proprietors grants (captaincies), each to be developed at the expense of its proprietor, who in return was given almost sovereign rights over his land. Each captaincy was based on a strip of coastline 150 miles (50 leagues) wide, to extend inland to the Line of Demarcation. The number of captaincies varied from nine at the beginning to seventeen after two centuries, and several were never taken up. Inevitably then, today's political map of Brazil does not conform closely to the regular pattern proposed at the beginning of its history. Further complications were interposed by nature. A suitable harbor rarely articulates with a navigable river, which alone could furnish easy ingress through the coastal rain forests at the beginning of settlement. Some rivers became boundaries between captaincies. Elsewhere spurs of the interior mountains were natural divides adopted as political boundaries. In the rugged interior, the Line of Demarcation was nowhere translated into an inland boundary line. Rather, ranges or rivers serve.

Where the plan did not too rudely violate nature, it has left its impress. In spite of modifications the original grants can be traced in the sea frontage possessed by every one of the States which stem from early settlements. A few States retain a coastline not far from 150 miles long. The long axis of several runs east-west, in spite of the overlapping of claims cornering behind Cape São Roque, and the obstacle of rugged mountain along the whole hinterland (an obstacle which even today has been surmounted by railroads in only six of the fifteen coastal States).

During the first phase of colonization, settlement was most successful in the Northeast. There the rain forest could be cleared to make way for sugar plantations, yielding a commodity increasingly in demand throughout Europe, where it was shifting from a luxury to a necessity. Negro slaves from Portuguese territory in Africa solved the labor problem, and Brazil, meaning the Northeast, supplanted the Orient in Portuguese esteem. The initial system of proprietary grants, a device inherited from the conquest of Moors at home, proved unadapted to the colony, and gave place to direct colonization by the government, the first royal captaincy being established on the superb harbor of Bahia. So commodious and protected is this harbor that it is known simply as "The Bay" and the name is persistently applied to the port city as well, although its official title is São Salvador. With Bahia made the capital of all Brazil in 1549, the Northeast embarked upon a spectacular career of plantation agriculture, so different from the typical preoccupation of Spanish America that it recalls the contrast between the home countries — Portugal the maritime and agricultural state; Spain the country of interior highland, devoted to grazing and mining. Eager to obtain a share of the wealth, both French and Dutch adventurers attempted to plant settlements on the coast, but all those south of the Amazon were driven out, leaving only the no man's land between Amazon Portuguese and Orinoco Spanish settlements to the nations of northern Europe.

The first serious threat to the supremacy of the Northeast came with the discoveries first of gold, later of diamonds, in the highland of the

Center. Although the earliest Portuguese settlement in America had been made along this coast (at São Vicente across a small island from the later Santos), the region had made little progress. The narrow coastal plain is sandy and not suitable for sugar cane, and the climate is no more inviting to Europeans than that of the fertile Northeast. The " Rio de Janeiro," although a glorious harbor with several recesses adequate to shelter ships of every size and in large numbers, proved to be not a river but a bay, behind which swampy flats and steep mountain ranges bar the way to the interior. The still more precipitous escarpment back of São Vicente had the virtue of leading to a plateau where cooler climate and mixed woodland and grassland provided a habitat suited to Europeans. On this highland grew up a generation of mixed Portuguese and Indian descent who pushed their way across the plateau in every direction from their center at São Paulo, near the seaward edge of the highland and immediately behind São Vicente. Disregarding the Line of Demarcation, these hardy Paulistas, as they were called from their capital city, planted the flag of their country far to the west. To the northeast they took part in the discovery of gold near the end of the 17th century, and of diamonds a generation later. This was the mineral wealth which led to the creation of the first inland State, Minas Geraes (General Mines). Down their principal river the Paulistas followed a broad valley which skirted the highland of Minas Geraes, and intercepted the route connecting it to the sea at Rio de Janeiro. In the course of generations, these energetic colonizers found varied uses for their own part of the highland, which their descendants made the chief coffee producer on earth, followed by oranges, cotton, and a variety of other crops.

The magnet of the mines drew thousands of men from Europe, and the Center rapidly came to have a moderate population. The later plantations of coffee attracted others to the plateau, chiefly from Italy. The three easiest outlets from the Center, the ports of Santos, Rio de Janeiro, and Victoria, became welded, along with all the back country, into a well-tempered unity. So vigorous did the Center become with the mining boom, that in 1763 the capital of Brazil was removed from Bahia to the central port town, Rio de Janeiro. The feudal captaincies, which had flourished only in the Northeast, were extinguished. These changes signalized the shift of the center of political gravity. While the economic life of the Center was flowering, plantation sugar was falling on evil days. Long continued importation of slaves infused a large Negro population, and for two centuries groups of slaves escaped into the forest, where they became practically independent of the authorized government. The prolonged conflict over the abolition of slavery was attended by insurrections and crowned by emancipation only in 1888. The large Negro element, now for half a century part of the body politic, has given to the Northeast a distinctive political character, which its isolation from the more active areas to the southward has tended to emphasize. Revolt is always possible in the Northeast, and the beginnings of political overturn in Brazil frequently germinate there.

The far South lagged behind the Center, in spite of its possessing the climate most favorable in all Brazil to European settlement. Unable to raise any of the standard plantation crops, and lacking mineral wealth, the southern end of the highland, including its coast, was further handicapped by lying west of the Line of Demarcation, a line which the earlier Portuguese settlers respected. Not so the Paulistas, however. They initiated explorations and settlements which took the Portuguese power to the banks of the Plata at Colonia by 1680 (Fig. 66). Thenceforth, until the very end of the wars for independence in the Spanish colonies, Uruguay remained a bone of contention between Spanish and Portuguese forces. An element in the creation of the Viceroyalty of the Plata was the reversion of the Banda Oriental to Spanish hands and its attachment to the new administration. The victory was celebrated by destroying the Brazilian outpost Colonia, so long a menace to Buenos Aires, and was followed up by a partial conquest of the southern highland, almost to the Line of Demarcation. A generation later, the conflict between the Spanish settlements on the two sides of the Plata estuary permitted Brazilians to regain all the highland and to push their conquest to the Plata itself. This extreme position it held only a dozen years, when the long conflict was compromised by the installation of Uruguay independent of both major powers. The boundary line is drawn some distance south of the precipitous and densely forested escarpment of the plateau margin, but it lies within the zone intermediate between rugged highland and lightly rolling Pampa. Brazil has retained the lowland where half a dozen streams, navigable in their lower courses, mingle their waters in the great lagoon which borders the coast for 170 miles.

At about the time the forces along the Paraná succeeded in pushing Brazilian power back from the Plata, the South began to receive a vigorous impetus from immigration, mainly from Germany, but also from Poland and Italy. For a century the region grew quietly, adapting the agricultural life of Europe to the exigencies of a subtropical upland environment. Unaided by strikes of mineral wealth or by a fortuitous plantation crop, this section made its political power felt for the first time in 1930 when, supported by the Northeast, it overthrew the domination so long exercised by the Center.

Now at last each of the three principal sections of the country has had its turn in the seat of power. As in cases of sectional cleavage the world over, sentiment is not solidly regional, because some interests cut across sectional frontiers. For example, coffee plantation owners in the Center have much in common with sugar and cacao planters in the Northeast. Increasingly the residents of the big cities of both the Center and the South find their interests similar. Nevertheless each section comprises a grouping of States which corresponds roughly to regional unity. This is accentuated by diversity in origin of the population — a heavy infusion of Negroes in the Northeast, predominance of Italians on the nearer central plateau, Germans in the southern part of the country, and smaller settlements of Japanese, Russians, Poles, and others in areas now or lately on the frontier. Half a dozen or more immigrant groups have maintained their individuality by congregating in solid and isolated settlements which retain their mother tongue and stamp the landscape with a culture pattern brought from the old country.

The federal organization of Brazil facilitates this differentiation among the component States. State feeling is strong enough to nullify regional unity in many cases. It is possible for States to erect trade barriers against their neighbors, and they currently do so. At the same time States which feel themselves to have common interests can and do combine politically. Furthermore, border States, torn between two sections because they share the natural environment of both, can readily shift from one side to another. This is especially easy for States physically set apart by empty lands along their boundaries — a usual condition in Brazil.

In the sense that there is much unpeopled land under the Brazilian flag, the country is immature. The only settlement of consequence is that which began on the coast and is pushing inland from the established centers of the highland. As people flow into the new territory it is politically organized into new units of the federal system. The characteristic types of pioneer boundaries — rivers and geodetic (surveyed) lines — form all the divisions between these newly organized States. Railways accompany the advancing frontier. One of the three rail nets in Latin America is that of Brazil — Center and South. Although the Brazilian highland is both dissected and mountainous, no very large areas are so rugged that railroads cannot be built as soon as the density of population warrants. It appears that all the drier interior, as far north as the rain forest, is likely to attach itself by rail to the highland, rather than to follow downstream to the sea by way of the Amazon or Paraná.

The political unity of Portuguese America contrasts strikingly with the separatism of Spanish America. The difference is rooted in nature. Brazil is more compact, less broken up by variation in surface configuration, and less diverse in climate. Much of the interior remains wilderness, the abode of untouched indigenes. Until these parts become objects of desire on the part of people of European outlook they will not be subjected to the tests of political affiliation that other sections have passed.

Thanks to the removal of the Portuguese king to his American colony in the 19th century, the restraining hand of tradition held Brazil in its grasp two generations after mainland Spanish American countries had severed their connection with European governance. Throughout the life of the Brazilian republic, it has been subjected to no major conflict, either internal or external, sufficient to disrupt its sections.

Until the era of railroads the populous regions were linked loosely by sea. With rails, motor roads, and airplanes, the relations of the several parts are becoming more intimately juxtaposed. It is too early to determine whether this will increase friction among the United States of Brazil and lead toward breakup, or whether it will bind them into a coherent unity akin to that of the United States of America.

## CHAPTER FOURTEEN

# Latin-American Boundaries and Capitals

## CRITICAL BOUNDARIES

AS in all " new " continents, a large percentage of the boundaries in Latin America are lines agreed upon antecedent to settlement. Some were determined in Europe, preparatory to sending out colonists. Others were drawn in the unpeopled zones between nuclei of settlement. The last-named are likely to coincide, at least roughly, with barriers. This is particularly true of lines which restate boundaries already in force between groups of Amerinds.

In Latin America all the coasts were attacked by settlers almost simultaneously, and the boundaries have tended to converge in the centers of each land mass. In South America this is conspicuously true, both because of the large area and because the interior is for the most part repellent to Europeans. Much of the center has not yet been occupied, some of it not yet explored.

As people have come to settle the area from bases on the coast, the boundaries projected on crude maps have been demarcated on the ground. The need to mark boundary lines arises as a region fills with people or as its resources come to have value. The desire to gain possession of farmland, timber, minerals, routeways, and other advantages, real or imagined, has engendered successive crops of Latin-American wars. The vague language of treaties and royal grants, the inaccuracy of early maps, and the military inequality of claimants all lead inevitably to disputes and frequently to invasion of the desired territory by armed force.

So long as the potential wealth of an area is imperfectly known, the contestant countries hesitate to have boundaries precisely defined, lest they later discover that they have abandoned valuable resources to a rival neighbor. That definition is occurring, even in the depths of the interior lowland between Venezuela and Argentina, is perhaps the

451

clearest proof that this exceedingly difficult territory is a frontier on the threshold of development.

The longest of the back-country boundaries, that of Brazil, lies, throughout most of its length, in the zone where up-river versus down-river penetration brought Spaniard and Portuguese face to face. In

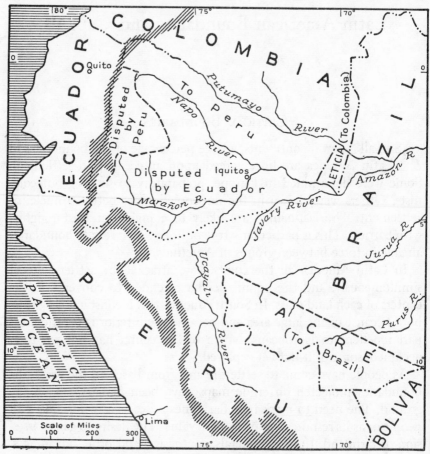

FIG. 68. Boundaries in the upper Amazon drainage.

The crosshatched belt represents the east front of the Andes; this is approximately the zone of cloud forest, the real barrier of the region.
Streams are shown only as far as the head of launch navigation.

the Amazon Basin, not only the masterstream but also the titanic tributary rivers easily carry mariners upstream as far as the first falls or rapids, around which small boats can portage to penetrate farther inland. The northern tributaries are still only partly explored, and the watershed has been accepted as the boundary on the north. On the east the barrier is the cloud forest and the precipitous eastern slope of the Andes, a narrow zone nearly everywhere traversed by Spaniards before Portuguese reached it (Fig. 68).

Spanish penetration downstream from Peru, in the west end of the Amazon Basin, fixed the boundary there some distance below the lowest impeding rapids. Movement down-valley is always natural, and both Cajamarca, the scene of the initial triumph of the Peruvian conquistadores, and Cuzco, the Inca capital, lie well within the Amazon system. Spanish explorers early traced a number of Amazon tributaries from their Andean sources well into their lower courses, in spite of the hazards of heat, humidity, and disease. The resultant boundary of the Peruvian Viceroyalty has been adopted by the succession republics as their frontier toward Brazil. Except for a few river ports the territory on both sides of the political boundary is largely wilderness touched lightly by rubber gatherers for three or four decades before and after 1900. During the height of the ravaging for rubber both Bolivia and Brazil strove to attach the revenues from the border territory known as Acré (Fig. 68). The product of the forest inevitably moved downstream into Brazilian territory, and a shortlived attempt of the local people to set up an independent republic ended in military conquest by Brazil, afterward legalized by payment to Bolivia for the disputed territory.

The land between the Marañon and the Putumayo has long been fiercely contested by Peru, Colombia, and Ecuador. The two streams and their tributaries are navigable closer to the Andes than any others, hence their especial value. During much of the colonial era most of the territory was administered as missionary country from Quito, which had the advantage of direct passes through the difficult region of cloud forest to the main headwater of the Amazon, the Marañon itself. The advantage was diminished by the presence in the area of fierce, head-hunting Indians, who kept the route closed much of the time. The more roundabout routes from Peru via southern tributaries of the Marañon, being unhampered by inimical tribesmen, led Peruvians to settle the back country. Before the end of the colonial period, government of the area was transferred to Lima. This advantage was redoubled with improvement of overland routes and restriction of water travel to power vessels. The only route much used today utilizes the railroad from Lima to the Puna, and by means of motor road strikes a tributary of the Ucayali River almost due west of the Peruvian capital. Colombia's one route of access follows the Putumayo River.

The dispute between Peru and Colombia has placed armies in the Putumayo district during the past decade. Prompt decimation by tropical diseases of highland troops sent into the lowland appears to have averted war and led to the cession to Colombia of its claims as far as the Putumayo line and in addition a tongue of land giving frontage on the Amazon.

The issue between Peru and Ecuador, although still outstanding, promises to be settled by mediation.

Neither Colombia nor Ecuador has made appreciable use of its interior lowlands, but both anticipate their utilization as pastoral and plantation lands, and cherish the hope that petroleum may also be discovered. Some forest products, gathered mainly in Peru, find their way to the Peruvian port Iquitos on the Marañon. Peru maintains for political reasons regular bi-monthly sailings between Iquitos and Callao (Lima), via the Panama Canal. Presumably this is the most roundabout ocean ship line on earth.

In the Paraná drainage the positions of Portuguese and Spanish are reversed. From the Brazilian highland the down-valley routes all point toward the Paraná (Fig. 60). Where the upper rivers are not navigable, their valleys provide guide lines and minimum gradients for overland routes. The chief center of expansion has been São Paulo, where the little Tieté beckons in the direction of the Sorocaba region. From there the Tieté and its masterstream the Paraná were followed, and easy overland routes from headwater to headwater led to almost simultaneous penetration to all the left bank confluents of the Paraná. Several of these rivers are navigable in parts, and the portages at the intervening rapids in many instances became starting points for overland routes between the several rivers. By these routes fluvial and overland, the Portuguese worked their way downstream until they met the Spanish up-tide, in Paraguay and in Uruguay. The frontier zone toward the Paraná is only now being effectively occupied, by Germans and Poles in the south, and by Italians and Japanese in the north — all these along with Brazilians from the more populous sections of the country. Before Spain withdrew from America, the monarchy handed over to Portugal a piece of land claimed by Asunción (afterward Paraguay), in return for Colonia on the Plata opposite Buenos Aires. The principal members of the Paraná waterway are internationalized, an advantage for Paraguay and for the interior lowlands of Brazil and Bolivia. Yet Bolivia loses out (here as well as in the Acré district farther north) because nowhere does Bolivian territory touch the Paraguay River, westernmost of the navigable Paraná tributaries (Fig. 69). Above Corumbá, head of navigation for small river ships, the boundary between Bolivia and Brazil lies 6 kilometers (ca. 3¾ miles) west of the river. Below that place Paraguay holds the left bank, confirmed by a prolonged war to which Bolivia lately referred its counter claim.

Bolivia has been a contender in two of the severest boundary wars ever fought on the continent, and in several minor struggles as well.

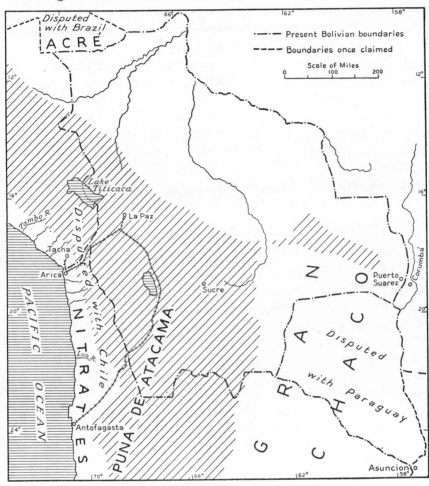

FIG. 69. Bolivian boundary disputes.

All of them are the heritage of the separation of the Puna along the break caused by Lake Titicaca. This cleavage left valuable coastline and lowland interior to the southern Altiplano, a bleak highland unequal to the task of coordinating and exploiting a rich and diverse territory.

Of the major boundary wars, the one concluded recently was a struggle against Paraguay for the disputed part of the Gran Chaco. Except for a little dyewood, thus far useless because inaccessible to the overseas market, the region has no certified resources whatever. Traces of petroleum have been found in the Andean foothills immediately west of the Chaco lowland. The Chaco itself is a barrier zone, because no navigable streams cross it and overland routes are severely handicapped — by seasonal inundations over wide expanses of the flat plain, alternating with parching drouth during the rainless months. Its northern margin is a sterile plateau behind which rises a range of high hills, easternmost extension of the Andean uplift. Along this ridge runs the one long-established route from inner Bolivia toward the navigable Paraguay River. Routes from the Altiplano lead down to the base of the wooded Andean foothills, where they are connected by a lightly travelled trail paralleling the mountains. Adjacent to the foothills is the driest belt of the Chaco, thorn bush with some spots of grassland. Into it the streams from the Andes disappear. The eastern half of the Chaco is grassland dotted with trees, interspersed with many lagoons. In the wettest years all this belt is inundated except islands of dry bush, and for thirty or forty miles from the Paraguay River hardly a spot of dry land remains. And yet the rainfall is so irregular that in some years the river scarcely leaves its banks and the lagoons become saline. Attempts have been made by Paraguayans to graze cattle and even to do a little farming in the eastern zone; the experiment has been inconclusive.

On this front Bolivia has lost; with four-fifths of its population highlanders, its army is unadapted to fight at sea level. For mountaineers addiction to pneumonia is added to the usual scourges of rainy lowlands — malaria and dysentery chief among them. The boundary as defined following the war of the 1930s awards about three-fourths of the Chaco to Paraguay and leaves Bolivia blocked off from navigable water on the Paraguay River. The new boundary has the advantage of traversing sterile country — the naturally marked boundary zone between the rival nations.

Bolivia and Argentina still have an open boundary question although their confines lie on the high and forbidding Puna except for a short march across foothills and Chaco. Barring possible minerals, this border territory has no conceivable value. Nevertheless the Argentine press in 1935 was taking notice that some of the questioned area had been occupied by Bolivian troops. Any unsettled boundary is a potent germ of war.

The western boundary of Bolivia has been the source of another major boundary war, a conflict which left a heritage of disputed territory for half a century. The coastal lowland immediately in front of the Altiplano is a zone of transition. In the north, the desert slopes to the sea and is traversed by valleys carrying water enough for small-scale irrigation. In the south, the desert is hemmed in between Cordillera and Coast Range. Across it few streams can struggle, even intermittently. No naturally marked barrier crosses the desert in this transition zone. Farther south a tongue of the Puna de Atacama approaches the coast. This gradually came to be recognized as the boundary zone between colonial Peru and Chile, and the line was inherited by Bolivia when it became independent of Peru. The northern border, being unmarked by nature, has shifted southward. When Charcas was separated from Peru, the boundary through Lake Titicaca was continued to the coast in a direct line, in such a way as to include within Charcas the irrigable valley of the Rio Tambo. By stages it was moved southward until Peru reached the Rio Loa. It was also pushed inland, across the western Andean range to the margin of the Altiplano. Presumably this occurred because the settlers in the irrigated valleys of the coast use the mountain pastures, whereas most of the people of the Altiplano live in its easterly half, where the mines are.

So long as the minerals of the Altiplano remained the only wealth of Charcas and were forced by Spanish law to leave the continent by way of Lima, the desert coast immediately below the plateau held no economic or political importance for the Altiplano. The declarations of political independence and technological changes initiated not long after, upset the political status and made this hitherto neglected region a *casus belli*. Independent Bolivia, seeking the most direct outlet for its mines, found Arica the most convenient. It was Bolivian territory, behind it lie relatively easy passes through the Cordillera, and it possesses a roadstead somewhat protected by a cliffed promontory on the south, the direction from which the most severe storms come. The port provisions itself from the nearby oases, of which Tacna is the largest. While Bolivia was finding a direct outlet across its desert, rich lodes of silver were discovered near the southern end of the dry coast. These finds were developed progressively northward by Chileans, from their ancient base at the end of the trade route across the Puna de Atacama (Fig. 65). The value of the silver, however, was eclipsed by the value of fertilizers — guano on offshore islands of the Peruvian coast and nitrates in the almost rainless basin behind the Coast Range in Bolivian territory. Chileans, accustomed to pass along that coast in reaching the outside world, a route increasingly used with the advent of the steamship, swiftly established ports in Bolivian territory, on available roadsteads from which the nitrates could be worked and shipped. Peru, apprehensive of this rapid economic penetration toward its border, joined Bolivia against Chile in the War of the Pacific. Chile, having command of the sea, first occupied the guano islands, a major source of Peruvian income. Then the Chilean navy invested port after port on the mainland, including the hill defenses of Arica. Finally Chilean arms repeated the feat of a half century earlier by capturing Lima. With each port fell its hinterland, and the treaty of peace confirmed the Chilean occupation of all the nitrate desert, both Bolivian and Peruvian.

The treaty pushed the Bolivian boundary from the coast to the mountains (Fig. 69). It left open the ultimate disposition as between Chile and Peru of the port Arica and the nearby oases of the district of Tacna. This disputed zone is the most direct outlet for Bolivian overseas commerce, by way of the port of Arica. Although lacking in mineral wealth, the 2500 irrigated acres of nearby Tacna can furnish subsistence for the nitrate fields to the south. Or it might sustain a small army capable of threatening continued control of the nitrates by the seapower of Chile.[1] As arbitration of the Tacna-Arica dispute has turned out, the port has been separated from most of its irrigated hinterland. Chile retains the port and the railroad to the Altiplano, Peru holds the inland oasis, and Bolivia remains cut off from the sea. The harshness of these provisions is ameliorated by providing free zones in the port of Arica for both Bolivia and Peru. The railroad built by Chile to link Tacna with its port is now an international line, and one of the few inhabited districts in 2100 miles of coastal desert is crossed by the one national boundary in the whole stretch. It is thus that human greed flies in the face of natural design and sows the seeds of further dissension. Ironically, the production of nitrates in the northern hemisphere as a by-product of steel-making and by electrolysis from the atmosphere, has during the past decade reduced the value of the Chilean deposits to hardly more than the cost of their production. Few firms are working, and Chile triumphs in a Pyrrhic victory in the contested area — except that Chilean Arica profits from the foreign trade of Bolivia.

Railroad construction has fixed the grooves of traffic between the Bolivian Altiplano and the sea in terms of Chilean interests. The first line to be constructed was an extension of a route from the port Antofagasta to silver mines in the coastal desert. Two decades later the ancient trail from Arica to the vicinity of Lake Titicaca, still in use in spite of the competing rails, was supplanted by a railroad. Solution of the transportation problem does not necessarily assuage the political urge of any state to control its own seaports, an urge redoubled in Bo-

[1] The next considerable coastal oasis north of Tacna is Ica-Pisco, 500 miles away by sea.

livia's case by its position as one of the two important tin-mining regions on earth, and the rising exports of that metal to a world needing ever increasing quantities of it. It is Bolivia's misfortune that, dependent upon overseas trade, its only transit zone to the ocean should have been strewn with valuable mineral resources which could be more readily contrólled from the sea than from the highland.

There is no naturally marked boundary on earth more conspicuous than the narrow, single range of the Southern Andes (Fig. 65). On the Chilean side especially, the front seems to spring at one leap to stand, a magnificent, almost vertical, snowy wall, incredibly high. Toward the southern end of the Central Chilean Valley the range is lower, and the wall, while still abrupt, is broken here and there by low passes. It is easy to understand how such a range should have been accepted on paper as an indisputable boundary *line*. That it gave rise to one of the most bitterly contested disputes in all South American boundary history, is one more proof of the rarity of precise linear demarcations in nature.

The treaty between Chile and Argentina on which the boundary was based assumed that divide and crest are identical. In the center, between latitudes 30° and 40°, the " main range " does rise to the " highest crests " and also forms the " watershed." There alone the two nations could not misinterpret the treaty. Oddly, the two sides of this section of the Andes had traditionally been associated. Both Incas and *conquistadores* occupied the Central Chilean Valley from a base in Cuyo on the east flank of the mountains. North and south of the center, the three terms in which the treaty is couched are not synonymous. If marked on the ground they would form three braided lines. In the north, where the Puna de Atacama offers isolated peaks for crests, saltpans with no outlet for watersheds, and no main range anywhere, the country is remote from the centers of population, and three-and-a-half centuries of eager prospecting had failed to discover mineral wealth. This section of the boundary was arbitrated, and the scheme of drawing straight lines between the outstanding heights was accepted by both countries. To demarcate such a line in these mountains is difficult but not impossible.

The serious dispute arose in the south, where there is no main range, but where the highest crests generally lie well west of the watershed. Naturally the Argentine government bespoke the crest line, whereas Chile insisted upon the watershed. For two decades the dispute waxed ever hotter, until at the beginning of the 20th century both sides were in full preparation for war, even to the conscripting of troops. At this juncture arbitration was agreed upon, and a British commission was appointed, composed of explorers and headed by a geographer,[1] to delimit the boundary line. Their adjudication was accepted by both parties, and war was averted. The difficulties of the commission arose from the wild character of much of the country, through which no trails had been run, and from the zonal character of natural conditions: small lakes and marshes which discharge to both oceans, and glaciers which lie on and conceal watersheds; bifurcations of the ranges; settlements here and there all along the boundary, which might be ruined if cut off from their sole means of access. As determined the line follows ranges or clusters of lofty mountains wherever possible. Chile has an uninterrupted Pacific borderland, although a few lakes which discharge into the Pacific are cut in two by the boundary. Argentina is given possession of many areas of excellent grazing land, mainly on moraine associated with the lakes, in former geological epochs tributary to the Atlantic but now discharging to the Pacific.

Despite the problems of fixing upon a linear political boundary, the Andes remain a real barrier. The present-day communications between Chile and Argentina demonstrate their barrier character. Except for a little local traffic, such as the movement of livestock, only three passes are in use. Two of these lie in the southern, broken section. From near the south end of the Southern Chilean Valley four lakes, alternating with automobile roads, carry passengers from the end of the rails in Chile across the Perez Rosales Pass to the end of the rails in Patagonia. This route has the virtue of being perennially open, for the pass is low, 3300 feet, and its approaches are easy. In winter, when the snow lies deep, horseback riders can always get through. It is roundabout, 48 hours by rail from Buenos Aires to its Argentine end, two days more across the mountains, and a fifth day to Santiago. The seven changes in mode of travel (eight in winter) further handicap the route as a promoter of freight. Except in the height of the summer tourist season only one trip weekly is made. Some 150 miles to the north, about where the broken ranges of the south mount to the loftier, continuous ranges of the center, lies another pass, not as yet implemented with regular service, but making contact between the newly developed irrigation district along the Rio Negro and the heart of the South Chilean Valley. The third pass, the Uspallata, on the direct line between Buenos Aires and Valparaíso, is high (about 13,000 feet), but its approaches are easy. For two decades it has been tunnelled by a railroad line which reaches no higher than 10,452 feet. The difficulty of maintaining con-

[1] Col. Sir Thomas H. Holdich. For a statement of the work of delimiting the boundary, see his The Countries of the King's Award, London: Hurst & Blackett, 1904.

nections is illustrated by the situation which has prevailed since 1934, when part of the line in the entrance gorge on the Argentine side was washed out, along with the fluvial terrace on which it was built. Since then half the traject through the mountains has to be made by automobile, and in the worst of winter weather the road is blocked for many weeks. Even in late spring and early autumn passengers are frequently turned back at the transfer point from rail to motorcar by snow or freshet. (Here and there the motor road lies in stream beds.) Under these conditions only weekly service is advertised. With luck, it takes two very long days to make the trip between Buenos Aires and Santiago. In recent years the airplane offers tri-weekly service and has become the " common carrier " between Chile and Argentina for passengers, mail, and express. Even this service is interrupted whenever weather makes flying especially dangerous. The planes, like road and railroad, utilize the Uspallata Pass because they thereby minimize the problem of lifting into the very rare air over the main crest of the range, more than 20,000 feet high in that vicinity. Even so the rise from the piedmonts on either side is so swift and the altitude so lofty that oxygen is laid on at each seat in the plane for the benefit of passengers and crew. Projects for improving connections between the two countries move slowly because of the staggering cost entailed in tunnelling for railroads or even in building and maintaining roads.

That so real a barrier as the Chileno-Argentine Andes should so narrowly have escaped precipitating the two countries into war shows how unsatisfactory it is to substitute boundary *lines* where nature has been content with *zones* of transition. As an evidence of their gratitude for the peaceable settlement, citizens of the two countries have erected a colossal " Christ " at the crest of the Uspallata Pass. Standing at the most commonly crossed point on the boundary line, the statue is rarely seen. Most voyagers pass beneath it in a tunnel, the rest fly high above it.

## CAPITALS

The location of capitals in Latin America tells a story of the strong pull of the ocean, in the administration of overseas colonies and in the ocean trade of a pioneer world with older centers. Yet only five of the seventeen mainland capitals are ocean ports. Other chapters in the story relate to violent contrast between highland and lowland, to the remoteness of some centers of population, and to the political landscape which existed before there was an overseas connection. The sites of the capitals tell a still more complex tale of history and geography.

Mexico, the earliest seat of European government on mainland America, is a capital of conquest. Any European colony settled in this region would establish its seat somewhere on the highland. The rainy, Gulf lowland of entry is uncomfortable, not highly productive, and, until the 20th century was pestiferous as well. The less rainy Pacific coast is too remote from European centers to serve. On the highland triangle any one of several intermont basins might do, but one near the east side has the advantage for maintaining sure connections with the home country. The fertile and well-drained basin on the brink of the plateau, now known as Puebla and Tlaxcala, seems to possess all the requirements: the part of the highland nearest to the harbor of ingress; easy connections with all the other basins of the highland triangle; a broad and fertile plateau fitted to support a large population. Its advantages were early recognized and an attempt was made to establish the capital at the town Puebla, on one of the two ancient routes from the coast to the Aztec seat in the Valley of Mexico. The plan fell through, and the capital has remained where Cortes placed it in the heat of conquest — on the site of the Aztec power — as a convincing demonstration to the Indians of the Spanish succession. The cathedral, largest church in the Americas, rose on the foundations of the dismantled Aztec temple; the governor's palace was built on the site of the " Old Palace " of the Aztec rulers; the administrative seat of the Viceroyalty (National Palace) replaced the " New Palace " of Montezuma; the municipal government is housed in the colonial building which supplanted the abode of the commander-in-chief of the Aztec army. This array of buildings, grouped round an open square, has remained for Mexico what it was for the Aztecs — the heart of the state.

The floor of the intermont basin known as the Valley of Mexico stands some 7500 feet above sea level. Its bottom is partly surfaced with a shallow lake, remnant of more extensive water. On all sides routes must climb a thousand feet or so to cross the surrounding ranges. The site of the city was chosen by the Indians for its defensibility. Legend says it was a rock in the lake; perhaps it was a mound of higher ground rising above the water. There the Aztec capital was founded, and it grew slowly by diking, ditching, constructing streets on causeways, and paving buildings and patios at the artificial level. Until the end of colonial days water surrounded the place, except for ribbons of embankment roads leading to north, west, and south. High water inundated the place on an average of every twenty-five years. Now the lake has been drawn off to a safe distance by drainage through the encircling mountains, leaving an expanse of unoccupied marshy land between it and the city. In the dry season it shrinks, and the winds fill the city with swirling dust picked up from the lake bed. Most of the heavy buildings, including those started by the *conquistadores*, have settled into the artificial ground and farther — into the soft, water-filled, lacustrine deposits beneath, leaving uneven floors and cracks in the fabric. However valuable the site may have been in Aztec military strategy, it lacks many advantages for a modern national capital. The political, and consequent economic, magnetism of the city has drawn to it railroads from all parts of the country. Other basins, Puebla and Celaya, have become railroad centers without political preferment. Mexico is a neat example of an outmoded defense point maintaining its political leadership in the face of a radically changing economic world, supported only by vested interests and a location near the geopolitical center of gravity.

Cuzco of the Incas (Fig. 63) was treated by the Spanish conquerors almost exactly as was Mexico of the Aztecs. The perfectly fitted masonry of the Inca capital made foundations for Spanish churches and palaces, and unweathered, pre-Conquest walls still define many streets of the city. Where the stones were thrown down, they have been re-erected crudely with mortar into European superstructures — a conventual church atop the Temple of the Sun, the cathedral on the central square, seat of Inca government, and barracks, schools, prisons, and palatial abodes everywhere. Nevertheless, for the *conquistadores* and their successors Cuzco could be no more than a subcapital. Whether approached from overseas by the direct Inca road or by the circuitous modern railway, it is tucked into a recess of the Amazon drainage. To reach it one must cross the thirsty coastal desert, surmount the steep and breath-taking face of the Andes to nearly 15,000 feet, traverse either the Altiplano, by turns semidesert or awash with rains, or the rugged Puna, and finally drop into the Cuzco Basin at 11,500 feet, below the bleak *páramos*, but well up in the *tierra fria*. As administrative center of an overseas power, Cuzco lost out in competition with the coast, thereabouts salubrious as well as accessible.

To serve as seat of the Viceroy of Spain, Lima was created. Lima has two advantages over any other site on the coast adjacent to the High Andes. At that point the Rimac River, debouching onto the coastal plain furnishes the water to make one of the largest arable patches between the Gulf of Guayaquil and the Central Valley of Chile. By good fortune, just at the mouth of the Rimac stand offshore islands and reaching toward them a long gravel point. These features make a north-facing roadstead, free from the steady rollers that pile in upon that shore from the southwest, and somewhat protected from all storms except northers, rare in that latitude. The combination of a large oasis and a superior harbor is unique on that coast and therefore mandatory to anyone seeking a coastal site for a capital. The climate is at once propitious and objectionable. It rarely rains, and yet for eight months the city is blanketed in low cloud except for occasional memorable afternoon hours. The sun is hot. In cloudy weather vigorous exercise is needed to keep warm, but when the clouds vanish, during four months when the sun is highest, desert heat leaps down. The sun's rays are mitigated by the sea breeze, a regular daytime visitor, but in the cloudy season, indoors and especially at night, a sharp chill penetrates the marrow. Only a dozen degrees from the Equator, Lima is exempted from the usual chief penalties of lowland climate within the tropics. Considering everything, it serves better than could any other point as capital of the combined desert coast and Puna which constitutes the Peruvian ecumene.

All the other mainland capitals within the Spanish-American tropics which have become capitals of national states stand on highlands except Panamá City.

The function of the Isthmus of Panamá is to serve as a lowland crossing (Fig. 67). Hence its life has always adhered closely to the trade routes, of which there have been three, all crossing near the narrowest point. The capital city lies on the slightly less rainy Pacific side, although the principal trading was done at the Atlantic terminal during Spanish domination. Its elevation from an administrative arm of Colombian authority to be a national capital is due to the world's need for an interoceanic canal and the failure of the government in remote Bogotá to read the signs of the times aright. Its good health is due to sanitation in the Canal Zone, an example which spreads its influence into the adjacent Republic of Panamá. In every respect it is an exception to the norms for tropical Spanish-American capitals. It stands instead as the fulfillment of a special human need.

Guatemala City is the 18th century successor to an earlier capital which lies sixty miles to the west and was repeatedly flooded by water and mud from Volcano Agua. The present city sits astride a saddle dropped between a rugged and lightly populated mountain mass to the southeast and the long volcanic range with well-settled lower slopes stretching northwest to the Mexican border. Easy routes down to both coasts and roads into the volcanic region make it the obvious focus of the Guatemalan Republic, except for the Mayan lowland of the northeast, which physically belongs with the Yucatan Peninsula, of which it is the base. The city's elevation of 4900 feet places it on the border between tierra templada and tierra fria, and cold winds draw across the open plateau during the cooler season, thus giving it more variation than true templada climate.

The four capitals of the other Central American states have much in common. Each lies on a highland, not high enough to be in the zone of the fria, and Managua is in the upper band of the tierra caliente. Not having been capitals in colonial times, and perhaps in part because they have suffered repeatedly from earthquakes, none is distinguished by buildings of architectural merit. Each is linked by a road to the nearest coast, and three possess railroads as well. Tegucigalpa has no railroad, and only San José is in touch with both coasts by rail. Being capitals of small provincial populations they can scarcely be ranked with political centers of either first or second magnitude.

Colombia, the northwesternmost state of South America, is a composite of diverse lowlands and highlands, which, with minor deviations, have retained allegiance to the highland of which Bogotá is the chief city (Ch. 13 and Fig. 64). Like Mexico City and Cuzco, Bogotá was a pre-Conquest capital, and like them it was rebuilt for Spanish administration, ultimately becoming the seat of the Viceroyalty of New Granada. Its domain was all the land too remote to be retained directly under the administrative machinery of Lima. With increasing population its political status was augmented and its tributary area diminished. The city stands at 8500 feet, in the tierra fria, the rigors of its climate intensified by winds which sweep across the flat, grass-carpeted intermont basin at the edge of which it rises. The site, where an adequate water supply tumbles out of the encircling hills, has for its core a piedmont alluvial plain. Ribbons of settlement reach out along roads which cross the basin, and straggling lines of houses cling to steep slopes above the urban center. Formerly relying on trails and on the Magdalena River for contact with the several parts of the land which it administers, Bogotá now has rail connections to the river and also to other basins of the highland on which it stands. Motor roads, river steamers, and airplanes are utilized for connection with the remoter regions and with the outside world.

The two highland sections of the colonial Viceroyalty of New Granada which have facile connections with the coast, have converted their provincial administrative centers into national capitals.

Caracas, capital of Venezuela, lies only 6½ miles from the sea, but its elevation makes the railroad which connects it with its port 23 miles long. The altitude scarcely lifts the city above the *tierra caliente*, but its climate is varied by alternating dry and humid winds. The intermont basin on the margin of which it stands and which gives it life, is intensively tilled. It has the further virtue of being easily linked by road to adjacent highland basins to east and west, and to the Orinoco lowland to the south.

Quito, capital of Ecuador, lies in the largest and most abundantly watered of the arable basins which alternate with moorlike *páramos*, in the depression between the two lines of volcanoes which there rim the highland. That it should be the largest and leading upland town is natural. Its low latitude, only 14' south of the Equator, is compensated by its high altitude, 9350 feet, which lifts it into the cold zone (*tierra fria*). It lies at the foot of the western range, at a point where a stream brings down water enough to supply the city, a site functionally akin to that of Bogota. But because the valleys which furnish the water are deep ravines, the hilly town and its surroundings do not in the least suggest the Colombian capital. The only through connection with the coast is via the railroad, although a road is being built down the mountain face. A road links all the basin towns, and extends northward beyond the basin and the country into the Cauca Vale. The rugged border zone between the intermont basins of Ecuador and the Cauca momentarily or for some functions has sometimes been administered from Quito. All these intermediate highland fragments apparently might have become appendages of either Quito or Bogotá, with a slightly different turn of events at critical moments. It is conceivable that the Upper Cauca Vale itself might be a part of Ecuador if Quito had had political and cultural prestige equal to Bogotá's.

Sucré, 9300 feet above sea level, in the *tierra fria*, is the traditional capital of Bolivia (Fig. 63), anciently the Spanish *audiencia* of Charcas, and it is one of four cities officially designated to be capitals of the national state of today. Since 1898, however, the *de facto* seat of government has been La Paz, one of the other official capitals. The map proves that Sucré is the more central, but because 80 percent of the Bolivian population lives at altitudes above 10,000 feet, i.e., on the Altiplano, La Paz, near the Peruvian border but an Altiplano town, is less to one side than it appears. The treeless, windswept Altiplano, with its wintry nights, is so unpleasant a site for towns that only the mining camps and railroad junctions stand on the open plain. La Paz, for protection against the worst of the cold blasts, is dropped down 1500 feet into the head of a gulch. On the steep sides of this bare canyon and along the rushing torrent in its bottom, clamber the streets of this Puna city, at an altitude of 11,800 feet. Although originating as a camp for mining placer gold, first worked by the Indians, the modern city is the creature of politics. Besides makeshift buildings housing government agencies, the place has drawn to itself a certain amount of trade and even manufacturing, in spite of the cost of moving people and goods up and down the canyon wall. The fastest trains take almost an hour to make the descent and longer to climb out of the hole. Automobiles can make slightly better time, on the recently completed road. There is no exit down-valley, for the open gulch becomes a narrow impassable gorge less than a dozen miles below the town. The events which made La Paz the capital turn on local (provincial) politics within a country made up of very diverse regions, but the result may fairly be said to represent the status of the body politic: a population resident chiefly on the Altiplano; an environment so unsuited to urban life that its only towns are mining camps; the capital on the only site offering some mitigation of the harsh conditions of the Puna climate.

Asunción, although it lies a little outside the Tropic of Capricorn, shares with all of Paraguay a low-latitude lowland climate. The capital stands at a critical route point — a broadening of the Paraguay River, locally called a lake, where down-river and up-river boats transfer goods (Fig. 66). On high ground in a region subject to inundation, it is also in a district which was already tilled by the Indians when the Spanish arrived. Kept alive by its excellent site for military defense and by its remoteness from more powerful centers, it might easily have suffered the fate of similar Jesuit missions farther south — total annihilation. Indeed 70 years ago the Paraguayans were reduced by a sanguine war from about 1,300,000 to some 221,000 people. Lately the country, numbering about 800,000, has defeated Bolivia, a state of 3,000,000. In both cases, the natural environment fought for the Paraguayans. To its tropical diseases, its inundations, its unreliable rainfall, and the paucity of its products, the country owes its independence, and Asunción its status as a national capital.

The capitals of the three countries of middle-latitude Spanish America are free from the impulsion to seek habitable sites at high elevations.

Montevideo is fittingly the capital of " The Eastern Shore of the Uruguay." It stands on an elevated, rocky point which forms one side of a well-protected harbor recessed in the sea-like estuary of the Plata. Across the harbor stands the hill, crowned with its fortress, to which the city looks for protection. The town was established as a foothold against the fierce plains Indians of the hinterland and as the outer military bulwark of Buenos Aires, defenseless on its low terrace. Once the Indian enemies and their successors the Portuguese had been driven off, the town became the capital of a border state, too deeply affected by years of Portuguese rule to be whole-heartedly Spanish-American, but resolutely opposed to becoming Brazilian. As the chief port in a country which lives entirely by overseas trade, Montevideo has remained the logical capital. Indeed, every city in little Uruguay lies on the border, and Montevideo, the oldest, has never lost its leadership. Upon it focus the railroads — few, but adequate for a country devoted exclusively to livestock ranching.

Buenos Aires, today more than twice the size of any other city in Latin America, or in the Southern Hemisphere, was slow in getting started. Its location is far from the Spanish colonial routes, and the products of its hinterland interested the mother country but faintly. The first attempt at settlement was dispersed because the countryside could not feed a town, and the wretched Indians, hounded to bring in food when half-starved themselves, rose in reprisal. When cattle and horses, introduced from Europe, had converted the grassy Pampa into a larder, the refounded settlement had to fight an Indian population much increased in numbers and power, now mounted on horseback and nourished on hearty beef. Spain, fearing that silver might be smuggled out by this back door, decreed that all overseas trade must move via the deserts and the Andes, the Pacific and Panamá. The settlement on the Plata was hampered by lack of any market for its bulky products and by outrageous charges for imports, which had to stand the cost of this politically enforced route of ingress. That the place survived appears to be due largely to smuggling with the aid of French, Dutch, and English ships which refused to recognize the broad and inviting Plata as a locked door. When Buenos Aires was made the seat of a viceroy, near the end of Spanish domination, it was in recognition of the fact that this entry to South America could not be debarred from ocean trade.

On seaborne commerce the population has surged to its present level. Small ships could come within gunshot of the shore, but nowhere on the shallow western side of the Plata is there a harbor, and much of the coast is debarred from the sea by a wide amphibious zone of foreshore flooded whenever high tides and east winds combine to hold back the turgid Paraná. At Buenos Aires a low terrace forms a landing place, as exceptional as it is inconspicuous. There the first and luckless settlement was planted, and there its successor took root. Flat land to the horizon provides room for any required expansion. Increasing wealth enables the city to maintain harbor works commensurate with its overseas trade.

During its early years Buenos Aires was made a minor administrative center because it stood at the small end of the funnel of the Paraná River system, from which trails led across the semiarid country to the oases of the northwest (Fig. 66). With the growing European demand for food and leather, the grazing land known as the Pampa overhauled the older hinterland. The semicircle of the Pampa focuses on Buenos Aires no less surely than does the river system. To grow it must trade overseas, and to trade overseas it must find a harbor — difficult indeed on that unbroken coast. What more natural than that paths should be beaten to the already established metropolis! Railroads and refrigeration complete the concentration upon Buenos Aires. The uncannily flat grassy Pampa, etched only lightly and rarely by rivulets, is the foreordained paradise of the railroad builder. The finespun web of railways which radiate from Buenos Aires is the symbol of that city's uncontested predominance in the life of its country. The capital is the chief point of contact between the world overseas and a land which, pent up by political repression for two centuries and lacking in harbors, is now a leading exponent of a world order based on exchange of exports.

Santiago, Chile, in contrast, is the inland capital of the country which ranks first on earth in ratio of shoreline to area (Fig. 65). A country, moreover, which has almost no close connections with other parts of the South American continent, and even carries on much of its internal business by the convenient and cheap sea route. The railroads between Chilean ports and Bolivia are Chilean only in the sense that they cross Chilean territory and link some Chilean minerals to the sea; and the " longitudinal " railroad functions chiefly as a local line, its only important through traffic being confined to the Central and Southern Valleys.

The ecumene of Chile lies in the central part of a long chain of intermont basins between the Andes and the coast ranges. Up to the 19th century only the Central Valley and its adjacent coast (the series of intermont basins blessed with dry, subtropical climate) were effectively occupied. The initial settlements in the Southern Valley were extirpated by the fierce Araucanian Indians, and until toward the end of the 18th century no effort was made to replace them.

Santiago, lying squarely in the settled Central Valley, has always been in close touch with the bulk of the population, as no point on the precipitous coast can be Nevertheless, it stands near the northern end of the original Chilean ecumene. As population has spread, chiefly southward in spite of mining and irrigation in the northern desert, Santiago's location has become increasingly excentric. It remains the capital, because in addition to the inertia which always opposes removal, it has an advantage that has been a steady counterweight to shifting population. Its basin is linked by a low saddle with the next basin to the north — smaller and less productive, but the nexus of the longitudinal highway with the principal east-west route of the country. From the east, along the Aconcagua Valley and over the Uspallata Pass, both Incas and conquistadores crossed the Andes into the Central Valley from Cuyo and high Peru. Later this route became the chief connection with the plains of the Plata region. To the west the Central Valley makes its principal contact with the sea and the outside world through the port of Valparaíso. Partly by way of the Aconcagua Valley, which debouches somewhat north of the harbor, routes follow relatively easy gradients to the north-facing roadstead, protected from the southwest storms by a hilly spur of the mountains, to which the port city clings.

PORTUGUESE AMERICA

Nearly two-fifths of the people of Latin America reside in Brazil, a country about the size of the United States. To discuss its capital locations on the same scale as those of Spanish America, therefore, takes this inquiry into the realm of States within the nation. There is justification for this course, since Brazil is a federation of States, in contrast to most of the Spanish-American Republics, and the individual States possess considerable autonomy and express the regionalism of a large country. Most of the State capitals follow the pattern of the capitals on the Plata — being fixed on the favorable harbors along the coast (Fig. 60). From them settlement moved inland, and through them the plantation products characteristic of this coast have always been exported and financed. Every part of the Brazilian coast is hot all year and rainy at some reasons. Hence the location on the lowland of the capital of every coastal State save two, runs counter to the rule for capitals in the Spanish colonies and corresponds rather to their ports of contact, such as Vera Cruz, La Guaira, Cartagena, and Guayaquil. The interest of Portugal in plantation crops rather than in minerals long kept attention riveted to the coastal lowland, and even today most of the northern States have done little to develop their upland interiors. The early importation of Negroes to the coast and the mixed blood of succeeding generations have made it easier for the inhabitants to maintain permanent homes in a climate trying to European stock.

A number of the coastal capitals stand on offshore islands or peninsulas. Either is a characteristic location for a political base from which to colonize a continent. Such a site furnishes a haven behind the island or point in direct touch with the homeland via the seaway; it is easily seized from and defended against inimical natives because of its small size and sea-girt borders; from it can be undertaken either military or naval operations against the less tractable mainland; to it refugees can retire before the sporadic fury of dispossessed aborigines. On the rainy Brazilian coast, islands and peninsulas are more open to refreshing winds than the unrelieved forest of the mainland. Island sites which fulfill the specifications for capitals of colonization are Recife in the north and Florianopolis in the south. Their harbors still accommodate their shipping, but both have outgrown their confining cradles and have been linked to the mainland by bridges. At first Recife, on malarial offshore bars, was port for a capital five miles back on high ground. After a period of occupation by the Dutch in the 17th century, administration was transferred to the port city. Today the ancient hill capital is a suburb of the port metropolis. Maranhão, once the administrative center of all the Amazon country, now capital of one of the larger coastal States, stands on an island in a deeply incised estuary. It remains without bridge connection to its mainland.

Two capitals stand on peninsulas which serve the purposes of health and defense almost as well as islands. Bahia, for more than 200 years the capital of all Brazil, and still the capital of the largest coastal State outside the Amazon Basin, faces a superb harbor which its peninsula protects, and from which it takes its name. The original settlement, on low ground, is defensible from a tableland which rises steeply behind, and which now is the residential quarter, breezier and more open than the business center below. Pará, on a peninsula in one of the estuaries of the Amazon, is protected in the rear by the dense forest of an equatorial plain. It succeeded Maranhão as capital of the Amazon Basin, and retains that function for an immense territory of the lower river and its tributaries.

Fortaleza, a fortress town as its name indicates, is unique among the ancient Brazilian administrative capitals in occupying a mainland site. Facing an open roadstead and lying among sand dunes, it is merely the least disadvantageous landing place on a stretch of harborless coast. Fortunately storms are few in those latitudes and the dry climate of the district, found nowhere else on the Brazilian coast, relieves the mainland from the handicap of excessive humid heat suffered everywhere else. The lack of natural protection for the infant settlement was offset by man-made defenses.

Four small States of the Northeast have as their capitals river-mouth towns. Bars across the outlets of these streams delayed settlement. Natal and Parahyba, like nearby Fortaleza, were outpost forts, established from Bahia fifty or seventy-five years after the initial settlements. Maceió and Aracajú are 19th century foundations. During that century three of the four were made capitals of newly created provinces.

The four remaining lowland capitals face almost landlocked waters. Porto Alegre stands at the head of the lagoon-like, freshwater Lake Patos, near the confluences of five navigable streams which penetrate Rio Grande do Sul, the southernmost of the Brazilian States. Its connection with the sea by way of the long shallow lake is mediocre, and it was made the capital only after its predecessor, at the outlet of the Lagoa dos Patos, had been captured by Spanish forces sent out from the Plata.

Victoria, capital of Espirito Santo, the most northerly State of Central Brazil, is set in a long, narrow bay amid " sugarloaf " hills of bare rock, like its more famous neighbor, Rio de Janeiro. The partially submerged flanks of the hills plunge steeply into deep water and so provide a safe though narrow entrance to the harbor. Their picturesque crests make a cordon of defense points around the town, which sits on a small island, now connected with the mainland and railroad station by a short bridge. Nictheroy, capital of the State of Rio de Janeiro, succeeded in that office to the city of Rio de Janeiro in the 19th century. It faces its predecessor across the immense and famous bay, of which its harbor is a reentrant, guarded and well-protected by sugarloaf hills.

Rio was among the later of the first spate of Portuguese settlements in Brazil. This has mystified historians, who see in its magnificent harbor and the fertile and diverse tributary area the nature-ordained center of the country. Its advantages were less obvious in the pioneer days. The bay shore is difficult to occupy, because such of the low ground available for wharfage as is not wide marsh requiring costly drainage, lies scattered in small pockets of terra firma. These are hard to defend with a small force, because they are dominated by encompassing hills, themselves overlooked by a range of low mountains rising abruptly behind them. The first attempt at settlement was made by Frenchmen, and the Portuguese occupied the site with the object of preventing its being effectively occupied by foreigners. The immediate hinterland, a plain alternately marshy or sandy, stretching from the bay to the wall of the coast range, twenty miles inland, is useless land even today, and held no inducement to early settlers. The nucleus of the city is a pocket of low ground facing a small island which sheltered ships from the waves of the huge bay. On all sides rise hills which were early fortified, but the still higher ground behind is too extensive to have been manned by a budding settlement. In time the hinterland beyond the coast range contributed to the growth of what had been little more than a naval base. Toward the end of the 17th century, Rio became the capital of the southern captaincies. After that, it was again taken by French forces. Gold, found in the highland north of the town at the end of the 17th century, enhanced its importance. In 1762 it came into its own, superseding Bahia as the capital of all Brazil.

The capital it remains, a compromise location between the waxing, upland South and the waning, coastal Northeast. The city and its neighborhood have been segregated into a federal district. Rio probably comes nearer than any other place could to representing the diversity of interests that make up Brazil. Its port gives it easy access to the whole coast and instils in its inhabitants an appreciation of port problems common to all the harbors along the coast and on the rivers. Its connections to the interior ramify more widely than those of any other port, and lead to regions producing all the upland plantation crops, to the chief mining sections, and into the nearer livestock-rearing country of the interior grassland.

Three States have their capitals well up-river on streams; two of these possess no coast. All the upper Amazon is administered from Manaos, the confluence town near the downstream end of the State, to which all traffic drains, and a port accommodating good-sized ocean vessels. The watershed between the Amazon and the Paraná drainage had its capital first on a headwater of the Amazon (Matto Grosso on the Guaporé), but for more than a century it has been at Cuyabá on the river of the same name, a tributary of the Paraguay, navigable by canoe. (Cuyabá was the initial settlement of the region, established as a placer gold-mining camp.) The State of Piauhi in the Northeast, has placed its capital, Teresina, well inland on the navigable Parnahiba River. The interior of this State is more fertile than its coastland, and the few miles of sea frontage do not embrace a harbor.

The four States which have capitals inland but not on navigable streams, are the true highland States. Although two of them possess seacoast and ports, the coastal zone is narrow and infertile, and the steep and high face of the plateau is choked with cloud forest. The plateau itself, on the contrary, is high enough to be notably less hot than the coast, and its alternating dry and rainy seasons, modified by rugged terrain, lend diversity to the vegetation. This highland is the most salubrious part of Brazil.

The original capital of the whole of it is São Paulo, today almost as large a city as Rio de Janeiro. Standing on a wide expanse of plateau at about the 3000-foot level, São Paulo appears to have a location no more favored than any other place near the top of the road which leads up from the island that shelters the harbors of São Vicente and its successor, Santos (Fig. 70). All the land for many miles on every side is unused, or utilized only for a little grazing and for occasional poverty-

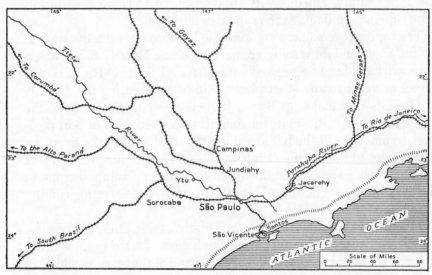

FIG. 70. The focal location of São Paulo on the plateau of South Brazil.

stricken farms. The site, on hilly ground above the marshy Tieté valley, was pleasant and appropriate for the monastery which was the original European settlement. Today it forces a city of a million inhabitants to scramble up and down steep slopes in the business quarter and to pay the cost of constructing long and high viaducts between the various upland sections.

On several lines radiating inland, an hour and a half to two hours by fast train, a semicircle of towns appears to account for the continued predominance of the city of which they are outliers. During the decades while the highland was being explored and seized these towns were advance bases from which expeditions moved along all the naturally marked routes radial from São Paulo. Today each of them is the center of a productive district. The railroad system conforms to the same radial pattern and utilizes the outlying metropolises by making them junction and division points, and in some cases terminals. Eastward, down the broad vale of the Parahyba toward Rio de Janeiro, stands

Jacarehy in its rice fields. Thence a route takes off toward the mining camps to the northeast. Northward, Jundiahy is the starting point for gold placers of Goyaz away to the west; beyond Jundiahy, Campinas, metropolis of the coffee growing district nearest to São Paulo, is a further junction. Westward, Ytu, near the Tieté, points the way to all eastern tributaries of the Paraná as far away as remote Matto Grosso. Southwestward, Sorocaba, today in an orange belt, is the traditional outfitting point for the south; from there little bands of resolute Paulistas carried their standards against the Spanish.

Today the rails are creeping along the routes of the explorers, radiating outward from these advance bases, and converging inward on the original center. Quite possibly increasing utilization of land now on or beyond the frontier of settlement may reduce the relative importance of the advance bases in the geopolitical structure of the highland. In contrast, barring further subdivision of the State, the capital promises to be aggrandized by expansion of settlement.

For two centuries São Paulo administered all the highland country westward to the frontier of the territory disputed with Spain. Then in the mid-19th century, Paraná was separated (Fig. 60). Its capital is Curityba, like São Paulo at the transportation center of its upland, in a basin of no marked productivity but handy to the difficult route to the sea and port.

Minas Geraes, heart of the mineralized highland, was carved out of the territory of the Paulistas much earlier. It was this loss which turned them toward the west and south in search of other sources of precious minerals. The first capital, Ouro Preto, is an early mining town in the heart of the mineralized country. Its cramped site has led the State to develop a new site on the open plateau at about 3000 feet altitude and fifty miles northwest of the old capital. On the expanding frontier, it represents the faith of the people in the interior grassland, and is appropriately named Bello Horizonte.

Patterning after Minas Geraes is another inland State — Goyaz. Its capital, bearing the same name, is a mining camp close to the watershed between the Paraná and the Tocantins, most easterly tributary of the Amazon.

In the State of Goyaz, but on the border of Minas Geraes, Brazil has set aside land for a Federal District and a future capital. This reservation anticipates intensive development in the vast interior plains, and a density of population thereabouts, of which no foreshadowings can be discerned.

## Latin America Geopolitically Immature

From the foregoing survey of critical boundaries and of capitals in Latin America, it seems clear that much of the area is geopolitically immature. Many boundaries in the interior are undetermined or have recently been in process of demarcation, and boundary quarrels and wars have been rife ever since the close of the colonial era. Many capitals remain on the coast, or as near the coast as may be while obtaining the climatic advantage of high altitude. This is typical of overseas colonies. A few capitals occupy early centers of European dispersal. Others stand in the pre-Conquest ecumene of the territory they administer.

The qualities of immaturity Latin America shares with the other new continents, where the current mode of occupance has likewise had a short life-span. The parallel to colonial areas, such as Africa, is masked by the political map, because the sovereign status of nearly the whole area lends a superficial appearance of political maturity. With a few exceptions, Latin-American independence of European dominion is not the outgrowth of a favorable combination of environmental elements on which independent states are commonly founded. It has resulted rather from the self-assertiveness of the United States of North America in cooperation with an open-door policy on the part of Great Britain. Indeed, continued political independence of the nations of Latin America is likely to remain entailed in a continued willingness of the United States to fight for it.

Increasing population will inevitably be accompanied by shifts in the relative importance of regions within most Latin-American states. Some boundaries may perhaps be altered to avoid transecting newly settled areas, but the experience of North America suggests that boundaries demarcated antecedent to settlement are likely to hold, because the inflow of settlers conforms to the established political lines. Antecedent boundaries appear to be more stable than lines laid down subsequent to occupance, such as those of East Central Europe, determined at the close of the World War and already altered or questioned.

Shifts in population may also entail agitation to remove capitals to points more central or more accessible to the whole people. Such removals of the seat of government have occurred in regions politically immature, including Latin America itself. Nevertheless, a modern capital is rendered immobile by heavy investment in buildings, and is moved only if the new location and site are incontestably and vastly superior to the old.

## CHAPTER FIFTEEN

# The Antecedent Boundary Between the Americas

THE continent of North America is generally recognized as terminating at the Isthmus of Panamá, all but the most southerly of the Caribbean islands being included. The physical geographer may properly accept this demarcation. For a realistic political geography, the division between the two continents must be drawn much farther north — along the southern boundary of the United States, exclusive of its Caribbean possessions. That boundary lies within or close to the critical zone of cleavage between the middle latitudes and the tropics, between the peoples with Anglo-Saxon traditions and the peoples with Iberian and Amerindian backgrounds. Climate and cultural antecedents combine to make a geographic transition of the first order of magnitude. North of the border zone all the inhabited country, except for a discontinuous fringe along the northernmost coasts, lies under a unifying net of rails, and most of it is further integrated by excellent motor roads; south of the border zone railroad nets are scattered, small, and wide-meshed, and many areas can be reached overland from their neighbors only by pack trails. More to the point, still, political North America is divided between but two sovereignties, and might be a single state but for the historical accident of the American Revolution, which separated the United States from Canada on grounds of sentiment unsupported by nature. In contrast, political Latin America is parceled into seventeen mainland states, three island republics, four mainland colonies, and scores of islands divided among four foreign powers — almost all separated from each other by effective natural barriers.

These and many lesser contrasts, natural and cultural, locate the line between the two geographical Americas somewhere in the Northern Gulf of Mexico and in the desert which reaches westward across the

477

continent from the Gulf to the head of the Gulf of California and the
Pacific Ocean. The entire boundary zone is uninhabited or lightly
peopled. Yet the demarcation of a line through it has not been dictated by nature; rather it has been gradually determined by the repeated concurrence of complex forces.

## CLEAVAGE AND COHESION IN THE CARIBBEAN

It will probably be generally agreed that the Gulf of Mexico plays a
natural role as a dividing sea, setting off the Caribbean archipelago from

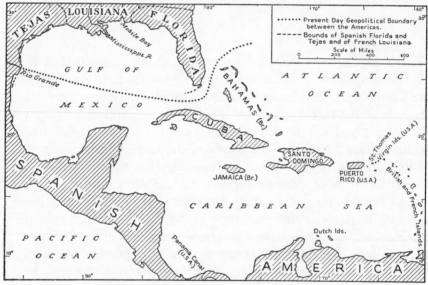

FIG. 71. The Gulf of Mexico as a political divisor.

the North American mainland (Fig. 71). Nevertheless ceaseless forces
urge union. The landlocked gulf furnishes a ready highway for communication between its mainland shores and the Caribbean islands.
While Spain monopolized Mexico as the world's chief colonial prize,
Spanish footholds in Florida and at the mouth of the Mississippi were
maintained to keep the Gulf of Mexico a Spanish lake. When Dutch,
British, and French freebooters and colonists began planting settlements on the mainlands of the two American continents, notably on
the Mississippi delta and along the Guiana-Brazil coast, they seized as
many Caribbean islands as they could. Such of them as are held by
European states today are remnants of lost empires, retained when the
mainland possessions had to be abandoned. Such also was the status of
Cuba and Puerto Rico, the last American holdings of Spain, until they
swung into the orbit of mainland United States at the end of the 19th

century. Today most of the islands owing fealty to European states, perhaps all of them, are fiscal liabilities to their political sovereigns. The British group alone fits into a functional colonial pattern, and that because of its reciprocal trade with Canada. That is to say, trade made easy between middle-latitude mainland and low-latitude islands which are fortunate enough to belong to the same sovereignty.

The mutual advantages of exchange between low and middle latitudes can be utilized to the full only when the economic attraction is facilitated by political ties. This has accentuated the tendency for powerful continental states to magnetize offshore islands, and has repeatedly entangled the history of the United States of America with that of its insular neighbors. Annexation of one or another Antillean island has been prophesied and striven for since the inception of the federal union. Conversely, the Monroe Doctrine has been frequently called out to fend off further acquisition of Caribbean territory by foreign states, especially by waxing powers such as France, Britain, and Germany.

For half a century after the union many public men assumed that the possessions of the waning colonial countries would in due course gravitate to the United States. When the expansionist movement of the mainland republic gained momentum enough to surge into Caribbean lands, the slavery issue had become entwined with it, and prevented the acquisition of islands where the plantation system was as well entrenched as in the South itself, and where slavery either existed (as in Spanish colonies), or might be reestablished. Emancipation of slaves in the United States set free imperialistic aspirations from the bogey of increased slave territory, but left them trammelled by an idealistic attitude, shared by many Americans, which opposed all expansion — at any rate beyond the continental limits of " manifest destiny." After the close of the Civil War the American executive undertook to purchase the three Danish West Indian Islands. One of them possesses a commodious and strategically placed harbor which had been used to the detriment of the Union forces during the conflict. The treaty could not be ratified because of apathy of the American public, coupled with opposition of the anti-expansionists. A few years later, efforts to annex Santo Domingo failed.

These summary rejections of political affiliation came to be nullified by the forging of economic bonds based on the exchange of mainland foodstuffs and manufactured goods for insular plantation crops. Every decade saw increases in investment of United States capital in several of the islands, notably the nearby Cuba and Santo Domingo-

Haiti. An illuminating barometer of change in public opinion can be read in the attitude toward the two 19th-century insurrections of Cubans against Spain. In each conflict bands of Cuban guerillas, abetted by sympathizers in nearby United States, fought organized and authorized armies of the mother country. The earlier revolt, breaking out in 1869, dragged on for ten miserable years and was finally put down, the rebels having received no official support from the United States. The insurrection of 1895 led to American intervention three years later, declaration of war upon Spain, and peace terms which included surrender by Spain of Cuba and Puerto Rico — all her remaining possessions in the Americas. During the earlier and unsuccessful rebellion Cuban trade with the United States was not large, and it actually increased slightly, the rebels being unable to seize a single port. Moreover, not enough American capital was lost to cause much outcry. During the later rebellion trade fell off sharply, being less in 1897, two years after the outbreak of hostilities, than for four preceding decades. American investments in Cuba, by 1895 swollen to a large figure, suffered severely, and pressure of interested citizens upon the United States government went hand in hand with propaganda calculated to incite American public opinion against Spain's colonial government.

With Spain eliminated, it seemed that Cuba would at last gravitate to the political orbit of the United States as it had already come to circle in its economic orbit. This consummation was thwarted by a self-denying resolution passed in the United States Senate on the eve of the war, and Cuba was constituted an independent nation, subject only to intervention to avert destruction of property. Pursuant to this provision, armed forces of the United States were landed in 1906, 1912, and 1917. In 1920 a single arbiter was substituted for detachments of marines, and more lately the American minister has served as the mouthpiece of American requirements. In 1934 the United States Congress surrendered its legal right to intervene in Cuban affairs. Cubans who had been galled by foreign supervision hailed the new political status as marking the beginning of independence. In reality, no political device can emancipate the island from the adjacent mainland, so long as Cuba depends for a living upon the sale of sugar to the United States and in turn buys therefrom much that it uses. Climatically reciprocal, the two regions inevitably share a common economic lot, and many an American law, perhaps enacted without reference to Cuba, is bound to affect the legally independent sister republic as vitally as though it were a colony of the United States.

Although Cuba remains politically independent, the United States does possess colonies in the West Indies. While the larger Spanish island, the cynosure of public opinion, was being guaranteed independence, the smaller, Puerto Rico, was quietly annexed. A generation of dominion has made this island as dependent upon the step-mother country for a livelihood as Cuba, but it has effected no correlative rapprochement between the clashing societies of the ruled and the ruler. Instead, it has engendered a vociferous party which demands independence, a political ideal as incompatible with geographic reality as is the legal fiction of independence already operative in Cuba.

Shortly after the absorption of Puerto Rico, the Danish government, which had long since ceased to have vital colonial interests, agreed for the second time to sell its Caribbean islands to the United States. More than a decade and a half elapsed before the purchase was consummated. This annexation was another evidence of the pull exerted by the mainland upon the islands. The expenditure was justified on the ground that it would prevent an uncomfortably proximate harbor of capital strategic value (St. Thomas) from falling into the hands of a strong European power. As in the cases of Cuba and Puerto Rico, the transfer failed to improve the economic position of the Danish islands, which had seen their most prosperous days more than a century before. Cotton had reached its peak in 1797, sugar in 1812, and even the World War increased output only slightly in these marginal producers. The population maximum was registered in 1835, double the figure of 1930. The shipping business, centered in the harbor of St. Thomas, throve during the days of sailing ships and declined only moderately from its peak in the 1830s to about 1875; since then it has fallen off more rapidly. When the floating drydock sank in 1924 it was not rebuilt. The substitution of oil for coal as fuel reduced the number of ships stopping, and electric cranes for coaling cost the long queues of Negro porters their jobs. The United States spends far more in the islands than Denmark ever did, and both countries have incurred annual deficits.

Before the extravagance of owning Caribbean islands became apparent the absorption of others seemed imminent. To protect property of its own investors and to avert intervention by European governments concerned for their nationals, the United States since 1916 has administered the customs of both the republics of Santo Domingo. Customs officials were backed by forces of marines which governed the two countries outright — the Dominican Republic to 1924 and Haiti until 1934. By constitutional revision both states have now regained *de facto* sovereignty, barring the collection of customs under a supervisor who must be a citizen of the United States. Foreign capital invested in the island must once more make the best of the local governments.

Relinquishment of the legal right to intervene in Cuba, withdrawal of marines from Santo Domingo, and efforts to satisfy the demands of denizens in Puerto Rico and the Virgin Islands indicate a reversal of the trend toward political domination of the Antilles. Yet the basic economic attraction persists. Neither the dissatisfied island possessions, the republics, nor the United States itself can unweave the web of economic bonds which unite them. On the contrary, the colonies of European nations are being increasingly affected by the tightening threads. The winter tourist business has grown to large proportions, not only in Havana, but also in Jamaica, Barbados,. and particularly the Bahamas, which have become an adjunct of the nearby Florida winter resort. For this purpose their attractiveness is heightened by their British nationality.

The more distant islands are of interest to the United States chiefly, perhaps solely, as potential naval bases which in time of war might jeopard the Panama Canal. Since the close of the World War there has been unofficial talk of transferring certain British and French Antilles to the United States in payment of war debts. The possibility is remote. United States capital is as well protected in British or French territory as in American; the tourist attraction is heightened by foreign connections, so long as no passport nuisance is imposed; and sentiment in the islands is strongly against transfer. Like the Danish Islands, most of the other Lesser Antilles have been floundering in chronic depression for a century or more, regardless of political affiliations, owing to changes in the larger world. Their fiscal status would be only slightly affected by annexation. The gossip, which persists in the face of objections, leagues with overt acts of the United States to demonstrate the permanent mutual attraction. Here is an illustration of the principle that islands which fringe a mainland power lie within its field of economic force and may fall subject to political domination as well.

The fluctuating status of the Antilles with reference to the United States has no parallel on the mainland north coast of the Gulf of Mexico. That region, being subtropical, was fantastically outside the experience of British immigrants to North America. Yet nearly a century before any Caribbean island fell to the United States, men of British stock wrested the mainland from its Spanish occupiers.

The funnel-like outlet of the vast Mississippi Basin was, in the days before railroads, the most critical spot between the Appalachian and the Rocky mountains. Either the power established astride the deltaic outlet to the navigable system of waterways must control the otherwise landlocked basin, or the power ensconced in the basin must break its way out to the Gulf. With the more productive half of the interior in the hands of the United States, by virtue of the treaty which closed the American Revolution, that country was faced with the alternative of obtaining control of the Mississippi mouth or abandoning its hold on its trans-Appalachian lands. Spanish monopoly of the Gulf of Mexico, impaired by the cession of Louisiana to friendly France, was ruptured when Louisiana was purchased by the United States (Ch. 16).

The seaboard, called Florida, between the original United States and Louisiana, fell under American sway a few years later. The appealing simplicity and the military value of an uninterrupted oceanic boundary drew the rising American nation irresistibly across this country, at the time almost useless — a sandy coastal plain, either swampy or pine-covered, extending well into a humid low-latitude climate. Long after Florida was purchased by the United States, occupance and development was slow, partly because of its infertile soil and sluggish drainage, and partly because its new owners of North European extraction had no experience of tropical climates. Despite this lag in settlement, the political grip on Florida was never relaxed, once the territory had been annexed.

## THE BORDER ZONE IN THE TEXAS COUNTRY

While the northern and eastern Gulf coasts were changing hands, Spanish Tejas was evolving haltingly along the western shore of that body of water (Fig. 72). Tejas was an outlying province of Mexico which had been settled from the sea in the early part of the 18th century, like the mouth of the Mississippi itself. The first settlements, missions planted 200 years after Cortes conquered the Mexican highland, lay in country that could only be considered an extension of Spanish Louisiana, because it possesses the same climate, landforms, soils, and natural vegetation. Beginning some four degrees of longitude west of the Mississippi, provincial Tejas was outlined on the south and west by stations on Corpus Christi Bay and inland as far as the present San Antonio. These posts lie on the southwest margin of that geographic realm which every American recognizes as " The South." A line connecting them and swinging northward in a crescent to the Red River,

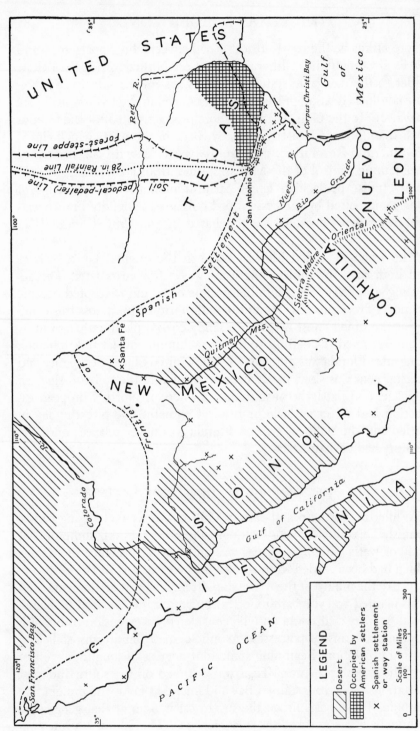

Fig. 72. The mainland boundary region between the Americas prior to delimitation.

closely corresponds to noteworthy transitions in the natural landscape: the annual rainfall line of 28 inches, approximately the contact between humidity and semiaridity in this latitude; the line separating lime-accumulating soils from lime-leaching soils; and the boundary between prairie grass and oak-hickory woodland to the east, and mesquite and desert grass to the west. This zone of interrelated environmental transition is one of the most critical demarcations in the North American continent. It is therefore illuminating to find that a line marking it was drawn by the earliest Spanish settlers of the country — a line which they considered the political boundary of their province. This they did, notwithstanding that it left an unsettled and a politically unorganized belt of terrain 250 miles wide between them and the nearest Mexican province, the northern limit of which corresponded with the plateau which is buttressed by the Sierra Madre Oriental. This wide belt of dry country was recognized as hunting ground of the nomadic Indians by sedentary residents in surrounding tracts organized by the Spanish as Coahuila, Nuevo Santander, New Mexico, and Tejas. As late as 1834 travellers reported it as used only seasonally by wandering tribesmen. All these bordering provinces had long been occupied before the first Spanish settlement was set down in the desert lowland between the Mexican Highland and Tejas-New Mexico. It was launched in the irrigable valley of the lowest Rio Grande. That small strip of delta is even today the only populous district in the whole vast borderland belt, the remainder being livestock ranching country of low carrying capacity and a barrier to intercourse.

In sharp contrast was the northeast boundary of Tejas. With all but the Tejas fragment of the Mississippi Basin joined to the United States, and no break in the character of the country between the two sections, this outlying bit of Spanish Mexico was more likely to receive increments of settlers from the northeast than from the southwest.

By the time Florida had been incorporated in the United States, cotton growing by slave labor had swept westward to the Tejas border, and the demand for more cotton land was echoing to the accelerating pace of the Industrial Revolution. Some land-hungry cotton planters entered fertile Tejas, but shortly thereafter Mexico declared its independence from Spain and wrote into its republican constitution a prohibition against slaveholding. This law, and political turbulence throughout Mexico during the years which followed the declaration of independence, checked the flow of immigration but did not stop it. Few slaves were entered as long as the Mexican government remained the sovereign of the country. The United States government made vigorous but vain efforts to purchase the territory. Texans of United States origin became increasingly restive after their State was consolidated with Coahuila, its ecumene far away beyond the desert, on an intermont plateau.

In 1835–36 these dissatisfied Texans revolted against the Mexican government and set up an independent republic in which slaveholding was declared legal. In both these acts they had the sympathy of many United States officials, and the new status of independence and slavery attracted an increasing immigration from the slaveholding States east of the political boundary. Figures prior to the United States Census of 1850 are unreliable, but estimates show a swiftly rising tide of settlement: 3000 in 1828, 6000 in 1831, 20,000 in 1833, and 100,000 in 1846. The official figure for 1850 is 212,592, of which 58,161 were Negro slaves. Practically all the increase was due to immigration from the United States. In 1821, when the first colony was established, the Spanish settlements in northeast Tejas had been destroyed and there remained only a meager handful of missionaries and traders along the marginal belt from Corpus Christi Bay to San Antonio. Between 1821 and 1836, 30,000 people are supposed to have entered from the United States, and Texan independence in the latter year accelerated the movement.

High tariffs on cotton moving into the United States reduced profits of Texas planters, however, and after 1839 the price of cotton was discouragingly low. Texans redoubled their efforts to join the United States, abetted by many Americans. These efforts met with rebuff from anti-slavery groups in the prospective foster-mother country. They succeeded for nine years in postponing the admission of a large slave State, despite well-grounded fears that Great Britain might convert disgruntled Texas into a cotton growing colony. The activity of British agents in Texas reversed the attitude and brought about a hasty admission as one of the United States, slavery and all.

The issue of the boundary between Texas and Mexico came to the fore with the declaration of Texan independence. Early Spanish Tejas had been bounded along the critical line of transition in climate-soils-vegetation, and the few settlements in the very dry country southwest of that line had been made from Mexico. Yet the political attachment of Tejas to Coahuila, and some still earlier official documents, lent color to the claim that Texan territory extended to the Rio Grande. In its lower course this stream roughly paralleled the margin of inhabited Texas, although at a distance of 150 miles and more. By all odds the longest and largest river of the whole border zone, its all-year flow makes it even more conspicuously the prime linear feature of the landscape. In new and sparsely settled regions, political boundaries tend to be drawn along notable linear items of the natural environment, and the Rio Grande was no exception to the rule. In its lower course, trending southeast, it flows in a narrow, deeply etched valley, devoid of irrigable floodplain except for inconsiderable and widely separated reaches, chief of which is the final hundred miles. Therefore no sedentary population of consequence had to be reckoned with in allocating the boundary. The Lower Rio Grande, from the point where the river enters a gorge to cross the Quitman Range, possessed several qualifications of a satisfactory boundary laid down antecedent to settlement. It passed through inhospitable, semidesert country, it provided little scope for irrigation, it was clearly marked on the natural landscape, and it could be conveniently crossed at only a few places.[1]

Independent Texas claimed not only the lower valley as boundary, but the middle course of the stream as well. In its south-flowing segment the river traverses a series of structural basins, in each of which it has deeply incised a flat-floored, irrigable floodplain (Fig. 73). The gorges between the basins range up to 20 miles in length, and in extreme cases force the overland valley route onto the upland. The arable floodplains and the road connecting them had long been the seat of population in the Spanish province (and succession Mexican State) of New Mexico.[2] From the southernmost of the floodplains the route continued to Mexico City via Chihuahua. At El Paso del Norte, the short narrows between this plain and its neighbor next upstream, easy routes at relatively low altitudes, to northeast, to southeast, and to west, cross the north-south river highway. There trails west from San Antonio and from northern Texas naturally crossed the Rio Grande. El Paso, by virtue of this focusing of routes, is one of the most strategic spots in the whole borderland, and was crucial in the boundary quarrel between independent Texas and Mexico.

When the annexationists won their cause and Texas became one of the United States, the larger sovereignty inherited the dispute over the Rio Grande boundary. Annexation was a signal to the Mexican government to sever diplomatic relations with the United States, but no attempt was made to recapture any territory north of the Nueces River

---

[1] It has not proved an easy line to defend in wartime. Sam Houston criticized it on this score at the time it was established.

[2] In established parlance, this part is known as the " Middle Rio Grande " despite the fact that about half the valley is thereby consigned to the " Lower Rio Grande " and only a tenth remains to the " upper " river.

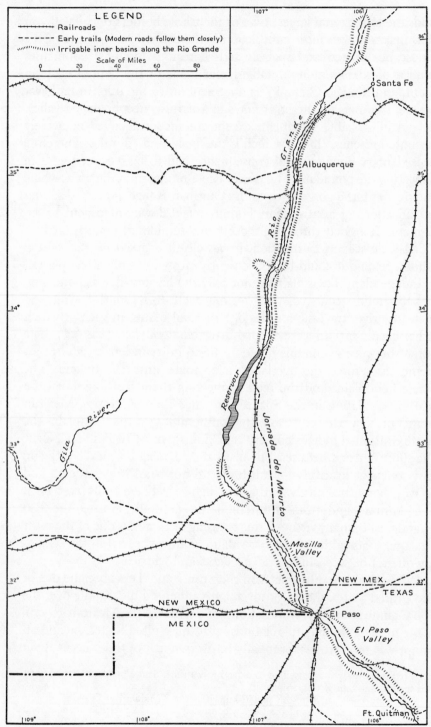

FIG. 73. The critical boundary in the region of El Paso.

(Fig. 72). This stream had become the symbol of the environmental demarcation between the well-endowed farming country indisputably Texan, and the ranching country of the border belt, which Mexico claimed. Only when American troops moved to the valley of the Rio Grande did they meet resistance from the Mexican army. The success of American arms in the struggle which followed confirmed not only the annexation of Texas, but also its right to the Lower Rio Grande as the boundary.

## NEW MEXICO AND CALIFORNIA

The Texan claim to the land westward to the Middle Rio Grande was considerably weaker than that to the lower river. If admitted, it would cut into two ribbons the irrigated floodplains, give to Texas two-thirds of the population of New Mexico, including the critical Jornada del Muerto, a two-day, dry-camp road connecting the two lower basins with the five upper ones, and even the traditional capital of the State of New Mexico (Fig. 73).

Before hostilities broke out between the United States and Mexico over the Texas boundary, an offer had been made to purchase New Mexico, on the ground that it was a remote province, isolated from other settled portions of Mexico by the Chihuahuan desert, and difficult to defend properly against the Indians of the uplands adjacent to the Spanish settlements in the middle course of the Rio Grande. These Indians were warlike nomads, and it was averred that unless held in leash they might cause trouble in neighboring territory of the United States. Behind the proffer to purchase lay claims against Mexico by American citizens who had lost property in the course of twenty years of revolutions. These claims the Mexican government could not hope to reimburse in cash, and American authorities hoped for a territorial bargain from which they might pay the private claims.

The American offer to purchase territory extended likewise to California. Cut off from the core of Mexico by the Sonoran desert (Fig. 72), California was in similar case to Texas. It was occupied sparsely by missions and by livestock ranches, but was clearly a country of more promise than most of Mexico north of its central plateau. Its possibilities must have been better understood by Mexicans than by Americans, since it is the natural counterpart of eastern and southern Spain and in no way like eastern North America or North Europe. Whether its potential value was appreciated or not, it faced the ocean. It was therefore vulnerable to sea power, and Great Britain was suspected of having designs upon it. To complete the parallel to Texas, Americans had begun to filter into the country around and behind San Francisco Bay.

When Mexico rejected the opportunity to settle claims of United States citizens for money, an American force was dispatched overland to Southern California by way of Santa Fé, the capital of New Mexico. At the same time an American naval force headed into San Francisco Bay. Before either arrived, Americans resident about the Bay had proclaimed independence from Mexico under a flag on which a bear was depicted, thus paralleling the history of Texas with its " lone star " flag. When American authorities soon afterwards took possession of the California ports, the " stars and stripes " was substituted for the " bear."

These military operations in the tier of Mexican States adjacent to the United States were followed by the occupation of several capitals of the range of States next south. Then a United States army, advancing from Vera Cruz over the Jalapa route (Cortes's march followed this way more than three centuries earlier, Ch. 13), forced Mexico City to capitulate.

The offer to purchase the northern belt of Mexican territory was then renewed and the boundary was ultimately drawn through the deserts of Chihuahua and Sonora. It assured to Texas the line of the Lower Rio Grande, and it severed Upper and Lower California at the delta of the Colorado. The intervening (New Mexican) boundary was drawn along the Gila River (Fig. 73).

Peace had scarcely been declared before the boundary between the Rio Grande and the Colorado was called into question. The easy east-west route across southern New Mexico takes advantage of the low saddle at El Paso, runs up the valley for some distance, and crosses a low divide to the Gila, which it follows along the south bank to its confluence with the Colorado. By the terms of the peace treaty, this route remained in Mexican territory. For Mexico it was a small district beyond the desert and useless except as the habitation of a few irrigation farmers. For the United States it provided the route of minimum gradients between the east and newly acquired California. Its value was multiplied by a project to construct a railroad across the continent, a scheme called into being by the annexation of territory cut off from the older United States by deserts and mountains. It was argued that for such a line the notable gap at El Paso and the gentle gradient of the Gila Valley were exigent, on the ground that low altitudes coupled with southerly location insured freedom from snow as compared to any crossing of the mountains within the United States. Finally, the then dominant Southern leaders intended to push the transcontinental line westward from some Southern city, presumably New Orleans. At the same time a treaty clause permitting the United States to charter a railroad on Mexican soil was scouted as undesirable. Closer study of the terrain showed that the Gila route, suitable enough for a trail, would prove awkward for a railroad, even if the line were built mainly in Mexico to take advantage of minimum gradients. The most feasible rail route lay somewhat south of the Gila Valley, on the broad interstream upland.

The issue was brought to a head by the American governor of New Mexico, who threatened to take military possession of the Mexican side of the Rio Grande Valley north of El Paso on the ground that the Chihuahuan government did not protect it against Indians. The clash over this bit of territory played into the hands of the railroad promoters, who planned to use it for their route (although it turned out that no line has ever been built there). It also represented a larger problem which affected the whole border country from the Gulf of Mexico to the Pacific, but which was most acute in the central segment. This was the practice of bands of Indians to raid sedentary settlements.

In the view of the nomadic Amerinds, whose homelands were either the northern Sierra Madre (both Oriental and Occidental) or the plateaus of the Colorado Basin, raids upon settlements were ethical and normal activities. All the chief cities of the northern States of the Mexican Plateau were victimized at one time or another, as far south as San Luis Potosí. The most frequent incursions took toll of settlements in the desert and semidesert between the Mexican Plateau and the outlying settled cores of California, New Mexico, and Tejas. This was traditionally hunting country of the nomadic tribes, who were incensed as they found their preserves disturbed by whites. The newcomers generally seized spots of arable, lowland soil for irrigation agriculture and, thus isolated, made easy prey for the Indians.

The treaty line which closed the Mexican War ran the boundary through the heart of this Indian hunting ground and cut much of it off from some of the most vigorous tribes, notably Apaches and Comanches, whose usual haunts were on the semiarid Colorado Plateau. They were leagued with Navajos and other nomads whose domiciles were farther north, but who disposed of plunder obtained in Mexican territory. By terms of the treaty the United States took upon itself the task of keeping its new Indian wards on their own side of the political boundary. This reversal of an age-long adaptation to natural conditions

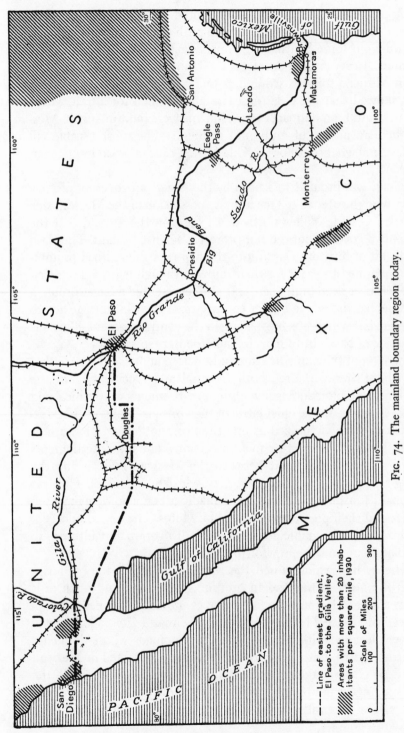

FIG. 74. The mainland boundary region today.

The shaded area next west of the Colorado River is the Imperial Valley irrigated district.

Line of easiest gradient, El Paso to the Gila Valley

Areas with more than 20 inhabitants per square mile, 1930

Scale of Miles

0    100    200    300

492

proved impossible, and the difficult problem of controlling the Indians was rendered insoluble when the Mexican government, still smarting from wartime invasion, refused to permit the United States cavalry to pursue raiders across the border and likewise disarmed sedentary settlers in all the border Mexican States. In a vain effort to fulfill its treaty obligation the United States posted a large fraction of its army along the frontier. In spite of this precaution, the number of claims by injured citizens of both countries against the United States government rapidly mounted. Proponents of a railroad paralleling the border argued that without it no pacification of the Indian troubles would be possible. Five years after the close of hostilities, a new treaty was drafted whereby the United States purchased a strip of territory south of the Gila extending to a maximum of about 100 miles (Fig. 74). The new boundary traverses desert for about three-fifths of its length, with a strip of slightly less arid country (the traditional Indian trekway) associated with higher altitudes between longitudes 109° and 111°. In this belt have been built the only north-south railroads traversing the political boundary west of El Paso. Although it did not move the boundary far enough south to reunite the whole desert hunting country, it provided suitable ground for the transcontinental railroad, on the upland. As events turned out, railroad construction was delayed, and the first transcontinental line was built west from Omaha, after the Civil War had shifted the political center of gravity from the South to the North. When finally built, the El Paso route was the railroad of lowest altitudes among all the transcontinental lines in North America, a distinction which it retains to this day.

THE BOUNDARY AS A GEOPOLITICAL FORCE

As revised, the boundary is probably as satisfactory as any which could have been drawn between the power dominant in humid eastern North America and the power dominant on the Mexican highland. It lies more or less midway between the cores of Anglo-American and Ibero-American settlement; it traverses the country of least resources (and therefore of least population) to be found in the zone of contact.

All the border belt is climatically either desert or semiarid. Except for irrigated strips and patches, the desert shrub and the steppe grass support nothing more intensive than ranching, with its attendant sparse population. Sedentary settlements based on irrigation have grown up astride the border, on the deltas of the Colorado and Rio Grande and in the southernmost floodplain of the Middle Rio Grande.

Valuable minerals have given rise to mining camps, chiefly in the mountain section. There mining operations entail sites on both sides of the boundary.

Routes paralleling and crossing the line have been built to exploit the resources. Their pattern faithfully traces the most accessible ways to the highly localized spots favored by nature. The principal international railroad connects San Antonio, on the southern margin of humid North America, with Monterrey, principal oasis at the northeastern foot of the Mexican Highland. It traverses steppe and crosses the Rio Grande at one of the rare floodplains of the lower course of the stream. The alternative rails cross on the edge of the desert at the irrigable floodplain next upstream. Much farther west a minor line traverses the Chihuahuan Desert by a route used by the Indians (including the river crossing at Presidio).

In the mountain region, all the newer railroads have been constructed primarily to haul ores from Mexican mines to smelters in the United States, located at El Paso and Douglas to take advantage of the superior political security afforded fixed capital by the United States. The railroad which closely parallels the border between these towns is likewise a mineral road. The lines focusing on El Paso traverse the Chihuahuan desert and were built only after the sinking of deep wells to supply the locomotives and crews with water. The routes farther west stay within the belt of steppe between the Chihuahuan and Sonoran deserts. One of them has been extended to the Mexican Highland and has become the second ranking international line.

In two places a railroad connecting the Lower Colorado Valley with San Diego swings into Mexican territory; in one case to serve the irrigated land of the Colorado Delta; in the other case to avoid rugged terrain. The lines which cross the Rio Grande Delta at Brownsville and run up both sides of the valley are likewise for service to irrigation farmers. All these desert and steppe railroads follow routes which were predetermined by the distribution of water supplies, sometimes on the surface, more usually deep underground.

Highways conform to much the same pattern as railways, but because they are cheaper to build and less bound to conditions of terrain, they can be more numerous. The first through motor road between the Mexican Plateau and the United States has only recently been completed, and it parallels the pioneer international railroad.

Thanks to increasingly efficient transportation, a nomadic habitat has been transformed into a sedentary one. In a real sense the location of the political boundary in this arid zone between the thickly settled cores of the two countries has been justified by substitution of a sedentary for a nomadic mode of life. This happy outcome was the result of accident, because there is no evidence that either of the boundary treaties was negotiated in the expectation of a fundamental alteration in the mode of human existence. On the contrary, it has been asserted that the present Mexican-United States boundary represents merely a compromise between the forces favoring annexation of all of Mexico and the forces urging no territorial aggrandizement. The seizure of approximately half the Mexican territory lends color to this view, but it must be remembered that the half annexed was very lightly settled by Mexicans at the time.

The slowly expanding web of communication lines is an index of increasing intercourse across the boundary and consequently increased opportunities for friction. In the decades since its establishment, the border zone has experienced occasional tenseness, but the causes of friction have changed, and some of them have lain outside the border belt.

### BOUNDARY TROUBLES

The revised treaty absolved the United States government from responsibility for Indian depredations south of the political boundary. Nevertheless, raids continued for many years, both from New Mexico into old Mexico, and from the Sierra Madre Oriental into Texas. It required a generation of fighting to quench the border forays, but they came to be considered local affairs, until finally railroads brought in sufficient settlers to convert the Indian hunting ground into livestock ranching country, spotted with irrigated bits of valley and with mining camps. The Indians were then rendered innocuous by being relegated to reservations.

Lawlessness on the border was not confined to nomadic Indians. Cattle ranching was long a risky business because rustlers found it easy to drive the animals they stole across the boundary to immunity. For a few years certain Mexicans made a practice of guiding runaway Texan slaves to free Mexican soil. The long distance and the inhospitable country must have restricted the number liberated, and in any case this annoyance ceased with emancipation.

A more prolonged source of trouble has been smuggling. The Mexican tariffs on most goods are high, thus making it profitable to smuggle from the United States across the long, unpopulated, and undefended border. In the early days this illicit business was centered in Texas, and the border men frequently took the law into their own hands. Improved policing has reduced this annoyance. Smuggling from Mexico has been confined mainly to the persons of Asiatics, who are excluded from legal entry into the United States.

Temporary border difficulties have arisen because of internal strife in one nation or the other. During the Civil War the blockade of southern ports caused a violent boom in the exporting of cotton from ports at the mouth of the Rio Grande. Not only were neutral Mexican ports unaffected by the blockade, but by treaty the Rio Grande had to be left open to commerce. This cause of friction between the two countries terminated with the cessation of hostilities within the United States. The mushroom growth of the port towns at the mouth of the river was followed by rapid decay when the war was over. Half a century later the outbreak of the Mexican Revolution was followed by repeated escape and pursuit across the boundary on the part of warring factions. The United States government thereupon stationed troops at all the strategic points along the border. In obeying their orders to prevent incursions, the border forces engaged in numerous skirmishes.

All these evidences that the border is not ideal have been minor causes of friction compared to that generated by conflicts over water. Of the total boundary, 68 percent is formed by rivers, all but 20 miles of this being the Rio Grande.

The Lower Colorado is rated as navigable, including the 20 miles of international boundary. Advocates of a port for the United States on the Gulf of California have recurrently pressed their demand. For a generation after the cession of California and New Mexico the claim was supported by periodic visits of a ship carrying provisions to an American fort near the mouth of the Gila River. With the coming of the transcontinental railroad, the Colorado ceased to be navigated even in this minor degree. Since then the repeated demand for a port on salt water has had no practical foundation.

Of the Rio Grande only the last few miles (to Brownsville and Matamoras) have ever been used for shipping. The entrance to the main channel is obstructed by shoal water, and the Brassos Santiago Lagoon is the normal outlet. It took the high prices due to war and blockade to bring the stream into use, and well before the first railroad entered the lower valley craft had ceased to ply the river.

The critical use of water in both the Colorado and the Rio Grande is for irrigation. The Colorado reaches the sea through a delta which it has built across the narrow Gulf of California near its head.

Prior to the Mexican War no boundary across the delta between mainland and peninsular California had been suggested. When the line was drawn (from the mouth of the Gila to a point south of San Diego), it cut across the grain of the country, and traversed the delta of the Colorado River somewhat north of its crest. For many years this was savage country, devoid of human occupance except for a few Indians, and its discordance with easy routes and with irrigation canals appeared too late to raise serious question of alteration. The north slope of the delta comprises a large share of the only region of low-latitude desert climate within the United States. During the 20th century it has been converted into a gigantic market garden, purveying to the whole nation. Mexico, over-endowed with this type of climate, uses only a part of its portion of the delta and makes cotton the leading crop. Water for both countries is diverted from the Colorado within the United States, but the principal canal, adhering to the contour of the delta, crosses the international boundary twice. To ransom this hostage to a foreign government, the United States has recently completed a costly canal wholly within its own territory, in part through sand dunes and in part in an elevated aqueduct. This undesirable and costly work, requiring undue maintenance charges, is another case of a political boundary superimposed athwart the most efficient utilization of the land. It reappears in the pattern of overland transportation. In order to build a railroad between the Lower Colorado River and the nearest Pacific Coast port (San Diego) the only route which could be justified on economic grounds requires two deviations into Mexican territory. The easternmost avoids as much sanddune as possible by following the contour of the north flank of the delta. The western loop crosses into Mexico in order to obtain the easiest gradient.

As a cultural feature the boundary on the Colorado Delta is easy to trace (as it is also in the Lower Rio Grande Valley). The style of architecture, the intensity of cultivation, and the character of the crops all disclose the political division line to the casual observer.

Possession by Mexico of the final few miles of the course of the Colorado gives that country a lien on some of the water of the stream. With the impounding of water upstream the question as to Mexico's share is brought to the fore, and decision is complicated by the far more troublesome apportionment of the water of the Rio Grande.

The simplicity of the Rio Grande as a boundary line ceased when railroads brought the arable floodplains and delta into economic reciprocity with the ecumene of the two possessor nations. Thereafter irrigation farmers made increasing inroads upon the meager supply of water, which now is known to be inadequate to cover the irrigable floodplain and delta land of the river and its principal tributaries.

The irrigable string of basins in the Middle Rio Grande is supplied with water from sources wholly within the United States (Fig. 73). The basin farthest downstream, which lies between El Paso and the Quitman Mountains, is divided between the two governments, the larger part of the floodplain lying on the Mexican side. To protect the farmers there, a treaty guarantees delivery of a fixed amount of water from impoundings in the United States.

In the whole 1300 miles of river which forms the international boundary, there are few spots of irrigable floodplain and terrace between the basin immediately below El Paso and the delta, which begins 100 miles above the mouth of the river and widens to approximately 80 miles at the coast (Fig. 74). The canyons and negligible floodplains of the " Big Bend " lie squarely in the Chihuahuan Desert and receive no tributary waters. Because all the dependable water of the upper course of the stream and its chief northbank tributary is diverted into irrigation ditches, the channel between Fort Quitman and Eagle Pass is dry except in times of flood.

The floodplains near Eagle Pass and Laredo, and the much larger delta, are irrigated primarily by streams which rise in the Sierra Madre Oriental of Mexico, and additional water supplies must be derived from these sources. The arable lands, particularly the delta, lie in low enough latitudes to be used for winter vegetables and delicate fruits. As on the delta of the Colorado, the two sides of the valley present sharply contrasted landscapes: north of the river intensive fruit and vegetable growing for sale to the northern city markets; south of the river cotton growing, for the mills of the Mexican Plateau, but not very intensive. This strip of valley will develop in accordance with future allocation of water, since there is not enough for intensive development of all the arable acres. Irrigation has progressed much faster on the United States side of the river than on the Mexican side, although works on the Salado River, one of the principal Mexican tributaries of the Rio Grande, are tapping sources of water which formerly fed the masterstream. Unrestricted expansion of diversion in the tributaries would destroy the American gardens and orchards nourished by Mexican water. The relations of water supply and irrigable lands to the boundary makes the entire Colorado and Rio Grande systems subject to international bargaining, and potentially a source of dangerous political friction. The risk is heightened by the fact that the United States is deficient in the vegetables that the irrigable lands can be made to yield, whereas Mexico has a plethora of such lands.

Whenever an international issue becomes acute, dormant legal entanglements are likely to be cited. Diversion of water for irrigation has been the logical and progressive means of utilizing the river resource. Inevitably it has affected navigation adversely by diminishing the volume of water and intensifying sedimentation in the channel. This has occasioned no economic damage, because river trade never amounted to much, and for years before the beginning of the present century, when the deltas were tapped by railroads, there had been no navigation on the streams. Ships never ascended more than some 25 or 30 miles from the mouth. Unfortunately, the potentiality of navigation has impeded the progress of irrigation, because by treaty (dated 1848), "navigation . . . shall be free and common to vessels and citizens of both countries; and neither shall, without the consent of the other, construct any work that may impede or interrupt, in whole or in part, the exercise of this right. . . ." Here is a neat exemplification of the tyrannical hold of international agreement in checking a desirable evolution in the utilization of natural resources.

To make matters worse, the Rio Grande has proved a freakish boundary line. The international frontier is defined as the " middle of the river, following the deepest channel." Like all streams, and particularly those which traverse steppe and desert, it suddenly rises from a trickle to a torrent, only to subside as quickly. In this process the channel frequently shifts. On the floodplains and the delta particularly, the stream, flowing at grade, is continually cutting off meanders and thus transferring land from one side of the " deepest channel " to the other. This is annoying enough as a physical inconvenience; when a shift in the course of the river also transfers land to a foreign country, the situation becomes intolerable. With augmenting investment of capital in irrigation works and farms adjusted to the widely different markets of the two countries, the incidence of these shifts had to be minimized. In 1894–95 treaties created a permanent commission to deal with the impermanent boundary. Its first task was to eliminate transfers of sovereignty when the stream changed its course (generally by abandoning meanders). It has adopted the postulate that gradual planing away of a bank involves a parallel sideward shift of the channel boundary, but that quick and marked changes, such as the cutting off of meanders, leave the boundary in the deepest part of the forsaken channel. Each case is adjudged on its merits, and of nearly 200 complaints against the willful river about 170 have been settled, most of them in the delta, where few cut-off oxbows remain to be adjudicated. As cases are determined, markers are substituted for the deserted channel. Damage caused by the river's plowing a furrow through a farm and the inconvenience of having farmland on both sides of the stream are beyond the powers of the commission to remedy. The use of increasing quantities of water for irrigation and the construction of dikes tend to stabilize the channel.

Most cases have concerned farmland only, because townsites are typically on high ground or well back from the river. The one exception concerns a part of El Paso and has proved the most awkward case of all, because people, as well as land, are involved.

The work of the commission is turning increasingly to flood control, as is shown by the execution of a treaty in 1933 authorizing it to deal with this problem in the El Paso section. Two fundamental questions which remain to be solved are interrelated. The fiction that the Rio Grande and the Colorado are navigable streams interferes with free use of their waters for irrigation and should be abandoned. The question of how much of the water originating on one side of the boundary may be used by residents on the other must be settled.

Conversion of raw floodplains and deltas into farms, and development of mines and smelters on or near the border, have brought to the fore new boundary problems arising from movements of populations. Not nearly so many Mexicans lived in the territories annexed in 1848 as inhabit the United States side of the border today. Increasing Mexicanization has become a crucial problem. Mexicans perform the heavy labor in city and country, especially during peak seasons, as far north as the Los Angeles Basin in California, everywhere in the former New Mexico, and to the ancient line between arid and humid Texas. It is a striking fact that Mexicans are preferred to Negroes by the cotton growers of south Texas, and several counties along the Rio Grande are essentially Mexican in their social structure, except for a small group of United States ancestry which shares ownership with long-settled Mexican families.

## STATUS OF THE BOUNDARY BETWEEN THE AMERICAS

Along the southern margin of the United States a boundary line of diversified character exemplifies the flux of political issues which surges along any such linear cleavage of nature's unit areas and zones of transition.

Even where a clear-cut break is made by the Gulf of Mexico, increasingly intimate bonds have brought the nearby islands closer and closer to the mainland power. The riveting of these bonds has been accompanied by a rising tide of protest in the islands against economic discomfort, all of which is laid at the door of the political connections.

Along the land boundary, far less signally indicated by nature, technological improvements and the utilization of unforeseen resources have narrowed the zone of barrier waste land. Railroads and motor roads have brought the cores of the two countries closer together and have unlocked mineral and agricultural opportunities adjacent to the boundary line. In order to utilize these resources, population along the line has increased from a few hundred to more than half a million, with resultant manifolding of points of friction. The riverine portion of the boundary, which was the most easily agreed upon, has created thorny problems that are being settled peaceably only because the two governments have created a unique body — a permanent commission empowered to adjudicate differences. The part of the boundary which consists of arbitrary surveyed lines has given the least trouble. Most of it has the merit of lying well away from resources which have generated dense populations, and along it there is no joint possession of high value, as is the case of irrigation water in the rivers. That no greater friction has been generated may be attributed to the establishment of both the fluvial and the overland lines antecedent to settlement. As people moved into the boundary zone they accommodated themselves without strain to the existing political line. In the process the boundary itself has become a cogent feature of the landscape.

At no point does an authentic and significant contrast in natural environment coincide with the political line. Yet few transitions in cultural landscape are so sharp as along the more closely settled reaches of the boundary. No one could have the least difficulty in locating and tracing the line wherever buildings, farms, or roads exist. Only in the aspect of mining camps, owned and operated by Americans, is the contrast lacking. The distinctive appearance of a Mexican hamlet or town, with its Amerind and Spanish antecedents, is not to be confounded with the wholly different United States village or city, bespeaking a North European background even where the architecture patterns consciously after the " mission style."

The permanency of this boundary has been questioned. It is already of respectable antiquity, as international boundaries go. Paradoxically, the fire-eating temper which clamored for all of Mexico at the end of the war more than 90 years ago, has waned with the increase in points and planes of contact between the two peoples. In the Western Hemisphere the past century has seen progress in the peaceable solution of boundary problems. Because problems arising between Mexico and the United States have thus far been settled without altering the established line, it appears unlikely that the boundary will be shifted in any predictable future.

In review, it seems clear that the boundary between Latin America and English-speaking America is as satisfactory in its general location as any which could be drawn. In detail it presents awkward spots and strips, and dispassionate study might suggest relocation here and there. No boundary line can hope to sever completely the groups of people which inhabit its opposite sides, and problems must occasionally arise as the changing modes of human occupance bring to the surface latent resources, the use of which must be allocated.

The present boundary problems are merely the issues of today. They did not appear above the horizon of 1850 or 1900, and they may disappear below that of some succeeding generation. Today they stand out as being these: (1) The problem of investing United States capital in plantations on the Caribbean islands, and in ranches and mineral resources in Mexico. (2) The problem of allocating the water of the Rio Grande and the Colorado systems to irrigable lands on the two sides of the boundary. (3) The problem of infiltration of Mexicans into the country north of the boundary, and their assimilation into the life of the United States.

## CHAPTER SIXTEEN

# The Geopolitical Structure of North America

IN contrast to Latin America, English-speaking North America [1] has gone far toward political consolidation. Only the Australian continent is more completely unified, and it is smaller in area and in population than either of the two larger political units of North America. Excluding large but insignificant Greenland and two tiny islands near Newfoundland, two sovereignties split the whole area into somewhat unequal halves (United States and Alaska about 3,500,000 square miles; Canada and Newfoundland about 4,000,000).

This political distinction should not obscure the fact that the two share a single ecumene originally peopled by uniform British stock and traditions. Even the exceptional French Canada (the Lower St. Lawrence Valley), was settled mainly by Normans and Bretons, close kinsmen of the English and Welsh on the opposite shore of the Channel. In analyzing the geopolitical structure which has arisen in North America, Canada and the United States can be treated as two parts of a whole. The rest of the continent may be disregarded. Alaska is an adjunct to the United States, its present resources being restricted to extractive products. Newfoundland was included in the plans for the Dominion of Canada, and its pinched environment and small population may be considered as an extreme phase of typical Canadian conditions.

As in Iberian America, the nations of North America have been erected by people of Western European origin in the novel natural environment of the New World. In both continents of the Western Hemisphere colonies were planted and in the course of time sloughed off their colonial status. Over a period varying from a century and a half (in the case of the United States) to seventy years (Dominion of

[1] Including French Canada. In order to steer between cumbersome and inaccurate designation, the part of the Western Hemisphere lying north of the Mexico-United States boundary is referred to as " North America." The justification for this course in a discussion of the political geography of the Americas is stated in Chapter 15.

Canada) America has independently practised the European system of government in novel settings. The results of Iberian colonization in a region of diverse natural environment, much of it handicapped by low latitude (Chs. 13 and 14), afford instructive contrast with the outcome of British colonization in a continent no less diverse but handicapped chiefly by high latitude.

## PROSPECTS FOR COLONIZATION

North America was colonized late. For sailing vessels from Europe its one accessible coast lies off-side the path of the trade winds (Fig. 59), and its humid, and alternately hot and cold climate was inhospitable to the Mediterranean peoples who took the lead in American colonization. These disadvantages were not offset by compensations. It lacked sedentary societies which could be bent to the conquering Europeans' demands. Its indigenous denizens knew of no deposits of precious metal which by minting could be transmuted into European money. Its none too fertile coastlands held no promise of becoming producers of spices, pepper, and sugar — vegetable commodities which a rapidly rising demand in Europe might make profitable in competition with remote South Asia.

When at last the rising seapower of the nations of Northwest Europe enabled them to enter the colonial field in earnest, they found that North America was the nearest and the least unpromising land not already preempted by strong states.

The vast and as yet unexplored interior possessed one extractable resource — furs. To this interior two water-gates give access (Fig. 75). The Mississippi Delta, far to the southwest, lies in a hot and humid climate uncongenial to North Europeans. It can be approached only through the straits which flank Cuba, where Havana, the capital of the "Spanish Main," long stood guard against threats to Spanish monopoly. The St. Lawrence estuary is rather more approachable. Lying near the natural landfall for ships on the Great Circle route (Fig. 59), it leads to a river navigable far inland, although ice-blocked more than half the year and marking the northernmost land on the eastern coast capable of sustaining a dense population.

Between these gates (Fig. 75) stretch more than 3000 miles of sea frontage, punctuated with short streams which lead a few score miles inland to a barrier of mountains. At one point, where streams of a bygone geologic period carried water from the continental ice sheet to the Hudson Valley, the barrier is breached — by the Hudson Valley

FIG. 75. Water-gates to interior North America, and the zones of early settlement.

The boundary between Spanish Florida and French Louisiana was not delimited, nor were those between the English coastland and Spanish Florida and French Canada. The Appalachians constituted the undefined barrier between the English coast and the French interior.

and its connections the Mohawk and Champlain troughs. Neither of these troughs carries a stream throughout its length.

The coastland appeared to 17th-century eyes to possess but two possible values — trade in furs and land for farms. North of Chesapeake Bay the best that could be expected of the climate was subsistence agriculture akin to that of Northwest Europe itself, but carried on under handicaps of cold and snowy winters and depredations by barbarous Amerinds. Along the southern seaboard, at least as far as sandy Florida and its jealous Spanish warders, optimists hoped to establish plantations of subtropical crops. To this end " companies of adventurers," most of which were compelled to be adventurous indeed, were sent out from France, England, Holland, and even Sweden, to trade and plant.

For both interior and coast the outlook was poor as compared to Iberian America, where gold and silver, tropical crops, and Indians who could be made to labor for the invaders all combined to induce early exploitation. Only remote and insignificant Chile and the long-retarded Plata region and southern Brazil appeared to be so ill-favored as the whole vast continent north of the Mexican highland. Nevertheless, this area, larger than all Europe including Russia, incorporated a region more extensive than Western and Central Europe combined, that finally proved well-suited to settlement by European stock.

This potential ecumene is bounded on the north by long, severe winters. East of Lake Winnipeg, this heavily handicapped region is carried southward of the climatic barrier by ice-scoured, sterile, crystalline bedrock — bare or mantled with thin soil — and capable of bearing nothing more productive than scattered forest. On the southwest the ecumene is bounded by desert and steppe. Westward beyond both the cold lands and the dry lands, mountains further cut off the huge, Atlantic-facing ecumene from small Pacific basins. The Pacific slope is the only part of the continent in which the climates and associated vegetation are true counterparts of those of maritime Europe. The northern interior and the Atlantic slope are more akin in climate to Central and Eastern Europe, although their vegetation and landforms cannot have been very strange to newcomers from Britain or France. In the south half of the humid east, long summers and high temperatures create climate, soils, and natural vegetation unfamiliar to Europeans and known, among advanced civilizations, only in China and India.

Into the mold of this continent European pioneers and their American descendants poured successive generations of their plastic life.

Each stage of colonization occupied a segment of the continent delimited by barriers which temporarily arrested expansion. The mode of occupance in each of these areas tended to become set in a form which represented the optimum utilization of the natural environment compatible with the tools and the training of the settlers. Some regions could be utilized at once; others have had to await inventions before realizing their opportunities. For instance, cotton was unprofitable in the " Cotton Belt " until the gin for extracting the seeds was devised; rich black soils of the subhumid west had to await railroads and harvesting machinery before they could be turned into wheatlands.

The social structure of the land of origin has made its impress upon the new continent, no less than have the material instruments of society. The feudal seignory of the Lower St. Lawrence expresses itself in the close-set " stringtowns," each dominated by its one huge church. The large estates sown sparsely over the plantation South depict the life of English " county families " transferred to the new continent, and the plantation house with its slave quarters is essentially like the English manor house with its village of farm laborers.

The political experience and temper of the newcomers likewise played its part in each stage of settlement. English, French, and Spanish colonies differed in the use they made of the land, because the land systems they imported, the degree of local government to which they were used, and their forms of government were unlike. Generally speaking, the Spanish and the French colonies were planned in some detail in Europe, and the home government kept them under watchful and restrictive care. The English colonies were subjected to varying degrees of control, depending on the value of the colony in the eyes of the mother country and on the degree of autocracy being practised in England. On the whole, they enjoyed a large measure of home rule, and some of them were politically autonomous for long periods. Thus they could profit from economic union with Great Britain without suffering from administrative mistakes growing out of European incomprehension of conditions of life in America. The range and diversity of political forms is illustrated by comparing a southern colony with a northern one. Rural Virginia found it easy to set up county government. Its governor, assigned by higher authority, and its House of Burgesses, representative of the propertied classes, reproduced on the new soil the legal form of the English King in Parliament. This system had grown up in rural manorial England, where the king enjoyed his station by right of inheritance, while the Parliament was elected by a restricted franchise. In antithesis to Virginia, Connecticut was quasi-urban from the first, with its area subdivided into "towns," its people living in farm villages or in market towns or port cities, and its government carried on by the talkative town-meeting, a pure democracy.

The natural environment furnished the ground on which fell the varied seed of governmental forms, political attitudes and technical proficiency. In most parts of North America the European folkways were but little affected by American precursors. Apart from game and wild fruits pioneers from Europe found no important food in their new habitats but maize, although they learned novel uses of beans and squashes. Even the American potato and turkey were Middle American in origin, and reached North America as reimports via Spain from England and France. The Amerinds themselves could not be incorporated into a Europeanized society. Except to gather furs they refused to work for the white men. On the contrary, they periodically destroyed European farm settlements, because the sedentary husbandry of the pioneers seized upon the Indians' crop lands and destroyed the game on which they mainly relied for a living. In the earliest years the immigrants came to the viewpoint that " the only good Indian is a dead Indian." This maxim they relentlessly enforced, and with superior weapons. As a result few Amerind populations of any considerable size remain, and these are confined to the sedentary oases of the Southwest, the forests of the North, and a few reservations in the steppe country. None of these regions lies within the North American ecumene. The indigenes merely survived in natural refuge areas until their relinquishment of war and a growing humanity in the white community ended their persecution.

The swift elimination of the indigenes from all the lands best suited to Europeans made North America a *tabula rasa* of natural resources on which the European impress could be stamped with little modification other than that produced by the natural environment itself.

While in the large the North American continent differs from that of Western Europe, in detail every group of immigrants from across the Atlantic has been able somewhere to find a familiar scene. This was easy in the few regions which in climate, soil, and vegetation parallel Western Europe. Spaniards and Italians have in turn made themselves at home in California with its " Mediterranean " climate; parts of the Puget Trough are as English as old England. In other areas nature has compelled some adjustments to novel conditions. Men from the limestone lowland of Normandy early adapted themselves to the limestone valley of the Lower St. Lawrence, in spite of its cold and snowy winters; Portuguese fishermen are numerous in the mild southeastern corner of New England; Scandinavians have become major groups in heavily glaciated regions where lake-dotted moraine and ice-scour dominate the landscape; Dutch settlements cling faithfully to boggy lands requiring drainage; Prussians can find sandy glacial outwash; and central Europeans any degree of humidity and rugged terrain to which their homelands have accustomed them; even Basques find their place in transhumant grazing lands of the West, and Jews in congested cities. In spite of this natural tendency of peoples to seek familiar landscapes, most emigrants to North America have adapted themselves to environments different from their homelands. The degree to which they have impressed their ways upon the new land and the degree to which the new land has gently or peremptorily changed their habits have not been sufficiently studied to permit conclusions to be drawn. Undoubtedly both action and reaction have been continuous.

The initial settlements were not guided by the wish to recreate the homeland in the New World. Rather they were economic ventures calculated to make maximum profits from unexploited resources. Both France and England began their attempts to plant colonies at various points along the coast toward the end of the 16th century and succeeded in attaching permanent settlements to the new soil in the first decade of the 17th. The objectives of the settlers were the mixed motives of every time and clime: quest for riches, religious ardor, hope of improving a miserable existence, and love of adventure. Both governments granted concessions to private individuals and to companies, leaving the risk to the concessionaires.

## FRENCH COLONIZATION

From the first, the French grants concerned the fur trade, and the French settlements in the St. Lawrence gateway to the interior source of furs outstripped their contemporaries, also French, on the peninsula of Nova Scotia. Few Frenchmen desired to leave home and few were needed to serve an extractive industry in which the indigenes did all the work of killing and curing the pelts. The small base required was amply furnished by the Lower St. Lawrence Valley, a narrow strip of moderately fertile soil punctuated by strategic points on the river (Fig. 76). All the land used for farms is served by the river highway. The arable strips which flank the stream are narrow and abruptly bounded by the infertile soil of the adjacent crystalline and ice-scoured uplands.

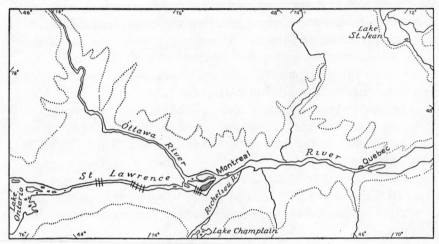

A. The upper course of the stream.

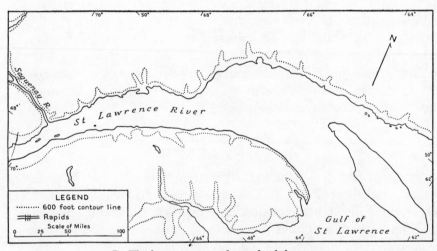

B. The lower course and mouth of the stream.

FIG. 76. The St. Lawrence gateway to the continent.

The chief military position was Quebec, at the head of the broad estuary. There a narrow strand of foreshore lies at the base of a 200-foot cliff, behind which rises a mesa of still higher land. This site controls passage between the estuary and the narrower river, and is nearly impregnable. Montreal was founded on a narrow, steep-sided ridge which stands thirty feet above both the river and a small tributary valley. Its site is defensible, but the place derives its significance from its location at the foot of the final rapids of the river, and near the confluences of the Ottawa, direct river route to Lake Huron, and the Richelieu, outlet of Lake Champlain and the trough leading to the Hudson Valley. Montreal is the chief concentration and distribution point for all the land tapped by the St. Lawrence system, and goods following the main stream itself have always been transshipped there.

Nature has provided for this tightly constricted Lower St. Lawrence region but one easy line of expansion — upstream. Concomitant with establishing the fur trade, the French government, just then nearing the peak of its period of centralized absolutism, forbade settlements inland. Instead, it built a chain of forts at critical confluences, portages, and narrows of the interior waterways. These were calculated to serve as trading stations and to protect the handful of men engaged in collecting furs, as well as to hold the country against foreign nations. The terrain lent itself to this procedure. From streams tributary to the Great Lakes, easy portages lead across gentle plains to the drainage basins of Hudson Bay and the Mississippi River.

A century after the Lower St. Lawrence was first occupied, French traders entered Mobile Bay and other coastal waters westward to and including the Mississippi Delta. On the delta they repeated the form of settlement already employed in the Lower St. Lawrence. Ribbon farms reached from the river highways to the marshes. Settlement ramified along all the distributaries, but was forbidden above the head of the delta. Northward, forts made contact with the Upper Mississippi and the Hudson Bay country. New Orleans, a dry site farthest upstream of such places served both by the river and by lagoons leading directly to the open Gulf, has been the strategic and commercial focus of the delta ever since its founding.

The French mode of occupying the country was admirably suited to glean its extractable resources. The Amerinds favored it because it brought them blankets, weapons, and gewgaws from overseas at no cost except the sport of taking the furs — goods without value to them. The French concessionaires ran great risks and stood to gain fantastic profits. The Roman Catholic Church was given all facilities for proselyting among the heathen indigenes. The national government, which closely controlled the whole system, gained in prestige and pocketed a high percentage of the financial profits.

## ENGLISH COLONIZATION

Between the gateways to the interior lowland occupied by the French, the first English settlements were made by chartered companies intent upon ransacking the country for extractable wealth, and raising crops salable in Europe. Except for a few furs, no readily extracted goods were found. English interests were then directed toward the subtropical part of the seaboard, where within a few decades four export crops, tobacco, indigo, rice, and sea-island cotton, came to dominate the agriculture. The whole coast claimed by the English was at first chartered to two companies. As these companies failed to fill out their grants of coastline with settlements, other charters were dispensed.

At first the lands were granted " from sea to sea," i.e., from the Atlantic to the Pacific. Every charter to land south of the Potomac contemplated expansion to the Pacific. In this southland of plantation agriculture, most of the streams flow in an easterly direction (Fig. 77). They therefore correspond roughly to the east-west ribbons of land which the charters laid out, and their drowned mouths, swept by tidal currents, provided coastal bases for the pioneer settlements. Because the export crops had to move out by water, and the rivers constituted the only easy routes of penetration into the back country, the grants were not serious misfits, as far inland as the mountains. In two cases rivers were substituted for geodetic boundaries without detriment to the economic life of the colonies.

From Chesapeake Bay northward the streams and their estuaries trend south, rather than east (Fig. 78). In a time when all heavy transportation was confined to waterways, the sea-to-sea charters ran across the grain of the country. Only two such charters were granted in that section, all the other colonies being limited or having undefined boundaries on their landward sides. The lines of the navigable Connecticut, Hudson, Delaware, and Chesapeake became axes of settlement, and the pattern of political units evolved as a checkerboard rather than a series of strips. Two colonies were reduced to a few miles of mainland coast and one, after energetic struggles to dominate a neighboring foundation, relinquished its ocean frontage, although it maintained an outlet via a broad estuary.

Except that all the charters were granted by the British authority, there was no uniformity in either the stated objectives of the colonists or the legal provisions of the instruments of government. There was equally little community of feeling among the groups of settlers. Several religious sects were represented, and a number of the settlements were theocracies. Some of these were schisms from older American foundations. A few colonies enjoyed virtual independence, others were directed by private proprietors or by governors appointed under royal authority. All had elected assemblies to legislate local matters, subject to executive veto in most cases.

Even the economic interests of the several colonies were rival, or at best reciprocal; they were rarely coincident. The northern settlers, unable to grow any exportable crop which could not be produced in the mother country, had little in common with the southern planters of cash exports. Instead, they subsisted on their corn (maize), small grains, beans, squashes, and livestock, and undertook to turn a cash profit from the sea — by catching fish for the British colonies southward to Barbados, and by building and sailing ships to carry goods, both British and colonial, which could pay for transportation across the Atlantic or along the American coast.

One problem all the seaboard colonists shared. Unable to force the nomadic Amerinds to work for them on their farms, they were compelled to build up their settlements with immigrants. The more successful the colony, the greater its need for labor from outside, although natural increase was rapid. Successive waves of immigrants were attracted from England, Netherlands, Scotland, and Germany, as well as individuals from all the other countries of Northwestern Europe. Each group as it arrived tended to occupy the first choice unsettled land its leaders could find. The Dutch, who came early, filled the inviting valley of the Hudson River. Germans, entering much later by way of the Delaware River, found that valley occupied and trekked overland to the westward until they discovered a basin-land of oak woods and glades similar to the country of the Middle Rhine from which they had come. On the fertile limestone soils which the deciduous woodland had signalized, these folk, set apart by religion and language, have remained to this day a prosperous and distinct group, the " Pennsylvania Dutch." Scots, arriving still later by the Delaware approach, pushed into the longitudinal valleys of the eastern Appalachians and were led southwestward behind the subtropical seaboard, into an environment where altitude and remoteness compelled them to practice subsistence agriculture.

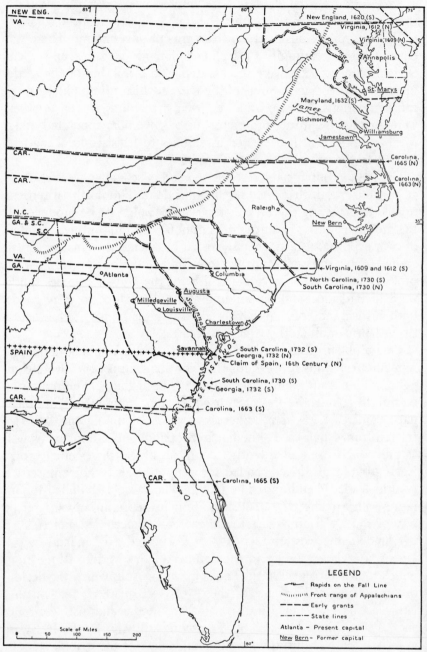

FIG. 77. Conformity of early grants and later States to terrain south of the Potomac River.

514

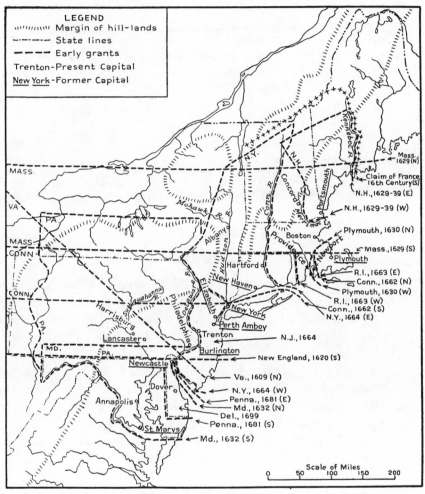

LEGEND
............ Margin of hill-lands
—··—··— State lines
— — — Early grants
Trenton-Present Capital
New York-Former Capital

Mass. 1629(N)
Claim of France 16th Century(S)
N.H.,1629-39 (E)
N.H., 1629-39 (W)
Plymouth, 1630 (N)
Mass.,1629 (S)
Plymouth
R.I.,1663 (E)
Conn.,1662 (N)
Plymouth,1630 (W)
R.I., 1663 (W)
Conn.,1662 (S)
N.Y.,1664 (E)
N.J.,1664
New England, 1620 (s)
Va., 1609 (N)
N.Y., 1664 (W)
Penna., 1681 (E)
Md., 1632 (N)
Del., 1699
Penna., 1681 (S)
Md., 1632 (S)

Scale of Miles
0    50   100   150   200

FIG. 78. The checkerboard of nature and culture north of the Potomac River.

515

Meantime the southern seaboard planters found it difficult to obtain from Europe enough labor willing to toil on the hot, humid, malarial coast. They solved their special problem by importing Negro slaves from the similar environment of African Guinea. In the north and in the highlands of the southern Appalachians no export crops of value could be raised, and the summer climate permits European colonists to work in the fields without undue discomfort. There Negro slaves, who had to be warmly housed during the winter, proved uneconomic. Whether the new settlements were white or mixed white and black, they were made up of colonists in the strict sense of the term — incomers who abandoned their old homes and made new ones in the New World, supplanting the aborigines.

## TERRITORIAL EXPANSION

The stages in settlement of the American continent, the location of the coastal bases, and the direction of movement inland fit its regional structure.

### OCCUPANCE OF THE SEABOARD

The first settlements, whether Spanish, French, or English, adhered closely to the coast and the lower valleys of the rivers. Along the Gulf of Mexico harbors are few, except in the river mouths, where shallow estuaries or lagoons behind offshore bars make contact with broad but silt-laden streams. Of the whole length of coast the delta of the Mississippi is least unfavorable to shipping, and its river system taps the largest basin on the continent. Natural deterrents were intensified by the Spanish and the French occupiers, because neither of them encouraged settlement of the interior. The Spanish developed small ports on a few harbors, for strategic reasons connected with their interests in the Gulf of Mexico. The French founded New Orleans to carry on trade with the indigenes of the interior.

On the Atlantic Coast, northward from Florida, the harbors become more and more closely spaced and furnish progressively superior conditions of shelter and depth of water, and the larger ones indent the coast deeply. At the north limit of land fitted to support a dense population, the St. Lawrence estuary and lower river can carry large ships to the lowest rapids, 600 miles inland (Fig. 76). Early settled by the French, the narrow ribbons of limestone soil bordering the stream were turned into continuous farmlands. Isolated by rugged and infertile terrain on either hand, except where two or three tributary valleys permit tongues of settlement to reach west or south, the French settlements were further restricted by laws which forbade farming in the interior, to which the valley gave access unequaled anywhere on the coast. Cramped by nature and by inescapable laws, the St. Lawrence farming and trading people solidified into the most compact and static society on the continent.

Between the St. Lawrence and Florida many streams reach the sea, but none of them penetrates beyond the watershed formed by the Appalachian Mountains. The lower courses of all the larger rivers are navigable, their upper reaches are beset by falls and rapids.

Between the Gulf of St. Lawrence and Chesapeake Bay (Fig. 78) deep and broad estuaries, sounds, and bays are numerous, due to recent drowning of the lower courses of the streams by seawater. There the coastal bases of settlement are generally on bays. In the era of initial occupancy, the small seagoing ships of the day could enter scores of harbors along this coast with impartial ease. The ports located at the inner ends of the longest deep-water harbors generally became the commercial metropolises, and in most instances the political capitals as well. Most original grants to the seaboard settlements laid out their boundaries to westward from the seaboard, which was conceived in Europe as running north-south. As elsewhere, streams formed the natural lines of penetration to the interior, and all the larger streams of this section flow south. The grain of the country tended to counteract the east-west strips of the colonial grants, and to create political units of various shapes. That several of them retain their long axis east-west is in part a tribute to the force of boundaries laid down antecedent to settlement in molding the subsequent occupance. It is also due in part to the interrupted courses of most of the streams by shallows and rapids of glacial origin. Failing navigable waterways, pioneers moved overland across the grain of the country on the coastal lowland. The south-flowing Hudson, which is tidal as far as the confluence of the Mohawk and furnishes an easy route almost to Lake George, drew settlement northward. At the same time the north-south alignment of the mountain ranges that mark its eastern watershed effectively checkmated the east-west political trend of New England. Similarly although less strikingly, the broad Delaware formed a north-south axis of settlement.

East of the Hudson-Champlain Trough expansion inland soon stalled against rugged hill-land overspread with sandy outwash and bouldery moraine derived from crystalline bedrock. This is a region of long, cold winters better suited to footloose Amerind hunting tribes than to sedentary European farmer-pioneers. In the Hudson lowland itself the swift expansion to the confluence of the Mohawk was as abruptly arrested there. This one real breach of the Appalachians, made by troughs which extend north to the St. Lawrence and west to Lakes Ontario and Erie, was blocked by the Iroquois, the best organized and most powerful fighters among the indigenes of eastern North America. They were less hostile to English colonists than to French, but they brooked no encroachments upon the land they claimed.

From the Delaware southward (Fig. 77) small ships can navigate most of the rivers to the Fall Line, where traffic is interrupted by rapids and low falls as the streams tumble from the ancient crystalline bedrock of the piedmont to the softer sediments of the coastal plain. The Fall Line set a limit to the first field for colonization, especially south of the Potomac. The easily worked, light soils of the coastal plain produced tobacco and indigo, the irrigable bottom lands rice, and the inshore " Sea Islands " cotton — all of which found a ready market overseas. All the streams flow southeast and aided the early settlements in pushing inland more or less parallel to their east-west grants.

Along the entire coastline the tidewater settlers remained in touch with the Old World by the slow but inexpensive ocean route. After the first years they never felt to the full the isolating and barbarizing effects of the frontier. Insofar as their wealth and their experience permitted, they reproduced in the new continent the life of the old.

Gradually the vacant lands along the coast were taken up and the several colonies came into contact with their neighbors. As need arose, they sent representatives to confer on common problems. The first political union was created in New England. There the early settlements lay close together, and were much alike in origin and aims. Almost at the outset they found themselves pressed by Indians loath to share their lands with the newcomers. Before long they became aware of rivalry from the French, settled on Cape Breton Island and expanding southwestward along the Gulf of Maine, and from the Dutch, who, from their base on Manhattan and Long islands, were endeavoring to establish trading posts on the mainland streams which empty into Long Island Sound. For a decade the four (of six) colonies most akin joined in a formal " United Colonies of New England," to facilitate unified action against threatening neighbors, red and white.

As outside danger waned, their bonds dissolved and were replaced by two permanent unions. Within a decade the Connecticut River settlements absorbed New Haven, which was faced with the alternatives of joining its Puritan neighbors or being merged with Anglican New York. A generation later the Plymouth colony, stagnating on its sandy moraine, was annexed to thriving Massachusetts Bay, which benefited from fertile soil, and especially from trade and fishing facilitated by its superior harbors. These were the only lasting results of the early New England Confederation and of subsequent plans of the home government to unify all the American colonies from Delaware Bay to Nova Scotia. Effective union could come only when the Atlantic slope was more densely settled.

By the time the more accessible seaboard was fully peopled, the tide of settlement had begun to flow inland. Gradually it overspread the country above the Fall Line in the south and filled valleys and basins in the north which lay well inland. This marks the second stage in colonization. The new lands constitute the first American " West," often called the Old West.

In the north expansion was restricted so long and the available country is so inhospitable, that the Old West is unimportant. It was not until the French fur-trading interests had been ousted from the continent that this section was sufficiently free from Indian depredations to be opened to the limited settlement which its environment permitted. Between the Mohawk and the James rivers a series of limestone valleys, parallel to the coast and intercommunicating, furnished homes and productive subsistence farms for a rapidly growing population compounded of families from the coastal settlements and the immigrant groups of later colonial times, chiefly Scottish and German. Southward from the Potomac, between the Fall Line and the first ridge of mountains, stretches the Appalachian Piedmont. Deprived of unbroken water communication with the outside world, it is also unsuited to sea-island cotton, indigo, and rice. It gradually evolved a a modified régime of plantation crops, subsistence crops, and livestock which made it a transition, buffer zone between the aristocratic tidewater plantations and the democratic subsistence farms of the inland basins.

Throughout the Old West the frontier exerted a powerful leveling force. Pioneers had to leave most of their goods at their old homes when they trekked overland in search of new ones. Everybody labored at much the same tasks. The most successful were those who could wrest a livelihood from the forest with gun, ax, and plow. Ingenuity and handicraft contrived shelter and clothing, as well as food, from the new environment. Initiative, inventiveness, and adaptiveness were virtues having direct survival value. If they were accompanied by roughness, coarseness, and heartiness, nobody objected — society being widely scattered and opportunities for intercourse too few to justify squeamishness. Equal economic opportunity has bred social equality and political democracy on each successive frontier.

By right of the grants under which they were founded, most of the seaboard colonies had claims to their respective hinterlands. While such of these claims as read " from-sea-to-sea " had never been staked out in the interior, which was ruled by foreign countries, nobody had challenged them east of the Appalachian Mountains. Thus the Old West, unified by its common lot on the frontier, was legally divided into arbitrary segments, each of which was yoked with a segment of seaboard. Only a minority of the pioneers to the new country came from the immediate seaboard settlements. Many were immigrants, who may have paused briefly in a port while on their way from an old European home to a new one in the west. Others entered North America far from the homes they ultimately chose. This was particularly true of those who filed down the long valleys of the eastern Appalachians from some remote entry in Pennsylvania or Maryland. Once these people had become backwoodsmen, they were still further differentiated from the coastal lowland by the frontier itself. Held in unwilling partnership with the seaboard, they were disregarded by their aristocratic compatriots of the coastal plain, until by the might of more rapidly growing population they were able to demand either independence or a fair share in the colonial government. For all their demands, the up-country folk really wished to retain connections across the adjacent seaboard to the coast, because with few exceptions, their readiest line of access to the outside world lay that way. With both sides in favor of union, practically all the colonies remolded their governments in the forge of political strife. The new order took shape chiefly in two outward phenomena: the back country received its proportionate share of representatives in the colonial assembly; the capital was moved from its original seaboard site to an inland location, generally on the border between the sections (Figs. 77 and 78). Both these moves were facilitated by the independence of thirteen of the sixteen British colonies, which were thereby enabled to adopt new frames of government without reference to a possible veto from overseas. Of the new capitals, five moved from a seaport to the head of navigation on a river and four from a seaport to an up-country location not in direct water connection with the colony's seaboard metropolis. Many years later two more States consolidated governmental activities at the interior of two coordinate capitals, while only one seat of administration has remained at the original seaboard site. The thirteenth had early shifted to a more central but still seaboard location.

### TABLE 7. MIGRATION OF CAPITALS

New Hampshire — Portsmouth to Concord, 1808.
Massachusetts — remained in Boston.
Rhode Island — consolidated in Providence, 1900.
Connecticut — consolidated in Hartford, 1873.
New York — New York City to Albany, 1797.
New Jersey — Elizabeth to Perth Amboy and Burlington, 1686; to Trenton, 1790.
Delaware — Newcastle to Dover, 1777.
Pennsylvania — Philadelphia to Lancaster, 1799; to Harrisburg, 1812.
Maryland — St. Mary's to Annapolis, 1694.
Virginia — Jamestown to Williamsburg, 1704; to Richmond, 1779.
North Carolina — New Bern and others to Raleigh, 1791.
South Carolina — Charleston to Columbia, 1790.
Georgia — Savannah to Augusta, 1786; to Louisville, 1795; to Milledgeville, 1807; to Atlanta, 1868.

By acceding to demands of the Old West, the seaboard retained its political hold westward to the mountains. The incorporation into political units of distinctive social groups occupying different environments could be accomplished only by compromise. This is in the British tradition (Ch. 5), and foreshadows the continuous adaptation which has marked the political consolidation of North America.

Political integration as between coastal and inland settlements was powerfully aided by the Appalachian mountain wall — a landward buffer of successive ranges and dissected blocks, tangled with the undergrowth of heavy deciduous forest. Only three lowland routes lead from the Atlantic seaboard to the interior. At the north the St. Lawrence breach was the center of French colonial activity. At the south end of the mountains a broad piedmont and coastal plain was inhabited by well-organized Amerinds, resolute in their determination to hold their hunting grounds against the whites. They were supported by the Spanish on the coastal plain, intent upon keeping the north fringe of the Gulf of Mexico free from European settlements which might jeopard the Mexican trade. The Hudson breach was blocked by the energetic and warlike Iroquois. Thus dammed along the whole west front, from the French settlements in the Lower St. Lawrence to the Spanish military hold on Florida, each English colony remained compact, kept in touch with seaports, and learned how to create a framework of government sufficiently elastic to encompass a moderate degree of regional differentiation, based on representation of the several sections in an elective legislature seated at some central point.

While each of the colonies was welding its sections into unity within the boundaries staked out for it, movements were on foot to bring them into closer relations with one another.

From the distant viewpoint of the mother country, the colonies were all of a piece, and whenever the English government was relatively free from civil disruption, it undertook measures of consolidation. With minor or ephemeral exceptions, these schemes failed. They disregarded the fact that every colony faced the sea and was in direct communication with the outside world, whereas roads were so few and unkempt that overland communication was awkward. This isolation from each other had accentuated the distinctions which began with the initial settlements, and which had sharpened in cases where natural environment had led to antithetic economic and social life. It would have been difficult to impose political union upon the long string of colonies even if they had been granted large autonomy in a loose federation. Unluckily for the plans of the royal government, they were based on abrogating the charters under which the colonies had been founded, and were intended to quench the representative, republican forms which had grown up during the formative years. The most the home government could do was to bring the separate colonies under governors appointed by the crown, leaving to them their representative assemblies. Two colonies never lost their republican charters, and even kept them as State constitutions after ties with the mother country had been severed.

Effective union ultimately came from the colonies themselves. At the very time when they were resisting unity by royal imposition, able provincials were proposing measures of consolidation, and a number of informal intercolonial conferences were held on matters of common concern. When the threat of war with the French loomed, most of the colonies north of the Potomac sent representatives to confer with the Indian allies of the English. This conference drew up a plan of union. It was rejected by the constituent colonies, but some of its creators were active in achieving union a score of years later, again under the stress of external war.

Reconstitution of the colonies to harmonize the interests of the seaboard and the Old West, and a drift toward union of neighboring colonies, at least for purposes of defense, were symptoms of a coherence of the British population unequaled elsewhere in the colonial world. The Atlantic face of North America had become a transplanted bit of Western Europe, modified by the special problems of location overseas and on a wilderness frontier. The Amerinds had all but disappeared from the country between the sea and the mountains before the flood of colonization burst the Appalachian dam, to sweep down the " western waters " into the New West.

## THE STRUGGLE FOR THE INTERIOR

Before the central lowland of the continent could be comfortably occupied by settlers under the British flag, the French had to be dislodged from its natural outlets on the mouths of the Mississippi and St. Lawrence rivers, and their Amerindian allies had to be dispossessed of their hunting grounds. Once the French were eliminated, the indigenes could be disposed of tribe by tribe.

Seen in the large, the Anglo-French struggle for possession of the interior was one aspect of an important match in the world-wide elimination contest among the colonial powers of Europe. (The struggle has been in progress ever since Spain and Portugal endeavored to settle their disputes by appeal to the pope to draw a line of demarcation between their rival claims.) Looked at with North American eyes, it was, for French settlers, a war to keep hold of the lucrative fur trade, and for English settlers a chastisement of the Indians who, abetted by their French friends, were destroying communities all along the frontier.

In the contest British America had the advantage. Its uninterrupted block of settlements, reaching almost to the mountains, provided an ample base for a British army, and the settlers themselves, skilled in Indian warfare, contributed valuable contingents to the army. In defense of their homes these men fought willingly and ably, and the laissez faire policy which had generally characterized England's governance had taught them to stand on their own feet. Under the duress of Indian wars colonies ordinarily contemptuous or jealous of each other were accustomed to join forces. Migrations to successive frontiers had done much to intermingle people of different origins. Besides, on the frontier hardships of the common and inescapable lot levelled all distinctions apart from the innate character of the individuals. Great Britain and its colonies could put up a formidable and fairly unified front, notwithstanding the haphazard backgrounds of the British community.

The nature of French occupance of the New World handicapped French arms in the contest. The restricted European settlements were scattered and small, and not even the Lower St. Lawrence colony was strong, apart from support furnished by the mother country. None of them was habituated to defending itself. For manpower France had to depend on European troops, unused to woodsmen's warfare, and on Indians, eager enough for scalps, but unable to comprehend the necessity for prolonged resistance. The only usable French ·base was the St. Lawrence Lowland, the Mississippi Delta being remote from the scene of fighting.

Defeated, France ceded its North American mainland: the part east of the Mississippi to Great Britain, the part west of the river to Spain, including the outlet at New Orleans. By this division, the sea-to-sea grants claimed by some seaboard colonies were automatically truncated at the Mississippi. This caused no grumbling in the colonies, because the extreme claims of the early charters had been generally recognized as unattainable. For practical purposes the colonial western boundaries ran along the Appalachian Mountains, and there is evidence that the colonies would have accepted the mountain limitation, had the transmontane lands which England received been opened to settlement. Quite possibly some such scheme was contemplated for the future. For the time being, ejection of France from the North American mainland left the British government in the mood to enforce stricter supervision upon its own somewhat self-assertive colonies. The peace was followed by a royal proclamation setting the inland limit of the seaboard provinces at approximately the line of settlement, and reconsecrating the territory beyond to the Amerinds and the fur trade. This attempt to perpetuate the French mode of occupance and to restrict westward expansion was restated in a more explicit law a decade later. Coming at the moment when the Atlantic slope was at last covered by settlement, and frontiersmen were in process of pushing into the forbidden area, these moves were among the chief incitements to revolt of the seaboard colonies against British authority. The growing resentment and independence in the cities was matched by settlements defiantly planted in the Mississippi drainage basin by frontiersmen who pushed through the maze of valleys and gaps leading to the headstreams of the Tennessee, the Cumberland, and the Ohio. An ominous coincidence for the European power which had just come into possession of those lands!

The first tentacles of settlement reached out along the upper courses of Tennessee River tributaries, several of which rise east of the crest ranges in the long, troughlike, limestone valleys of the Eastern Appalachians (Fig. 79). From these springboards, settlement leaped across the rugged and infertile Western Appalachians by way of Cumberland Gap to the limestone lowlands which came to be the nuclei of Kentucky and Tennessee. This part of the Ohio Basin, besides being fertile in soil and not too rigorous in climate, was unpopulated by Indians, except at times when tribes from north and south went thither to hunt game or to war upon each other. When the dissatisfaction of the seaboard flamed into open revolt, the settlers on the " western waters " were largely instrumental in holding the Ohio country for the rebel cause.

## UNION AND FISSION

The revolt of the thirteen mainland colonies involved settlements reaching along the coast from the Kennebec River in Maine to the St. Mary's in Georgia, and inland at one point as far as the Bluegrass of Kentucky. It did not involve the British colonies in the Antilles, nor those in and about the St. Lawrence waterway.

The Caribbean islands were then at the height of their prosperity as producers of sugar. Jamaica was one of the most prized of all the British colonies, its governorship being as juicy a plum as that of India. The European settlers were few, they sold plantation crops to the mother country at a good profit, purchased in return all their requirements even to staple food, and were satisfied.

The northern settlements had been founded by France. The Lower St. Lawrence Valley was the French base for the interior fur trade and was solidly settled by conservative Catholic, French peasants who had nothing in common with the schismatics of British origin, particularly the Puritan merchants and artisans who dominated New England, their nearest, but still very remote, neighbors. The small and scattered settlements on the peninsulas and islands about the Gulf of St. Lawrence were likewise French foundations, except for parts of Newfoundland. They had been established in connection with the banks fisheries or as strategic outposts for defense of the approach to the St. Lawrence Valley. Nova Scotia and Cape Breton Island ranked high in military value and were seized by British forces half a century earlier than the St. Lawrence and the interior. Their population remained dominantly French and agricultural, and their value strategic. Neither the peninsula nor the islands were vexed by the regulations issued by the govern-

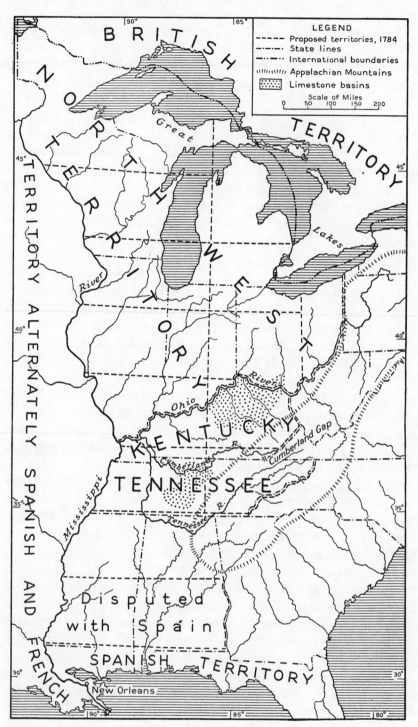

FIG. 79. The New West.

ment in London, because as military French settlements they had been strictly regulated from the beginning and knew nothing of representative government. Being subsistence farmers, the colonists had little trade that could suffer from increased taxation on goods in transit. Finally, the country had never attracted many immigrants, and the few settlements felt no need of expansion. Such border troubles as they had were harryings of the coast between the St. John and Kennebec rivers, which Nova Scotia disputed with Maine. This served to intensify the distrust of each for the other. Clearly, quondam French colonies were segregated from their neighbors to the south by social and economic gaps no less wide than the broad belt of wilderness which separated them physically.

The thirteen intervening British colonies had coalesced into a continuous line of settlements along the coast and had pushed inland to, or even beyond, the Appalachian crest. They stood in a relation to the mother country unlike either the Caribbean islands or the regions first settled by the French.

Little attention had been paid to the earlier foundations by the sponsor government, which was fully occupied during much of the 17th century by civil war at home. Besides, the North American mainland yielded no ready riches, and the " merchant adventurers " who sent out settlers generally lost money. The pioneers, hard put to subsist, turned over no profit and were therefore permitted to create whatever economic life they could. When finally the colonies became firmly established, they depended on the mother country only to the extent of participating in empire trade, free from restrictions imposed on foreigners. They practiced local self-government with only sporadic interference from overseas, and evolved political machinery fitted to local needs. The exigencies of the expanding frontier stamped society with increasing democracy and permitted the continuous rise of new wealth, as new resources were tapped. To begin with, each colony was planted in the wilderness, and every subsequent migration into the back country increased the weight of the frontier in the body politic and economic, and heightened the antithesis between America and England.

In a very real sense the revolt was led and supported by " new men." The rank and file of enthusiasts was provided by the back country — democrats by virtue of training on the levelling frontier — and by workingmen in the cities who were imbued with democratic ideals and had no objection to seeing their aristocratic employers lose out. In the southern colonies the tidewater soils which had been their wealth were wearing out and were losing out to the fresh and generally more fertile piedmont soils. It was planters of the piedmont who headed revolt in the South. On New England, which depended upon trade, fell the brunt of the restrictive laws by which the mother country planned to absorb an increasing share of the profits of imperial business. This threw many wealthy merchants into opposition.

Revolt of any individual colony would have been fruitless. The presentation of a common front was facilitated by practice in self-government, and by a custom of organizing representative congresses to consider common problems and especially to prepare for joint resistance against the ever-present danger of attack by Indians. Of this nature was the Continental Congress which acted as the head of government during the war that followed the colonial declaration of independence.

Once the war was on, the rebels had certain advantages. The tradition that every man should be able to shoot, fostered by generations of Indian forays, made a trained militiaman of every citizen, except some denizens of the larger seaboard centers. Guerilla tactics, the rule in Indian fighting, was the source of American success in the very first battle of the war, and was resorted to on subsequent occasions with telling effect. The frozen winters of the north and the muddy country everywhere were more serious handicaps to British regiments than to bands of American militiamen. The revolt took on the character of a defense of home and family, whereas its suppression had to be achieved from a base across the ocean. The British government was entangled with greater affairs of state, chiefly the necessity to fight France for the valuable Caribbean sugar colonies. In the contemporary English view, the outcome of the contest in mainland North America was of little moment. It could not be foreseen that success of the rebellion would set the stage for dividing English-speaking North America into two sovereignties, and for launching critical experiments in governance.

One of the direct results of the war was the creation of Canada, apart from the French-speaking foundations. By no means all the residents of the rebellious colonies favored independence. Perhaps a third opposed open rebellion, and among them were many of the wealthy and powerful families of the older settlements. The most ardent loyalists to the British cause were exiled or fled from their homes, generally to lands still British. Of such lands the most accessible and at the same time the most habitable for people of European extraction, were the wildernesses beyond New England. The country between the mouth of the Bay of Fundy and the Gulf of St. Lawrence was thinly peopled, although it had been British for decades. So rapidly did loyalists flock to these parts that in Nova Scotia and Prince Edward Island the balance was shifted from French to English speech and population, and New Brunswick was carved out of mainland Nova Scotia as a new colony. In the limestone lowland of the upper St. Lawrence and the lower Great Lakes country other colonists found arable land heretofore reserved to the fur trade. This was the seat of another new colony, Upper Canada. It became and has remained an English makeweight for French Quebec, or Lower Canada as it was styled. Still other immigrants filled into the hill-land of southern Quebec, giving for a century a marked British tinge to that stronghold of French culture. To these ardent partisans of Britain, Canada owes its separatism from the overwhelmingly more populous nation which originated with a revolt against Britain.

If Canada received such an impetus from the American Revolution as to be virtually refounded, the war and the peace treaty made a unit of the thirteen wrangling colonies which had fought it. The war, once launched, had to be carried on. As an aid to joint action, the congress of the colonies set one committee to drafting articles of confederation while it put another to work on a declaration of independence. Fifteen months later a plan for union submitted to the constituent governments had been adopted by all save Maryland. This small colony, confined by specific boundaries, refused to permit the operation of the confederation until its neighbors which had sea-to-sea or indefinite territorial claims agreed to relinquish them, beyond lines already indisputably occupied. By these enforced cessions all the revolting colonies acquired a joint territorial stake of undetermined, but supposedly high value, before the transfer of territory to the federal union had been completed. The acquisition was confirmed when Great Britain yielded to the newly recognized United States all the territory south of the Great Lakes, north of Florida, and east of the Mississippi.

This relinquishment of an astonishingly large tract of wilderness reflects the British ignorance of its possibilities and the optimism of influential Americans, many of whom were already financially involved in western land schemes. As a fact nobody knew whether or not the continental interior could furnish a suitable base for colonization, but faith in its future, widespread in the settled Atlantic slope, was a major influence in keeping its thirteen bickering joint owners attached to the united cause. As it turned out, the New West was very like the Old West in natural environment, except that all its conditions are somewhat more extreme. The climate is hotter in summer and colder in winter, the plains are larger, the streams are wider and subject to greater fluctuations, and above all the routes to the outside world are longer and more arduous. The ax-woodsman technology for subjecting nature, devised on the seaboard, could be carried without modification into the deciduous forest which stretched to and beyond the political boundary of the new nation. Only in the part later known as Illinois were there extensive tracts of grassland, then universally believed (although erroneously) to be an indication that the soil was too infertile to produce trees.

To the rosy view of Americans of the time, this wilderness, when settled, should not differ from the already existing States, themselves carved out of a similar wilderness not so long before. A frontier area hotly disputed between New Hampshire and New York had begun to assert its political separatism during the Revolution, and became Vermont, the first addition to the original thirteen States. Already the two fertile limestone basins south of the Ohio River were in process of settlement by courageous pioneers. They took shape within bounds of colonial origin. Kentucky was the westernmost county of Virginia, and Tennessee was the part of North Carolina which lay beyond the crest of the Appalachians. The land south of Tennessee was in dispute with Spain. By these deductions the joint domain was reduced to the territory northwest of the Ohio (Fig. 79). For this wilderness, congress provided administration as joint property in units of convenient size and arbitrary, generally rectangular, shape, until such time as the population of each territorial unit warranted constitution as a new State within the federation. The States which evolved in pursuance to this plan were less numerous and less arbitrarily bounded than originally contemplated. Instead they were shaped gradually by their settlers. They, and others subsequently admitted from territories having humid climates, were so bounded as to give them access to navigable streams or lakes. Every one of the States that emerged in the part of the country having a humid climate took form before it was penetrated by railroads.

The federal union came into legal existence and national recognition on a wave of land cessions. The backwash of that wave carried the thirteen sovereign states into the " more perfect union " in which they submerged a part of their sovereignty and to which they admitted coordinate additions as fast as was warranted by the growth in population on the frontier. The plan was plausible, but it might not have worked. In turned out to be effectual because the New West was sufficiently like the Old West to permit enlargement of political concepts to keep pace with territorial expansion and the problems it entailed. Nevertheless, it was different enough to require a high degree of flexibility in governance.

## THE NEW WEST

When the United States came into possession of its territory between the Appalachians and the Mississippi there were several vigorous, small settlements in the limestone valleys of the tributaries to the Tennessee and in the larger limestone basins of the Middle Cumberland and the Middle Ohio. These had grown from a trickle of migration following the passways provided by the upper James and Roanoke rivers into the mountain valleys of the Upper Tennessee. Thence the Cumberland Gap opens a narrow but fairly direct way to the fertile valleys of the plain. With the peace, plans for western settlements were pushed. Alternate routes from the Potomac and Susquehanna valleys to the upper tributaries of the Ohio soon carried a flow of pioneers to the limestone basins and also to the fertile soils of glacial till north of the Ohio itself. The stream of settlers was interrupted only by winter weather.

As soon as these folk had established themselves on farms, they began to seek a market for their surplus. The mountains, which so grudgingly passed emigrant pioneers, empty-handed save for a gun and a kettle, were an insuperable bar to shipment of the bulky frontier products, chiefly corn and hogs, to the populous East. The Great Lakes drainage basin is little larger than the lakes themselves, and was still in the hands of Indians. Besides, the St. Lawrence waterway belonged to Great Britain. The natural outlet for all the occupied interior leads down the rivers of the Mississippi system to their focus at New Orleans, guardian of the sole Mississippi water-gate to the outside world. Spain once again held this portal as well as the whole north coast of the Gulf of Mexico, and Spanish colonial fiscal administration was notoriously unmindful of economic principles. The western settlements unceasingly demanded that their government break the political dam which stopped sales or sharply reduced the value of their surplus products. Accustomed to stand on their own feet, and disheartened by the inaction of the federal government, some of them undertook to deal directly with Spanish officials by attempting to get a reduction in customs duties at New Orleans. At least four " sovereign " governments were set up on the western waters without consent of the federal congress, thereby repeating, a stage farther west, the independent establishments of the American Revolution. When decadent Spain ceded New Orleans and its hinterland west of the Mississippi River to rejuvenated Napoleonic France, the annoyance of exorbitant tariffs was supplanted by the danger of a powerful rival of the interior American settlements, a colony which would hold the key to prosperity on both sides of the boundary river. Spurred to action by this threat, the United States authorities redoubled their efforts to purchase New Orleans. The French government refused to subdivide its holding — logically, because to do so would place its interior in the unenviable position from which the Americans were trying to extricate themselves. In the end the United States purchased the west half of the Mississippi Basin in order to secure an outlet for the east half. Once again France was eliminated from the North American mainland. At a stroke the already vast area of the United States was more than doubled.

The Mississippi Basin is far too large to be a unit, except as a drainage system. In early days the surface waters which reach the Gulf via the delta floated the commercial life of the area, and the Appalachians stood as a barrier against the Atlantic lowlands. For some decades commercial unity and isolation made of the scattered settlements of the New West a geographic region which expressed itself politically in sectionalism. Together with the north and the south halves of the Atlantic slope, differentiated from each other since the first days of colonization, the three regions embarked upon the eternal seesaw which is the foundation of a successful federation (Fig. 80).

As the West grew in population, the unity of its youth was weakened. Peace was made with the Iroquois tribes of the Mohawk Trough and the northeast thereby gained for the first time a direct route of emigration to the west. By virtue of its broad, low level and its connection with the navigable Great Lakes, it is a much easier route across the Appalachians than any other, and it channelled great numbers of New Englanders into the region north of the Ohio River. This migration was redoubled with the construction of a canal in the trough.

While the northern interior was being populated with northeasterners, the lands south of the Ohio and Missouri were even more solidly filled with families from the southern seaboard, who swept around the southern end of the mountains. The invention of the cotton gin a decade after the New West was opened to settlement turned all the more fertile lowlands to plantation agriculture as far north as cotton can grow, i.e., the line of 200 days free from frost. Within a quarter century the southern New West lost its identity, to become an inseparable part of the Atlantic-facing South. Like the older South, the eastern Gulf slope consists of a coastal plain reaching to a fall line, behind which lies a piedmont. Both coastal plain and piedmont merge into the broad alluvial floodplain and delta of the Mississippi, a banner cotton country surpassing any district farther east. Beyond the lower Mississippi, only 120 to 200 miles away, lay the boundary of Spanish territory, soon to become Mexican. Scarcely had cotton growing swept to the Mississippi Delta and converted the territory into the States of Louisiana, Mississippi, and Alabama, when Florida was wrenched from

**THE NORTHEAST,
THE SOUTH, AND
THE NORTHWEST**
IN THEIR SETTING OF
PLAINS, MOUNTAINS
AND HILL-LANDS

Scale of Miles

FIG. 80. Sections in eastern United States.

The divisions are arbitrary median lines passing through zones of transition between the sections.

The base is Lobeck's *Physiographic Diagram of the United States,* used by permission of the author and the Geographical Press.

Spain and cotton planters were making settlements in Texas to the west of the international boundary. The sandy soil of Florida proved inhospitable to the dominant crop, and migrants to Texas found themselves handicapped by Mexican laws.

Meanwhile the northern interior was being settled relatively slowly. No crop that could grow there promised immediate and reliable return, and even the construction of a canal through the Mohawk

Trough gave the farmers only a slow outlet to the East. Their best market remained the South, where devotion to cotton induced farmers as well as city folk to buy much of their food. The fan shape of the Mississippi Basin and its political reflection, the Louisiana Purchase, insured to the North a long reach westward, while the South felt unreasonably pent within narrow confines. At the same time it was not recognized that west of the 100th meridian, north and south, the country is semiarid and doomed to sparse population. It was obvious that eastern Texas was suited to cotton, and the flood of emigration burst across the international boundary. Before the last units of land east of the Mississippi had been granted Statehood, this outlying State of Mexico had declared itself independent and then had been annexed to the United States.

THE FAR WEST

The seizure precipitated war with Mexico. Its outcome was the elimination of Spanish-speaking governments from all the mainland north of the broad band of steppe and desert which reaches from the Gulf of Mexico to the Gulf of California and the Pacific Ocean (Ch. 15).

Nearly the whole immense addition of territory lay south of parallel forty, approximately the boundary between the South and the North in the east. The opportunity thereby afforded the South was immediately matched by dividing the Pacific Northwest, hitherto occupied jointly with Great Britain, along the 49th parallel. (This was the line already established for the United States-Canadian boundary between Lake Superior and the Rocky Mountains.) At a stroke the national domain was pushed to the Pacific Ocean along the whole frontier (Fig. 81). At the same time, the way was opened for Canadian expansion parallel to and to the north of the United States.

As it turned out neither the South, the North, nor Canada was able to occupy the newly acquired land by simple extension from regions already established in the East. The western quarter of the Mississippi Basin and the prairies west of Lake Winnipeg are too dry to fit into the agricultural systems of the humid east (north or south). Beyond the steppes rise the great ranges of mountains, which themselves constitute a formidable double barrier between the sedentary regions of the east and those of the Pacific basins and seacoast. South of the international boundary the Great Basin enclosed by the mountains is largely desert. The Canadian section, for all its drainage into Hudson Bay and the Atlantic Ocean, is cut off from eastern Canada by an in-

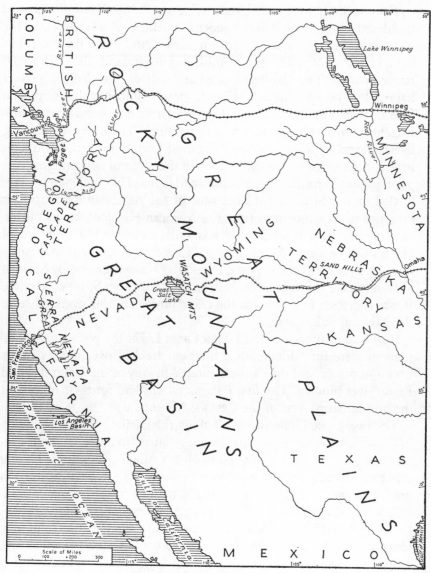

FIG. 81. Western North America.

tractable wilderness north of Lake Superior. The new acquisitions were not densely peopled, even by indigenes.

The southerly valleys had been subjected to Spanish influence. In the deserts of the Great Basin sedentary Amerinds already knew the technique of irrigation when Spanish missionaries found them inhabiting a country not unlike the Spanish interior upland, although much larger in scale. The California coast and valleys provided the perfect habitat for the Spaniards. Its climate closely simulates that of littoral Spain, its streams can be made to supply irrigation water, and its unirrigable plains will support wheat or livestock. The indigenes, lacking livestock and staple cereals, were the most primitive on the continent, having been unable to advance beyond the stage of collecting edibles provided by the restricted native flora and fauna. That this coast was not settled by the Spanish until the time of the American Revolution is evidence of its remoteness from the Mexican Highland across blistering deserts. That ultimately it was settled overland is evidence of Spain's lack of seapower on the Pacific, by way of which it may easily be reached from Mexican ports. Even after being occupied by Spanish missionaries, California received little aid from either Spain or Mexico. It was therefore easy prey for the rising power pushing overland from the Mississippi lowland.

In the country west of the Upper Great Lakes the precursors of settlement were fur traders. Some of them trekked overland by canoe from Ottawa or St. Louis, others entered by way of the Columbia and Fraser river mouths. The first folk-migrations had for their objectives the humid basins west of the Cascade Mountains.

The new coastal settlements all along the Pacific constituted highly individualized regions, and they were isolated from the national ecumene to a degree unprecedented in North America and rarely on any other continent. To retain its new provinces the United States ran mail lines, and promised the construction of a transcontinental railroad which should traverse the unpeopled deserts and the lofty mountain ranges. In Canada a similar lure was held out to British Columbia, separated from Upper Canada by a wide neck of forested wilderness as well as mountains and an expanse of grassland. In order to bring these hopes to fruition the Canadian provinces, all having attained local self-government under the British crown, were consolidated by Parliamentary authority into a federation. The Dominion of Canada became the prototype of other self-governing British dominions and thus completed the political evolution begun by the declaration of independence of the Thirteen Colonies. Although Canadian sentiment is strongly British, the Canadian government is fundamentally hardly more colonial than is that of the United States. Both north and south of the international boundary, federation provides the means whereby large and diverse regions have been able to work out their complex and sometimes incompatible problems with minimum friction.

English-speaking domination of the continent was completed by the United States in its purchase of Alaska from Russia.

By coincidence the United States extinguished the Russian title to North American territory in the year of Canadian federation. These events may be regarded as signalizing the end of colonial tutelage in North America. In the United States people felt that the country had attained its "manifest destiny" when, two decades earlier, it had set the American flag on the Pacific Coast. Yet it was not until after the purchase of Alaska that the first transcontinental railroad was completed from Omaha, near the western margin of the humid east, to San Francisco, outlet of the Great Valley of California. Then for the first time a segment of the Pacific Coast was effectively joined to the national ecumene.

## SECTIONS

Neither the fear on the part of the older settlements that the Pacific Coast might secede, nor the construction of improved lines of transportation to avert secession, was new when the first transcontinental railroad was built. North America, like every other continent, is an aggregation of complementary or conflicting regions. In all the other continents except Australia, these regions have gradually taken form as political sovereignties or as colonies of older states. In North America most of them have been resolved into sections of two very large states. The section is the political version of the region. The federal components are always the engines of sectional interests, and State or province boundaries outline the sections. A few of the political units, such as Quebec and California, incorporate whole regions. In most cases, groups of States or provinces join forces in giving voice to their regional attitudes. This repeatedly appears in the Prairie Provinces, in New England, in the South, and elsewhere.

Sectional boundaries, i.e., State and provincial lines, are determined by political expediency and compromise, and are framed as precise lines defined in legal documents. It is rather rare that they coincide with regional boundaries, which are lines only by exception because they usually take the form of transitional zones of natural phenomena. The discrepancy has been of less moment than have been political clashes within regions arising from internal subregional distinctions. This is in sharp contrast with Europe, where regional borders, lying on or near boundaries of sovereign states, repeatedly become causes of war. In North America the inevitable zonal character of boundaries, instead of being accentuated by attributes of sovereignty, is minimized by federal laws which apply to all regions impartially, and by federal judicial systems which provide legal machinery for resolving border disputes. Scores of State boundary issues have thus been amicably settled. This is not to say that regions have been extinguished by legal devices. On the contrary, regional unity is so tenacious of life that State and provincial boundaries which do not happen to coincide with definite regional breaks are blurred in dozens of minor ways by the daily intercourse of communities on opposite sides.

The first critical sectioning of the continent appeared in the struggle between the seaboard and the Old West (pp. 519–23). Its successful settlement — reconciliation of the sectional interests of the several colonies — paved the way for repetitions of the clash on larger stages as the country expanded westward.

The New West constituted a section so long as it remained isolated from the Atlantic slope and unified as a frontier area interconnected by the navigable Mississippi system. With the expansion of short-staple, upland cotton and the increase in demand for tobacco, the part south of the Ohio-Missouri rivers differentiated from the north, and became merged with the southern Atlantic slope in one of the most strongly marked sections on the continent — the South. Its well-ramified navigable streams carried its export crops to their world markets, and the uniformity of its economic life laid the foundation for a patriarchal society and a political outlook dominated by a few wealthy planters and their professional associates.

The northern interior was much slower to conform to the pattern of the North Atlantic slope. Its isolation in the heart of the continent was broken down very slowly. Superior in soils to most of the Northeast, it evolved as a producer of food for both its neighbors — the one a section devoted to trade and increasingly to manufacturing, the other to raising inedible crops. Shipment to the East was difficult because of the Appalachian barrier. Even after the route through the Mohawk Trough had been smoothed with a canal, the Great Lakes, to which it gave access, had to be connected with the Mississippi riverways by other canals, before the bulk of the northern interior was effectively attached to the Northeast. Communication between the Ohio branch of the Mississippi system and the eastern seaboard necessitated not

only canals in the upper valleys of the Atlantic streams, but also highways over the mountains. Pennsylvania, on the most direct line between the coast and the confluence which forms the Ohio proper,
constructed a canal which provided for hauling the barges up the Al-
legheny Front on an inclined plane. The National Road was built with
federal funds to give access to the heart of the northern interior. The
question of " internal improvements " — canals, stage roads, and other
means of communication — constantly agitated the government of the
United States for a generation.

The problem was solved by railroads. They minimized the barriers
of distance and mountains. Specifically they modified and crowned the
new regional pattern that was foreshadowed by roads and canals built at
public expense. In the South many navigable streams and little fast
freight discouraged construction. The lines built welded bonds already close, thanks to a uniform mode of life. As connections between
southern and northern interior they merely paralleled the waterways
with a faster but more expensive mode of travel. In the northern interior they promptly replaced roads and canals as links between the
Great Lakes and the Mississippi drainage. They pushed their tracks
along the Mohawk Trough and through every other suitable pass in
the central Appalachians. For the northern half of the United States
the railroad completed the downfall of the Mississippi riverway as a
regional prop. In the new alignment, the Northeast drew the northern
interior into a measure of reciprocity never before achieved. Foodstuffs
from the Middle West could now move upgrade across the Appalachians, and manufactured goods, either locally made or imported,
could as readily be sent west from the Atlantic seaboard.

The railroads could also carry increasing numbers of immigrants into
the northern interior from the northeastern section. These people
found farms on the deep black soil of the prairies which constituted
the western half of the Upper Mississippi Basin. These lands had been
considered infertile, and in any case it had been impossible to break
the heavy prairie sod until the invention of the steel-shod plow with a
self-scouring moldboard. At about the same time harvesting machines
were devised and rails were pushing west. These technologic advances
brought immediate return in bumper crops of wheat and other grains
grown in the virgin soil, which proved to be the most fertile yet en-
countered. The grain could find markets both in the manufactural
Northeast and in the plantation South. The Middle West, year by
year a bigger prize, held the balance of power between the sections.

As the expanding frontier demanded to be set up as coordinate

States of the federal union, struggle after struggle was precipitated in Congress. Until the middle of the century new States were invariably admitted in pairs, one north one south. Then the territorial handicap of the South began to tell, and only the northern interior, continuing to grow, presented further candidates for Statehood. The regional issue was thus squarely placed upon control of the Middle West. If that section should adhere permanently to one or the other side, the favored choice would become paramount in the federal government.

The Middle West was becoming more urban and less agrarian as trade and manufacturing sprang up along the Lower Great Lakes, the inland seaboard of the country. This brought it into line with the East, but at the same time made it something of a rival of the older manufacturing region. More political weight was exerted by the growing cleavage along the Ohio-Missouri line over the issue of slavery, which came to be the chief emotional issue of sectionalism. Although few realized it, slavery merely typified the " irrepressible conflict " between a mode of life which could thrive in a humid subtropical environment and an antithetic scheme of things suited to higher middle latitudes. In the end the issue was precipitated by the demands of still other regions: the coastal basins of the Far West, and the intervening steppes and deserts.

Beyond the line of semiaridity, population was not inclined to go until the humid country had been preempted. For a long time to come the acquisitions of Mexican territory beyond eastern Texas, and even the western part of the Louisiana Purchase, promised to remain in the hands of nomadic Indians, except the basins and valleys along the Pacific Coast (Fig. 81). There humid climates, counterparts of those of Western Europe, invited settlers, who began their treks across the plains and the mountains just at the time that the sectional friction in the humid eastern half of the nation was generating an uncomfortable degree of heat. With the discovery of gold in the Sierra Nevada, California swiftly advanced from a sleepy, outlying, pastoral province of Mexico to a roaring mining camp peopled with the most ruthless and bold North Americans to be found anywhere. At the same time the Willamette Valley, the most fertile lowland of the humid northwest, was more slowly filling with American farmers in search of opportunity in still another arable west.

The energetic Californians brooked no delay in being admitted to the Union. As neither the Mexican grazers nor the American miners and townsfolk possessed slaves, California was sure to come in as a free State, although all its populated area lies south of the latitude generally accepted as the sectional boundary in the east. It was already apparent that slaves were unlikely to be held in any territory too dry for cotton growing, and the only such land not already admitted to Statehood was the Indian Territory, inhabited chiefly by tribes which a few decades before had been dispossessed of their aboriginal hunting grounds in the eastern cotton belt. If California were admitted to the union as a free State, there would be no counterbalance of slave territory. The fear lest delay would cause the isolated Californians to declare their independence overcame sectional apprehension, and gave the free States a majority in the federal Senate, for the first time since the admission of Tennessee more than half a century before.

Whatever the political status of the Far West, it was clearly recognized by all that it must be bound to the eastern half of the country by lines of communication and transportation. Mail and light commodities were carried by the " pony express " operated by the federal government. Its relays covered the immense distances in astonishingly short time. The railroad held hopes of a still faster and cheaper schedule, and a transcontinental line to be built with federal aid was projected before the United States held full title to any part of the Pacific Coast. During the decade following the admission of California and the territorial organization of Oregon, unceasing efforts to provide for the desired railroad were checkmated by sectional rivalry. None of the competing eastern termini — New Orleans, Memphis, St. Louis, and Chicago — could obtain intersectional support in the federal Congress. That body could not even agree upon territorial organization of the country through which the line must pass between the western boundaries of existing States and the eastern boundary of California, because neither section was willing to permit natural conditions to determine the future of slavery in the federal holdings. It was an effort to organize the trans-Missouri territory, to the end that a railroad might be authorized, that brought out the first open vote of what might be termed a " solid " South.

This vote was one of a series of indications that the forces which make for national unity were cleaving along the intersectional boundary zone. Each of the popular evangelical churches had already broken into northern and southern independent units. It took a decade for the last national tie to loosen. Then, at about the time the South was voting almost solidly in favor of opening the Nebraska Territory to slavery, the northernmost fringe of States gave birth to movements which coalesced in the Republican party, dedicated to the abolition of slavery. In a few years this party pushed its control almost to the Ohio

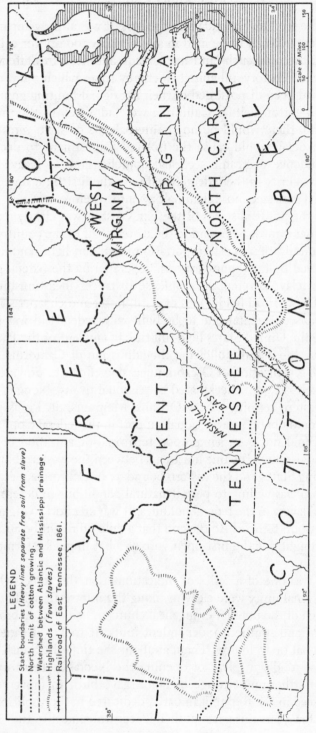

FIG. 82. Sections in the border zone between North and South.

LEGEND

State boundaries (*Heavy lines separate free soil from slave*)
North limit of cotton growing.
Watershed between Atlantic and Mississippi drainage.
Highlands (*Few slaves*)
Railroad of East Tennessee, 1861.

River, signalizing the effective union of the East and Middle West. This political cohesion was the final outward sign of economic and social solidarity which had been growing up over a period of decades. The election of a Republican (sectional) President precipitated the secession from the federal union of the eleven States which comprised the South. This move was an effort to keep control of its cherished and peculiar institution, slavery, now that it was indubitably blocked by cold at the north and by aridity at the west. The opposed system of free labor, triumphantly expanding northwest to Minnesota and Oregon, and even southwest to California and Kansas, had captured the federal government by means of sectional realignment.

As is usual in sectional conflict, a transitional border zone declared itself between the unequivocal North and South (Fig. 82). Of the five slave States which bordered on free soil, four failed to secede. The fifth, Virginia, was rent by internal sectionalism. The part lying next to free-soil is a land of mountains and high valleys facing the Ohio Valley and distinct in origin, in economic life, and in customs from the Virginia beyond the watershed which parts Ohio from Atlantic drainage. Supported by federal troops dispatched from adjacent Ohio, the Ohio Basin Virginians seceded from their State and set up as the State of West Virginia within the federal union.

In all the border country from the Delaware estuary to the big bend of the Missouri River, save for the southeast corner of Missouri, cotton is ruled out by the climate, and slavery was not really profitable. In the highlands — Ozark and Appalachian — slavery never had a foothold. Along the eastern mountains a tongue of union sentiment thrust deep into the seceding South, but was rendered ineffectual by the physical and political structure of the area. The highland section of North Carolina is too small to offset the combined piedmont and coastal plain, by this time indissolubly linked in plantation agriculture. In Tennessee the major sectional conflict was reproduced in miniature, and the struggle for supremacy was close. The mountain-and-valley east, a sectional outlier of the North, was offset by the west end of the State, an extension of the cotton-growing Lower Mississippi region. The balance of power resided in the Nashville Basin, the centrally located, traditional core of the State. Its rural economy was a combination of crops characteristic of both sections, on land worked by slave labor. In the end Tennessee seceded. The eastern section, unable to maintain contact with the North, was swept along with the center and west. It opens at its north end to the piedmont of Virginia by way of the James and Roanoke river valleys; at the south end to the piedmont of Georgia and Alabama along the Tennessee River. Cut off by nature from easy access to Kentucky and West Virginia, it was peculiarly in pawn to the South when the crisis arose, because the one railroad then in the district followed the lines of easiest gradients to Virginia, Georgia, and Alabama.

Secession of the eleven southeastern States was followed by a war to maintain the federal union intact. Success of the Union cause may be attributed to the superior resources of the North. Aside from unexpectedly sudden emancipation of the slaves, the only issue permanently settled by the Civil War is the question of secession. It demonstrated that no minority section can withdraw from the federal union against the will of the majority. Instead, it must attain its desires, if at all, by alliances with other sections to give it a majority, at least on the questions involved. An immediate but temporary geopolitical result of the war was the abrupt shift of sectional (regional) domination from the South to the North. Gradually, as new resources have become available, the South has moved to new levels of economic and political power, and the sectional combinations and permutations have long since been resumed. An effect has been the weakening of sectional political solidarity, both north and south, which was a heritage of the Civil War. The solid South in national politics is the expression of racial coherence in the presence of the Negro. It is not different in character from the solid minorities which vex the governments of Europe. It may vanish in elections for representatives of localities, such as congressmen and State legislators, and it does not apply to the border southern States. As a fact, the solid North is almost as much a reality as the solid South. It consists of the northernmost fringe of humid States, and has been uniformly Republican in national elections except in large cities, until very recently.

The dynamic urge of regionalism has continued unabated since the Civil War determined that sections must manage to function within the framework of the existing union. The peopling of the country beyond the line of the Missouri River has introduced new regions characterized by fresh sectional interests. During the sectional conflict between North and South, several transcontinental railroads were at last chartered. With the South in revolt, the southern route of low altitudes (Ch. 15) was inevitably neglected in favor of lines which would have for their terminals cities in territory loyal to the federal government. Political expediency fitted in with regional common sense, because most of the railroad mileage of the country was in the North and during the decade before the Civil War broke out Chicago had become the principal rail center of the nation. From it lines running almost due west made Omaha on the west bank of the Missouri River, and close to the steppes of the Great Plains, the logical place for commencing the new railroad (Fig. 81). The route follows, with only one deviation, the relatively gentle gradients and low passes across the plains and the Rocky Mountains which pioneers had traversed on their way to the goldfields of California. It runs the length of Nebraska and crosses the widest part of Nevada, two territories of small population which had been admitted as States just before and just after the close of the sectional war in order to increase the voting strength of the northern extremists in the federal Congress. It was rightly believed that the railroad would increase population along its line. Its construction was financed by grants of alternate square miles of land in a 20-mile strip on either side of its right-of-way, and this land the promoters proposed to sell to settlers. The Territory of Wyoming was formed after the railroad had brought into the region its first permanent groups of settlers. The line had the further advantage of touching the oasis at the western foot of the Wasatch Mountains, where, a score of years earlier, the Mormons had created a prosperous community based on irrigation agriculture. In spite of its political backing and its easy route through the Rockies, the line crosses much country unproductive of traffic. In central Nebraska it skirts the Sandhills, the most sterile part of the Great Plains. From the Great Salt Lake to the foot of the Sierras it crosses the widest part of the intermontane desert. Its climb across the Sierra Nevada is beset with stiff gradients, and on the pass with very heavy snowfall. In requiring government aid, the first transcontinental line was not unique. No transcontinental line was built without land grants, until finally the Great Northern was financed on wheat along the northern margin of the United States, where there is no intermontane desert and where the steppe can be tilled in moist periods.

The Canadian Pacific is a political double of the Omaha-San Francisco line. It was built under government guarantee to retain for humid, eastern Canada the isolated and well-watered Pacific Coast (Fig. 83). The intervening grassland and forest was purchased by the British government from the Hudson Bay Company in the year the first American transcontinental railroad was completed. The subhumid grassland of the Red River Basin, with its deep, black soil, was opened to settlement and at once became a promising wheat country. An all-Canadian line of rails was undertaken soon after, but a decade was required to push it through the rugged and forested waste

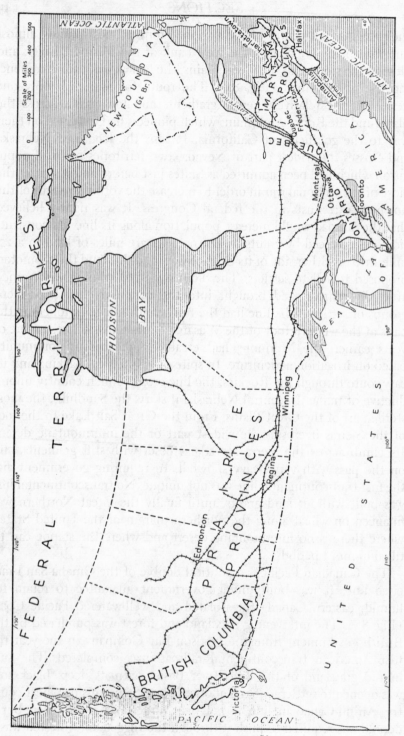

FIG. 83. The separate centers of settlement in Canada.

of ice-scoured crystalline rock between the Georgian Bay and the fertile Red River Basin. There it tapped the rising spring wheat region and was carried to completion on the Pacific Coast two years later. In its crossing of the intricate mountain ranges it surmounts stiff gradients, chosen in preference to the easy pass farther north (later followed by a second Canadian transcontinental railroad) to save mileage, i.e., to reduce cost of construction.

All the transcontinental railroads have to traverse wide belts of country able to provide but little traffic. Nearly all those which have remained solvent derived some advantage from the generous grants of land from the two federal governments. In the long run the barren mileage has to be supported by business originating in the productive regions. In the United States these are the terminal humid Mississippi Basin and Pacific basins. In Canada they are the four separate centers of population — the Pacific shore, the Spring Wheat Prairies, the St. Lawrence lowlands, and the Maritime Provinces. Quite possibly too many lines have been built across the lightly peopled regions, in view of the total available traffic. The last two western systems, completed shortly before the outbreak of the World War, have never paid their way. The one in the United States has been financially embarrassed almost from the day of its inception, as was also the one in Canada until the federal government took it over.

Without the railroads the western half of the North American continent would have been far more difficult to attach to the political systems of the East. The transcontinental rails and the telegraph wires alongside provided comparatively rapid communication between the Pacific Coast settlements and the East and thereby reoriented them to face both east and west, instead of west only, as do the Pacific states of South America.

In the course of this achievement, the new lines opened to settlement all the country between the navigable Great Lakes and Lower Missouri and the hinterland of Pacific ports. Until the coming of the rails, this vast region was virtually inaccessible because its streams were few, fluctuating, and unnavigable, and much of it was cut off from both east and west by lofty ranges of mountains.

In this region territories and States were given surveyed lines for most of their boundaries, instead of the natural features predominant in the East. Use of geodetic lines as boundaries is as old in America as the earliest charters, and of the original constituents of the two federations, only Prince Edward Island and peninsular Nova Scotia are without at least one such boundary. Nevertheless, rivers and bays, mountains, crests, and bounds of local governments superseded a good many of the charter provisions. In the territory between the Ohio, Mississippi, and Great Lakes, the original plan of subdivision called for sixteen units as nearly square as the irregular confines of the area permitted. Later the number was reduced to five. Even on so uniform a plain rivers and lakes were utilized along many lines, chiefly in order to give each new political unit access to navigable waters. Similarly, Florida was truncated in order to give a bit of shoreline to both Mississippi and Alabama. West of the Mississippi River the straight line begins to take precedence, although even there rivers are followed in many cases where rainfall makes them actually or potentially navigable. Beyond the Missouri and Red rivers there are few boundaries other than geodetic lines, and each of the exceptions is related to settlement prior to the railroad. The Rio Grande and Colorado are inherited from Spanish provincial boundaries. The watershed range of the Rockies in northern United States is the historic boundary between French Louisiana and the jointly claimed Anglo-American Northwest Territory. In Canada its continuation marks the limit of the territory trapped by the Hudson Bay Company. The Columbia River boundary indicates pre-railroad settlement in a humid region where all demand access to navigable waters.

On the whole the geodetic boundaries have occasioned rather less litigation and controversy than boundaries marked by natural features. Ready acceptance of a boundary line has little to do with its relation to natural features. The most satisfactory line is one which traverses country sparsely occupied due to meager resources, and which, once surveyed, remains static. The charted lines which reach through deserts and mountains of the West best fulfill these specifications. A potent additional advantage accrues to any sort of boundary which is laid down antecedent to settlement, provided it does not shift thereafter. People coming into an area adjust their lives to the established political line no less than to the climate. Many natural features are less fixed than are surveyed lines, because they may shift irrespective of human volition. This is particularly true of streams.

### SECTIONS IN NORTH AMERICA TODAY

The political subdivisions of the country have always been the standard bearers of sectional interests. Rarely do they correspond exactly with geographic regions.

In Canada the coincidence is considerable, if the international boundary is accepted as a fixed regional limit (Fig. 83). British Columbia is the region of Pacific-facing valleys and the mountains which cut them off from the interior. Quebec is the region of the Lower St. Lawrence, occupied by French-speaking people and severed from Ontario by the neck of crystalline rock that connects the outlying Adirondacks with the great mass of the Canadian North Country. Ontario is the lake peninsula, a triangle of dense population. Between these two provinces the political line lies somewhat east of the infertile zone. It is noteworthy that the district which is politically in Ontario but physically akin to Quebec, is becoming more and more largely French-Canadian. The remaining Canadian Provinces fall into two groups, each of which has acquired regional recognition — expressed as a name in current usage. The three which border the Atlantic and its gulfs are called The Maritime Provinces. The three lying between the rugged crystalline barrier toward Ontario and the Rocky Mountain barrier toward British Columbia, are termed The Prairie Provinces. The five populated regions of Canada are therefore readily distinguished by their character, and are marked off from each other by almost unviolated barriers of wilderness. Their regionalism expresses itself constantly in sectional voting in the federal parliament. Talk of secession is not uncommon, especially in the terminal regions.

In the United States the regions are neither so fixed nor so sharply set apart. Only one State, California, corresponds at all closely to a regional unit, this being the North American area of dry-subtropical climate. The sectional character of California is well known. Elsewhere sectionalism may be deduced from repeated segregation of the same States in successive political crises. This repetition is classic in New England, which began to band together within two decades of the first settlement. Its members stood shoulder to shoulder during the Revolution. When the Second War against Great Britain was being prosecuted, the New England States sent delegates to a " convention " which proposed amendments to the federal Constitution and threatened secession. In the successive crises over slavery, New England led the opposition to the South. In recent years it has been customary for New England governors and representatives of various interests to meet regularly or on call to discuss matters of common interest. Even the urbanization of the southern part of the region has not destroyed the sectional community of feeling in these six northeastern States.

Sectionalism of the South reached its climax in the Civil War. Twice before its appeal to arms it had expressed its unity in conspicuous political utterances. In remonstrance against federal laws which abrogated the right of free speech, Jefferson and Madison advanced the rights of the States to nullify obnoxious laws. These statements were embodied in resolutions of the legislatures of Kentucky and Virginia, respectively, at the end of the 18th century. A generation later nullification of federal laws by States was transformed into a mode of action by Calhoun, a South Carolinian, in a report adopted by the legislature of his State in protest against an unpopular tariff. On this platform was erected the doctrine of the right of secession, first applied by the same South Carolina. After both nullification and secession were stifled by the strong hand of war, the South was confirmed in its sectionalism by the presence of the Negro, and by poverty induced by warfare and emancipation of the slaves in an agricultural region where soil was rapidly deteriorating. In recent years manufacturing, specialized fruit and vegetable growing, and tourism have furnished the South with new bases for creating a life interwoven with that of the rest of the nation. Its sectionalism is therewith being modified.

Of the clearly defined major regions of the country, the humid northern interior has displayed less flamboyant sectionalism than any other. Its large size, its central position and ready connections with other sections — east, south, and west — and its abundant and varied resources have combined to make of it the heart of the nation in the political as well as in the geographic sense. Its primary need has always been improved transportation to the outside world, and for roads, canals, and railroads it has looked to the federal government. Only in the opening years of exploitation, while its expanding frontier fell short of adequate transportation, and yet had to depend on distant markets for its one or two crops, has this region as a whole fallen under the spell of political panaceas for economic growing pains. As the economic base broadened, such shiny schemes lost their appeal.

Farther west, in the regions where insufficient rainfall and remoteness make a single crop the economic mainstay, the hope of improving the economic lot by political means alternately lies dormant and bursts into clamor.

The semiarid steppe is incessantly appealing to the federal government for legal surcease of its difficulties — difficulties which arise from changes in density of population, new material technology, and cyclic changes in the character of human occupance that occur as a result of the occupance itself. Originally sparsely inhabited, the steppe came to be used by Amerinds as nomadic grazing country as soon as they obtained the European horse. Under the conditions of nature in such climates, water supplies run dry before the herbage has been over-grazed, and the migrants are forced on before they destroy nature's balance. The white man made laws to encourage settlement in this region. He dug wells, established permanent ranches and cities, and above all shot the country through with railroads. The strong demand for cheap money for building the railroads and establishing the home-steads created vociferous sectional movements. The Greenback Party of the 1870s and the Granger movement a bit later were centered on the frontier of the humid region, in alliance with the steppe. The drier regions came into their own with Populism and a demand for a bime-tallic or even a paper standard of coinage in the 1890s.

Once the new technology, introduced from the humid lands of their invention, had been established, evil effects appeared in the semiarid landscape. It permitted overgrazing, and even stimulated it by furnishing a vast outside market for livestock products. In favored districts, at least during normal periods of more than average rainfall, wheat came to be grown. As good fortune gave way to bad, sectional politics again arose, this time in the Farmer-Labor movement at the close of the World War, when the price of wheat fell from its wartime heights. This movement has been longer-lived than its predecessors, because the adversity has been more prolonged. Post-war prosperity was followed by worldwide economic depression. This synchronized with destruction of the natural herbage by the teeth and hoofs of ex-cess stock and exposure of bare soil by the plow. As a consequence cropless years and dust storms which destroyed the soil plagued the country during the succeeding normal period of less than average rain-fall. Many inhabitants have been compelled to emigrate, and a cycle of human occupance has been brought to a close. Recently federal laws have been formulated to restrict grazing to the carrying capacity of so much of the area as remains in the public domain, and plowing and grazing on private holdings may in future be similarly regulated.

In the desert region between the mountains, sectionalism is nulli-fied by the conflicting interests of mining, grazing, and irrigation agri-culture, and by the close economic alliances of each of these interests with market regions in other parts of the country. Wool growers are affiliated with manufacturers of the Northeast, cattle grazers with meat packers of the Middle West, miners with factories near the Great Lakes or the Atlantic Seaboard, and fruit farmers with the urbanized market regions. The Pacific Coast draws continually nearer to the humid East. As it puts more and more of its arable land into fruits and vegetables for the eastern market, and as it attracts an increasing number of seasonal tourists and retired persons from lands of cold winters and monotonous landscapes, its dependence on the nation's ecumene grows.

Sectionalism in the broad view of regional antithesis, is often masked by internal clashes arising from the existence of subregions. Nearly every intermontane State contains the three economic interests — grazing, irrigation tillage, and metal mining — generally in separate districts. The opposition of the southern Appalachian highlands to the lowland portions of their respective States has already been discussed.

Every State which includes one or more large cities tends to develop a sectionalism as between urban and rural areas, or a rivalry between two sections, each containing a large city. This is often accentuated by the common practice of making streams and lakes serve as State boundaries. Because they and the ocean also serve as arteries of commerce, most of the major cities of the country have grown up on or near State lines. Excentric location stresses their failure to typify the State. In Massachusetts, Michigan, Illinois, Wisconsin, Louisiana, Nebraska, and Oregon the metropolis frequently finds itself opposed by the rest of the State. New York City counterbalances and clashes with the whole " Up-state," even though the interests are dominantly urban from one end to the other. Rival cities lead rival political factions in Pennsylvania, Ohio, Missouri, Washington, and California.

In both the United States and Canada the complex pulling and hauling of the sections and subsections in their unending efforts to obtain their individual ends has proved a salutary check upon excessive centralization of political power. The danger of centralization in areas so large and so diverse as these nations is real. Even the vaunted transportation and communication which has so markedly shrunk both countries, especially the United States, leaves them distinctly divided into regions. So long as regions exist, sectional clashes are bound to occur. The large degree of regional autonomy permitted in the federal organization has been the secret of political success in both nations. Substitution of centralized government can work only if the governing group effectively represents the relative strength of all the sections. That such a governing group can live in the central capital and preserve its regional diversity has not been demonstrated, either in North America or elsewhere.

## North American Capitals

Political authority of the two national federations of North America and their component States and provinces, nearly threescore in number, is exercised from capitals which profusely exemplify requirements of states in process of expansion and diversification.

The initial settlements along the seaboard became *ipso facto* the capitals of the nuclear colonies, as the landfalls of European political authority on the North American continent. All were ports and in every case it was hoped that a favored spot had been chosen. In the colonies which persisted, surprisingly few removals were made throughout the colonial era. In each of the exceptional cases, exceptional circumstances were responsible for the shift. The first settlement in Maryland, St. Mary's on the drowned St. Mary's River, six miles above its confluence with the Potomac, lies near the southern tip of the domain (Fig. 77). Efforts to remove the capital to a more central site bore fruit after the revolution in England which unseated Catholic James II. St. Mary's, a Catholic settlement, lost out to Annapolis, a Puritan foundation which had the obvious advantage of lying on the Chesapeake Bay, central thoroughfare of the colony, about midway between its head and the southern Maryland boundary. In Virginia the insular site of Jamestown, subject to erosion by the James River, after nearly a century was abandoned for Williamsburg nearby on a level plain central in the narrow peninsula between the James and York rivers. New Jersey's capital migrated uneasily with the shifting fortunes of the colony (Fig. 78). The original seat of government, Elizabeth(town) on Newark Bay remained sole capital only a score of years, although the legislature occasionally met there in subsequent decades. Partition of the colony created two capitals, one at Perth Amboy on tidewater protected by Staten Island, the other at Burlington on the Delaware some distance below the head of navigation. When Great Britain took Acadia from the French and renamed it Nova Scotia, Port Royal on the coast of the fertile but recessed Fundy Basin was abandoned for Halifax, a strong defense point on a deep harbor opening directly off the Atlantic (Fig. 83).

Toward the end of the 18th century a general transfer of capitals from the seaboard to inland sites occurred. The new stations lay along the border between the Tidewater and the Old West. Desertion of the coast was evidence that intimate connection with the mother country was at an end. Selection of the margin of the " West " signalized that colonial servitude had vanished and recognized that an expanding frontier had to be courted lest it secede.

As the New West was staked out, seats of territorial administration fluctuated but tended to remain close to the center of population. When the territories one by one qualified as States, the sites selected for capitals were almost invariably central. In the States occupied by a more or less even spread of settlers, the locations lie close to the centers of both population and area. Along the northern fringe of the country coniferous forests on sterile, sandy soils repel settlement, even today. The capitals of those States lie well to the south of the areal centers, although close to the cores of dense population. This rule holds for all the provinces of Canada except Prince Edward Island, which because of its shape and uniform fertility can have a central capital, and Alberta, where the capital lies near the north margin of the ecumene.

With the organization of the steppe of the Great Plains into States the same principle held. In the range of States from Texas to North Dakota, three capitals stand well east of the areal centers and within the humid regions of dense population. The other three lie not far from the areal centers. In two of these the population spreads the length of the State and the capital is reasonably central to the ecumene; only in South Dakota does area take precedence over population. Washington and Oregon likewise exhibit the seat of government central in the humid ecumene.

In the dry and mountainous States of the West the capitals are on irrigable lands, and generally occupy sites in alluvial valleys or piedmonts. Centrality to either area or population appears not to figure in these vast units of small and scattered communities. Both Florida and Louisiana use capitals far off center with respect to both area and population. Each lay within its ecumene at the time it was selected. Tallahassee is reputed to be the spot reached by rivals representing West Florida and East Florida who started out at St. Augustine and Pensacola and raced along the Spanish trail until they met.

In only ten or a dozen cases is the capital also the commercial metropolis of its political unit. On the contrary some capitals, chiefly in the mountainous west, do not even lie on main lines of railroads. Only one, Atlanta, Georgia, appears to have been selected with reference to its function as a railroad center. In that case the temporary military government also influenced the choice. A considerable number of capital cities have become railroad centers in part because, when railroads came to be built, they were drawn to the capitals by the weight of State governments.

The two federal capitals exemplify a novel phenomenon — a seat of government selected for the purpose without regard to economic considerations. Both Washington, D. C., and Ottawa, Canada, lie in critical political boundary zones.

Ottawa was chosen to avoid ill feeling which would have resulted had any of the four candidate cities been selected. It stands on the Ontario side of the boundary between Upper and Lower Canada (Ontario and Quebec), the two chief Canadian provinces at the time of the federation. It likewise marks the edge of French-speaking territory within Ontario as well as in Quebec, and is divided into two almost equal linguistic sections. Therefore it is as nearly neutral ground as can be found. It lies near the northern margin of the most considerable population in the country, but its offside position is justified by its location on principal railroad lines leading to all the other provinces. It has the further merit of marking the end of a canal connecting Lake Ontario with the Ottawa River. This canal was built as a military measure to give the Great Lakes an all-Canadian water outlet.

Washington is on the Fall Line — demarcation between two principal societies at the time of its selection. It stands almost midway between the southern and northern boundaries of the original States and only 50 miles from the Mason and Dixon Line, boundary between slave soil and free. Its summer climate is hotter than the optimum for urban life, but hot summers cannot be avoided at any central location east of the Rockies. Supplements to United States territory and the growth of population throughout the west have left Washington very excentric, both areally and in the ecumene. Today a point between Lafayette, Indiana, and Topeka, Kansas, would split the difference between population and areal centers. On the other hand the urbanization of the Northeast has left Washington on the border between a dominantly commercial and manufactural region and a region largely rural. In view of the increasingly important part played by city and country in sectional rivalries, the borderline location of Washington in this respect is fortunate.

## CHAPTER SEVENTEEN

# Earth Impress on Political Thought

THE political structure erected by every group of people is, ideally, a device for facilitating the economic and social life of the community. It is most successful when it neatly fits the conditions of the natural environment in the area where it functions.

This is not to say that political order is merely an adaptation to nature. The preceding chapters have shown that in every region the mode of government results from a concurrence of forces, environmental and human. Moreover, the active agents are generally the technological equipment and the social attitudes of the inhabitants, brought to bear upon more or less passive nature by the enterprise of individuals and groups. Among the active elements political concepts rank high, perhaps first. Their cogency is indicated by the heated arguments so readily generated by political topics of conversation. In the schisms which have cleft social groups in twain, the last tie to break is invariably the political. The Roman Empire was maintained as a fiction for centuries after the fact of political unity had vanished. In the bitter antagonisms of the Protestant Reformation people sacrificed their homes and their kin, but not their state, which as a unit either remained in the Roman Catholic fold or adhered to one of the new sects. It was the débâcle of the government that precipitated the French Revolution, some time after the economic causes of it had been formulated into a program of revolt. Regional antithesis between the northern and the southern United States of America cracked and broke one symbol of unity after another, but civil war was postponed until the structure of government melted in the heat of dissension and recrystallized along sectional lines.

While recognizing the power and vitality of political concepts and forms, it must be kept in mind that the natural environment ceaselessly conditions the operation of all human forces. Political forms and concepts are among the institutions and attitudes overtly or subtly modified by the compulsion to function within the limits set by nature. As material technology advances or recedes, the scale of political operations changes and the incidence of conditioning nature alters. It never disappears.

## CONTRASTING LEGAL SYSTEMS

Every political system is the summation of laws which people make in order to extract a livelihood from their habitat. It follows that the political concepts held by any group derive from their natural environment. The more niggardly and harsh the natural environment, the narrower the limits set for political operations. The doctrine of environmental determinism receives the support that gives it verisimilitude from backward societies which are narrowly circumscribed in their environmental opportunities. Most of these people are in some degree migratory with the seasons, following a mode of life forced upon them by nature. Such folk wander from place to place and live under a political order based on the unfixed human unit, rather than on a fixed piece of territory. The character of their migrations varies in detail with their natural environment.

Amerinds in the unexplored nooks of the rainy Amazon Basin and the most backward tribes of hot, humid Africa and New Guinea follow game, fish, and the fruiting of their forest fastnesses. Desert dwellers from Mongolia to the Sahara migrate with the sporadic rains which provide forage and drink for their flocks and herds. The extension of French power across the western Sahara, of Soviet Russia into inner Asia, and of Italy in the central Sahara, has broken up the nomads' practice of raiding sedentary settlements and trade caravans, but it has effectively altered the life of the people only in the small spots where nature can be persuaded by drilling of wells or extension of railroads to provide the means of sedentary livelihood. Outside such spots the roving desert folk retain their allegiance to the tribal mode of government. The groups of people scattered along the Arctic coasts of North America and Eurasia have been left to their own ways less because they are difficult to reach than because their resources are too meager to invite domination. The United States, Canada, Denmark, Norway, Sweden, Finland, and Russia claim political suzerainty over the varied Arctic groups, but none of these countries has interfered with their mode of life, beyond introducing firearms and some diseases. The Eskimo move at will along the Arctic coasts of North America. The Mongoloids of northernmost Siberia have been brought into contact with the outside world only with the attempt of Soviet Russia to expand its ecumene into this harsh wilderness. With the demarcation of linear boundaries between Norway, Sweden, and Finland, international treaties guaranteed to the transhumant Lapps the right to transgress the national lines, and as the Scandinavian frontier has pushed northward, encroachment into the Laplanders' range has been accompanied by revisions of the treaties, in the direction of specifying seasonal limits for migrations and of fixing areal limits for nomadic groups.

In spite of interference from more favored parts of the earth, most nomadic and transhumant people continue to live a life which consists of one everlasting moving-day. Their productive property is restricted to the most mobile of natural resources, animals. True, these beasts consume herbage and water, and so depend on the same elements as does the livestock of sedentary populations. But their masters cannot occupy permanently the vast acreage needed to maintain the flocks and herds. Able to subsist only by repeated removals, these wandering peoples, whether in rain forest, in deserts, on mountain ranges, or along the Arctic Ocean, keep their menage down to essentials. Home and its entire equipment can be packed on the backs of a few animals. And with the home moves the law and the state. Government is tribal, and the member of a tribe is subject to its law wherever he may be.

Communication with the outside world is difficult, slow, and irregular, in spite of recent innovations of European governments which lay claim to the territory over which the tribes move. Legal modes prevailing in most such areas do not touch outsiders, apart from adventurous spirits who go out of their way to travel in those regions. The one exception is the belt of dry lands which reaches across Africa and Asia. Inhabited by true nomads, this vast zone lies between the cores of occidental and oriental civilization, and casts its nomadic, tribal government between their sedentary, territorial systems. Throughout the whole broad and uniform zone, with insignificant exceptions, the tribal mode of government has been stabilized and integrated by the adoption of Moslem law. Evolved in the desert, Moslem law eminently suits the conditions found there. It provides for whatever degree of political unity strong chieftains may from time to time assume over the scattered tribes, and it gives their political ambitions powerful and permanent support from religious solidarity. The Koran is both the Holy Book and a guiding star of government for Moslem society. As a political instrument it is a standing and familiar negation of the concept of government held by sedentary populations the world over.

In passing from niggardly environments to those better endowed, the conditioning effects of nature on political concepts become less clear-cut. Throughout the rainy low latitudes, and even in many parts where seasons of drouth alternate with the downpours, indigenous society has been organized tribally from time immemorial. This apparently conforms to the practice of shifting the location of villages in such environments once in a few years, when the easily exhausted soil accessible to the settlement has been depleted and must be left to nature's reclamation. Most of these regions, lying as they do in low latitudes, have been subjected only recently to contact with the concept of territoriality. Yet already the ideal of the state as coincident with a fixed territory has begun to take root. Improved methods of farming and fixed railroad transportation have diminished the amount of shifting, both of crops and of villages. Landholding in common by the community, an essential feature of tribal government, is giving way to individual properties. The notion of fixed political boundary lines was not suggested by the natural environment nor thought of by indigenes. But when imported as a part of European administration, the fixed line is as adaptable to natural conditions within the tropics as anywhere else. Finally, the tribes of the rain forest and jungles are separated by impassable wilderness and have remained segregated from each other in customs and in beliefs.

Many believe that sedentary society, with its concept of territorial limits to the state, evolved on irrigated farms in oases. Certain it is that early and apparently unrelated sedentary groups arose in deserts of the low and lower-middle latitudes — in the basins of the Nile, the Tigris-Euphrates, the Indus, the Hwang-ho, the Colorado, and on the coast of Peru. The preciousness of irrigated land, the hard work needed to prepare it, and the permanent use of the same fields, perennially fertilized by flood-borne silt, must have compelled attention to landmarks and bounds. In any event, the state as a territorial unit is associated with sedentary societies, whether in irrigated regions or in humid middle and subtropical latitudes.

The territorial state coincides with a fixed portion of the earth's surface, and its laws operate within that area. Persons finding themselves within the prescribed area are *ipso facto* subject to its laws; conversely any who leave the territory leave the state, presumably to enter another. This concept of government is made possible by the continuous occupance of the given area by a single group of people. It is made necessary by the immovable but easily destroyed property which is the basis of sedentary human existence. Foremost among fixed possessions are crops, which annually provide much of the food, some of the clothing, and more or less of the shelter for the population. Tree crops and

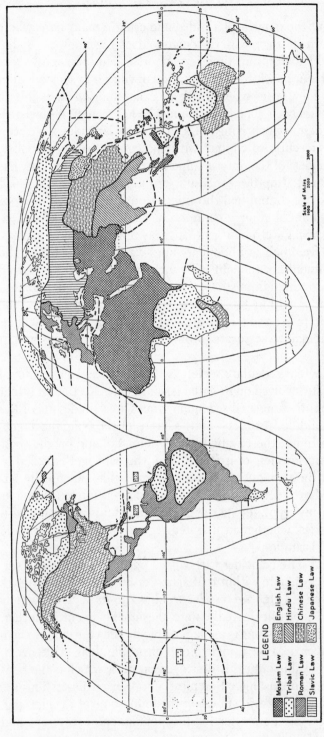

FIG. 84. The earth's legal codes.

Except for Tibet and interior Liberia the tribal codes have been overlaid by either the Roman, English, Slavic, or Japanese law. To a less degree this holds also for Moslem law in areas controlled by European states. In India Moslem and Hindu law are intermingled.

Suggested by a map by John H. Wigmore: "Present Day Legal Systems of the World"; Geographical Review 19 (1929), facing page 120.
The base is the homolosine projection, used by courtesy of the University of Chicago Press (J. Paul Goode's series of base maps; H. M. Leppard, editor.)

LEGEND

Moslem Law
Tribal Law
Roman Law
Slavic Law

English Law
Hindu Law
Chinese Law
Japanese Law

natural forests are as vulnerable as annuals and take longer to replace. Other resources are critical in varying degrees. Domestic water supply may be interrupted or defiled. Minerals and soil are less easily annihilated, although the World War proved that even they are subject to partial or complete destruction, at least in small areas. Buildings are most vulnerable of all and represent concentrations of human investment. Within the edifices themselves much of their equipment is fixed — plumbing, heating, and lighting systems, heavy machinery, and embellishment, such as sculpture in stone or in wood and wall painting. As material technology advances, the stake in fixed property increases. The city is the climax of this trend, and the modern city, sustained by routes of transportation and means of communication for the most part fixed and readily destroyed, is the tenderest plant on earth. Little wonder that a society possessing fixed investment should protect it by territorial law.

Every sedentary society does evolve such law. Even in the Old-World desert the large oases have codes differing from the law of the circumambient nomadic tribes. In the humid regions of Eurasia several legal codes, ranking with the Moslem legal system of the deserts, have evolved into systems. Three systems exist today on each side of the arid belt (Fig. 84).

In South and East Asia distinct systems were devised in the two extensive lowlands, China and India. In the course of time each of these spread into the intervening region of local codes. On the offshore islands of Japan a legal code arose, differentiated from those of the mainland. In Europe the Mediterranean World rose to great power under Roman Law which spread into northern and central Europe, supplanting local codes. In eastern Europe, Slavic law has stood its ground. Insular England devised its own system, very much as did Japan off the opposite coast of Eurasia. In detail each of these new systems is found to have many features which grew naturally out of the environment of its origin. Nevertheless in growing from a local code to the stature of a system spread over different natural regions, each became to a degree cosmopolitan.

With expansion overseas from Western Europe, the two systems there in force were carried to the far ends of the earth. Where settlement colonies of Europeans were planted overseas, chiefly in the middle latitudes, the Roman or the English law prevails, altered only as it proved to be unworkable in novel environments. Where European government has been imposed on small and disseminated tribes, as generally in the low latitudes, the local code may be supplanted, or it may be retained as private law for the indigenes, whereas public law and private law for persons of European extraction are Roman or English, as the ruling power determines. In East Asia the Roman law and in South Asia the English law have contributed some features to the systems there in vogue. Parts of India and the East Indian archipelago had already been invaded by Moslem law before European systems were introduced. Both the innovations have left their marks. It is evident that the spread of legal systems is part and parcel of the extension of political domination, and also of strong economic influence even when unaccompanied by the imposition of sovereignty.

A by-product of this situation is the legal status called extra-territoriality. In regions where government was supported by local law only, Europeans overseas have generally been able to establish themselves without let or hindrance, in port towns if no further inland. They naturally set up their own legal system in the districts thus preempted. In parts of the world fortified by well-articulated indigenous legal systems, the native authorities resent the creation of European sovereignties within their own. At the same time Europeans are usually unwilling to abide by decisions handed down under other codes, which rightly or wrongly they consider less conducive to justice than their own. In such places political conquest may guarantee European law to Europeans, as the English law in India and Dutch (Roman) law in Java, while the conquered people continues to be governed under its own code. Failing of political conquest, treaties may be negotiated whereby Europeans are permitted to set up their own courts with jurisdiction over nationals owing allegiance to states of European origin. Such extra-territorial courts have been in operation in many countries south and east of the limit of Roman law. One by one they have been abolished as the countries have adopted legal safeguards adequate to secure justice to nationals and foreigners alike. Today few remain.

The abandonment of extra-territoriality has been one manifestation of a pronounced swing toward uniformity of the world's legal systems. Without discarding traditional form and procedure, the more parochial systems have enlarged their scope, especially in matters touching world trade. This is in line with legal procedure generally — to expand with new needs. Thus English law during the 16th and 17th centuries incorporated maritime law, and since then has continued to parallel the growing unity of an interdependent, worldwide, economic society.

In the years since the World War this tendency for legal systems to march together has been thrown into reverse in some parts of the world by the upsurge of unbridled nationalism. Where, as in Italy, this movement is a result of an unsatisfactory internal structure of government, and finds inadequate support in the moderate and ill-balanced natural resources of the country, it would seem out of tune with nature and unlikely to continue unabated for very long. Moreover, the age-long practice of Roman law there tends to retard the adoption of a legal system fundamentally at variance with general occidental practice.

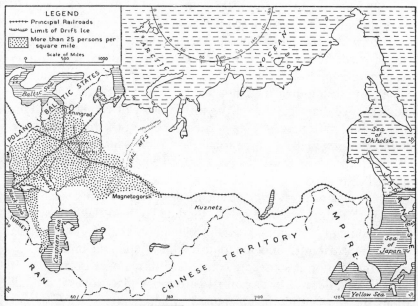

FIG. 85. The Soviet state.
For the natural vegetation of the area, see Fig. 8.

In Eastern Europe exclusive nationalism has more hope of becoming established as a permanent ideal. In so far as it succeeds, the legal system is bound to be modified accordingly. Recognizing Germany as a transition country, both drawn toward and repelled from Western Europe (Ch. 7), it would be rash to predict the effect on German (Roman) law of its present move in the direction of unrestrained nationalism.

The nation in that quarter most likely to achieve its goal is Soviet Russia. Under the flag of the hammer and sickle is aggregated one-sixth of the earth's land surface (Fig. 85). The Russian state lies along a margin of the inhabited earth, cut off from neighbors on its long north coastline by perennial ice, that most formidable of terrestrial barriers. Much of the country has little or no present value, being bleak and boggy Arctic tundra, scattering, stunted forest, or waterless desert. The fraction readily utilizable — a triangle based on Russia's western neighbors with its apex one-third of the way across Siberia — is a land of violent contrasts between hot summer and cold winter, and of monotonous plains, fertile only in the southern half. Here and there the Soviet lands are well endowed with water power, and with coal, petroleum, and iron — the mineral triad on which modern industrial society rests. No humid area so vast can fail to comprise the variety of products needed for a large measure of self-sufficiency. If the denizens of Soviet Russia are willing to stay at home and accept the rather low standard of living imposed by the limitations of their resources, they may continue to experiment unhindered with any form of government they please.

The basic structure of the Russian legal system is Slavic, somewhat modified since the beginning of the 18th century by Roman law. This system has been imposed on many tribal groups of the tundra and the desert. (Only 77 percent of the total population is Slavic, but no non-Slav group comprises more than 4,000,000 people, and they all live in scattered districts outside the ecumene of the Soviet state.) The government is making every effort to anchor desert nomads and wandering groups within the forest and on the tundra. To them the legal system of the dominant Slav group is applied whenever possible, although as in all such cases it must undergo some modification in the process.

No other nation is so deeply committed to national isolation as is Soviet Russia. Because of its natural barrier boundary zones it is of all nations the most nearly invulnerable to military attack, except at its eastern and western ends. Both these borders are being converted into military zones. From a strip 1500 to 3000 feet wide along the frontier, the populace is being moved inland, thus clearing the border for military maneuvers. To guard against loss of vital industries, should the boundary defenses fail, manufacturing cities are being developed deep in the interior. The state has established automobile works at Gorki (formerly Nizhni Novgorod), 300 miles east of Moscow, the capital, and tractor works at Stalingrad, a similar distance east of the Donetz coalfield. A steel center has been begun on the iron mines at Magnitogorsk, on the Asiatic side of the Ural Mountains near their southern end. Another is planned in the coal basin of Siberian Kuznetsk, 1500 miles still farther east. Russian armies, if compelled to retreat from either the western or the eastern border, will fall back on their sources of supply, and progressively shorten their lines of communication.

The resources within the Soviets are suitably located and sufficient in amount and variety to make feasible the isolationist policy which has been pursued by the government for more than a score of years. The

Soviet state is founded on a political philosophy directly opposed to the political philosophy of the rest of the Occident, and a permanently isolated Russia is almost certain to evolve a legal system having many distinctive features. Its interior location and its vast size make Russia the natural protagonist of the centripetal point of view, which tends to take political form in a self-sufficient nation. This is diametrically opposed to the centrifugal view of maritime Western Europe. The clash of outlooks rests on a permanent base — the distribution of lands and seas. In the long run it promises to generate one of the most irreconcilable fundamental issues in the political affairs of mankind. This issue has already appeared from time to time, but it has never been sharply drawn, apart from other opposed views. It underlay the struggle between Napoleonic, continental Europe and maritime Great Britain. A century later it figured in the World War. In both cases Russia was arrayed on the side of the maritime powers, and Central Europe, in the transition zone between maritime and interior Europe, stood for the centripetal political machine which unalloyed is represented by Russia alone.

## NATURE AND LAWS

If legal systems in broad outlines are images of the regions in which they function, sometimes faithful and sometimes distorted, individual laws in detail mirror the society and the habitat by and in which they are created. Because humanity occupies its habitat dynamically, laws tend to become outmoded. When this occurs they are usually revoked, sometimes they are disregarded, occasionally they are given new meaning.

Studies in the mutual interplay of geography and the law are few and deal with small and specific instances. Many more are needed to furnish an adequate base for comprehensive treatment of the subject as a whole. This approach to such a treatment must await the accumulation of years. A less precise approach suggests itself as the survey of a code or other specific body of law in its environmental setting over a period of years. Such a survey ought to disclose modifications of the legal outlook that evolve with the passage of time and the concurrent shifting in values of the natural environment. At the same time it ought to uncover instances in which the law has modified the utilization of earth resources. An attempt to outline this sort of survey follows, in the form of a consideration of the constitution of the United States of America in the changing setting of its 150 years of existence.

EARTH CONDITIONS AND THE CONSTITUTION OF THE UNITED STATES

The impress of earth conditions on a fixed body of law is nowhere so well exemplified as in North America, particularly the United States.

From the outset, settlers of British origin on the American continent made a practice of banding together to carry on corporate life in emergencies. When the Pilgrims made their landfall at Cape Cod, they found themselves outside the area granted by the charter under which they had sailed. They promptly united themselves into a body politic to maintain orderly government. This " Mayflower Compact " was succeeded by many another spontaneous political agreement. Cohesion of small and isolated groups of people amid the uncertainties and possible dangers of new regions is natural, because it obeys the law of self-preservation. But repeatedly American pioneers adopted well-planned and effective regulations for self-government with an earnest ease which betokens a familiar habit of thought as well as the urgency of the frontier. The tendency to band together for a common purpose appears to have grown out of a political philosophy of the times — the individualistic and self-determinant attitude which evolved along with the expansion of mental horizons introduced by the Renaissance and the Discoveries. While all Europe was affected by the new knowledge, " rugged individualism " in political affairs is most conspicuous among the peoples who, pursuant to precepts of John Calvin, habituated themselves to the making of covenants — with each other, with their leaders, and with their God.

To men accustomed to live by covenants based on faith in inherent rights of the individual, orderly government lay ready to hand whenever and wherever needed. It is perhaps not a coincidence that the extreme frontier, the zone habitually troubled by fighting, has been from the first a favorite abode of sectarian individualists who readily pooled their interests in political covenants to match their religious creed.

In reciprocation the frontier has ever been a potent supporter of democracy, both in colonial times and later. So long as free land remained to be had for little more than the price of hard work and initiative, it was impossible to cast society into a mold of economic and social classes. On the frontier itself everybody was rated on his ability; in the older and settled country emigration to the frontier kept labor at a premium, stimulated the invention of labor-saving devices, and forced the established members of the community to admit to their ranks capable individuals from all walks of life. Thereby the democratic ideals bred by the frontier indirectly enforced a degree of democracy upon the older settlements, preventing them from crystallizing economically and socially, and insuring the perpetuation of democratic forms of government.

The growth of continent-wide democracy out of the variety of political forms established at the outset of settlement along the Atlantic seaboard germinated in the colonies from the moment of their foundation. Whether organized in the form of a proprietary monopoly or as a stock company, every British North American colony during the first century of settlement was primarily organized in order to trade. No matter what the formal charter under which they were licensed to engage in trade, the early emigrants to the new lands were forced to rely on their own capacities for social and political organization, as well as for economic prosperity. In the case, first of Massachusetts Bay, later of some other colonies, the charter was brought out from England and served as an instrument of government, a sort of constitutional frame within the stated limits of which the local assemblies made laws and the local authorities administered government. In this process the intention of the charter might be altered, especially when conditions of the new land compelled the authorities to construe it loosely or else face annihilation.

Yet it must not be supposed that government in the new world was merely the hammering out of formal charters or spontaneous agreements on the anvil of a novel natural environment. The instruments under which pioneers took up life after crossing the ocean were generally cherished as evidences of contact with the familiar world left behind. In so far as harsh nature permitted, the new life was fitted to the imported frame of government. Thus the charters came to stand for stability in the body politic, and they were respected so far as possible. As a rule the legislation of colonial representative assemblies was drawn to conform to the charter. Generally the governor, as representative of the proprietor, company, or king, had the power to veto legislative acts. Sometimes he did so on the ground that the act ran counter to the charter. Occasionally the courts, in deciding cases under the laws, found them irreconcilable with provisions of the charter. In such cases the charter took precedence over the legislation.

In another respect the colonial charters acquired special sanctity which laid the foundations for government under a written constitution decades later. They came to be regarded as the bulwark of local political privileges and " natural rights " against usurpations by the home authorities in England. In the efforts to keep their charters the colonies lost more often than they won, because single-handed they were no match for the mother country. Threats of ever closer supervision from overseas finally led thirteen adjacent colonies to band together to form a compact in the same free fashion as their pioneer forefathers and contemporaries had been wont to do. The articles of confederation proposed were intended to be fundamental law for the united colonies, just as the charters had served as fundamental law for the several individual colonies. Both as a device for carrying on unified government and as a means of organizing a state independent of established sovereignties, the Declaration of Independence which launched the revolt against the mother country and the Articles of Confederation under which it was concluded closely paralleled the current political philosophy of covenanters in the British Isles. Isolation from the homeland gave scope to the political tenets these documents advanced, and long practice in self-government on a problem-posing frontier gave them reality.

The original frame of government adopted by the revolting United States turned out to be practically powerless, once the fighting was over. It was superseded by a more wieldy instrument, called a Constitution. The nation which adopted it consisted of a long, narrow string of settlements east of the Appalachians, which possessed jointly the vast unpeopled trans-Appalachian interior between the Great Lakes, Florida, and the Mississippi River (Fig. 79). Some of the States which combined to set up the Constitution were small, others were large; some were exclusively agricultural, others were partially urban; some were devoted to patriarchal plantation agriculture using Negro-slave labor, others were lands of small farmers and tradesmen where both slaves and Negroes were rarities. Out of the compromises of conflicting interests such as these the Constitution was formulated. Because of its moderation and its ambiguous phrasing, it was adopted by states which were still so jealous of their individual sovereignty that they immediately wrote in an amendment reserving to the several States all powers not specifically delegated to the central government.

After the incorporation of amendments entailed in its adoption and a few to legalize necessary changes in procedure, it proved extraordinarily difficult to amend the document formally. Nevertheless, it soon had to be amended or discarded, because the country had an almost unequaled opportunity to spread across a vast area of diverse regions, in an epoch when material technology was advancing at a pace never before approached. No human ingenuity could have provided for such undreamed alterations in the national life. The Constitution has been retained as the frame of reference for the nation's laws by the device of construing its provisions loosely. This procedure was not established without much political friction, because for three-quarters of a century Americans did not realize that the territorial and economic expansion they desired was impossible under strict construction of the document. The outcry and kicking are now seen to have been growing pains, natural to a lusty and thriving infant nation whenever it felt the pinch of a political garment its economic body was incessantly outgrowing.

Fortunately the Constitution provided the basis for a federal system geared to any conceivable expansion, at least within middle latitudes. This is the provision that the representative lawmaking body may admit new States on a parity with the original constituent members. It was not foreseen that in order to create working unity among the States the federal government would have to exceed its specified powers. All three branches of the federal government severally or jointly found themselves forced to interpret their prerogatives broadly.

Loose construction was made inevitable by the astonishing success of the embryo United States in obtaining the "west," an unsettled region two and a half times the area of the original States, as a condition of peace after the Revolution. The ink on the last legislative ratification needed to put the Constitution in operation was scarcely dry before pioneers in the new country, cut off from Atlantic seaboard markets by range on range of mountains heavily forested and tangled with underbrush, were threatening secession unless their natural outlet via the Mississippi drainage was opened to them by political means. Events marched swiftly to their conclusion, and the federal executive, without constitutional warrant, found himself in possession of the mouth of the Mississippi and the major part of the grassy Great Plains to boot, a land very unlike the forested country that theretofore had comprised English-speaking North America. The legislative Congress appropriated the sum needed to complete the purchase, and so took its turn at loose construction. At one leap the United States had more than doubled in area.

The impulse to acquire territory grew like a rolling snowball, and the tropical flats of Florida, the deserts and lofty, bare mountains of the West, the Mediterranean climate of California, and the giant forests of the rainy Puget Sound region were all added within two generations of the inauguration of the Constitution (Fig. 81). The habit of territorial expansion had become second nature, and the United States had become ten times the size of the original thirteen.

At this juncture a vault across British territory to Alaska seemed to many to be unconstitutional, but was finally justified on the ground that the new acquisition was all within North America. The first step outside the continent took another full generation, but the incorporation of Pacific and Caribbean islands involved far more than extra-American interests, although those monopolized attention at the time. Including Alaska, the area overseas is nearly one-fourth as large as continental United States, most of it being very remote in time as well as in miles; all of it has climates unmatched in the United States; and the population comprises 12,000,000 people utterly alien in race and culture to the Americans, hitherto a remarkably homogeneous group, considering the size of the country.

The mere expanse of this nation-empire compels the loosest possible construction of the Constitution, if all its component sections, both within and without continental United States, are to have government reasonably suited to their peculiar needs. The diversity of the natural environment intensifies this compulsion. Quite possibly one of the severest tests the Constitution has ever faced is now confronting it — the need to give satisfaction to the low-latitude peoples incorporated since the opening of the 20th century. For all its tested flexibility, it has not been stretched to apply the federal principle fully to any territory not adjacent to the original thirteen States, and a repercussion of this is heard in the clamors of Puerto Ricans and Filipinos for a greater measure of home rule. Their complaints rest upon remoteness from the center of government, racial differentiation, and a totally distinct natural environment with its own economic and social life, developed through long centuries of adaptation. When the Constitution shall have been extended to care adequately for these most recent territorial acquisitions, it will prove itself to be the most flexible and therefore the most remarkable political document ever penned.

No less than thirteen out of some fifteen major types of lowland climate found on the earth are represented in the territory under the American flag, to say nothing of countless subtypes in mountainous regions. Probably all the scores of known landform types are present in one or several examples, and no major soil group is lacking. As an inevitable consequence of this diversity of climate, landforms, and soil, the vegetation types range from almost barren deserts to deep forests of the largest trees alive. And of leading minerals, only potash, tin, nickel, manganese, and chromium are absent or if available, at costs too high to compete with supplies under other flags. On this broad base of natural environment a multiplex economic and social life is evolving. The political framework must be adapted to it, in the future as in the past.

Along with territorial expansion, the Constitution has been modified by progressively centralizing authority in the hands of the federal government. Not long after the President and Congress chose to construe the document loosely rather than forfeit the national property in the Mississippi Basin, the Supreme Court of the United States took a similar stand. It laid the foundation for its subsequent career as the interpreter of the Constitution by declaring that the federal government has the implied power to do anything not expressly prohibited in the Constitution, so long as " the end be legitimate [and] within the scope of the Constitution, and [the] means appropriate." [1] It was then in a position to range itself with the President and Congress by declaring the purchase of Florida constitutional, and by implication all other acquisitions to territory, accomplished or to come.[2] The constitutional provision for federal control of transportation and communication between the States was upheld by the Supreme Court at the expense of State regulations.[3] In this field, as in some others, the national government can function more efficiently than the individual States. Such tasks it performs, often invoking an incidentally mentioned power granted by the Constitution to cover a major activity. Up-to-date transportation is essential to our vast and diverse nation. The nature-made lines of communication trend north-south, whereas the movement of goods and people is predominantly east-west. Hence under the proviso that it may establish post roads, the federal government subsidizes the construction of canals, railroads, motor roads, and air lines. In this instance the Constitution has been modified to further the all-important cause of efficient transportation in a large country which could hardly have maintained its unity without improving its communications.

Once begun, the centralization of authority under the Constitution has no logical limit. Encroachment of federal power on the power of the States has never ceased. Only its rate has fluctuated.

The frontier has generally opposed centralization. Despite the fact that loose construction has been supported by the federally constituted territories and the newer States in such matters as acquisition

1 McCulloch v. Maryland. 4 Wheaton, 316.
2 American Insurance Co. v. Canter. 1 Peters, 542.
3 Gibbons v. Ogden. 9 Wheaton, 1, 190.

of additional lands and construction under federal auspices of transportation and communication lines, the pioneer is an individualist. He endures the hardships of the frontier for the sake of " elbow room." His occupations, chiefly farming, grazing, or small-scale mining, are most successfully carried on by individuals. The isolation of sparsely settled country breeds self-reliance. Representatives in the federal Congress of each successive " west " have generally been on the side of States Rights, even while demanding that the federal government do something to diminish the isolation of their region. More remarkable, jurists appointed to the Supreme Court from the West have normally delivered opinions, in close divisions, opposing laws which would have the effect of increasing the central authority. This tendency has persisted into our own time, although the frontier, in the sense of free, government land obtainable by the individual, disappeared twoscore years ago.

Obviously time is on the side of the older, settled areas, and in the machine age on the side of the regions which possess the minerals on which manufacturing is based, the ports and inland metropolises in which goods are made and through which they are dispatched, and the rich farmlands which feed the urban populations. The individualism of the frontier as such is bound to diminish. For two or three generations the " liberal " jurists on the Supreme Court have been those whose opinions have furthered the power of the central government to regulate life in densely populated sections, heavily urban.

While the influence of the frontier is passing, that of the section remains. Minority sections are by nature opposed to federal authority. If they are intimately bound up with dense, urban populations and the economic pursuits which can best be undertaken in common, or which ramify throughout the nation, their sectional opposition is ephemeral. New England, which threatened secession over the Second War with Great Britain, became staunchly nationalist soon after. The sectional conflict which brought about the Civil War was debated in Congress on constitutional lines a generation before the war broke out. The South, a strictly rural region, took its stand on the ground that sovereign states had created the United States and that they could, if they chose, secede. The Northeast, yearly growing more urban, championed the philosophy that in relinquishing some of their sovereignty to the federal government, the constituent States had formed an indestructible union. The northern Mississippi Basin, retaining the flavor of the frontier long after the southern segment had lost it, refused to ally itself with the Northeast until it began to partake of the life of the seaboard. Even then the West was precipitated into the alliance by the moral issue of slavery, an institution unsuited to its economic life. Lasting foundations for the union of East and West were provided by the rapid growth of manufacturing cities between the Great Lakes and the Ohio River, after the Civil War was over.

The South has remained the traditional stronghold of States Rights and opposition to centralization of power in federal hands, just as it has remained primarily rural. Nevertheless critical decisions of the Supreme Court since the seceded States regained their full privileges in the federal system show the South actually rather more favorable to centralization than the West. The rise of manufacturing in certain parts of the South may help to account for this.

The success of the North in the Civil War vastly increased the central authority. In itself the war outlawed secession as a constitutional mode of action. As a result of it the Constitution was formally amended for the first time since its authors had passed from the scene. Two of the three amendments then adopted expressly prohibit the States from enacting certain specified legislation. Hitherto the document had contained no such wording. At this period the old custom of using a plural verb after " United States " was abandoned in favor of the singular — a telling commentary on the shift in public thinking.

By subsequent amendments and interpretations the federal prerogatives have continuously encroached upon those of the States. The greater the environmental diversity, the greater the need for articulation of the parts, and the greater the spread between the favored· and the handicapped regions. The existence of effective central authority implies the power to collect taxes and distribute funds throughout the whole territory of the state. Notable modifications of the American landscape have resulted from the habit of distributing to backward and to pioneer areas money collected from prosperous regions. This is, in other terms, a transfer from sections favored by natural environment to sections laboring under temporary or permanent disabilities. The Tennessee Valley reclamation is a spectacular recent example, but the principle has long been in operation, thanks to loose construction of the Constitution. Much of the irrigation of land in western States has been paid for from federal funds; the federal government provides aid in building routes, especially in sparsely populated regions; many railroads have been similarly aided, wherever they have been trajected through difficult or unpeopled territory. Federal tax money collected chiefly in lowlands goes for objects which make habitation of the highlands possible. Many forests and recreational preserves in handicapped regions are maintained by the central government. Some regions, prosperous enough to support themselves in local affairs, can benefit greatly if given aid from the central government on specific problems which transcend a single region. Flood prevention in the Mississippi Basin is too comprehensive a task to be dealt with effectively by any existing political unit smaller than the United States. So is the utilization of the waters of the Colorado and Rio Grande rivers, although in this case the interest of Mexico throws the problem inevitably into the federal purview (Ch. 15).

By being construed loosely, the Constitution has become the basic law of a well-integrated national state instead of a frame within which certain delegated powers of sovereign states could function. In recognizing the advantages of loose construction, it should not be forgotten that in a country of uncommon regional diversity the federal organization of government is useful — perhaps essential. The recurrent insistence upon States Rights regardless of its futility, calls attention to the advantages of variety in laws to fit diversity in natural conditions. An example of unsuccessful national legislation compared to successful State legislation is furnished by the arid and semiarid west.

As settlement swept inland from the humid seaboard into the humid Middle West, a federal homestead law fixed the size of an individual's claims to unappropriated public land at a figure which had proved satisfactory in the parent States. Conditions being much the same in the two regions, the law functioned smoothly. Farther west, in subhumid regions, where tillage has to be extensive, and still more in regions so dry that only grazing can prosper without irrigation, application of these laws predestined homesteaders to hopelessly inadequate holdings. The common practice of allotting alternate sections of the land to railroad companies as an inducement to extend the rails, further complicated the pattern of landholdings. After the error was realized, successive laws increased the acreage allowed, but they came too late to benefit most of the stock-raising country. It has been found difficult, often impossible, to piece together from abandoned claims and the rigid checkerboard of railroad holdings, enough land with the proper balance between winter and summer pasture and with suitably spaced waterholes, to make a successful stock ranch. As a result some land is overgrazed while other land is not used to its capacity, or is occupied without legal right.

In contrast to federal control of land allotments, is State control of the use of streams. English law, born in a humid lowland where placid rivers merge almost imperceptibly into tide-swept estuaries, insures to abutting owners the right to unimpaired flow of the water for purposes of navigation. This legal doctrine of riparian rights fitted conditions in the English North American colonies, and in the humid Mississippi and Great Lakes basins. Where rapids and falls could furnish water-power, dams might legally be erected, if provision were made to carry boats around the obstruction. In most such cases, a dam and a lock actually improved navigation. In the dry and rugged West streams are few, fluctuating, and even intermittent, and many never reach the sea but sink into thirsty sands. There riparian rights, if adhered to, would have prevented the installation of irrigation works, without serving any useful purpose in regions devoid of navigable streams. It is not sur-prising that no less than twelve western States have by law rescinded riparian rights. They have substituted laws to safeguard irrigation farm-ing, by guaranteeing to users a fixed minimum diversion of water in the order of " first-come-first-served." Here, near the Pacific, across two continents and 3000 years from its Mediterranean home, the use of water is again regulated by laws which closely parallel the Roman code.

Evidences of the lag between settlement and application of suitable laws appear here and there. In the dry-subtropical San Joaquin Valley of California litigation between landholders who wished to maintain riparian rights and those who desired to divert water for irrigation, retarded for decades the evolution of agriculture normal in dry-sub-tropical climates. Even today not all the irrigable land is under ditch, and in each irrigated district the crops grown are dominantly those which promised profit at the time when legal controversies happened to be settled. These evidences of geopolitical immaturity bid fair to disappear in time.

If States have been slow in altering their fundamental law, how much more difficult would it be to obtain desirable national legisla-tion, with three-fourths of the States and a still larger percentage of the population satisfied with the existing code!

Flexibility adequate to the satisfaction of regional idiosyncrasies in an area so vast and so diverse as the United States is scarcely possible under any political system yet devised, except the federal. It is true that improved communication has done much to draw the different parts of the country together, and increased use of the air for planes and radio ought to knit them still closer. At the same time, swift transporta-tion is even more effective in integrating each region, thereby empha-sizing its unity. New England is developing a closer community of opinion and action than ever before, but its sectionalism is not dimin-ishing. If anything it is becoming more sharply defined, as the differ-ences between it and other sections of the country become better known. And likewise with other regions.

### REARRANGEMENT OF ADMINISTRATIVE UNITS

Both in the United States and elsewhere, rearrangement of internal administrative units has recently come to the forefront of discussion. The problem is not new. On the contrary, it is typically incidental to the growth of a state by accretion. It becomes an acute issue whenever the traditional and inherited subdivisions become misfit. Reasons for maladjustment vary. Groups of people accustomed through long habit to think and act in the frame of accepted territorial units may disturb the balance of a state which absorbs such units. At certain periods rapid advance in means of transportation and communication render ancient administrative subdivisions anachronistic. The texture of long-established administrative units is exceedingly cohesive. It usually takes a political upheaval, such as a revolution or a realignment of boundaries, to break them down.

In the modern world the earliest notable case of general rearrangement of the political map occurred in the fundamental reorganization of political France during its revolution. For the 37 ancient provinces with their varying size and diverse rights, privileges, and obligations, were substituted 83 departments of about equal size. Each ideally comprised a uniform number of administrative subdivisions, and its chief town lay within a day's travel by horse from every boundary. In this rearrangement most of the interprovincial lines were altered, although a few barrier boundaries remained unchanged. This frank recognition of the importance of communication in the political structure of the state, while doctrinaire, is a notable example of theoretical principles of government put into practice. To obliterate memory of the superseded provinces so far as possible, the new departments were given names derived from rivers, mountains, and other local natural features.

Napoleon's enforced reorganization of much of Central Europe was in the nature of consolidation of sovereign or semi-sovereign units, rather than administrative reorganization. Nevertheless, it had the effect of reducing many states, particularly those of Western Germany, to units less absurdly out of harmony with the modern world than the feudal chaos that antedated the Napoleonic conquests. Amalgamation of German territories continued during the 19th century, especially in the successive conquests of small states by Prussia.

The second comprehensive rearrangement of administrative districts in Europe has occurred since the close of the World War. The general unsettling of boundaries by the treaties which closed the war has been followed in many states by the substitution of absolutism for representative government. In a number of instances, notably Soviet Russia, Yugoslavia, and Rumania, the traditional subdivisions have been replaced by new patterns. In Italy and Germany the ancient lines are more or less in abeyance and plans for formal rearrangement have been set on foot in Germany. In Italy the operation of the corporate state, in which economic groups rather than areal units are the components, should automatically eliminate the historic provinces. In Soviet Russia the component units vary greatly in size and in resources. Many of them appear to bear the stamp of divisions current before the Russian Revolution. In this case the state is so vast that a certain degree of federation is permitted, even in a political system which functions as an absolutism.

In the new continents administrative reorganization has not been precipitated by thoroughgoing revolutions which involve fundamental alteration of the political structure. Chile has adopted a new pattern of subdivisions in the interests of simplicity in administration. This has been made possible by the traditional unitary character of the state and by the practice of absolutism under the forms of a republic.

In the United States there has been active discussion looking toward an increased correspondence between administrative units and earth conditions. Possible rearrangements might be made in different orders of magnitude. The pattern of States might conceivably be redrawn. As proposed, such a change would substitute sections of large size for the present somewhat smaller units. The geographic problem of laying out units satisfactorily representing sectional (i.e., regional) interests begins with the question as to suitable size, and goes on to more complex issues: such as whether a region should consist of a single type of human occupance of the land or of reciprocal types; where the boundaries shall be drawn; whether regions should be about equal in size, in population, or in value of natural resources. The political problem of substituting regions for States arises from the constitutional guarantee against subdivision without consent of the area to be dissected. This is backed by State patriotism which thus far in American history has precluded subdivision even in areas where it would be economically advantageous. Texas, which possesses the right to subdivide itself, and which consists of strikingly contrasted regions, frequently discusses the possibility but never seriously acts upon it. Quite clearly it will take a revolution in the political affairs of the country to alter the present pattern of States.

A more practical possibility is the elimination or amalgamation of lesser administrative subdivisions, such as counties or townships. Both derive their legal status from the several States. Most of them were laid out antecedent to settlement, and, west of the Appalachians, largely in terms of the rigid rectilinear land survey, and to specifications providing little or no variation of scale. It is inevitable that townships and counties of essentially equal size cannot fit natural conditions equally well in a nation of continental proportions and corresponding diversity of natural environment. This came to be realized in the arid west, where counties are likely to be very large. Nevertheless, even there, and more strikingly in the lands of the northern tier of humid states, both counties and townships are likely to be incapable of sustaining themselves, because the natural environment will not support enough people to pay for roads, schools, and other necessary facilities maintained at the public charge. Elsewhere, particularly in regions of extractive resources or areas subject to drouth, political units once thriving have dwindled in population until they are liabilities to the States.

Whatever the cause of the misfit of local administrative districts to natural conditions, the result is heavy expenditure by central governments, in this case both the States concerned and the federal government. To eliminate needless political officers it has been proposed to reduce the number of counties or townships. Little has been accomplished. In a few cases where townships are practically empty they have been recast into the public domain of the State. Where certain lands are wanted for specific uses, a way has generally been found to eliminate useless political machinery. This is true of townships taken over for public reserves, such as national or State parks. It has occurred here and there where a city expands over several townships, and the local governments can be legally superseded by the municipal government.

All efforts to rearrange administrative units face the inertia of established structures and the resistance of beneficiaries of the existing system. Little wonder that it generally takes a revolution of the first magnitude to alter even minor subdivisions!

With internal reorganization being discussed or carried out from one end of the earth to the other, marches the attempt here and there to form permanent combinations of sovereign states. In this practice there is no violation of the geopolitical theory that the state should match the status of communication. Moreover it is not a new practice. The whole history of Europe since it resumed the line of progress after the dissolution of the Roman Empire, has been gradual coalescence as rapidly as permitted by improved transportation and kindred economic advance. Latterly it took shape in the national state, the mode of political organization which happens to dominate the scene today. The efforts of the Austro-Hungarian monarchy to construct a national state in the Middle Danube region and of Germany and Russia to reduce the number of political entities on the North European Plain were in the tradition of the centuries. They happened to be incomplete jobs when the World War knocked down the scaffolding and disclosed deep fissures in the fabric.

These fissures conformed to ancient cleavages along linguistic lines. Language, because it is the vehicle of mutual understanding, is the engine of the emotion patriotism, or nationality. When the defection of Russia and the defeat of Germany and Austria left the terms of peace in the hands of peripheral European powers, they eagerly seized upon resurgent nationalities of East Central Europe as handy devices for reducing the strength of their erstwhile enemies. By substituting ten states for three, the peace treaties had the effect of carrying to the Baltic Sea the political atomization characteristic of southeastern Europe, the area just emerging from centuries of Turkish (Asiatic nomad) rule (Ch. 8). Whatever one's sympathies for the " right of self-determination," it cannot be gainsaid that this act runs flagrantly counter to the saecular trend. Proof of it resides in the resumption of normal evolution as soon as the war was over.

Germany, already a powerful state, although small in area by comparison with new states such as the United States, Russia, or Brazil, has been able to mount the band-wagon of " nationalism " and thereby to annex Austria, a fringe of German-speaking peoples on the borders of Czechoslovakia, and Memel, the most northeasterly German-speaking city. In these acts Germany resumes its effort, checked by the World War, to expand to a size suited to the modes of life in the 20th century. Yet if all the Germans contiguous to present-day Germany were to be incorporated, the state would still fall short of being one of the group of very large sovereignties.

Where then shall such expansion stop? Quite clearly, not at the confines of German speech. Disregarding the non-German minorities forcibly taken into Germany in its first wave of expansion, Slavic Bohemia and Moravia, unluckily almost enveloped by Germans, have been annexed, and Slovakia, although it projects far beyond the extreme boundary of Germanic speech, has been placed under a German " protectorate." If the remaining German minorities in other neighboring states are to be rendered unto Germany, in strict accord with the principle of self-determination, will that be only a prelude to seizure of those states *in toto?* Self-determination has proved a powerful entering wedge for aggression by large states. It is no defense at all for small ones, unsupported by area and resources somewhat commensurate with those of adjacent sovereignties.

Whether they like it or not, small states are faced with the alternative of federating among themselves or being incorporated into their more powerful neighbors. Such federations are the antithesis of combinations intended to achieve a balance of power and so fated to result in war. They are in line with the trend of the times, *i.e.*, the creation of states large enough to function comfortably in a world in which the units of movement are swift and the units of production and consumption large. No such federation has yet occurred in the contemporary world, because of mutual jealousy, fostered by nationalistic propaganda and thriving on the distortions of understanding inevitable among different language groups. In an earlier stage of European history, the Swiss nationality, compounded of German, French, and Italian groups, evolved from common geo-economic interests. Switzerland therefore is the prototype of fusions that might well take place elsewhere, but on a larger scale. Diminutive Switzerland, befitting an age of slow transportation and correspondingly small territorial units, falls far short of the ideal size for a state today.

Some combinations among the small states of Europe which find they have common interests, suggest that they are aware of their danger. The post-war Little Entente was the successor to the pre-war Balkan alliances, although both groups coalesced only in hate and fear of specific enemies. As originally constituted the Little Entente was an unsound areal unit. Its successor, the Balkan Entente, is somewhat more in concordance with earth realities. The " Oslo Group " of small maritime states in North Europe recognizes the discrepancy between their tiny areas and the feasible size of a powerful state in the contemporary world. These are small beginnings but they may result in federations effective enough to prevent absorption by one or another of the Great Powers.

Many small states owe their sovereignty to their position among powerful neighbors which checkmate one another's greed. Who can say how long such a balance of forces will last? It was the protection enjoyed by Ethiopia until France withdrew its interest, leaving Great Britain the alternative of fighting Italy or acquiescing in Italian conquest of the African highland. It has been the protection of Switzerland, but now Austrian and German jealousies are merged into a single political intention.

Nationalities circumscribed by narrow confines suffer from political concepts that derive from the railroad train, the motor car, the airplane, the telephone, and the radio. All these instrumentalities function best in large units. They easily and swiftly transgress circumjacent national borders in peacetime, they can be used as propaganda for war, and they amplify the scale on which war may be prosecuted.

Quite possibly all the states of Europe west of Russia are too small to fit the conditions of the 20th century. Without exception the nationalities on which they are based evolved in an age when each part of Europe subsisted almost wholly on its local resources, and when trade among the parts was merely a trickle of luxury goods. Indeed, the political concepts of governments so new as those of the United States and Australia are based on a society devoted chiefly to hand agriculture. Most of the authors of the American Constitution were suspicious of the small cities of the Atlantic seaboard they knew and ignorant of machinery other than the simplest sort. Their swiftest locomotion was the galloping horse and the careening sailing vessel. The political ideas underlying Western European governments are rooted in still older soil. Political unity in an area so large and populous as France was a miracle in the 17th century, accomplished only through unscrupulous destruction of localism by a ruthless centralized autocracy.

The society in which small states harmonized with rural life and snail's-pace communication was transformed between the middle 18th century and the World War into an age of machine production and machine locomotion, based largely on extension in the utilization of minerals. By virtue of aggregation of mineral resources unequaled in any other continent, little Europe became the seat of five of the half dozen most powerful states on earth. It is not strange that these states feel themselves crowded, even if they possess safety-valves in the form of undeveloped colonial territory. National boundaries so remote from nuclear cores that few were demarcated earlier than the 17th century have become resistance coils burning their way into the consciousness of whole nations, for which they make frontiers too proximate.[1]

The effect of this transformation on the thinking of the nations is not reasoned. For the individual it heightens the emotional tension called patriotism, and prepares him to support his government wholeheartedly in any program which promises to relieve the discomfort. Upon the government it urges the obligation to expand.

[1] The line between Germany and France is an example.

As a means to obtaining the enlarged space wanted, restrictions upon political action by the constituted authorities are discarded. For democratic forms and two-party government is substituted autocracy under the specious symbolism of a single party. Absolutism, in capable and ruthless hands, is the most efficient form of government ever devised. Autocracies created the national states to which the world has become accustomed during the past two or three centuries. Dictatorships have blossomed almost everywhere in Europe, since the World War threw into flux the painfully established boundaries of that continent. It is possible that they are destined to create fewer and larger states, political entities more neatly fitting the existing economic form than the nations which flowered from the seedbed of subsistence agriculture.

The danger in thus abruptly refashioning Europe's political garments lies in war. The interdependent economic structure reared by the aid of complex machines is fragile. It might be destroyed by the very attempt to readjust political life to suit it.

If it is true that a government can succeed in the long run only if it approximates (although perhaps crudely) the requirements of the people and the area over which it presides, then the governments of the present day will have to take on a gloss of the machine age in order to persist. In view of the inability of most occidental governments to solve many of the problems posed by a mechanized society since the close of the World War, it is fair to suspect them of lagging behind the times. The experiments being tried in the parts of Europe least adjusted to the machine age may face in the direction of progress.

Soviet Russia, the most backward part of Europe a generation ago, has embraced the mechanisms of material existence with enthusiasm, and has undertaken to create a state dominated by the interests of proletarian, urban elements in society. Avowing as its guide the work of mid-19th century writers on economic society, men deeply affected by the earlier manifestations of the machine age, Russia is trying to telescope into a few years the economic evolution which required five centuries in Great Britain, and to advance its political structure beyond that reached by any national state in the older tradition. It is too early to judge its success. Indubitably it is proceeding by the method of absolutism. Thus far, only Mexico has shown a pronounced proclivity to follow the same path. In Spain, forces with kindred ideals have seized upon Catalonia, the only mechanized part of the country. During peacetime this section betrayed no stamp of political alteration other than a change of masters. Its defeat in civil war has checked its course, at least for the time being.

In Italy absolutism has been adopted without reference to either economic or political theory. For the present discussion the interest of the Italian (Fascist) experiment lies in its substitution of economic classes for areal districts as the basis of representation in government. Until the newly constituted representative government gains an opportunity to function, it will be impossible for the scheme to have a fair test.

In Germany, the machine has been installed for a century. Steps toward democratic government lagged behind mechanization, until destruction of the political order in the cataclysm of the World War thrust republican forms to the fore. After a brief trial, the republic succumbed to a dictator. The adoption of absolutism appears to have been essentially a resurgence of the fundamental concept of government in vogue before the war, now untrammelled by the alien forms of democracy. Representation in the real sense has been abolished, and rights and privileges of the federated components of the state have been abrogated. Otherwise the government simulates 18th-century German absolutisms like Prussia. The other highly mechanized countries of Europe (Great Britain, France, and the two Low Countries) retain the forms of democracy, although in the effort to protect themselves against the aggressions of the new absolutisms they have been compelled to adopt measures that would have seemed high-handed to the pre-war generation.

The time has not yet come to assess equitably the political concomitants of the machine age, beyond reiterating that representative democracy is having to give ground to absolutism, in an effort to create a suitable frame of government for the new economic order and its social products.

## INTERNATIONAL CONVENTIONS

In the fires of rekindled autocracy many an international treaty has shriveled to ashes. The invasion of Belgium in 1914 by Germany, a state which had been a signatory to Belgian neutrality, was justified by the violators on the ground of military necessity. It has been followed since the war by several similar disavowals of treaty obligations on the part of newly risen dictatorships. The wholesale repudiation by Soviet Russia of all the obligations of its predecessor state is justified in Russia on the ground that the new national concepts need have no traffic with the old. Numerous arrangements entered into between nations to solve problems created by international boundaries have been abrogated. An example is Rumania's action in refusing to recognize longer the international character of the segment of the Danube which lies wholly within Rumanian territory.

The tacit understandings known as international law are even more readily dishonored than are treaties. Japan wages war year after year without declaring war. Germany marches unprovoked into adjacent sovereign states. The findings of the League of Nations are flouted by its members.

All these moves are related to machine technology generally, as applied to the practice of warfare. The declaration of war, the adherence to treaty obligations, the abridgment of sovereignty by international agreement — all these acts put the aggressor at a disadvantage in a type of warfare which depends on mass destruction before the unready opponent can rise to his own defense. Redoubled emphasis on the central authority and on the national ego is at the same time the result of outgrowing agrarian governments and a means to find a new adjustment more in accord with mechanized society. International arrangements are inherently weak in that they fail to satisfy the deep instinct that government should be coherent and unified, not a patchwork.

If and when a new concept of the state emerges from the experiments of the times, it will succeed to the degree that it fits the economic and social structure of mankind. It is to be hoped that our civilization will not have to walk through the valley of the shadow of death, as did that of classical antiquity, in order to find renewed life.

## CHAPTER EIGHTEEN

# Earmarks of Political Geography

## THE POLITICAL AREA

THE kernel of political geography is the political area. Every political unit describes an areal pattern of nuclear core, constituent or administrative regions, problem areas, vulnerable zones, capitals, strategic spots, and boundaries — all affecting its success even if not vital to its persistence. These features take form with respect to specific conditions of the natural environment. Commonly they harmonize with the earth conditions and the peopling of the place at the time of their origin. Once established they tend strongly to perpetuate themselves. It is a truism that maladjustment between a political feature and its natural setting may gradually increase for generations before it is rectified. The political areas which endure longest are noted for making frequent alterations by law in order to keep their institutions abreast of changing times. Where maladjustment is permitted to go on, it may have to be corrected by the dire expedients of revolution, disintegration, or conquest. In the meantime failure of the political pattern to fit the natural features which condition human existence causes friction. Indeed, the vise of crystallized political forms may distort the normal geographic design.

This is not to say that political areas are predestined subdivisions of the earth's surface. They may expand or shrink with the passage of time. Military conquests, folk migrations, discoveries of new lands, and changes in material technology have more than once altered the size, shape, and character of political areas. They may even lose their identity, although regions which have once stood out as leaders in political affairs are likely to reappear after longer or shorter eclipse. In the long view it must be conceded that the political significance of any area bears a well-defined relation to its climate, landforms, and natural resources. This relation remains unchanged, with the momentous exception that human ability to utilize and cope with nature advances or recedes and by so much alters it.

A factor in the persistence of those political areas which retain their identity is the pertinacity of the past in the realm of government. Political feeling is one of the strongest of all human emotions. Political attachments are correspondingly tenacious, and some part of the heritage of environmental conditions long vanished remains in the political order of every period. The political geography of few, if any, areas can be understood without recourse to their past. Study of the present-day political landscape must be supplemented by a review in their original setting of such relics of past landscapes as survive in the patterns of today. The present can be set in its perspective only by reconstruction of the fragmentary records of history, and in some places the still more meager remains of archeology.

It seems likely that when a thorough canvass of the earth's political areas has been made, it will be possible to group them into well-defined categories, each characterized by specific inherent traits. This has been the line of advance in the study of natural regions and of economic regions. No such thorough canvass has as yet been made. Hence no satisfactory statement of the inherent traits of political areas is in the purview of the writer. At this stage it does seem possible to submit a crude catalog of major geopolitical designs.

1. Political areas tend to cohere about easily defended highlands, often folk-fortresses.
2. Conversely, others focus on fertile lowlands, particularly a natural nexus of rivers or other easy routes.
3. Margins of an inland sea may be rivals if they are alike in natural environment, or allies if they are reciprocal by nature. In any case they strive among themselves for political power.
4. Coastal footholds with penetration to the hinterland is a pattern commonly found in backward areas.
5. Jointure of strongly contrasted and reciprocal resources is urgent where the cleavage is sharp and no major barrier exists. The combination of a lowland with an adjacent highland is a common form. Another is the union of contrasted climatic regions.
6. Expansion over the whole of a unit area of climate is possible where desert or grassy vegetation predominates.
7. Transit lands find it difficult to remain independent and even to cohere, but they strive to achieve both objectives.

A crude outline of the elements in the study of a political area is suggested below.

1. Ecumene (often also the nuclear core).
   a. Natural environment, including size and shape, climate, landforms, and natural resources.
   b. Cultural structure — people, language, economic and social life.
2. Components — accretions to the ecumene or relics of territory once held.
   a. Relation of natural environment of each to that of the ecumene.
   b. Subordination of peripheral cultural structures.
   c. Unitary or federal character of the aggregate components.
3. Problem areas and friction zones.
   a. Natural and cultural items in the problem or friction.
   b. Relation of each district to the ecumene and to its immediate neighbors.
4. Capitals.
   a. Central — related to the whole area or to the ecumene.
   b. Peripheral — related to a defensive or offensive frontier, or to relict position.
   c. Subcapitals — of constituent members of a federation, and of administrative districts.
5. Boundaries.
   a. Naturally marked or otherwise.
   b. Antecedent or subsequent to current occupance of the area.
   c. Density of settlement and degree of interpenetration along each distinct segment of the boundary.
   d. Strategic reaches and points.
6. Allied areas and dependencies.
   a. Contiguous or separated.
   b. Character of separation — land or water.
   c. Cultural structure and the degree of subordination to the dominant area.

## THE LAW AND REGIONS

The agent whereby the political structure of any area is constructed is the law. Like any other human concept, the law freely flits from one region to another. Laws are frequently enacted which are so at variance with nature in the political area affected that they have to be rescinded or they remain among the statutes as dead letters. Others, while somewhat inharmonious, manage to operate; to some extent they modify utilization of earth resources. In time the fundamental law in each political area becomes roughly suited to the few compulsive conditions laid down by nature. A large body of law, even when introduced from outside, falls within the range of tolerance established by earth conditions. The legal forms which guide most human activities may vary considerably without doing violence to human living. At the same time they may produce contrasts in man's use of identical environments. Variations in culture patterns in uniform environments on opposite sides of a political boundary are common, and prove the possibility of modifying the landscape by political means. The operation of law can be traced only through patient study of the incidence of individual laws. Few such studies have been made.

The legal structure of only a few political areas today is wholly consequent upon local natural environment. Four basic legal structures may be recognized:

1. Migrant. Personal law inhering in the unfixed tribal group.
2. Sedentary. Territorial law adhering to fixed areas.
3. Transhumant. Territorial law extended over seasonally vacant spaces, in many cases by special agreement among groups concerned.
4. Commensal. Government by agreement or by domination divided between a sedentary and a migrant group.

The last two of these may be thought of as variants of the first two, and in any case affect a small portion of the earth and a still smaller fraction of its inhabitants. All the categories are too broad to correspond to any legal systems established in the contemporary world, although they include the practices of some small and isolated groups.

Most of the great legal systems of the earth are so flexible and adaptable that they operate in a considerable variety of regions. In some cases they have been transferred from their original homeland by colonization. Or they have been superposed on an existing regional society. In either case the adaptability of any broad system saves it by permitting necessary modifications. Even in the region of its origin every legal system is subject to continuous alteration to conform to changes in density of population, new material technology, and the cyclic changes in the character of human occupance of a region which occur as a result of the occupance itself. The interplay of law and regions is incessant. Each affects the other and in the process is itself modified. As in every other aspect of geography, earth conditions permit a wide range of laws in most regions, and at the same time set limits that nullify laws which stand outside the permitted range.

## GEOPOLITICAL FORCES

The forces which give to earth conditions their expression in the law have been much discussed but are imperfectly understood. Doubtless some of them remain to be discovered. The tables of contents of most works on political geography abound in touchwords with which the authors endeavor to give tongue to these intangible forces; e.g., space, the ground, situation, natural domain. How many of them designate valid concepts is not known, because most of them have been deduced from theories of the state and of its relations to the earth.

An alternative approach to the veiled subject of geopolitical forces suggests itself, in the processes which entail interplay of regions and law. One of these is the functioning of political parties. Parties appear to be fundamental to any government, although they obtain free play only in democratic societies. One function of a political party is to give voice to regional interests; another is to exert its influence on lawmaking. Another pertinent process is administrative. Executive officers of government work within a legal framework, but their acts frequently exceed the specific instructions of laws. One of the reasons for this is the eternal divergence between law, which once passed is static until revised, and nature, unceasingly dynamic. A third process adheres to the third branch of government, the judicial. Laws are subject to interpretation by judges, although the freedom of action of judicial officers is narrower in most countries than in the United States.

To obtain a clear view of the geopolitical forces the earth processes must also be studied. Chief among these is the earth's inexorable march from causes to consequences. Laws flagrantly unsuited to regions where they operate ultimately destroy the resource which they govern; e.g., the state which taxes timberland annually soon finds on its hands denuded and worthless tracts which have reverted to the state because of non-payment of taxes. There is more than a little reason to believe that the current insistence in some states on national self-sufficiency at the level of world interdependence is depleting soil, upsetting the balance between nature and society, and undermining the state itself. Scarcely any considerable alteration can be performed upon the face of nature without unexpected repercussions. Most such operations are possible only to governments. The dams built in Egypt since 1900 have already made it necessary for Egyptian farmers to import fertilizer for fields which had got on very well without it for at least 7000 years.

Perhaps studies of these and other processes in which laws and regions figure as protagonist and antagonist will render tangible the geopolitical forces, as yet so little understood.

### OBSERVATION IN POLITICAL GEOGRAPHY

Doubtless political areas, the interplay of law and region, and the underlying geopolitical forces can and should be studied from every conceivable angle of view. The utility of multiple working hypotheses in arriving at sound conclusions is well understood and needs no restatement here. Unfortunately the growth of modern geography has been retarded by a tendency of its sponsors to generalize on the basis of insufficient evidence. This has perhaps been true of the youth of all sciences, but human geography is so young that it still suffers from overzealous devotees, who claim for it a body of " laws " in advance of their proved validity.

In no sphere of geography has the disproportion between observation and speculation been so great as in political geography. This is natural. Political theory has been a favorite intellectual calisthenic from early times. Its application in the realm of geography is enticing, and the painstaking testing of its validity is hampered by three major difficulties.

The chief of these is observation of the facts *in situ*. It is axiomatic in geography that its data must be gathered from the field. Techniques for the study of physical geography are well established, and economic geography is becoming equipped with facilities for effective field observation. As yet the remaining branches of systematic human geography — social and political — almost totally lack recognized field techniques. Political forces generally etch the landscape but lightly, and still oftener their effects are inextricably entwined with phenomena of economic geography. The patent observable features of political geography are boundaries, capitals, administrative components, and a few areas of political friction or unquestioned strategic importance — no others. Its many further ramifications must be sought in the economic and social impress of laws upon the landscape, in the vestiges of political and military contests, and in the ephemeral man-made structures whereby government is facilitated. The observer in the field, confused by the complex intertwining of political, social, and economic patterns in the landscape, and perhaps thwarted in his efforts to trace any evidence whatever of political forces, can show only meager and piecemeal results of his efforts. These compare poorly with the splendid façade built up of theory spun from a few well established facts.

Political geography also thrusts strong and deep roots into the past. The emotional character of political thought holds communities and states to traditional patterns and practices long after their original connection with the natural environment has been forgotten. Sound political geography therefore must trace these relict forms and procedures to their source, by means of observation in the field, a duty which has too often been neglected. Even when undertaken, the quest in historical and archeological records may prove barren, for lack of adequate historical or archeological data or because the circumstances are recorded without reference to their environmental setting. Without the exact knowledge of place which comes only from observations on the spot, the most carefully gathered records of the past are likely to be geographically meaningless.

A further difficulty faces the political geographer, i.e., his political fealty. Nowadays every occidental person is born into a national state, the validity of which is accepted without question. It is easy to lose sight of equally valid rival claims of other states, especially if they conflict with axiomatic loyalties, accepted from earliest recollection. The shaping of political geography to serve the ends of statecraft is a natural human tendency. It inevitably vitiates any claim to scholarship. Unfortunately it has found such widespread expression in the years since the World War that a whole literature of books and papers has been published in support of the environmental rightness of political claims. Many of these biased statements can be distinguished from unprejudiced studies in political geography by the designation " geopolitics," commonly used by German proponents of the earth-based claims of their nation. They are not, however, confined to German writers, but may be found in chauvinistic work appearing in every country. Here again, the chief check against mistaking national aspirations for geographic truths is rigorous observation in the field. The field alone is uncolored by the prejudices, conscious or unconscious, of human minds.

In an effort to escape the dilemmas inherent in the present status of the subject (or perhaps because they are unaware of its central problems), some students have attached the name " political geography " to discussions of the economic or regional geography of political areas.

This is nothing but reversion to the " general geography " current in the 19th century, and abandoned with the growing recognition of the paramount significance of economic phenomena and regional associations as compared to the mere outlines of states, as frames for assembling geographic data. The relapse to an outworn procedure is the more lamentable because it diverts the term " political geography " from its accepted sense. The mere fact that most compiled data needed by geographers are arranged by political units is no palliation of the sin of debasing a recognized and useful appellation. It should be noted that observation in the field promptly discloses the unreality of political lines as the fundamental subdividers of the earth.

## SERVICES RENDERED BY POLITICAL GEOGRAPHY

The study of geography, more than any other discipline, should inculcate a sympathetic understanding of political groups inhabiting all the varied regions of the earth. It emphasizes the long view, the persistent conditioning of human life by nature-made surroundings, and the difficulty any group of humankind has in seeing beyond its geopolitical horizon.

Just now the volcano of national ambition seethes and heaves. Postulates of government long regarded as axioms are being cast into its crater. In several parts of the world long-established structures of government have been fused and remolded in its intense fires during the past two decades. It appears unlikely that any state on earth can escape unscathed the stresses produced by its force — ungovernable by human agencies, when once unleashed. The familiar political world may conceivably recrystallize into wholly new political forms. Nearly all the nations of today grew up as political manifestations of small, isolated regions, separated from each other by barriers to intercourse. They now find themselves in a world made narrow and uncomfortable by express-train transportation and lightning communication; a world, moreover, in which mining, manufacturing, and a host of specialized professions have come to take their places alongside the ancient occupations of farmer, priest, and soldier. Inevitably they suffer from friction with their neighbors. Growing divergence between the parochial political pattern of the earth and a worldwide economic pattern, evolving ever more rapidly as material technology advances, is bound to disrupt the accustomed stability of social groups. Unfortunately nationality is even narrower in its compass than the political pattern. At the same time it is the dominant current expression of one of the most powerful human emotions, and has been made the touchstone of every interest which desires to alter the political map. The world therefore finds itself in the awkward position of using nationality, the narrowest of all acceptable bases for the state, as the instrument with which to broaden the base to conform to an economic pattern which exceeds the scale of all but a very few contemporary nations. Little wonder that values have become distorted.

Among the cross-currents of political, social, and economic streams the only fixed points for guidance are found in the natural environment. Within broad limits human society must always shape its political order so as to facilitate economic life. As man's skill in utilizing earth resources improves, his political horizon must widen. The alternative may be destruction of the material technology which carries group interests beyond their local regions. To reshape the political world wisely requires all man's ingenuity. Success is to be measured by the degree to which states harmonize with the regional pattern of the earth. Political geography provides the needed facts. Its calm outlook in the world of governance can provide salutary release of the high emotional charge which politics usually carries. If it is to function effectively, its practitioners must hold to the impartial study of political groups in their regional distribution. Otherwise they will drift into the mystical realm of propaganda, serving only the selfish ends of narrow national emotions. Sound political geography must always take the long view afforded by history and archeology, because in the political realm much of the past coexists with all of the present. At every step, its findings should be checked in the field, *i.e.*, on the ground, lest they prove to be unsupported by earth conditions, and so fail to be geography at all.

# Bibliography

THE writer of any book obviously factual is under obligation to disclose his sources. He may document his work with footnotes, he may append a detailed annotated bibliography, or he may acknowledge his debt in general terms.

It will be apparent to all students of political geography that I have drawn freely on both general works and detailed studies in the specialized field. In a few instances the careful investigations of predecessors have been indispensable to my treatment of particular areas. But taken as a whole, works specifically in the field of political geography have been equalled in value for my purposes and exceeded in quantity by studies in economic and regional geography, and in history. I have likewise drawn slightly upon archeological evidence.

It becomes apparent that documentation or even a complete bibliography of all these items would defeat its own purpose, by its very mass, and by throwing out of scale the references specifically drawn on as compared to items equally fundamental but not directly citable. The alternative, of referring only to those predecessors who gave me considerable blocks of digested data, would unduly emphasize half a dozen works in a long list of studies which have contributed scattered facts or basic viewpoints of signal importance, but which cannot be singled from their fellows at the end of two decades of pondering the subject.

Citation of references to publications, and to a less extent the listing of them, lies open to the further objection that it overemphasizes the printed word in comparison to field studies, on which the book is so considerably based. Indeed, a chief justification for publishing this book is its steadfast endeavor to correlate its facts in their areal (distributional) relations. Without personal observations in the field these correlations would possess little geographical reality.

To the student who wishes to pursue political geography beyond the confines of this volume, there is the vast bulk of writings on history and archeology as well as on economic and regional geography. More specifically there is a considerable array of books and papers dealing with political geography as a whole or with specific areas or topics.

Most of them have been made readily accessible through recent and current guides cited below.

The standard bibliography of the subject is an annotated list of more than 3000 titles, arranged topically and regionally, together with an index of authors. This occupies three-quarters of the *Geographisches Jahrbuch*, Volume 49 (1934), 79–325; Gotha: Justus Perthes, 1935. Its compiler is Walther Vogel; its title, " Politische Geographie und Geopolitik." This list naturally stresses German work, but because the Germans have made many more studies in both political geography and geopolitics than all other groups combined, the emphasis is not undesirable.

A source of citations that more fully covers work in French and English output is the *Bibliographie Géographique Internationale*, published annually since 1923 under the auspices of a group of seven geographical societies, and previously in the *Annales de Géographie* (Paris: Armand Colin). Each volume contains a section on " Géographie Politique," in which both books and papers are cited with brief annotations.

A particularly valuable survey of the evolution of the subject, particularly in its later phases, is " Recent Developments in Political Geography," by Richard Hartshorne. This appeared in the *American Political Science Review*, Volume 29 (1935), 785–804, 943–966. It is elaborately documented.

# Glossary

WHILE this book has been written in non-technical language, the wide range of its subject-matter entails the use of some terms that may not be familiar to all readers. Also, for convenience, a few words and phrases are employed in a special sense; they are defined on the occasion of their first appearance. For ready reference all words likely to puzzle any reader are collected here.

Amerind — American Indian.

Cloud forest — the dense forest of seaward-facing slopes in the rainy low latitudes, bathed almost constantly in clouds.

Core, or nuclear core — the area in which or about which a state originates.

Crystalline rock — a mass of rock in crystalline form, generally hard and yielding relatively infertile soils.

The Discoveries — the discoveries of the Orient and the new continents by European voyagers in the 15th and 16th centuries.

Ecumene — the most populous region of a state, particularly that part most closely knit by communication lines.

Edaphic — pertaining to soil conditions.

Fault (line) scarp — the slope marking a line of slip in the earth's crust; often significant in mountain ranges and in routes of transportation.

Folk-fortress — a district of natural defensibility in which a political group girds itself either for defense or for expansion.

Geopolitical — politico-geographic.

Hill-land — a region of rugged but low relief. Used in contrast to plains and to mountain land.

Hinterland —— the tributary area lying behind a port or other coastal center.

Karst — rugged landforms created by foundering of the surface into limestone caverns.

March — a border district established to defend a frontier, particularly against a people of a less advanced technology.

Rain forest — the dense forest of rainy low-latitude lowlands.

Relict — pertaining to a survival from a past geographic epoch.

Rift valley — a lowland formed by the foundering of a block of the earth's crust; its margins are fault lines.

Settlement colonization — colonization in the classic sense, of transplantation of people to new homes.

State — when not capitalized, a sovereign political unit; when capitalized, a member of a federation and legally so styled.

The Straits — the Bosporus and the Dardanelles, taken together.

Technology — the state of the arts.

Tierra caliente ⎫ The three temperature bands — hot, temperate,
Tierra fria ⎬ and cold — commonly found on plateaus and
Tierra templada ⎭ mountain slopes in the low latitudes.

Unitary — the form of government in which power derives from the centralized authority.

Modern place names are consistently used, regardless of the period to which reference is made. This reduces slightly the place names, inevitably numerous in a wide-ranging treatise on geography.

# Index

WORLD AFFAIRS: National and International Viewpoints
An Arno Press Collection

Angell, Norman. **The Great Illusion, 1933.** 1933.

Benes, Eduard. **Memoirs:** From Munich to New War and New Victory. 1954.

[Carrington, Charles Edmund] (Edmonds, Charles, pseud.) **A Subaltern's War.** 1930. New preface by Charles Edmund Carrington.

Cassel, Gustav. **Money and Foreign Exchange After 1914.** 1922.

Chambers, Frank P. **The War Behind the War, 1914-1918.** 1939.

Dedijer, Vladimir. **Tito.** 1953.

Dickinson, Edwin DeWitt. **The Equality of States in International Law.** 1920.

Douhet, Giulio. **The Command of the Air.** 1942.

Edib, Halidé. **Memoirs.** 1926.

Ferrero, Guglielmo. **The Principles of Power.** 1942.

Grew, Joseph C. **Ten Years in Japan.** 1944.

Hayden, Joseph Ralston. **The Philippines.** 1942.

Hudson, Manley O. **The Permanent Court of International Justice, 1920-1942.** 1943.

Huntington, Ellsworth. **Mainsprings of Civilization.** 1945.

Jacks, G. V. and R. O. Whyte. **Vanishing Lands:** A World Survey of Soil Erosion. 1939.

Mason, Edward S. **Controlling World Trade.** 1946.

Menon, V. P. **The Story of the Integration of the Indian States.** 1956.

Moore, Wilbert E. **Economic Demography of Eastern and Southern Europe.** 1945.

[Ohlin, Bertil]. **The Course and Phases of the World Economic Depression.** 1931.

Oliveira, A. Ramos. **Politics, Economics and Men of Modern Spain, 1808-1946.** 1946.

O'Sullivan, Donal. **The Irish Free State and Its Senate.** 1940.

Peffer, Nathaniel. **The White Man's Dilemma.** 1927.

Philby, H. St. John. **Sa'udi Arabia.** 1955.

Rappard, William E. **International Relations as Viewed From Geneva.** 1925.

Rauschning, Hermann. **The Revolution of Nihilism.** 1939.

Reshetar, John S., Jr. **The Ukrainian Revolution, 1917-1920.** 1952.

Richmond, Admiral Sir Herbert. **Sea Power in the Modern World.** 1934.

Robbins, Lionel. **Economic Planning and International Order.** 1937. New preface by Lionel Robbins.

Russell, Bertrand. **Bolshevism:** Practice and Theory. 1920.

Russell, Frank M. **Theories of International Relations.** 1936.

Schwarz, Solomon M. **The Jews in the Soviet Union.** 1951.

Siegfried, André. **Canada:** An International Power. [1947].

Souvarine, Boris. **Stalin.** 1939.

Spaulding, Oliver Lyman, Jr., Hoffman Nickerson, and John Womack Wright. **Warfare.** 1925.

Storrs, Sir Ronald. **Memoirs.** 1937.

Strausz-Hupé, Robert. **Geopolitics:** The Struggle for Space and Power. 1942.

Swinton, Sir Ernest D. **Eyewitness.** 1933.

Timasheff, Nicholas S. **The Great Retreat.** 1946.

Welles, Sumner. **Naboth's Vineyard:** The Dominican Republic, 1844-1924. 1928. Two volumes in one.

Whittlesey, Derwent. **The Earth and the State.** 1939.

Wilcox, Clair. **A Charter for World Trade.** 1949.

TEXAS A&M UNIVERSITY-TEXARKANA